Janie's Journal

VOLUME 3

1992-1996

Also by Janie Tippett

Four Lines a Day

Janie's Journal
Vol 1: 1984-1987
Vol 2: 1988-1991
Vol 3: 1992-1996
Vol 4: 1997-2004
Vol 5: 2005-2009
Vol 6: 2010-2015

Janie's work appears in
the following anthologies:

Talking On Paper: An Anthology
of Oregon Letters and Diaries

Crazy Woman Creek:
Women Rewrite the American West

Janie's Journal

Volume 3

1992-1996

Janie Tippett

Lucky Marmot Press

www.luckymarmotpress.com

Wallowa, Oregon

JANIE'S JOURNAL, VOLUME THREE: 1992-1996
was originally published in the weekly Agri-Times NW.
These columns are collected here with permission of the publisher.

All photos were taken by Janie Tippett as part of her photojournalism
for Agri-Times NW, except where noted in the captions.
All photos are used with permission.

The cover photo of Doug and Janie Tippett was taken
at the home place on Prairie Creek outside Joseph, Oregon.

ISBN 978-1-7334833-4-6 (paperback)
ISBN 978-1-7334833-7-7 (ebook)

This volume was collected, digitized, edited, and published by
Lucky Marmot Press in Wallowa, Oregon.
https://www.luckymarmotpress.com

*Brandon "Bubba" Nobles, 3, son of rodeo clown J.D. Nobles, comes bustin'
out of the chute in the popular mutton-riding event at the Joseph Junior
Rodeo in May 1992.*

1992

January 5—It is 11:20 a.m. The rain has stopped for the time being. I am seated in a chair in front of a small typewriter table, typing (or attempting to type) while my gaze wanders across the American River canyon toward El Dorado County.

Out on sister Mary Ann's deck, geraniums, primroses and pansies bloom in wooden planters. Pigeons, blue jays and chickadees visit a bird feeder, pecking at seeds which scatter upon the deck railing. Camellia bushes droop with buds, nearly ready to open, and oak and digger pine march down toward the river.

Out of my line of vision and to the west are the subdivisions, acres of them, miles of them. The nearest and the newest, Falcon Crest, is composed of pretentious three-story affairs, some of which resemble castles...all for a single family? They are constructed of beautiful wood, brick, stone and glass...lots of glass; so their occupants can look out over the once lovely, oak-dotted hills upon other houses, like their own.

As you've probably guessed by now, Doug and I are on our yearly pilgrimage to Placer County, California. When potatoes are safely stored in temperature-controlled cellars, and Ben and Steve can manage the daily feeding of cattle, we are able to take a January break from the ranch and pretend we are semi-retired rancher-farmers.

Having left Wallowa County on Friday morning, January 3, and driven to Farewell Bend, we lunched at the spot where, after 330 miles, those pioneers who had been following the Oregon Trail left the Snake River behind.

During construction of the new interstate highway, which replaced the Old Oregon Trail highway, large earth movers uncovered a burial site where a man, woman and two children had been buried in a wagon box. The remains were reburied in a new grave site, marked today by a plain concrete post, located within the angle created by two forks of the frontage road on the west side of the highway. Doug and I are fascinated with Oregon Trail history.

   The roads were good, no snow and ice to contend with as we sped through the lonely Owyhees. A passing ranch sign read, "Pardner, you're in Cattle Country U.S.A." I gazed longingly up a dirt road leading to Leslie Gulch; it beckoned. Here sage was frosted with frozen fog. Watercolor landscapes whizzed by my window; white frozen creeks wandered, fringed by brush stroked with ochre, rust, burnt sienna...Cattle Country's cattle looked good. Most ranchers hadn't broken into their haystacks yet, as there was plenty of natural feed left, with warm water springs for stock water.

   We pulled into Jordan Valley where I watched Doug down a slice of black walnut cream pie, baked that morning in the old Basque Inn's kitchen. We motored through painted rocks and down across the sluggish Owyhee at Rome, watching a desert storm rising as we continued our southwesterly course.

   The far-off Steens floated ghost-like above the sage, their white peaks appearing above a layer of purple fog. We made our usual bet on who would spot the first antelope, but none appeared. Soon desert dusk fell and we pulled into McDermitt. After a cup of tea, we hurtled on through the black desert night to the 74-mile distant city of Winnemucca, a cluster of twinkling lights set smack in the middle of the Nevada desert.

   We waited in line with returning college students and weekend fun-seekers for a table at the Red Lion restaurant. The meal was worth the wait, and the bed felt heavenly. The next morning, we were eating breakfast there when we recognized Donna, Chris and their two boys, friends from Hermiston. They were on their way home after visiting relatives in California over the holidays.

   We stopped in Lovelock to gas up, then drove the long straight road leading to infinity, speeding by snow-dusted purple mountains, varied-colored tumble weeds, olive sage, yellowish-white alkali flats, and old abandoned cars, claimed by the desert, taking on desert colors. Sunlight streamed through breaks in dark clouds. The thermometer in our van registered 40 degrees.

   Storm clouds continued to build in the distance over the Sierra, and our radio warned of a winter storm due to hit Donner Summit and Truckee Meadows by nightfall. The traffic's tempo increased...Reno, the biggest little city that's not. High-rise Harrahs, Harold's, and Circus Circus loom over lesser buildings. Today, a breeze blows away the smog.

   Taking the Sacramento exit, we look out at the new subdivisions, clone houses. "NOW RENTING," scream banners tacked over new windows, but the houses are all vacant.

   Where are the people? Where will they find enough water for all these households? If families ever do occupy them, will they lose their identity living in a home exactly like their neighbor's? Bedroom to bedroom, springing up like mushrooms against the sagebrush-sprinkled hills that form the eastern slopes of the Sierra Nevada.

We ate lunch at Boomtown amid a mix of old pioneer relics and modern people up from the valleys of California for a weekend of gambling. Atop every casino gaming stool perched modern humanity in all its forms: obese women, skinny yuppies, Mexican Americans, Orientals, truck drivers, white-haired grandmas, long-haired cowboys—all with a cigarette in one hand and slot machine handle in the other, clinking coins, flashing lights, and buzzing buzzers while silent wooden cowboys stared around them.

After a sandwich with Doug, I escaped to our van to read *Refuge*, a new book by Terry Tempest Williams; my refuge! After satiating his gambling urge, Doug reappeared and we ascended into the mountains, up past Donner Lake into the high Sierra.

Fast-moving storm clouds continued to roll in from the west, and last night's snow lay piled along Interstate 80; 33 degrees at the summit, but warm to us! Man-made snow at Boreal Ridge, skiers waiting in long lift lines to zoom down their favorite runs. Actually, very little snow covered the higher Sierra ramparts. Much more is needed for the snow pack which must supply water for the multitudes below. We voiced our thoughts about the ill-fated Donner Party and how they would surely have made a successful crossing in a winter such as this.

Near Nyack, far below, lay Bear Valley, its mists rising from frozen meadows. We exited at Colfax to visit a remembered antique shop. The proprietors were discussing the big storm coming, hoping it would.

It was sixty degrees when we arrived in Auburn and parked in front of Mary Ann's Riverview Drive home. New grass was greening under the old, and oranges hung on backyard trees. Red Pyracantha berries decorated landscapes everywhere. And amazing orange-red leaves clung to maple trees.

For Sunday morning breakfast I cooked sausage gravy and biscuits, using some sausage we'd brought from home. The expected storm arrived, preceded by a wild wind that flailed the digger pines and made them sing. A gentle, warm rain fell on into the night. Leaving Doug to visit lower Auburn's antique shops, I zoomed over unfamiliar roads with M.A. in her little pickup, to find a once familiar road where, as children, we lived briefly during the late '30s when daddy was herdsman for Cloverton Ranch.

At a corner of that country road we stopped to purchase Granny

Smith apples freshly picked from an adjoining orchard. *Serve yourself*, the sign read, as M.A. weighed apples, leaving money in a coffee can and making change in a coffee pot.

January 6—I walked down the hill, past houses built along Skyridge to Sacramento Street, where my mother lives in an apartment with her husband, Bill, overlooking Auburn's sprawl. Doug drove down later and together we were given a private showing of my 81-year-old mother's watercolor paintings. We were most amazed at her creative and prolific outlet. Her paintings were full of color and expression. After my stepfather left for his exercise class and Doug went up town, mom and I were left to discuss our lives. It was a very special time.

Doug and I returned to M.A.'s by way of Bell Air Market, where we purchased some beef shanks and vegetables to make a good soup. It was fun selecting from such a variety of fresh vegetables: parsnips, parsley, leeks, Chinese cabbage, and celeriac, to go with canned tomatoes in the soup pot. I began typing my column while the shanks simmered.

Took a welcome break from the typewriter to have lunch with Mary Ann in the Old General Store-turned eatery in Auburn. While munching a wonderful salad full of artichoke hearts, eggplant, lettuce, garlicky white beans, and tomatoes, all sprinkled with feta cheese, we got into a deep conversation about our childhood. Soul-searching stuff.

January 7—It rained today, a steady drizzle soaking into the foothills and greening up the grass. After M.A. left for Sierra College, Doug and I chose that day to "do" the antique shops in Roseville, which took all day. I escaped with several books; Robert Service poems, an original edition of Jack London's *Call of the Wild*, a Mormon cookbook, a rolling pin for my collection, and two soup bowls.

Returned home and used a cookbook recipe to prepare a salmon casserole for supper. The rain moved on, the California sun warming us and the landscape.

January 8—The sun rose over the distant blue El Dorado ridge and clear skies prevailed. I took a long morning walk around the neighborhood: west on Riverview, east on Poet Smith, north on Carolyn, west on Sacramento to Maidu. Here I found postcards in a drug store to send to grandchildren in far away Wallowa County whom I miss dreadfully.

Returning on Carolyn, I glimpsed small dogs peering from picture windows; pets left alone all day. No children, no toys in the yard, no laughter or crying…nobody. Roses bloomed; camellias, in lovely shades of pink were opening their buds; frost lay along the shaded sidewalks and a nippy breeze played with my hair. Exercising at 1,000 feet elevation is much less strenuous than 4,000 feet where we live, and I chugged right up the hill in no time.

Since it was such a nice day, Doug and I then drove down to the Mt. Pleasant area, to the old ranch where I was reared. Only, the old ranch isn't, really. It is what I refer to as a ranchette, which the present owner works out to support. We visited with my brother's wife, Joyce, who was watching their small, twin grandsons.

Jim and Joyce have done a great job of maintaining what is left of our old ranch. They run a few cattle, and so far manage to keep ahead of rising property taxes. Down the lane, in the woods, stands the small house daddy and mom lived in at the time of daddy's death. One of Jim and Joyce's twin daughters, Jeanette, lives there now with her husband, Don, and their twin, boys.

Leaving Joyce and the boys, we climb a fence and traipse through dormant star thistle, skirt huge granite rocks covered with moss, and pass grazing cattle to a long meadow that borders Doty's Ravine. Here three black tail deer flee from where they have been nibbling fallen acorns, and disappear behind a low hill.

Along Doty's Ravine, the stream of my youth, Doug pans for gold. Sunlight sifts through ancient black water oaks, a blue jay screeches his warning that we are afoot in his territory, water gurgles from the creek, and Doug's shovel slices into a gravel bar to fill the sluice. I read, perched on a sunny bank, feet dangling above the creek. We eat lunch there, and later, returning to our car, find wild turkey feathers, which tells the story of an encounter with a fox or coon. From the looks of things, the varmit won!

We drive down to where daddy and mom used to live. Doug and his gold pan head for Ditch Creek while I walk through daddy's runaway garden, photographing. His cement creations and out-of-control ivy, pots spilling over with succulents, the cactus garden, a wild area where old plow shares and desert relics compete with desert cactus, varieties so lovingly transplanted from his travels.

Colorful old bottles swing from tree limbs, ivy chokes the trees, and creeping myrtle covers every inch of ground beneath my feet. I have to step high to keep from becoming consumed by the stuff. Old harnesses hang from oak trees. Miner's tools, old buckets, and tea kettles take on grotesque shapes, weathered and consumed by the innards planted there years ago.

Daddy's presence was there; his spirit spoke.

"I live," it said, "in this garden."

I remembered his voice describing the different plants or explaining what each cement sculpture represented—a Greek grotto, the sculpted head of a woman, a perfect round granite rock, carefully balanced and centered in a concrete form. I wondered how many love notes to my mother lay entombed in those cement shrines. Once he had intimated that such existed.

Shafts of sunlight filtered through the jungle, a rain forest, after the rain. Washed of dust, every ivy leaf glistened. I wandered over to the old patio, overgrown with Bermuda grass, past the rock wall and cement table and benches. The weathered Navajo beehive oven was still there where, during our last visit before he died of cancer, he baked my sourdough bread. The oven had been heated with an oak wood fire, then scraped of coals, and the bread carefully placed inside with a long wooden paddle, the door sealed, and the round, golden loaf baked to perfection. How he loved the entire process.

I walked among the cedar, catalpa, and persimmon trees he planted. Clinging to the bare branches of the persimmon were brilliant orange fruits, overripe and partially eaten by the birds; too, there was the mulchy, wonderful compost he'd made and spaded into the shallow granite soil where he raised his wondrous onions and vegetables. Overgrown with weeds, the place is raising twin boys now; no time for a garden. The boys sleep in his bedroom, looking amazingly like him, big and strong, growing up in his dream, just not knowing it yet.

I walked down through the dark oak woods to join Doug, still panning. He had added a few more hard-won grains of yellow stuff to his growing collection. After reading some more, I went for a long walk that led to the other side of the ranch, following Ditch Creek, activated now by the rain, to Wally Allen's old place. A gray squirrel swirled through the woods and up a tree. Wild grape vines, dark and bare, hung in a Tarzan sort of way from the water oaks.

January 13—We have been here in Northern California over a week now, catching up with endless relatives and friends, and seeing new country with every passing day, each so full of adventuresome experiences that time and space limit description.

January 14—Spanish music, black and white cows, clanking stanchions, the rhythmic pulse of milking machines, fresh warm milk, flashing red numbers above each cow, recording pounds of milk. One hundred cows per hour...and only one man! Startch would be in shock. I am.

Doug and I are standing in the milking parlour of the Gnos Brothers modern dairy facility. Ernie, Rose and their partner, who is from Holland, are giving us a tour. A Spanish-American milker pulls a lever that carefully lowers a monitored feed ration into each cow's trough.

Before the cows enter this parlour they must stand under jets of water, which spray their udders clean. The milker then walks up and down this double row of Holstein bovines, eye level with all those teats and massive mammary systems, wiping udders with a paper towel. Again, up and down, "priming" each udder; a squirt from each teat. Then *swup, swup, swup, swup,* on go four teat cups, and the pulsating begins. A quiet *chish, chish* as milk flows like white honey until each cow is stripped dry. In unison, teat cups retreat automatically, like satiated leeches, and fall back into their designated place.

Again, the milker pulls a single lever, and out march the cows, like girls in a chorus line, step to the right, turn to the left, in perfect time to the music.

It is beautiful. Some cows are so relaxed they are actually chewing their cuds. When the parlour is empty, a flood of water comes swooshing down to clean feeders and floor. While this is going on, the next bunch, a curious and closely-knit cluster of first-calf heifers, stares at us. Their expressive faces reflect anticipation of grain and relief from swollen udders as much as the novelty of us.

Six hundred cows, three times a day, one man each shift, around the clock. WOW! Ernie and Rose, you remember, were the friends who appeared at our kitchen door with that huge box of tomatoes, which we made into salsa. We had been invited down to their faun setup near Dixon to spend the night, and take a tour of their 2,000-acre farming operation. The obvious success of such a large enterprise is due, in part, to family cooperation. Even the hired help is treated like family.

We were introduced to Ann, the office secretary, who had been a friend of daughter Ramona and son-in-law Charley when he was employed by the Gnoses several years ago. Then there was Sam, the young man from Holland, whom we had met in Wallowa County. On the office wall hung a large map showing the color-coded location of each field. Each color represented what crop was planted in what field; sugar beets, corn, alfalfa, walnuts, wheat, tomatoes and other agricultural products. Mind boggling, to estimate the amount of food produced here.

We are impressed by the lagoon that stores run-off dairy waste which is, in turn, spread on nearby fields. A lush grass mixture, already knee-deep, will be chopped for silage come spring.

Replacement heifers, looking healthy and clean, were housed in portable wooden pens; we began with baby calves, then progressed to the yearlings, and lastly came to first-calf heifers. As we drove past the maternity pens, three cows were at that moment calving. Each corral has its own run-off gutter, which is flushed daily into the lagoon. When the lagoon becomes too full, it gravity-flows through pipes to another holding area, where it is used to fertilize other crops.

Alfalfa hay for the dairy is raised on the ranch, all part of the partnership arrangement. We returned to Ernie and Rose's spacious, modern home and were treated to a most delectable supper. Ernie, the chef, prepared crab Louie. Fresh shelled crab, piled on a bed of lettuce and garnished with marinated artichoke hearts, asparagus, hard boiled egg slices, tomatoes, lemon, parsley, and red pepper. We crunched San Francisco sourdough french bread, the real stuff, and sipped white wine. It just doesn't get any better than this.

We were joined for supper by Charley's parents, Jack and Charlene Phillips, who also farm nearby. We two grandmas did a lot of picture exchanging of grandchildren and such.

The next morning, before leaving, we treated Rose and Ernie to breakfast in Dixon. We ate at a little family-owned eatery where local farmers gather each morning at a round table to discuss and cuss the weather and the government. Ernie and Rose loaded our car with tangerines and oranges just picked from citrus trees growing ire their patio next to a swimming pool. A short distance down the road Doug stopped to pick some fallen black walnuts. He had in mind me making some ice-box cookies. We also drove by Spice Islands farm where we gazed out on a field of thyme.

We pulled into Rio Vista where "Humphrey" the whale had come swimming up the Sacramento River in that confused voyage of his. Today there is a stone plaque dedicated in his honor near the river. Thick fog enveloped us as we drove slowly through the fertile delta. Every so often, through the gloom, we spied long-legged white egrets standing among the tules. The dark bodies of hundreds of swimming ducks, geese and other waterfowl were visible through the murk.

We could see mile after mile of delta farm land, rice and corn fields... all under water. California might be in a drought situation, but there is water here in the delta. We were heartened to see so many acres of productive agricultural land where, by choice, farmers have held onto their lands and kept developers at bay. But filling the spaces between towns and freeways are the subdivisions... stretching forever and ever.

Still in fog, we arrive in Lodi and pass acres of vineyards. Out in the country we locate the Lauchland vineyards and find Mrs. Lauchland and her sister working in the shop. The women are clipping dead wood off grape vines that will be used for grafting. The variety they are working with is Chardonnay. We have been hearing a lot about this family from our granddaughter Tammy, as she and Matt Lauchland are seeing a lot of each other. Tammy and Matt will both graduate from Cal Poly in June.

Naturally, grandma wanted to meet the family, who proved as delightful as Tammy said they were. They are another family-owned operation where the two sets of grandparents still live on the farm.

Our days are so full. On the way home from Lodi we stop to visit my 83-year-old uncle John, who lives in North Sacramento. So many memories, seeing that old house where grandma raised her seven children. Uncle John, like my mother, is still creating after age 80, composing musical scores for complete productions.

Last Sunday, we drove farther up into the Sierra foothills to where my girlhood chum Sandra and her husband live. They took us on a picnic over near the Oroville Dam. The California sunshine felt so good as we picnicked above the back waters of the Feather River.

We crossed Bullard's Bar, another dam, which holds back the waters of a fork of the Yuba River.

Then it was back to Freddy's "Drunk Duck," which had been roasting slowly in wine, and done to perfection. I'm telling you I don't know how much more of this life we can stand! And I haven't even mentioned our trip to South Lake Tahoe to visit Uncle Marshall and Aunt Billie, nor our visit to the Roseville auction.

January 15—A few clouds in an otherwise clear sky welcomed us this morning. I baked a batch of icebox cookies using some of those black walnuts Doug so patiently cracked with his antique nut cracker. I'd forgotten how good and easy they are to make. After getting my column in the mail, M.A. and I met sister-in-law Nancy for lunch in Auburn. Doug had gone to Doty's Ravine again to continue his gold panning.

M.A. dropped me off after lunch at Lee's Photo on High Street and I walked several blocks, or miles, to my mother's apartment, where I left the portraits I'd taken of her and my stepfather, Bill. Leaving these two young senior citizens to pick out which shot they liked best, I walked back up to Riverview. The jaunt was just what was needed after typing all morning.

January 16—Up to fix sourdough hotcakes, bacon and eggs for Doug, M.A. and me. Have been somewhat neglecting Doug's breakfast on this vacation, and he appreciated having sourdough again. M.A. produced some mineral water to mix with the starter, because city water contains chlorine, which kills the desirable bacterial action in sourdough.

Still in a cooking mood, I mixed up sponge for a loaf of sourdough french bread. Sister Caroline showed up during her lunch hour, so we pigged out on salad and warm-from-the-oven bread, after which we went for a short walk before she returned to work.

I walked down to mom and Bill's to play Scattergory all afternoon. Still in the mood for some creative cooking after, I prepared a hot beef salad for supper, and eggplant, baked slowly with olive oil and garlic cloves, which was then spread on the sourdough bread; fresh persimmon puree over vanilla yogurt and icebox cookies for dessert.

Doug returned from antiquing in Sutter Creek just in time for supper.

January 17—With my youngest sister Kathryn accompanying Doug and me, we left for a planned trip to Bridgeport to visit the old mining town of Bodie. Unfortunately, M.A., who was in charge of logistics and itinerary, wasn't able to join us. Her daughter, Lori, was expecting a new baby, and grandma might be needed at home.

It was cold and raining as we left Auburn, but the rain ceased when we drove up into the Sierra. In no time we were at Incline Village on Lake Tahoe's north shore. We lunched at a place called Mesquite Chicken, where mouth-watering chickens and tri-tip beef roasts revolved on a spit placed over mesquite coals.

Wind-made waves splashed against the rocky shoreline of Tahoe and ribbons of deep turquoise were visible to us from the car. It was snowing lightly as we drove over 7,141-foot Spooner Pass, and breezy gusts soon created a mini-blizzard. We zoomed down into the great Carson Valley and onto dry roads, where we spent some time in Carson City, a bustling Nevada town on the eastern side of the Sierra. Here K. and I discovered the Comstock book store where we spent the better part of an hour going through second-hand books.

Soon we were driving through cattle country that surrounds the small town of Genoa, still set in that big valley. We saw deer and wild geese mixed with cattle and sheep, the habitat of one enhancing the other. At dusk we came to Minden, Nevada, and secured a motel in its sister town, Gardnerville.

The decor at our motel was hot pink, even the outside doors. But inside the lamps were fire engine red and the bedspreads brilliant orange. We ate that evening at the old Hotel Basque restaurant. Never have we been that full! Homemade old country soup, served in a tureen; red wine, the hearty kind; french bread, salad, family-style stew, fried shrimp, potatoes and ice cream. Oh, my!

K. and I went for a walk afterward to shake down that excellent Basque cuisine while Doug checked out the local casino.

January 18—Absolutely clear, cold and beautiful. The snowy mountains rose abruptly from the valley floor in that sparsely settled high-altitude area. It reminded us of home.

We ate breakfast at a friendly little bakery close by before driving south on 395 to Bridgeport, located back in California. High country wandered through Walker Canyon and bordered the wild Walker River. In Bridgeport, a town not much bigger than Imnaha, we found a motel with a view of the snow-crusted mountain; picnicked there and then took off for Bodie.

Just a short way out of town we came to the turnoff that led up a narrow 13-mile winding road to even higher country. Signs read 6,000 feet, 7,000 feet, and at nearly 9,000 feet the pavement ended and we found ourselves on a snow-covered dirt road. And there it was. In the dead of winter, the mining town of Bodie, which in its heyday boasted 10,000 souls.

Nestled among sage, scrub juniper, rabbit brush and rocks, this snowscape resembled pictures of some high Tibetan plateau. On the way up we'd looked behind us to see the awesome crest of the high Sierra, which was now out of sight. Now we were on a tree-less high rolling divide. Bodie, which we had read so much about, slumbered in the January afternoon sunshine in a state of arrested decay. Our car thermometer registered 34 degrees. The air was pure, cold and stimulating.

K. and I got out of the car and walked the final half mile into the abandoned ghost town so we could photograph the clustered buildings from a distance. We ambled over the snowy main street of Bodie, which had been known for its wicked climate and bad men.

On a hill opposite slept the bad men as well as the innocents. We were taken with the old Methodist church, its wooden boards colored by searing summer heat and frigid winter cold. Wood so rich, saturated in clear desert air, flooded with snowlight, took my breath away. My photographer's heart took over. The silence was all-consuming. Clumps of blue sage stuck up through the snow, old windows gleamed, and my camera clicked and clicked.

We wandered on up the street, peering through cracked windows to see dusty furniture, dishes and tools left just as they were by Bodie's inhabitants, who simply walked out. We peered in the windows of an old school with cast iron bell still in the tower, a blackboard with chalk marks on it, wooden desks, a crude wooden globe, hand-carved and faded, and a small torn flag.

An immense metal mining structure loomed on a hillside above the town, housing all the equipment needed to mine the millions of dollars worth of gold extracted from the nearby hills. Other buildings, many of which were about to succumb to time and weather, contained old wagons, homemade wooden skis and all manner of handmade tools and furniture. As planned, we met sister Caroline and her husband Duane walking down the main street of Bodie.

The last frame on my film, taken by another tourist, shows all of us standing on the steps of the old church. That night, back in Bridgeport, we ate beef at the BUM (Bodie Union Mining) Co. restaurant.

It appeared we were the only guests at the motel, if not the town. Sister K. thought we should take advantage of the motel's Jacuzzi. At 7 p.m. it was 16 degrees! We watched the moon through pine boughs and soaked outside under the stars. It was wonderful!

After a quick trip back to our rooms, we slept like babies. The next morning, in a clear and crackling cold six-degrees, we breakfasted on homemade buttermilk pancakes at the only place in town open, then headed for Mono Lake.

January 19—"Whoa!" hollered sister Kathryn. Doug braked the van and we came to a sudden stop. Below us stretched a panorama that took our breath away. Cold air met the warmer brackish waters of Mono Lake and created a fog that floated over the lake. It was like looking down onto piles of soft, velvety clouds. The eastern crest of the Sierra rose magnificently to the south and west; snow-covered, silent, and unpeopled.

Highway 395 descended, curving along the lake shore, then disappeared into the Mono mists. Driving down into that picture post card, we, too, disappeared in fog. At Lee Vining the morning sun burned through enough to show us those mountains, at the foot of which frosted sage glistened in that high altitude air. It was 16 degrees.

Kathryn and I were having a film fit—we were out! At the small town of Lee Vining we were able to purchase some and had our cameras loaded before taking a five-mile, snow-covered road to the lake, where a sign read, South Tufa Towers. Caroline and Duane followed and joined us on our one-mile walk from where our parking place on the lake shore to Tufa Towers. Carbonates of the salty lake water mixed with calcium from fresh-water springs create tufa, or calcium carbonate. Some of these towers of tufa are estimated to be between 200 and 900 years old, forming over many years of springs welling up through the alkaline lake water. At one time Mono was an ancient sea.

Describing the Mono country is hard to do. John Muir did it better: *A country of wonderful contrast, hot deserts bordered by snow-laden mountains, cinders and ashes scattered on glacier-polished pavement, frost and fire working together in the making of beauty.* How true. Perennial snowfields and glaciers at 13,000 feet overlook a dry, sagebrush-covered desert.

The lake covers about 60 square miles and is truly ancient, at more than 700,000 years old. It has no outlet. It is fed by the Eastern Sierran streams, but since 1941 the city of Los Angeles has been diverting four of the seven streams that feed Mono Lake for its domestic water supply. Streams that once provided 65% of the lake's annual water supply now provide 17% of Los Angeles' annual supply. Consequently, Mono Lake has dropped approximately 40 feet and doubled in salinity, and the Tufa Towers can now be seen, which, prior to 1941, were submerged beneath the waters of Mono Lake.

As we walked among the frosted sagebrush, our breath hung in the morning air. Weirdly shaped tufa, eroded and left high and dry, took on ghostly shapes in the lifting fog. It was cold and silent, save for the soft lapping of the water along the alkaline shore. There was an eerie feeling there in the lifting fog, breathing that salty air and seeing Tufa Towers all around. The sage, in yellow bloom, was sweet smelling. Rabbits skittered from rabbit brush to rabbit brush; their droppings littered the snowy trail. As sunlight burned holes in the scene we began snapping pictures until, numb with cold, we retreated to the warmth of our cars.

Back on the road, we lunched at Topaz Lake, on the Nevada border. Caroline, K and I walked down toward the lake and were delighted to see hundreds of quail inhabiting the yards of the lakeside dwellings.

Saying goodbye to Duane and Caroline, we headed north toward Gardnerville, then up over the high Sierra through Luther Pass and down into snow-covered Hope Valley. Climbing up Echo summit we looked back to see Lake Tahoe gleaming in the evening light.

Almost on top, we came to a dead stop. Cars ahead were bumper to bumper clear over the summit. We could imagine the pile-up behind us. After a two-hour stop-and-go delay, we descended two-lane Highway 50 to Pollock Pines where we learned the reason for the delay: so homeward bound skiers could enter the flow of traffic as they exited Sierra Ski Ranch! That's a typical Sunday evening for you in California's recreational areas.

That same highway, remembered from my youth, has changed drastically in 40 years. Back then it was used as a stock driveway for my cousins and other El Dorado County ranchers to trail their cattle to the high Sierra meadows near Meyers.

Remembering the peaceful meadows, with the Truckee River ambling through, is gentler on my mind than what I see now. A golf course and a luxury all-weather lodge are being constructed where I slept in the bunkhouse and where the ranch headquarters used to be. Grazing cattle with Mt. Tallac rising in the background provided a far more peaceful scene than this one in 1992.

Progress!

January 20—M.A.'s daughter Lori hadn't had her baby yet, so M.A., though happy we'd had such a good time, was really sorry she hadn't come with us. To cheer her up, we took her to a place she'd suggested for gold panning and hiking. It was a lovely day and we picnicked in a wild, rolling oak-covered tract of land that for some amazing reason hadn't been "developed."

We took Caroline with us and we three sisters hiked and traversed the bouldered banks of Coon Creek. We heard cow bells, and soon several cows and calves ambled out of the brush to give us curious looks. It was a lovely wild area there along the creek and we explored while Doug panned for gold.

For us sisters, the area was gold in itself, still in the same state most of Placer County was in during our girlhoods. The familiar flora and fauna; live oak, digger pine, decaying logs, cottonwood, granite, birdsong, toyon berry, buckeye, red bud, black-tail deer and the gurgling sounds of Coon Creek singing its song off down the steep canyon, forming pools and natural bathtubs over the ages.

Even the belled cows fit right in. I fell asleep on a flat rock in the warm sunshine and awoke refreshed. Such a perfect day.

Tonight we treated M.A. to Italian cuisine at Pasquales in Auburn. Yum...

January 21—On one side of the morning a yellow moon glows bright in a clear sky, and on the other side a pomegranate sky bleeds into daylight. Smog and fog do create spectacular sunrises.

Today we visited my cousins in White Rock, the Smiths and the Mehrtens, who continue to operate a cattle ranch within a few miles of the cancerous growth of Folsom's subdivisions. It was so good to see all of them. They are through calving already, but haven't seen the sun in 26 days! Nothing but fog and smog.

Tonight an eight-pound girl was born in Sacramento and M.A. welcomed her first granddaughter.

January 22—Tonight we invited my brother Jim and wife Joyce over for supper. I spent all day cooking, using what was on hand in M.A.'s kitchen and what we brought from Oregon. Pomegranate salad, baked squash, sourdough bread, antelope stew, pheasant baked with rice, pumpkin pie, and persimmon pudding with lemon sauce.

Although the menu took most of the day, I managed to squeeze in a final walk with Caroline.

January 23—Twenty-eight degrees and stagnant, foggy and frosty as we packed up and left, turning our eyes northward from Lincoln, following old 99-E to Red Bluff, stopping at fruit stands to purchase dried apricots, peaches and pears.

On past Shasta Lake to Weed. No snow and no fog. Over Siskiyou summit and down into OREGON, to the land of Madrone and evergreen and oak, where we spent the night with our Roseburg friends.

January 24—We "antiqued" our way up the Willamette Valley, taking the back roads to Cottage Grove and on into Salem, stopping to visit daughter Linda and grandson Jordan.

January 26—Arrived in Portland on this Sunday night, to attend the potato conference.

January 27—Seagulls, gray like the rain and the pewter waters of the Columbia River, swoop and glide above the waves as I gaze out the window of our fourth floor room here at the Jantzen Beach Red Lion on Hayden Island, in Portland. Doug is attending meetings of the Oregon Potato Commission held in lower level conference rooms. The 25th annual Oregon Potato Conference's opening session begins at 1 p.m.

Last night we drove into the city and secured a room at a Best Western near Portland Meadows. I am amused at the decor in some of these motel rooms. Paintings that grace the walls seem to have one criteria—to match the bed-spread and drapes. Nothing else matters. Our bedspread and drapes had big splashes of pink, pale yellow and avocado green on them, so the two paintings, expensively framed, were splattered with brush strokes of pink, pale yellow and avocado green. No shape, no suggestion of any subject, just color. They matched.

Then, this morning we walked into a large dining room where a free breakfast buffet was laid out for motel guests. Lovely. Five kinds of coffee, tea, milk, juices, fruit, sweet rolls, bran muffins, five kinds of cold cereal, yogurt. Bowls were clear glass, eight-sided, and I couldn't corral that last bite of Special K and milk! The glasses were four-sided. The tablecloth matched the paintings, the apron on the waitress matched the painting, and everything was in order. Precise.

A pilot from the nearby Portland International Airport walked in, poured himself some Columbian coffee and complained because it was too weak. He didn't match the painting! And neither did I, with my corduroy pants, red plaid Pendleton shirt, and white tenny runners. A mother and daughter walked in wearing jogging suits, their hair still wet from showering. I felt better. Many miles have passed since I last sat at this typewriter, so I'm taking time today to catch up.

January 28—All conference attendees were bused to Timberline Lodge on the south slopes of Mt. Hood for the final banquet. There at 6,000 feet elevation, the snow was piled up outside the windows of that grand old lodge. Built in the 1930s during the Depression, by Civilian Conservation Corps and Works Progress Administration, this work displays the talent of enduring workmanship. Those workers working in a time of no jobs were amateurs who through a labor of love became artists. The sight was worth seeing.

After a gourmet meal "inundated" with potatoes, we boarded buses back to Portland. I could write an entire column on Timberline Lodge, but am running out of space, and I must get us home.

January 31—We arrived home on Prairie Creek to a gale wind and our well pump burned out, and the next day we were without power because of the high wind. What was left of the snow on the ranch quickly melted in the Chinook.

February 11—Each day the mother cows' bellies swell even larger, and udders begin to fill. The first calves have already appeared on the Imnaha and Alder Slope. The mild weather has been ideal for calving, and most days there is the warmth of sunshine for the new babies to doze in. With the exception of morning frosts, our days resemble spring rather than winter.

Soon the men will be readying the equipment needed for shipping seed potatoes. Steve and his crew began sorting some this week. Ben, who faithfully feeds the cattle each day with Steve's help, kept the ranch in good shape during our absence. Like I've so often said, the success of any operation depends on good help, and we are blessed with the best.

A damp, spring-like fog curtains the mountains this morning. Earlier, a sudden Prairie Creek breeze tousled the dark cloud bank forming over the eastern hills. After the wind died down, swirling mists crept in from the lower valleys, curling around our hills and draws in cold silence.

Moving like chilled smoke, the fog now envelops all.

It is a good morning to write. Because the weather has been so warm and sunny, I have been doing a great deal of walking. One day last week I rang up my old chum Scotty, who thinks nothing of walking six miles in a single morning, and asked her to join me on a hike. After throwing together a lunch for our day packs we drove to upper Prairie Creek and left the car at the Irwin's. Friend Linde is visiting her family in Germany.

Scotty and I struck off up a dead-end road toward a timberline mountain meadow, then into the woods. Crunching along snow-crusted trails, we followed the rancher's elk fence until we emerged from the trees onto the ski run road. From there on we left the snow and made a big loop, returning to the car. Six miles, according to Linde, who walked the same route during my absence.

From this road we could see lower Prairie Creek and the eastern hills stretching northward, snowless and quiet. No activity, save for the feeding of cattle. No farming, no tourists, just a great silence over the February land. Sunshine warmed us, but the air was brisk enough to make walking a pleasure.

Stopping at noon alongside the same road that the Appaloosa riders took last spring, we sat down upon two accommodating rocks and ate our lunches. Simple pleasures. In a nearby stubblefield, a large resident population of honkers filled the air with soft gablings. We walked up the lane to Timberline Ranch and paid a brief visit to neighbors Van and Betty Van Blaricom. After settling the world's problems, we hiked the pine-lined gravel road to our car.

Chief Joseph Mountain's snowfields gleamed a blinding white in the mid-day sun as we drove back to the ranch.

February 8—Awoke to hoarfrost on everything. "Fog whiskers" covered weeds, raspberry canes, fence rows and animals. A kettle of beef and vegetable soup simmered all morning on the old Monarch, and most of it was delivered to an ailing friend.

Since our return, I have been baking bread again. My stepfather gave me a delicious whole wheat bread recipe that makes three loaves: one for our friend, one for the freezer, and one for the supper soup.

Behind us, last week, is the yearly income tax bookwork. Hurrah!

One night Doug and I attended a basketball game in Enterprise, where we watched the Savages beat the Prospectors, who traveled all the way from John Day. Before the game we partook of a baked potato feed sponsored by the senior class to raise money for its drug-free graduation party. The potatoes, donated by Tippett potatoes, served with different toppings, were very tasty, especially because Mrs. Tippett didn't have to bake them.

Also, last week, I stopped at the Wallowa County Nursing Home to visit old-timer Cressie Green, who has been in a nursing home in La Grande for some time. Welcome back to Wallowa County, Cressie.

February 9—This evening, I made valentines for all of my grandchildren. Using pictures clipped from magazines and seed catalogs, I fashioned each valentine to fit the personality of the child. In so doing I not only amused myself, but helped defeat the growing commercialism being aimed at Valentine's Day.

After returning from our trip I couldn't wait to have my grandchildren over, so we could pitch the backpack tent I had purchased at an Auburn flea market. We set up camp in our living room and pretended we were in the mountains, and that night we slept in our sleeping bags.

Doug was attending the Washington Potato Conference during most of these goings-on. We made homemade waffles for supper and ate them in our "camp." The next morning, we constructed telephones out of baling twine and tin cans, made willow limb bows and arrows, went for long walks, and generally had a rip-roaring good time.

However, my ordinarily-placid Barred Rock hens were glad to see the children leave. James, especially, is becoming deadly accurate with the willow bow.

February 10—Doug and I and family attended a play put on by the Enterprise High School drama club. Granddaughter Carrie played Little Victoria in the old-fashioned melodrama, "The Shame o Tombstone," which we thoroughly enjoyed. All of the young actresses and actors were perfectly cast and put their hearts and souls into their roles. It was a superb job of acting.

We have experienced some disappointment and sadness since our return, but seeing these high school students with their zest for living has given us a lift. There is nothing like energetic and talented young people to buoy the spirits.

February 12—The angry roar of the wind consumes all of Prairie Creek today. The horses and mule line up, head to tail, enduring these terrific gusts, which are the result of what our weatherman refers to as the Pineapple Express colliding with one from Alaska. Whatever the cause, the effect is rather violent. It is as though spring wants to make an early entrance, but winter won't open the door.

Warm bursts of sunlight stream through my windows onto a potted salmon-colored amaryllis that I am "plant sitting" for an absent friend. Boiling black and blue clouds roll across the prairie sky and the Wallowas are inundated by falling snow.

We leave tomorrow for a brief trip to Jackson, Wyoming, to meet daughter Lori and her husband, Tom.

February 14—We had good roads all the way to Jackson, and storms that painted the horizons black parted to let us through. Our friends Bud and Ruby Zollman traveled with us. It was a relaxing time for them, and gave them a vacation from their hardware store.

On Valentine's Day we pulled into Jackson just ahead of a snow storm, and met Lori and Tom at a motel where they had made our reservations.

February 15—Large feathery flakes of snow sifted quietly down upon the 6,000-foot resort town of Jackson. Muted were the sounds of traffic and the red-green stop lights as we drove to breakfast at a local pancake house. After a pleasant visit with our young family, we walked up and down the boardwalk streets of Jackson, where we spotted an old-time photo shop.

Bud and Doug finally consented to having their photos taken with Ruby and me dressed in those outlandish western outfits. We had a hilarious time squeezing into those old 1800s clothes, which were provided by our petite blond photographer.

Doug donned a coonskin cap and fringed buckskins, and sporting a long-barreled rifle, posed with yours truly, who was attired in the outfit of an early-day dance hall girl. Bud looked wild and woolly in his cowboy garb, and Ruby, along with me, felt positively naughty in feather boas, tight-laced bodices, black mesh stocks, and plumey hats.

We all got into the act and entertained the photographer no end. Lori and Tom, too, were greatly amused at the antics of their elders. While our photos were being processed, we walked to "The Bunnery," where we enjoyed steaming bowls of beef-barley soup, and freshly baked buns.

The sun came out and melted the icicles, which began to *drip, drip, drip* from every roof. After a good laugh over our old-time photos, we drove out to a nearby ranch where the Cutter races were already in progress on a snowy meadow-turned-race track. In past years son-in-law Tom has participated in this event, which attracts 3,000 people.

In two days, 40 teams of fast horses pulling chariots fly down a snow-packed quarter-mile track, heading for the finish line. Enthusiastic bettors lay down their cash, the proceeds of which are donated to the Shriner's Hospital for Crippled Children in Salt Lake City.

Two gutted-up teams of nervous thoroughbreds were prancing and straining at the bit, ready to race, when we arrived. Some of the horses were decked out in brightly colored harness and created quite a contrast against the snow-filled meadow. Rugged mountains rose up all around, and the sight of all those cheering people was one to remember, as the sweaty teams came pounding down the track, snow flying in every direction.

Outriders on a dead run must catch the horses after they cross the finish line and disappear around a bend. At that point, every team is a runaway, before the outriders reach down and grab their bridles to slow them down. Quite often there is a wreck, but thankfully, none while we watched. The sun came out periodically, but everyone was dressed for cold. Pretty exciting stuff!

After the races were over we drove up to Teton Village. Ten miles from the town, this ski resort is tucked at the end of a long valley known as Jackson Hole. We are spectators only at this swanky resort, watching skiers zoom down various mountain runs, clad in the latest skiing fashions, which are very colorful.

Nearby ski shops offer the latest in ski wear, and we guessed that between purchasing lift tickets, eating and lodging there, one would need a pocketful of money. It was interesting to see how the other half lives, and wonder at it all.

Driving out, we looked across to see a lone coyote loping along a long meadow that stopped short of the bustling Teton Village, perhaps hunting for a leftover hot dog discarded by some skier.

Between Teton Village and the town of Jackson lay acres of open space and an occasional ranch. Pleasing to the eye. There were also beginnings of expensive homes being built in that outlying area. Reading an article in the local paper, we understand there is mounting concern about overbuilding, and future emphasis will be given to leaving this space open, and encouraging more ranching.

The article went on to say that the beauty of the area is what attracted people in the first place, and if that attraction is removed by over-development, Jackson Hole will lose its charm.

The entire area is already experiencing monstrous "people" problems: elevated living expenses, and soaring rent and real estate costs. The bulk of the jobs are provided by service industries related to tourism, and those incomes don't allow for high rent or home buying. A lesson could be learned here, and I hope other areas will take heed before they, too, make the same mistakes in the name of promoting or boosting their economies.

We were surprised to see three moose right along the road. In fact, they were walking around a house in deep snow. Their heavy dark winter coats stood out against the whiteness of the landscape.

That evening we experienced Saturday night in Jackson. It was an eye-opener. We feasted on buffalo stew, served in round loaf bread bowls, and watched in amazement as Jackson filled to overflowing with throngs of people.

At 10 p.m. we left for wont of air to breathe. We saw everything, including men in coonskin caps draped in the garb that we had donned for our photos. On the wall I noticed a painting depicting one of the early-day rendezvous in Jackson Hole.

Here, I thought, was Rendezvous 1992. Everyone but us had on hats and boots. We ranchers wore tenny runners! For heaven's sake, mamas, don't let your babies grow up to be Jackson Hole cowboys.

February 16—We wait in line to eat breakfast. More people problems, but the food is worth the wait.

We check out of our motel, give hugs and kisses to our family, and drive out to view the vast Jackson Hole elk herd being fed breakfast, which is hauled out to them by four teams of horses pulling sleds over the preserve.

Hungry coyotes prowl the perimeter of the herd, gnawing on the bones of the young, old and sick, while ravens hang back waiting for the last bites of leftover flesh. The scene is primeval and resembles, in a way, instincts resurfacing in the would-be mountain men we saw roaming around in Jackson Saturday night.

On the way out of the valley, we stop along the Snake River so I can photograph another herd of elk feeding in an open clearing that borders barren hills. We descend the Snake River canyon to frozen Palisades Dam, where ice fishermen dangle lines into their fishing holes.

After a long drive to Boise, where we spend the night, we arise to a warmish morning to continue our journey homeward. Arriving back at the ranch we find a good inch of new snow has fallen.

February 20—Was just returning to the mainstream rhythm of ranch life, grandmotherhood and community, when along came the first winter Fishtrap Writer's conference. Naturally, I had been one of the first to sign up. This meant having to add to an already full daily routine, even more juggling, to create time for this gathering, which kindles my spirit among kindred spirits.

February 21—Quite a day: cloudy and raining, with light winds blowing when it wasn't raining. I was up before dawn to feed the horses, mule, chickens and myself. Doug was out of town, attending a meeting and an auction.

While two loaves of sourdough bread were set to rise, I baked two apple pies and cooked a kettle of beef-vegetable soup. The two youngest grandchildren arrived at 9 a.m. and, between more baking and adding to the soup, we made slingshots, told stories and ate lunch.

In the afternoon I loaded the children in the car, along with the soup, two loaves of bread and one pie. All of the food with the exception of one loaf of sourdough bread was left with an ailing friend. The other loaf was to be donated to the CattleWomen's silent auction that night at Cloverleaf Hall in conjunction with the annual family potluck. I left one of the apple pies at home for Doug.

I amused the children until daughter-in-law Angie returned home from work. Then I dashed home, checked the calving cows, donned boots, and slopped through deep corral mud to feed the young bulls. All of the men were out of town.

A bit breathless, I finally got myself up to Vali's at Wallowa Lake, where Fishtrap was already in progress. After consuming delicious slices of pizza, baked by Mike and served by a smiling Maggie, we regrouped at the nearby Eagle Cap Chalet.

Seated in the new conference room, surrounded by western writers and readers, I finally relaxed, and entered another world, a world in which 45 others and I listened to the soothing written words spoken by the ones who wrote them: Terry Tempest Williams, Kim Stafford and Charles Wilkinson.

Terry evoked tears, Charles made us think, and Kim made our hearts sing. When I reached home, Doug had returned safely with his newly purchased cultivator in the back of the pickup.

February 22—Today began in much the same way, except that by 8 a.m. I was seated in the Eagle Cap Chalet conference room chatting with new acquaintances over Anne Bell's great catered breakfast. Mere written words cannot describe her array of home-baked quiches, breads and jams. Writers need food to fuel their souls, and Anne's lunches and breakfasts provided the necessary food for thought.

Then the sessions began. We weren't just talked to, we were participants and given assignments to write. At one point we were told to go off somewhere for an hour and write. The air was cool, but not unpleasant. I could hear the sounds of the Wallowa River and was drawn to it. After crossing a wooden bridge, I sat down on a damp stump, beside the water, and listened.

This is what I wrote, a short essay entitled "My Song":

The Wallowa waters drew me; they wooed me, and soothed me. The waters filled my senses with the movement of their running, their simple sound of falling, their scent of melting snows and touch of icy coldness.

The waters sang a song of seasons, singing about their birthplace and of their destiny. The river rocks were eroded with water stories, stories that echoed down the ages. They told of snow-filled crevices, roaring avalanches, blinding blizzards, and sterile cold.

One rock, worn smooth by the telling, spoke of rolling thunder, lightning, and flash flood, while others spoke of searing summer heat, topaz skies, shimmering moonlight paths and alpen glow. Some stones remembered red fish brushing against them, and sun-colored leaf shadows moving above them. Every rock spoke of patience.

The water song was composed of memories. High alpine cirques, glistening lakes, seeping bogs, star-dusted meadows, elk wallows. Born in beauty, its gift, beauty. The water's song was my song. We shared the same experiences. My pen writes with water, so my grandchildren's children hear MY SONG.

Listening to and telling stories is an old as time. "We who write in the West have been taught by the west itself," Charles Wilkinson says. "We are part of that, all of us. Western writers are a pretty special group with no professional jealousy, a giving group."

I will expound more in future columns about Fishtrap, including some exciting new ideas with regard to sustaining the West's rural resources, which would include community, people and agriculture.

I leave you with this thought by Terry Tempest Williams:

"Do something that won't compute. Laugh. This is not a time to hate, but to love."

February 24—Life goes on. The phone rings all morning. Everyone wants something of me. It is warm, nearly 50 degrees.

I go for a long walk to burn out the cobwebs, and discover for myself the first buttercups—and five bluebirds, two Hungarian partridges, and a pair of mallards. May our hills always harbor birds. They are as necessary to our landscape as they are to our souls.

February 25—After answering my phone yesterday, a cheerful voice from the other end of the line said, "I saw the first buttercup!"

"All right," said I, who had just returned from a walk over the hills in search of same.

Returning from town this morning, I watched a small brown, furry body brake to a stop in front of my car. The squirrels are out. Then, across the way in a neighboring field on this 50-degree morning, a wet, wobbly newborn calf searched for his first taste of life.

Spring, it would seem, is all but here, except for those of us who have lived through such false alarms and therefore aren't as easily convinced.

The men are sorting our mother cows this morning. The ones closest to calving are put in a pasture handy to the road where the sweep of a floodlight can scan during the night. A hiking friend from Walla Walla, Maryann Deck, who trekked with me to LeGore Lake last year, had given me some tulip bulbs, which I planted in a large blue enamel-ware pan.

Placing dried leaves over the dirt-covered bulbs, I carried them into the bunkhouse to spend the winter. That planter is now next to a sunny window in the living room, where green shoots are fairly leaping up. Soon I will have a blue panful of blooms.

It has been so warm lately that the first crocuses have already appeared along the house, and buds have begun to swell on the young Northwood maples. Along Little Sheep Creek and the Wallowa River, blood courses through the veins of the Red Ochre dogwood.

Due to this late February mildness, all that snow we found upon our return from Jackson Hole is gone, retreated once more to timberline. 'Tis the season of mud; not even enough frost to curb that seasonal malady, which is in itself a sign of spring.

February 26—Glittering frost crystals whiten Prairie Creek this morning, until an unseasonably warm sun breaks over the eastern hill and dissolves them. Nary a cloud mars the deep blue hues of the late February sky.

After walking out our lane to the mailbox to post my column, I begin some long-neglected yard work, raking up winter's refuse, which seems to take refuge on our lawn. Old Jake, the ranch dog, drags all sorts of treasures and deposits them there. Remnants of former roasts, steaks and chops, which nearly fill up the wheelbarrow.

Fierce Prairie Creek winds have pruned the willow trees, whose dead limbs lay strewn among the bones. The raspberry patch prunings, the discarded Christmas tree, and the withered sunflower stalks are hauled off to be burned.

This afternoon Doug and I took a trip to the hills to see how things fared there this winter. Such a contrast to previous Februarys. The rolling, dry grass-covered hills were completely devoid of snow. A faint tinge of green peeked through the old grasses.

Deep silence, broken only by soaring hawks and eagles that swooped down to snatch at the numerous ground squirrels that were scurrying around in search of the first green shoots of spring. If one would, and one should, one could hear the rush of soaring wings. It was that kind of silence.

On a high, partly pine-studded butte, we spotted more than 30 elk grazing. And close to thornbush thickets and aspen trees that clustered in the draws, several mule deer does and their yearling fawns watched us pass.

We drove to the old red barn. It is not red anymore, just weathered and old. The roof has been deteriorating for several years, and that means that one of these winters the old barn will succumb to the elements. Before this is allowed to happen, Doug decided to give friends Pat and Linde the opportunity to tear it down and use any lumber that could be salvaged. Perhaps the old red barn will rise again, in the form of a smoke house, a smaller barn, or any one of the innovative uses these two are capable of creating.

When we arrived, Pat was atop the roof ripping off rafters while wife Linde was pulling nails out of weathered boards and stacking them. A wall tent complete with sheepherder stove and plastic cover was pitched not far from Salmon Creek, which meanders on down the draw between the hills.

"All the comforts of home," says Linde, who invites us to stay for supper. The barn provides scrap fuel for our meal. And Linde and I provide words to fuel the conversation that flows as freely as the waters of Salmon Creek. We haven't seen each other in two months.

We catch up while we prepare supper. I make a salad-in-a-kettle and fry potatoes with onion while Linde grills pork chops and opens a jar of her home-canned green beans, to which she adds bits of bacon, and soon all is sizzling and boiling over the open fire. We season the meal with more conversation, and feast in the open on campfire cookin'.

After we finish with the dishes, the stars pop out, brilliant in the clear nighttime sky. All around we are hemmed in by the hills whose dark outlines are etched above us. We speak of stars, and question why it is that we don't seem to be aware of the wonder of them until an opportunity like this presents itself. Why, when they appear so often, and are always there?

Although Pat and Linde have a new home that they enjoy, they agree there is something satisfying about living out like this, though something hard to define. Perhaps it is the simplicity of it all.

They work hard all day, ripping apart that which early-day home-steaders worked so diligently to build, and in so doing perhaps that pioneer pride rekindles itself in them. We marvel at the sturdiness, endurance and simple beauty of this early carpentry. Built in the early 1900s, these old structures are just now beginning to show the effects of the harsh Eastern Oregon winters and time itself.

We will still refer to this parcel of land as the red barn pasture, and hanging on our wall at home is an oil painting that Doug's brother, Bob, painted from one of my earlier photographs. We also have a watercolor painted by Doug's sister, Barbara, of this same scene.

Pat built up the fire while we talked of Lewis and Clark and how it must have been for their expedition. We know very little about either subject, but wondered out loud about them for some time. Linde told us how they were serenaded each morning at dawn by the coyote choruses.

Driving home in the pickup, all talked out, our silence matched that of the hills, as Doug and I returned to the ranch over the long, winding gravel road. Smelling of campfire smoke, I envied our friends being able to stay lost out there, tucked away among the vastness of the Zumwalt hills.

February 29—I boiled up a panful of eggs, fixed lots of egg salad sandwiches, and soon we rumbled and lurched out to Salmon Creek in the old '64 Chevrolet truck with the dozer loaded on the bed. We ate lunch in the sunshine near Linde's "kitchen," and left the dozer so Pat could pile the leftover rubble. While driving slowly in the old truck, we saw 20 head of mule deer, and rock chuck (marmot) and more raptors.

During the final hours of this Leap Year day, grandson Chad has won the state championship Class 2-A wrestling title in the 168-pound division at Western Oregon State College in Monmouth. Clear across the state. Congratulations, Chad. And all you other Sourdough Shutterbugs, I am proud of every one of your accomplishments.

March 2—Neither lamb nor lion would accurately describe March's appearance yesterday, although it would seem the day leaned more in favor of the lamb here on Prairie Creek. Our cows are really into calving now, and that alone usually triggers a storm, but the most that has happened so far has been a fine drizzle of warm rain.

Last evening a heifer went into labor and it soon became apparent that her calf was entering the world backward and crosswise. After driving her into the calving shed and assessing the situation, Doug hauled the heifer with calf attached into town. He returned some time later with cow and calf detached.

This morning, aside from showing a clipped area across which a neatly stitched incision lies, mom seems content with the world. And baby, a clone of mom, acts as if that was the way all calves come into being. Thank goodness for doctors of veterinary medicine like Dr. Lathrop, who respond even on rainy Sunday nights in March.

March 9—The vibration of my typewriter causes a shower of delicate white sarvisberry petals to fall upon my kitchen table. This wild bouquet, a small handful of sprigs plucked by granddaughter Mona Lee and given to grandma as we hiked the Imnaha canyons together yesterday, brings the memory of it back today.

Here "on top," skies were overcast and cool as neighbors Linde and Pat rode down along Little Sheep Creek with me yesterday to church. As we approached the mouth of Lightning Creek, the sun broke loose and the canyons vibrated with color. Farther down we were gladdened by the sight of fruit trees in full bloom; apricot, peach, plum and brilliant splashes of yellow forsythia.

After church, we drove up to daughter Jackie's and partook of her crock pot beans and sourdough bread, the traveled downriver with grandson Buck and granddaughter Mona Lee for a hike. Leaving the car parked along a dirt rimrock road, we took off on foot to locate an old cave. Buck was our guide. Hidden in the dry bunch grasses, we spied yellow bells and tiny pinkish-white starflowers.

As we climbed the steep canyon hillside, giant white clouds floated in the blue, disappearing only to reappear from behind high rock rims towering overhead. Refreshed by a cool March breeze, we paused to catch our breath and looked down to see the Imnaha flowing north, its course wandering through neatly-kept small ranches, where lambs frolicked and fruit trees blossomed.

Across the river, on the steep grassy slopes, bloomed the sarvisberry. Brush strokes splattered up and down the draws, snow white in sunlight.

We could hear the river sound far below, the waters rushing toward the Snake. On the opposite bank we watched the small tributary of Fence Creek tumble down to mingle with the Imnaha. Several pairs of chukars screeched and whirred downhill away from us. The children laughed and chattered, running free; out of school, out of church, excited with the taste of adventure! As were we.

Presently Buck rounded a bend and disappeared up a small brushy, rock-filled draw. "I found it, come up this way." So we followed, scrambling upward through the humble of rocks to where Buck stood next to a narrow cave entrance. We lit our small candles and one by one crawled on hands and knees until we came to a place where we could stand.

The old mine tunnel was narrow and damp. We marveled at how long it must have taken early miners to dig through the rock with only the crudest of tools. Suddenly the tunnel forked and we took a right turn, which dead-ended. Then we backed up and started down the other dark passage that led far back into the hillside.

Buck described it best: "It was awesome." Mona Lee and I were the first ones out. Thinking of cougars, rattlesnake dens, and hibernating bears, we quickly retreated toward the entrance light.

On the way up I'd picked up several pieces of copper-bearing rock. I surmised that perhaps the early-day miners were searching for copper. Many unanswered questions began forming on our lips. Returning to the small settlement of Imnaha, we stopped to visit 92-year-old Ferm Warnock, who has descended from some of Imnaha's first settlers.

We found him there in his modest house along the river, eager to share what knowledge he had about the mine. It had, indeed, been a copper mining venture, he said, only the copper wasn't of the proper grade and so the mine was abandoned. Amazing was the fact that the miners had had to pack in by way of Trail Creek, and then cross the Imnaha and climb the hillside. No small feat. At that time Trail Creek was the only access to that area.

Ferm, eyes a-twinkle, said he suspected the mine had been salted, and probably the only profit realized from the venture was in the selling of bogus shares to outside investors…A common practice at the time. We so enjoyed our visit with Ferm, who says he has seen many changes occur along the Imnaha, but none so drastic as in the past 30 years.

When asked if he remembered a mild February and March like we are now experiencing, he recalled one, way back, when in May came several feet of snow! Perchance that could happen again?

After reading Roger Pond's recent "Gutter talk" column, I couldn't resist more udder-gutter reminiscing. Having also grown up on a dairy, I can relate to what Roger recalls of his boyhood. Before rural electricity came to our small ranch in the foothills of Northern California, our first milking parlour was simply a part of the hay barn.

Memories here are dim, but the wooden gutter must have been there too. The milk from these cows was separated with a hand separator on the porch, and the cream left in five-gallon cans, wrapped in wet gunny sacks, and placed on a wooden milk stand under an oak tree along the country road for the milk truck to pick up in summer, we hoped, before it got too hot.

Being very young at the time, my clearest memories are of the new grade B dairy facility built later. Cement walls, wooden stanchions and a cement gutter. As Roger says, gutters couldn't accommodate the length of every cow, so consequently most missed. Especially first calf heifers, which were understandably more of a nervous nature than mature matrons.

In addition to being a stripper, which is another story, my job was to wash the barn, to rid walls of splatters that didn't fall into the gutter. After much scrubbing with a stiff brush, the entire barn was hosed down with water so that all of the, 'er, manure ended up in the gutter, which was the last to be flushed out.

This gutter muck conveniently drained into a lower reservoir built to capture irrigation runoff from the permanent pastures that grew above the barn on open hillsides. This was pretty efficient, really, and this stored water, along with the gutter goop, combined to create a nutrient-rich liquid fertilizer that was used to irrigate the flat below. This leveled, checked bottom land produced a variety of forages for our milk-cows.

As our dairy herd grew, so did our family, which included 100 cows and five children. Seventy-five percent of the herd consisted of registered Guernseys, which qualified us to ship Golden Guernsey milk. At that time, a premium was paid for this high butterfat product, as cholesterol was in then.

By this time we were a grade A dairy with DHIA testing and modern, for the '40s and '50s, milk house facility. Mama was in charge of the "dairy work," which meant washing and sterilizing all those buckets and surge milking machine parts. We always knew when things were going smoothly in the barn, as daddy's melodious voice would float out into the open air.

Then again we might hear something akin to what Roger's Earl used to utter over the gutter after being kicked by a first-calf heifer. It never ceased to amaze me that such romantic melodies could emanate from the interior of a milking barn. It must have been the acoustics. They were wonderful!

All during this time daddy was teaching me about cows. I entered every 4-H dairy cattle judging contest I could. Giving oral reasons was my specialty, and I would happily rattle on about level top lines, spring of rib, high wide udder attachments, evenly-spaced teats, levelness between hooks and pins, sharp smooth shoulders, smooth tail heads, dairy character, and mammary systems.

But before this subject gets utterly out of hand, I will close. Fun though, isn't it Roger? The remembering.

March 11—We shipped the first semi-loads of seed potatoes today. I had been concentrating on sleeping arrangements for our impending company when Doug called from the potato cellar in Joseph. One of the workers couldn't be there today; could I come right in? I quickly donned old clothes, put together a lunch, and headed for the cellars.

The day was warm, hot even, and dust from last fall's dry fields still clung to the spuds. All day we stood in line with this moving conveyor belt in front of us, removing damaged seed, seed that was too large to ship, and the occasional rock from the potatoes being loaded into the waiting semi.

Three semis later, covered with dust that lodged in our eyes, noses and hair, still seeing potatoes move past in front of our eyes, we wobbled away to return home. No picnic, simply a job that must be done. I had a hot shower, prepared supper, and was in bed by 7:30 p.m.

March 12—Returned to the housecleaning and cooking for our company, who really did appreciate a home-cooked meal and clean beds after such a long drive. Somewhere during that busy day I attended our monthly CattleWomen's meeting and did some grocery shopping.

March 13—I have spent this morning cooking and baking again, this time for a family moving from a large Nevada ranch to Imnaha, where the father will be employed on a Wallowa County ranch. Just thought it would be a neighborly thing to do, to make them feel welcome after journeying all that way with their three children to a home they had never seen.

In a sense, we still have pioneers in this day and age. Different circumstances, but the same challenge: it is an ongoing struggle for today's cowboys and their families to continue living their unique lifestyle. I'm betting on them. We need them. And real ones are hard to come by.

March 16—The robins are back! And today finally feels like March. Dark rain clouds hover over the purple-white mountains and temperatures have plummeted to the more normal 30s and 40s. The frost has long since left the ground, and things are becoming so dry that I watered the young maple trees yesterday, along with the emerging tulips and blooming crocuses.

March 14—It has been quite a week.

Daughter Lori, her son, Ryan, 41/2, and mother-in-law, Joan, arrived late Thursday evening. Lori had driven out to interview for a postal job in Pendleton and had to be back in Thermopolis Monday morning. After leaving Wyoming, however, Ryan broke out with the chicken pox. By the time they arrived here, he was a sight.

People have been burning dead grass all over the valley, and large smoke plumes rise into the air. Doug torched some dry stuff around the machinery yard yesterday, during those nearly 70-degree temperatures, which always makes me a little nervous.

That Friday the 13th night, around 11:30, a smoldering fire thought to be out, suddenly took off. For some unexplained reason, I had awakened then, and spotted the glow from the window. The blaze, dangerously close to a diesel tank, was quickly extinguished by Doug, whom I awakened from a sound sleep.

Grandson Ryan, who woke up during all the commotion, was running around the house wearing a red plastic fireman's hat over his bright red hair. Added to that was his covering of bright crimson chicken pox spots.

We were able to laugh this morning, but things weren't too funny at the moment it happened. Ryan was still wearing his spots when they all left today.

The cows are shelling out calves right and left, and every time I go for a walk down the road, several more babies have appeared. My two milk cows, however, are not even close to calving. Luckily, we have had a 100% calf crop with no orphans yet, and I hope this luck continues, or I will be feeding bottle babies.

March 17—St. Patrick's Day dawns cloudy and cold, and all the upper Prairie Creek country wears a blanket of March snow. The frosted, forested slopes of the mountains remind us that we still live in a high altitude valley, and spring, although not far off officially, will probably take just as long as it always has.

It rained during the night here, and muddy puddles in the lane are a welcome sight after such a prolonged dry spell.

Remember Blanche Strey, the woman who back in the '30s and '40s wrote a ranch woman's column under the pen name of "Dorcas Jane" for the Wallowa County Chieftain? Well, Blanche and I have continued to keep in touch, and another letter from her appeared in yesterday's mail.

More coincidences: she writes how she enjoyed reading the little essay written while I was attending the Fishtrap Writers' conference at Wallowa Lake. She writes,

When we lived at the Buttes, we did not spend a lot of time at the lake. (As you can well know.) After we sold the ranch, we lived for a week or so in the Strickler cabin, that was in November 1944, and we had some of those golden days that only Wallowa County can dish out.

*And I recall sitting at the water's edge and being wooed even as you.
It has been fun looking up what I wrote then. I don't know the lay of the
land, but a stream flowed by the cabin.*

It just so happens that nearly 50 years later this Blanche (Jane) wandered in front of that same (Strickler) cabin and sat at the water's edge
there, to write of the place. The stream, a fork of the Wallowa River,
heads high among the Eagle Cap snowfields of the Wallowa Wilderness.

Perhaps the waters were singing Blanche Stray's song back then,
and simply retelling it for me. I hope that 50 years hence, yet another
generation can be soothed, and so inspired to keep that song alive.

March 18—Yesterday's St. Patrick's Day storm didn't amount to
much, and our dry, warm weather pattern has resumed, with clear frosty
mornings and nearly 70-degree days...this is highly unusual.

Farmers are out working their fields, leaving dust in the wake of a
variety of harrows being towed by a variety of tractors over the manure-
poxed winter feeding grounds. In complete juxtaposition to our pregnant
cows calving on snowy pastures in the past, this March they sink com-
fortably down upon dry ground, covered with old and new grass, to give
birth amid the mildest conditions we can remember. No chilled, frozen
calves carried in out of a blizzard to thaw out in front of the old Monarch
this year!

Taking my daily walk to check on the cows yesterday, I noticed a
young cow lying prone on the grass, apparently in the final stages of her
labor. Presently, thinking it was all over, she rose to her feet; whereupon
the slippery calf dangled downward, its head nearly touching the ground.
Then suddenly mom whirled around to take a look at the result of her
labor when...*splosh, thunk!* Welcome to the world.

By the time I returned from my walk, the "dumped" calf, licked by
its mother's tongue, was standing on all fours and nursing. A cow's life
is so simple.

At times, it seems, our lives become so entangled with those of our
families and friends, it is as though life itself is acted out upon a large
stage and we are all actors. However, no playwright could ever come up
with a script to equal some of these real-life dramas.

Some comedy, some tragedy; all part of real life experiences, which
must be, inevitably, dealt with as best we can. It is therefore necessary, in
order to cope with these complexities of modern life, to escape to where
it is quiet, where one can perhaps talk to a friend and sort everything
out in an atmosphere conducive to clear thinking, until some semblance
of order is restored.

The West Fork of the Wallowa River flows past the Strickler cabin.

March 20—Today, on the first day of spring, the day of the equinox (Latin for "equal nights"), the day when, everywhere on earth, days and nights are of equal length, Linde and I dropped everything and celebrated the day for what it was. As if we needed an excuse.

The morning sun radiated an unseasonable warmth and soon melted the early frost. After packing my day pack with some huckleberry scones I'd risen earlier to bake, along with some leftover fried chicken, Linde and I were off to Alder Slope.

Leaving our car parked at a friend's place, we were soon hiking up toward the timbered slopes that flank Ruby Peak. We shed our jackets on an open slope, leaving them hanging over a fence to retrieve on our return. The Seven Devils mountain range was visible to the east, the town of Enterprise sprawled below, and above towered the snowy Wallowas. From our high field we could see the moraine of Wallowa Lake. The rolling hill country, just beginning to green, stretched seemingly to the northern horizon.

Brightened by the sun spilling upon them, waxy yellow buttercups bloomed profusely in moist, open clearings. It was strange not seeing any snow at that elevation, but the ground was still damp under the tamarack needles, although the trees looked like they could use more rain soon. The birds were happy, and the flash of bright blue as a Western bluebird winged its way into the woods made us happy too. All our cares began to slip away. The exertion of climbing the gradual, steep slopes made us feel alive as only outdoor exercise can. It was a perfect day, with only a hint of a breeze to cool us now and then.

We came upon a large elk track, fresh in the damp trail. No doubt we'd spooked him out ahead of us with our noisy approach. We caught a fleeting glimpse of six mule deer threading their way through the thick stands of timber. The snowy summit of Ruby Peak, which loomed close but yet so far, tempted us.

We wandered aimlessly, heading in a northerly direction, until we became curious as to our whereabouts. Simply by going downhill we eventually came upon the fringes of civilization, where we located the upper Alder Slope irrigation ditch that led us back to our jackets.

Feeling enormously refreshed, and pleasantly tired, we ate lunch with our friend, then returned to the 1992 rat race.

March 30—It was with a new-found awareness that I hung my wash out on the clothesline this morning. This ordinary, necessary, timeless task performed down through the ages by women has been elevated to an art form. As a matter of fact, the entire subject of laundry has opened

Clotheslines provide an interesting subject for the photographer. This photo was taken several years ago at Red's Horse Ranch, a wilderness dude ranch on the Minam River.

up unlimited creative possibilities. Therefore, I would like to share this revelation with others who might have their spirits lifted when they realize all along they have been artists.

This new awareness came about after friend Linde and I attended a program presented by folklorist Joanne Mulcahy, who talked to us about "The aesthetics of women's everyday lives," made possible by the Oregon Council for the Humanities and our Wallowa Valley Arts Council.

After introducing herself, she showed us the documentary film "Clotheslines." The title alone was fascinating. So it was with rapt attention that a small group of Wallowa County women viewed this 30-minute film, and as we became lost in the story, our own stories began to surface.

From the small TV screen, clothes flapped on clotheslines that were strung all over the world, accompanied by women's conversations. Words tossed in the breezes of time. Lines of words. Laundered words that connected us to the scrub board and the wringer washing machine and the flat stone at the river's edge.

The photography was creative, and the conversations of women that accompanied the clothesline images evoked a wide range of emotions. Lives themselves were aired in the sun and the wind. Every woman's personal statement was clothes-pinned to her line.

When the film ended, Joanne asked if the group had any interesting stores to tell about their own "clotheslines." And then the fun began. Like many other women in that pre-electricity era, Hope told of scrubbing clothes on a wash board.

After the birth of her son Erl, she said, her husband, Harold, bought her one of those noisy, gas-powered, motor-driven washing machines. Hope would put a load of laundry in and Harold would step on the starter of the cumbersome motor, which would roar to life and begin the agitating...Until Harold was out of sight, at which time the motor invariably died. Hope could never get the thing going again, and time after time, she told of having to remove the dripping soapy clothes from her new washer and revert once more to the scrub board.

One day Hope had had it! Taking out all her long pent-up frustrations on that scrub board, she beat it to death and threw the splintered remains where her husband couldn't help but notice. Apparently this strategy worked because, after that, Hope's husband stayed close by on wash days. Hope, a folk artist in her own right, sews lovely patchwork quilts and weaves rugs in addition to being a farm wife on Alder Slope.

It was clear and sunny when I hung out my wash this morning. A robin, searching for nest-building material, watched me from the yard fence. Out in the hay field behind the house, "Spread with Ed" Jones' fertilizer crew is fertilizing; Ben arrives to feed the cows and I have already finished my chores early, so I can steal time at the typewriter.

In addition to haying the horses, mule, and two milk cows, and tending the chickens, I have been this past week feeding two orphan calves bottles of milk replacer night and morning.

Now, as I type, large thunderheads fill the sky and my wash is threatened. My artfully-hung shirts, socks, towels and jeans must be brought in and thrown in an unsightly heap on the bed. But there is hope. These objects of art must be folded and tucked neatly in drawers. I began thinking about other "ranch wifely" tasks in a more creative light.

What about the loaf of sourdough bread I just took out of the oven, or splitting kindling, starting a fire in the Monarch, butchering chickens, and raising calves and lambs? What about growing flowers and vegetables and raising kids? Perhaps as our society of instant this and instant that progresses, or digresses (whichever way you look at it), these tasks of the past will one day all be considered folk art.

I remember, as a very young bride, bending over the bathtub, washing sheets. We didn't have a washing machine, or even a wash tub, and the kitchen sink was too small for sheets. I remember how heavy those dripping wet clothes were to carry out to the clothesline. Then, when I finally got a wringer washer, how wonderful it was. The nearest town was 60 miles away, and I couldn't drive, so laundromats were non-existent in my case.

I loved those wringer washers. There was something satisfying about letting the clothes agitate as long as you wanted; the grimy work clothes seemed to come out cleaner, somehow. There was an art to putting the different shaped clothes through the wringer. One learned by trial and error. The novelty wore off when, four children later, I began to think my sole function in life was washing, hanging out, bringing in, folding and putting away all of our clothes. Sometimes my mind would reel with miles and miles of diapers blowing in the wind. Stacks and stacks of them being folded.

After the children grew up and moved out, I began to enjoy laundry again. Being out in the open air, hanging up clothes. Even though today we have a dryer, I hardly ever use it, preferring to hang clothes in back of the wood stove on rainy days or during a snow storm.

That documentary film "Clotheslines" has inspired these lines. Lines hung with women's stories, as well as laundry. Next time you hang out the wash, do so with pride. This thankless task is finally being recognized.

April 1—Lofty blue ridges, only faintly visible through veils of snowy mists, separate themselves in ever-changing hues as cold snow squalls swirl over the Wallowas. It would seem our high, mountain valley has returned, at least somewhat, to normal.

April 2—Perched high on the limbs of ancient willows that grow in our bull pasture, a pair of Barred owls *hoo-hoo*-ed into the April Fool's night. Often these owls predict a weather change; snowy weather usually. But today dawned bright and clear, with only a touch of frost along the bottoms.

By mid-morning it was actually hot again, so I let the fire go out in the old Monarch and opened all the doors and windows to air the house out. I even got carried away enough to sweep, mop and wax floors. After helping load a semi of seed potatoes, Doug spent the rest of the day repairing fence on our summer range. A happy meadowlark sang to me all the day long.

Since Doug didn't return until dark, I walked along our country road picking up trash thrown out by passersby. It's amazing what some people throw away.

April 3—Clouds formed by afternoon and "whiskers" appeared on the mountains. Maybe the owls were right after all.

We invited neighbors Linde and Pat over for supper, and later we couldn't believe our ears—the sound of rain on the roof!

April 4—The rain turned to snow overnight, and by morning all of upper Prairie Creek and Ferguson Ridge was covered with snow again. A branding we'd planned to attend at Imnaha was canceled, Doug was off to a farm equipment auction in Walla Walla, and Linde's husband, Pat, left for a search and rescue survival training campout. There was only one thing for Linde and me to do: go for a hike.

Deciding there was no better time than the present to do a little exploring, and since the mountains lay under a blanket of fresh snow, we turned toward the warmer climes of the Imnaha canyon country. Hiking in the canyons is an adventure in itself. One never knows what will turn up. We had in mind searching for and then researching two early homestead sites.

The coolness of the day kept the rattlesnakes hidden and refreshed us as we negotiated that steep terrain. We found the first yellow bells all along the deer and cattle trails, and hot pink Bird-bills, which were called Johnny-Jump-ups where I grew up. The previous night's rain had freshened up these wildings and greened the bunch grasses and dampened the dusty trails.

Large clouds cast moving shadows across the greening canyons. A perfect day to be out. We stumbled onto an old weathered cabin, falling in on itself, located in a secluded draw. A small sheepherder stove, rusting away, lay among the remnants of old bedsprings and ornate bed posts. Rotting horse harness stuck up out of the ground. All of these things painted a picture of hardship and struggle.

Another cabin, which has haunted me for years, lay a considerable distance uphill from Little Sheep Creek. Searching for but not finding a place to cross, we decided to wade the creek.

So, rolling up our jeans and carrying our shoes and socks, we struck out across the swiftly flowing, icy-cold snow-melt stream toward the opposite shore. We had come hunting adventure, and we were getting it.

Our feet turned numb with cold, and we were barely able to keep our balance on those slippery rocks, but we made it. Not wanting to bother with the putting on and taking off my hiking boots again, I opted to climb the hill barefoot. Not bad at all. The ground, damp from the rain, felt good to my cold feet, and the exertion of climbing warmed them up again. The effort was worth the agony of de-feet, and we were able to find out more fascinating history of the place.

It seems the homesteader had built his cabin at the farthest corner of his 160 acres, which was also the closest to the creek. In my mind's eye, I could picture him hauling two 5-gallon milk cans of water from the creek on his pack mule up that steep hill to his cabin.

What the cabin lacked in conveniences, it made up for in its magnificent view. The canyons continued down along the meandering course of Little Sheep Creek, which wound its quiet way through a spring-green meadow. Wildflowers bloomed profusely near the cabin, and tall ponderosa pines grew overhead and below. Besides the creek, the only sound was birdsong. The homesteader probably never got rich, but then, he didn't have to, he was already rich, in a sense.

These things we pondered as we looked around, seeing through the eyes of that early homesteader. After fording the stream again we dried our cold, wet feet with our socks, donned hiking boots, and headed down the road anticipating further adventure. Turning into Bear Gulch we visited with the Moore brothers, who live there, where the small creek that flows out of Bear Gulch joins Little Sheep Creek.

Nearby we had noticed several beavers working on the alders and aspen growing along the creek banks. The sun came out as we struck off up the gulch, following the remains of an old wagon road, which now alternates between a road and a trail. This old road once connected the Divide country with the Imnaha.

As it was past noon, we decided to select a suitable sunny spot to eat our lunches. We hadn't walked very far when we came to a small feeding ground for a bunch of first-calf heifers. Forming a half circle around the log we sat on, a collection of contented, cud-chewing cows with calves curiously cogitated and contemplated us. Holy cow!

Leaving the ranch behind, we followed the splashing, happy creek, opening and closing three gates, and climbing higher toward the Divide. The fresh scent of new leaves on cottonwood and alder smelled of spring. High up, under wonderful rock formations, glowed golden clusters of the sunflower-like blooms of the balsamroot plant.

On a bench above a seeping spring, we spied a patch of purple-blue larkspur. In a stagnant pool, we watched mud puppies (salamanders) and knew myriad microscopic life teemed there, though we couldn't see it. We crossed and re-crossed the creek, which varied in width due to numerous springs that fed into it. A sudden breeze came up and the clouds overhead thickened.

It was late afternoon and the sun had already disappeared over a high rim, when we turned around and headed back down the gulch. We caught up with the sun again and marveled at the sight of those last rays of an April day filtering through the gauzy green of new-leaved cottonwood and alder.

Figuring we had hiked more than 12 miles, including our homestead hunting, we drove out "on top" and looked down upon the snowy Wallowas. Returning to our ranch on Prairie Creek, Linde started up the big John Deere and I fed bales of hay to the calving cows. Then we grained and fed the bulls hay before Linde left for home.

After hauling 10 gallons of water to an ailing cow in the field, haying the horses and mule, and feeding the orphan calf his bottle, I was ready for a hot bath. Doug returned, happy with his purchases at the auction in Walla Walla, and happy that the chores were done.

And now, as I type, Prairie Creek is covered with a good three inches of snow—good wet snow that will add much-needed moisture to the ground—and April is back to where it should be.

April 5—We set our clocks ahead and at dawn arose to see the ground covered with snow. Spring snow, which quickly melted under the warmth of a spring sun. The morning continued unsettled as we finished our chores and left with friends to attend a country estate auction up the South Fork of the Lostine River.

By the time we arrived, throngs of Wallowa Countians had already converged on the old Wynans place, which is also a trout farm. The people were colorful, the setting was colorful, and the weather matched. The auctioneer was into his sing-song chant, standing outside next to a row of garden tools that leaned against the weathered boards of an old barn.

"Choice 'em for $5," said the auctioneer, and people went up, as they had bid, and picked out an ax here, a shovel there, until all the tools were gone. Looking south up the Lostine canyon into the mountains, we could watch the little blizzards being born, and knew it was only a matter of time when gusty winds would carry them down to us.

The auctioneer moved quickly through piles and rows of "stuff" that had been accumulated for years. Today it would be shifted around and mixed with the neighbors' growing accumulations.

People do this every spring, this "junk shift," moving treasures from farm to farm and house to house. No doubt some of these same items will be unearthed from the dusty interiors of old barns and house closets to be sold at future estate auctions. But it's so fun.

Doug decided he couldn't live without an old horse-drawn potato planter, and then he and Arleigh Isley made a "deal" over two sets of tire chains. Included in the deal was that Arleigh would haul home a pine captain's bed that I purchased for grandson Bart. Cardboard boxes overflowed with dusty pocket westerns, canning jars, and assorted kitchen utensils.

Neighbor Pat had the winning bid on two old lanterns with red glass mantels. Arleigh's wife, Glenna, got her three oak chairs, and gradually the accumulated wares were carted off. Only the hardy remained after a sudden gust of wind, mixed with fine feathery flakes of snow, spilled down out of the Wallowas and engulfed us.

We pulled our collars up under our chins, but soon forgot the weather when the irresistible aroma of frying onions and hamburgers assailed us. We perched on an old trunk and savored the simple fare, and watched as the bidding continued into the afternoon.

April 13—Out north, in the direction of our hill range, a curtain of deep purple has drawn across the afternoon sky. Scattered April showers have been wetting Prairie Creek between interludes of warm-winded sunlight. Every shower, and every hour that advances toward May, transforms the land.

The magic time is here! The green is deepening and spreading. The meandering courses of creeks are colored pale, willow green, and the lawn is in need of mowing. Pairs of mallard ducks and wild honkers fly overhead at dawn; Hungarian partridge and pheasants hide out their nests in tall, dead grass and brush. The rhubarb pushes its red curly leaves through the dried horse manure, and the chives have been snipped off more than once for a salad.

My red tulips, recovered now from the snow, have just begun to open alongside the house. On the hills just east of us, pale, pink grass widows wave in the breeze. I went for a walk among them yesterday. Through the din of bawling cows and calves I can hear the creaking of a metal gate, as the fall calves are separated from their mammas. Tomorrow morning, early, Mike McFetridge and I will begin trailing the cows to the hills. A two-day drive.

This afternoon I take frequent walks down to the corrals to shout various messages from potato growers and truck drivers, over the bawling of cattle, to my husband. Who, in turn, must make frequent trips back to the phone to coordinate three loads of seed potatoes that will be shipped tomorrow.

Between typing this column, I am cooking a beef-vegetable soup that can be warmed up for tomorrow night's supper. After 17 miles and eight hours in the saddle, I won't feel much like cooking. Pork chops tonight and then I must attend the annual meeting of the Alder Slope Pipeline Association. In addition to water business it is a chance to visit my Alder Slope neighbors.

April 15—Back at the typewriter again, after surviving the trailing of our cows to the hills. Each year my bones protest louder, but how can I complain, when riding next to me is 85-year-old hand Mike McFetridge? Who never complains.

Wishing I hadn't eaten any of that blackberry cobbler I baked last week, I climbed aboard my faithful mare for the first time since last fall. Those few added pounds do make a difference. Once in the saddle, it felt good; that is, until around 2 p.m. when I was wishing for a break.

Ben and Doug, on Hondas, helped us drive the cows away from their calves. Ben stayed with us until we left the valley and began the long drive out the Crow Creek road. Aside from a few anxious moments when two full-uddered cows made a dash back toward the ranch in search of their calves, we proceeded without incident to the "pink barn" at the old Dorrance place, where the cows were corraled for the night.

We didn't push them, just let them drift and graze the new shoots of green grass alongside the road and water up when there was some to drink. The last of the buttercups bloomed among the grass widows. Hawks hunting ground squirrels were everywhere, and the meadowlarks and other birds sang to us. It even forgot to snow as we climbed up and over Crow Creek Pass. Mike and I remembered last year, when wind driven snow plastered our eyelashes shut.

About halfway the cows ceased their bawling and trying to turn back, and seemed to focus their attentions on the succulent bunch grass pastures they would soon be grazing.

"The calves will wean good," said Mike. "The sign is right."

Ranchers hereabouts castrate and wean their calves by the sign of the zodiac, as given in the Old Farmer's Almanac. Ben was waiting for us in the truck as the last of the cows trailed into the corral. Mike and I read the unspoken look in each other's eyes. We had made it, one more time.

April 16—This morning Mike and I returned to the cows, climbed stiffly up into the saddle, and trailed the cows up Dorrance gulch and on out past where the old Dry Salmon Creek school house used to stand. Dry Salmon was wet, and that dark purple cloud I mentioned earlier appears to have dumped its contents over the Zumwalt hills overnight

The crisp, clear morning was perfect for trailing cows. You could see forever over the rolling bunch grass hills. Arrowleaf balsamroot and cous (biscuitroot) sprinkled the area with golden blooms. Beyond the Pine Creek road, we split the herd: 61 to the Johnson pasture and 62 we drove to Butte Creek.

Looking back, we could see the crest of the snowy Wallowas and watch new storm clouds form. Ben, who had been hauling salt to both places, was there to haul us and our horses home. The count was right.

"We didn't lose any cows," joked Mike. And now I type while sitting on a soft pillow, and my column will be a day past the deadline. Spring is definitely here.

April 17—Today dawned cold and windy. While snow clouds emptied their contents over the mountains, rain and sleet fell here on Prairie Creek. Throughout the day, our faithful and hardy potato crew, working outside under those miserable conditions, hung in there and filled four more semis.

The two youngest grandchildren arrived this morning to color Easter eggs. At first the eggs emerged from their small cups of dye decorated with pretty pastel colors, until James became more creative and began mixing several colors until only brown and black eggs resulted.

By late afternoon the sun pierced those dark rain clouds, and our "resident rainbow" arched over Hough's field before quietly fading into the air. The children fed the little twin his bottle of milk replacer and named him Buster.

Returning from taking the children home, I found son-in-law Tom here. He and his family are moving from Thermopolis, Wyoming, to Pendleton, Oregon, after the first of May. Tom had supper with us and, after breakfast the next morning, he was on his way back to Wyoming.

The snowline was midway on the mountains again when Tom left.

April 18—Our crew loaded four more semis of potato seed on this Saturday, and the Chief Joseph Days court riding trials took place at the Harley Tucker Memorial arena. Cold or no, the show must go on, along with the work.

High wind gusts blew wheel lines over fences and sapped moisture brought by recent rains.

Doug and I attended the 11th annual Queen's Coronation dinner at the Joseph Civic Center. This popular event draws more people every year, and becomes even more elaborate. The three court members were nervous because a new queen would be crowned later in the evening.

After a hardy dinner that featured baron of beef, Dave Yost, president of the Joseph Chamber, introduced master of ceremonies Butch Knowles, of Heppner. Butch is a past winner of the Harley Tucker Memorial Award, a champion saddle bronc rider in the Columbia River Circuit, and a sports commentator for ESPN on television.

And guess who received the honor of being chosen grand marshal for the grand parade during the 1992 Chief Joseph Days? None other than our old hand and friend Mike McFetridge. He received a standing ovation as he made his way to the stage for the presentation; then told how in 1946 he helped build the bucking chutes for the first rodeos, which were the forerunners of the first Chief Joseph Days rodeos, Those early rodeos were held in a natural bowl, high between the two east moraines of Wallowa Lake. Today the last of the old chutes are crumbling away.

Butch related the following story about Mike: Not long ago Mike was riding his horse along some back country Wallowa County road when a friend passing through the cattle Mike was driving stopped to chat a spell.

"Do you know what you're doing?" asked the friend.

"No," replied Mike. "But my dog does!"

Born on Elk Mountain in 1908, Mike has outlived all of his many former employers, Doug's father included. Modest, as always, about his long cowboy career, he said much of the ongoing success of Chief Joseph Days should go to Dave and Darlene Turner, who, he said, "Have stuck with the event all down through the years."

When Henry Kinsley's local country-western band began to play, Mike was one of the first ones on his feet, swinging his daughter-in-law around the dance floor. A surprised Jessica Olsen, 17, of Enterprise, was crowned queen of the 1992 Chief Joseph Days, and her court princesses, Kristal Botts, of Joseph, and Jodi Bacon, of Lost Prairie, smothered her with happy hugs.

April 19—Easter Sunday—Up early to feed all my critters so I could attend the Joseph Methodist Church sunrise service and cantata at 7 a.m. The sun rose over the eastern hills into a clear sky and soon melted the frosty valley. Pale cloud shadows slid silently over the face of Chief Joseph's snowfields as I drove to town.

Inside the old church the morning sunshine streamed through stained glass windows and created a golden glow among the wooden pews and altar. Blooming white Easter lilies brightened the stage. Every seat was taken and extra chairs had been placed at the end of each pew. Members of the cantata filed down the center aisle, took their places up front, and began to sing.

The early-morning sunglow, diffused by the lovely stained glass, shone now upon the faces of the singers, who raised their voices in the songs of "Calvary's Love." I recognized many familiar faces among the singers: neighbors, town mayor, Imnaha school teacher, my daughter and her husband. I smiled at my two grandchildren across from me.

Driving back to the ranch, I felt a wonderful feeling of community.

Bouquets were heaped on Chief Joseph Days Princesses Kristal Botts and Jodi Bacon, and Queen Jessica Olsen, at the coronation dinner-dance.

Seeing those wondrous Wallowas so close, looming above this church that is more than 100 years old, and all the people streaming out into the sun to go about their Easter Sunday get-togethers made me feel again how lucky we are to live in such a place.

That wonderful, special Easter service won't make the headlines in any newspaper, but I'll write about it because it proves the world isn't all doom and gloom, and as long as a few people are willing to donate their time and energies toward producing such a cantata as we witnessed that day, there is hope.

Returning to my kitchen, I made a fresh strawberry topping for a cheesecake I'd baked yesterday for granddaughter Carrie's 15th birthday. A ham that had been baking in the oven all morning filled the house with Easter smells. After Doug and Steve finished feeding the cattle, we headed to Imnaha and drove up Camp Creek, where we joined our large family for an Easter picnic.

After gorging ourselves on ham, turkey, salads, deviled eggs, beans and sourdough bread, we had the birthday cake, followed by an Easter egg hunt. Then all the rest of the long afternoon we got into a baseball game on the flat alongside the creek. Young and old alike, everyone had a turn in the batter's box (a plastic feed sack) and in the field. When the ball landed in the creek, everyone joined in the search.

Horses and cattle grazed nearby, and the greening rimrock canyons soared above it all. The day couldn't have been more wonderful. Weary children clutching crushed colored eggs and melting chocolate bunnies were loaded into cars and, except for the canyon family, returned to their homes "on top."

I remembered to deliver my photograph to the Joseph Civic Center before 6 p.m., as the Wallowa Valley Festival of the Arts begins Friday evening.

Home to feed the calf and gather eggs while Doug does the evening feeding. Tomorrow our crew will load four more semis of seed and, as usual, the busy spring week will slip quickly into history. But for one day we did take the time to savor the lilacs that drenched the canyons with their sweet, purple fragrance.

April 20—What a week this last has been! After moving the fall-calving cows to the hills and recovering from two days in the saddle, I finally got around to mowing our lawn. And, after drooping under a heavy frost for several mornings in a row, my bright red tulips have finally burst into bloom.

Four semi-loads of seed potatoes have been leaving our cellars on a daily basis, and the weaned fall calves have ceased their bawling. Bull buyers arrive to look at or purchase our bulls, and I am constantly kept busy on the phone relaying messages to Doug at the cellar.

April 23—Our porch thermometer registered 20 degrees. Everything was frozen. There was ice in the hoses, ice on the chickens' water, the tulips went limp, and the apple blossoms, ready to open, didn't. Then along came a dry, warm wind that took what moisture there was with it.

After spending the morning attempting to reduce the size of my "letters to be answered" pile, I mowed the lawn. Later that afternoon, I drove into Enterprise to pick up granddaughter Carrie, who had stayed after school for drama practice. That way I could watch some of the rehearsal of "Pirates of Penzance," a musical production in which Carrie plays a leading female role and grandson Chad is cast as the pirate king.

I was so impressed with all of the students. What talent! What fun! And what work. These dedicated young people manage to juggle school, sports, FFA, 4-H and homework and find time to practice this musical. I learned that they sometimes practice at 6:30 in the morning or until 9 p.m. These young actors are very fortunate to have instructors who inspire and encourage them to their finest efforts.

Watching my grandchildren there, I remembered when these two were born, one 18 years ago and the other 15. Both have April 18th

Cows and calves breakfast on hay on the Tippett ranch. Beyond Prairie Creek can be seen the moraine of Wallowa Lake, and the Wallowa Mountains.

birthdays. How swiftly time passes. One of the real joys of living has to be watching one's grandchildren grow into such fine young people. Every one of them is a plum in my bonnet.

Doug says I'm just another one of those SOGWPOGIP (silly old grandmas with pictures of grandchildren in purse).

April 24—We woke to a clear, frosty 25-degree morning. Frost and lack of rain will not make grass grow, and in the cattle business grass is priority. After a busy day for both of us, Doug and I actually got our work done in time to attend the artists' reception of the Wallowa Valley Festival of Arts.

As in past years, a large crowd gathered to view the art, which was artfully displayed and allowed everyone to walk among sculptures, paintings, photography, pine needle baskets, blown glass and fibre arts. In addition to many local artists, there were entries from all over the Northwest.

Earlier I had put together a fruit tray to add to the finger food table. We nibbled tasty tidbits, listened to live music, and visited friends while we viewed the art. Doug didn't know if he could handle that much "culture" in one night.

Alice Warnock, rancher's wife from Baker City, was there with her brushes and watercolors to create a whimsical pig during the quick draw contest. Each participant had just one hour to complete a piece of work, after which a silent auction was held to sell the work just completed.

Alice also won an award on her lovely watercolor painting of Holly Hocks. At an age when many women retire to the armchair, Alice is becoming an accomplished artist. Which reminds me of another artist, my 81-year-old mother, who just recently had a private showing of her watercolors in Auburn, California.

At 9 p.m. the awards were announced by the judge. As in the past, I was amazed at the amount of local talent. Artists continue to come out of the woods and canyons and valleys. Living here must inspire and make artists out of us all.

April 25—Doug saddled up his gelding and drove down to a branding at Imnaha, while I went another direction to take grandchildren on a promised fishing venture. Trout season in ponds and lakes opened this morning. After feeding a pail of night crawlers to the fish, losing several hooks, eating a picnic, and getting our feet good and wet, we managed not to catch a single fish.

Fishing, defined by different people in different ways, is a state of mind. Personally, I count the day successful without any fish. Just being there, next to a mountain lake or a pond with children is enough. They never have any trouble amusing themselves while I untangle lines, tie on hooks, or photograph.

This evening I treated granddaughter Chelsie and her friend Analise to dinner at Vali's Alpine Delicatessen at Wallowa Lake. This promised birthday treat for Chelsie has become an annual tradition. Usually we do lunch, but this year we decided to make it dinner. Because all three of us were pretty hungry, we savored broiled steaks, homemade rolls, baked potato, and salad, prepared by Mike and served by his friendly wife, Maggie.

It's always a treat to eat at Vali's, which has become so popular that one must make reservations far in advance. Granddaughter Tammy graduates from Cal Poly in June and grandsons Chad and Shawn graduate from high school in May. Keeping up with these young people makes for an extra busy spring. We'll start the cows and calves to the hills this week, and we hope it will rain soon. For the benefit of everyone living in the North-west, think rain.

April 27—The dandelions are back. Their bright yellow splotches punctuate green Prairie Creek this morning. Why fight 'em? Enjoy 'em!

Dark clouds form over the dazzling white Wallowa snowfields, and we all pray for rain.

Out in their cultivated fields, farmers stir up great clouds of dust as they seed their spring grain. Ponds, normally full this time of year, are either dry or close to it. Lesser creeks, which rely on melting snow banks to feed them, are waterless. Guess we'll have to do a rain dance, or wash the windows, or something.

April 29—This afternoon, I climbed aboard my mare and helped Ben and Doug sort out 20 pair of cows and calves. The cows will later be AI'd (artificially inseminated). The remainder of the spring calves and their mammas would be started to the hill range the following day.

While we sorted, a beef roast cooked slowly in the oven, and that night we enjoyed our first taste of fresh asparagus, from some that Doug had brought home the day before from Hermiston. The roast beef would provide sandwiches for the next two days on the trail, and one more supper. Black clouds formed out north, the wind blew, but only a few sprinkles of rain fell. Nothing to brag about.

April 30—The last day of April dawned dark and foreboding. A moaning wind rose before sunup and thunder rolled off the mountains. After chores and breakfast, we saddled up and began the long day that stretched before us. Old hand Mike McFetridge arrived to help gather the cows and calves and then turn them out onto the county road.

The scent of rain, followed by the rain itself, and then, through a shaft of sunlight, the pastel colors of a rainbow framed the entrance to Hurricane Creek canyon. Our long, yellow slickers shed the rain, and the morning air was fresh and clean. It was a perfect day to trail cattle.

We headed north. Our friend, Scotty, now in her 71st year, had expressed an interest in going on the trail ride, but she didn't show up. Suddenly a car pulled up behind us, parked alongside the road, and out jumped Scotty...a-foot! She said she wanted to walk the 13 miles to East Crow with us! Scotty proved to be of good help, as we always need someone to help push the tail end calves along.

There we were: Mike, 84; Scotty, 70, Doug, 60, and yours truly, 58, following a bunch of cows and calves down the road, in a spring storm. Ben, a-horseback, and Steve on his Honda, were there as well. Steve and Doug stayed with us until we got lined out on the gravel Crow Creek road, then Steve rode back to the ranch and drove out a pickup to load Doug's horse in, leaving Mike, Ben, Scotty and I with the herd.

We were to experience all types of weather. When the sun came out, we'd consider taking off our slickers, at least until it would commence to rain again. We made it up over Crow Creek Pass again without a blizzard developing, but it soon began to hail. Our horses walked sideways, attempting to turn their backs to the stinging storm.

Scotty, using a long willow stick to prod the calves on, plodded steadily onward. As dark clouds raced across the sky, a sudden wind blew so hard we had to hold onto our hats to keep them from blowing away. The cattle preferred to keep moving so we ate while leading our horses behind them.

There was virtually no water along the route, so we watered up at Circle M, where we let the cattle rest awhile before resuming the drive, which ended at East Crow. Here we turned the herd into a holding pasture for the night, where Ben, who had been in the lead, was cold. He'd been waiting there, in the wind, for us to bring up the stragglers.

Wearily we unsaddled and turned our horses loose with the cows and calves, and soon Doug and Steve showed up to give us rides back to the ranch. Scotty, who turned out to be a real trouper, was tired. She figured she'd walked more than 13 miles, taking into account the back and forth trips it took to encourage those lagging, foot-sore calves.

Due to lack of moisture there weren't many wildflowers, and already the grass looked stressed. The little rain that fell was waved away by the wind. There wasn't a drop of water in East Crow, and a pond there, usually full in May, was bone dry.

After a supper of warmed-over roast beef, mashed potatoes and gravy, and a hot bath, it was bed at 7:30 for me.

May 1—Clear, cold, and frosty. We take bets on whether Scotty will want to finish the drive today; she does, of course. Our breath hangs in the frosty air, as we saddle and feed our horses before gathering up the cows and calves.

I sense the colorful scene we create on this early morn; cowboys, green hills, bawling cows and calves. I bring my camera along today in one of the saddle bags, in hopes of recording some of it. However, the best shots present themselves when I'm chasing an errant cow out of the roadside brush, or climbing a steep bank to push a calf along.

A logging truck, loaded with logs, makes its slow way through the herd. Cattle and timber, beef and houses, but I am too busy keeping calves out form in front of the truck to record Wallowa County's two important industries. Just a few miles up the road, we water the cows in Crow Creek. Since the road was "improved," it isn't an easy thing to water a large herd of cattle. The only access now is down a steep embankment, where only a few at a time can drink. The cows drank greedily. It was the first water they'd had since yesterday afternoon.

The morning is perfect; Mike says so. He is in his element. In the saddle, behind a bunch of cows, out in the country he loves. When we are nearly up the grade, Doug drives down to tell us there is a mix-up on top. It seems our cows went through an open gate and got mixed up with the neighbor's cattle.

Leaving Scotty to hold the drag, I rode up to help Ben and Mike sort them. We got everything straightened out, eventually, and resumed the drive. As the day warmed up, the smallest calves began to lag even more. Scotty, too, looking weary herself, gamely kept up. She refused to ride my horse.

At the bottom of the final hill, I got off my mare to help push the cluster of little calves through the wire gate into the Deadman pasture. Once inside, all the little calves immediately laid down.

After the evening chores were finished, we went to town for a steak dinner. Must be getting in shape, not so tired tonight.

May 5—Heat waves shimmer over Prairie Creek as unseasonably hot temperatures climb toward 80. A repeat of yesterday. New seedings, pastures, and hay fields begin to wither under the rays of a high altitude sun. A sun normally doesn't have this much strength until mid-July.

Ordinarily, during the spring rush of working cattle and planting potatoes, we don't have to contend with irrigation; but this is definitely not an ordinary year. At our potato cellars this morning, one of the last semis is being loaded. Norchips; destined for the Willamette Valley, to provide seed for a crop that will end up on the supermarket shelves in the form of potato chips.

May 7—Doug and I attended the 62nd annual Enterprise FFA banquet this evening. After partaking of the traditional roast beef dinner, topped off with strawberry shortcake, we watched the well-organized awards program.

As always, we were very impressed with these fine young people. If they are an example of other FFA chapters across the state, our future is in good hands. Again my heart swelled with pride at the accomplishments of grandsons, as well as members of my 4-H Sourdough Shutterbugs.

Seated across from us were Mr. and Mrs. Melvin Thorpe, who used to live out at what is referred to locally as "The Buttes." They left the area there, which lies northeast of Enterprise, around 1946. Married for 53 years, the couple had been neighbors to Blanche and Bill Strey, whom I've often mentioned in this column. It was a pleasure to get to know them. Melvin, an honored guest, was a charter member of the Enterprise FFA 62 years go.

May 9—Our weather turned cold. Our crew loaded out the final semi of seed potatoes yesterday, and now the cellars and equipment are being cleaned for the next harvest. After all those hot, dry days, it seemed odd to start a fire in the old Monarch again.

I picked up my friend Grace Bartlett this morning, and we drove high up on Alder Slope to visit old-timer Emory Crawford, who, with his wife, Alma, had driven over from Milton-Freewater to visit their son and family for the weekend.

From a well-worn leather brief case, Emory drew forth old black and white photos that depicted his early life in the remote Snake and Imnaha canyons. The pictures brought reality to Emory's words. The old prints were priceless in that they recorded an era that will never be again.

Emory rattled off names of places—Spain Saddle, Lightning Creek, Cow Creek, Tryon Creek, Lord Flat, Eureka Bar—as well as names of early day stockmen—Joe McClaran, Jim Dorrance, Warnock, Litch, Spain. Several photos showed Emory pulling pack strings of mules over incredibly steep canyon trails.

That morning, we were transported back to a time where hard work was the name of the game to survive... though it still is. For the few of us still in ranching, the future will be full of challenges, but looking at and listening to men like Emory, Mike, and Joe McClaran, still alive, reminds us that it wasn't easy then, either.

Two nights in a row, I've watched the Enterprise High School Drama Club stage its production of "Pirates of Penzance." Very entertaining to a grandma who had two grandchildren in leading roles.

May 10—Mother's Day—And this mother and grandmother was thankful for no more than the privilege of being just that to such a wonderful brood. Daughter Lori and her family are now settled in Pendleton, where she is working nights at the post office. Tom, who is playing "Mr. Mom" at the moment, rides herd on Lacey and Ryan while mom gets her *zzzz*'s.

They drove over yesterday and we had a belated birthday celebration for Lori. I had baked a Black Forest chocolate cake filled with cherries and frosted with whipped cream. Lacey was in charge of the candles and we all sang "Happy Birthday" to a sleepy Lori, who hadn't gotten enough sleep that Sunday.

Dr. Sam Morgan, a local veterinarian, is here this morning to Bangs vaccinate our replacement heifers. Knowing I will be horseback the next three days, I must get this column in the mail by tomorrow.

Since I hadn't seen my youngest grandchildren in a while, I stole some time before grocery shopping this morning to take them to the park for a picnic, where I joined other grandmas who were doing the same.

Adele and I took James to his kindergarten class, and then I took her home. All too soon these little ones will grow up and become involved in their own activities, like their many cousins are doing. So if I want to enjoy them, better do it now.

Last week I dropped in on my neighbor Ardis Klages, who has been recuperating from a lengthy illness. Because Ardis likes to read, I've kept her supplied with books from my library. She was just taking a fresh, warm pie from her oven when I walked into her country kitchen.

"Rhubarb," she said, "Harold's favorite."

After returning to our ranch, I looked at our "pie plant" and decided there were enough red stalks to make a rhubarb pie for us. And pretty soon that pleasant mouth-watering aroma of pie filled my kitchen as well.

It was like July here this week, with days in the 80s and nights so mild we've been leaving the bedroom windows open until daylight.

One evening I went to the chicken house and plucked five of my Barred Plymouth Rock hens off their roost, tied them securely in three gunny sacks, and transported them to Mike and Joyce McFetridge's hen house. They needed some laying hens, and I don't need 20 eggs a day. Mike reported that the hens apparently didn't slow down a bit. They laid five big brown eggs the very next day.

May 12—Looking like shards of shattered crystal, ice hangs from electric fences and heavily weights a lower power line connected to an automatic watering trough in the pasture. As the sprinklers make their *chish, chish* rounds, jets of water freeze everything they touch on this 20-degree morning.

Dandelion blossoms, encased in clear glass bubbles, wait patiently for the sun's warmth to free them from their icy prison. Looking up Prairie Creek, I see our neighbor's wheel lines marked with paths of white ice! Ben and his son Seth arrive around 6 a.m. to change pipes. Cold hands! The little twin calf comes running to me for his bottle of milk.

Birds sing and, cold or not, the prairie comes to life for another rainless day. Yesterday morning, clouds hung low over the mountains and teased us with the promise of rain. But none came; only the merciless winds can be relied on to appear.

Every day the grasses cry out for rain. More creeks turn to mud and then dry up in the incessant winds. The last cows have calved, so today we hauled those tail-enders to the hills. Ben and Doug hauled the cows in separate cattle trucks, while I followed with a pickup full of bawling calves.

It is sad to see the hills looking so dry, especially when the grass had such a good start. Luckily our stock ponds are full and we have two live streams running through our range areas, but if no rain comes, that, too, will change.

Tomorrow morning Mike and I will start the fall calvers in from the hills, a three-day drive, to their high moraine summer pasture, where they will begin to calve in August. Pat has been plowing fields in readiness to plant seed potatoes, a job that looms all too soon. We must brand the spring calves and, owing to these unusually dry conditions, irrigating has become a full-time job.

Doug, like every rancher in the valley, is busy from dawn till dark. The season of long days and short nights is here. Flood gates are opening all over the valley, pipes are being laid out, ditches are running full of precious water—irrigation ditches that have been constructed by past generations to bring water to this parched land. If it weren't for these irrigation set-ups, our prairie valley would resemble the sage hills that adjoin us.

Stored snow runoff provides this life-giving ingredient. Numerous ditch companies were formed early on, with colorful names like the Farmer's Ditch, Silver Lake, and Moonshine. Ditch walkers patrol the ditches to make sure every one of the waterways receives its fair share. My friend Linde and her husband are ditch walkers on upper Prairie Creek. By the end of the season, Linde may be known as "the Ditch Witch."

If we don't receive the normal spring rains, many creeks flowing out of the mountains will dry up earlier than usual. Kinney Lake and Wallowa Lake will have to carry those fortunate enough to be under them.

May 13—We rolled out of bed to face a succession of days that began early, ended late, and would find us trailing our fall calvers from the hill range to the lake moraine. Many hours were spent in the saddle by Mike, Ben and yours truly. After three days and more than 35 miles we got the job done. The men were busy preparing the fields to plant seed potatoes.

May 16—Following another busy day, Doug and I drove the 30 miles to Imnaha to attend the annual Cow Chip Lottery. It was a lovely evening. Jean Stubblefield and Don Marks were frying ham and eggs, hotcakes, and hash browns on a grill set up just outside the little two-room school. People were eating at picnic tables scattered on the play-ground, and nearby, chewing her cud, was a young Holstein cow corraled in a small space that had been marked off in squares.

It was a pleasant setting: the children running around playing, the cow, the people visiting and eating their simple breakfast-dinner fare. Colorful jars of Imnaha women's jams and preserves decorated the tables to be were smeared on the hotcakes. Apricot, peach, wild blackberry...

No sooner had Doug and I purchased several squares for the lottery, when the anticipated event took place! The cow went!

"The cow is going," yelled Jean Stubblefield, as she turned another pancake. All eyes turned toward the Holstein, who had made her deposit not in a gutter but on a blank square. No one, it seemed, had purchased that particular square. The cow was given another chance, but because she was never again so moved, it was determined that the closest square to the chip would be the winner of the $100.

Lots of fun for a good cause. Proceeds were donated to the Jack and Harriet Finch Memorial scholarship fund, in memory of two of Imnaha's former teachers, who were well-loved in the community. Larry and Myrna Moore of Bear Gulch loaded up the cow, which was ready to return home. The school under the rim rocks emptied of people and we returned to Prairie Creek under a full May moon.

May 17—It warmed into the 80s and Doug spent the entire day irrigating. Sprinklers were sending out jets of water all over the valley. Doug took time to hook the roto-tiller up to the tractor and work up my garden spot.

I spent the morning interviewing Jimmie Weaver in his home on Alder Slope on the occasion of his 100th birthday. That long, hot after-noon I typed up my story on Jimmie and thought about grandsons Chad and Shawn, on their Senior Sneak, floating the Snake River.

May 19—Mike, Ben, Doug, Linde and I spent another long day in the saddle sorting cattle out on Salmon Creek. After turning the bulls in with the sorted bunches, we rattled home over the long dirt road to the valley. Meanwhile, back at the ranch, Steve and his potato crew began planting seed.

The next two days we returned to Salmon Creek and branded and worked all of our spring calves. The weather continued hot and dry.

Somewhere in there we managed to get into Joseph to vote. Between night and morning I was able to bake a ham, put together a macaroni salad, and make a chocolate cake to feed our branding crew.

When we weren't in the saddle gathering in another bunch from the large hill pastures, Linde and I took turns pushing the big, husky calves down the chute and working the gate. One day Linde's husband, Pat, helped, which gave us a little break. Pat also helped mend a section of fence that the bulls had torn out.

May 22—We spent today packing our gear preparatory to participating in the re-creation of a segment of the Oregon Trail, which was being staged to help commemorate the opening of the new interpretive center on Flagstaff Hill near Baker City.

My two grandsons, Buck and Josh, plus Linde and Pat and old friend Scotty and I were signed up as walkers. Tanned and sturdy from cattle ranching duties, we pulled out of Enterprise and headed for another wild "adventure."

We spent that night at a friend's ranch in North Powder. Expecting to throw our sleeping bags out in the yard or on the floor, we were surprised when Barry graciously turned his entire house over to us, and he slept in the bunkhouse. We ate supper at the Haines Steakhouse, and our comfortable accommodations at North Powder would quickly come to an end... The next night we would be out somewhere in the middle of Virtue Flat sleeping in bedrolls in a sage-brush bedroom that boasted a star-studded ceiling!

May 23—Arising before dawn this morning, we packed up and drove to Baker City, where we were bused to the beginning of our trek in Pleasant Valley. Here we join over 200 other walkers, and that many horseback riders. We are all dressed in period dress. Linde, Scotty and I look like pioneer women in our long skirts, bonnets, aprons and hiking boots! The men and boys look like those who trod the trail, holes in their pants, old hats. There are many children, just as there were in the 1800s.

We watch, fascinated, as mountain men decked out in buckskins and beards, wearing coyote headdress and carrying black powder rifles, pass to and fro in the melee. Our guide, a 64-year-old local woman clad in long dress and bonnet, starts up the trail.

Our Wallowa County contingent follows her at the head of the procession as we leave Pleasant Valley and begin walking along a dim road following a sagebrush-strewn draw. Willow trees growing there would be the last shade we would encounter during the two days on the trail. A female hawk circled above, screeching in alarm. We could see her nest made of sticks in the willow tree. We were told this was the worst tick season in 20 years, and to watch out for rattlesnakes!

The dusty trail continues up a narrow, grass-strewn road and approaches a creek that is slightly boggy, but not running. Because of the dust, we are thankful that the riders will approach tonight's camp by a different route. We keep up a pretty good pace and climb a rather steep hill, from which we can view the far-off Eagle Mountains on the other side of which lie our own Wallowas.

From here on, we are following the actual route of the old Oregon Trail. I have been reading some early journals and diaries jotted down by the pioneers as they traveled this part of the trail. It isn't hard to imagine what the immigrants experienced.

The land looks the same, unchanged from when they, too, must have paused to gaze out upon the vastness of the undulating sagebrush hills toward the snow-capped mountains. We see nary a sign of human habitation. A breeze stirs the drying grasses that are struggling to live during this drought year on Eastern Oregon's high desert. We, too, pause on this high hill to drink in the view. We can look down toward Virtue Flat, and up in the direction of Flagstaff Hill.

Behind us, the walkers have strung out in the sagebrush. We decide to eat our lunches there and are joined by a 60-year-old woman who lives not too far from here, she says, on a ranch. She herds sheep on foot, having moved here years ago from Salinas, California.

"Everything is here," she says. "Peace and quiet." I take her picture and do an interview for an article. Because the other walkers are so spread out, we are quite alone, and we know what the woman speaks of. The pungent sage fills our nostrils and heat waves shimmer over the vast desert. Our skirts are covered with dust, which also sifts up our legs; sweat forms under our bonnets, which shade our faces from the blistering desert sun.

How easily we fall into the pioneer woman's role, and we feel how it was: the lonely, unfamiliar, homeless land; parents left far behind; worry about children; praying to get through one day at a time. Soon we are walking downhill toward Virtue Flat, an immense plain that fills an entire valley. Wilted wildflowers droop in the mid-day heat as we come to a lonely child's grave, marked only with a blank slab of rock; a victim of the trail. We bow our heads in silence.

Off in the distance a six-horse hitch pulling two covered wagons comes into view. It is an unforgettable sight, with the mountains still rising up in the distance. We shoot lots of film.

Dusty and hot, we finally walk into a circle-up of 25 covered wagons. We can smell the delicious aroma of buffalo stew being cooked in enormous black kettles over open fires.

A covered wagon pulled by a team of oxen joins the circle of wagons on Virtue Flat to camp for the night along the Oregon Trail. Mother kettle holds savory beans. Men trail-tenders stir the beans and stew with huge, hand-carved wooden spoons. The sun burns down with a summer-like intensity, while all over the Northwest records are being broken for heat.

Josh and Buck have run ahead of us down the hill into camp and already located the gear wagon, and have our bedrolls ready to set up our sagebrush camp on Virtue Flat. Soon the 200 riders descend the hill in a cloud of dust and the first eight miles on the trail is over.

Inside the circle-up of covered wagons there is much activity. Large teams of draft horses and mules stand quietly beside their wagons, harnesses draped over the wagon tongues. I am fascinated by a team of oxen, huge, sullen, long-horned beasts. Oxen were used more than horses on the trail due to their strength and endurance, and because their meat was more palatable than horse meat when game became scarce.

The water we carried these eight miles was gone, so we were glad to find the water wagon and quench our thirst. Looking up toward the long hill we had just descended, we watched as more than 200 horseback riders single-filed down toward camp. The riders trailed clear back toward the skyline of the hill where we had eaten lunch. A long cloud of dust rose out of the sagebrush and followed them. Halfway down, a panicked horse reared and unseated his rider, but others soon caught the runaway and rescued the rider.

The final walkers straggle in. The end of eight hot miles! And not a speck of shade. Pat and the two boys locate some old fence material and construct a crude shelter using Linde's Indian blanket. Shade! We watch the drama of a covered wagon camp unfold as the long, hot afternoon wears on. All the riders and walkers have arrived and watered their horses, but there is great confusion because of so many horses. Inside the circle-up of 25 wagons, we go crazy photographing. So much to record and hear. A rooster crows. Two wagons have chickens in cages strapped to the wagons' sides. One wagon has a yearling Jersey heifer tied to the back. She bawls and bawls, looking at the two oxen, which seem to be the only other bovines in this equine world.

Mules bray, a goat bleats; a stuffed, mounted coyote stands motionless outside the perimeter of the circle of wagons. The bearded ox team driver snaps his whip. He is trying to drive the oxen off onto the flat. One ox

From left, Scotty Doyle, Jan Bailey, Janie Tippett, Ulrike Straus, and Marilyn Goebel of Wallowa County joined the official Oregon Trail Wagon Train at La Grande and in the next two days walked to Emigrant Springs.

does the pulling; the other puts his head down, sullen. They lurch and take off. My camera clicks.

A new wagon rolls into camp. A young Hereford cow and her calf are led into the melee. The loose calf follows the cow, and a herd of children follows the calf. Little girls, looking like prairie wildflowers in their colorful, long dresses and pretty bonnets, gay and laughing. A long-legged boy jumps on the cow and rides her around camp. The calf nurses the cow. The children are from Jordan Valley, a fun-loving group of kids raised in the sagebrush and very much at home here.

Some of the wagons have plows, cross-cut saws, axes, shovels, pulleys, and water barrels strapped to their sides; tools needed to begin homesteading the Oregon country. One wagon has a cradle made of wicker willow that has been in the family for generations. The cradle, in fact, traveled the Oregon Trail with a baby in it. The Jersey heifer is tied to this wagon, which is pulled by a wonderful, gentle team of matched black mules.

Outside this wagon, cast iron kettles hang from a black tripod. A wash basin sits atop a handmade wooden stool. Furniture in the wagon is authentic. The young family has two little girls. Next to them stands the U.S. Cavalry wagon with its team of mules. An American flag waves in the desert breeze. Men wearing the blue and gold cavalry uniforms act as trail bosses and camp tenders.

In the heat and dust, the roosters crow, the children laugh, the Jersey bawls, the teamster scolds his oxen, a team of large draft horses runs away, and is caught inside the circle-up. The buffalo stew bubbles away, and soon men roll up their sleeves and begin to mix huge pans full of bannock, pan bread, dough. A fire has been built in a long narrow trench and the dough is slapped into waiting greased fry pans, which are then placed at an angle near hot coals in the trench. Soon the bread turns golden brown.

The entire camp, more than 500 people, lines up to be served from the large steaming black kettles of buffalo stew, beans and hot-from-the-pan bannock with butter melting over it. We sit there in the sagebrush and eat the hearty trail food. Buffalo stew spills on my flour sack apron. Now I know why the women wore those long aprons. The long dresses and bonnets are cooler than jeans, but sure get dusty.

The sun sinks lower. The land is so immense it absorbs the noise of our large encampment. We visit and smile at each other, and I am so glad my grand-sons Buck and Josh are having this experience. There are many children in camp, and as the hot day ebbs they come to life more, making new acquaintances, chasing rabbits through the sagebrush, and talking about their horses.

The scent of sage intensifies with the coolness. A breeze wanders over Virtue Flat, and we look up toward Flagstaff hill six miles away. It is so warm and mild that we hardly need even a light sweater, but the women return to their camps and drape shawls over their long dresses. We walk around the circle-up and talk to the wagon people, listening to their stories.

Mike and Linda Hanley from Jordan Valley are there with a six-horse hitch pulling two wagons. Where the riders water their horses at long water troughs, I steal some to rinse the buffalo stew off my apron, then hang it on our tripod shelter to dry.

At twilight, with the mountains rising blue and far off, I crawl into my bedroll, take pen in hand, and write in my trail diary, like those who came before. My thoughts are of my great-grandfather, Isaac Wilson, who came across the plains with the westward migration. When my grandson Buck becomes hot and weary on the trail tomorrow, I'll tell him to think of Isaac also.

As I write by the last light of day, sitting here on my bedroll, the air is heavy with sage and blessedly cool after the heat of the day. After the children have been called to bed, the stars blink on, and a powerful quiet descends over the desert.

The Sesquicentennial Wagon Train pulls out of Spring Creek camp in the Blue Mountains just after sun-up. This crossing of the Blues was a rugged part of the Oregon Trail, but also pleasant for the pioneers, because of the trees after a thousand miles of desert and plain.

From left, Jim Conner of Fruitland, Washington, gets acquainted along the trail with Barbara and Keith Petrie of Sandy, Oregon.

May 24—I sleep soundly next to the earth until awakened in the early morning hours by a wild chorus. Coyotes...in stereo! Are they investigating their still-life compadre? I drift off to sleep again as a deliciously cool breeze wanders over the Flat.

Dawn steals over Virtue Flat; birds twitter and a mauve sky backgrounds purple sage and far off blue mountains, on the other side of which is home. When the emigrants passed this way, the other side of those mountains was relatively undiscovered by white settlers, except for an occasional mountain man or trapper...But it was home to Chief Joseph and his Wallowa band of Nez Perce Indians. Due to its geographical isolation, it was bypassed by the Oregon Trail and even by Lewis and Clark, who passed to the north with their "Corps of Discovery."

I muse upon these things as the morning sun burns over the horizon, igniting a wall tent to the east, which glows in sunlight. A Cavalry man crawls out of his tent, and lifts a bugle to his lips. Reveille. A rooster answers! The camp awakens with the sun; a horse snorts, a mule brays, and the Jersey resumes her bawling.

I look down at my dusty skirt and apron, after only one day on the trail; what did the women look like at the end of three months? Sitting up on my bedroll, I stretch, and welcome the sun and the day, knowing the cool won't last.

The children, weary from yesterday's excitement, sleep a little longer, at least until Josh smells breakfast. Soon Buck, Scotty, Linde, Pat and I join the long chow line with Josh. Ham slices sizzle in dutch ovens, flap jacks, golden brown, eggs sunny-side up, served in the sun. We find a block of fire wood to sit on and hold the food in our laps while we eat.

Have I mentioned the baby? No, one wasn't born along the trail, but a young couple walked the eight miles yesterday carrying their baby, a chubby little girl about five months old or so. Wearing a bonnet and dress, the tot rode in a shawl slung from her mom's shoulder. This morning the babe seems none the worse for wear, and appears to be adapting quite well to life along the trail.

After breakfast we pack up our bedrolls and stow them in the gear wagon before gathering for a non-denominational church service. Grouped around inside the wagon circle on this Sunday morning, a retired Army chaplain explains to us how it must have been on such a Sabbath along the Oregon Trail.

"Even today," he says, "it is too painful to talk of the deaths of the little children, and of the suffering from heat, cold and hunger." We repeated The Lord's Prayer, which must have been spoken many a time by many a pioneer to provide the needed faith it took to get through each day.

It is REAL here in the morning air, under the immense sky. The service is simple and effective. We sing "Amazing Grace," and pay silent homage to those who came before, so we can be here today. The American flag flaps in the breeze from the Cavalry tent, and even the mules bow their heads. Our motley group of modern pioneers begins to break camp, but not before the Jordan Valley children sing, play the fiddle, harmonica and Jew's harp.

There follows a great flurry of activity as teams are hitched, gear is stowed in wagons, and riders and walkers choose which wagon they will accompany. While waiting for our wagon to line up, I perch on a stump of wood near the makeshift kitchen and jot down more notes, when an elderly gentleman approaches me and begins to ask several questions.

He says his name is Jim Evans, 48 years old—though I later found out from his daughter along the trail that he is 84! Jim is Baker County's historian and a reporter and writer for the Baker City Herald newspaper. He, too, has been taking notes while walking the trail.

Finally, order emerges from chaos and the outriders take their places; walking families find their wagons; and "Wagons Ho!" yells wagonmaster Stan Wellman. Josh says we are a family: "Two grandmas, a mother, a father, and two boys."

We decide to adopt the wagon with the Jersey tied to it, and the old willow cradle attached to the rear. Twenty-five wagons begin to roll. Their wheels creak, the dust rises, the oxen strain, the horses plunge, and the mules plod faithfully on. The dust will be with us until the end.

We make our way up a gentle rise and down a washout. Wagons lurch and sway, and several teams of horses have problems. One breaks its harness and there is a delay while it is repaired. The young mother and father with the baby are in our group. When we stop, after a hard pull out of the rocky washout, the wagon driver invites the parents to place the baby inside the cradle for the remainder of the trip. So from now on the baby rides in the jolting, swaying willow wicker cradle that held a baby so many years ago along this original route. The day warms and the unrelenting sun blazes down upon the wagon train.

Pulling the last wagon, the plodding oxen bring up the rear and pull into another circle-up on a level spot for lunch. Not an inch of shade left; all of the wagons have people sitting in every speck there is.

After lunch we begin the ascent of Flagstaff Hill. Jim Evans walks beside me and never complains, even though the heat and dust become worse. After six miles are accomplished we are told that we must walk another 3-and-a-half miles to where buses will transport us back to Baker City! This, too, is REAL! A little too real, as we thought the end was nearer.

Buck and Josh, who had friends in two wagons, were invited to ride the final miles, and Jim Evans was finally persuaded to accept a ride in a covered wagon. The woman sheepherder, Kathleen, and I trudged wearily on, as did Scotty, Linde and Pat. Once returned to Baker City, we were too hot and tired to visit the new Interpretive Center. Instead, we headed for home with Oregon Trail dust still clinging to us.

"Home," beyond those mountains!

May 26—Its raining! In fact it looks as if it must have rained most of the night here on Prairie Creek. After all those hot, dry days, any semblance of May weather is most welcome. Even the thirsty hills look refreshed this morning.

A heap o' livin' has occurred in our lives these past busy weeks.

June 1—Yesterday four friends and I worked all day on a hiking trail that follows the old stock driveway to Murray Gap. Wielding pulaskis, bow saws and pruning shears, we went about restoring this historic trail blazed years ago by sheepherders.

This route, which leads to the secluded Silver Creek country and beyond, offers some of the most spectacular scenery found anywhere. The trail is steep and, from several high rocky ledges, the sight literally takes your breath away. The rewards are worth the extra effort it takes to get there.

In the early 1900s this "stock driveway" was used to trail hundreds of sheep to high mountain meadows that provided them with summer grazing. Aged, decaying stumps left along this high ridge top provide mute testimony to those early herders who cleared this pathway through the trees.

On the sunny openness of this narrow ridge grows the wild huckleberry and grouse whortleberry. On either side, yawning forested canyons, dense with underbrush, provide habitat for elk, deer, coyote and bear. We saw signs of all four along our trail. Way up in the saddle, or gap, we saw numerous signs of mountain sheep.

Small, orange butterflies were feeding on purple penstemon. The water, flowing along the irrigation ditch dug by hand so many years ago by local farmers, cascaded through the gap in a wonderful waterfall, falling to irrigate the slope below. At our feet lay the fertile valley, the rolling hill land, the Seven Devil Mountain range, the breaks of the Imnaha and the Snake, the towns of Joseph and Enterprise, and the shades of green farming circles that dot the hills north of Enterprise. We had an eagle's eye view.

Across from us rose the back side of Ruby Peak, its snows melting away in the unseasonably hot sun. Our legs know they've had a workout today, but we feel good about improving this old trail so others, too, can enjoy it.

Grandsons Chad and Shawn graduated from high school last week. Can it really be that they are that age already, and soon off to college?

The next night, grandson Rowdy graduated from 8th grade in Enterprise, and then there was the Imnaha end-of-school program, in which two more grandchildren took part. Imnaha school graduated one 8th grader. Somewhere in there, the same night as high school graduation, I fixed an anniversary supper in honor of daughter Lori and son-in-law Tom's 10th wedding anniversary.

June 8—June is the season for wild roses. This spring the delicate blooms that line the country lanes are pale pink rather than deep pink, due to the lack of rain. But in some of the forested glades, where the moisture has been preserved by deep humus, the wild roses wear the true, deeper hues.

"Life is just a bowl of cherries," or so the saying goes. However, when one purchases 20 pounds of ripe ones, like I did, one must then do something with them! So, before I was able to sit down at the typewriter, I reduced the box of Bings to seven jars canned, a batch of preserves, a huge juicy pie, and some given to friend Linde.

Now my blue-stained fingers wander from this column to the bowl on the table, full of cherries left fresh to nibble.

The precious mountain snow continues to melt. When it is gone, so, too, will be the water. "Tucker's Mare" has shrunk to a barely discernible shape of a horse as the mountain snows evaporate before our eyes.

Neighbor Melvin Brink has hay down, and the Eastern Oregon Livestock Show opens this week in Union. If it doesn't rain for these two historically "dampened" events, we'll know this drought is pretty serious.

[Editor's note: It rained.]

Our potato crews are in the final stages of planting three fields of seed. Normally, when we receive the much-needed June rains to sprout the spuds, we don't have to contend with irrigation to bring them up. Not so this June. Weary agriculturists must deal with pipes, wheel-lines, and flood irrigating on top of an already over-burdened spring workload.

As a result, there are many weary, overworked ranchers around this area. Have you hugged a rancher lately?

June 22—Inside the thermometer, nailed to one of the posts that holds up our clothesline, the mercury is rising toward 90 on this long, hot afternoon. Hay fields, pastures, flowers, lawn and gardens, given a boost by the recent rains, are once again beginning to wilt under the rays of this high-altitude sun.

Oregon's drought, even after over an inch of rain fell here in our valley, continues...

June 11—Daughter Ramona, son-in-law Charley, two of their children, Shawn and Carrie, plus Doug and me, piled into the car to drive to Pismo Beach, California. The reason for this trip was the spring commencement exercises at Polytechnic State University (Cal Poly) located in San Luis Obispo.

It turned out to be quite a trip. Getting away from the ranch was the hardest part. After that it all fell into place. How relieved we were, when we called home two days later, to learn that it was raining. Even raining enough to turn the sprinklers off in the potato fields.

On the road early that morning, we drove without incident to Jordan Valley and lunched at the Old Basque Restaurant. After watching in wonder as Shawn downed two pieces of homemade pie, we headed south with stops at McDermitt, Winnemucca and Lovelock.

It was late evening when we pulled into the small Sierra Valley town of Loyalton to spend the night with friends of Ramona and Charley. It was old home week for Shawn and Carrie, who attended school here before moving to Oregon. And could it already be four years ago that we drove to Loyalton to attend Tammy's high school graduation? I remembered the nostalgic side-trip my three sisters and I took to visit Sardine Valley where our great-grandmother Electa taught school so many years ago.

We hit the road again the next morning, joining a fast freeway that takes us through Auburn, Sacramento, Stockton and on down south through the vast farm lands of California's central valleys. From I-5 we watch acres and acres of cropland whiz past our windows, plus acres and acres of houses, and towns-turned-cities which, over the past ten years have grown to cover much of that early farm land.

We turn southwest at Kettleman City and drive through rolling, dry, grassy hills dotted with oak trees, to Paso Robles. Expensive real estate here. The freeway bypasses San Luis Obispo, and 10 more miles brings us to the ocean and Pismo Beach, where Ramona has made reservations, far in advance, at a condominium called the Sea Gypsy.

We are surrounded by humanity and traffic, but find the place and pack our bags into the apartment we will share with other relatives. Charley's folks, along with Aunt Molly, pull in right behind us, having driven from Dixon, California.

Is this REAL or what? We open sliding glass doors to view a long sandy beach, and hear the roar of the blue-green Pacific. Seagulls swoop down off the roof top, looking for a handout. A cool sea breeze, refreshing and salty, fills our room. After all those long hours in the van, we relax.

Soon our Tammy arrives from the nearby college, and joins her family. My mother and her husband, Bill, have arrived safely and are staying in Paso Robles. We go shopping at a nearby market and bring back fixin's for supper and breakfast. We prepare a light meal, relax, and hit the hay. Shawn and Carrie are out on the beach after dark, hunting little crabs that crawl out across the sand during the night.

Ramona awakens me in the middle of the night to come look out at the ocean. A bright path of moonlight shimmers over the dark Pacific's waves. To us high mountain valley dwellers this experience is quite a novelty.

June 12—I can't wait to walk the beach before breakfast the next morning, to collect shells and do some photographing. It is very relaxing and enjoyable. Ramona and I walk out to the end of a large pier and watch a fisherman cast his line into the ocean. There weren't too many people on the beach, and that makes it nice.

Mom and Bill join us and we walk around the touristy shops, ending up eating clam chowder and sourdough rolls at noon in a small eatery not too far from the beach. Pismo Beach boasts some of the largest clams in the world.

In fact, it was a little on the cool side during our entire trip. Early in the morning, before the breeze came up, one could walk the beach without a sweater, but later some sort of covering was necessary.

After walking back to the Sea Gypsy, we dress and get ready to attend the graduation ceremony, which is scheduled for 4 p.m. Since this is such a large affair, with so many people attending, Tammy insists we go early to secure seating. The logistics of parking and then walking from point A to point B are mind-boggling; not at all like going to Harley Tucker arena in Joseph, or Cloverleaf Hall in Enterprise.

Everywhere...people and cars converging on Mustang Stadium. By some miracle we all arrive as a body and stay together as we climb to the bleachers and wait. Then Shawn says: "Here they come!" I climb to the top row of seats where he is, and look back up the road from whence we came, to watch a sea of moving caps and gowns. Two thousand students, a river of energy flowing into the stadium from both sides. Soon, they, too, are seated, and the ceremony begins.

Speeches...applause. No diplomas given. En masse, the schools stand when called. The School of Engineering. Cheers! The School of Liberal Arts. Cheers! And finally...lastly, the School of Agriculture! Followed by a great roar from these students, making a noise to a world that is increasingly ignoring and failing to understand their reason for being.

Our Tammy, in their midst, one of many, but special to us, who came so far, to celebrate her moment of achievement. Our small-town country girl, graduating from a big-town college. After the graduates marched out to music, we collected everyone and drove to the Embassy Suites in San Luis Obispo where the agriculture students had reserved a room for their reception. Here we visited and partook of fancy finger food and a huge cake decorated with the graduates' names, and in a much more personal atmosphere, got acquainted with some of Tammy's friends.

The students introduced their families and when we said we were from Joseph, Oregon, no one knew where that was. Leaving the younger generation to dance until midnight, we older folks retired to our apartment over the beach.

June 13—This morning found me on the beach, strolling along with other early beachcombers, enjoying sky, surf, sand and sun. Eighteen-year-old Shawn, just graduated from high school, rented a surf board and headed for the breakers. A first for him! He does just fine for a mountain boy.

Later, we pack and drive to San Luis Obispo to help Tammy move four years of accumulated college "stuff." We drive behind as she and sister Carrie head for Lodi, where Tammy will finish out the six weeks of required courses to receive her BS degree in animal science.

After spending the night in Lodi with Tammy's friends, we wake to find ourselves in the middle of a vineyard just down the road from the Sebastiani Winery.

June 24—It was 90 degrees before noon. Our men were all ag-bagging, making silage out of green-chopped meadow hay and mixing it with some leftover potatoes, and changing pipes in the potato fields.

"Don't hay until after the 4th of July." That used to be the rule Prairie Creek farmers followed for years. Then along came the drought and changing weather patterns; hay matured earlier, was cut and cured, no clouds appeared, and June rains were few and far between. The hot sun shone down day after day and many ranchers have their hay stacked by the 4th of July.

So, during this normally wet time in our high mountain valley, after days of unseasonably hot temperatures, with no rain in sight and the scarcity of water looming all summer-long, much of the ready-to-cut hay fell to the swathers. When one, long, double-thick plastic "Ag Bag" was filled and sealed for winter feeding, Ben swathed 15 acres of meadow grass to be cured and baled for hay.

June 30—The weather returned to normal a week ago—normal meaning June rains, and it's been "normal" ever since. The ground is saturated, the grass is lush, my garden is growing in time with the weeds, and the wildflower patch is riotous with Icelandic and California poppies, bachelor buttons and daisies.

A few industrious and lucky souls managed to get their hay off the field but, for the most part, paths of yellowing windrows color the hayfields while second cuttings grow greener by the day around them. And daily the thunderheads build to dump their contents on the soggy hay! Does this mean El Niño, or global warming, or whatever, is over? Who knows!

The hay lies forlorn in the green field, all for the want of a PTO for a truck, which has kept us from making silage out of the now ruined hay. In all of Wallowa County there seems not to be a PTO for this old truck.

Doug spends all morning on the phone trying to locate one, and finally enlists the help of Bryan Wolfe, a Wallowa County boy, whose son, Jeff, is coming this way and will bring us one. We hope!

Meanwhile, our neighbors are calling, wanting us to make silage out of their wet hay. But how beautiful the country is now. The forests are no longer in fire danger, the hills perking up, and the wild grasses growing again. The streams flowing, the wild flowers blooming, the air cool and fresh, and wondrous clouds floating over all.

Bursts of sunlight spill through and rainbows form during the thunder showers and the glorious mix of June is here today and gone tomorrow.

For tomorrow is July. Weary ranchers and farmers rest when it's time for Hin-mah-too-ya-let-kekt. Rest is the gift of "Thunder-rolling-over-the-mountains."

June 25—Out of bed shortly after 4 a.m. and heading out toward the Zumwalt country to pick up my Appaloosa mare "Foxy," who was then at the old Steen ranch on Chesnimnus Creek, 30 miles from here. Taking along some mountain bread and a jug of water for breakfast, I savored the ride in the cool dawn of a cloudy day.

Since Doug needed the pickup that morning, I was back with the mare by 7:30 a.m. As dawn gave way to daylight, the sun turned the cloudy eastern sky into a stained glass window. Although it appeared I was the only human traveler at that early hour, the country was alive with animals and birds.

Mule deer bounded across the road in front of me; wet does, coming from ranchers' stock ponds, returning to fawns tucked away among the Imnaha's breaks. Cattle, in cattle country, silhouetted against hilltops; two cow elk and their yearling calves stand and stare, their new calves perhaps hidden in the timber that borders the ranch at the Steen place. In sheltered draws I glimpse weathered homesteads slowly succumbing to the hills, persevering and enduring in their final years like those who lived there.

There are mallard ducks in every man-made stock pond, ducklings trailing behind, and hawks perched on every rockjack and fence stay, watching me with their wild eyes. Because this is the rancher's land, it is the wildlife's land, and it shows. Because it is rancher's land, it has remained relatively unchanged for more than 100 years—except for the "improved" road, a new fence here and there, and lately, new owners.

The drought has taken its toll on the natural feed, but hopefully these delayed rains will help bring the country back to life. It is a special place, this high plateau where sky meets hills on the edge of the breaks of the Imnaha. I waved to the ghost of big Dan Goertzen, whom I never knew but feel as if I should after listening to tales about him from Doug. Dan's one-room shack tilts crazily, open at one end, roof sagging, on its last legs, waiting for a strong wind to deal the final blow.

The long, winding gravel road wanders past the town of Zumwalt. Town? Well, once it was a post office, and there was the school house just up the road. This morning the gray, weathered boards of the bell tower lay in a fallen heap atop the old one-room school building. Many a time on horseback, from our Butte Creek pasture to the west, I would look across the country to see the old bell tower outlined against the sky; a familiar landmark, a sort of silent sentinel in the lonely hills. As its boards decay into the ground, the memory of the old building is all that remains.

To the east rises the jagged crest of the Seven Devils Mountains in Idaho. After entering a timbered area, I finally come out onto a wide meadow at the end of which lies the old Steen ranch headquarters. Although during the last 25 years many owners have come and gone, the place is referred to locally as the Steen place.

Smoke curls up from a branding fire at the corrals. The cowboys are out early, perhaps anticipating another hot day. I am greeted by a young cowboy wearing chaps, hat, boots and spurs. His name is Steve Bronson, and he is the one who knows my mare best. He tells me she is in a pasture alongside Chesnimnus Creek.

Armed with a small bucket of grain and a halter, I tell Steve to return to his work and I will track down my mare. After climbing a well-worn trail that leads to a high ridge top, I find her. She is easy to catch and I lead her down past the old log house, now more than 100 years old, and load her into my pickup. It has been a long time since I've seen her. She is out of my mare Cal, the horse I ride when trailing cattle, but has been in the canyons all winter at Tulley Creek. When the cowboys trailed the cattle through the steep breaks to their summer grazing, I decided to pick her up.

Foxy is 12 now, having been foaled in a pasture here in May 1980. Thanks to all the cowboys who have ridden her during the intervening years, which includes a son-in-law and a son, Foxy is now a well-broke cow horse.

June 27—We moved some 40 cows from the east moraine to the lake side this morning, and I rode Foxy. It was a pleasure, and she definitely knows about cows! Because this mare's mother is 22 years old and won't be carrying this old lady over too many more trails, it's nice to have Foxy home. In appreciation for riding my mare, I baked Steve and the other Steen ranch cowboys a loaf of sourdough bread and a mincemeat pie yesterday, and daughter Ramona rode out with me to deliver it.

The rains have transformed the hills into green again, and carpets of brilliant pink clarkia blanket the area. We drove under a sea of billowing clouds, which opened up over us as we drove into the ranch.

The far-off Wallowas revealed themselves in a peek-a-boo fashion through misty rain curtains. It was a lovely drive. Home in time to put sourdough biscuits to rise in a cast-iron skillet for supper.

Later, when my grease-stained husband returned after a frustrating day of attempting to repair the old truck, he was cheered by the aroma of sourdough biscuits hot from the oven. Likewise, the wet cowboys at the Steen ranch were no doubt surprised when they rode in, unsaddled their horses, and walked into the old log house to find a loaf of sourdough bread and a warm mincemeat pie.

July 2—While Doug and Steve attended the seed lot trials in Hermiston, I drove off in our mini-motor home to Imnaha to collect daughter Jackie and her 4-H Photography Club members. We headed upriver, stopping along the way to photograph. It was a lovely morning, fresh after

Members of Jackie Matthews' Imnaha 4-H photography club eat lunch at a campground at Indian Crossing along the Imnaha River.

the rain and all. Huge, billowy white clouds floated in a sky cleansed by the storms.

We photographed old log buildings, sunflowers along the banks of the rushing muddy waters of the Imnaha, and horses and mules backgrounded by rim rock canyons. Passing by Barbara and Grant Warnock's tidy ranch, we stopped to photograph their lovely garden and yard in its canyon setting.

We followed the river up toward the Pallette Ranch, where we glimpsed several mule deer does in the old apple orchard there. Up past the Imnaha River Woods we went to Ollokot campground, and then on to our destination at Indian Crossing. Don't you love that place's name? All the while, the building clouds threatened to dump another storm on us. The ground was saturated and the tall grasses glistened with moisture. Wildflowers, given a boost by the storms, were riotous; the country was green and lush.

We pulled into the campground and soon had camp set up, and lunch time was upon us. We ate there in a bright green clearing using one of the provided picnic tables. Because it was so warm and still not raining, we decided to hike two miles up the Imnaha River Trail to the Blue Hole. The trail wound through many wonderful groves of pines, and the scents and sounds of the forest enveloped us.

The upper Imnaha River is wild country, and soon we were inside the wilderness boundary, walking beside patches of lush brake ferns and prolific blue daisies that grew on the sunny banks next to the river. Always in earshot of the river, we hopped across two small creeks activated by the rains. We heard distant thunder and watched dark purple clouds form, but not a drop fell on us.

Presently we came to the enormous gorge where the Imnaha flows through the Blue Hole, only it was brown. We could envision the water spouts and resulting mud slides up in the higher country that had caused that color change.

We returned to camp via another route that took us past Isley's old pack station headquarters, where 15 years ago I cooked for a fall hunting camp. It was there at Indian Crossing that we loaded up the pack strings and rode, me leading two mules, up the nine mountain miles to the big deluxe camp along the North Fork. The memories of younger years.

Back in camp, we faced the challenge of starting a cooking fire in the round metal pit provided by the campground. The ground was muddy and a huge thistle grew in the center of our "stove." Obviously, we were the first to use the facility this season. After sending the 4H'ers on pine cone gathering forays, and breaking up some good limb wood, we got a good fire going. s We consumed a goodly portion of burned hot dogs, followed by S'mores, a sinful combination of roasted marshmallows placed against a chunk of chocolate bar and the whole compressed between graham crackers, and it began to rain. We all fled to the shelter of the mini-motor home, where the six of us sang songs until the rain ceased.

The boys spent the night in a tent, and the girls slept in the back of Darla Marks' Toyota pickup under a canopy. Jackie and I had the motor home all to ourselves. From the surrounding forests came several mule deer does, curious and hoping for potato chips. They wandered unafraid about our camp.

July 3—A big-eyed doe stuck her head into the open end of the girls' bedroom and woke them up!

The morning sky was clear and sunny except for a few hazy clouds. Jackie supervised the breakfast, cooking up hotcakes, bacon and eggs on her large cast-iron griddle, which she set up over the metal grate of the cooking fire. The young photographers got some good shots of golden brown flap jacks and sunny side-up eggs. Good subjects.

We were packed and ready to leave by 9 a.m., cameras at the ready for what might come along…And what did were two obliging sheepherders who posed their pack string of mules for us. Farther down the road we spied the sheep, hundreds of them, flowing down the hillside, the morning sun streaming onto them and filtering through the pines. The sheep grazed as they came like a river of wool, bleating ewes and lambs with an occasional black lamb among them. A photographer's dream.

These 4-Hers should have some good prints to enter in the Wallowa County Fair.

July 4—Rainy weather didn't dampen the spirits of our large extended family's 4th of July activities. We all gathered at our neighbors', the Irwins, and had a great celebration. Just before the picnic got under way, a passing thunder shower wet things down, but the food was taken to the barn and laid out on long tables. After that it didn't rain again all night.

Pat built a nice cooking fire and a large bonfire. We ate while visiting family and friends. The children ran around like children do, and a good time was had by all. I had mixed up the makin's for two batches of homemade ice cream, chocolate and vanilla custard. That was a hit. Homemade ice cream is a family tradition on the 4th of July.

All the youngsters plus the young at heart, Doug included, ignited their fireworks, and the rest of us *oohed* and *aahed* from the sidelines and wrapped blankets around the younger ones to keep them warm.

July 5—Doug and I and a guest, nephew Mike, drove to Imnaha to pick apricots in Inez Meyer's orchard. The fruit was so ripe that I canned and preserved it immediately after we returned to the ranch. Twenty-one quarts canned, one batch of pine cot jam put up, three pie fillings frozen, and a fresh cobbler baked. I was tired when bed time came.

July 6—Caught up on weeding the garden so I could attend a Fishtrap Writer's conference workshop by 1:30 p.m. at Wallowa Lake.

July 7—Clouds, big, soft and wet, glow over the Wallowas in the early, intent sunlight, and Mt. Joseph's ridges displayed the fresh new snow that fell during last night's storm.

July snow! Is it June in July? Not really, just the return of normal haying weather in Wallowa County. The hay, discolored and limp, continues to lie in wet windrows.

Finally, just this morning, the truck needed to auger the chopped wet hay into the ag bags to make silage has been repaired. Locating parts for old trucks is never easy, but thanks to the combined efforts of many, the truck is now in service. I hear the roar of its engine now as it passes through the field. Our men will attempt to salvage our soggy hay, and in so doing remove it from the field so the second cutting can grow unimpeded.

Meanwhile, out in our seed potato fields, the faithful roguers turn up for work amid the wet and muddy conditions that prevail each morning. Daughter Ramona and daughter-in-law Annie are among them. While it has been a bit frustrating trying to get on with the ranch work, the past week nevertheless has been full of activity.

July 16—All last week my energies were directed toward the workshop I took, which was part of the annual Fishtrap Gathering writer's conference held at Wallowa Lake.

This week has been devoted to catching up, only I haven't, because my priorities lie with grandchildren and gardens, which both needed tending after a week's absence. My column just didn't get written.

As a result of taking Alex Kuo's workshop, "Writing and Photographing the West," I did produce quite a lot of written material as well as photographs. The fruits, so to speak, of my labors are now on display at the Skylight Gallery in Enterprise. However, I did compose a poem on Monday of this week.

This poem, inspired by my wildflower patch, doesn't have a title.

Children are like gardens.
You must tend them every day
cultivate, weed, nurture, provide warmth, love, protection.
You will weep over failure
rejoice over success
be surprised, disappointed, proud.
Given a good year, in summer or late fall,
the product of your labors will ripen and mature.
And, after many summers
grandchildren will give you flowers,
to wear in your graying hair.

The photos are leftovers from the photo essay I did for the class on that place-in-the-heart known as "The Imnaha." They depict a small bit of the upriver character; Barbara and Grant Warnocks' lovely garden, sheep grazing the lush forests, and a weathered cabin. The photos were taken when I helped daughter Jackie with her 4-H photography club's assignments. The members made me proud, by the way, and have some wonderful shots to enter in the Wallowa County Fair.

An old weathered cabin on the upper Imnaha River.

Grant and Barbara Warnock's well-kept garden is situated along the river and watched over by a scarecrow couple, backgrounded by the Imnaha canyon country.

A large band of sheep grazes lush grasses near Coverdale on the upper Imnaha River.

July 18—One evening this spring, I snatched six of my Barred Plymouth Rock pullets from their roost and delivered them in gunny sacks to Mike and Joyce McFetridge's chicken house. Mike turned them loose with some half-grown Rhode Island Red roosters he'd recently acquired at our local feed store.

"When the roosters are ready to butcher, I'll trade you six for the pullets," said Mike.

So last week a grinning Mike appeared at my kitchen door clutching three squirming sacks of roosters. "They're ready," he said. "Joyce just dressed out three."

I dumped the contents of the three bags into my chicken pen, whereupon "Chester," the small but mighty barfly rooster, threw out his chest, began to crow and then flew at the poor unsuspecting roosters in apparent rage. The young roosters got the message. Chester still ruled the roost!

Tonight I write myself a sticky note. "Butcher Fryers," it reads.

July 19—The note greeted me Sunday morning. Since I was quite alone most of the day, I decided it was now or never. The canning kettle was put on to boil water, to heat to scalding stage. This simple act of turning on the burner under a kettle of water sets chicken butchering in motion. It is not a fun thing, but it does allow one time to think.

As I accomplished this unpleasant task, I remembered the first fryers I ever butchered, how I closed my eyes when I chopped off their heads, and breathed through my mouth so the smell of hot chicken feathers wouldn't gag me. Butchering chickens is not something one learns in college. Kind of like writing—you learn by doing.

Hatchet in hand, wheeling an old wheelbarrow, I march to the chicken pen. It is a lovely morning, hay bales lay in long rows, and the air is heavy with the scent of sweet clover blossoms.

I hold on to these pleasant thoughts as I proceed with what has to be done, for what has to be done is not as easily accomplished as it was when I was 30. Now I must use brain, instead of brawn, to outwit these birds. Because before I can lop off their heads—ugh—I must catch them.

Ever watch one of those chicken scrambles at the county fair, where they turn about 10 unsuspecting chickens loose in the arena along with 30 children who run them down and tackle them? I mean throw their bodies down upon the birds? At age 58, this method has lost its charm, although after 20 laps around the chicken pen in my hot overalls, I am about to resort to childhood tactics. I am desperate.

Finally, after cornering one, I look the red rooster in the eye, all the while holding out both arms, to bluff his escape. Very slowly I close in before encouraging his escape along the fence, which is within the grasp of my outstretched right arm. Zoom! Red feathers fly past. I clutch at a wing. I have him!

"Squawk, squawk," hollers the rooster.

"Squawk, squawk," answers Chester.

I carry the rooster upside down to the chopping block. As I position his head sideways on the block, I avoid looking him in the eye and concentrate on sending this hapless bird to his reward as painlessly and swiftly as possible. Chop! It is done.

I hold on to the bird until it relaxes. Blood spurts from the severed neck. When the last muscle ceases to twitch, I toss him into the wheel-barrow before repeating the process. After wheeling the three headless roosters down to the porch, I dunk each one into the hot water to scald them, so the feathers will release easily for picking.

Out on the lawn, I pluck them under the cool shade of a willow tree, then plunge the bodies into cold water to cool them. After they are picked clean, I pull out their innards, dress them, gut them.

From then on the task isn't all that unpleasant. I separate the membrane from the gizzard, observing what the bird ate for breakfast, which includes a lot of grass. Chester hasn't been letting them eat at HIS hens' feed trough!

The Rhode Island roosters are healthy, not too fat, unlike those Cornish-cross fryer types, and will make tasty fried chicken. I save one for Sunday dinner and throw the rest in the freezer.

Just as I am cleaning up the mess, Doug returns from the potato fields. He has no comment except "Good morning." To him, I am doing what every ranch woman is expected to do. No big deal.

July 20—As the "Thunder moon" wanes, the thunder remains. Yesterday afternoon it boomed and echoed over the valley like Nez Perce drums, well into the lovely evening. It was accompanied by a soft wind that stirred the bright Icelandic poppies and exercised the rows of half-grown corn in my vegetable garden. The rain fell, refreshed the wildflowers, dampened the hay and released its alfalfa fragrance.

The Canadian thistles are nearing maturity. No matter how hard we fight to be rid of them, they always win. The long rows of baled hay march toward the mountains, lying in green fields all over the valley.

Sunday is a day of rest for the Houghs. Their haying came to a halt late Saturday evening, after they worked until after dark in a race against building storm clouds. The small tractor with the hay rake attached is parked at the edge of the field. The behemoth hay compressor that spits out "bread loaves" is silent now, until the hay dries out enough to continue.

This weekend, at opposite ends of the county, two "cultural events" took place. Friday and Saturday, Wallowa Lake was the scene for the annual "Jazz at the Lake" thing...2,500 people expected, according to the paper.

Down in Wallowa town the annual friendship feast and powwow, staged by descendants of the Wallowa band of Nez Perce native Americans, was being held. I didn't attend either one.

I enjoyed the day on Sunday, which was not advertised in the papers, here on Prairie Creek. Most of the day I was alone, Doug having to change sprinklers, as he gives the hired men Sunday off, and then make a 60-mile round trip to the hills to check on water conditions and put a wandering bull back in his pasture.

After attending Fishtrap, which Marc Jaffe calls a "family reunion" (and he is absolutely right), I have been inspired to begin my book, which my editor, Virgil Rupp, says is long overdue. After meeting with writers from all over and being exposed to some wonderful stuff, like "thinking," and taking the time to think, it is time I get on with it.

Yesterday, alone, I did a lot of it. I will continue to write this column, although some weeks it might not get written, as I will be working on my book.

Chief Joseph Days begins this week, and our small cow town of Joseph, which isn't a cow town any more, will overflow with thousands of visitors coming to taste the "Wild West," while the real West continues on its quiet working way in the rural areas, away from and beside Highway 82, where the action isn't, but is, really.

Sweaty men and boys haying, irrigators in muddy hip-boots, cowboys riding the fence lines, putting out salt, checking on water. The women doing same, others cooking big meals, taking food to the hay field, running children here and there. Wallowa County youths working at summer jobs, saving money for college; weary men sinking into easy chairs at the end of the day, exhausted, but getting up at dawn to continue with what has to be done to keep the ranch or farm—the West that most people never see.

July 30—The zucchini is ready! I picked the first two this morning. After days filled with the sound of thunder and accompanying storms, our summer has returned. The vegetable garden and flower beds bask in a tropical paradise. Everywhere it is green, even the hills, normally burned and toasted by July's end, are wearing a greenish tint. The irrigated valleys and meadows wear spring shades of green. In July.

How I love the freshness of those first vitamin-giving vegetables: new red potatoes, peas, swiss chard, lettuce, and the early cabbage. We are enjoying them all. Caring for a garden isn't work; a garden feeds the body and soul of the gardener.

My wildflower patch is riotous with color, especially the Icelandic poppies, which just keep on blooming and blooming. The California poppies add their golden touch, and the assortment of seeds I sowed this spring are all but ready to burst into bloom. I can't wait for the old-fashioned varieties to open...zinnias, marigolds, sweet William, petunias, snapdragons, and cosmos. The cosmos have been in bloom for some time. The aptly named "Sensation Mix" is full of color: bright pink, lavender, pale pink, white. A row of calendulas shading from pale yellow to bright orange glows among my wildings.

My gardens provide solace and an escape from the hectic routine of a Wallowa County summer. Each warm day, followed by warm nights, brings the 140 acres of potato plants in our three fields closer to maturity. The long rows have filled with foliage now, and some earlier plantings are nearly seed size already. The fields have required constant attention; cultivating, irrigating, applying pesticides, and rigorous inspections.

Between raking, baling, and stacking hay and the seed potato operation, Doug, Ben and Steve spend little time doing anything else.

Ben's son Seth is here each day, weekends included, to change the sprinklers. Ben swathes, irrigates, loads and stacks hay, checks cattle, and attends to all those myriad details that are part of ranching. Doug bales, sometimes into the night, and rakes hay, irrigates, and changes wheel lines. Steve spends all of his time in the potato fields. There is little time for rest.

And fall calving time is here! Ben reported the first two in the lower field this morning. Doug rode the Honda up to the high moraine pasture this afternoon and found several cows had already calved there too!

Chief Joseph Days has come and gone, and all those people, too, who smothered our small town of Joseph for three days, and left in the wake of the annual celebration...countless paper cups, beer cans, and wrappers of every sort. Under the grandstands of the Harley Tucker Memorial arena, tons of trash. I spotted old-timer Gilbert Marlin last Monday morning, quietly and slowly picking things up and putting Joseph back together. Countless other volunteers have been doing same. The tipis have been taken down from where they stood along the creek, next to the rodeo grounds. I miss them and look forward each year to their return.

According to reports, the visiting tribes had a wonderful time this year, carrying on with their traditional ceremonies and dances. They are to be commended for holding on all these years to their culture, their heritage, and their pride.

I always sense their caring for one another as a group, rather than for just themselves... They love their children and respect their elders. They are family. Whether it be community, or tribe, or an encampment at Chief Joseph Days, they conduct themselves with quiet dignity and a slowness of purpose that we could all learn from. These native Americans simply enjoyed being together and doing things together.

Our extended family was in a world of its own after the rodeo on Sunday, when the official Chief Joseph Days ended. There were thirty-one of us! We practiced a little tradition too: the gathering of the clan.

We picnicked outside in the yard on that lovely summer evening, eating homemade ice cream, freshly-baked wild blackberry cobblers, and watermelon. We played games, from the youngest to the oldest, in a circle, laughing a lot, until way after dark. Some left earlier, as they had a long way to drive home. Some came earlier than others and some later, from their hay fields where they had been baling.

Come as you are. Be as you are. Family. Like the native Americans, eat, play, work. Live and hold on to tradition and roots. As I see it, the loss of what I am saying here is why there are so many troubled souls in our increasingly complex society. Family can be community, city, or the entire Northwest. We should uphold what we value the most and strive to keep what we all live here for.

Off the soapbox!

Some time ago I received a letter in the mail:

Dear Janie, Hope you've told prospective visitors to come another day, because three of us hope you'll do Maxwell Lake at 10:00 a.m. Tuesday July 28, meeting where the road up the Lostine turns off the highway. Then we could follow you home for a glimpse of a real Oregonian at work play and!! Fan mail.

Maryann, you remember, was the gal, I took to LeGore Lake two years ago. She reads my column sometimes, she says, when a friend gives her a copy of Agri-Times. So, I sticky-taped Maryann's letter to the calendar and went. Actually friend Linde and I met the three: Karen, MA's daughter, and her friend, Elaine, waiting there as planned.

After driving the 17 miles up the graveled South Fork road to the Maxwell Lake trailhead, it was nearing noon when we shouldered our day packs and struck off up the trail. The elevation at the trailhead is 5,520' and we would be climbing 4 miles to Maxwell Lake at 7,760'.

Eagle Cap came into view, and the Fast Fork of the Lostine, with its huge white waterfall visible through the evergreens, spilling down to join the South Fork. How I yearned to go on and on to see once again the lovely East Fork, with its wind-flower-filled meadows and its crystal-clear stream meandering through it all.

Remember, any of you, the scenic view prints of the West that Standard Oil Company handed out when you purchased gas at their stations? Somewhere in the late 1940s or early '50s. Anyway, they were great prints. "THE GLORY OF THE WEST." Full-color photographs taken by such well-know photographers of the day as Ray Atkeson, Ansel Adams, Joseph Henry Jackson, Bernard DeVoto, and J. Frank Dobie.

Well, one of those prints was of the Wallowa Mountains. The photograph, taken by the late Ray Atkeson, showed a pack string of horses and men making their way up a lovely glaciated valley, backgrounded by the Wallowas. On back of the print, writer Ernest Haycox wrote,

It is in many ways the most rugged chunk of Oregon, and the stranger it seems that these hulking mountain chains and great granite-glittering peaks have fashioned a land without direction or pattern. But, by one canyon or another, the trails lead upward through odored aisles of timber and along yard-wide ledges hanging over space toward the Basin.

Haycox went on to describe the high lakes, and how it is to camp beside one. That poster and those words haunted me; I was 14 then, and a young married mother. The print hung on our wall and I wanted to crawl into the picture.

Thirty years later, I would be there, and recognize that very spot where Ray Atkeson must have set up his tripod. Leading a hike for my 4-H group, I would stop in wonderment after searching the Wallowas for years find the place. The East Fork hasn't changed in all those years, and neither has Maxwell Lake, which I hadn't visited for 16 years, and then in deep snow.

This time, I was able to see this lovely area in Alpine springtime. You can be sure the lake will draw me there again.

August 7—It's the same story every year. I say to myself I'm going to cut down on summer activities, like the Wallowa County Fair, for instance. I'll just watch my grandchildren show their market animals and stroll leisurely around the grounds taking it all in, visiting neighbors, eating a hamburger at the food booth without working in it. You know, stuff like that.

Then August rolls around and once again many of us are smitten with what I call "fair-itis," a malady that afflicts young and old alike, and virtually all former 4-H'ers, myself included. Like malaria, once in the blood, the disease is there to stay.

We not only continue to participate, but seem to involve ourselves more and more with each passing year. We have all those years of experience, after all. Can't let them go to waste. So here I am, sitting down at my kitchen table, surrounded by canned peaches, staring at my typewriter, three days past my column deadline, wondering what to type.

I spent most of yesterday and today at the fair. Yesterday morning, bright and early, Linde and I took our photos down to be entered in the open class photography exhibit at Cloverleaf Hall. Then returned that afternoon to work on our photography club's booth. In the interim I rode herd on four grandchildren while daddy supervised the clipping of Josh's steer. The children, full of the energy that I lacked, talked me into taking them fishing.

So there I was, trudging over the hill to the creek, worm pail in one hand and a handmade stick pole in the other, dodging sprinkler pipes but getting soaked anyway. The fish were biting, and four fish later we trudged back to the house, where I fixed lunch.

Then little hands picked the raspberries and bore them proudly to me.

"Bake us a cobbler, grandma." So I did and, between dad and his brood, the fresh warm dessert was inhaled in less time than it takes to tell about it.

When the children left, I returned to the fair, and there was Nancy Carlsen stapling American tradition—red, white and blue—all over Cloverleaf Hall. And here I was again, my 23rd year at the Wallowa County Fair.

I'm not alone, however. Many have been there much longer. Familiar faces, back again every year. *Fair-itis.*

August 8—This morning found me in the cool of dawn, in the garden, gathering zucchini, snow peas, lettuce, cabbage and potatoes to enter in the horticulture division. Why? I simply couldn't help myself. The fair premium book is forever imprinted on my mind. I remembered, as I picked three cosmos, three single Shasta daisies, three calendulas, making sure the specimens were uniform in size and color, blowing off the ants and removing the extra leaves on the stems.

I loaded the flowers in cans of water into the car, along with the vegetables and more props for the photography club's booth: a wagon wheel, some potted blue lobelia, an American flag, and a large bouquet of Shasta daisies in a white enamel coffee pot. Linde pulls in the driveway. I can tell she has fair-itis too. All of the tell-tale signs are there. Her car is loaded with blooming red geraniums and more props for the booth.

Down at Cloverleaf Hall, the wonderful scene is the same as it has been for years. A small boy stands dutifully holding two huge sunflowers in each hand, waiting for his mother to enter them. Another boy walks in carrying a frosted cake, a wheat league cake recipe entry for his mother, who is carrying more baked goods. She has been up before dawn, baking.

Proud gardeners bring in their best cabbages, onions, potatoes, green beans, and raspberries. Many enter from as far away as Imnaha, bearing Wallowa County's bounty. I sense a pride here in our valley, and a desire to show off what our dirt produces.

There are volunteers everywhere. People helping people amid lots of laughter. Reatha McCormack hanging quilts, Hope McLaughlin donating her time. Familiar faces. This is what makes our fair tick. I spot a few younger faces coming in now, taking over where some have dropped out or left us.

This morning Chris, Linde and I laughed until we cried, trying to prop up a stuffed "man" we'd created to pose over this tripod taking photos. We named our man "Walt" after our local master photographer, Walter Klages, of whom we all are very proud. "Walt" kept falling over until we secured him to the tripod with baling wire. After the last prop was in place, we stood back and approved our handiwork.

Now, back to reality and the typewriter.

August 3—Monday—This past weekend was the Tippett family reunion, and the last of the family stayed until today, which was nice, except for me it became a day of washing towels and sheets and generally cleaning up.

After having 16 here Saturday night for dinner, with many sleeping in every bed in the house, plus two tents and the sheepherder wagon, things were in a state of disarray.

August 5—Inez Meyers called from Imnaha last evening, to say the early Elberta peaches were ready. So, this morning early, Linde and I drove the 30 miles to Imnaha to Inez's pretty little place there along the Imnaha River to pick those lovely peaches to can.

By noon, one canner-full was finished and a fresh peach cobbler bubbled away in the oven.

Also received a letter from sister Mary Ann, from the Caribbean island of St. Lucia. She writes of her life on a tropical island and her training for her Peace Corps assignment on Dominica. She sounds a little homesick.

Every time I mention not writing a column, I receive letters from people. Like the one that came this week from Kohler Betts of Adams, Oregon. Kohler is concerned about my determination to write a book, as he thinks this task will rob me of time to continue my column. He says he might not be around to enjoy the book when it is finally finished. Because of Kohler's wonderful letter, and for others like Blanche Strey of Lacy, Washington, I'll carry on as long as I can.

Marc Jaffe will be pleased to hear I have begun my book, even though it has been put on hold due to fair-itis. Perhaps we'll have one of those old-fashioned winters again, with deep snows, so I can hole up and write. Now, here in Wallowa County, we must make hay while the sun shines.

August 17—Having just smashed my fingers in the pick-up door this morn, my two fingers on my right hand are not usable at the moment, so am typing this with my left hand!

I included some photos I took of the fair, which just ended. WHEW! Hope they can take the place of my column for this week. And if my fingers aren't broken, I'll have a column next week. There's no shortage of things to write about, which means there's just NO time.

I have an antelope tag. Season opens in morning, and it is the Cattle-Women's and stockgrowers annual meetings all day! I must cover it for the Beef Producer! Oh my.

We've had a granddaughter from Pendleton here all week on top of the fair every day, and apples to sauce. Granddaughter is now peeling apples. Doug will deliver this when he takes Lacey back to Pendleton.

My garden is wonderful. Want some zucchini? You should see my wildflower patch. Want to go into Red's Horse Ranch, but if I go antelope hunting I can't until following week. Would love to just go to the mountains and hibernate, but far too much going on here.

August 21—Awakened from a sound sleep Wednesday night by the ringing of our bedside phone...the voice of daughter Ramona at 12:30 a.m. Did we know Mt. Howard was on fire?

Doug and I staggered sleepily out of bed and made our way to the kitchen, from which vantage point we would look out to what resembled an erupting volcano. The mountain, named after General Howard, whose army captured the fleeing Nez Perce of Chief Joseph's Wallowa Band before they made their escape into Canada, is directly in line with the window over the kitchen sink.

Great streamers of fire catapulted down the steep mountainside. Dead and dying timber and other dry fuels fed the fire as it shot upward in a pitchy holocaust. In the dark it was hard to tell exactly where on the mountain the fire was located, but I guessed it to be about a mile or so from the Mt. Howard Tramway terminal. The sky above reflected the redness of flames, which continued to explode and move on with terrifying speed. Burning snags fell, starting spot fires that took off below the main fire in the timbered steep terrain.

Earlier that evening, as I lay in bed listening to the thunder and watching flashes of lightning play upon the walls, I remembered how hot the preceding days had been and knew the forest was tinder dry.

Doug and I, weary that evening, had retired early and slipped into a deep sleep, having just that afternoon returned from a rushed antelope hunt. That's another story. Ramona's late night call had transpired because grandson Shawn had been called up to help man the gondola, which was being operated to transport firefighters to the summit of Mt. Howard. As an employee of the Mt. Howard Tramway all summer, Shawn had been earning money to help finance his enrollment at Blue Mountain Community College in Pendleton.

Then, Ramona got to thinking about our fall calvers, which are, in fact, now in the process of calving up there in their 1,000-acre pasture, which runs up the lower slopes of Mt. Howard. Given a high wind or lack of fire suppression in such steep terrain, there was a chance the fire could race down and become a very real threat to our cows. Needless to say, I didn't get a lot of rest that long night. Doug, however, promptly went back to sleep.

Morning came, bringing prevailing winds in our favor. The fire was now eating its way up the mountain and down into the draw on the southern side. Luckily it was also traveling away from the gondola's summit terminal. Soon helicopters were scooping great buckets of water from Wallowa Lake and emptying them over the fires.

By mid-afternoon weary firefighters had the blazes under control. Just in time, because our 90-degree heat had returned and a dry wind had materialized out of the south. Not so good news from the fire raging in the Payette Forest in Idaho, which lies just across the Snake from us. In the heat of yesterday afternoon great billowing clouds of smoke formed and boiled away under white thunderheads in the east.

Other than a few spot fires resulting from some 80 lightning strikes here in our county that Wednesday evening, we seem to be all right, at the moment.

So, while Wallowa County holds its breath, we worry about our less fortunate neighbors in Idaho. As I type, the smoke from those Idaho fires fills our valley. The mountains are but dim smoky outlines, and through the haze we see more thunder clouds building over our valley. But it is cooler. Already there is a feeling of fall in the air here on Prairie Creek.

The morning sun rose hazy yellow, sifting through gilded dark clouds on the eastern horizon. Mt, Howard was wreathed in sleeping smoke. A yellow pallor colors the morning, the autumnal golden light intensifying the pinks of cosmos, yellows of marigolds, and the varied colored wildflowers. Hough's bread loaf hay is stacked against the winter, the sprinklers continue to irrigate the second cutting of alfalfa. The cattle graze the pastures that lay close to the toasted hills.

It is a lovely time. The intense heat is gone. The burgeoning, tropical vegetable garden is lush, its growth heavy and rank. I can scarcely make my way through it. The first sunflowers have opened, the purple string beans hang in clusters, snow peas beg to be picked, Blue Lake green beans come on, ripen overnight; beets, carrots, lettuce, onions, potatoes all have reached maturity. Corn rows form silky ears. Everything is pregnant! Yellow and green zucchini.

August 30—OH MY GOSH! My name was drawn for an antelope tag in the Beulah unit, where I bagged my antelope some nine years ago, and where Doug shot his last August. Naturally, the short season is open during one of the busiest times for us ranchers. Opening morning fell on the annual Stockgrowers and CattleWomen's annual meetings last Saturday, and then the potatoes had to be rogued, because OSU field inspections were scheduled for Tuesday.

After the inspection, it was nearly dark when we pulled out of the county. At the summit of Dooley Mountain we parked our mini-motor home and tried to catch some sleep. It was 11 p.m. We were exhausted from the hectic summer schedule, and it was so hot. Finally a cool breeze wandered over the mountain top and the absolute stillness lulled us to sleep.

At 4:30 I awoke with a start that roused Doug, and soon we were driving down off Dooley Mountain. Daylight seeped into the peaceful bottoms near Hereford as we followed the Burnt River to Unity. Mule deer and fawns scampered in front of us on their way from the alfalfa fields. Little cottontail rabbits ran everywhere.

We were surprised at how green everything was. The springs looked healthy and, thanks to the ranchers, hay fields were green. Newly baled hay lay in the fields or was just being cut. The scent of newly mowed hay came to us in the dawn, full of dew and fragrant in the morning air. It was a quiet, peaceful ranching area; cattle, horses and ranch buildings. Nice. The small settlement of Unity dozed, not a light was on, even the Water Hole" was silent at that early hour.

As we drove out of Unity, two yearling buck antelopes crossed from the unit I couldn't hunt in, and scrambled up the bank into the Beulah unit! It was cool and peaceful in the pale daylight before sunup in the fragrant sagebrush hills, where I stalked and bagged my little buck. He was fat and the meat looked good. After driving to a nearby campground, Doug skinned the buck while I cooked breakfast along East Camp Creek.

This campground is like home away from home to us. We have used its facilities each time we come antelope hunting. Hanging from a tree limb, the meat chilled out in the crisp morning air. The morning sunlight came filtering through the forest. The little stream gurgled, birds sang, the air was pure and fresh, and a herd of Simmental cross cows and calves came up to the fence to say good morning before making their way down the road or ambling slowly through the trees, grazing. They were fat, sleek, and resembled our own range cattle in all colors.

"Injun cattle," Doug calls them.

Not another soul occupied the campground, which boasted picnic tables, trash cans, and clean outhouses. Several empty log trucks drove by, up into the mountains. Some returned, loaded with logs. The drivers honked at the cows and calves. Compatible.

A Forest Service pickup pulled in. A woman about my age got out and began to clean the toilets and empty the garbage cans. I walked over and struck up a conversation with her, opening with how impressed I was with the cleanliness of the campground, and how my husband and I enjoyed seeing the cattle and the log trucks; how it was healthy to see the economy going here, like it belonged.

She looked at me with incredulous eye. "Really," she said, "most people object to both." I liked her immediately. She had the look of an Eastern Oregon ranch woman about her. She was sunburned, hard, muscled, healthy, outdoorish, with common sense stamped all over her. I wasn't surprised when she told me she had been a local rancher until her husband just died.

Rather than move to town and work at a job there and live away from the country she loved, she opted to stay in the country and maintain the campgrounds for the Forest Service. We had a nice visit. I think I would rather clean toilets than live in the city myself.

September 22—Pear butter *blurps* away on a slow burner; spicy smells fill my kitchen-office with "essence of fall." The calendar my sister Mary Ann gave me for Christmas says today is the first day of autumn. Already? What happened to July, August and most of September?

I look again, unable to read the days of the months because so many words are written over them. That's what happened... those words translate what's happening to my life. As I reflect on those busy days, I wonder why? Some business was necessary, but most was not.

It is a warm, golden morning here on Prairie Creek. Blackbirds hold concerts in the yellowing willows; frosted, withered cornstalks rattle in the breeze; under a topaz sky, heavy-headed sunflowers, browned by frost and starved for moisture, droop forlornly. Nothing survives in the wildflower patch, save for the sky-blue cornflowers and a few scraggly poppies.

The "Oregon Spring" tomato plants next to the south window are dead, and the last of the smaller, shriveled green tomatoes cling to the vines. The three young Northwood maples have flamed and died; the hills are colorless and grassless due to the drought and earlier frosts. Red geraniums, which spent those frosty nights in the living room, are now enjoying a return to summer or, perhaps, the coming of Indian summer.

Two saddle horses wander around, allowed now to graze the tall golden grasses that have grown between the house, garden and chicken pen. The air is soft and sunlight falls at different angles now. This morning it rests a while on my bookcase, full of books, which tempts me away from this typewriter.

Fall is here. My time. Only I am so busy I have only time for small sips of it. My soul, however, is seized with that now-familiar wanderlust that pulls me away to the mountains, hills, canyons, the outback. The vagabond spirit.

Pulling in the opposite direction is this seasonal urge to preserve everything in sight; press apple cider and make sauerkraut; can pears, apples, and tomatoes; pickle beets; preserve jams and jellies. Not to mention store dried "keeping" onions, red potatoes, and carrots, and put a few heads of cabbage in cold storage. It all tastes so good during our long, cold Wallowa County winters. Kind of like opening a jar of summer or fall and tasting the autumn sweetness again.

When it is 20 below and snow covers the frozen landscape, just the sight of my canning cupboard warms the spirit, but today it is supposed to climb into the 80s. Yesterday was a soft 70 when we made apple cider with an old wooden press on Alder Slope, beneath Ruby Peak. It was work, but worth the effort. By the time I wearily returned to the ranch, bearing several jugs of sweet cider, it was after 6 p.m. and my day was long from over.

After preparing a hearty pork chop supper for Doug, son-in-law Tom, who arrived here to help with the potato harvest, and 5-year-old Ryan, I tended to the apple cider, washed the dishes and fled to bed with a good book.

Yes, our seed potato harvest has begun. Somehow, I find it ironic that we have in excess of 20 workers (two daughters, a son-in-law and a son included), yet back in the ranch house, yours truly, the woman-of-the-house, has NO help.

HELP!

It's nothing new. For generations our role of ranch women would stagger most imaginations. We do grandchildren, can, garden, chickens, cooking, sewing, mending, washing, baking, housework, and community work; we help neighbors and our husbands, provide a telephone answering service, run myriad errands, not to mention actively work on the ranch itself. We do bookwork, coordinate workers, trouble shoot, grocery shop, and attend meetings to become informed on issues that affect our very way of life.

HELP. And if you are a ranch-wife-writer, heaven help you! This year I am not working on the digger, but I have a a hot, hearty meal ready at the beginning and ending of each long, dirty day, for those who do. Don't get me wrong. We all love our lifestyle. But when you figure the average age of ranch women today is 60, who is going to want to take our places? Granted, there are a few out there, but their numbers are dwindling and many of them have the added burden of working off the ranch to support it.

Hopefully, in about three weeks, depending on breakdowns, help, and weather, the potato harvest will end. Then it will be time for yours truly to cook up a big supper for the annual harvest get-together in our shop, which is our way of saying thank you to those faithful workers who helped make the harvest possible. Without them, we are sunk! And with each passing year, good help is becoming increasingly difficult to find.

After the potatoes are all dug, our beautiful fall will be gone. Indian summer will have blown away in the final flutter of a withered aspen leaf. Then the familiar cold winds of winter will sweep across Prairie Creek, and the old Monarch will gulp seasoned tamarack and cook our meals, and we will spread thick pear butter on our whole wheat toast for breakfast.

So, today I steal a few sips of fall. I savor the cinnamony smell of pear butter. I listen to the blackbirds through the screen door, step out into the golden sunshine, pat my dog on the head, and listen to the young roosters crow, as I haven't had time to finish butchering them. I feel the soft September breeze upon my cheek. And in this month of my 59th birthday, I gaze longingly up toward the slopes of the mountains and see that the cottonwoods and aspen thickets are yellowing, and the tamaracks are just beginning to lighten.

Will the elk still be bugling on Sheep Ridge? The clock *tick-tocks* over the mantel. The enemy, TIME, flows, like Thoreau's stream, toward eternity. Again I look at my scribbled calendar and ponder. It is called living. Coping. "Taking each day as it comes," says my husband. Some days are a little harder than others.

The yellow Joseph school bus drives by now. Our road is a quiet one, really. A few ranchers passing by, saddle horses loaded in old trucks, Mark Butterfield hauling loads of hay to Imnaha, an occasional hunter passing early of a morning. Most are neighbors, and we wave.

It is quiet here on the ranch today, removed from the leased potato fields. Ancient trucks, laden with their full loads, rumble on into our Joseph cellars now, the newest cellar here having been filled last week with our own seed.

For the first time in weeks, I have time to sit down and resume this column. For the sake of all those nice people who have stopped by to visit, or phoned or written letters, I will attempt to keep writing. However, you must understand that, in spite of the most disciplined organization, my time is not my own. And not unlike my many contemporaries out there on ranches and farms all over the West.

I REALLY wanted to write about our grouse hunting trip, our pack trip into the Wallowas, the pit barbecue birthday get-together on Alder Slope, the Labor Day CattleWomen's steak feed, and all the other events that shape our everyday lives, but somehow, I got off on the wrong trail.

Three weeks ago, Linde and I stole away and hiked eight miles up the lovely Hurricane Creek trail, and on another occasion, taking Betty Hammond with us, we drove to Paradise and picked apples and pears.

This winter, when I drink a golden glass of cider, I'll recall those happy times. Contained in that sweet elixir will be the combined memories of Paradise, Prairie Creek, and Alder Slope.

September 27—Last Sunday evening I rode up to the high east moraine of Wallowa Lake with Doug when he hauled water up there to our fall calvers. As the water from the tank gurgled and filled the big water trough, Doug and I listened to the quiet below. Alpenfest had just ended, and the Mt. Howard gondola was coming down for its last ride of the season. The tourists had all gone and the lake was ours again. Spidery filigree floated silently through the air; the quietness was so soothing. The lake, due to drought, was very low, lower than I can remember.

I thought about grandson Shawn, who worked all summer at the Mt. Howard tramway, saving his money for college. He would leave after work to attend Blue Mountain Community College in Pendleton.

September 29—This morning, 84-years-young Mike McFetridge, Mike's grandson, Tim, and yours truly tended to the cattle ranching detail, while our potato crews kept busy at the Joseph cellars and digging in the fields. After driving the long miles out to our Butte Creek place, we unloaded our three saddled horses and began to ride the big pasture to gather 95 pair I helped move there a month ago.

Thankfully, we still have water, but the grass is fast disappearing, and from now on the cows won't milk as good, and therefore their calves won't do as well.

Doug was having us cowboys trail the herd to Deadman, which is closer to our corrals, so it will be much handier to gather, sort and ship the calves when we wean. When the calves have gone over the mountain to Hermiston, we will trail the mother cows into the valley and begin to feed them hay because of the drought, which is now entering its seventh year. Many years in the past, there has been sufficient feed to allow the cattle to stay out there until December.

On such a lovely fall morning I guess there was no place the three of us would rather have been than out under those wide autumn skies, gathering cows and calves among those quiet, rolling, unpeopled hills.

"Daisy," my newly acquired Border collie bitch, was in her element as she eagerly followed along; enjoying one's work, the secret of true happiness.

Twenty head of mule deer does and fawns blended so well with the tawny color of the hills, all we could see was the movement of white beneath their tails. Tim spotted them first, then a buck and, off to one side, a coyote slinking along.

Butte Creek glinted in autumn light. A riparian area, beautiful in spite of, though perhaps because of, cattle, which have grazed it for many years. Fall color in ninebark, aspen and thornbrush. Alongside the "crik" are green carpets of grass, shaded by thornbrush thickets and tall ponderosa pines. A haven for deer, elk, coyote, cattle...providing water, shade, grass, and cover. Precious dry bunch grass upon the hills. The cowboys are careful not to overgraze, and to leave grass there to winter over, providing protection for the new growth, and feed for wildlife when the snows come.

The bulk of the herd was across the crik, grazing a steep hillside. I took that side. Mike rode tip the creek. Tim rode the opposite hill. What a picture it made, though I had no camera, save my mind's eye: 95 pair, all streaming up out of the creek bottom and coming off the hills right and left to form one bunch. A cowboy's dream.

We drove them up the bottom, and thence up the fence line to the far gate. Morning sunlight lit up the backs of those sleek Simmental crosses and the dust sparkled and muted the scene. A shame, but this cowgirl-photographer didn't have time for picture-taking; she had to ride on ahead to get a count as the cattle flowed through the opened gate onto the dirt road. So, she here paints you a "word picture" instead.

Quickly the morning warmed, and by the time we. had the cattle halfway to Deadman it was downright hot. Our far-off, snow-splotched Wallowas were always present to remind us how vast was this outback, an outback watched over by the cowboys, today, as it has been all during "old hand" Mike McFetridge's life. If left in the hands of these "men of the land," the hills will remain cared for. These men and women, whom you don't see often in town, are the ones who repair the fences, develop water holes, check cattle, and take care of the grass. They truly love the hills; the real reason for good stewardship.

More than 100 years of this kind of caring has allowed this vast grass land to remain intact, preserved, if you will, by experts. Long live the cowboy! The unsung hero of the hills, valleys, canyons and mountains.

When we got the cattle strung out on the road, and Mike loaded his horse in the truck and drove to Salmon Creek. He left the truck there and rode back in time to help us turn them into Deadman. We ate our lunches after riding back to the corrals, then loaded up our horses and headed back to the valley ranch. It was 86 degrees on Prairie Creek. I unsaddled my mare, gathered eggs, and prepared an enchilada casserole for the "potato men."

Ryan returned from his day on upper Prairie Creek, full of vitality, vim and vigor. His daddy and grandpa weren't that lively, and they were covered with dirt and sweat.

I feel sorry for the gals on the digger. A dirty job, and so tiring, and then they must go home and prepare supper, do housework, tend to families and get enough rest to climb aboard the digger the next day. Such is agriculture. Next time you enjoy steak and taters, remember what it took to bring these popular foods to the table. Ditto for all the other farm commodities grown in our diminishing agricultural communities.

September 30—There now, I've sat myself down at the kitchen table in front of my trusty, little Smith-Corona and typed out the above date. It has taken me since dawn to be able to do this. After fixing breakfasts for Doug, son-in-law Tom and five-year-old Ryan, making lunches, doing dishes, watering trees, feeding dogs and cats, checking on my two very pregnant milk cows, feeding my mare some withered corn-stalks, tending to the chickens, answering the phone (an all-day job in itself), writing letters, taking meat out of the freezer for supper, making lists of errands to run in town, and reading last night's paper, finally I am ready to write.

The morning is all but gone. Perhaps because I took time to contemplate the changing autumn weather and pick a handful of sweet peas so I could savor their sweet perfume while I type.

Mini-vacations! A busy person's secret to survival and peace of mind. As a warm, dry wind moves mare's tails across an autumn sky, the smell of smoke drifts into the valley from the forest fire we hear is burning near Cornucopia in Baker County, over the mountain southeast of here. The fall wind's hot breath shrinks the new snow, which fell over the high places during last week's cold spell.

This month brings a yo-yo mix of weather; cold and heat, separated by hours, and never a gradual change.

And now, at noon, it is already 80 degrees.

The warm winds have torn loose what little fall color Prairie Creek had, and sapped what little moisture we received during last week's brief storm. Most of the ancient willows and cottonwoods along the farmers' ditches are still green. Others, away from the water, have lost their leaves altogether. The colors in Joseph were lovely last week but, due to the heat and dryness and earlier frosts, have passed their peak. The huge maples that line the end of Main Street are shedding their leaves, and great golden mounds of them are piling up along the sidewalk and on the dried lawns.

The drought shows no signs of abating. Out in the hills where most of our cows and calves are, the range is burnt brown by frosts and heat. The land wears the colorless, lifeless look of a lack of rain. These are coyote, mule deer, cottontail, and rockjack colors. It is so sad for us who live close to the land.

We pray for rain, even though it could mean a delay in the potato harvest or, for others, a disruption of grain harvesting or late cuttings of hay. Just let it rain, and rain, and then let it snow all winter to save our hills, canyons and valleys, and give our thirsty forests a long-awaited drink.

Sunday, we will trail the cows and calves on the moraine home, and turn them in hayed-over fields. Hopefully, the potato harvest will end next week.

October 3—This Saturday morning might have been the opening of general mule deer buck season in Wallowa County, but it was potato digging as usual on this ranch. Since it was also daughter Ramona's birthday, and she was working on the digger, grandchildren Adele and Ryan "helped" me bake a cake, and make a corsage of sweet peas and bachelor buttons, and a picnic lunch.

At noon we piled into the car and transported our "birthday party" to the potato field. Because it was windy, cold and sprinkling rain, all the workers were huddled in their rigs warming up. We held our party there in the dirty field and lit the candles away from the wind. The dirt-covered smiles made it all worthwhile.

I was remembering back in 1951, having just turned 18 and giving birth to this daughter.

Later that evening, Ramona, her husband Charley, and I attended "Landmark," a theatrical magazine for rural America, at the OK Theater in Enterprise. I had so hoped Doug could attend too, but it was 6:30 before he returned from the potato field, and then the bulls got out!

The Vigilante Theatre Company, which produces "Landmark," believes that its theater should relate to the lives of the people where they live. They searched and researched for the material, some they wrote themselves, and the result is this wonderful production. Four young men and women staged a drama of how country life is today. They deserve a wider audience.

Quoting from a note from the editor, printed in the program, *Less than 100 years ago over 80% of the people in our nation were directly involved in agriculture. Today the figure is near 3% or less. However, it is still the largest industry in the state of Montana and important to their entire region and the world. People come and go. The world grows smaller. And though the natural joys and difficulties are still present in farming and ranching, the country life just ain't what it used to be. Theatrical material on this new kind of life is not exactly abundant.*

The Vigilante Theatre Company is sponsored by the Montana "Agriculture in the Schools" program and believes its efforts "provide a better understanding of the contribution of agriculture to our lives and to the nation's economy." Through the medium of singing and acting, this small traveling theatre troupe brings more understanding to our city cousins.

It was good to see our local farmers and ranchers in the audience. During these times all of us need a little ego boosting and a good laugh.

The change in the weather and the much welcomed moisture made for a successful buck season weekend for our family. Grandson Buck shot his first muley on Imnaha, Uncle Charley hunted his own place and bagged a buck, and grandson Shawn, home from college for the weekend, got his venison somewhere in the vast outback of Wallowa County, as did son Todd. Todd took along his two sons, who, with their cousins Shawn and Buck, have some good huntin' stories to tell.

Cousin Rowdy shot his buck during bow season. Yes, we have a lot of young'ns growing up who love being out in the outdoors and love the taste of venison. Eighteen-year-old Shawn, who is doing his own cooking at college, will welcome the addition of some meat to go with his Top Ramen noodles.

October 4—Sunday morning early found old hand Mike McFetridge, Doug and me riding the steep moraine to gather our fall calving cows and their new calves. Only they didn't want to be gathered. What a time we had, riding and searching that wet and cold timbered tract, which runs halfway up the side of Mt. Howard and down along the east moraine of Wallowa Lake.

This 1,600 acres of high mountain meadow and timber is enclosed on the bottom side by a 16-foot-high elk fence, to keep the elk on the mountain and out of the ranchers' fields on upper Prairie Creek. The mountains and the lake below were obscured by an all-enveloping layer of cloud and fog, which lent an eerie feeling to the morning. Riding alone, all I could hear was the scolding of blue jays and camp robbers.

After many hours of hard riding, we turned the herd into a hayed-over field here on the ranch, and then went back after the truck and a calf that got away from us near Green's. Doug roped the husky little red calf, then tied him to a post and brought him home in the truck.

Who needs aerobics when you live like this? Must be in shape, as I'm not a bit sore today! Another plus for our lifestyle. It's a heifer!

October 5—It rained! Not much, but enough to dampen the ground and calm the dust in our potato fields, and enough to make frost on this clear, crisp fall morning.

I watched an early weather report on TV and, as usual, the coldest spots in the Northwest were not recorded. Walking out in the frosty grass to peer on the post that holds up the clothesline, I see that our temperature is 28 degrees. The coldest on TV was 30.

But then, Joseph isn't on the map, at least as far as weather is concerned. It is beginning to be, as a burgeoning tourist area and a haven for an influx of artists, but the truth about our weather is seldom found in travel brochures...If that fact were known, perhaps our rural county would not be invaded by all these new people who want to live here. Would they still want to do so when, in fact, on many occasions we have had the chilly distinction of being the coldest spot in the nation?

As I finish the final typing of this column at my kitchen table, I make frequent visits to the cow pasture or look through my binoculars. Startch seems to have picked this beautiful blue-and-gold autumn day to calve. I'll keep you informed.

Currently, the big concern in our rural areas is the continuation of our rights as private landowners. We ranchers, as part of the entire Western agricultural community, are under the gun, so to speak, in managing our natural resources. We are the buffer against a changing West. We hold the last frontier. Like our cattle during a storm, we are backed up in a corner. The biggest challenge of our time, and the future of our young agriculturists is on the fenceline. Which way to turn? What choices? What decisions? How to proceed? Up the fenceline, cross it, go back.

I have faith in us. Agriculturists have handled crises before. It is not "just luck" that we people of the land have managed to stay in business through droughts, depressions, and other numerous disasters. It took commitment and work and plenty of smarts. Now is the time for all of us to show that we can manage, have managed, and will manage the resources entrusted to us in such a manner as only people who love the land can. And so will our young agriculturists of the future.

But this will not come about without sacrificing time. We must keep informed, and that is hard when we need to be home doing the work. Because if you don't stay home and do the work, you can lose your ranch that way for sure. Oh my! Most importantly, it is a time to be united, not divided, for if we are to save what we value most, we need all the help we can get.

I feel a new breeze blowing over the West, a refreshing breeze called hope. Former National CattleWomen's president Gerda Hyde of Chiloquin, Oregon, has always stressed, "Tell our story. Let those masses of people, generations away from the farm, know who we are, where we've come from, and where we are going." Chances are, most of them have come from the same roots, and it's only generations of city life that has made them forget.

We must inform and educate. It is our only hope for survival. It's about preserving a way of life that could possibly be the salvation of our

entire country. Some of us are going to have to clean up our act, and our
water, and do a better job of managing our lands to show that we can.
We must set good examples; stay home and do the work. Perhaps some
good will come out of all this, if we all work together.

Alright, off the soapbox.

Barring unforeseen breakdowns or other numerous complications,
our potato harvest just might be finished as early as tomorrow. Yeah!

October 6—Yesterday, I mentioned that Startch, my large Simmen-
tal/Holstein milk cow, chose a gorgeous blue and gold day to give birth
to a heifer calf. Well, it was a heifer, but she didn't have it in the midst
of an Indian summer day. Far from it. Rather, it was born sometime
between midnight and 3 a.m. this morning.

It was a night to remember. Startch, who spent the previous afternoon
in obvious distress, still had nothing to show for her labor as night fell
over Prairie Creek. I checked her before I went to bed, and every hour
after that, until midnight. No front feet protruding, no contractions. I
began to worry, and even thought about calling the vet, but because this
cow is so big and roomy, I refused to believe she couldn't get the job
done on her own. Wrong!

At midnight, my big, black and white cow was still standing, nervously switching her tail. I went back to bed. At 3 a.m. I woke up with
a start. Heavy frost on the meadow grass glittered in moonlight as I
ran, flashlight in hand, to where I had last seen her. When I reached the
farthest end of the cow pasture, my heart nearly stopped.

In the pale moonlight I could see her white face and then all four of
her white-stockinged feet sticking straight up! Dead. But no: a sound, a
low moan. Beaming my flashlight in her direction, I could see the cow
was in a real jam. Apparently while calving, she had rolled down a slight
rise, which sloped down toward a fence. Unable to get up because of the
fence, she lay there totally helpless.

A white movement caught my eye to the left of the cow. Her calf!
The long, lanky black and white heifer, covered with amniotic fluid, stood
shivering in the fence corner. As fast as my clumsy rubber-booted feet
could carry me, I ran back to the bedroom and shook Doug awake. Then
back out to my cow, telling her to "hang in there."

After what seemed like an eternity, Doug appeared, assessed the
situation, then went back for the pickup to pull her out. I stayed with the
poor cow, who still couldn't get up and had rolled down next to the fence
again. There she was, huge udder sticking out from under her largeness.

Returning to the house for a suckle bottle, I managed to squeeze enough milk from her swollen teats (through the fence) to fill the bottle. The calf drank hungrily and butted me for more. Just as daylight seeped into Prairie Creek, a chorus of coyote puppies wailed from the dry hills. The cold creek gurgled and far up in an old cottonwood an owl hooted.

I walked back to the house and sank down on the sofa for a brief nap. When we could see better, Doug and I returned to the cow and cut the fence that was keeping her from getting up. Then we rolled her over on her other side downhill to a flat spot near the creek. She was so exhausted from her all-night ordeal that she didn't even attempt to stand. I was still worried about her, and didn't like the glassy look in her eyes.

Back in the kitchen, I fixed breakfast, and then had to drive to Alder Slope by 7:30 to pick up granddaughter Adele. She and brother James would be spending three days with grandma. On the way home, Adele and I stopped by the vet's and asked him to pay our cow a visit.

The vet soon determined that the cow had given birth to a backward calf, and therefore he suspected she had damaged herself inside. After some expert doctoring and more rest, Startch lurched to her feet. Hoorah!

Adele helped grandma bring the calf into the barn and named her "Happy."

October 12—We held our annual harvest dinner in the shop this evening, inviting all our potato workers and their families. I had more help this year. I did spend the entire day in the kitchen baking up a storm, but daughters Ramona and Jackie and grandchildren made it less work for grandma.

It has been freezing hard at night lately, and two days ago we had a slight skift of snow dust the high country. Clouds formed yesterday, and swirled over the Wallowas like cold smoke.

I made a final batch of salsa out of some of Jackie's Imnaha tomatoes, and canned some ripe prune plums. Just can't bear to see anything to to waste.

Last week I was rolling out a crust for a deep dish apple pie when Doug came into the kitchen and asked if I could help sort cattle and then drive them to another pasture. Sure. So, I invented "Cowgirl's Apple Pie." Here's the recipe:

In a pre-heated 425 oven, bake a deep dish pie for 15 minutes, then turn oven off. Saddle up, ride across the fields; gather, sort, and hold cows and calves in the lane; drive them to another pasture, return three hours later. Remove pie from oven. Delicious!

I watched the October full moon, the hunter's moon, rise over the dried hills Sunday evening, and watched it again from the cow barn

Monday morning as it dipped out of sight over Sheep Ridge.

October 14—Better enjoy the quiet while I can. The cowboys are hauling in our spring calves to be weaned. By nightfall that familiar wall of sound will well up from the corrals, as tenors, sopranos and altos form a bovine chorus: *Maaaaaaa...ma!* And mamas will be doing the same, far out on the lonely reaches of Salmon Creek.

October 15—It's been a week since Startch calved, and she is her old self again. The calf, which Adele helped tame, is growing like a weed. So is the little bull calf, which is also nursing. This milk maid, however, isn't faring quite as well, because, in addition to everything else in her busy life, she must now deal with this gargantuan udder twice a day.

We had company for two days, and that meant cooking for eleven that first evening after a sleepless night. Oh well, that's life. So now, on this Thursday, it is 5 a.m. and the only time I can find to type. Hopefully, today I will acquire another calf, because even after two calves are full, the kitty dish overflows, the dogs drink, and the chickens, and I milk for house milk, there is still milk. Help!

I complain, but really don't mind. I find it comforting to tuck my head against the warm flank of a cow and milk. Guess it was because I was reared on a dairy, and the smell and feel of a milk cow get in one's blood. We all look back on pleasant times in our childhoods, and this was mine. I raised registered Guernseys for my 4-H project and showed them at all the county, district and state fairs, and the Cow Palace in San Francisco. Like my daddy, I loved my cows.

On the wall in the cow barn hangs a metal sign with the ideal Guernsey cow and bull painted on it. An antique, they say. It was the original logo for the American Guernsey Cattle Club for years. My sister Mary Ann gave it to me as a gift. Speaking of Mary Ann, she is serving two years in the Peace Corps, on the island of Dominica. Way out in the Lesser Antilles, somewhere in the Caribbean. Her letters are fascinating. What an adventure!

October 16—Grace and I drove to the lower Imnaha and traded potatoes for some of Inez Meyers' wonderful winter squash. The ride down into the fall canyons is always pleasant and the reds and golds followed the draws and watercourses. The morning was crisp. Yesterday, it had gotten down to 16 degrees here on Prairie Creek. Imnaha, at a much lower elevation, had experienced only 32 degrees.

October 17—Today was a busy day for us cowboys and cow-gal! Out early on Salmon Creek, we caught our horses, saddled up and rode more of those large pastures to gather a different bunch of cows and calves. The morning quickly warmed into the 70s, and in spite of everything being so dry, recent light rains in the Zumwalt country have started new grass growing.

The dry bunch grasses must contain valuable nutrients this dry year, because our calves are weaning at heavier weights than ever. Some husky spring calves are going over 800 pounds! Mama cows, too, are in good shape. Cows and calves were widely scattered, and didn't want to go anywhere. They just wanted to stay there in those rolling hills. Can't say I blame them.

After some more hard riding and plenty of "Hey, girls, git along there," we finally got them all into one bunch and corraled into dusty corrals, where the bawling of cows and calves was intense. After Ky and Ben pulled out with the first two truckloads of bawling calves, Doug and I ate our lunches, and then sprayed the cows. We returned to the ranch, leaving Ky and Ben hauling calves.

Because they were so much larger this fall, not as many calves would fit into the old stock trucks. They were bulging at the seams and Ben's truck got a flat tire.

Shortly after we got home, daughter Lori and her husband, Tom, and their two children were here with their horse trailer to load up Lori's piano.

This evening Doug treated all of us to dinner at Cactus Jack's in Joseph. The steaks were wonderful and renewed our strength.

October 18—We listened to more of the "bawling calves concert," as the first bunch we weaned had finally ceased. Later this afternoon, we borrowed a horse trailer and drove to Wallowa, where we loaded my secondhand piano and hauled it home. Now I won't miss having a piano to play. This one is an old upright, like my grandmother's. By the looks of it, many little fingers have played upon its keys, which only adds to its charm.

Framed photographs of myriad grandchildren smile down from the top of the old piano as I steal a few moments each day to play. Music is soul food! The only thing left in my fall garden is a partial row of carrots. I dug some of the sweet vegetables the other day and placed them around a lamb brisket with potatoes and onions, then grated three cups and made a carrot cake. Doug's favorite.

There hasn't been any time left in these shortening fall days to do any hiking, but I do steal time to do a little photographing. The golden tamaracks call, but I can't seem to walk among them.

I often think of sister Mary Ann, now serving in the Peace Corps on her 29-mile-long Island of Dominica.

She writes: *Hot water is again a thing of the past! And I'm now a resident of Portsmouth, Dominica. Not that hot water and Portsmouth have any connection. It's just that after two weeks of hot showers in Roseau at Ruth's house on Cork Street, this morning's cold shower reminded me I'm now on my own!*

I wonder if I'll ever truly understand the value of having lived for all those seven weeks with West Indian families. They taught me so much. Most of the learning came gently and in the context of day to day living. But I'm also just as sure that I have no conception of the lessons still to be learned.

Our biggest challenge now for we four PC ENCORE volunteers is to get to know our areas, the people, their problems, and let them know us. Saturday we plan a raft trip up the Indian River, next will be a hike through the Cabits National Park with its ruins of Fort Shirley, a probably-wet trek up Mt. (Morne) Diabiotins and maybe Mt. Aux Diables, plus I'm dying to see the rugged Atlantic coastline of Dominica. And due north of Portsmouth are reportedly excellent snorkeling waters.

Speaking of snorkeling—I did! I put mask and snorkel on, face in the water and became lost as I floated through an unknown world for over an hour! Black fish with bright yellow stripes, cobalt blue and turquoise, plaid fish, polka dotted fish, translucent fish with their skeletons showing through, green on top and clear on the bottom, then reversed.

The sun would strike their colors and I thought of the effervescence of the humming bird. Mother Nature and God are incredible. I'm hooked!

Sounds as if my sister, 19 months my junior, is having quite an adventure. We are surely enjoying her letters, and we understand Agri-Times is finding its way to the Caribbean.

October 22—Cool stars glittered brilliantly in a rain-washed morning sky at 5:30 a.m., and a cool breeze freshened the air before frost formed, sometime between dawn and daylight, on the rain-dampened meadow grasses. As daylight lightened our world, I could see new snow dusting the high Wallowas. From now on, the snow-line will creep slowly down toward the valley with each new storm. And I hope we receive many storms.

It began to rain just as daughter Ramona and I pulled into La Grande yesterday afternoon. We made the 140-mile round trip to visit an old friend who recently underwent surgery. It was an enjoyable ride. Fall color along the Minam River was especially lovely.

The tree-lined streets of La Grande flamed with color, the maple and sumac leaves created a mixture of fall palettes that ranged in color from pale yellow to red ochre. We lunched at the "Fickle Fox," a delightful eatery on Main Street, owned by former Oregon CattleWomen president Jeannete Knott. The food is delicious and attractively served. Jeannete told us they are also serving dinner now.

The Grande Ronde Hospital was decorated for Halloween, and the bright rooms looked out on hills now wearing their fall colors. Nice to know our friend had such cheerful surroundings.

On the way home, we stopped on the way to Island City to shop at the recently opened Walmart store. It was so immense, I lost Ramona right off.

Returning home, we ran smack into the end of a colorful rainbow near the town of Elgin, and the wonderful rain just kept pouring down on our thirsty country. Yeah! As usual, it was good to be home on the ranch again, even if there was supper to fix and a milk cow to contend with. Things are much easier now at the barn. Three calves do most of the work.

We have been enjoying day after day of beautiful Indian summer weather, but welcomed the rain, which is long overdue.

October 24—One sunny morning early, with frost still glistening over Prairie Creek, I rode with Doug, Ben and Ky to gather our fall calving cows and their calves. The cattle moved well for a change, and we easily drove them to a hayed-over meadow grass field near the house.

After that, I rode over the hill to help Ben and Doug cut out and move some bulls. We cut out two yearlings without incident, but one bull became ornery, or playful, so I got tough and hollered loudly at him while turning my mare into the bull's oncoming charge. Whereupon my mare laid back her ears and went to bucking!

For the first time in my life, I got bucked off! Doug, watching this performance, said it was beautiful. Luckily, except for my wounded pride and a few sore spots, no damage was done. Thank goodness my abrupt landing was on soft pasture.

November 3—Puffy, white fog banks wreath the snowy summits of Chief Joseph Mountain on this sunny November morning. The air, cleansed by the scouring of yesterday's snow squalls, is sweet and fresh. And now, we have MUD instead of DUST. Hoorah!

Fall windstorms have stripped the faded yellow leaves from the willows and cottonwoods along the creeks, and the morning air is filled with the sound of honkers again. Due to the moisture there was a heavy frost over all this morning, and ice over the chickens' waterer.

The mud in the barnlot had a crust of ice over it when I opened the milking parlour door to let "Startch" into her stanchion. If I dawdle doing this, my big black and white cow pushes me inside...with her head! At 6 a.m. it is still dark. I switch on the light (a bare bulb attached to the ceiling), then push the wooden block that locks her into the stanchion. The two hungry calves, waiting beyond a small gate, are let in to nurse, and then I scoop from the grain bin a coffee can full of rolled barley and dump it into her feed box. Startch eagerly slurps the grain and begs for more. She would "kill" for rolled barley!

Her own heifer calf and an orphan bull soon drink their fill, and I turn them back into their pen and pasture before milking what is left. And what is left is a full bucket! Five barn cats form a ring around me, meowing in anticipation of their warm, frothy breakfast.

It is cozy there, bundled up in my old scarf, overalls and boots in the warm ring of light. Startch gives off her own warmth and keeps my hands from becoming too cold while squeezing away on those large teats. After applying bag balm to her teats, to prevent chapping in cold weather, I let the cow out, throw her some hay, and check her grown daughter, now a third-calf heifer herself, who calved two weeks ago. Another fine heifer calf, also born at 3 a.m. No problems.

Last week, I took the third calf I had on Startch and necked it together with this new baby, and now, after three days, mama has accepted the orphan. Because I still have too much milk, Doug has hauled in yet another motherless calf, which I will graft on Startch beginning this evening. *Later note: Success!*

And so it goes—every morning and evening, I traipse out to the cows barn and perform this task. Chores. I like chores. They keep me fit, and provide a break from housework. It has been an eventful past few weeks.

November 4—It's snowing! Feels like winter has arrived. I envy friend Linde, who is encamped with husband Pat up on Sour Apple Flat helping Jim Steen with his elk hunters. I would imagine that the wood stove in the large wall tents will feel pretty good today up there beyond Hat Point, on the breaks of the Snake River. What country and what adventure.

Our company arrived this week. Sandra, an old school chum, and husband Fred, who come up every fall to spend their vacation on our ranch. It is a working vacation, as life on this ranch goes on as usual. The day after they arrived, Doug scheduled the digging-up of our old septic tank and the replacing of a new one, which all took place in the middle of our lawn.

Doug announced that evening that no one could flush or even run water down any drain.

Of course, the next morning I came down with the flu. Fever, runny nose, headache, the works. Ugh. All I could do was lay on the sofa.

My friend Sandra took charge, and I concentrated on getting well. The septic system was restored and we were able to drain and flush. Hoorah! Although Sandra and I were both reared in the rural foothills of California, she is not what you would call a ranch gal. In other words, cows aren't her thing. So I struggled out twice a day to "do" the cow.

Except for one evening. I was just too sick. Doug and Fred disappeared into the night to meet the cow barn challenge. What seemed like an eternity elapsed until they returned. It seems that Startch wouldn't come in for them, but after some gentle persuasion and lots of patience, she reluctantly entered the barn to let the calves nurse. Doug, looking thoroughly disgusted, didn't have much to say about the incident, and I was able to handle the chores from then on.

Milk cows are creatures of habit and routine, and like the same person to handle them. Let a stranger show up and things invariably go awry. Cowboys don't milk cows. They sure do love to pour that sweet cream on their raspberry cobblers and oatmeal, though.

It is such a pleasure to have whole milk to cook with again. I made a wonderful old recipe for rice pudding the other day. Hard to beat whole milk for those old-fashioned desserts.

After I got to feeling better, Sandra and I picked up Linde and drove down to Imnaha last Saturday. We spent a leisurely day photographing, and visiting old friends. We picked Golden Delicious apples at Mary Marks' pretty place upriver. Mary had been out splitting wood and invited us in for a nice visit.

A fall storm moved in and wild winds blew leaves off the cottonwoods. We stopped at the Imnaha Store and Tavern, ordered chicken gizzards and Jo Jo's, and washed them down with blackberry tea. The old barrel stove was warm and cozy and the place was decorated for Halloween.

We celebrated Sandra and Fred's 41st wedding anniversary on November 2nd at Vali's Delicatessen at Wallowa Lake. What a perfect ending to a perfect day: char-broiled steak, baked potato, salad, Mike Vali's homemade rolls, and a Black Forest cake. Maggie Vali kept snapping Fred's suspenders, as well as those of other guests in the small eatery, which made everyone feel like family.

November 7—Fred and Sandra just left yesterday morning.

Life is never dull around here. The men branded and worked the fall calves. Then Doug purchased more weaned calves and, of course, they had to be worked.

The rest of the previously weaned calves have been shipped over the mountain to Les Marks' Beef City, where they will be grown out this winter in a warmer climate.

The general hunt for Rocky Mountain bull elk is on, and our county is filled with hunters of every description. Sunny Hancock (cowboy poet from Lakeview) rolled in last evening with his hunting party. They left their horses here overnight and this morning showed up to head out toward Chesnimnus Creek.

November 9—The soft silence that accompanies falling snow is all around on Prairie Creek this morning. Dog and cat prints criss-cross our lawn, telling stories—Daisy and old Jake chasing a cat up a tree—and the tell-tale tracks of a skunk lead to and from the dog dish.

November 8—Doug and I drove out to Salmon Creek to check on our cows this morning. It was snowing out there too, a wet snow, not sticking. The cows were contentedly grazing old bunch grass, and even mixing a few bites of green with it.

We stopped to visit some elk hunters who were enjoying, or perhaps enduring, a November camping experience in Wallowa County. Just off the Zumwalt road, we happened upon two hunters skinning out a freshly killed bull elk. It was a cold sight seeing them there. An icy wind blew across the barren hills, and the snow was sticking by then, which makes for cold fingers!

We drove into the old Steen ranch and left two 100-pound sacks of potatoes in the house for the cowboys. No one was about, not even a barking dog. And the snow just kept falling.

It fell on the small bunch of saddle horses munching hay by the log corrals. It fell softly on the branches of the tall Ponderosa pines along Chesnimnus Creek, and covered the bare willows in a delicate, white tracery. The old log ranch house, now a cow camp, is more than 100 years old, and still serves the purpose of shelter from the cold. Over the years it has been home to many cowboys.

We drove on down the creek and passed two more successful hunters. The freshly gutted bulls were still steaming in the cold air. Presently we pulled into Sunny Hancock's camp where his party of seven was holed up. One fellow was standing out in the falling snow, tending a large campfire as Sunny and Ernie emerged from the cook tent and bade us welcome. We entered the tent to find Ernie hanging the wash on a line strung across the top poles, and Sunny had a big pot of beans cooking.

Out of the storm, it was warm and cozy by the camp stove, stoked fiery red and full of seasoned tamarack. Snow piled up on the tent, then slid off because of the stove's heat. I loved it. The simple cook tent evoked memories of my former elk camp cooking experiences far up on the Minam, at Elk Creek, when I cooked for Red's Horse Ranch. Doug and I ate our lunches, relaxed and listened to the stories told by these cowboy poets, who were delighted to have an audience.

Since they had been assigned to the camp chores, our arrival provided a break in the monotony of a snowy day. They were well-qualified to tell stories. Sunny was a former cow boss on a large spread out of Paisley, Oregon, and Ernie puts on a poetry gathering in Carson City, Nevada, and drives and trains teams of draft horses. Sunny told tales of a life that has all but disappeared, tales of mules hitched to single-sickle mowers to cut meadow hay; tales of outfits that ran 6,000 head of cattle, and of riding through drifts on the desert in below zero weather. Tales about the Sycan marsh and an old barn that used to be there, but isn't now.

It was homey there, way out on Chesnimnus Creek in the storm. Garlicky and delicious smells came from the pot of Sunny's beans on the stove, from the steaming laundry and the popping fire. We ate our sourdough bread sandwiches filled with smoked salmon, washing them down with lots of hot tea and coffee.

Before we left, I photographed Ernie's team of draft horses, which were munching hay in a small roped-off area across from the tents. A small rubber-tired wagon was parked by the road. Sunny and Ernie drove the team to gather wood for camp and were on call to haul in any elk the hunters might bag. The younger hunters (kids, Ernie and Sunny called them) were all out hunting, while these two seasoned camp tenders kept the home fires burning.

Returning over those long miles through the cold, lonely Zumwalt hills, Doug spotted a herd of 30 elk! No horns, all calmly grazing and bedding down on a snowy hillside, oblivious to the storm. Typical elk. Like our cows, they are at home on these vast ranges that lie between the breaks of the Imnaha and the timbered country to the west.

Phone calls that night enlightened us on our own family's elk hunting successes. Son-in-law Bill and grandson Buck rode horse-back up a remote side canyon where Bill shot his bull. By the time he shot it, early darkness was coming to the canyons and Bill only had time to take care of the meat before running out of light to pack it out. The next day, daughter Jackie and her husband rode back up the canyon and packed their meat out on a mule.

Daughter Ramona's extended family bagged two bulls on opening day somewhere on the upper Imnaha. More stories. Partly due to the cold, snowy conditions during this second season bull hunt, reports of lost or injured hunters are now filtering in. Son Steve has been involved in a couple of weekend rescues.

How I envy friend Linde, who has been cooking at a remote hunting camp up near Sour Apple Flat, beyond Hat Point on the breaks of the Snake. Although road conditions getting to and from that place are a bit hairy this time of year, the rewards outweigh the risks.

Linde, who shares the same excitement I feel toward the outdoors, was telling me about a ride out on Sleepy Ridge. "It was beautiful!" she said. "You could see the Wallowas in the distance and the views were spectacular." And I bet it was, Linde.

Although I've never seen Sleepy Ridge with snow on it, I remember when, several years ago, I took my 4-H group up to Hat Point for a cook-out, camp-out and photographing jaunt, and the next day we delivered a sourdough chocolate cake to grandson Buck on Sleepy Ridge on his third birthday. We bumped and jolted over a mere cow track to find the wall tent that was home to daughter Jackie, son-in-law Bill and Buck and little sister. The wall tent provided a summer cow camp for the family when they were tending Wilson Wilde's cows over a vast range that stretched nearly from Imnaha to Hat Point.

What a wonderful life for those children growing up. They had packed in with horses and mules. How we ever got that old Dodge pickup in there was a miracle. The chocolate cake was a bit messed up when we got there, but the grin on Buck's face when we lit the candles and sang "Happy Birthday" made the effort worthwhile.

Meanwhile, life and November rolls on, and soon it will be Thanksgiving, which arrives while our elk hunt is on. Doug and I have cow tags for the Chesnimnus unit, beginning the 21st. Linde, who also has a tag, thinks we should plan a Thanksgiving meal in an elk camp. A great idea, but too many chores tie us to the ranch.

November 18—Perhaps this story should appear in "What's Up By Rupp" instead of "Janie's Journal," but here goes anyway,

Once upon a time a petite, sparkling-eyed blond by the name of Tammy met a tall, handsome prince…'er fisherman named Matt Lauchland. These two young people, now in their early 20s, got acquainted while attending Cal Poly in San Luis Obispo, California.

Last June, Tammy received her B.S. degree in animal science while

Matt was awarded his in crop science. Until Matt got involved with Tammy, his main interest in life was fishing. Actually, it still is. Since this couple has been seeing a lot of each other for two years or so, Tammy's and Matt's parents have been anxiously awaiting news of an engagement. Okay, mostly the moms. But nothing happened.

A year ago last fall, the couple was visiting Tammy's parents here in Wallowa County, and Doug took Matt steelhead fishing on the Grande Ronde River near the small settlement of Troy. No luck.

Then, when Doug and I drove to San Luis Obispo last June to attend the graduation, we stopped on the way home in Lodi to visit Matt's family and, of course, Matt took Doug fishing on the Delta for bass. No luck.

As time went on, it became an ongoing challenge to simply catch a fish, and a sort of unspoken tradition grew between these two fishermen.

Last week Matt and his family rolled into upper Prairie Creek where they would spend the next 10 days elk hunting. Tammy, who had been vacationing with her parents, was glad to see Matt, of course. Fishing was put on hold, as on opening morning of the second season Rocky Mountain elk hunt their party bagged two bulls somewhere on the Imnaha. That meant tending to all that meat.

After a few more days of trudging up and down mountains and canyons after more elk, as Matt hadn't filled his tag yet, it was decided they would pursue, or rather resume, the steelhead fishing thing.

So, early one cold November morning, Doug took the party down along the winding canyon road to Cow Creek, where they fished the Imnaha Gorge. Tammy went along too. They fished all day, and the only one to catch a legal steelhead was Doug. The jinx was broken, but Matt's fishing prowess was still to be proven, and the challenge continued.

Now, Novembers are cold down there along the Imnaha, and chill winds often sweep up the gorge from Eureka Bar, where the Imnaha joins the Snake. Tammy, a good sport, followed her man and offered support. That night, Doug returned to Prairie Creek triumphantly bearing his fish and telling his story.

Later in the week we had the entire family over for supper. With great skill Doug barbecued his steelhead outside in the cold fog while I took four cast-iron frypans full of sourdough biscuits from the oven, and Matt's dad, Cliff, carved a leg of lamb. Friend Linde had contributed a Greek salad, and I'd made a big wild blackberry cobbler that morning. Over much merriment we devoured the good food and sampled wines made from grapes raised by Matt and his family in Lodi. As the biscuits disappeared the fish stories got more and more out of hand.

Then last Saturday, on a cold, damp, foggy, 33-degree morning, Doug went fishing on a friend's pond where there were some large trout needing to be caught. Not so much as a bite! The next morning, Matt willingly took up the challenge. Tammy, freezing through two hours of watching her prince charming fish, witnessed the catching or not one but two 20-inch rainbows!

That evening, we all met at Vali's Alpine Delicatessen at Wallowa Lake for dinner.In the kitchen, Mike turned out his famous steaks and potatoes and Black Forest cake.

Matt waited until all were seated at one large table before he brought forth with a flourish those two large trout. The look of wonderment on Doug's face wan just great. And Doug, who had bet Malt a dollar he couldn't catch any fish in the pond, paid off then and there.

Maggie Vali, bearing a tray of salads, thought she was losing it for sure when Matt proudly displayed those two rainbows right there in her restaurant. At my suggestion, the fish were quickly whisked to the cold car outside for safekeeping. Maggie, a good sport, said she liked our rowdy group and made everyone feel special by her friendly kidding.

On the last night, before departing with his family back to Lodi, back to the grapes, leaving Wallowa County behind with its fish and fish stories, Matt proposed to Tammy. She had passed the test, standing by him in his moment of failure and success, cheering him on as he fought and landed his fish and nearly froze to death in the process.

Always true to her mate, Tammy is sworn to secrecy when it comes to telling which lure Matt used to catch those fish. In my opinion, Tammy isn't too shabby a fisherman herself. She caught her a husband, hook, line and sinker. And it wasn't easy landing him, either. End of fish story, but the beginning of another one...Matt and Tammy's.

At Matt's request, the fishing story was NOT to be upstaged by the engagement. Priorities. I am sure all of these goings-on will keep going on, and continue to keep all our lives interesting. And now we understand the wedding is planned for June.

On Monday morning I took Matt and Tammy's photo there on upper Prairie Creek with snowy Chief Joseph Mountain rising beyond them, before the fog rolled in again, before they left. Goodness! This means there are prospects of my becoming a great-grandma. That is good.

November 20—This evening daughter Jackie, son-in-law Bill and their two children, Buck and Mona Lee, were here for a steak supper, after which Doug and I drove to Joseph and joined other family members at the high school to watch the drama class perform Shakespeare's "Midsummer

Tammy Phillips and her "catch," Matt Lauchland.

Night's Dream." An excellent dramatization.

Leaving Shakespeare, we returned home to greet Bryan Wolfe, who had driven over from Hermiston to join us in an antlerless elk hunt in the Chesnimnus Unit tomorrow.

All in all, this Friday had been quite a diversified day in the life of the city of Joseph—Dave Manuel moved his museum to its new location, which took two hours. Because Dave's family and friends chose to stay inside the building and it was cold outside, a fire had been built in the massive stone fireplace so the occupants would stay warm during the move. Consequently, as the large log building moved slowly down Main Street, on dollies pulled by professional movers, smoke curled out of the chimney.

Wanda Sorweide stood on the balcony and waved to the crowds who had gathered from all over their county. I must say it gave me quite a start upon returning from Enterprise to see this huge log museum blocking Joseph's main street. Our out-of-the-way community is never lacking for excitement.

November 21—After finally hitting the sack last night, we didn't have a "Midsummer Night's Dream," but rather dreamt of antlerless elk in a winter setting.

All too soon, 4 a.m. came, and I was up frying sausage on the Monarch before heading out into the black, cold morning to find my black and white cow. Startch thought I was losing it when I turned on the light and called to her in the darkness. From afar, she stumbled sleepily past me into the barn, where the calves, too, woke up enough to nurse.

Returning to the warmth of the kitchen, I heated up the big cast-iron griddle and baked sourdough hotcakes for us all. Linde and Pat were here by 5 to join us for breakfast. By dawn, we were far out on Salmon Creek. As daylight filtered through a cloudy sky and a chill wind picked up speed, we spotted a herd of elk at the head of a draw.

The wind was blowing furiously by this time, and it was anything but pleasant when we strayed out of the pickup. The stinging cold wind not only took one's breath away, it produced a headache!

Bryan shot a yearling before the herd escaped over the snowy hills to the east. We pursued, but never caught up to them again. Noon found us still in our pickups and overlooking the breaks of the canyon country. We ate our lunches in the warmth of the four-wheel drives and watched the wind-shipped snow squalls dance over the country like gauzy curtains tossed about in the storm. The elk had vanished into the safety of those vast canyons, and it was so cold we were almost glad we didn't bag anymore that day.

We returned to the ranch and, while the men skinned out Bryan's elk, Linde and I built up the fire and rested. Later, everyone fell asleep. After gathering the eggs and doing the "cow," I warmed up the big pot of beef and vegetable soup, prepared the day before, and we dipped sourdough bread into the nourishing broth and supped supper...And recounted the day's hunt, and planned the morrow's.

November 22—The next morning, same deal. Only this time we approached our elk from the bottom. The wild windstorm of the day before had blown trees down across the Imnaha highway, and there was a sheet of black ice on the pavement. We stopped to remove one tree that lay across the road so some unsuspecting early hunter wouldn't skid coming to a stop to avoid it.

It was pleasant there in the canyon at daybreak. The leafy remnants of fall lay in the draws and creeks, which gurgled cold and clear, smelling of rain and cleanness, and greenness. Quite a contrast to the snowy world on top, which could be easily glimpsed on the high rims above.

We hadn't traveled very far until we ran into the elk...Only they were safe, and they knew it, bunched up, grazing those high snowy hillsides above us. We got ahead of the herd and Pat led us "women" across the creek and up a steep embankment to a large rock outcropping where we waited for the elk to appear. Pretty soon, here they came, single file, along their high well-traveled trails, but out of rifle range! Somehow, it didn't seem to matter. Just gazing up, watching those elk in that wild, lovely canyon, counting more than 100 head trailing along, was enough. I'm sure it created a sight we will forever store in our mind's eye.

We then drove out of the canyons over a slippery, icy, snow-filled road that brought us out on top again, just in time to see our elk emerge from those bottoms, traveling a familiar route that takes them to their high, grassy plateau in the Zumwalt hills.

After much confusion created by us humans, the elk continued to do as they pleased, at least until they were intercepted by several hunters. Then the herd split into smaller bunches. Finally, one of those splintered groups of elk headed back toward us and began slowly walking up a nearby draw. Elk hunting is 90% luck, and that element was with us, because we waited, crouched down out of sight in the snow.

"Here they come," said one of our fellows, and we held our breath as first one cow, then another, came into rifle range. On that cold snowy ridge in the storm, I filled my cow tag. She was a dry, and very fat.

Others got their meat as well that day, there in the cold silence of the area known as the Buttes.

We drove the long snowy roads back to the Prairie Creek ranch, where the men skinned my cow while I gathered eggs and did the barn chores. Then, Linde and I heated up the soup kettle on the wood stove again. Meat for the winter, and stories for a lifetime.

November 24—It was a mere 6 degrees when I left the cozy warmth of the old Monarch and ventured forth to the cow barn in this morning's cold, clear dawn. The frozen snow crunched beneath my boots and the cats left a trail of paw prints as they ran in front and to the side, always in my way, meowing in anticipation of their warm bowl of milk.

Stars faded from the clear sky and light seeped in over the eastern horizon as I walked back to the house with my pail of milk. Fall has given way to winter here in Wallowa County.

November 25—Now zero degrees.

A hunting update from friend Linde and son Steve, who filled their tags yesterday. Grandsons Rowdy and Chad got two 5-point bulls on opening morning of bull season.

We start the cows home from the hills right after Thanksgiving, which is tomorrow. Thirty-one people will crowd into our home for turkey day. We have so much to be thankful for.

Our elk hunting stories never seem to end. Doug drove out yesterday to chop ice so the cows could drink, and ran into, or rather, as his story goes, several cow elk ran into him! Consequently, he came home with his tag filled. Actually, it was no small feat, because he was alone and loading such a large game animal by oneself is quite a chore.

November 26—Thanksgiving—Daughter-in-law Angie and husband Todd drove all the way out to the hills to find those cow elk again, and Angie filled her antlerless tag. Friend Linde and son Steve bagged theirs after an all-day ordeal, which involved dragging two elk a considerable distance to their parked rigs. We are all going into the winter with plenty of elk to fill our large family's larders.

Somehow, I survived the day. Actually, it was pretty wonderful. In addition to our own large, extended family, we opened our home to three other families who didn't have family living here in the county. In other words, we shared our family. And that is what Thanksgiving should be about: sharing and spreading around what we often take for granted.

My day had begun early when son Todd and his wife, Angie, had dropped off their four young ones at grandma's so they could go elk hunting. Adele and Becky helped me milk the cow and feed the chickens. It was bitterly cold, too, around 10 degrees. After straining the milk, I scrambled eggs and made toast and hot chocolate for the children before returning to the huge bowls of bread dressing. The 20-pound turkey finally got into the oven and the children helped decorate the tables with pretty fall leaves I'd pressed earlier. Mom and dad returned with the elk, and a child came carrying the dripping heart into the kitchen for me to tend to! Such is life in Wallowa County.

Big families can be a blessing—that is, when everyone gets along. Our herd of "kiss'n cousins" like nothing better than an excuse to be together. We had little ones, pre-teens, teens and two home from college. It was a pretty proud moment for this matriarch (what a word) to look upon such a brood, watch them heap their plates, eat, and know that they were all feeling a common bond of "belonging" to all of us. Just squeezing 31 bodies into our modest home was something else, but it all worked out, and the conversation and food spilled over into the darkening afternoon.

Then, because all of them are "country folk" too and chores must be done, everyone left and our house settled back down into our quiet routine.

December 1—November slipped away in the cold, quiet night. This morning's December brings more snow and cold, though not as intense as it has been. The preceding days of freezing have caused the subtle changes to occur in the ground, hardening the soil surface, and with each passing hour the frost penetrates a bit deeper into the earth.

No song does the land sing now. No bird song, save for a few noisy crows and magpies that occasionally flap about. The sound of winter in the country is silence, cold silence. Except for the cattle; their bawling is such a familiar presence in my life, I can't imagine what it would be like without it.

Listening to a mother cow call her calf this morning, I realized how much this sound has been with me throughout the years. Having been born into it, raised with it, and hearing it all of my adult life, I am so conditioned to "cow sounds," it is the norm. A sound synonymous with quiet places. For cows, like me, function better in quiet places. That place and space we call home is important to all of us, and those familiar sounds of such a "place" contribute to a feeling of security and well-being.

While on the subject of "mooing," there is more of it around here now, because the spring-calvers are in from the hills; and when our fall-calvers hear the old yellow silage truck start up, they begin their calling and run to meet it. It took two days to trail the herd in from its summer and fall range, and now they are on a daily ration of hay.

Doug and I cut and wrapped my elk the other evening, and we gave some away to other members of the family. Our two dogs are getting fat on the scraps left on the bones.

And now life has slowed somewhat, with the advent of snowy weather. I am enjoying the luxury of reading by a crackling fire, and even finding some time to write. I always look forward to winter–a time to rest–until the calendar begins to fill up with holiday activities. Linde, Scotty and I are hoping for even more snow, so we can break out the cross-country skis.

Doug and I have opened up our home to an old friend, a bachelor fellow who has been living alone for years. Bill George has had a run of bad luck this winter. After having just recovered from intensive radiation treatments for cancer, he fell and broke his hip. After three weeks in the hospital he returned to Wallowa County, only to come down with pneumonia. So it was back in the local hospital for another week, then back here.

Now Bill is recuperating nicely, and getting around with the aid of a walker, eating good food and sleeping well. If he keeps up his present progress he will soon be returning to his cabin. I can remember, as a child, being aware of many households where "old folks" were just a part of everyone's lives. They were respected and honored members of the family, and looked up to. Nursing homes were places where only ones without any family went.

Bill has no family, save for one son, who resides in another state. He had no one, and the nursing homes and even foster homes were non-existent in his case, as they were all full. So we told him he was more than welcome to stay here and regain his strength. Now in his 79th year, Bill say he had looked forward for years to the "golden years," and how wonderful it would be.

"They lied," he said. "It isn't all golden, but fraught with health problem, which in turn bring about the endless frustrations caused by our present health care system."

Bill is a trouper, however, and Doug and I are trying to make his recovery and life a bit easier. In turn, Bill enriches our lives by telling of his life's experiences. Over meals we listen to tales of marching in the Army in Europe during the war; the horror and futility of it all, the cold and hurting of marching in winter; frozen feet, hunger and cold.

We listen with rapt attention to stories of his younger days spent in Arizona and New Mexico when he cowboyed in the age of Mexican steers, roping with rawhide riatas in a time of no corrals, and riding all day in rough country that covered two states; of breaking horses and existing on hardly any pay; of eating beans and bacon and biscuits day after day. In an era most of us only read about, Bill lived it.

He possesses those rare qualities imbued to those who live alone. He has time to think. He is a man of integrity and expects that same quality in other men, and is disappointed when he doesn't find it, which is typical of people in his age group. Isn't it a shame there aren't more like him? Especially in leadership roles. Many of his thoughts dwell on life and how one must accept with quiet dignity what it dishes out.

In the meantime, we do not consider him a burden, but rather an honor as we try to glean some of his wisdom. Guess that's why I enjoy having children and "old folks" around—they teach you so much about life.

December 7—Linde drove down from upper Prairie Creek and helped me peel and chop apples to make mincemeat.

I remembered last night to thaw out a gallon of that sweet cider we pressed last fall. This morning, the cider is put into a big kettle with cooked, ground-up neck meat of elk, chopped apples, raisins, spices, vinegar and honey, and allowed to simmer all day on the old Monarch. The house smells of mincemeat—Doug's favorite pie.

As winter settles in here on Prairie Creek, the ranch work falls into a steady routine. One that centers around the care and feeding of livestock, and for me the caring and feeding of menfolk. Actually, I do both, and the act of going from a hot kitchen to a cold cow barn has not been conducive to my recovery from a nasty sinus infection. But I am slowly on the mend, and I hope I'll be healthy for the holidays. It seems a lot of local folks have had the same malady.

Pete Donovan tuned my piano last week. What a joy it is to sit down and play, if only for a few minutes. Cooking takes much of my time these days, and it's fun to peruse my large collection of cookbooks and prepare something from scratch.

My favorite recipes are the very old ones. There is something satisfying and comforting about clinging to some of our older traditions, especially now in the hectic '90s. If ever there would be a visionary hope in my thinking of the future, it would be that we all SLOW DOWN! Easier said than done, but what if we would eliminate many of those so-called time-saving devices that clutter up our lives? Instead, do things with our hands again, knead bread, plant a garden, read to children, listen to the elderly, help someone in need, watch more sunsets, breathe deeply of the morning air, savor quiet, enjoy good music, cultivate friendships.

Life is for living, not just for scurrying around in a dither to accomplish God-knows-what. Read a good book. Granted, there is some terrible writing these days, but there is also some very good stuff out there. Visit your local bookstore and seek it out. Enrich your life and improve your thinking. Goodness, listen to me. The one who is constantly on the go, telling others how to slow down, but those who really know me understand what I am trying to say, and know that I do practice the aforementioned...and that is how I cope. It works.

Last night, as I ventured out into the dark to the cow barn, the nearly full December moon was muted. Its lemon glow shone through a soft, gauzy layer of clouds. From the far hills floated the ageless wailing of a lone coyote, hungry perhaps, and wishing he could follow the scent of the elk rib cage on our lawn, and share a meal with old Jake and Daisy.

Most of my laying hens went on strike. Too cold, I suspect, although four of the Barred Plymouth Rocks continue to keep us in fresh eggs. I have begun writing the annual Christmas letters, which will be mailed with our cards. It is fun to make the yearly contact with those many friends who live so far apart from us.

Our friend Bill continues to improve on a daily basis. Good, nourishing food, rest, and regular exercise in a home atmosphere are making this happen. Sometime next week he will return to his cabin, and we will miss him. Bill lives simply in his humble abode and is the envy of many because, although his life is outwardly poor, it is inwardly rich. By rich I mean he enjoys each day for what it brings, and enjoys his solitude. In other words, he has come to grips with both life and himself. Many people spend an entire lifetime and never get to know themselves, much less the world out their front door.

December 8—Cows, their calves pushing ahead of them, huddle next to the fence corner. A low, moaning wind stirs the grasses sticking up through the snow and tosses the bare limbs of willows along the creek. I observe all this from inside the barn through a large crack in the old wooden door while I am perched on a three-legged milking stool. It is 7 a.m. and the winter sun will not appear today, because of a layer of thick, snow-laden clouds. It looks as though the snow will fly before the wind any minute, and the cows must think so too, but no snow falls and only the wind continues. Its lonely roar drowns out all other sound, Snow is falling over the Wallowas, and that is good.

As I walk back to the house with my pail of milk, wild gusts of wind lift surface snow, sifting it into small drifts here and there. As that loose snow blows away, it exposes hard-packed icy layer, a threat to both man and beast. Yesterday our previous below zero mornings were replaced by a welcome rise in temperature. This morning the thermometer registers a balmy 30 degrees, and the wind has lost its bite.

December 9—December means bazaars in Wallowa County. The Handcrafters held their annual event last weekend. Cloverleaf Hall was all a-buzz with the sights and smells of Christmas. The Imnaha Grange ladies spent hours baking pies, and their menfolk pitched in to help serve chili and sandwiches for lunch.

Last Friday evening the Grange served its "All you can eat roast beef dinner." In spite of the below-zero temperatures that brought bitter cold to the valley, the populace for miles around turned out for this annual feast. It always provides a place to visit old friends, chat about the crafts displayed, and even purchase many of the items offered for sale for Christmas giving.

When winter comes to the snowy world of Alder Slope, many of those inhabitants become very creative. Jim Blankenship was there again with his beautiful rawhide, braided horsehair reins, and other leather tack. So was Annie Nash, who had her booth next to Jim's and displayed her unique Santas, all handmade and all different. And it just wouldn't be a bazaar without Harold and Hope McLaughlin, sharing Harold's lovely wooden creations and Hope's beautiful handmade quilts. Other booths offered fudge, cookies, aprons, needle work of all kinds, and ceramics, all colorfully displayed. Wallowa County's Old Time Fiddlers fiddled some happy music, and good cheer warmed everyone's hearts in spite of the cold outside.

December 10—Linde and I took carloads of CattleWomen up and over snowy hills on a stormy day day in the Leap country. CattleWoman Connie Dunham opened up her ranch home for our annual Christmas party. The lovely large home was aglow with Christmas spirit, and good food. Outside the many windows, the snow fell, softly at first, then slanted against the panes, blown by a furious wind. Our world shrank. We were just us, out there in the hills. The other world didn't exist.

Instead of participating in a gift exchange, we donated canned meats and stews and soups to our local food bank.

That same evening, friend Linde hosted the Photo Club for its annual Christmas party meeting. Seated around the cozy fireplace sipping egg nog and spiced cider, and nibbling more traditional holiday goodies, we felt lucky indeed.

The cold came down in the snowy woods and settled hard on Prairie Creek, which lies beneath the winter-locked stillness of the Wallowas.

December 16—It is Wednesday already, and normally this column is in the mail by now. Somehow, I simply couldn't sit myself down and begin. Perhaps I'm not with it because we moved Bill back to his cabin yesterday. After nearly two months of doing things for him and taking care of his place and dog, I felt the need to relax and read, and that's exactly what I did. I finished William Kittredge's new book, *Hole in the Sky*. Great writing.

When we took Bill back up Alder Slope to his humble little cabin, and saw that he was settled in, we were definitely in the spirit of Christmas. Doug had gone up earlier and installed a cordless phone, so he could answer the phone easier from different areas of his home.

Then Linde and Pat gave him a TV, something Bill has never had, and Linde hooked it up. We carried wood in for him and did his grocery shopping. Doug made a stand for a small Christmas tree, which we placed in the front room. The floors were scrubbed clean and bachelor quarters put in order. Bill was so pleased. The look of happiness and surprise on his face just made our day.

Knowing someone cares is better than any medicine to make old folks "all better." Who knows, perhaps one day we too will need this kind of caring. So, here it is, nearly 5 p.m., and I'm just now sitting down at the kitchen table to type, yet I know not what.

This evening there are only two baked potatoes in the oven, and two steaks thawing out. Where Bill's chair sat on its platform, our newly decorated Christmas tree twinkles with cheery lights. In the darkening gloom of evening outside the big picture window in our living room, behind that Christmas tree, the snowy hills that form the eastern flank of Prairie Creek give off a luminous glow under a purple sky, a sky that holds promise of more snow. Arctic air, driven by a rising wind, sucks and pulls at the loose snow, curling it into drifts.

The wind took my breath away when I went out to chore after supper, and the fine, stinging snow sandblasted my face. Startch was grateful for the temporary shelter of the barn, and the three calves nursed hungrily. I opened a bale of straw and scattered it around for the calves to bed in before I headed back to the warmth of the house.

'Tis the season for the school Christmas programs. But before they began, the Enterprise drama class put on the production of "I Remember Mama." Granddaughter Carrie played the role of Dagmar. She needed a live cat for the part, and Carrie, who is a cat lover, just happened to have one, named "Elizabeth," which just happened to be the name of the character cat in the play! Elizabeth fit into her role purrr-fectly. During the many weeks of practicing, she got so used to jumping into the car to travel to town, she began to look forward to this new-found diversion from country life.

Then, one fateful day, Elizabeth got under the car, and you guessed it. So, Carrie's gray kitten, "Buster," was substituted, which worked out well until Buster, on one cold morning, decided to climb under the hood of a warm ranch rig, and eventually succumbed to fan-itis, a malady that is fairly common here during our cold Wallowa County winters. But the play had to go on, and so it did, with another cat.

But, alas, there is more to the story of these ill-fated Elizabethan felines. Before the third performance, the Boyd family volunteered its family pet. And wouldn't you know. Yep—a log truck! Weary of sorrowing over dead cats, the cast broke into uncontrollable laughter. After all, 'tis the season to be jolly and, besides, young people can't be sad for long. Wallowa County still has an abundance of cats.

"I Remember Mama" staged by the Enterprise High School drama class was absolutely tops. The actors were perfectly cast, the stage setting professional and innovative, and the costuming and makeup people did a splendid job. Those of us lucky enough to see it were impressed.

Acting out stories of other people's lives helps young people better understand their own. All of us have the need to understand other life situations, to make our lives more meaningful. Hats off to those young people, the tireless parents who supported them, and the drama teacher who made it all possible.

It is also time for joyful singing, for cantatas and Messiahs, the kind that makes our souls soar. I attended our countywide cantata twice. Having seven members of my family among those voices had something to do with it, of course, but the pride felt was for all of our community. Singers were from Imnaha, Joseph, Lostine and places in between. It was the voice of Wallowa County, raised in praise. Joy showed on their faces and was reflected in their songs.

December 18—And now it is Friday, and still very dark at 5:30 on this 10-degree morning as I sit here in my kitchen-office, still at that typewriter.

I arose very early, woke up Startch to milk her, let the calves nurse, cleaned up a bit, and left the ranch by 6:30 to make granddaughter Chelsie's junior high Christmas choir breakfast at the Enterprise school. It was worth the effort. Grandmas, such as Hazel Johnson, were already there helping prepare a breakfast feast of fruit, rolls and juice, all attractively served on a table complete with lighted candles.

The junior high staged its little program, and music teacher Gail

Swart, who taught many of these children's mothers and fathers, carried on as she has so ably done in the past. Not looking any older herself, she accompanied their skit at the piano.

Afterward I drove up the snowy road to Bill's to check on him. I took in his mail, filled the wood box, and found him puttering about in the kitchen, stewing up apples he'd stored in the root cellar.

One o'clock found me back in Enterprise, seated along with other proud parents and grandparents in the high school gym to watch the grade school's program. James, now in first grade, waved at me. Gail Swart was there too, coaching yet another generation of Wallowa County youths. As the crowd spilled outside into a full-scale blizzard, the town of Enterprise was all but obscured.

By 5:30 Doug and I were following the snowplow down the winding 30-mile road to the canyon settlement of Imnaha to watch the two-room school's annual Christmas program. Grandchildren Buck and Mona ran to meet us all excited, as were all the children, at the prospect of performing for their relatives.

December 23—The yeasty, cinnamony aroma of Tannenbaum Brot (Christmas tree bread) fills our warm kitchen. The morning's warmth is created by the wood stove oven and enhanced by bright sunshine that streams through our window. Close by, looming south and west, Mt. Howard, Bonneville and Chief Joseph mountains reflect their white brilliance against a blue sky.

Forming wavering, dark lines upon their snowy pastures, our cattle munch their daily ration of hay, which has been fed by Ben, before sunup. The scene is being repeated all over the valley now—A slow-moving tractor pulling a low hay wagon heaped with baled hay; ranchers cutting twine and looping it over one arm before kicking flakes of hay off both sides to the eager cattle.

We have enjoyed a brief respite from the cold lately. Yesterday and today could almost be described as balmy. By mid-morning, as the snow began to melt, our county roads were covered with a slick glaze of ice. While traveling up toward Alder Slope yesterday, I noticed a small pickup heading my way, going a bit too fast for the road conditions.

In less time than it takes to tell it, that light little rig spun around and came to a sudden stop in the borrow pit, facing the opposite direction. If I had been a few feet behind, we would have collided. It was so slick, there was no way to stop, and I didn't even try. Besides, I had a car following me, which by some miracle missed being hit as well. Whoever the driver was, he learned the very same lesson on the very same corner that taught me years ago to slow down.

My reason for traveling to Alder Slope was to deliver Christmas boxes of goodies to family and friends. Doug had sacked potatoes to deliver also. After leaving a sack of potatoes at Wilmer and Mary Cook's back door, I knocked and was invited in to visit a spell.

Mary had spent the morning making Christmas candy with her daughter Joyce, who had driven up from town. Her counter was full of rocky road, peanut brittle, and divinity.

Wilmer said, "Mary, hunt up those pictures so I can show Janie."

Mary rummaged around until she found an envelope of snapshots taken this fall by Joyce during deer season. There was Wilmer, 80 years young, grinning over a nice mule deer buck he'd bagged way out in Wallowa County's back country. There were other pictures, too, including one of grandson Willie with his buck that won a prize in the big buck contest, and more photos of happy youngsters posing out there in the forest. A familiar young lad turned out to be my grandson Rowdy, who is a friend of Willie's brother Ryan. The photos were wonderful, capturing those carefree, happy faces in moments to be treasured as the years roll on.

More important than the hunting was that Wilmer and Mary do things with their family, together; things they all enjoy. Building traditions and building families, something we can't all do enough of, extending our own family to include those who do not have anyone to take pictures of them. As I see it, this is our only hope to rescue a society that is headed in the wrong direction. Our youth is our future. Their hurt hurts us all.

Farther up the Slope, I pulled into a snowy lane where son Ken and his family live. It was good to see Grandson Chad there, home for the holidays from college. Rowdy, his brother, took me out to see his new litter of baby pigs. As we approached the barn, a large red sow ambled out to greet us. She grunted contentedly as she walked beside Rowdy, nudging him with her head. When she got his attention, she lifted her head up so Rowdy could scratch under her double chin. The sow obviously adored Rowdy; she never left his side.

Under a heat lamp in a bed of clean straw, the little piglets wriggled and uttered mini-grunts—*woof, woof.* They were adorable, of all colors. After one more scratch under the chin, the sow walked into where her babies were. What a family. Rowdy has always had a way with animals. Chickens, dogs, horses, sheep, pigs, you name it, Rowdy has it.

I drove up to check on Bill and found him doing just fine, except for a tinge of cabin fever. Understandable, for one who isn't supposed to drive yet. I hope he will be able to regain enough strength so he can get in some cross-country skiing this winter.

Returning home to Prairie Creek, I found Max Gorsline in the living room visiting Doug, so I joined them a while before doing more Christmas baking. Today was a day well spent visiting old friends and seeing family. What more could anyone desire? Happy New Year!

December 24—Our snowy winter weather has created great conditions for cross country skiing. I dropped everything this morning and joined Linde and Teresa, an exchange student from New Zealand, on a skiing jaunt to a mountain meadow. We made our own ski trails up and down a hill. Great exercise! Snow crystals sparkled in sunlight, and there was no wind. The evergreens wore frosted covers, and Chief Joseph Mountain was etched clean and bright against a topaz sky. We were skiing into a Christmas card!

We laughed a lot, when, for one reason or another, we fell in the soft, downy snow. The sun was warm and the air fresh. Forgetting that it would be Christmas Eve tonight, I returned home with just enough time left to bake a batch of rolls before we drove to upper Prairie Creek, to partake in dinner and Christmas Eve at daughter Ramona's house. Once again, our family gathered and the small farm house under the east moraine of Wallowa Lake rang with merriment.

December 25—Christmas morning dawned bright and clear. After chores, I was mixing some dressing for our roast duck dinner, when the phone rang.

If I wanted to photograph Santa Claus feeding cattle, I was told, I could do just that, across the road from our ranch, at neighbor Dwayne Voss' place. So Steve and I jumped into the car and tracked down Santa. He and Mrs. Santa made quite a picture out there with the cattle against the snowy background of the Wallowas. Those Voss children will remember this Christmas for many years. The cowboy who was Santa turned out to be friend Linde's hubby, Pat, who caused quite a stir around Prairie Creek on Christmas morning.

Later, we all enjoyed drunk duck (duckling roasted in wine), after which the adults draped themselves around the living room furniture and the children went out to go sledding. It was turning cold, about 14 degrees, and already after 3 in the afternoon. But not to worry, Grandma took them all sledding on Alder Slope.

After delivering packages to two more grandchildren, and dropping several off at their home, I returned with Buck and Mona to find granddaughter Tammy and her fiance in our living room. Tammy and Matt had traveled all the way from Lodi, through fog most of the way, to be with family. As darkness fell on another Christmas night, this grandma was fading fast, but very thankful for all the blessings bestowed upon us during the Christmas season.

There was a bit of sadness thrown in with our family's festivities this year. A well-loved uncle passed away on Christmas Eve. Uncle Reid Nunn, whom we especially remember this time of year, suffered a stroke, and quietly passed from this world as he was talking to his family in the living room.

When my brother and three sisters and I were children, living on the small dairy ranch in the foothills of Placer County, California, it was uncle Reid and auntie Carol who would drive from Sacramento on Christmas Eve to take us and mama to grandma's big white house in Rio Linda. Daddy, who had to stay to milk the cows, never got to go, as I remember.

However, so we country bumpkins could experience that traditional Christmas at Grandma and Grandpa Wilson's, this kind uncle and equally kind aunt would drive, often in fog, clear out in the country to transport us to grandma's house. At that time, all we had in the way of transportation was an old ranch pickup, and in winter we children couldn't very well ride in back. We were treated to a real car and sang Christmas carols all the way to grandma's. It was a special time. Grandma always served hot chocolate with marshmallows and there was this big, magical tree with gifts under it for all.

There were many other cousins and aunts and uncles who always said, "My, how you've grown!" Those aunts and uncles really cared about us, watching as we really did grow up. We took it for granted then, but now I realize it was their caring that gave us the stability needed to cope with our lives. So we all appreciate your gift, uncle Reid, and auntie Carol too, a gift that has kept on giving down through the generations of our family.

Today, there is a whole new set of uncles and aunts who care about their nieces and nephews like you did.

December 26—Doug and I braved icy roads and blowing snow to travel over the Blue Mountains to Pendleton to spend the day with daughters Lori, Linda and their families. It was like changing seasons to drive down off Cabbage Hill to green grass and balmy temperatures. Returning tonight, it snowed so hard between Lostine and home that we could scarcely see the road.

December 27—I drove over snow drifts to friend Linde's, where she and I and Pat donned cross country skis and headed up through the snowy woods, emerging onto the road to ski down those drifted lanes to visit our snowbound neighbors.

Returning after four miles, we slided and glided along, all but lost in the blowing snow. We looked and felt pretty small and insignificant out there, lost in the storm. We made it safely back just before dark. A great way to spend a Sunday afternoon, visiting neighbors and keeping our bodies in shape.

Returning to our warm home, I found Doug watching his football game on TV. He says he's fed too many cattle in too many storms to be out in them for the fun of it.

December 28—There is no sky, mountains, hills or fields. Even at mid-day there is very little light, and that light is dull. Our world is in wind-powered motion. Snow flies past the windows, resting only briefly before being picked up again and swept away. Neighbors, whose homes lie at the end of east-west country lanes, are snowbound. Their roads are drifted in. Those who must drive out do so by traveling across their fields, which are swept clean of snow. Winter has come to Prairie Creek.

The old Monarch gulps wood. Flames fanned by the ceaseless winds send sparks flying up the stovepipe to disappear into the motion of the storm. Christmas is over and the new year looms. Cattle huddle in bunches, their backs to the storm. Most of their hay has blown away to be consumed by the dull, swirling whiteness which is their world as well as ours. The five calves on my two milk cows are having it a bit easier than the fall calves on the hill. They can wait out the storms in the barn by entering a creep hole. Inside, dry and sheltered from the wind, they happily nibble grain and hay.

Tepee at Dug Bar, on the Snake River, looking toward Idaho.

1993

January 5—After an unusually heavy snowfall last week, followed by a wild wind last night, drifts piled up everywhere on Prairie Creek. I tromped through those drifts this morning, sinking to my knees with every step, to feed my animals. Snow had blown through cracks in the old barn and plastered pretty patterns against the walls. It was piled in mini-drifts in the corners.

We are leaving Wallowa County tomorrow, heading south for our yearly jaunt to California, which always provokes mixed feelings. I love winter. Even though it does bring discomforts, it also brings a peacefulness and tranquility. I will even miss my chores!

I said goodbye to the calves. The heifer that Adele named Happy came up for her usual scratch under her throat latch. Ben and Steve will be in charge of my chores until we return.

January 6—Winnemucca, Nevada—It is 9:30 a.m. I am seated not at my kitchen table on Prairie Creek, but at a tiny table provided by the Red Lion Motel in downtown Winnemucca.

Staring through a window beyond the bare, snow-dusted branches of a small tree, I look down at a parking lot full of travelers, people like ourselves, heading south or north. Cars, with engines running, warming up so their drivers can take off down the long stretches of high desert that connects the sparse Nevada towns.

We drove through a picture postcard as we left winter-locked Wallowa County via the scenic Miriam canyon. Numerous elk and deer browsed the canyon sides, searching for grass sticking through the snow or nibbling twigs. The winter will be hard on the wildlife this year, as ice has already formed along the river and the boughs of evergreens drooped under the weight of blobs of snow.

When we negotiated Ladd Canyon out of La Grande, we left the icy pavements behind and, luckily, followed only bare roads to Winnemucca. After a brief stop at Farewell Bend, we sped on toward Ontario, where Doug made reservations for the Oregon potato conference, which we will attend on our way home.

On to Jordan Valley and homemade pie at the Old Basque Inn. Leaving town, I spied a young cowboy, a daddy, holding the hand of his very young son, just learning to walk. He smiled broadly at us. It left us with a good feeling for this little cow town. It was already dusk when we wound down over the Owyhee River and passed through Rome, and dark when we looked down that long, straight road that leads to McDermitt. Far out in the snowy sagebrush flat we could see two tiny pin-pricks of light. Probably a rancher's pickup covering the lonely miles to home.

Jackrabbits fled before us as we drove onward through the dark to McDermitt. Lost in the night, just us, the bunnies, and the moon, which rode along beside and illuminated snowy hills to the west, beyond which rose the far-off Steen's Mountain. We rested at McDermitt and drank some hot tea before continuing on toward Winnemucca, its blinking casino lights on the horizon, attracting travelers out of the night like moths.

We found the old Winnemucca Hotel, noted for its Basque hospitality and hardy home-cooked meals.

The owner motioned us into the dining room. "Come in," he said. "We feed anyone who comes in off the street." He hollered in the direction of the kitchen and held up two fingers. A slim, dark-haired girl laid a hot tureen of soup before us even as we slid out of our coats. She returned a few seconds later with thick slices of french bread, which we soaked in the beefy vegetable broth. Then this girl poured red wine into our glasses and set out a large bowl of lettuce salad, tossed with a tasty olive oil and vinegar dressing.

As we were helping ourselves family-style to the food, we were joined by two fellows who had ambled in from an adjacent room. Seeing as how we were family, we inquired as to their whereabouts. Speaking with an accent, the bigger fellow, opposite me, said he was from Idaho, and the one sitting across from Doug was from the local area.

When the girl brought in platters of steaming rice, beans, potatoes, cabbage cooked with chorizos, and a hearty stew, I commented, "Guess I'd better go out and find some sheep to herd, to work off all this food."

At this, the fellow from Idaho perked up, and said, "Do you have any sheep?"

"No," I answered, "but when I was young I raised some…but I do own a sheepherder's wagon!"Do you have any sheep?"

"Yes," he replied.

"How many?"

"Too many…7,000 head!"

And then we got to talking about his life, and became so enthralled with his story that we forgot to ask his name. Twenty years ago, as a young lad, he came to America alone from Spain. He hired on herding sheep for a "very nice man," he said, in Wyoming who owned a large sheep outfit. For years he worked faithfully for his employer, saving his wages and beginning to build up his own band. Sometimes the owner would pay him in sheep, and over the years helped the fellow get established with his own sheep operation.

"He was a nice man," he kept saying. Just talking with this sheepman, we could tell the owner had the same feeling for his faithful employee. Today our newfound friend summers his own sheep in the Soda Springs area of Idaho, where they graze national forest lands in the mountains. The sheep are wintered in Bakersfield, California.

"The sheep must be trucked a long way," he said, and added fondly, "I love the mountains. I don't like cities."

We mentioned that we were acquainted with several Basque families in our own country in Oregon, and that they used to own the Cherry Creek Sheep Company, and what respected sheep ranchers they were. When we spoke of Joe Onaindia, he said with surprise, "Oh, I know Joe! He is good lamb buyer in California." And it turned out that the Joe he spoke of was none other than the son of our friends, Marge and Joe Onaindia. Small world: out there in Winnemucca, eating at a long table with strangers, who weren't, really.

About this time, the Basque girl brought four huge steaks, still sizzling, hot off the grill, and we just kept on talking and eating, in the Basque tradition. More people came in, and were treated in the same manner.

"No one goes away from here hungry," said the owner, a twinkle in his eye. Neither do they go away hungry for companionship, I thought, which is just as important as the food.

Our newfound, nameless friend was headed for business in Reno, he said, and as we talked about our cattle and seed potato business, the other fellow, who had remained silent through most of the meal, added some comments of his own.

He said Winnemucca used to be a big potato growing area, but is mostly planted to alfalfa now.

Earlier on TV, watching winter storm warnings for the Tahoe Sierra Valley, I wondered if we would be snowbound in Reno tonight. Meanwhile, I've called our relatives in California and assured them we are getting closer. I also think of our large, extended family left behind in

Wallowa County and wonder if it did get below zero, as it was predicted. How are they all making it?

Meanwhile, for us, it will be onward, over the snowy Sierra, to the foothill city of Auburn. I harbor this illusion that I will be working on my book, holed up at a niece and nephew's house in Auburn. Will it happen?

January 13—My typewriter and I have finally landed in Auburn, positioned, again, at a kitchen table. It is 8:30 a.m. and I have this large, new modern house all to myself, although I am surrounded by evidence of those who live here.

Cheerios from year-old Kayla's hurried breakfast remain scattered on the high chair. A cozy oak fire burns in the family room, started by Kayla's daddy, Tom. Five-year-old Kyle's kindergarten drawings are taped to the fridge. Lori left to drop off Kayla at 6:30 at the day care before driving to her job at the bank. Tom left earlier for his job of managing the complex system that supplies water to cities in the surrounding area, taking Kyle to kindergarten on his way.

It isn't the kind of life our families lead in Wallowa County, but a life many young people lead these days. At night, house becomes home again, filled with family, who have been scattered in different daytime directions. Kayla is a happy, toddling little presence and Kyle shows us what he made in kindergarten. Tom and Lori prepare supper and tend to the needs of their children.

On this rainy morning, Doug has driven off in the direction of Sacramento in search of an antique mall. Hope Sacramento isn't flooding. Outside the windows of Lori's spacious kitchen, barren oak limbs writhe and digger pines thrash in the gusting winds of a warm California storm. Lots of moisture here, rain in the valleys and snow in the mountains.

When I was growing up here in the Sierra foothills, this area around Auburn was steep rolling terrain covered with a wild mix of oak and Digger pine. Wild blackberry, Toyon berry, Buckeye and Chaparral grew on the grassy hills. Ravines, creeks and rivers that once sluiced gold from placer mining claims laced the land, creating a vast watershed that served the fertile Sacramento Valley.

Only a few of those oaks and Digger pines remain now. The rain, driven in sheets by the wind, runs down new pavements of steep streets and into drains. Very little moisture is soaked up by roots of trees, shrubs and grass. At the moment, the street out front is a river of falling, rushing water. Hope the drains below don't become clogged.

Lori is sister Mary Ann's daughter. As you know, Mary Ann is on the island of Dominica, serving two years in the Peace Corps. Normally, we stay with M.A. when we come south each January. We miss her, but understand Agri-Times eventually makes its way to her tiny island in the Caribbean. Perhaps she can read this and weep, because we know she misses her family.

Arriving here last night, we looked for the first time upon little Kayla, who was born on the day we left last year. We hugged Kyle, ate Tom's tacos, and listened to a tape prepared by M.A. on Dominica. It was the next best thing to visiting her in person.

She held the recorder so it would record her island sounds: rain hitting the tin roof of her flat, roosters crowing at dawn in the village of Zicak, musical sounds of frogs and insects that occupy the lush tropical rain forests, yipping puppies, noisy children, and M.A.'s Dominican friends speaking in many dialects and Creole. It wasn't hard to detect a note of homesickness in her voice, speaking to her family so far away. Kind of choked us up too. Even made us feel sort of guilty here in this comfortable home, enjoying her grandchildren.

After spending Thursday until Monday at a friend's ridge-top home above Auburn, we drove to Lodi to visit granddaughter Tammy. Daughter Ramona was there too, making wedding plans. We got together with the future in-laws before we left, over dinner at Pietro's. Am invited to my mother's apartment for lunch. Her husband, Bill, will provide taxi service.

We understand it got down to minus 17 on upper Prairie Creek after we left. I think often about my calves and how the barn cats are making out. We haven't had a winter like this one for quite some time. All of this moisture surely ought to pull our West out of its long drought.

We brought the sourdough jug with us and a bowl of dough is working away. Biscuits for supper! From now on, while we are staying with Lori and Tom, I will do the evening meal. Fun, in such a modern kitchen; that is, if I can find anything.

Better get this column in the mail so it can begin its long journey northward to Pendleton.

January 19—Saturday dawned clear over the Auburn foothills, setting the stage for our annual adventure. We three sisters look forward all year to being together. I say three because M.A. is still on her island of Dominica.

By mid-morning, Caroline, Kathryn and yours truly were soon swallowed up by freeway traffic, heading down I-80 toward San Francisco. Clearly-defined Coast Range mountains and rolling foothills turning spring green put us in a good mood. Caroline exited at Napa Sonoma and we wound through countryside dotted with sheep and oak trees.

At Petaluma we shopped for fresh veggies and fruit, before lunching on the wharf at Bodega Bay, where we indulged in a bowl of that famous clam chowder. Off again, excited as school girls about seeing for the first time the seaside cottage Kathryn had secured for our weekend.

And suddenly, there it was—appropriately named "The Tides of Life"— a secluded little abode perched high on a cliff above the sea. Aged limbs of a gnarled cypress tree embraced the house and covered the stone patio. A wood pile leaned against a weathered fence, on the other side of which grew rank bushes. Orange-red hot poker plants flamed among the greenery threatening to engulf the wooden gate.

Numerous plants and succulents had taken root in the cliff, which was held securely together by a series of cascading terraces. Below a wooden, fenced-in deck that held a hot tub, ice plant spilled downward to the beach. And beyond the sprawling sandy beach boomed the Pacific. It took our breath away. Sea gulls sailed over the waves, and myriad birds chirped from the tangled bushes growing everywhere.

We unlocked the door, which in itself was charming: old, with wooden carvings and one of those old screen doors. As we turned the clear glass knob, we entered a small room full of antique furniture. Dated original oils adorned the walls, and the light fixtures were made of stained glass and wrought iron. It seemed a refuge for poets and artists, and we fell in love with it immediately.

Kathryn slid a tape in the stereo, and soft music floated throughout the cottage and outside. After unpacking and making the beds with sheets we had brought along, we picked our way down via a zig-zag path through the blooming ice plant to the beach below.

We wandered into the late afternoon, picking up shells, watching breakers spill their turquoise contents upon the sand, breathing great gulps of salt air into our lungs. When the setting sun glinted along a path of shimmering light, we returned to the cottage. After the sun sank into the western waters, we built a fire in the wood stove with Caroline's kindling.

K. got busy in the kitchen and soon we were eating stir-fry chicken and veggies in a charming little nook commanding a view of the sunset. We ate by candlelight, listened to music of sea and surf, and thought we must surely be dreaming.

K. and C. soaked in the hot tub under a now cloudy sky while I entertained myself by reading a "Tides of Life Journal" that we found in the drawer of an old cabinet. Most interesting, reading about the previous visitors' experiences in this special place. Many couples had used it for their honeymoons. We also got a kick out of reading the notes taped to the walls—near the heater thermostat, *Fuses in cellar*, and on the toilet, *Don't flush often, water shortage.*

This struck us really funny, especially when it poured all night and all the next day, and there we were beside a rushing creek spilling into the ocean. The water was stored in a big wooden water tank beside the cottage, and our fire proved sufficient in keeping us cozy, so we didn't risk blowing fuses and stumbling around the cellar for more heat.

I awoke often in the night as the wind threatened to blow us off our cliff. It did blow open the front door, which jerked with a bang when the chain caught it.

The next morning it was still raining as K. and C. poured bird seed into a wooden feeder outside our breakfast nook. While we dined on oatmeal, fresh fruits and freshly brewed coffee, my sisters happily identified Redwing and Brewer's blackbirds, house sparrows, California towhees, Rufus-sided towhees, golden crown sparrow, house finches, and American robins, not to mention the ever-present gulls and a lone hawk.

The refrigerator turned out to be dysfunctional and froze even our vegetables, so we found a package of dry bean soup mix in the cupboard, which I simmered until tender, then added the frozen contents of our frig. Voila! "Tides of Life soup."

It turned out so good that I immediately wrote down the ingredients: green pepper, fresh basil, tomato, mushrooms, cabbage, onion, carrots, added to the cooked bean mixture. A dash of rice vinegar for added zip, plus the seasonings provided in the bean soup packet. The soup was thick, and wonderfully tasty. We dipped chunks of sourdough-rye-cornmeal bread into the hot broth, and served fresh pineapple for dessert.

We called our missing sister, Mary Ann, but her line was busy. We so wanted to let her know she was with us in our thoughts. We made a quick trip to the Crab Pot for fresh crab and sourdough bread, which provided our evening meal.

Clouds, deep purple, velvet-piled, met the pewter sea. This place turns us all to poets. Another storm blew in off the Pacific. Foam, resembling frothy lace, edged huge waves that broke against the tide, as K. and C. climbed into the steamy hot tub. They tried coaxing me in, but having just recovered from a cold, I declined, content to read and stoke the fire. Listening to the rain drumming on the tin roof was pure heaven.

The next morning I awoke early enough to see a cleansing dawn break over the waves. Ever-changing light struck the rolling Pacific, which curled into long crashing breakers. The sky was clear. I ran for the hot tub, and through the steam I watched the muted morning. Feeling a bit guilty, enjoying such contentment.

The gals were soon up, feeding their birds, laughing and preparing breakfast, and we were sisters again, the years rolled back. Newborn lambs frolicked on green hills behind us, running to their moms, butting against swollen udders for nourishment. The surf was up, pounding and breaking over large black rocks that lined the shore.

We breakfasted in sunlight in our nook, eating fresh fruit, muffins and Caroline's leftover lemon bars. After tidying up the cottage, we sat outside, reluctant to leave this secluded place. The previous stormy days had discouraged tourists, so we had the place mostly to ourselves, a rarity in California.

We lingered on until nearly noon, then packed up, and left the "Tides of Life" behind, a shared experience tucked away in our busy lives, bonding us together. We lunched at the Tides in Bodega Bay, watching through the window of a restaurant alongside the wharf as a seal swam close to show off, and we purchased salt water taffy to take home.

Then, once again, we entered the flow of holiday traffic returning to Auburn.

Today the weather has resumed its damp, cloudy pattern, and here I am again, seated at the oak table in Tom and Lori's kitchen, typing out my column.

Doug is off gold panning, in spite of the dreary weather. His favorite panning streams are flowing bank to bank this year. He has spent most of his free time checking out antique shops and relaxing away from the responsibilities of running a ranch. Thanks to Ben and Steve, we are able to do this sort of thing once a year.

January 26—Ontario, Oregon—The January sun burns its way through a layer of frozen fog as I sit in our motel room in Ontario this morning. Doug is attending an early meeting of the Oregon Potato Conference while I begin the fourth column written during our absence from the ranch.

We pulled into Ontario yesterday afternoon, having driven in from Winnemucca. Our California stay ended Sunday when we bade goodbye to family. Under clear blue skies, we motored up and over the snowy Sierra to the snowy Nevada desert. After weeks of rain, wouldn't you know that the weather turned sunny just when we had to leave?

We were very grateful, however, for one special day, Saturday, which couldn't have been lovelier. Only a few high, thin clouds marred the otherwise blue skies. Caroline and Kathryn picked me up and we spent the entire day poking in and about our childhood haunts.

Because of the rains, the greening gave us a preview of the spring to come in the Sierra foothills. Caroline took the back roads from Auburn to the Mt. Pleasant District where we grew up.

We investigated a road where my school chum Sandra used to live, a road remembered well because she and I walked the country miles between our rural homes many times. On the very spot where Sandra's modest little house used to stand, a $300,000-plus mansion greeted us.

A country home? Every inch of its acreage groomed and immaculate. Nothing looked familiar. Turning around, we returned to Mt. Pleasant Hall, which did our hearts good. The old wooden building was still there, serving the community as it always has, and having recently been elevated to the status of historical landmark. We read the plaque, which told how the area used to be known as Hungry Hollow, and remembered daddy saying same.

Another sign, which read "Mt. Pleasant Hall 4-H meetings," stood next to the old building. I remembered that, after the war, it was my parents who started up the Mt. Pleasant 4-H Club again. And, of course, all of us Bachman children were members. As we drove over the hill to our old ranch, K. recited the "Head, heart, hands and health" 4-H pledge.

We ended up at brother Jim's, where he and his family continue to live. In spite of the fact that 15 homes are scattered about most of the original 150 acres, Jim still owns part of the old property. We parked near where daddy's neglected garden struggles to endure.

The garden has missed him since his death in 1984, but the things he planted continue to grow in their own haphazard fashion. Drought seems to have taken its toll on the ivy, but recent rains are bringing some back. A variety of succulents and cacti spill forth from collected bottles and kettles suspended from oak tree limbs.

His cement sculptures and miniature Greek temples choked with creeping myrtle. As always, we felt his presence as we tripped through a maze of creeping plants and fallen oaks. Once in a while some little treasure that he had purchased for pennies at the Roseville Flea Market would smile at us from the dead ivy tangle.

Wearing rubber boots, we traipsed through the oak woods and halted near a pond so K. and C. could watch two pair of wild geese through their binoculars. After crossing a tiny creek that flowed into the pond, we smelled wood smoke and soon found the clearing where Jim and his family, including twin grandsons, were cutting wood.

They had a grate full of hot dogs roasting over the coals of an oak fire. A small trailer attached to a tractor served as a picnic area. Thirty-month-old Beau and Brandon were helping load wood, as was their golden retriever. It was a family affair. After picnicking, C., K. and I strolled up a knoll to a remembered clearing where two old, weathered oak posts stuck out of the ground, all that remained of a round corral I helped a boyfriend build, when I was 16, so he could break a colt for me.

Then we followed the old dredger diggings where the '49ers dredged for placer gold so long ago. We wondered if the dredger ponds still held bull frogs, and if the oak scrub grown over the rock piles still provided refuge for deer, quail, coons and foxes.

We wandered in the sunshine of our youth and remembered... wishing for fields of golden California poppies and purple lupine, new, shiny leaves on white oak and cottonwood. We could envision Johnny-jump-ups, scrambled eggs, and baby blue eyes... the smell of those wildings. We knew black-tail deer had eaten most of the fallen acorns; we saw their tracks. Out on the soggy meadow, where great pools of water lay after the storms, we remembered catching polywogs and bringing them home in fruit jars, to turn into frogs all over the house.

Leaving the ranch we drove up and over the rolling foothills to where the trees were sparser and the settlements were few, to visit daddy's grave in the old pioneer cemetery. It was peaceful there, looking out over the wide open, greening pastures where cattle grazed and a pond filled with honkers glinted in the afternoon sun. In the silent cemetery, filled with pioneers who settled that country, we found daddy's headstone. The one I'd ordered made of local granite with a cow engraved on it.

Bright red Toyon berry bushes and stately oak trees grew among the grave markers. The oldest headstone, weathered and barely legible, was dated 1831. Several of daddy's friends and neighbors were buried close by. We noticed, some amaryllis bulbs sending their green shoots up through the red granite dirt on his grave.

Reluctant to end the day, we stopped to visit an old dairyman and his wife, who had just celebrated their 50th wedding anniversary. Caroline wanted to photograph two of their old Guernsey signs. More nostalgia. We remembered the sign hanging on an ancient oak at the entrance of our own dairy: "Oakcrest Ranch—Registered Guernseys—Matt J. Bachman."

We crammed the day with remembering, so didn't talk much. Didn't need to. Being together was enough. We called M.A. on Dominica when we got home.

Last week was spent visiting more relatives from Sacramento to White Rock. Uncle Reid's widow, Auntie Carol Nunn, fixed us a delicious lunch and Uncle Johnny, 87 years young, drove out from Rio Linda to join us, as did two of the Wilson cousins, Janet Feil and Patty Nunn. Amazingly, Uncle Johnny continues to write and compose musical scores for the Sacramento Children's Academy. A musician all his life, and now a historian, and published writer. Being creatively productive must keep him young at heart and happy.

We loved listening to Uncle Johnny tell about when his mother, my grandmother, and her girlhood chum Blanche drove a horse and wagon from Donner summit to Sacramento. We could picture those two 19-year-old girls stopping for the night at friends'. Their mother couldn't call in those phoneless days and ask, "Did the girls get there OK?"

He also regaled us with stories of his fruit-picking adventures during the summer. Driving their old "flivver," Johnny and his friend picked fruit from Newcastle to the Delta. Home was wherever the flivver was parked, and they cooked over an open fire and slept outside. They were 14!

We drove another day in a terrible wind and rain storm to visit the Smiths on their ranch at White Rock. Carson Creek spilled over its banks, and cattle backed up to the wind-whipped rain, which came down by the bucketful. The old three-story brick ranch house withstood the storm, as it has for years. More of the old-timers gone now, except for Agnes and George.

New subdivisions creep closer each year, and the pink glow in the night sky comes from El Dorado Hills—country clubs, a golf course, and elite homes. But the Smiths continue to live much as they've always done, simply, making their living from the commercial cattle business. Cows winter there at White Rock, near Folsom, and summer in the Sierra.

We looked at photos of fall gathering crews, old cabins, cow camps near Wrights Lake, and remembered names like the Barrett's country, Rockbound Pass, and Maud Lake. It is good to be returning home, where the book I am writing is still waiting to be written. Perhaps this digging up of my heritage will point the way.

January 28—Leafless raspberry canes protrude from five-foot drifts, a mound of hardened snow has buried our picnic table, and the beaten path to the chicken house isn't; all evidence of wild winter winds that blew during our absence. Bladed by the snowplow, great chunky piles of snow line the county roads here on Prairie Creek. But this bright blue and white morning is drenched with sunlight, and the ground hog will surely see his shadow, if, that is, he can dig his way out of a snowy burrow.

After munching hay and silage, the cattle soak up the warm rays as they meander to the water trough or holes chopped in the creek. The spring calvers, bellies swollen with life, are nearing their time. The year begins anew.

It is good to be home, seated at my own kitchen table in front of the trusty Smith-Corona, I must tell you, however, that Doug gave me at Christmas a new, ultra-light computer something-or-other, which waits patiently in its box for me to comprehend its complex personality. Help!

After perusing no fewer than five instruction booklets included in the box, I am more confused than ever. I think I'll need professional counseling before this "thing" and I become comfortable with each other. My husband's intentions were good, and I do appreciate his thinking that I could use a more streamlined method of producing a weekly column. Besides, that way he could use the Smith-Corona.

So, as I begin my tenth year of writing this column, readers beware, and hang in there. Perhaps I'll even get the hang of it, and become compatible.

My two milk cows and their five calves looked hardy and healthy when I resumed my daily chores, and the barn cats were all accounted for. I like to think that Daisy, my young Border collie, missed me, but she, too, was in good hands, having spent the weeks with Pat and Linde. Once again, she greets me every morning before sunup, happily leaping and running circles in the snow. Glad to be alive, in the way of joyful pups.

January 30—Linde called this morning. She and Gay (another Prairie Creek rancher) were going cross-country skiing. Did I want to join them? Chores finished early, I stuffed water bottle and a sandwich into my day pack and drove to Linde's. Foggy here on the ranch, hoarfrost covering trees, fences and livestock, but upper Prairie Creek glittered in frozen brightness under the bluest of skies. It was 14 degrees.

We drove over Sheep Creek hill, turned up Little Sheep to the summit at Salt Creek. Vapors of steam floated above Little Sheep Creek. If we didn't have creeks here, we wouldn't know how to get anywhere. We pulled into a bladed parking lot in a snow park, donned skis, slung packs over our backs, and slid off on a six-mile mountain loop, Nordic ski trail.

There were several rigs parked in the area, but no one about. It was so quiet, even the snowmobilers must've been far off. We slid and glided along groomed trails. Relaxing and effortless, until we came to an uphill section o the trail, and then we had to use those arm and leg muscles. The crusted snow made for perfect skiing, packed so it didn't stick to our skis. We were one; ski trail, forest and sky, drawing fresh air, pure and crisp, into our lungs.

We didn't meet another soul along the trail. Wallowa County's best-kept secret, we thought. Each bend in the trail brought new adventure, especially when we began descending a rather steep, curvy stretch that seemed to head down into a wooded canyon. Snowshoe rabbit tracks criss-crossed snowy openings and disappeared into deep woods. We skied silently, winding through stands of scorched, naked trees, grim reminders of the old Canal burn.

Nature's artwork surrounded us in the form of snow sculpted stumps and logs and even swirled around the bases of trees. We just kept repeating, "What a glorious day!" It almost seemed like we were the only three people on earth.

Around noon, our stomachs reminded us that it was lunchtime, so we slipped out of our skis, sat on our jackets in the snow beneath two spruce trees, and ate the contents of our day packs. We had been a bit concerned earlier, as the trail continued its downward trend deep into the canyon, and we knew what went down must come up. Come up we did, but thanks to the trail engineer, ascent wasn't as steep as descent.

Since we still consider ourselves amateurs at this sport, we took some rather undignified dives into deep snow on steeper terrain. It took even more undignified maneuvers to get on our skis again, as we chuckled at the indentations in the snow where we had fallen, which resembled more the foundering tracks of a bull moose.

It was late afternoon and the shadows lengthened on the snow when we returned to the snow park. We could feel we had done all those miles. Fulfilling a promise to Doug, I made a "from scratch" lemon pie, warmed up some leftover antelope stew and sourdough biscuits for supper, and hit the bath tub to soak tired muscles.

January 31—Guess all those walks I took around Auburn in the rain kept me in shape, because today I wasn't a bit sore.

I baked a loaf of bread for grandson Shawn to take back to college, and gave him a care package of home-canned fruits. As today is Super Bowl Sunday, Linde and Pat appeared at our door armed with popcorn, chili and sourdough biscuits. We watched the Cowboys beat the Bills while we munched our way through Linde's great food.

February 2—Yesterday I caught up on myriad jobs, and now we are back in the swing of ranch living. It is another lovely "bluebird day" and, if we didn't know better, we'd think spring was just under the next page of the calendar. Soon we will be shipping seed potatoes, calving, and thinking about all the "spring things" that follow the seasons in rural living.

Ranchers and farmers hereabouts are happy with the snowpack in the mountains, hoping it is enough to fill our streams, ponds and springs with life-giving water.

February 9—Bare patches are beginning to appear between snow banks now, and this morning there is even a little mud. Wafting on February's milder breezes is that old familiar essence of feedlot: corral number 3.

In the canyons, February brings the smell of birth. New calves and lambs doze in sunshine, or bound wildly about for the simple pleasure of being. Friend Grace and I drove down into those canyons of the Imnaha one day last week, hoping to experience that first "feeling of spring" that always shows itself earlier in those lower elevations.

We visited briefly with 86-year-old Inez Myers, who is as much a part of the Imnaha as the river itself. Inez's modest house appears almost dwarfed by canyon rims, which rear east and west to the sky. Southward, the timbered upriver country stretches to the snowline, and northward, in the way rivers run here, the Imnaha rushes to join the Snake.

It is still too soon for the crocuses to bloom in Inez's old-fashioned country garden, but Mary Marks' snowdrops have been blooming since January.

We had a bite to eat at the Riverside Cafe, and met a woman who had returned for a visit after a 30-year absence. Cowboys gathered on the steep street of the small settlement. From here, the roads lead up to Hat Point or heads northward down to Dug Bar, where both roads dead end. But, like the old-timers tell strangers: "If you want to go to Mexico, take the upper river road, the one that turns across from the post office, between the Imnaha Store and Tavern, and the Riverside Cafe."

One afternoon I picked up the two youngest grandchildren, James and Adele, and brought them out to the ranch. They had missed their grandma and admonished me for staying gone so long. After hugs all around, which grandma needed too, we had a great time catching up.

Cross-country ski conditions have been tops this year, so we have been taking advantage of them. Even on cloudy days we are out and about on some new back country trail, discovering a new adventure. One of the advantages of Nordic skiing is its freedom, that of being able to strike out most anywhere. And that we do.

One morning, we decided to ski an old logging road, which came to an abrupt end at the top of a high ridge. Not wanting to return the same steep way we had skied up, we opted to take the plunge, so to speak, get ourselves to the bottom so we could ski back to our rig. Easier said than done.

On foot, carrying our skis and poles, we floundered downward through deep powdery snow, following a lone elk track, until we lit in the brush-covered draw. Here began a real challenge; we skied in and around and over logs and trees, and crashed into snow banks. We were testing ourselves a little beyond the norm, just to prove we could.

Finally, after crossing a creek, we emerged into a clearing and found our old ski trail. We were all pretty damp after traveling through such deep wet snow, and figured we'd traveled more than six miles. A warm fire and a cup of hot tea, and we were as good as new.

Doug is enjoying his own type of senior citizen recreation. He, Max and Bud drove to Dug Bar and spent the day steelhead fishing on the Snake River. Doug returned late that night with a nice fish, which I can't wait to cook.

Yesterday morning, Linde and I decided to check out the Ferguson Ridge Nordic Ski Trail. After chores and breakfast, we drove to the McCully Creek trailhead, whereupon we got a little stuck in some off-road snow. After hoofing it back for help we were considerably delayed, but not discouraged, and we skied up a packed snowy road to where a Nordic ski track dove off into a thicket of lodgepole and fir.

Using our arms and legs, we poled and slid up and over little hillocks that led to a wider trail and a sign: *Ferguson Ridge Nordic Ski Trail...Most difficult.* Undaunted, we took that trail, which we hoped would ultimately lead to the Eagle Cap Nordic Ski Club hut, which, in fact, we could see perched above us on a high ridge.

We began a long, gradual ascent that soon brought into view the valley and beyond. We recognized the Findley Buttes, the rolling Zumwalt hills, and the timbered country stretching northward as far as our eyes could see. The big cut leading down the canyon, following Little Sheep Creek, was clearly visible, as was the breaks of the Imnaha and the Snake.

On a familiar lay of land, I picked out our Prairie Creek ranch and home. An eagle's eye view. Presently we rounded a high bend and stared directly into the snowy ramparts of the Wallowa peaks, and their dazzling sunlit snowfields.

Below yawned the McCully Creek drainage. It was almost hot as we made our final sliding way to a hog's back on which sat the ski hut. Dead trees, charred from the old Canal burn, stuck out of deep snow farther up and below the ridge top. The shelter's entrance faced directly east on a level with Idaho's awesome Seven Devils Mountain range. The sight took our breath away.

While we ate lunch, we vowed to return before winter's end to spend the night. On our skis again, we faced yet another challenge: that of descending that which we had come up.

The course proved to be slick, steep and a bit tricky in places. We fell often, laughing, into snow banks until we emerged victorious at last to the road, which led to the safety of our unstuck car.

Back to the ranch to carry on where I left off, several times lately, in the housework department. The yearly headache of the income tax is behind us, the phone is beginning to ring with potato buyers, and soon it will be time to "get with" the calving.

In the meantime, this excellent snow won't last, and we must take advantage of it while we can. The years roll on, we never get any younger, and keeping in shape will prolong our chances of being able to pursue Wallowa County's outdoor activities.

In other words, it is best to do today what you would otherwise put off until tomorrow—with the exception of housework. Tomorrow may be too late.

February 15—Prairie Creek is reduced to basic black and white, so when Ben and the old yellow silage truck chug through deep snow, passing by the house on their way up the hill to feed the fall calvers, it adds a bit of color to my world. Once again, everything buried beneath a white blanket of snow that fell all night and into today.

Today was Valentine's Day and, after Doug and I exchanged cards, and my cows, horses and chickens were fed, he took me to Joseph for breakfast.

Returning to the ranch full of energy, which I attribute to our recent cross country skiing, I tackled myriad tasks. For starters I defrosted the refrigerator, which led to cleaning out counters and cupboards in the utility room. Now we can find the calf scour boluses.

After lunch I helped Doug unload a pickup of wood he'd hauled in for our wood cookstove. Then I squeezed a bag of lemons and froze the juice for future pie and lemonade, went for a walk, did two loads of wash, took oyster shell to the hens, typed up an article on my granddaughter's engagement for the local paper, and read a chapter in Ivan Doig's book *Ride With Me Mariah Montana*.

By 5 p.m. Doug and I were on our way to the canyon settlement of Imnaha, 30 miles away, where we had been invited to attend the annual Sweetheart banquet at the new church. Max and Millie Gorsline were just ahead of us as we wound down and around the curving road that follows Little Sheep Creek.

Daylight lingered in our lengthening days, and clouds hovered over the rims, but the temperature moderated as we descended into the canyon. The church reposes on a leveled rise above the old Pioneer Cemetery, looking out upon the cattle ranches that support the folks here. Everyone was in a jovial mood.

"Happy Valentine's Day!" they called, and greeted us with handshakes and hugs. To the sound of organ music, friends and neighbors crowded together in groups inside, many dressed in their Sunday best, while others had come in straight from calving or feeding cows. The long tables were decorated with pale pink crinkly ribbons and silk flowers, while cooking smells and the cooks' chattering drifted from the kitchen.

Platters on the lace cloth-covered tables were heaped with homemade rolls, crisp relishes, individual cherry pie turnovers, ice water in pitchers, real silverware, pink napkins, and heart-shaped candles. We sat next to a rowdy carload that had traveled down from "on top," like us. Presently here came the servers (ours was Ken Stein) carrying more platters: sliced ham, turkey, steaming bowls of scalloped potatoes, the ones we donated, and buttered corn.

After eating and eating until we could hold no more, the entertainment began. Pastor Smith, in a jovial mood, emceed the most incredible two-hour program, the likes of which one would never see outside of Imnaha. It was the kind that springs from the hills, canyons and valleys...from the very souls of those who live in the outback.

Steve Soderblom, the quiet fellow who worked for us in potatoes, held us spellbound, playing classical guitar. Marsha Harrington and Arlene Lovell, a duo on piano and organ. Pete Donovan, who lives with his wife and two children out on OK Gulch, played three waltzes, ending with Brahms, on the piano...and using no music! Jim Blankenship, from Alder Slope, told vignettes drawn from his colorful life as a Snake River rancher, sheep herder, and Imnaha mail carrier.

Wonderful stuff. Jim said that when he was asked to speak, he looked through an old journal he'd kept while ranching on Snake River, and read about those early years: "He'd sat on a rock...and thought. Then later, he just sat on a rock!" Jim then related the following tale.

"Returning to sheep camp on the Lostine one summer, I unpacked my mule, unsaddled my horse, and entered the tent." To my surprise there was this fellow sitting there, so I spoke to him, but the man said nothing. I said hello again. Silence. The hair stood up on the back of my neck, until I realized someone had played a trick on me and placed a dummy in my tent!"

Over the years, Jim, who has played his share of jokes on his friends, still finds them trying to get even...notably, old-timer Clyde Simmons, who sat right there in the back wearing a cat-eating grin. These old cowboys and sheepherders know how to have fun.

Cowboy poet Sam Loftus, born on Elk Mountain, another product of the canyons and mountains, strode to the front and recited a couple of poems he'd written about his life, describing special memories of a mountain meadow and how he'd found peace there.

Skip, Pam, Sarah and Mike represented a younger mix of herders, cowboys and literary types, who are also mothers and fathers and supporters of their community. Mike and Skip on guitar and harmonica accompanied the sweet voices of their gals. Clad in jeans, boots, leather, with golden hair, these beautiful young faces give no hint of the struggle it takes to live here. Their songs were full of pathos and humor. One said it all...the words, "Move to the country, raise kids and peaches, and find Jesus by yourself."

Another old-time canyon dweller, Norman Lovell, singing sorrowful Western ballads (shades of Ernest Tubbs). Pastor Smith's wife, Linda, halfway through her song when her computer music accompaniment malfunctioned. No problem—Pastor called on a cowboy poet who needed only the accompaniment of laughter. Daughter Jackie and her friend sang a duet of Amazing Grace," and the audience joined in.

In a weak moment Doug and I, Lois and Jim Blankenship, and two other couples agreed to participate in a skit, which was a hilarious take-off on the TV "Newly...and Oldly-Wed Game," all of which brought roars of laughter to those seated and red faces to us. Responding to a question about memorable honeymoons, one woman said they had spent theirs in a cattle truck.

The honor of 1993 Sweetheart was bestowed on Skip Royes. Rose Simmons received a bouquet of red roses for her support of the Imnaha Christian Fellowship, and Pastor Smith received a special phone call that afternoon from another Rose, across the miles, from Montana. Rose Glaus had called to wish everyone happy Valentine's Day and say how much she missed her Imnaha friends.

The world was held temporarily at bay there on that Valentine's evening, tucked away under the rims, alongside the Imnaha from the woes of modern society. Granted, many hearts in the small community were no doubt struggling with their own problems, but all seemed well that special night, when healing laughter pealed throughout the church under the rimrocks.

It began to snow at the mouth of Lightning Creek as we drove home, and when we topped out over Sheep Creek hill, the fat flakes spun crazily at us in the headlights.

February 16—Busy week coming up, what with CattleWomen serving free beef chili at Les Schwab's promotion, a photo club meeting and slide deadline for our 1994 color calendar, and the Winter Fishtrap Writer's Conference at Wallowa Lake beginning Friday evening.

This conference holds a special significance for our corner of the West. The theme is "At the Corner, Writing about Culture and Agriculture." That memorable evening at the canyon church last Sunday represented a goodly slice of Imnaha's culture and agriculture.

February 23—It is just beginning to snow again. Between storms, Linde, Gay and I have been out in the woods skiing on a daily basis. Out in the calving pasture, new calves are beginning to appear in the snow. Wobbly at first, they quickly come to life after that first suckle of warm milk. By day two they are racing around the field despite the cold.

Before calving is over I will be thankful for the colostrum milk saved and frozen from my two milk cows that freshened last fall. There will be times when it will spell life or death for a newborn calf.

The second Winter Fishtrap Writer's Conference was held at Wallowa Lake this past weekend, and many thought-provoking ideas were kicked around, related to the "Culture and Agriculture" theme.

Agri-Times editor Virgil Rupp drove over from Pendleton to attend this one, and Doug and I had invited him to stay here at our place, which he did. Attendees this year were, to say the least, a very diverse group, but they all shared a very strong interest in the West and its future. We were pleased to see the ranching community as well represented as the environmental one.

Many present were chroniclers of the West in general. There were historians, writers, editors, columnists, and readers. They all had something to say, a profound desire to express what they felt about the future of Wallowa County, which is, in fact, the future of pretty places all over the West.

Agriculture is in flux right now. There are national parks being proposed, and studies going on, as I write, about two large ones right here in Wallowa County, which would impact the lifestyles of the entire populace, especially the resource users, who supply food and fiber to the more populated urban community. There is a segment that would like to see our beautiful area preserved for all time, for all people, without regard to who will raise food or produce fiber for them.

Some say we are at a crossroads now, as we approach the next century. Which way to go? Some say we need to sustain our resources, manage wisely what we have, to provide for future generations, and at the same time sustain the beauty. One thing for sure: none of this will transpire if we are divided. We must agree on what we value most; agree, and then get about the work of maintaining and sustaining.

Because this was a writers' conference, it was hoped that everyone would appreciate the other views and that, quoting Rich Wandschneider, the director of Fishtrap, writers would be responsible for what they "write about cows, cowboys, trees and timber workers, fish and fishers." What the urban population perceives is what they read.

It was hoped a better understanding of where each of us is coming from, and going to, was achieved at Winter Fishtrap.

While driving to the lake Friday evening, I noticed a large sign, *Elk Trout Estates,* new and shiny, plunked down at the edge of one of the most beautiful views of Chief Joseph Mountain on rolling, glaciated hills adjacent to the monument of Old Chief Joseph. The sign and name were taken from a local stream and forest.

At the conference, we wrote on paper made from the forest and ate endangered salmon while sitting on wooden chairs and visiting over wooden tables; warmed by a cheery log fire, wearing leather shoes from cattle, we enjoyed the atmosphere of the old lodge, which was also a product of our forest.

It has been said we are using up our resources faster than they can be replaced. Ed Marsten, editor of High Country News, said to look around us and write about what we see. The entire West is in the midst of change, he said. "Fifty years from now historians will write about this time as being one of the most exciting times in the history of the West."

Caught in the middle of the "exciting" time is the rancher, who doesn't find it so exciting, but rather very frustrating, presenting an uncertain future to him and the generations who will follow. Ranchers now number less than two percent of the total population, and urbanites want their land for a playground.

The surviving ranching community is in a corner, resembling a frightened herd of elk or the dwindling salmon struggling up our creeks to spawn. Our rural habitat is increasingly controlled by outside forces. Those who depend on public lands to graze their cattle are groping for ways to hang on, a desperate attempt to preserve their culture and livelihoods, all the while producing food in an area where nothing else could be extracted.

In fact, they have been doing this while at the same time continuing to preserve and sustain the beauty that newcomers think they have discovered! For more than 100 years these Hells Canyon ranchers have managed to maintain and sustain this area. It is so attractive today precisely because it has been in the loving hands of those few, who for generations have been responsible stewards of that land.

Young, third-generation rancher Scott McClaran, whose very future depends on being able to operate like his father and grandfather before him, relies heavily on public land grazing. Meanwhile, the cows themselves, the object of so much present controversy, are now calving, unaware of all these goings-on here in Wallowa County, and the hired men and cowboys who rely on these ranches for their livelihoods are still out there, day in and day out, doing their job in all kinds of adverse weather.

Very few are recording this. They are too busy attending meetings, from which they go away more confused than ever about an already uncertain future. In addition to the valley's woes, developers eye our areas, and there are those who propose a wave of estates or subdivisions with dollar signs in their eyes. The very love of the land itself carries no weight here. Economics outweighs all else.

Locals who have moved here from other areas are worried. They have seen this happen in the communities they came from. Others think that landowners should have the right to do whatever they want with their land, and that present economics for the region is more important than long-term effects. There is no looking down the road.

Perhaps one day the trout and the elk will be gone, along with the cows and the cowboys, and all that will remain will be the Elk Trout Estates, inhabited by a new group of people from outside the valley, who, unlike the locals, have the means to purchase them.

Perhaps we should take another hard look at this fact. Do we want other signs to read Prairie Creek Estates, Cow Creek Acres, or Zumwalt Drive? Or do we want these last open spaces inhabited, as they've always been, by elk, cattle, coyotes, deer, horses, as some species have been even before the white man? Think about do it. Do we want prosperity or Place? Does prosperity bring peace? What do we value?

Look around, listen, read, and observe. Listen to the land, like the cowboys do, and perhaps you'll be able to think more clearly.

Hal Cannon, who organized the Cowboy Poetry Gathering in Elko, Nevada, emphasized the importance of culture, lest we become too political. Cowboys have souls too, and the expression of their poems an stories are as important to the West as its resources.

Alvin Josephy wanted to know what writers would write about this conference, after they went home. This writer, if I can call myself that, would like to say that I think this gathering proved that we could all sit down together and express our feelings, and respect those of others. That in itself was a giant first step forward.

Teresa Jordan, herself a fourth-generation rancher, lightened the course of the conference. She was wonderful! In real life situations herself that had affected change, she was a very real victim of that change. Now she is writing about it, and the Chugwater country in Wyoming that shaped her life.

I've been wondering, what is an elk trout anyway? Have the ODFW people gone too far? Do we have a hybrid cross here?

February 27—Saturday night—Doug and I attended a retirement dinner for Arleigh Isley, our former county agent and present county judge. With many others, we enjoyed a steak dinner at the local Elks Lodge and witnessed the roasting of Arleigh.

February 28—Our ranching community met again for the annual Stockgrowers and CattleWomen's potluck at Cloverleaf Hall this evening. After eating too much potluck, we tried dancing it off to the good country Western music of Henry Kinsley and Pam Smergutt.

Prairie Creek danced with Crow Creek and this writer thought she was in shape for dancing, but Crow Creek showed her a thing or two.

March 2—It was a warm 25 degrees before sunup when I went out to chore this morning. I say warm because, compared to a week of near zero readings, it seems almost springlike. Although the cold hasn't been too conducive to calving, cross-country skiing has been terrific. Linde, Gay and I have lately been spending more time in the snowy outback than in our homes, it seems, taking advantage of this excellent snow.

Remember the ski hut we visited, promising ourselves to return and spend the night? Well, we did last week. On a crisp, clear, cold bluebird day, we made preparations to pack into the mountains. Waiting until temperatures warmed to 10 above, we shouldered backpacks containing our food and sleeping bags and hit the trail. After the first mile we shed our jackets; in spite of the bitter cold, just the effort of skiing uphill with packs warmed us.

The snowy forests that Thursday were quiet and cold, covered with a fresh snowfall that sparkled underfoot. Feather-light flakes glittered in sunlight as we glided through open meadows and climbed into the mountains and across buried logs until we hit the main trail, labeled *Most Difficult.*

Linde and I feel like old pros by now. We've been skiing so often lately, we are in shape and able to maneuver much easier with each new experience. At first the packs did affect our balance, but once we got used to it there was no problem. We skied up a long switchback trail that overlooks the valley before turning a bend that brings into view the gleaming Wallowa snowfields so close.

We took our time up the final trail that ends at the hogback, whereupon perches the ski hut, and home. The outside thermometer registered 15 degrees, so we wasted no time kindling a fire. The homemade barrel stove had a flat top that accommodated cooking pots, so we promptly filled two with snow and began melting us some water. Let me tell you, it takes a lot of snow to make a little water. Pretty soon we had enough boiling for tea and coffee.

We had been given a key that was supposed to unlock two long wooden boxes that held foam sleeping pads and Coleman lanterns, only the key didn't work. No problem, not to worry, we would spread sleeping bags on wooden bunks and make do without. As for light, we had some small candles that would suffice.

After a brief rest we clamped skis on again, now free of those burdensome packs, and skied up the long hogback and practiced our downhill turns. Light powdery snow made it perfect for turning and we made about six ups and downs on that steep ridge.

When that weak February sun sank behind Mt. Howard, a bitter chill settled hard over the hogback. The thermometer went back down to 10 degrees, but inside our shelter, things were warm and cozy, and we were hungry. We nibbled on homemade bread while Linde fried some potatoes. When the spuds were done, I heated a fry pan and pan-broiled two rib steaks.

"It just don't get any better than this," we joked.

A peaceful quiet descended on the mountain, a wonderful silence except for the icy crack of freezing outside, the sizzle of melting snow in the kettle, and the popping of pitch in the fire. Gone was the noisy refrigerator motor, the blaring TV and the disruptive phone. It was pure bliss.

We lit a small candle and ate ravenously by its flickering light, with a hunger brought on by the cold and the exertion of outdoor life. We made frequent quick trips outside the tent to watch the changes taking place on the mountain, and were rewarded by the sight of a thin moon suspended next to a single bright star.

Far below lay the valley where our homes lay nestled among the glittering settlement of lights. Bundled up, we watched the night come on until the cold drove us back. When next we peeked out from the tent flap, the silver moon had disappeared over the mountain, taking the star with it.

The crisp, cold nighttime sky brought an explosion of stars, jillions of them filling the blue-black dome above us. Snowlight and starlight merged as stardust glittered on the snowscape.

Since it was still too early for bed, we found a game called Boggle and became a bit boggled as to how to play it until we made up our own rules. After which we found a deck of cards and played crazy eights until our eyelids began to droop.

After banking the fire and leaving a small candle burning, we climbed into our hard beds. I took the top bunk and caused quite a commotion dragging myself up, but finally accomplished the task. We lay there watching the shadows against the tent sides caused by the flickering flames of the candle and the wood stove, listening to the pitch explode in the stove and a faint breeze stir the canvas.

Our plywood "mattresses" were hard, but our tiredness gave way to sleep. We took turns getting up and feeding the fire, and during one of those times, Linde muttered "my bones hurt," but we endured and were thankful for the warmth of the shelter.

In the night we heard little chewing noises and several rustlings around the tent. Methinks a little woods mouse must have visited us; we found his calling card in the morning. We awoke to see an apricot-colored glow, and etched on the eastern horizon in deep purple, the jagged crest of the Seven Devils mountain range in Idaho.

Interesting that the thermometer still registered 10 degrees. We were to find out that it had gotten down to 10 below in the valley. Too much to see and do, we unkinked our hurting bones and began to putter around the hut and limber up. Soon the smell of coffee filled the tent and drifted out into the cold air.

We pushed a pot of simmering oatmeal to the back of the stove, then went outside to ski up an appetite, making a few more trips up and down that ridge top. By this time the sunlight had illuminated the snowy Wallowa ramparts, and the valley below was coming to life. I thought about my cows, calves, horses and chickens, and knew Steve would be feeding them this morning. Doug would already be on his way to Hermiston to sort our feedlot cattle.

Upon returning to the tent we added walnuts, raisins and brown sugar to the hot oatmeal and savored breakfast. We tidied up the shelter, packed in more wood, filled the kettle with more snow water, and closed the tent. On with our packs again, lighter now minus food, we slid down the trail to make the full loop back to the car. What a treat we were in for.

After reaching the shortcut route we had taken in, we kept to the main trail and skied to another high ridge, then glided down a series of curving hills to a road that brought us abruptly up to the terminal of the Ferguson Ridge T-Bar. We finished snapping our rolls of film, and skied around to finish the loop.

March 7—I took two of my grandchildren to the OK Theater in Enterprise this evening, to see the movie "Homeward Bound," a Walt Disney film, portions of which were shot here in our own Wallowa Valley. What a thrill to see our gorgeous scenery, which is often taken for granted, as a backdrop for this excellent, all-family entertainment.

March 8—For almost a week now thick valley fog has enveloped us. Cold, unmoving air imprisons the frosty vapors here on Prairie Creek. Lengthening days bring warmer air, which hovers over the frozen ground, coaxing mists which accumulate and hang low over the low-lying valleys. Just above us, on upper Prairie Creek, our neighbors have been enjoying clear, blue skies and warm sunshine.

Sometimes these March mists recede to expose the dark, ghostly shapes of cows and calves, their breath expelling steam. Winter-weathered barns and ranch houses swim in and out of the swirling fogs. The high country's deep snows are settling and softening. It is avalanche time.

Baby calves are coming thick and fast now; pastures are full of placentas, which attract scavenger crows. Late at night, hungry coyotes wail and sneak down from the hills to supplement mousey diets with bovine afterbirth. Hearing them, ranch dogs, perhaps responding to their own primal past, point their noses skyward and begin to raise a ruckus here on Prairie Creek. Skunks, too, have been active lately. One in particular has moved in with the barn cats.

Pheasants can be seen along the country roads, pecking at the wheat spilled by the grain trucks. Grandson James asked yesterday, "Grandma, did you know the geese are back?" I did not tell him that some resident geese have wintered here; better be it that my boy thinks of spring and its harbingers. Never discourage a child's zest for life.

My Barred Rock hens, responding to longer daylight hours, or perhaps to whole wheat that I throw out for them to scratch in, are now laying 11 eggs a day. Even Chester, the banty rooster, struts around and crows with an air of spring importance. The five calves on the two milk cows are as big as their August-born contemporaries. After being calved in late fall they have caught up. All the extra milk and TLC might have something to do with it.

Doug attempted to drive out to the Salmon Creek hills yesterday, to check on some horses and a mule we have wintering out there, but he made it only to the top of Dorrance Gulch, where the snow was sinking enough for him to become good and stuck. He is out there again this morning, having taken the four-wheeler along in hopes of making it all the way to the ranch.

The ridges are pretty free of snow this winter, and now, with the melting, there should still be plenty of feed. These animals are used to pawing through the snow for the nutritious bunch grass that sustains them throughout the long winters. Range horses are a tough lot and learn to survive if they have access to good grass beneath the snow.

Even though the signs of winter are still around, there is something in a March that makes us think of spring. Linde and I were at the Grain Growers Feed Department the other day, and we couldn't resist the urge to purchase vegetable seeds. Telling ourselves we wanted to have a good selection of green bush bean and Early Sunglow corn seed, we came home with both.

Last Monday, taking Linde and Grace with me, I traveled to Wallowa, where I showed the "Wallowa Story" to Jennifer Isley's grade school history class. The students, several of who are descendants of Wallowa County pioneers, were most interested in the history of their area. It was most gratifying to see their reactions and listen to historian Grace Bartlett answer their questions.

Called my mother and stepfather the other evening to see if they had returned safely from a trip to Dominica to visit sister Mary Ann, who is serving a two-year stint in the Peace Corps there. Mom, 82, said it was quite an experience taking a cruise ship, island-hopping in the Lesser Antilles, then hopping onto one island and finding your daughter there. Although their stay was brief, M.A. was waiting there to show them a little of her present, different world. The trip was an anniversary present.

Last Thursday, in an effort to escape the dreary fog, Linde, another friend and I headed for the high country and smack dab into another adventure. The story of my life.

After putting together a nice lunch of antelope steak sandwiches, prune-nut cookies, oranges and a bottle of water each, we were off. We left the car at the McCully Creek trailhead and donned skis to slide off up the trail. Our original plan was to take a shortcut to the ski hut, which stood on a high ridge a short distance away.

As the crow flies, it was only a short distance, but actually arriving there would prove to be quite a different story. Both the story and the route are long, so here goes the story...

Somehow missing the ski track we should have taken, we got onto the trail to McCully Creek basin, which also has as its destination a ski hut, only after a much longer trek. As we merrily skied along, I happened to glance up to the eastern ridge and spot our intended hut, only we were across the creek and heading in a southerly direction toward Aneroid Peak!

We realized that we had chosen the wrong route and our shortcut was about to become a long-cut. After making the decision to leave the oft-used ski trail, we followed a snowshoe rabbit track that dove down an embankment and wound through a maze of brush, trees, and fallen logs to the creek.

At this point we could look across the creek and see the lone ski track we should have been following going up the bottom.

After much floundering around in soft deep snow, we found a way across McCully Creek, skiing gingerly over a precarious snow bridge. It was either that or a snowy log. The snow bridge held for all three of us, and then we faced a steep, looming embankment that had to be climbed or scrambled up or whatever to gain the top. Long touring skis are not built for this sort of thing, but after much grunting, panting, sweating and sliding, we sidestepped up the bank, holding onto tree limbs to pull ourselves up.

We found ourselves in a pretty, park-like meadow with frequent openings that were easy to ski through. We thought we had it made. Wrong. Far above loomed an old logging road, a road we recognized as leading to the trail directly below the hut. So we opted to go for it. Another wrong decision. We should have stuck to the single ski trail, which traversed the steep mountain ahead of us. Instead we soon found ourselves skiing horizontal on a vertical mountain. Our road proved to be so drifted over at that point, we couldn't find it at all. The snow was so deep that when we planted our poles, there was no bottom. So we stamped with one ski in front of the other to make a track that would hold up long enough for us to slowly inch our way to a ridge. Somehow I got separated from my two compadres, and looked up later to see them already on the ridge.

Each time I took a sliding step with the ski, a mini-avalanche tumbled from the fall line. It was really quite beautiful, the round whorls of snow rolling down the mountainside in brilliant sunlight across the sparkling snowfield. I felt like Hilary ascending Everest, mesmerized, in an alien world. It wasn't until later that I realized my danger.

Making my snail-like way to a draw, I found the zig-zag ski trail made by the short-cutter and joined my skiing friends. While we herringboned our way up to the main trail, the sun's warmth melted the snow, which began to stick to our skis. Slipping was no longer a problem on the steep mountain. We finally attained the trail and wearily skied up to the hut.

Sitting in front of the tent, we took frequent sips of water and ate our lunches. An outside thermometer registered 45 degrees as we soaked up sunshine and watched clouds shift above the Seven Devils.

Before we got too comfortable, we waxed our skis to accommodate the softening snow, then slide back into them and returned via the long loop labeled *Most Difficult,* which was a piece of cake compared to our trailless route in. This experience taught us to check out a route before taking it, and to keep our cool. By using our heads and not panicking, we turned an otherwise bad experience into a learning one.

March 15—March's capricious weather is upon us. This morning's warm wind blew in a warm rain that melted snow drifts and caused little rivulets of water to seep from underneath into the earth. In the flat meadows the water is pooling into large lakes of manure-colored melt.

By early afternoon that rain is transformed into fat flakes of snow falling slant-wise, not yet sticking, but the back of winter is broken, and snow drifts and hay stacks are disappearing. It is pretty miserable for all the little newborn calves out in their soggy pastures. Lucky are the ones born in the sheltering canyons where they can find refuge on the drained slopes and enjoy a warmer, drier climate.

The first shipment of seed potatoes left our cellars this morning. Like our little calves, the sorters must endure the Ides of March. Seeking out more springlike conditions, Doug and I escaped into the canyons last week to do a little fishing. While driving down along the Imnaha, thence to Dug Bar on the Snake, we noticed the first signs of spring.

We passed red osier dogwood with blood coursing through its veins, the sap beginning to rise, that unseen force working in nature is asserting itself. Near Thorn Creek we spotted waxy buttercups, and past Cow Creek tiny yellow bells hidden among sage and bunch grass. We watched from afar some wild sheep and numerous mule deer.

Dug Bar looked faintly familiar, though changed from when Doug owned it. The alfalfa field has gone to weeds, and the buildings are all painted a Forest Service color. It is still a thrill looking down at the blue-green Snake after winding around that rim-hugging dirt road.

After checking on our boat parked there, Doug took two fishing poles stored there and we headed back to the Cow Creek Bridge. It was warm and mostly sunny when I took off by myself down the gorgeous Gorge trail.

Even now, in colorless March, the place is haunting. Rock formations seem more vivid, no longer having to compete with the leaves on willows and thornbrush. And the riversong fills my senses. I took some colored slides of buttercups and the first pussy willows that grew next to the water, taking my time for closeups.

Doug, not wanting to hike that far, fished closer to the pickup, while I trekked to a remembered hole where I had hooked and lost a big steelhead two years ago. I was feeling good about myself, in shape from all that cross-country skiing, and hiked along at a pretty good clip. Returning, I wouldn't be quite that chipper!

About two miles into the gorge, in the heart of the canyon, I arrived at my fishing place. A large rock shelves into the river here, and waters whirl and pool around another large rock in the middle. Standing on a sloped rock, I cast out into the current and let the line drift around the rock...and immediately got a bite.

Reeling in slowly, I cast again, and get another something.

On the third cast, *whammo!* I had a big steelhead on, and became so excited I forgot about being careful. Slipping on the wet rock, I lost my footing and pitched headlong into the swirling, cold waters of the Imnaha.

Coming down hard on both knees, I put out my left hand to catch myself as the other hand, holding the pole, went *crack* as the pole broke in two. My face slid into the water and I lay there, the shock of cold rushing over my upper body, wondering whether to concentrate on the fish or just what to do.

Meanwhile, the fish took advantage of my precarious situation and see-sawed his way free on the large rock that stood in midstream. Away he went, heading downstream toward Lewiston, one of Doug's black and white Mepps in his mouth. Gulping down a mouthful of water, I crawled to a sitting position and assessed my smarting knees.

Knowing Doug wouldn't come looking for me until later, I decided to get myself back up on the trail and drag to the pickup. So you can see I was not the same sprightly and fully confident, trouping down the trail earlier. But rather a dripping wet, old woman carrying a broken pole and trailing fish line, both pride and my knees hurt. Luckily, my camera, which had been in my daypack on my back, survived.

Slowly I made my way back to the Cow Creek bridge, just as Doug was about to settle down in the pickup for a nap in the warm sunshine.

"What happened to you?"

So I told him my fish story, about the one that got away. And while I dried out, we drove upriver where Doug fished and I nursed my wounds. My knees were pretty swollen by the time we stopped at the Imnaha Store for supper.

I entertained myself by reading signs on the wall. One in particular struck a familiar chord: *Early to bed, early to rise, fish like H... and make up lies.* Only I swear this tale is true, and I have black and blue knees to prove it.

While Sally Tanzey fried up some chicken and french fries, we visited with friends who trickled into the small store. Writing at the end of that day in a daily log I keep, I tried to recapture the feeling of walking down the trail before my misfortune; feeling the place, hearing the ancient murmur as the waters dash through the rugged gorge, carved of ancient rock, over eons.

The gorge is a great leveler, I thought. Like all of Wallowa County, it shapes you mentally and physically; you wear the scars forever, but you can't really be hurt by something you love. I will return.

Last Saturday Grace and I paid our friend Bill a visit in his cabin on Alder Slope. He produced some fresh bottom fish that his son had recently caught in the ocean, and I poached it in butter and lemon juice, then ventured out to the root cellar to bring in some potatoes and carrots, which were scrubbed and cooked.

Feasting on the sumptuous fare, we listened to some old records I recently purchased at the Cressie and Paul Green estate sale. It was wonderful. Italian troubadors, songs like "O sole Mio," Sousa marches, old waltzes, Nelson Eddy singing "Rose Marie" and "Indian Love Call." All the while we thought about Cressie growing up on Elk Mountain and how she loved music, too.

That evening while Doug was attending an out-of-county meeting, I drove alone to Cloverleaf Hall in Enterprise and joined a gathering of Blue Mountain old-time fiddlers, and proceeded to sit back and soak some more music into my soul until 11 p.m.

Don Norton of Imnaha announced the program, "and now from Lewiston Idyho we have..." and the players took their places on a small stage. Not much fanfare, just good music. I tapped my toes till they were numb. The gathering was organized by local people Charley Trump and Leonard Samples. Fiddle players came from Washington, Idaho and Union and Wallowa counties.

Why, there were people I didn't even know played the fiddle there. Like Feryl Laney, the little cook we met at Red's Horse Ranch and later at Minam Lodge, and local cowboy Dave Murrill, who also played the mandolin. My heart leaped for joy when teenager Clara Wieck, who is growing up on Swamp Creek, tucked a fiddle under her pretty chin, tossed her golden mane, flashed her bright eyes and let fly with something like "Orange Blossom Special."

It was touching to hear Charley Trump dedicate one of his pieces to his wife, Ella. "Cricket on the Hearth," as it was her favorite. It was even more touching seeing Ella herself play the fiddle for the first time since her stroke. Then Helen Stonebrink took up her bow and the strains of Annie Laurie, soft and mellow, floated through the hall. Tunes came out of their heads: Blackberry Blossom, Wildwood Flower, Peach Pickin' Time in Georgia...

A black-haired gal from Union County fiddled "The Milk Cow Blues." Oldsters fiddled and youngsters, too, all with music in their hearts. It was a wonderful evening. Where old-time fiddlers gather, there are always homemade pies. We took a break after 9 p.m. and fueled ourselves to stay awake. Driving home alone late that night, I couldn't get those tunes out of my head, and I swear all that toe-tapping helped heal my knees.

March 22—Buttercups, found on a neighboring hill by my grand-children yesterday, float in a small bowl of water on the kitchen table this morning as I write. James and Adele, ages 6 1/2 and 5, spent the past three days with us. Only the barest minimum of housework was accomplished during their stay, while grandma became a kid again. A talent known by grandparents.

On Saturday, to celebrate the vernal equinox, better known as the first day of spring, the children and I fled to Imnaha. Up Camp Creek, we sat ourselves down in green grass and consumed the contents of our picnic basket. After munching down egg salad sandwiches and homemade raisin cookies, we struck off on a tramp along the creek, accompanied by grandson Buck's new puppy.

On our way through daughter Jackie's yard, we spied the first yellow and lavender crocuses blooming alongside the house, and noticed forsythia about to burst into showers of yellow blossoms. Above marched the always-present canyons, wearing their high rocky rims like crowns. The cloud shadows swept slowly across their narrow draws and greening sides. Light and dark, like life itself.

We hiked up one rocky hillside in search of a small resident herd of wild goats. James discovered a cave and found some interesting rocks, so the trip was not completely unproductive. We did find tracks along a well-worn trail, but no goats. James, akin to the goats we were tracking, scrambled over the rocks with energy known to 6-year-old boys, while Adele, wearing clumsy rubber boots, gamely kept up.

Afterward we drove down to the Imnaha store for a cold drink. We walked across the bridge that spans the Imnaha to the school where the children played on the teeter totter and the swings. While grandma watched at the river, running high with snowmelt, and enjoyed the spring day. Hundreds of baby calves cavorted on the benches above the river, also enjoyed the weather.

Grant and Barbara Warnock, upriver ranchers, raked the school yard of fallen locust branches and limbs. Barbara drives the school bus and cleans the school building, all in addition to raising a big garden every year. As we visited, she said she could hardly wait to plant the first onions and radishes.

Returning to Prairie Creek, we were greeted by a yard full of feathers! Barred Rock feathers from my laying hens. I had let the chickens out so they could scratch for bugs and worms while we were gone. On previous days the dogs seemed not to pay any attention to them.

Apparently, from what we could reconstruct, Ben's Border collie pup along with Daisy and old Jake, had a real fun afternoon. Luckily, no dead birds lay among the feathers, but later we did find one defeathered hen still quaking with fear, wedged between two garbage cans in the carport.

Even Chester didn't escape the onslaught, and is now considerably less cocky with all of his tail feathers missing. This is nothing new to Chester, however; he'll survive. Must not have affected the hens too much. They laid 11 eggs that day and 10 the next.

Yesterday afternoon the children and I went for a hike over the snow-splotched eastern hills, and that is where we found the first buttercups. Our destination was a large frozen stock pond about a mile distant from our house, as the crow flies. Large patches of snow lay on the shaded norths and wet melt seeped out beneath them, forming rivulets trickling down the draws, watering the buttercups.

The air was soft, the breezes gentle, and we marveled in the day. Wandering over the hills, watching them awaken from the long winter's sleep. It will always be a sort of magic to watch this transformation. The children scrambled over gnarled, old leaning willow limbs and gazed out upon the frozen pond, the edges of which were beginning to break up, fresh water appearing here and there.

Walking along the snowy shoreline we could hear the faint cracks and groanings as floes of ice broke away from the larger surface ice and floated free. Later the wild Canada geese would come here to nest, lay eggs and hatch their downy goslings; in the summer, when the young learned to fly, great flocks of them would wing their way over our ranch to land in this pond. We talked of these things as we walked back home.

The children returned home last evening, and without their happy chatter it seems quite lonely today. To keep from missing them too much I tore into my neglected house, sweeping, vacuuming, dusting, mopping, all the while dreaming of our two yesterdays, which felt like spring. Today it is cloudy and a brisk south wind blows, a chinook, melting even more snow among our hills, so more wildings, grass widows and yellow bells will follow the buttercups.

Last week, Linde and I hiked up a snowy road that was too soft and slushy to ski or even drive, to visit with and invite some phone-less friends to a St. Patrick's Day dinner. A heavy fall of soft spring snow the night before had deposited wet snow on all the evergreens, adding to the accumulated winter's pack.

Dick and Billie answered our halloos, and opened the door to their small trailer, their home while they build a road to a house site in the middle of their 15-acre timber tract.

Later they led us along a snowy trail deep in the woods to show us where they plan to build. It was like walking through a fairyland. New snow transformed every limb, log and tree into something out of a picture postcard. Even McCully Creek, which flows through their property, was buried beneath snow bridges. We walked carefully across the creek on a log, stamping the snow flat with each step. In a clearing about a quarter-mile distant from the trailer, we stopped to imagine their future home.

Billie and Dick made it to the dinner that St. Patrick's Day, along with lots of other friends and neighbors. Linde's homemade corned beef brisket was superb. We all brought salads, bread and desserts. I'd spent the morning baking lemon meringue pie and Irish soda bread. While listening to Irish music, we feasted and visited around the blazing stone fireplace, and reminisced about our cross-country skiing trips, which are all but over for this year.

The two college grandsons migrated home for spring break, and we are still shipping seed potatoes and calving.

One day last week, Doug and I sawed and split a load of wood and delivered it to our friend Bill up on Alder Slope.

This morning I ordered 25 barred rock pullet chicks from the feed department of our local co-op. After our recent harrowing experience, my hens are living on the brink of disaster. Must plan for the future eggs, and in this instance, the chickens come before the eggs...that is, if you don't count your chickens before they hatch.

March 30—March is marching right off the calendar, about as lamblike as it can get, this morning, anyway. Snow fields gleam so bright they nearly blind you, the air is full of birdsong, and a canopy of robin's egg blue sky hangs over all. There isn't even enough breeze to move the clothes pinned on the clothesline. However, "puffer billy" clouds appear as I write. Perhaps they've escaped from a storm heading north of us.

Last week Linde and I wanted to show our new friend Billie some of our canyon country, so we packed lunches into our daypacks and headed for the Cow Creek Bridge. Billie was pretty calm as we wound around those high dirt roads, and didn't say much as she peered down into those yawning open spaces to see the waters of the Imnaha glinting far below.

Only once did she ask, "How much farther is it?"

Leaving Linde's Bronco parked at the bridge, we struck off down the five-mile trail that leads to Eureka Bar. On the way to Imnaha we had noticed Little Sheep Creek running bank to bank with rusty colored snow-melt, which swirled and churned down the canyon until the creek was swollen even more by the waters of Big Sheep.

When the current carried the two Sheeps' combined flow into the Imnaha, the big river's color changed to malted milk, and the waters roaring past us were frothy like a milkshake as we hiked the gorge trail. That cool lower canyon air was just right for hiking, and recent rains had dampened the trail.

Quite suddenly, and happily, we came upon profuse patches of "Dutchman's Breeches," small, pale pink petals shaped like Dutchman's britches, puffed out in small branched clusters above soft, fern-like bluish-green leaves. They were everywhere, spilling out of rock crevices, nodding alongside the trail, in clumps or singly. There was so much to see, hear and smell. We filled our senses with whatever happened around each new bend in the trail.

Alders were just beginning to bud into shiny new leaves; the cranberry color of red osier dogwood edged the river. We were gladdened further by dainty yellow bells punctuated by a few hot pink shooting stars, which Doug calls "birdbills".

We paused briefly to look upon the place where I'd done a number on my knees a couple of weeks ago. The water was so high here it covered the entire rock I'd been fishing on. We walked deeper into the canyon until we were across from the gaping dark hole on the opposite bank, the entrance to the old Eureka mine, one side of which opens onto the Imnaha, and the other, the Snake.

Here the trail climbed higher before winding down to the Snake. Waters, churned by the gorge, flowed out in a chocolate ribbon into the channel of the Snake. We draped ourselves under the low sprawling branches of a dormant hackberry tree, and ate our lunches, after which I placed my camera on a rock ledge, set on automatic, and hurriedly scrambled down to join Linde and Billie.

Click! We were to be positioned under a blooming sarvisberry, only I didn't quite make it in time. So this slide will record a blurred action shot of me attempting to join my laughing friends. Sarvisberries' white clouds of blooms graced every draw, marched to the sky, spilled and cascaded from rocks, and clustered on greening hillsides. These are the traditional harbingers of canyon springtime.

Because it was a long hike back to the rig, and an even longer ride out to civilization, we didn't spend much time at the confluence of the two rivers. We arrived none the worse for wear back at the Cow Creek Bridge around 5 p.m.

On the way out past Corral Creek, we watched five wild mountain sheep graze just above a herd of cows and calves. The sure-footed sheep looked right at home with the cattle and scampered up those rocky ledges like goats.

We stopped at daughter Jackie's, up Camp Creek, just long enough to pick bouquets of forsythia, which were set to burst into golden blooms.

The snow is all but gone here on Prairie Creek, but much remains at timberline, where Linde and Billie live. Our hills are clothed in pale green dress, and more buttercups appear daily.

Hard to concentrate on household chores on days like these, and even harder to put my mind to the typewriter. In fact, Linde is on her way down, my lunch is packed in the daypack, and soon we will be driving out to Salmon Creek to check on our horses and mule that have wintered there.

Doug has been unsuccessful in his attempts to reach the ranch because of several large snowbanks that filled the road. Perhaps we'll have to hike in. I will hopefully return to the typewriter with renewed energy.

March 31—I and my renewed energy are again seated at the typewriter. Yesterday's experience was splendid. Another day spent in the pursuit of really "living." As the teenagers say, "It was real!" The road had been recently plowed, a pleasant surprise, and we were able to drive to the ranch. We felt again like the only two people on earth, because in all that vast expanse of hill and sky, we saw only hawks, meadowlarks and red diggers.

The three mares and "Maud" the mule were doing just fine and pricked up their ears like a band of wild horses at our approach. We hiked to a small creek and were glad to find clumps of the biggest buttercups we'd seen in years. We ate our lunches alongside a gurgling creek, soaking up sunshine, and seized the day.

While sitting there in that special place, the words of Robert Louis Stevenson's poem came back to me from childhood: *The world is so full of a number of things, we should all be happy as kings.*

April 5—April showers on Prairie Creek are apt to come in the form of snow flakes, and that's what it's fain' to do right now. Snow flakes on crocuses, greening hills, and noses of newborn calves; it flutters against the window panes.

Last night's moon glowed cold and bright, and this morning's heavy frost hardened mucky barn lots, laying a film of glass over the mud puddles. Our mother cows are nearly through with their yearly chore of producing calves. Pain forgotten, their only concern now is the year-round one of stuffing enough forage into their mouths to keep their three stomachs churning. And yearning, perhaps, if cows do indeed yearn, for summer grazing.

Grass! Speaking of rangeland and grass, Doug and I attended the annual Hells Canyon Grasslands Workshop last weekend on the lower Imnaha River system, with a camp pitched on the banks of the Snake River at Dug Bar. Friday morning found us loading our pickup with sleeping bags, tent and other camping supplies. Meals would be provided during the tour itself.

It was one of those splendid mornings, as only April in the canyon country can dish out. It can also be windy, cold and rainy, but that morning it was pretty near perfect, maybe a tad on the cool side, with clouds creating an interesting backdrop to the greening canyons.

Lunch was served at the McClaran ranch up Cow Creek. Jack and Scott McClaran, their families and cowboys had prepared tasty barbecued beef sandwiches. While ranch wives Vickie McClaran, Mary Ann Yost and Betsy Henry served salads and a large "Welcome" cake, Jack, Scott and Cal Henry dished up the beef.

Everyone congregated under the big hay shed and ate on bales of straw. The canyon filled our view in all directions. Recent warm rains were soaking into the bunch grasses and providing a greening sight that warmed the heart of all cowboys.

Taz Conner, a descendant of Ollokot, the brother of Nez Perce leader Chief Joseph, talked to us about the Native American culture in Wallowa County.

"The people were, and still are," meaning those who inhabit the country now, "Strong. Strong hearts, bodies and minds; the mountains and steep canyons made them so." They were "dreamers," said Taz. They were one with the land. The land was their mother.

Those of us who live here now also have this link with the land, I thought, gazing up into the rimrocks, seeing spring transform the land. Sarvisberry bushes hanging heavy with white blooms, bright pink clarkia nodding among clumps of bunch grass, cows grazing the steep grassy sides, their cloven hoofs cultivating and stimulating the soils.

Taz told about the herds of horses and cattle that grazed here when the Wallowa band of Nez Perce inhabited this country. Scott McClaran, a third generation rancher on the ranch, spoke to us while the fourth generation, his and Vickie's three little girls, played around the hay shed. He spoke of the family patriarch, Joe McClaran, who will be 100 in November. Strong minds and bodies...Taz was right.

Scott said it was difficult to make long-range plans while running a cattle outfit in that steep, rugged canyon. For instance, he said, "One morning this winter, we awoke to 16 inches of snow here at this lower elevation. Decisions must be made to fit the moment...wise decisions."

The Imnaha and Snake River terrain is so steep, cows sometimes fall out of their pastures! Scott told how it had taken years of experience to learn how to manage the range, and to deal with the unexpected such as weather, which Scott's mom refers to as a "given". And if anyone knows about that, Marge McClaran does.

Scott named a few canyon cowboys who could answer questions on canyon history, among them native Sam Loftus, who has worked for most of the cow outfits during his lifetime, and presently manages a large one at Corral Creek.

"Doug Tippett cut his teeth on the canyons, too," Scott remarked, and he named many more sitting on those bales of straw whose lives were being shaped by this landscape.

Leaving the lunch stop, many went on tours to "experience" the country, while others, including us, snaked our way up the winding narrow dirt road that leads to Dug Bar on the Snake, where the road ends, unless you want to swim the river.

This amphitheater-like classroom at a grasslands workshop overlooks the Imnaha river drainages and the Nee-me-poo trail.

Charley Johnson, range specialist on the Wallowa-Whitman National Forest, conducts a workshop in Hells Canyon.

When we crossed the cattle guard that used to be Doug's old permit, winter range, Doug let me out. And I walked what is known now as the Nee-me-poo trail, the Nez Perce "Trail of Tears."

Shouldering my daypack, which contained my trusty camera, I climbed the high ridge that leads to the trail at Lone Pine Saddle. After scrambling up the rocky ridge, I stood in awe at what fell before me.

The saddle, where I could look both ways, to the breaks of the Snake or to the sweeping view of the dinosaur-back ridges that separate Cow Creek, Lightning Creek and Horse Creek. I could see Haas ridge, and the high grassy benches that become the cream of cattle country. I felt as free as the hawk circling overhead, and felt the spirit of the Nez Perce. The trail was aptly named. If I were retreating from this beloved country, there would again be a trail of tears.

The old pine tree that gave the saddle its name was down, its decaying trunk rotting into the soil, a victim of a wind storm several years ago. But two new pines nearby, one large and one small, were growing well. The April breezes strummed the needles softly, providing the only sound in all that vastness, save for the melodious notes of a meadowlark.

Great irregular cloud shadows swept silently across the greening canyons. The trail was damp, even muddy in places. The earth was fresh with growing things. Sarvisberry bloomed in great white sprays all along the trail. In the grasses at my feet lay yellow bells, birdbills, and profuse patches of Prairie Star flowers.

Lower down I found arrow leaf balsamroot in the protection of rocky ledges, their sunflower-like golden faces stirring in the breeze. For years I'd want to hike this trail in daylight, as the only time I'd traveled it before was in darkness, in late November, with ice and snow upon the trail, horseback, leading a saddle horse, following Doug ahead of me to Dug Bar, after trailing cattle all day from Buckhorn to Tulley Creek.

This ancestral Nez Perce trail was used for years to trail cattle into and out of the Snake River country, before Doug's father, Jidge, and other cattlemen built the present road. Its route follows under and hugs the high rims, dips down into draws that connect canyons, and leads upward to high saddles.

When the winding Snake came into view, roiling high with cloudy snowmelt, I thought again of the departing Nez Perce. Hiking down from a high divide, I looked back, trying to envision the old people, children, horses and cattle, when the river was like today, in spring flood. A herd of mule deer posed on a rim above me, their ears pricked up at my coming. No human tracks on the Nee-me-poo that day, the moccasin tracks buried and obliterated by time.

Only the cloven hooves and the depressions of horses' hooves kept the trail marked, and, I thought, kept it from eroding, as water pooled in prints instead of washing. Alabaster clouds grew, then gathered into a solid purple overcast. A pair of Canada geese honked upriver. Veering from the trail, I kept high, following a cow trail, and came out at the spring where water is piped to the house that Doug's brothers built so long ago, and to the cabins that Doug built.

Far below on the bar, the old hay field stretched out, the muddy Snake flowed, and already tents were being pitched in a haphazard fashion. I could see a lone tepee, which looked right and good there. Taz and his friends had put it up. Anyway, the tepee looked less complicated than the tent I tried to erect. Finally giving it up, I waited for Doug to return in his boat from taking a group of people upriver to Kirkwood Bar. I unfolded a chair, relaxed and contemplated the river.

Chuck Stertz showed up pulling a portable grill behind his pickup, and soon Bob and Terry Morse arrived, having driven all the way from Lost Prairie to cook thick steaks, the tasty product of our grassy cattle ranges. Potatoes, baked earlier by Barb Warnock and the Imnaha women, arrived via Grant Warnock, and we again feasted.

That night around the campfire, we listed to Ace Barton, author of a book on the Snake River, tell of early history, then Doug shared more early canyon lore. Tom Sheehy recited some cowboy poetry, and we fell asleep listening to the beat of a drum and the plinking of a banjo. Nez Perce and cowboy culture on Dug Bar!

Saturday morning we began the educational part of the range tour, and I wrote about the scientific stuff in an article for Agri-Times.

April 12—Although baseball season is well under way across the nation, our extended family "officially" opened it on Imnaha Easter Sunday. There are definite advantages to large families, one being able to come up with two complete baseball teams. Between spatterings of sleet-like rain shed on us from clouds that sailed over high rims, we played several games well into the afternoon.

We stood way back in the outfield when Uncle Todd and grandson Shawn were at bat, and even poppa Doug, who then fooled us by ticking the ball. Five-year-old grandson Ryan, wearing cowboy boots, skidded his way to first after hitting his first ball. James, 6, played third base and did some fancy pitching besides. Moms, aunties, cousins, uncles, and yep, even grandma, went to bat.

The green grass of the horse pasture was just right, providing the only level spot on the ranch to set out three "cowpie" bases. Situated alongside Camp Creek, with horses grazing nearby and Buck's puppy too full of scraps from the Easter picnic to get in the way, the field worked out fine.

A yellow glow emanated from the yard where old-fashioned forsythia bushes exploded in full bloom beside the old ranch house. Tulips that escaped the puppy bloomed red in rock terraces, and fragrant purple violets escaped into the lawn. It was a little on the cool side, but Camp Creek's lower elevation provided just the right conditions for a picnic and an Easter egg hunt.

Earlier we had all crowded into the old house to give thanks for our family's closeness. Today, such a closeness provides protection against the encroaching world and a haven of solace when something goes wrong, and glues us together with happiness when all is well. We feasted on ham, potato salad, fruit and tossed salads, Jackie's crockpot beans, and homemade bread.

Jackie, who had risen early, with her husband, Bill, and two children started the dough rising before driving 30 miles to Joseph to sing in the Easter cantata. Back on Camp Creek, she gave the beans a stir, punched down the dough, and took it with her when the family attended the Imnaha Easter service. Returning to her own kitchen, she popped the risen loaves into the oven, and voila! We all enjoyed hot bread.

Rural wives learn early how to organize and work around any given situation. Jackie's experience as a cow camp wife while on summer ranges near Hat Point taught her resourcefulness. She became adept at working with sourdough, baking in every kind of oven the camps could provide. Living in a small scale-house on Monument Ridge, a tent on Sleepy Ridge, or traveling to and from their trailer at the ranch on the Imnaha, always with two small children in tow.

Ranch women think nothing of their skills, but I suppose in modern society they could be listed as folk art today. Getting myself up extra early that morning, I fed a bale of hay to my two milk cows and five calves, threw a few flakes to the horses, packed water to my laying hens, fed them, filled the dogs' and cats' dishes, slipped out of muddy overalls and made the 7 a.m. cantata and the sunrise Easter service at the Joseph Methodist Church. It was worth the effort.

In this world of negative news, why doesn't something like this ever make the headlines? It should have, and I'm sure there were other services scattered across small-town U.S.A., but none could have compared to that one performed by our local citizenry, as the sun came up over the eastern hills, flooding through the lovely stained-glass windows of that old stone church. Sunlight illuminated the faces of the singers, created a glow on the polished wooden pews and softened the whiteness of the blooming Easter lilies.

We all felt it. Songs, sung from the soul, filling our souls with the Easter message. It was comfortable and homey knowing all of the singers. Cowboys, community leaders, housewives, businessmen and teachers and ranchers. Community, as it should be.

Back at the ranch Doug and I loaded the ham I'd had baking in the oven all night into the car with the deviled eggs, chocolate bunnies and colored eggs for the egg hunt. We enjoyed the ride down. Given a boost by the intermittent rains, the canyons are so green now. We ranchers hope for a good feed year and already the bunch grasses on the canyon sides and in the hills are lush.

Grandson Shawn, home for the weekend from college with grandson Josh in tow, climbed nearly to the top of one of those high rims. Grandson Chad, home from the University of Idaho, couldn't make it to the picnic; he had to return shortly after he arrived because of a college commitment.

The other morning we awoke to six inches of spring snow covering our world...again. When it melted later that afternoon, water poured off the eaves and formed a small river that ran down our driveway. No complaining, though. We'll take all the rain and snow we can get. Our thirsty hills can never get enough of that valuable necessity.

This morning's sky is mostly full of clouds, and sporadic snow squalls erupt over the Wallowas. Snow curtains, I call them, hanging gauzy from the peaks, and drawing over the valleys. Interesting to observe.

When the sun does come out, everything steams, and greens, and grows. We are shipping seed potatoes again today. Bull buyers drive in with horse trailers and trucks to pick up their purchases. Only a few cows have yet to calve. Son Todd shod my mare the other day, so I'm ready when the cowboys need me to help trail the fall calvers to the hills. I'm looking forward to being back in the saddle again.

Last week Pam Royes from Imnaha brought to me in a cardboard box, not a partridge in a pear tree, but a little wisp of some sort of exotic rooster, a plump and feathery-legged little banty hen by the name of Cheryl, and a Rhode Island Red pullet. The reason being that either I accept this menagerie or Pam going to do them in with her shotgun. It seems the little scratchers were bringing mass destruction to her budding spring flower beds.

The assorted fowl were an interesting threesome. Cheryl chose to lay her eggs in the crotch of a tree, 60 feet in the air. A crude ladder had been tacked to the tree trunk so son Luke could scramble up each day to gather her eggs. Whether Cheryl wanted to be safe from the numerous varmints that prowl the Imnaha's banks, or just what, no one could figure, but every day she flew to her perch and laid her egg up in that tree. The pullet, also laying, had thankfully chosen a lower elevation to deposit her eggs.

The minute black and white speckled rooster sported a floppy red comb, with the largest thing about him being his crow, which was really quite loud. When he was unboxed into my chicken pen along with sleepy little Cheryl and the confused red pullet, he turned into a tiny dynamo of feathers, and immediately went into a strut, keeping "his" two hens away from the others.

Just then, Chester, my banty rooster of fame, stepped into the scene! At first it was pretty comical, but it soon turned ugly. The two roosters flew at each other, hunkered down, necks stretched out flat to the ground, and staged a stare-down, after which the smaller fellow "whisped" over Chester's head. Chester blinked, then flew in blind rage, missing and finally striking the small one in the middle of his red comb. Red blood ran into the chicken pen and the little rooster keeled over.

Dead? No...a sign of life! A fluttering eyelid, and up and away into battle again.

I finally separated the two by banishing the victor to another pen. Chester continued to strut up and down the side of his enclosure, shooting daggers into the interloper's eyes. Three days went by and a big wind came up and blew down the gate between the two birds. When I discovered this I raced to the chicken pen expecting the worst, but Chester evidently gave the matter some serious consideration during his isolation, and peace had been achieved.

Now they get along great. Little Cheryl lays her small egg-a-day in the nest with the big Barred Rock hens, as does the Imnaha Rhode Island Red pullet. I've named the red hen Pam and the wee rooster Skip, after Pam's husband. Because of all these "layings" and "sayings," we had plenty of eggs to color for Easter, and a story to tell here.

April 19—This morning I transplanted two rows of Walla Walla Sweet onion plants and seeded a row of spinach into the fertile black soil of Alder Slope. My big garden will be planted this spring at a place we are leasing this year for pasture.

This April afternoon, with gorgeous cumulus accumulating overhead and a warm sun slanting between them, the family and friends of Joe McClaran stood at his grave and bade their last farewells. Joe would have turned 100 in November. The onions and spinach will root in the earth, and Joe's spirit will soar heavenward, but like the spinach and onions, his descendants will be rooted to the earth for generations to come.

At the funeral, held in the Episcopal Church in Enterprise, we received a small pamphlet. On the cover was an old photo of Joe astride his horse, his dog close by, there in the canyons he and his family loved. There, in the cream of cattle country, he and his family provided stewardship to this vast country of grass, river, sky and rimrock, caretaking a legacy to future generations. Even though Joe is gone, his stories live on. Grandson Scott won't let them die.

Local veterinarian Sam Morgan sang "Canyons and Trees," a song we recognized as having been written by another lover of the canyons, cowboy poet-veterinarian-rancher Fred Bornstedt. With a lump in my throat, I thought of Fred, who passed away in the prime of his life, doing what he loved most, riding a horse up Lightning Creek.

Grandson Scott, during his "celebration of life" presentation, gave credit where credit was due to the hired men and cowboys, who over the years held the outfit together. Remarkable men like Chet Lewis, an old-timer who still works for the McClarans, and Emory Crawford, who single-handed led a huge string of mules and packed in supplies from the boat landing at Eureka Bar, traveling those narrow, steep trails back and forth, providing the only link to the outside world for the ranch at Cow Creek and up Lightning Creek.

Under the photo of Joe and his dog were the dates 1893-1993. Pretty impressive. Scott said his grandfather was known for being a very successful businessman and someone asked him one time about any advice he could give.

Joe thought a minute, then said: "Produce something that people want!" and that's what his descendants continue to do. I think the probability of people wanting a thick, juicy beef steak will continue for many years.

Last week Grace, Jerry, Vivian and I treated ourselves to three days at the Warm Springs Indian Reservation Lodge, known as Kah-Nee-Ta. Mere words and limited space are deterrents to describing this special place. April is the month to experience Kah-Nee-Ta. At 1,500 feet elevation, spring is beginning to bless the land. They say all who visit this place have their spirit blessed. Whoever "they" are, speak the truth.

Originally, the main reason we traveled to Central Oregon was to visit the newly opened museum, which is near the town of Warm Springs. Since the lodge where we had reservations was 11 miles away in the rolling desert hills, we didn't get to the museum until the day we left. From the moment we arrived until the time for departure, all too soon, we were filled with peace. The setting was quiet, food was excellent, views superb, and swimming in those turquoise pools was wonderful.

Mineral water from the nearby hot springs bubbles up into the cool water pools, of which there are two. One is in the middle of the arrowhead-shaped lodge, and another down along the river near a tepee village. The lodge on the hill where we stayed was built in 1972.

We all swam during the days, and Vivian and I swam at night, the only ones in the pool, when underwater lights were turned on and the effervescent bubbles shimmered on the surface. Above us, stars exploded. Lighted doorways to each room, painted orange, cast a warm glow, like campfires burning, all around us.

The surrounding bunch grass and juniper hills were laced with trails, which we walked each morning before sunup. Grass widows, prairie star flowers, yellow cous and patches of pink phlox bloomed between the trails. Far below, the Warm Springs River snaked its way along the willowy, green meadows. Kah-Nee-Ta, which means "root digger," was the Indian name of the woman who owned the valley where the resort is now located, which is now owned by the confederated tribes of the Warm Springs, Wasco, and Paiute.

This reservation was created by the Treaty of 1855, signed on June 25, 1855. The tribes hold their annual Treaty Festival Days, Pi-Ume-Sha, in late June. The reservation encompasses approximately 800,000 acres and about 3,200 people live there. During peak resort season, about 230 employees work at Kah-Nee-Ta, of which about 50 percent are tribal Indians.

Indians also work at the tribal administration, lumber mill, apparel factory, and other tribal agencies, such as the construction department, roads, garage, warehouse, police, judicial system and educational facility. Their logging is on a sustainable yield program, which provides for future generations and not just for one individual's present gain.

We were impressed with the entire operation at Warm Springs. It all seemed to be working because, rather than individual gain, everyone worked for their community, which in turn benefited the individual. Perhaps a lesson could be learned here.

Hot Indian fry bread was served with huckleberry jam at the beginning of dinner. From the dining area we could look down upon the village with its pool and tepees, and the Warm Springs River winding between ancient rock formations. Large ravens swooped and cawed in the sky, along with squawking magpies and circling hawks. Myriad bulbs were in bloom at Kah-Nee-Ta and the village. Tulips, daffodils and hyacinths in brilliant colors punctuated the well-kept lawns.

After the kiss of a warm April rain during our second night there, the desert smelled of damp sagebrush and juniper. This we experienced through an open glass door to a balcony on our second story level. The structure was designed so that each room seemed alone, and looked out upon the desert hills where no other sign of habitation seemed to exist, save the wild things.

After a final swim in the lower pool, floating in the warm waters from the hot springs and gazing up to cliffs and caves overhung with blooming sprays of sarvisberry where carpets of yellow wildflowers ran between, we reluctantly tore ourselves away from Kah-Nee-Ta and drove to Warm Springs to visit the museum.

Built on the grassy banks of Shitike Creek and resembling more an encampment, the museum is both ancient and futuristic, simple and complicated. Primitives displayed in a modern atmosphere, but in such a way as not to lose its primitiveness and authenticity.

The physical part of the museum seems simply a way to express the Indian spirit. At the entrance a granite engraved Roman-lettered sign reads: *twanat,* Sahaptin for "way of life." A beautiful basalt rock wall surrounds the building, which is a sort of progression, architecturally speaking, that symbolizes the story of a civilization.

The museum flows in circles that sometimes confuse white men, who are used to coming to corners and turning them, but it is a restful place, and the life-like murals and displays give one an insight into the realness of bygone cultures and make us painfully aware of what is missing in many lives today. There was so much to see, we vowed to return.

Because it was warm and sunny on the grassy banks of Shitike Creek, we sprawled there and ate our lunches, which we had put together after purchasing fixin's at a nearby Warm Springs market. The drive home was long. We took the Antelope cutoff and, after chasing rainbows over endless hills, and driving in out of April storms, we finally arrived, via Heppner, in Pendleton.

After a thick, juicy steak at an underground cafe, we headed over the Blues to home. I sank into bed around midnight.

By 7 the next morning, Mike McFetridge and I were horseback, trailing behind our fall calvers, heading for the hills. The weaned calves' bawling back at the corrals faded into the distance. It was late in the afternoon when we drove the cattle into the old Dorrance corrals to bed them down.

The next morning, it was early up and out to frosty Crow creek to saddle up again.

April 26—During the past 24 hours there has been such a mix of weather, but that's April in Wallowa County. Yesterday's sunshine, although intermittent, had almost a summer warmth to it. Then clouds, billowy and beautiful, continued building until they seeped moisture enough to create a rainbow.

Later, here on Prairie Creek, strong winds began whirling and rattling around the house, which lasted into the night. This was followed by white flashes erupting from inky clouds—lightning. Then, in the middle of the night, silence. I peered outside...Snow!

Due to those cleansing winds and snow, this morning's air has been scoured and freshened, and blessed by rainbows. And perhaps last night's lightning storm awakened lethargic trout from their deep, dormant state down under the muck in ponds and thawing lakes, and electrified nightcrawlers, which worked their oozing way out of the moist ground this morning. Fish and worms. Better go fishing.

Yesterday Grace and I drove to our spring and summer range, where we walked beneath that land of cloud and sky under which wildflowers, too, responded in a lovely way to the storms of the season. Grass widows, shooting stars, yellow bells and cous were only a few we could identify.

Our main mission for being there, if one has to have a mission, was to put up bluebird houses. This we did, attaching them to dead snags, ponderosa pines, old buildings, and fence posts. On a far grassy hill we spied the cows contentedly grazing that Mike and I trailed out a couple of weeks ago. Motherhood was forgotten, although the calves that will be born in the fall grow in their bellies.

Stepping guardedly down a draw came a cow elk, her twin yearlings in tow, and in her belly, due to come into the world in June, would be her calf. She was heading to one of our ponds for a drink.

This high, grassy plateau is home to the sky-blue mountain bluebird. It is a never-ending joy to catch sight of his vivid blue feathers winging away above the bunch grass hills. Hoping to encourage more of them to the area, we are providing nesting sites that are safe from predators.

While there at the ranch corrals on Wet Salmon Creek, we heard friendly whinnying, and looked up to see my Appaloosa mare Cal, our white mule Maud, and two other mares, all of which wintered there, come galloping up the meadow to greet us. Looking healthy and strong, not having to work so hard for their feed now, they were already beginning to shed their winter coats.

It wasn't until we crossed Pine Creek and drove up over the hill that we encountered another soul. The Ketscher brothers were moving cattle out to their range. We parked there to eat our lunches, glass for elk, watch eagles and hawks dive for rodents, listen to meadowlarks, and contemplate the vastness of the Zumwalt country. Suddenly we became aware of a small Horned lark perched on a fence post next to us.

This small brown bird proceeded to let loose with jabberings that resembled people-talk, and it stayed and conversed all the while we were there. Was it lonely, or just wanting an audience for its twitterings?

Between bites of sandwich, we discussed a tribe of far northern Indians who believed that when one of them passed on, that person's spirit came back to earth as birds. Grace remarked that perhaps this little feathered friend was our deceased friend Cressie Green coming to pay us a visit in this place she so loved. A nice thought anyway, and these days not enough nice thoughts are thunked.

We passed the Ketscher truck pulling a loading chute and noticed yearling steers in Hinkley's range. We returned via the long Zumwalt road, watching the mountain-born storms spread their rain curtains across the valley. Our friend Bill, who lives alone on Alder Slope, has been wanting to move his chickens from their temporary quarters in a small greenhouse to the barn.

Managing fairly well on his own, he is still unable to do much heavy work. So after returning from the hills, I enlisted the help of two friends, and soon we were stapling chicken wire to his barn and wiring a gate, closing every avenue of escape we thought chickens could find.

When the pen was completed the fun began. After the honor of official chicken catcher was bestowed upon yours truly, as I had the most experience, all heck broke loose in the greenhouse. We three were suddenly standing in the midst of feathers, dust and straw. Chickens squawked, feathers flew, and general confusion reigned. Realizing the best time to pluck chickens from their roost is after dark, we nevertheless proceeded with what had to be done. It was now or never.

I reached a hand out to clutch at a chicken leg, caught a mad hen and stuffed her still squawking into a burlap bag held ready by Viv. Too late we realized the door wasn't quite closed, and one black hen escaped to safety outside. Well, actually, it wasn't exactly safety, but rather running for her life, with Bill's old dog, aided by my young dog, in hot pursuit.

My dog dutifully returned, black tail feathers stuck in her grinning mouth, tail wagging. We tied both dogs up and crept quietly up to a pipe trailer where the quaking hen was hidden. I made a blind grab and missed, but finally captured her. Then back to the coop to resume catching the other hens and one large, mad rooster that sported spurs.

I managed to connect with the rooster and the last hen with both hands at the same time. Carrying the bagged hens, the mad rooster, and the detailed black hen, we marched to the newly completed pen to release the bewildered birds into some fresh straw. We moved their water, feed and oyster shell, and they soon calmed down.

A pheasant in the nearby swamp let out a loud call as if to say, "Quiet down a bit, would you!"

We also cleaned out the garden, pruned raspberries, and forked out a pile of old cornstalks and bean plants. It had been quite a day. After fixing a pot of spaghetti for the chicken transfer crew, I drove home and spotted that rainbow against the snowy sides of Mt. Joseph.

Oblivious to the lightning, wild winds, and snow storm, my four-day-old Barred Rock pullets survived the night under their warm heat lamp cuddled in fresh straw—little black balls of downy feathers, eating, drinking and dozing, and growing. On the subject of chickens, I'm certainly not going to let my rooster "Chester" read the last issue of Agri-Times. At least not the article written by Joyce Edie, about her rooster "Spaz." Chester would just love to strap on a .44 magnum, and I don't pack a gun.

Before this column gets totally out of control, I'd better close.

May 6—The cold rain is on the verge of turning to snow as it falls outside on the green growing grasses. Such is May here in this high mountain valley. Between storms, a few beautiful, sunny hours ensue, like last Sunday, a good deal of which was spent along the shores of Kinney Lake, a nearby man-made pond, fishing poles in hand.

While Doug hauled in the catfish, James, Adele and I hooked our limit of rainbows. When a cool breeze ruffled the surface of the lake, and giant clouds cast their moving shadows, it created just the right conditions for hungry fish. Poppa Doug used a spinning rod to cast far out in the middle of the pond, while the children and I whipped an old fly rod, which sported an ancient hand crank reel, a frayed green line, a too-short leader tied on wrong, and one rusty hook that before the day was over hooked and landed no less than ten fish!

Often times James' casts were into the wind, and the old line curled around and swept back to him. A single lead sinker helped keep it out most of the time. But luckily, the fish were hungry and our nightcrawlers were irresistible.

Poppa Doug put his catfish in a bucket of ice water. After he left to go deliver a bull, we stuck our fish into an empty cranberry juice bottle. Pausing only a few minutes to devour our picnic, we immediately went back to fishing.

A large snowbank on the opposite shore, and the snow-locked Wallowas above us, chilled the breeze. Numerous patches of yellow butter-cups bloomed among the awakening grasses. A pair of honkers landed in the middle of the lake, and several pairs of nesting mallards could be heard along the shoreline, in the weeds. Kinney Lake, built by local ranchers to store irrigation water, is maintained by them, and provides a favorite fishing spot as well.

Last week, Linde's husband, Pat, dropped Linde and me off there at Kinney Lake, near the overflow gate that lets water pass into the irrigation ditch, so we could "walk" and clean the ditch. What a job! It was a cold blustery morning; mixed snow squalls and rain showers emptied out all over the valley. Beautiful to behold, but a bit cold to be out in.

Clad in all the old jackets, hats, and gloves we could find in Pat's pickup, and wearing hip boots, we struck off along the ditch bank. The small ranches that checkerboard Prairie Creek sprawled below the ditch. An old weathered barn, all that was left of an early homestead, stood near a large cottonwood tree.

We dragged limbs from the swiftly flowing water, which was milky with snowmelt; we trimmed willow scrub, fished out old boards and flotsam that had become lodged between rocks, and raked myriad smaller limbs out of the ditch-stream. It was hard work, and soon we weren't cold at all. We stopped briefly after noon, pulled up a dry board, sat right there on the bank and ate hungrily of corned elk sandwiches and savored two Nanaimo bars I'd baked the day before. These are delectable layered cookies that bear the name of a small village on Vancouver Island.

And while we lunched, the clouds merged and the wind increased. The day turned gray. The final section of the ditch was nearly overgrown with willows and clogged so with limbs that our progress was painfully slow. We gave out before we finished, deciding to call it a day.

Linde, the official "ditch walker" for the Prairie Creek ditch, gets plenty of exercise, walking miles of ditch throughout the spring and summer irrigation season. Her initiation into the job proved to be the ultimate challenge last summer, during the midst of severe drought conditions.

She quickly learned that there are also disadvantages to the job, especially when it came to dealing with ranchers who have done things their way for years, so water and tempers both ran short. Hopefully the dry years are behind and normal conditions will prevail this summer. Judging from all this snow that continues to pile up in the back country, we should be in great shape for the coming irrigation season.

Our cows and their spring calves were trailed to the hills this past weekend, and are now enjoying grass instead of their usual diet of dry hay. May 1st is the traditional "turnout" time and this should be a great grass year.

Last week I attended a play in Enterprise entitled "Tumbleweed", staged by granddaughter Chelsie's high school class. It was a take-off on an early Western mining town named "Grimy Gulch." The inhabitants were Chelsie and her classmates.

They did a great job under the direction of Gail Swart, who has put together these singing and acting programs over the years, first for my children's generation, and now my grandchildren's, all of whom are lucky to benefit from this extraordinary woman's talents. Gail makes them want to act and sing, simply for the joy of it. Not enough activities of this sort are available to youngsters today. Perhaps this is because there are not enough Gails to go around.

Having two of the younger grandchildren here all this week brings back memories of raising my own, especially when I must get six-year-old James up and off to first grade each morning. And then, when I and Adele pick him up in the afternoon, after which I go over his classroom work, encouraging his achievements and helping with mistakes. Little Adele stays home with me during the day and helps tend the house and baby chicks, which both children love.

After a warm soaking rain one night, we pick up nightcrawlers the next morning to fill the fishing bucket, and threw several into the baby chicks, which proved to be greatly entertaining. The resulting eating frenzy took place when the worms were used for a chick tug-o-war!

There are four places at the table now and the amount of food consumed by two healthy children is awesome. Just when I finally get into the swing of children again, they'll leave, and the house will feel quite empty. They are this precious age such a short time, and all too soon they will be claimed by their friends, school and other interests. Enjoy them while they're young.

While we were touring the museum at Warm Springs, I was impressed by an exhibit of a typical Indian family and their places in the family tepee. Mother, father, children, and a place for the grandmother.

The grandmother's role in Indian culture was of high importance. She was the one who raised the children, guiding them in the ways of their ancestors, teaching them with her wisdom, gained of having lived a full life, inspiring them, giving unconditional love, with gentleness and patience that only older women possess. While the young mother was busy with skinning, tanning, cooking, gathering and sewing clothes, and moccasins, it was the grandmother who cared for the grandchildren.

In our present fast-paced world, wouldn't it be wonderful if more children could benefit from a society where the grandmother was honored for her role? Perhaps we could empty some of our prisons by raising a generation of children who had at least one person in their lives who really cared. It is the simplest and yet, the most difficult challenge of our time, and it would save the taxpayers millions of dollars in dealing with delinquents, and subsequently adult criminals, who are poisoning our very culture.

May 11—For the third day in a row, the sun has shone down from a clear blue sky, causing temperatures to climb into the 70s and 80s. Yesterday and today a brisk southerly wind sapped moisture from the prairie, and licked at the high snowy ridges of the Wallowas. Avalanches tumble down steep chutes, leaving soil-stained rivers that streak the side of Chief Joseph Mountain.

Last evening I went for a walk up Tenderfoot Valley Road. The dry winds had calmed, and lush meadow grasses rested in the shape of their waving. Willows breaking out with gauzy green leaves stirred gently in the leftover wind's breath. The pastoral countryside was verdant green and teemed with the sounds of a May evening: clamoring honkers, nesting or landing on Waters' Pond; killdeers calling and robins voicing their final loud chirps before sunset.

The air was alive with red-winged blackbirds, noisy crows, swift swallows, and starlings. The distant barking of a farm dog and the low, steady hum of a tractor mingled in a familiar cacophony, soothing to the ear of a countrywoman. All is well, it seemed to say, and I could believe it truly was.

The Butterfields were still out late, farming their fields. Tractors pulling seeders droned softly, releasing a fresh earthy smell in their wake. Hockett's old barn and other Prairie Creek farms and ranches, being cared for like they have been for decades. Hough's cattle grazed the nearby hills that separate prairie from canyon. Black Angus dots against the brilliant green. Looking east and then north I could see familiar landmarks: Echo Canyon, OK Gulch, and Crow Creek Pass, evening shadows seeping into their folds.

Lori Butterfield passed in a pickup, probably on her way home after taking supper to husband, Dan, in the field, or trading off for her turn in the tractor seat. A young boy, a third generation Butterfield, follows his mother slowly, driving a four-wheeler.

With the exception of the modern farm equipment, the scene could be one from the early '20s and '30s, when horses pulled plows and seeders.

And the small boy would have been riding his pony down the country road, his dog following behind. Last night his big yellow dog tried bravely to keep up, but got left far behind, so joined my dog and me on our walk before returning to Dan in the field.

My tall shadow followed along and my little dog sniffed out meadow mice as we returned to the ranch. Walking off supper has become a nightly habit now, since the evenings have turned soft, warm and long.

Last evening's meal needed to be walked off. Just as I was putting a pot of Don Able's fresh asparagus on to steam, Ralph Tippett banged on the kitchen door. There he stood, holding a large brown bag full of calf brain mushrooms.

While Ralph, who had already eaten, polished off a bowl of fresh rhubarb crisp I'd just taken from the oven, I sauteed those mushrooms with a T-bone steak. Doug and I ate corn on the cob I'd taken from the freezer, green salad, and that fresh asparagus. Then we poured fresh cow's cream over that warm rhubarb cobbler. Better change the subject, as just writing about it makes me hungry again.

Last week my old friend Scotty and I boarded a bus at Lostine before 6:30 a.m., after I'd gotten out of bed at 4:30 to care for my animals and dress sleepy Adele, who we dropped off at Mary Ann McLaughlin's on Alder Slope along the way. James had spent the night with his dad so he could ride the bus to school.

Nine o'clock found us and other tour members in Haines, touring the excellent museum there. It was like climbing up into grandma's attic. The place was simply crammed with butter churns, mining equipment, early farming tools, and pioneer artifacts. An authentic-looking parlour and early kitchen was set up, complete with lifelike mannequins dressed in period wear. The building itself used to house the former gymnasium of the Haines High School. This tour, put together by Cheri Jo Carter, extension agent for Union and Wallowa counties, was a bargain.

After visiting the Oregon Trail Regional Museum in Baker City we lunched at Jimmy Chan's restaurant in Baker City before touring the Oregon Trail Interpretive Center on Flagstaff Hill. Total cost for the package was $16!

We had picked up more people in Wallowa and Island City along the way. Moffit Bros Transportation, of Lostine, provided the bus. Having visited the Oregon Trail museum in Baker City before, I hadn't realized that the collections were housed in a building constructed in 1920 as a natatorium, which means a place for swimming, plus a community activity center and a lovely ballroom.

After the old "Nat" was placed on the National Register of Historic Places, restoration, still progressing, was begun in 1977. The ballroom has been beautifully restored and is now used to display old quilts.

I was most impressed with the Cavin Warfel collection of rocks, minerals, fossils and semi-precious stones. Way back in the 1930s, the Cavin sisters, Elizabeth and Mamie, started collecting rocks, which turned into a hobby spanning 45 years. Mamie's old hiking boots, worn while collecting, are preserved in the museum. The displays overflow into several rooms and are mind boggling.

The youngest of nine children, Mamie, who was tubercular, was sent West for her health. She died just a few months ago at the age of 95. Her love of beautiful things is expressed in rocks, gems and beautiful butterfly collections that were accumulated over the years.

Although she was offered a fortune for her collection in California, she chose to donate it in its entirety to the Baker museum to be in the place she grew up and loved. How my father would have loved this marvelous exhibit. I plan to take my grandchildren to see it, so they can learn to appreciate more of our natural history, and perhaps their imaginations will be fired with the wonders of our earth.

Lunch at Jimmy Chan's was most welcome. We were all starved, having risen at such an early hour. Sweet'n sour chicken, pork chow mein, and pork fried rice went down very easily. Our bus wound up the steep road to Flagstaff Hill where we visited the National Historic Oregon Trail Interpretive Center.

With nostalgia, Scotty and I gazed down upon Virtue Flat, where we had spent the night in a circle up of covered wagons last Memorial Day weekend. We remembered the heat, dust and weariness, our sweat-soiled skirts and bonnets, and the welcome coolness of the high desert night. We looked out at the age-old wagon ruts of early travelers, then entered the immense new building that houses the interpretive center.

Although Doug and I had been here before, I took my time and tried to capture the essence of the pioneers, which is easy when the place is quiet, but this day there were touring school children and throngs of people. It was hard to hear the recorded voices reading from early diaries. Looking out upon the Powder River Valley, flanked by the Elkhorn range and leading north toward the Blue Mountains, I wondered what those early emigrants would think of this tribute to them today.

At 2 o'clock we were treated to a presentation by Jessie Benton Fremont, portrayed by author and historian Sally Roesch Wagner. Pretty obvious this lady had done her homework. At the end of her 35-minute monologue, Jessie answered questions posed by the audience. We learned facts about Fremont, her husband, never written about in history books.

Scotty and I walked the trail that led to the lode mine, just a short hike from the center. Old ore carts and tools could be seen at the entrance. A total round-trip of hiking trails wound through the sagebrush hills for four miles, but time limited our hiking them all.

Pink phlox bloomed and bunch grass, thanks to the rains, were the lushest I'd seen in the desert in years. Traffic in and around the paved trails was heavy. Future generations may be viewing the ruts left by today's tourists!

Last Saturday, other grandmothers and I braved a bitter cold, windy morning and afternoon to watch our pee wees perform in the Joseph Junior Rodeo. Mutton riders bit the mud instead of the dust. Speaking of grandmothers, one of our daughters sent me a Mother's Day remembrance. It was a hand-painted little grandma on whose bosom was printed, *Grandmas are antique little girls!*

May 14—During the early pre-dawn hours yesterday morning, I was awakened by a musical chorus. Coyote notes wafting from a nearby hill came through our bedroom windows. Thus began my three-coyote day.

It was out of bed early to fix lunches, do chores, saddle my mare and drive with the men to our summer range on Salmon Creek. Never have I seen wildflowers as lovely. We rode through fields of balsamroot, grass widows, bluebells, phlox, a few leftover yellow bells, acres of cous, sprinkled with lupine and, growing in marshy situations, tiny, hot pink birdbills.

I was astride my mare, climbing the hills into the Deadman pasture, gathering cows and calves, when a large dog coyote, light colored, trotted past me, then stopped suddenly. We exchanged glances before he resumed his dog-like trot over the grassy hills, disappearing as silently as he appeared, dissolving under cloud and sky. Number two coyote.

We gathered the scattered cattle, driving them into a corner near the corrals, where Mike and I held the milling herd for four hours while Ben and Doug sorted. First the yearlings, then yellow-tagged pairs, then white tags etc. Just when Mike and I began to think we'd be sorted next, Ben and Doug finished. It was dreadfully hot, and we were all glad to sink down in the shade of the old barn and eat our lunches.

After the yearlings were sprayed, we drove the long road back to the valley ranch, and I attended the Enterprise FFA pancake feed, where I purchased some of the chapter's greenhouse plants for my garden.

I remained in town to attend "According to Coyote," which was presented in the high school gym by Carlotta Kauffman, who is traveling over the U.S. performing her portrayal of "coyote." Coyote number three in my three-coyote day.

Coyote legend says, "I will give you a special power, Coyote. When you die, you will always come back to life. This will be your way, Coyote, afraid of no one. Go and do your work well." Native Americans attach great significance to seeing coyote. It means one will have good, or bad, luck. So far this week my luck has been good. Good luck and good health, and being able to enjoy life's simple pleasures. What more could coyote himself ask for? In legend, coyote was a "predecessor to man; he prepared the world for humans and taught them how to live by good and bad example."

At any rate, Carlotta presented a very interesting and extremely vigorous portrayal. No wonder that girl is in shape. She gave body and soul to her performance.

May 15—Last night, I dreamed of coyotes.

Early this morning found the cowboys and this cowgirl out on Salmon Creek again, saddling up at the old barn, riding out in the dew-laden hills, driving in cows and calves, corralling them, sorting cows from calves—*maw, maw, ba, ba*—a solid din, mixed with dust. Soon the smoke from the branding fire mingled with that of scorched hair, all under a merciless sun.

At noon I escaped to the cool banks of Salmon Creek and listened to the red wing blackbirds and swallows darting in and out of the willows growing there. Leaning back against weathered barn boards, I heard small chirpings above me. A bird house nailed to the side of the small barn held a nest of baby robins.

The long day wore on, the "oyster" bucket filled, and soon a pen full of calves wore the quarter circle brand. The last little doggie was pushed up the chute, the cows were sprayed, and evening fell. Huge clouds formed and pushed their shadows across the lush green hills. The last calf mothered-up and the bawling faded into the history of many brandings held on Salmon Creek.

May 16—Baked a double batch of Nanaimo bars, then drove to Alder Slope to work in the garden, fixed lunch for Doug, who was still farming, and watched huge dark thunderheads empty over the mountains and sweep across the valley.

By 6:30 p.m. Linde and I arrived at the Eagle Cap Chalets at Wallowa Lake with those Nanaimo bars, preparing for a "Chautauqua" there. The definition of the word Chautauqua escapes me at the moment, but the gist of it has to do with the bringing of drama, such as one-person plays and the like, to the sticks, to places like Wallowa County, where people must otherwise travel to Portland or Spokane to see such quality performing arts events.

Our local Fishtrap board sponsored this one, presented by Portland actress Kathleen Worley, who "illuminated the life and work of English novelist Virginia Woolf."

May 20—Spring in Wallowa County is full-blown, and then some! Apple blossoms drift through the balmy air, flowering crab, plum and every other blossoming thing is doing it. So are the bees. If it doesn't hail, freeze or dry out, there should be a bumper crop of everything.

Winter's accumulation of snow continues to melt in the high country, overflowing creeks and swelling rivers. Little Sheep Creek was on a rampage last Thursday when a carload of us gals from "on top" traveled to the canyons of the Imnaha for a CattleWomen's meeting. Pink phlox bloomed amid the rimrocks, and eye-catching balsamroot exploded, golden under a cloud-strewn sky that dappled shade and sunlight upon the green carpeted canyons.

We sat under an apple tree in a lush, grassy flat near the rushing, snowmelt-swollen Imnaha, eating our brown bag lunches and visiting Rose Glaus, a former Imnaha CattleWoman visiting from Montana. Unseasonably warm temperatures are causing everything to bolt. Rhubarb, lilacs, dandelions and quack grass, not to mention farmers and ranchers. After waiting those cold, wet weeks to work their fields or finish branding, the work came all at once.

Last week, as well as the early part of this one, local temperatures soared into the 80s. In spite of earlier rains, the ground is drying out and many ranchers have begun to irrigate. Our large garden on Alder Slope is growing. Peas, radishes, cabbages, onions, garlic, spinach and lettuces are all up. Swiss chard, parsnips, herbs and potatoes are planted. Doug is seeding the farm ground we've leased there to a mixture of grass seed, using barley as a cover crop.

After spending all of this morning gardening, I cut some fresh asparagus and baked a quiche, using fresh eggs and cheese. They say cowboys don't eat quiche, but Doug and Bill sure did. Son Steve, who has taken over the seed potato operation, began planting the leased potato ground yesterday. I hope this means Doug will have more free time...for fishing?

We have a new mule, a five-year-old molly by the name of Mildred. It is good to hear her friendly braying when I go out to chore each morning.

Such is life in Wallowa County—a three-coyote day, branding calves, gardening, CattleWomen, not to mention attending graduations and watching another granddaughter, who was cast as Dorothy in the "Wiz," topped off by Virginia Woolf.

Must get this typed so Linde, Betty and I can watch the "Quilters" tonight. It is continuing education just to live in this valley.

May 25—A warm wind blows over Prairie Creek, drying out the lushness, changing the very color of the landscape. The snows on East Peak are melting and the familiar shape of "Tucker's mare" emerges. This afternoon the horse has a long, flowing white tail.

Downwind from the blooming lilac bush, the air is fragrant with perfume. Two large trays of morel mushrooms are drying on the picnic table. Linde stopped by with a bag of them yesterday.

Doug and I laid out two lines of irrigation pipe on the new seeding up on the Slope this week, which means moving pipes twice a day until the field is covered. Doug set the line to send the jets of life-sustaining water over our large garden, as well as the fields.

In spite of dramatic cloud build-up all last week, not a drop of rain fell and the ground continued to dry out. This afternoon's clouds twine misty gray tendrils around the peaks. Perhaps we'll receive some moisture by nightfall.

The business (busy-ness) of spring is here. We and our neighbors wear that familiar frazzled look. So little time to get the work done. It is the same every year.

After setting sprinkler pipe, Doug and I stopped by a neighboring ranch where a goodly number of our family was helping brand. What a scene. Backgrounded by the snow-splotched Wallowas, in a corral full of bawling calves, was a mixture of cowboys, kids, cow ponies, dogs, young women and dust and smoke.

I recognized my oldest daughter castrating, while others gave shots, branded, ear-tagged and roped. A scattering of grandchildren, including Lacey astride her horse, here from Pendleton with her daddy, roping, taking a dally, and dragging calves to the branding fire. Outside the corral, other children, all horseback, rode around the ranch in the cool green afternoon. Little ones sat in the back of the pickup, getting sunburned. One wee little gal cuddled a border collie puppy.

Watching from the corral fence, I couldn't stand it, and soon this grandma, clad in tenny runners and floppy straw hat, picked up a loose lass rope and roped calves. Lucky for me there was always a grandchild or a son on horseback to dally around the horn after I made my ground catch.

Some of the braver children jumped on the calves and rode through the melee until they were bucked off. The day faded into evening before the last calf was worked. After changing pipes, it was home to supper at 8:30.

May 26—Early this morning, my mare was saddled and we were walking through the dew-washed hay field to the other side of the ranch to begin trailing the fall calvers to their east moraine summer pasture high above Wallowa Lake. Old-timer, cowboy Mike McFetridge and Ben's young daughter, Sarah, helped us.

Despite his 86 years, Mike continues to work cattle. Not just ride, but really work. Ben, Doug and I can attest to that. He shirks no task, no matter how difficult or dangerous. Riding the steep moraine to turn a bunch of cattle in thick brush takes skill and daring, and Mike demonstrated both last Monday. He will always be our "old hand."

As we drove the cattle past Voss' place, one of Dwayne's border collie dogs followed us. All our efforts to turn him back and make him go home failed. So we let him join my dog and Ben's. Between the three of them they managed to help us push the cows, which were pretty unwilling to go much farther by the time we reached the moraine.

Seventy-five head had to be driven to water on the lake hillside and they constantly took the uphill sides. Once, when Ben was driving a bunch of errant cows down off that steep moraine, Dwayne's dog blocked the trail. Not knowing the dog's name I called every one in the book: Bob, Skip, Pete, Jake…

The dog paid not the slightest attention, until, in desperation, I yelled, "Here, dog," at which he immediately rushed to my horse's side and sat! From then on, whenever I wanted him to come, I simply said, "Here, dog."

When we returned the dog to Dwayne, who was preparing to seed one of his fields, I asked out of curiosity what the dog's name was.

"Just Dog," he replied. "His name is Dog." A dog named Dog. It made my day, and this story.

After being in the saddle from early that morning, I was ready to rest and eat a bite.

This evening Doug and I changed pipes again, and another of those long spring days came to a close.

Last week neighbors Linde, Betty and I drove into town to attend the local production of "The Quilters," which was simply marvelous. According to the program, it was a musical mosaic of pioneer stories in tribute to the women who faced the frontier, assembled into a magical patchwork quilt.

Local women, many of whom we knew, were cast in the women's roles. Each scene was a separate flashback of what the women's lives had been. It wasn't your typical musical. The small cast and small set was just right. Under the professional direction of Louise Kienzle, the players' performance reflected hours of practice. In a time when so many are born into so much and take it all for granted, every young girl should see this. It was truly a tribute to our pioneer ancestors.

Scotty showed up at my door last week. After driving Doug up to the Slope to haul home a tractor, we stole away to the woods above upper Prairie Creek and hunted the wild morels. We returned with two brown bags full. It was so good to be out in the forest, even though it hailed on us for a few minutes. Sauteed in butter and fresh garlic, served with antelope steaks, they were a treat for supper. The remaining ones I stir-fried with onions, peppers, celery and marinated elk strips. Wild fare!

Our lawn is in need of mowing again. And all my bedding plants are set out. Why do we make so much work for ourselves in a yard? Must enjoy the fruits of our labor. Supper must now be planned around pipe changing, a task that will stretch into summer.

Western writer Bill Kittredge describes Eastern Oregon women's lives in his book, *Owning it All.* He writes,

This country fosters a kind of woman who never seems to bother about who she is supposed to be, mainly because there is always work, and getting it done in a level-eyed way is what counts most. These women wind up looking 50 when they are 37, and 53 when they are 70. It is as though they wear down to what counts and just last there.

Living the life he describes, day in and day out, I see what Kittredge means. Only hope I last till 70. Then there's old hand Mike, who puts us all to shame.

June 2—June... so soon? And summer only days away. This morning sure doesn't feel like summer, but rather a return to more familiar pre-drought Junes, the Wallowas swathed in mists and Prairie Creek damp after an inch of rain drenched the land during last evening's cloudburst. While thunder boomed and bright flashes severed purple clouds, I sat myself down to the piano and pounded out Beethoven's Für Elise and Strauss' Beautiful Blue Danube to the accompaniment of thunder and rain.

Linde and I spent yesterday morning up in the Alder Slope garden,

Newly crowned Chief Joseph Days Queen Katy Bothum, center, flanked by Princess Shelly Stillson, left, and Princess Erica Black.

seeding corn, beans, squash, carrots, beets, cucumbers, and setting out several tomato plants. Next to a row of corn, at the edge of the garden, I planted a row of giant sunflowers for the birds this fall.

A fine, warm rain fell as we worked in that moist, black soil. Perfect planting conditions. Just as the rain began to get serious, we finished. A good feeling, having it all planted. How I love to garden!

Saturday morning of the Memorial Day weekend, found Doug, me, Pat and Linde heading for Dug Bar on the Snake. It was cloudy and cool, and threatening rain when we left, but as we descended into the canyons the weather became much milder. The country was still green, and the air filled with the sweet orange blossom odor of wild syringa.

After traveling nearly 30 miles to Imnaha, we followed the narrow winding dirt road to Dug Bar....for 30 more miles. Blackberry patches at Pack Saddle Creek were about to blossom out, and cactus plants wore their annual colorful flowers. Tall native grasses waved in the breeze, and wildflowers grew everywhere. Rounding a high bend a large mule deer doe bounded out in front of our pickup and disappeared over the hill below.

"There's her fawn," exclaimed Doug, and we looked to see two tiny ears protruding from a clump of sagebrush. Immediately, I took to the steep hillside to photograph the spotted fawn. Only hours old, it lay, stretched out, head flat to the grass, its soft frightened eyes unblinking. Wild but instinctively still, scarcely breathing. What a thrill, seeing this newborn wild thing, so perfect in every way. The sighting of the wee fawn got our expedition off to a good start.

The road hugged the rugged rims under Lone Pine Saddle,and I gazed upward remembering my recent walk along the ancient Nez Perce trail. Presently the winding Snake came into view, far below, whitewater rapids visible even from that distance, and then we were descending the winding road to Dug Bar.

After transferring our camping gear into the boat, we roared off upriver. A great feeling, free from the care of an "outside" world, which suddenly became non-existent. Landmarks swept past. Lem Wilson's old place, Van Pools, Copper Creek. We passed a few floaters an a more boats on the river. Frothy white with blooms, the syringa marched up every draw.

When Doug pulled in at Somers Creek and anchored, we could see Ed Davis's tiny cabin, still intact, on a flat knoll above the river. The shore was rocky and littered with driftwood, which we would use for campfire and cooking wood. A picnic table sat near a huge mulberry tree. Hackberry, sumac, poison oak, and other native bushes formed a green area around the campsite. Somers Creek splashed, cold and clear, over rocks and ferns, racing from the draw above.

Numerous late-blooming wildflowers grew among the tall native grasses. An enchanting spot, just for us. A spring of wild mustard grew up through a crack in the picnic table. Since it was by then noon, we broke out the packboxes that held sandwich fix' ins.

While setting up camp it soon became apparent that we'd forgotten to put in our tent poles, which meant Doug and I would be sleeping on the tent, not in it, and in rattlesnake-infested territory! I envied Linde and Pat their snug tent.

A warm rain fell while we unloaded the boat; when the sun burst through the clouds, every leaf sparkled like tropical growth in a rain forest, and the sweet odor of the ever-present syringa intensified. Truly we had found paradise.

Leaving a package of hamburger to thaw on a shady rock, we climbed back into our boat and headed upriver. Doug negotiated the rapids that lay along the route with a practiced hand. He'd driven this same boat through these waters many times, when he was a river guide and operated the Dug Bar Ranch. We looked up to see the high trail on the

Idaho side known as Suicide, which lays across from Salt Creek on the Oregon side.

Doug anchored the boat at Kirkwood Creek and we visited the former ranch headquarters of Len and Grace Jordan. Grace wrote a book, entitled *Home Below Hell's Canyon*, which tells about their family's life there. Today an old log building has been turned into museum that houses memorabilia and artifacts of the Jordans, as well as that area there in Hell's Canyon. The ranch house Grace talks about in the book still sits along Kirkwood Creek, where the cherries will ripen on the trees growing there. The place is a fitting tribute to another era. Doug continued upriver to the end of navigation which lies between Rush Creek and Sluice Creek.

Treacherous rapids roar through the Hell's canyon gorge above here. Far above we could see the Hat Point fire tower. After turning around we later passed the Johnson place on the Oregon side, where Kenneth and Hazel Johnson operated a sheep ranch for many years. The boat rocked and splashed us with water as it churned through the boiling, whitewater rapids and returned us safely to Somers Creek and camp.

A lizard with a very full belly crawled out from under my package of thawing hamburger. We promptly named him "Harvey". Pat lifted the squirming reptile by the tail, placing him on his arms! At which the friendly lizard ran around Pat's neck, and took a flying leap landing on Linde's shoulder! Harvey hung around camp while we cooked hamburgers and watched evening descend upon the canyons.

Later, stretched out on my sleeping bag, on the tent, I couldn't sleep.

A chorus of crickets chirped above the roar of a high roiling river-sound. Because moonlight lit the nighttime sky, the stars were pale. Every movement in the grass was a snake, and every story I'd read about them crawling into people's sleeping bags for warmth came alive with vivid night time imagination. Ironically, a year ago, to the night, Linde, Pat, Scotty and two grandsons and I had slept out, under the stars, in rattlesnake infested sagebrush, on Virtue Flat. But that large wagon train encampment scared off all snakes, and I'd slept well.

I watched the moon until it disappeared over Somers Point. Its leftover glow soon faded and the Big Dipper shone brightly through the leafy mulberry. The sweet syringa scent was comforting, the Big Dipper moved out of sight across the sky, and, finally, I slept, just when the sky began to lighten.

The next morning we ate a late Sunday breakfast of sourdough pancakes, sausage, and eggs. While the men broke camp, Linde and I hiked up to Ed Davis's old cabin. According to Doug, in the late 1950s, Ed decided to become a recluse of the canyon. He didn't like paying taxes, so this little man picked this pretty spot to built a tiny cabin, using pre-cut used lumber hauled up river in a boat.

The cabin, as well as the outhouse were built very sturdy, and stand so today. Although Ed's possessions were few, he was rich in the things that counted. Doug said he eked out a tiny existence by gold panning.

June 8—Once again we live in an emerald green world, after nearly a week of storms that swept over the valley. They began with thunder showers and soon settling down to a steady dripping rain, leaving June's cool greenness in their wake. Waters runs and pools everywhere. Meadow grasses, urged to maturity by earlier warmth, wave their purple-hued heads and create a dark ocean above Prairie Creek's cool green landscape. The spinach on the Slope loves this cool wetness, and we've been glorying in fresh greens, steamed or in salad. Peas, lettuce, radishes and onions respond positively to the moistness.

I maintain that rain is Mother Nature's way of slowing down the frantic spring pace, giving weary farmers and ranchers a rest. Granted, many of them are out in their shops repairing or doing required maintenance on the old machinery, but the pressure is temporarily off. Seed potato planting also came to an abrupt halt.

School is out for the Wallowa County children, who, like my grandchildren, can't wait to go fishin'. So after a phone call about same, I picked up James and Adele one day last week, and between storms we went fishin'.

Although we didn't get so much as a nibble all day, we nevertheless had a great time in the outdoors. Plenty of exercise for grandma, who found herself leaning out over a pond, holding with one hand to an overhanging alder branch, retrieving James' hook. I escaped with only wet feet when the branch bent double under my weight and I managed to leap to shore, hook in hand, before the limb broke.

Later, safely from the shore, we watched numerous small birds skim Kinney Lake's surface in the cold wind, while wild wavelets slapped the rocks at our feet. We made only a few casts there before deciding it was more the sort of day to sit in the car and eat our sandwiches, watching the birds feed on insects and talking about former fishing trips.

Then we drove to Wallowa Lake and scrambled down a rocky trail to the water's edge. Adele and I used the faithful fly rod, using a battered fly baited with a section of nightcrawler. The wind wasn't as strong there, but on his third cast, James lost the whole deal: leader, spinner, fly, three-pronged hook baited with a nightcrawler. That boy comes prepared. The hooks had snagged on a rock submerged deep beneath the cold waters of Wallowa Lake. Grandma drew the line there; too cold for a swim.

Moving to the foot of the lake, where the wind died down to a whisper, we gave up fishing entirely while the children played in the sand, made driftwood boats and collected pretty rocks.

Children and water go together. Under the watchful eye of grandma they played contentedly for more than an hour. We were the only visitors at the lake that afternoon. After spending another hour or so in the secluded Joseph Park, which is really like being in the country, situated along a rushing river with swings and picnic tables, we ended our day at the Top Hand cafe sipping milk shakes.

The next day, before the next storm, Doug and I drove up to the Slope and repaired fence until noon. Then I fixed lunch and we watched the Belmont Stakes with Bill. We left in a sudden deluge of rain that pounded our garden and ran in wavering sheets across our windshield. White flashes of lightning sliced the darkness of clouds, and thunder echoed from the mountains. Some flooding occurred, while rain gauges filled up in minutes. Surely our drought is over.

Passing through Joseph on the way home, we stopped for a milk shake at Kohlhepp's Kitchen. The small eatery was crowded with antique car enthusiasts in town for the annual Wallowa Mountain Cruise. The electricity kept flickering on and off as soggy tourists and car owners streamed in off Joseph's main street, which was also a stream of water, to get under cover.

At home we discovered that the lightning had done a number on our TV. After I had just rented a video of the movie "A River Runs Through It." So, after frying chicken, steaming fresh spinach and baking buttermilk biscuits for supper, I went to bed with a good book.

On Sunday, after Doug left for Pendleton to attend an antique and gun show, I picked up Grace and we drove out north to see if the camas was blooming. It was. All of the low-lying great meadows wore a blue haze, and arrow leaf balsamroot grew in clumps alongside the roads or colored the hillsides yellow. It was cloudy and cool with an occasional burst of sunlight that illuminated the Krebs Brothers' two bands of sheep as they grazed the green meadows and hillsides. The herder's small sheepherder wagon was nearby, parked between the green hills.

After taking the Swamp Creek cutoff, we found ourselves off the beaten track, immersed in steep, rolling, wildflower-strewn hills where aspen thickets clumped together in the draws and ponderosa pine grew on the norths. Cattle grazed the lush spring grasses, a peaceful rural scene that mainstream tourists never see. Not much action here. No McDonald's, just country.

When we joined the Swamp Creek road, a white tail doe emerged from an alfalfa field, her white flag flying, stiff, upright, perhaps drawing our attention from a hidden fawn. Eagles and hawks soared over the land or perched on weathered rock jacks.

We parked on a slight rise overlooking an old farm, and lunched on cold fried chicken, biscuits and a fruit jar full of water. A dark and wet cloud approached from the mountains, and suddenly we were under it—more rain.

Later, armed with my movie, I dropped in on friend Scotty and together we enjoyed "A River Runs Through It," which is about fly-fishing and life, both of which are entwined in a most touching way.

My hens are laying well these days. I seem to always have an abundance of eggs, so I baked a custard, sprinkling nutmeg on top, for Doug when he returned. Among his purchases was a cookbook, *Cookery of the Prairie Homesteader,* for my collection. I wasn't surprised to find that many old recipes have endured the years. The custard I'd made, without a recipe, was basically the same.

It is cloudy and cool again this evening, but yesterday's wind dried things a bit so I took a walk after supper through our hay field. Standing there waist high amid the waving, maturing grasses with June all around, I felt a oneness with the land. It must have been like this for the homesteader and the lonely women who stood under cloud and sky, intimate with wind and meadowlarks, forgetting in such a June as this the cruelness of winter.

June 15—Take 25 people from diverse backgrounds, diverse interests, and diverse means of making their living, but sharing the common bond of living in Wallowa County, and place them for the better part of three days miles from the nearest town, without electricity, on a working cattle ranch along Chesnimnus Creek; for what reasons?

Well, for many reasons: to grow, to learn, to respect another person's ideas, to respect his or her right to be here as a member of the community, to understand where he or she came from and his or her dreams for the future, and to listen to his or her thoughts on how to achieve such a future community.

In more professional terms, this was defined as an alliance building workshop presented by Bill Proudman and Tim Bruan of Inclusivity Consulting Group, Incorporated, of Portland.

I looked up the word "alliance" in my thesaurus. It is a noun; *associ-*

ation, federation, league, combination, treaty, accord, marriage, connection. See cooperation, relation. At the end of those three days, there was definitely a combination of connection and cooperation that fostered an association of those present. Wherever our paths in life may lead us, we will forever be connected.

It was soon discovered that we were all linked together by a common thread, woven by a strong desire to continue to live in Wallowa County, and an equally passionate desire to work together to make this happen. At the bottom of the first page in our work sheet, the following words caught my eye, from Ron Kurtz, *The first step of a journey is more significant for the direction it announces than the distance it covers.*

We gathered in the spirit of the Philosophy of Inclusion, where everyone has a say, which appears simple but somehow seems to fall by the wayside as we grow older, as so-called "social conditioning" changes us from children to adults. We learn things like hate and fear, and not to trust one another, not even ourselves. After three days together we had all gotten back to the basics of communicating with members of our community, really listening to what the other person had to say. Speaking from our hearts, being respectful of others as well as ourselves; acknowledging differences and realizing that diversity brings in different perspectives that can be accepted and valued.

There, in that peaceful, rural atmosphere, in the old ranch house along the creek, looking out upon green ridges that were at that moment exploding with wildflowers, simply reaffirmed a commitment to this special place we call home, and strengthened desires to continue this quality of life for future generations, not just our own families, but other human beings, like us, who will choose to live here despite certain sacrifices.

There is something to be said about the basic goodness of being on a remote cattle ranch. People soon discover they don't need expensive conference facilities to function. Arising in the morning, going for a walk, gathering around a long kitchen table and visiting without feeling any pressure whatsoever; friendships are easily formed, new ideas are hatched, and neighbor begins to know neighbor.

And when Nancy's cooking fills the air with delicious smells, the gong is sounded, our places are filled, a spot is found to sit, and we are family. Nice!

Between group discussions and assignments we took breaks, which meant several jaunts for those of us who enjoy that sort of thing. During these hikes, some of which took us to the tops of high ridges, where we could view the distant Wallowas, we were always rewarded, not only by the scenery but by the input of our diverse neighbors. During these times it was most rewarding for me to see businessmen ordinarily so bogged down with their jobs that they never have an opportunity to actually get out and enjoy Wallowa County's outback. Witnessing the delight on their faces when encountering wildlife amid wild country is really a joy.

Members of the workshop slept in trailers, in tents, in the bunkhouse, or wherever they could throw a sleeping bag, sharing the facilities. Owing to the warm hospitality of our host, Doug McDaniel, and his people there on the B&H Ranch, we were comfortable and made to feel at home.

The first two days it rained on and off, then Sunday dawned clear and sparkled with sunlight. A bit of ice formed on the windshields in the big meadow, and frost whitened the grasses. On that final day, sessions were all held outside. A soft breeze stirred the fresh clean air, and the green fullness of a wet June along Chesnimnus Creek worked a sort of magic, which I'm sure had a lot to do with the success of the workshop. Looking back is likened to a dream of living in another place and time, but writing about those experiences brings back the reality of it all.

I savored every mile of the long drive back through tracts of un-peopled places managed by ranchers, where cattle grazed, wild roses bloomed along clean streams, penstemon displayed purple, lavender and pink, spilling from rocky crevices along the road, and grass grew belly-high to cattle and horses.

I passed a rancher riding a four-wheeler, perhaps checking fence lines or simply enjoying the day. Only one other vehicle did I see before I arrived at the junction of the north highway. Then those lovely, snow-splotched Wallowas loomed and beckoned. Arrowleaf balsamroot glowed golden upon the hills, camas bloomed blue in the long, wet meadows, where bands of sheep grazed under the watchful eye of a nearby herder.

It was a perfect ending to a special time in my life, shared by all, as they, too, traveled back to carry on with their various lives in the county. For those of us who participated in this workshop, the word "hope" will continue to fuel the long journey ahead for those who share a dream for the future of our county community.

July 1—Outside the church, the California heat shimmered over acres of tomato fields, corn, sugar beets and other row crops covering the vast farm lands that lie between the freeways and suburbia around the town of Dixon. Tomato fields stopped just short of the church, which was the same church at the end of the street, in which daughter Ramona and husband, Charley, were married nearly 24 years ago.

The hot sun streamed through colorful stained glass windows, moved from the old church when it was torn down, and installed there. Engraved at the bottom of one glass mural was the name of Charley's Aunt Molly's great-grandfather. Family roots dated deep in the fertile soil of Solano County. Inside the church, cooled by an air-conditioner repaired just hours before, gathered friends and family of the bride and groom, nearly 400 of them, from near and afar, to attend the wedding of my oldest granddaughter on that breathlessly hot Saturday in late June.

For those of us who traveled more than 800 miles, the occasion was also a family reunion. After being escorted down the aisle and seated in the front row next to Doug, I turned my head into a sea of smiling, familiar faces.

Mother and daughter shed a few traditional tears as the six lovely bridesmaids, two little flower girls, and a young ring bearer made their way slowly down the aisle. Then a hush fell as Tammy, slim, golden-haired, radiant in her long white dress, arm hooked through her father's, came gliding to the altar.

Memories came flooding back: my own wedding, her mother's birth, her mother's wedding, her birth (the first grandchild). All the joys and tears in between, jumbled together, entwined with hopes, dreams, and the final reality of life.

Another younger granddaughter, Adele, far from her Wallowa County home, held her basket of flowers, taking it all in. Grandson Shawn, tall, suddenly grownup, wore a tux. Granddaughter Carrie, singing again, this time for her sister's wedding. And Tammy's great-grandmother, looking younger than her 83 years, witnessing the continuation of life she brought into the world. The generations march on.

More grandmothers and grandfathers, on the groom's side, looking on as the young take their places. My two sisters and brother, perhaps thinking of our own father, gone now, wondering what he would think of all these great-grandchildren. The white-haired organist, the same lady who played for the bride's parents' wedding, gorgeous bouquets of flowers, and the ageless vows solemnly repeated. Another wedding, another young couple beginning life together.

The affair was the result of months of planning and went off without a hitch, except for the heat. Mother Nature does as she pleases. The reception was held in the country at the Glide ranch, where tables and awnings were set up on a wide lawn that surrounded a swimming pool. A tall, old wooden silo stood close by, and fields of tomatoes and corn stretched to the horizon.

While the bride and groom mingled with relatives and friends, gallons of punch and iced tea were consumed before everyone lined up for a tri-tip beef dinner. After the sun mercifully sank over the Pacific, the delta breezes cooled us off some and the band commenced to play. Old and young danced on the lawn into the night. Oregon cousins got acquainted with California cousins, and old friends became reacquainted. It was pretty special.

Most amazing to me was that our Oregon families, several traveling in old cars, had actually made it safely through the maze of freeway traffic and heat to arrive in one piece. Someone has to worry about such things, and that is usually yours truly. I was very relieved to have them make the trip down and back without incident.

Interesting to note that my branch of the family broke off from the California tree and emigrated, pioneer-like, 25 years ago to Oregon. And now that branch has grown a tree of its own, and my children and their children have settled into this far northeastern corner of Oregon and call it home, and chosen to live entirely different lifestyles than their city cousins, who tend to view our lives as romantic, as a choice to live without many of the amenities available to them.

A cowboy's paycheck hardly compares to most of their salaries, but after whizzing along a hot freeway, looking out upon miles and miles of subdivisions and country club estates, we were glad to return to our homes in Wallowa County.

While in Dixon, Doug and I were the guests of friends Ernie and Rose Gnos, who are part of a large farming and dairy operation there. The Gnoses' home is surrounded by farm ground; tomato plants in rows straight as a ruler, without a weed, some already bearing the first red crop. Farther down the road grows a field of fragrant thyme, owned by Spice Islands.

Next to their house, nearly hidden by giant walnut trees, sits a smaller house, where lives Johanna Gnos, Ernie's 93-year-old mother. I met Johanna early that first morning as I was out walking along the country road to beat the day's heat. She was walking too. We stopped to visit, and I told her we had come from Oregon to attend our granddaughter's wedding. Johanna says she goes for a walk every morning.

"Makes me feel good," she said. Her little dog followed close by. I was impressed by her robustness, her alert mind and general good health. The next morning after the wedding, I saw Johanna walk past the bedroom window, so I hurried to make the bed so I could join her.

But by the time I got to the road, she was gone. In the distance, I could just barely make out her pink blouse. She was stepping right along. When I finally caught up to her, she was surprised to see me, but happy to have someone to walk and talk with. She told me about the tomato crop and how her sons were good farmers.

"Notice," she said, "no weeds in their fields." They cultivate often, and keep them out. "The weeds cause problems in the mechanical pickers." Johanna knew about everyone who lived along that road, and told me of them. "Lots of old folks live here, and it is hard to get someone to care for them," she remarked sadly. Then I learned about her life.

One of 18 children, born in Switzerland, Johanna was one of 14 who survived. Her mother died at the age of 45, a year after the birth of her 18th child; and when four of the other children died, the surviving brothers and sisters were told that the mother came back and took them.

She spoke of her childhood, how poor they were, how they walked miles down off the mountain to the school in winter, and how the girls' skirts were frozen from the deep snows. How they were so tired and cold they didn't learn anything, and then had to hike home. She said the family existed on what money they got for cheese and butter made from milk from their cows, and their diet consisted of potatoes, cheese and bread, and very little meat. Sometimes a pig was butchered.

She emigrated to America and, up until just a few years ago, milked a cow and gardened. She still has a few chicks, and cracks walnuts, which she sells, and today her sons are successful farmers. It was a real bonus to become acquainted with Johanna. The morning we left, she brought two dozen of her fresh eggs over and ate breakfast with us.

Now back home in our high mountain valley, which is likened to Switzerland, I think of Johanna.

July 8—Through the open window of our spare bedroom, Virgil Rupp thought he heard someone playing a trombone this morning. Wake up call on Prairie Creek? You might call it that. The bawling of a big black baldy Simmental bull in a nearby pen did have a sort of trombone-like tremor to it. What we recognize as commonplace must sound foreign to one not used to country sounds, especially when the absolute stillness of night is broken only by the yipping of coyotes prowling over the connecting hills.

Virgil is staying with us while he attends the Fishtrap Writer's Gathering, now in progress at Wallowa Lake. Since his workshop doesn't begin until this afternoon, and because it was such a gorgeous morning, he made himself a meat loaf sandwich, filled his tank with gas in town and, armed with my map, headed his pickup out toward Buckhorn. Hopefully he'll not get lost. This is big country.

At noon I finished my workshop, which began Monday morning.

Thirteen writers from several western states signed up for Mary Clearman Blew's class—Writing From Life: A workshop on memoir.

None of us wanted it to end. Mary, who teaches writing at Lewis-
Clark State College in Idaho, is the author of such books as *Lambing Out
And Other Stories, Runaway,* and *All but the Waltz.* Her book *Balsam Root*
will be out soon. Mary writes about her life in Montana, and knows of
what she writes. Her great-grandparents arrived when it was a territory
in 1882. Her writings center around the Snowies, the Judiths and the
South Moccasins mountains and prairies that shaped her life. She is a
new generation of western writers who not only write but can teach as
well.

Our diverse group of writers, from different regions and backgrounds,
brought to Mary's workshop a mixed bag of ideas that stimulated con-
structive criticism and encouragement. Because of our diversity and
different perspectives, we all gained by the experience. After each of us
read our work, it was discussed at length by each person before Mary
gave us her opinions.

Our group included an editor of a weekly newspaper in Ashton, Idaho;
a published writer from Hood River; a young Nez Perce man from the
Colville tribe, who had been awarded a fellowship to Fishtrap; a young
woman from Seattle, originally from Brooklyn; a former Wallowa County
resident now living in McMinnville, Oregon, who is writing about her
mother, who was born up Lightning Creek on Imnaha; a rancher's wife
from Sumpter, Alice Warnock; and another book-in-progress woman,
from Idaho; a retired teacher-turned-writer who raises Limousin cattle
with her husband; and Mary Louise Nelson, who used to work for the
Wallowa County Chieftain, the only other local person.

Several in Mary's class, including yours truly, read at open mics held
each evening in the lodge. As each year passes, new acquaintances are
added to a growing list of friends. Marc Jaffe, editor-publisher of an
independent imprint at Houghton Mifflin, arrived yesterday to join what
he has termed a family reunion. Having attended every Gathering since
its beginning, I must agree with him—Fishtrap is a meeting of kindred
spirits.

Meanwhile, back at the ranch...Whoops! We all agreed not to use
cliches. Anyway, it is haying time. Actually the hay was ready to cut two
weeks ago, but the damp drizzly days of late June stretched into July and
kept that from happening. Consequently first cuttings are in the fields in
various stages, most of it still uncut, some in yellowing windrows, some
freshly swathed, some being raked again and again in an effort to dry it
out, some being baled, and some quivering and falling to the sickle as

I write. The temperature actually rose to 70 degrees today, after what seems like an interminable cool wet spell.

Our hay here on Prairie Creek is in three of the above stages. Ben is raking and Jim Stubblefield is baling. The seed potatoes are all up and growing.

My garden on Alder Slope is looking great, despite the coolness.

Peas are blooming, lettuce has been on our table for quite some time, and the radishes remain crisp. The corn and beans aren't growing as well, and cucumbers and peppers beg for warm nights and days. The apples on Bill's trees are simply loaded, and there is a good crop of plums and a few pears.

After Tuesday's workshop ended at noon, I fled to the slope garden to rest my brain, and before I knew it two hours had passed and I was able to hoe ahead of an accumulation of weeds.

Afterward. resting there in the garden, leaning on the hoe handle, I surveyed my handiwork. Great therapy.

Our early summer is more like late spring. Wild daisies run rampant along the irrigation ditches and their white petals with yellow centers dot every meadow and hillside.

Grain crops are lush, and the prolonged rains have created grass the likes of which we haven't seen in years. Cattle, horses and sheep glow with health.

July is the time for wild roses, and their pale pink blooms line the country lanes. How I enjoy my ride each morning to the lake. The wild, white froth of syringa grows along the lake shore and clumps of it spot the east moraine.

I watch for our fall-calving cows, which are due to begin calving there next month. They, too, are fat and sleek. I see them trailing back from their watering hole over trails that lead to and from the high places where they feed on the succulent bunch grass that grows on the steep moraine. Large Simmental-cross matrons, their bellies swollen with new life.

Returning from California, Doug and I took a different route this time. We headed out across that long, lonely road to Denio that ultimately took us through the Callow Valley. A vast high desert that I had read about, but had never seen. I was thrilled with its sheer space, as mile after mile of country whizzed past with only a few scattered ranches here and there.

We passed but one vehicle, a sort of library on wheels bringing books to that far-flung corner of Oregon. How the residents must anticipate the corning of the bookmobile. Other places I'd longed to visit included

Frenchglen, where a blue roan milk cow broke her tether and grazed near the store, and three roosters and several hens pecked for bugs in the street. It was so quiet!

We skirted the edge of the Malheur Wildlife Refuge and stared at the backs of Steens Mountain. We visited a carriage shop in Canyon City, gassed up in Prairie City—everywhere wildflowers, lush grass, fat cattle, ranches and farms; haying time there, too. We climbed Dixie Pass and down into Sumpter Valley, where we saw split rail fences and old mining towns.

We savored a steak dinner at the Haines Steak House and returned to Prairie Creek after dark. Oregon. Home. Even though my roots are in California, my children's will be here.

July 13—Our cooling trend continues. Day after day, white and fluffy clouds with dark undersides grow into changing shapes and move slowly above the landscape. Yesterday morning's frost reminds us that we still live in a high mountain valley, and even though the calendar says it is summer, this is normal.

Returning from granddaughter Tammy's wedding in California, I was faced with myriad tasks that seem to accumulate during one's absence, one of which was canning cherries. Jim McCormack had kindly saved me a box of Bings grown on his Grande Ronde River orchard. After mowing the lawn, weeding the garden, writing my column, and taking grandchildren to the Lostine Flea Market, I concentrated on the 4th of July, which was suddenly upon us.

We also had house guests, relatives from Pasco, who stopped in on their way to a family reunion in Bend, and ended up spending the 4th with us. Their three children went wild over my chickens, and the chickens went wild over them, as the children spent a good deal of time chasing around the pen. I spent most of my time cooking when more than 30 of our extended family gathered here to celebrate the 4th of July.

We consumed barbecued chicken, a leg of lamb, Basque bread baked in a dutch oven, salads, watermelon, pickled beets, sweet pickles, raspberry cobblers, homemade ice cream and even a birthday cake. Someone had a birthday on the 4th! The youngsters could hardly wait until dark and time for fireworks. It didn't have to be dark to shoot the potato guns, but that's another story.

As always, there was the satisfaction of having my brood together, strengthening ties, building memories for the younger generation to look back on. From the direction of Wallowa Lake we could see flashes of fireworks being set off up there. We were later to learn that the lake was crowded, full of tourists and visitors. We seem far removed here on Prairie Creek, and a gorgeous moon glowed brightly in a clear sky.

The next morning my "Fishtrap" writers' class began at Wallowa Lake. Driving up there I could see the trash left along the shore by last night's visitors. My heart was gladdened when later I saw some young people picking it up, stuffing the rubbish into plastic bags and hauling it off.

Mary Blew's workshop ended at noon Thursday, after which I returned to the ranch and managed to type some sort of column for Virgil to take back to Agri-Times; put a pot roast into the dutch oven and gathered the eggs. By the time Virgil and Marc Jaffe arrived, as I'd invited them to supper with Doug and me, I had time to take them on a quick tour of Alder Slope, which included a visit to Bill's to see the garden.

Then back to eat supper, which had been simmering in our absence: potatoes, carrots and onions cooked in the meat juices, freshly picked lettuce from the garden in the salad, and steamed spinach, also from the garden, plus french bread. After Doug demonstrated the potato gun to Marc, we left to attend the "open mike" in progress at Fishtrap.

The "Gathering" opened officially Friday evening when more writers converged from far and near to begin this sixth annual writers' conference. After a delicious baked potato bar, prepared by Jim Chandler and kitchen staff, we listened to readings that described "Western Worlds" created by each reader, unique to them; a tribal world, an ethnic world, a world of work, family and religion, told to us by writers David Duncan, Benjamin Saenz and Sherman Alexie. Pretty deep stuff, painting a word picture of their worlds through the wonderful medium of storytelling in poems and prose. The finale that evening was a play written and produced by J.T. Stewart's playwriting workshop. Wonderful!

Saturday morning found all of us mingling among and visiting with other writers over breakfast. Then New York editor Marc Jaffe moderated a panel discussion on "What defines and characterizes the West?"

Panelists Alvin Josephy, Native American writer Linda Hogan and Benjamin Saenz tossed around many ideas as they relate to the land, natural resources, indigenous populations, hopes and new beginnings, individualism. To lighten things up, Jim Heynen read from his latest book, *The One-Room Schoolhouse,* which is a collection of vignettes drawn from his rural Iowa roots. That evening we enjoyed a barbecue, followed by more readings, after which we sat back, relaxed and listened to Jim Wylie and his one-man show. Just Jim and his two folk guitars, one of which belonged to one of his grandparents. Marvelous!

Over Sunday morning breakfast this mix of voices blended into the most "multi-cultural" Fishtrap ever, a prediction made earlier by coordinator Rich Wandschneider) that has come to pass. The highlight of the Gathering for me, as well as many others I talked to, was Sunday's morning's round table.

After a week of cold weather, the sun shone with a welcome warmth, and the round table, which was square, was moved outside. There, surrounded by evergreens, amid the fresh air and in view of those mountains, with wispy clouds forming overhead, everyone gathered informally on the lawn and J.T. Stewart chaired one of the most gratifying, thought-provoking discussions I've ever been privileged to witness. Visiting writers sat around a long, low wooden table, kicking around ideas that centered on the theme "Visions of the Future: A working Western Community."

The audience, sitting on the grass, was later invited to join the discussion. I jotted down a few notes and quotes from some of the round table participants. J.T. Stewart, moderator, asked the panel, "What's at stake, what do we want to do, when talking of community in the New West?"

Linda Hogan suggested people have forgotten how to love, are out of touch with spirituality, rejecting this basic part of life and instead seeking it in other people. She also said we are connected to the land, that we share it with other creatures.

Jim Heynen spoke of a personal hunger for community, extended family, and lonely individualism. Nature is in our face here in the Northwest. When that face frowns, our souls suffer. He suggested we look at the faces of our kids and inside our hearts where real community begins; empower children with what we are doing; pay attention to role models.

Marc Jaffe comes to Fishtrap and Wallowa County to be revived and inspired. He envisions the future western community. What will happen? Historians of the future will give us the reality, past and present, interpreting the future by looking at the present. He asks, "What can I do for the West?"

Benjamin Saenz said he shared a room with four brothers when growing up, and remembers it as a good experience, even though they fought. "It provided me with a sense of belonging and loyalty for family," he said. "It taught us how to belong to each other." He considered how rural life is being erased, which is erasing a people and culture. How can we negotiate between each other when we don't appreciate each other's identity and very different backgrounds?

"We have to face these issues," he continued. Just because we all come from radically different places doesn't mean we can't be communicating.

We need to keep the river flowing. Exiling each other is a horrifying history we ought not to glorify. We are here and we aren't going to go away. The success of earth and its people depends on finding a way to belong to one another.

Afro-American writer J.T. Stewart found that a way to deal with her rage was to write and to learn about history, which helps us understand what is happening now, and to learn the importance of language. J.T. writes because she wants to change the world—a big agenda, but she says we cannot escape history, and so we should write about where we've been and what's happening, so others will understand. A community must embrace differences; migrations of people, all the time, on a global level have been taking place for centuries.

The underlying theme to me was this attempt to understand our neighbors, to learn why they act like they do, what do they want, how do they wish to achieve it? And to do this by communicating with them, forming family and community. We all need each other. We are a lot of us on the earth right now, and people are part of the environment, they aren't going to go away. Why not live together and respect each other, regardless of race, color or religion. It worked at Fishtrap!

July 20—Heavy, wet clouds wrap themselves around the mountains. Occasionally this mass of gray moisture parts enough to reveal a sunlit, snowy peak. Sodden hay lies yellowing in the fields, acres and acres of beautiful first cuttings being subjected to a daily thundershower. Water pools in every depression, and although it seems rather futile, sprinkler lines send out their jets of water all up and down the valley. Our lawn is littered with willow leaves, beaten down during last evening's hail storm. Hail the size of moth balls bounced off the roof, clinked against the windows, stung the horses and mule, and confused the cattle.

Suddenly, without warning, after a bright flash of lightning, then rolling thunder, the sky emptied over a narrow path of Prairie Creek. In a matter of minutes the ground was covered with ice balls. The mule and horses ran every which way trying to escape the pelting hail. Hough's Angus cattle ran to a corner, clustering and milling, bawling as the stinging ice pounded their hides. When it ceased, the ground was white, and Doug drove up the road to inspect the potato field.

Expecting the worst, he was surprised to find that the storm stopped just short of the first rows of potato plants! I called Bill on Alder Slope and was relieved to learn that our garden, too, was spared. It is a sad time for hay farmers and ranchers who, after rejoicing in one of the best hay crops in years, can't put it up. Heavy first cuttings, just beginning to cure and ready to bale, hit by yet another rain shower.

Most frustrating, but farmers and ranchers, or at least the ones still in business, take this in stride, never giving up, meeting each day as it comes and doing what has to be done. All are affected. The weather plays no favorites.

Last Sunday dawned clear, with rain-washed skies and a warm sun reminding us that it was, after all, summer. So after Doug and I repaired some fence on Alder Slope where our yearlings had broken through, I packed a lunch and we went on a huckleberry hunt.

We drove up Salt Creek Summit and down past Lick Creek. A shortcut road brought us to Skookum Creek, where we ate. Huckleberries in this area were thick on the bushes, but still green. Owing to all this prolonged wetness and coolness, wild flowers flourished. Brilliant penstemon grew out of rocky crevices, and Indian paintbrush made red-orange splashes protruding from lush grasses. Entire rocky hillsides were covered with the reddish purple of blooming wild onion. After lunch we drove to a spot along the upper Imnaha River.

It was peaceful there, overlooking a wide bend in the river. I stretched out in the grass and stared at the few clouds moving slowly through the azure sky. While Doug washed a few pans of sand for gold, my border collie dog Daisy and I went for a walk along the river.

Returning, we spotted a herder on horseback, driving some sheep back to the main band, which was grazing the lush grasses there in the Wallowa Whitman Forest. I was thinking the sheep were serving a purpose other than putting on weight. They were helping control a potential fire hazard, for, if the temperatures begin to soar, this grass will dry up, and a tossed cigarette would pose a real threat.

We turned up Gumboot, stopped to check a huckleberry patch near the road, and found it to be loaded with the first deep purple berries. We sat in filtered sun and shade, picking until early evening. Evidence that bears had been ahead of us began to appear when we found some bushes stripped of leaves and berries. The pungent odor of huckleberries and the damp forest smells filled the warm air there along Gumboot Creek. An entire day without rain! One to be savored.

Back at the ranch, our hands stained purple with huckleberry juice, I baked a batch of huckleberry muffins for tomorrow's breakfast.

Yesterday, after I'd hung out a load of wash between showers, Linde and Ulrike, a 16-year-old girl visiting from Germany, kidnapped me and took me to Wallowa Lake. We hiked up the Chief Joseph Trail to a bridge where we gazed down at the clear frothy waters tumbling down from the higher country, forming the Wallowa River's west fork.

On the way back we nibbled on ripe huckleberries that we discovered growing along the trail. We took another trail that offered a view of a turquoise-tinged pool boiling with foaming froth that fell from a waterfall above. What a sight of wild power and cleanness, all draining into Wallowa Lake, which is as full as I ever remember seeing it. Irrigation won't be a problem this summer, which is a dramatic turnaround from the drought years we've been experiencing.

Linde treated us to lunch at Russells. We ate outside on a picnic table under the pines, enjoying the rare bursts of sunshine, which lasted until late afternoon. Then dark clouds rolled in and that hail storm cut its path across Prairie Creek. Off toward Imnaha the skies were blue-black as the storm headed for the Snake River and Idaho.

Last weekend, during and between the ever-present storms, two diversified cultural events took place in the county, bringing floods of tourists. The Jazz Festival, held at Wallowa Lake, and the Indian Pow Wow Friendship Feast, held down valley near the town of Wallowa.

Meanwhile, on the Minam Grade, following orders from the powers that be (who never informed the local residents this was going to transpire), the state highway construction (destruction) goes on.

Traffic backs up to Elgin while giant earth movers decimate the once lovely entrance to Wallowa County. Blasting rocks where once grew the colorful penstemon, bulldozing trees to widen the road. For what? So more people can zoom down the grade at faster speeds, so no one will have time to gaze down upon the wild Minam River and its scenic canyon. And when winter's ice-covered roads greet all these people, who aren't used to winter travel, they'll come skidding and sliding and there'll be more wrecks than ever.

I watched this same thing happen in the California Sierra. The newer, wider roads encourage people to travel at such higher speeds, they can't take their eyes from the road to see the mountains they are traveling through. Winter is just treacherous there. We who live here wonder why we weren't informed of this monstrous waste of money. Is accessing Oregon going to be its ruination?

Chief Joseph Days begins this week, and the county braces for yet another influx of tourists. Meanwhile, the rancher struggles with his wet hay, so his cattle can eat this winter, and so the year-round economy can continue in this ever-changing West.

July 27—A single bright star glittered in the first faint light of dawn this morning. In a clear sky! For the first time in days, the sun came up and warmed the sodden hayfields. Its penetrating rays dried off the streets of Joseph after a wet and wild 48th annual Chief Joseph Days celebration came to an end Sunday.

Several local ranchers are contemplating chopping silage rather than baling their oft-rained-on hay. This is one way of salvaging winter feed, some say. There have been calls from neighbors wanting to borrow our chopper. Mechanically stuffing the hay into Ag Bags is costly and time consuming at this point, but perhaps a pit could be dug, or chopped hay could be stacked on the ground and covered. Knowing the ingenuity of these ranchers, they'll figure out something.

Meanwhile, in the dampened fields, second cuttings continue to grow around windrows of discolored hay. I can hear Ben raking ours again in an attempt to dry it out and hopefully get it baled before the weather should change again. Earlier I watched neighbor Lois Hough in the tractor seat pulling a rake over the tobacco-colored alfalfa field.

Later in the afternoon they were able to take the big stackers into the field and compress the big "bread loaf" haystacks. Huge billowing clouds of moldy dust followed in the wake of three machines as they roared down the rows. Make hay while the sun shines!

I went up to the Slope garden this afternoon and all is well there, except the corn, beans and squash would love several more days of this sunshine; they are behind schedule. Picked a big batch of Swiss chard and more lettuce, and noted that some little new beets are nearly ready to pull. Our two potato fields are lush and vigorous, with tubers sizing up. It has been ideal for them: fine misty rains, natural irrigation, and no heat-stressed plants. The rows are nearly filled and blooming.

Daughter Lori, husband Tom, and grandchildren Lacey and Ryan drove over the Blues from Pendleton to spend Chief Joseph Days weekend with us. We all attended the Shriners' breakfast held outside Saturday morning in Joseph, a traditional meeting place where old-timers and local folk gather to visit. The rain, although threatening, held off for the breakfast and the big parade, when the sun actually broke through the clouds and burned with enough intensity to remind us that it was, after all, the end of July.

We enjoyed visiting out-of-towner Bob Fauste, one of Doug's nephews, who reminisced about his growing-up years here in Wallowa County. Bob said that when he was 14 he worked for a sheepman by the name of Purcell who had a ranch on Cache Creek, near the Snake River. He said he was in charge of the mules when they drove the sheep to the high summer range.

"We used to drive the sheep through Enterprise," he said. "Then up the old stock driveway to Murray Gap, then down into Silver Creek basin, and up over Traverse Ridge to those high meadows for summer grazing." Having traveled that country myself, on foot, I can appreciate driving the sheep up that rugged route. But what an experience for a young lad. No wonder he looks fondly back on those times.

Wanda Soreweide's feet pumped the organ and her cheerful notes fell into the morning air, as folks visited over sausage and pancakes...all they could eat. Ryan was hungry and did the food justice. Continuing to visit, we found a place along Joseph's main street from which to watch the big parade, a great one, led by honorary grand marshal Joe Redthunder, Chief Joseph's great-nephew, and Icel (Edgemand) Miller, who was the grand marshal this year, as well as being the first Chief Joseph Days queen back in 1946. And she was riding a horse!

The large mounted group of Asotin Trail Riders came whooping and hollering down the street. They had ridden clear from Asotin, cross country, over rivers, up and down steep canyons, and across our hills to reach Joseph for the big doin's.

Another one of Doug's nephews, Wayne Tippett, and his family do a great job of organizing this popular annual event. After the parade, we hooked up with more friends and relatives and visited, which is what Chief Joseph Days is all about. Then Linde's friend Ulrike from Germany, granddaughter Carrie, Linde and I attended the Indian competitive dances, which were held inside the Joseph High School gym due to impending rain.

Here we entered the world of drum beats where dancers clad in beautiful beadwork, buckskins and eagle feathers moved to the rhythm of those drum beats. There were dances for the young boys and girls, men and women, according to age groups, and the last for the grandmothers. Everyone had an opportunity to dance and, at the same time, hold on to and preserve their traditional heritage. And how they enjoyed it.

The audience was invited to join in the Friendship dance, where the dancers formed two circles. We moved our feet in time to the drum, shook hands and smiled at those in the inner circle as they passed in front of us.

Sunday morning we awoke to the familiar sound of rain dripping off the roof. Another cold gray day. Doug and I drove into Joseph to eat at the cowboy breakfast outdoors, only it was deserted. A few people huddled under the roof of the serving-cooking shack, and the long tables, set with syrup, pooled with water from the steady downpour.

So we walked across the street and ate inside at the VFW breakfast, where we were served ham, sausage, pancakes and eggs. A few members of the Nez Perce Tepee encampment joined us to escape the rain. Afterward, Linde, Ulrike, Carrie and I joined more of our family at the Christian Cowboy Church service in the grandstand of the Harley Tucker Memorial Arena. During the service it began to rain again, fine at first, then settling down to a cold deluge that obscured the mountains and soaked into the already wet arena. From where we sat, we could see some of the tepees being taken down in the large encampment in back of the roping chutes.

Later the four of us drove to the lake to attend a ceremony to commemorate the new Nez Perce Park additions, one of which was the burial site of Old Chief Joseph at the foot of Wallowa Lake. It was very touching listening to Horace Axtell, a prominent Nez Perce elder from Lapwai, Idaho, who emceed the program.

A fire burned in the old stone fireplace, providing a welcome heat, after our outdoor church service in the rain. In rocks above the hearth the word "welcome" carried plenty of meaning that morning. There in that old historic lodge, listening to Indian prayers spoken in Nez Perce and talks by other tribal leaders, we were impressed, not only by a culture that was discouraged in the past, but also by the people themselves.

Well-known poet Phil George recited, and acted out in sign language, a very emotional piece he had written, having to do with the history of his people. The Nez Perce voiced concern for the uniqueness of the Wallowa Valley, especially where old Chief Joseph is buried. The spirits that live here will always be here, they said. It has been the ancestral home. The land must not be exploited. People can live here, but development must go hand-in-hand with sound planning so as to not spoil this uniqueness. This is a beautiful place, we agreed.

August 5—Summer finally arrived. The heat is on, weather-wise and activity-wise. These August days seem never long enough to accomplish all that we Wallowa Countians must do before winter sets in again. In the midst of it all comes our county fair, which began this morning.

Entries in the open class are down from last year, owing in part to the fact that the majority of exhibitors are farming and ranching families, and that means they are still trying to get that first cutting of hay up. Such frantic activity. Weary men, women and young people driving themselves from dawn till dark, some baling into the night. Thank goodness for these moonlit nights.

Here on Prairie Creek, Ben and Jim labor in the heat, deal with breakdowns, and try to steal a little rest before another day begins. Then, because of the heat, there are irrigation lines to change before and after haying. Because of all this sudden warmth, second cuttings grow lush between the yellowed bare spots left where hay, rained on for days, lay in windrows.

Enthusiasm remains high in the Junior Division of 4-H and FFA. A whole new crop of young people bring their livestock and projects to the fair for competition. The theme, reflected in all the exhibitor booths in Cloverleaf Hall, is "An Oregon Trail Tradition." Some of us Photo Club members put together a display there using relics that depict the Oregon Trail.

Outdoors, every berry that ever was is ripening. Doug picked wild blackberries at Pack Saddle Creek last week, which I froze. The raspberries ripen as I type, as do the gooseberries and bush cherries. I went over to Mike McFetridge's yesterday and picked pie cherries, which I pitted for pie and froze.

We have had a run of summer company, and they rave about the homemade pies and cobblers made from all of these berries. But why do they have to ripen all at once? And the peas in the slope garden are ready to pick, shell and freeze. Oh my. This has been such a busy week for me that this afternoon has been the first time I could sit myself down at the kitchen table and come up with any semblance of a column.

Last Sunday granddaughter Carrie, Linde, Ulrike and I, armed with a map drawn by Bill, carried signs to mark a trail and hiked up the old stock driveway to Murray Gap. We ate our lunches there in the high saddle that overlooks the valley where a waterfall spills down to form irrigation water that is diverted from Silver Creek. It is a very beautiful spot and a cool breeze refreshed us after a hard climb.

After resting, we began searching for old blazes on trees that marked the trail. At the meadows, the trail stopped each time so we put up our signs, which would eventually mark a route to Ruby Peak. It was fun looking for blazes, sometimes veering off course, then finding our way again by looking at our map and following landmarks, like "log across trail," "a large meadow with an island," "moderate climb from meadow," "stay on south side of creek."

That country up there in the Silver Creek basin is so lovely, but seldom visited, mostly because it takes considerable effort to reach it. The basin will only be visited by those who realize anything worthwhile must be earned. The trail follows Silver Creek, which runs clear and cold, fed by snowmelt and high mountain springs. Lush, emerald-green meadows abound with tiny shooting stars and buttercups (the alpine springtime is just beginning to flower).

Amid rocky situations where pink mountain heather bells bloomed near the last snowbanks, we put up our signs marking the trail to Scotch

Creek saddle, one approach to Ruby Peak. There are other routes for the more adventurous climbers, but this route is scenic and relatively safe, and allows the hiker to see some of the basin's beauty, its meadows and meandering creeks, not to mention a breathtaking view of snow-covered peaks that loom so close up there. Granddaughter Carrie, who hadn't ever been in the high country, is now hooked.

In a world that is most times confusing to our younger generation, the high country is a place to restore oneself. We did some pretty rigorous hiking over some rugged country by the time we circled back to Linde's Bronco.

The next day I took James (age 7) and Adele (age 5) on a long-promised overnight camping trip to Butte Creek. Fulfilling this promise turned into another adventure that taxed grandma's strength to the limit. But the effort was worthwhile, as usual.

When I'd originally planned this overnighter, far out on our hill land property, it was springtime, and cool. I had envisioned the three of us driving the miles there, parking our rig, and packing our camping gear down to the creek, just enough of a hike to get the kids used to carrying packs. Since we took the fall calving cows out of that pasture and drove them to their summer grazing on the high moraine some time ago, and after all that rain, the grass grew and grew.

It was so high we could find no semblance of a road, and going off the road meant hitting treacherous rocks, so we parked just inside the gate, shouldered our packs and tromped through that sea of grass, stickers and rocks in 80-degree heat. The kids were troopers, and each carried a small pack. Grandma staggered under the tent, sleeping bags, jackets and spare clothes. The children helped set up camp, which was at the bottom of a draw, down from a steep hill, alongside the creek.

Leaving them there to guard the camp, I returned to the car for our food. I trudged up that hot hill with an empty pack and returned a half-hour later with another load. We laughed a lot at my vow to stay until we ate all the food, because I wasn't packing any out!

After that second trip, I had worked up a sweat and was hungry and thirsty, so while I collapsed under a thornbush tree the children fixed me a sandwich. We were soon good as new and foraging around on the opposite hill under some old ponderosa pines for pine cones and firewood for our cooking fire that evening.

Everything about camping is fun for children. No one to say "clean your room, brush your teeth, mind your manners." But they kept a clean camp, brushed their teeth gladly, and were very thoughtful to grandma. Here we were, miles from civilization; as far as we could see in all directions, there was no sign of human habitation. The Wallowas loomed on the horizon, while eastward stretched the high plateau known as the Zumwalt Hills. We were quite alone.

We cooked our evening meal over the fire, and as the sun slipped over the hill in back of us, long shadows shaded our little meadow where the tent was pitched. We roasted marshmallows and made s'mores with crackers and chocolate bars. Yum.

We listened to the quiet and talked about the full moon that was soon to rise, and told stories until little eyes drooped. We crawled into our sleeping bags while it was still light. I told the children to listen for different birds and count how many songs they sang. In less than five minutes, they were both asleep.

Grandma watched the moon and counted her blessings.

August 9—Leaving our fair in full swing on this Monday, after a hectic day of photographing FFA and 4-H market beef and lambs, I joined four other gals and drove to La Grande. Arriving late in the evening we hunted up the official Sesquicentennial Wagon Train encampment. Marilyn Goebel, Jan Bailey, Scotty Doyle, Uhlie (visiting from Germany) and I pitched our tents and threw down our sleeping bags there at the edge of the encampment, and hit the hay early. We had to be ready to roll...'er, walk, at 7 a.m. sharp.

After such a long day at the fair, I was tired but too excited to sleep. I lay on my back peering through the open tent flap at a luminous moon slipping through velvet-piled clouds. We camped at the edge of a large grassy field, and the warm smell of August was all around.

August 10—Trail Journal, Day One—We awoke just at dawn and, with a chill breeze blowing, dressed in our long prairie dresses, aprons and bonnets. We wore hiking boots. Hurriedly we stashed our sleeping gear in the van and hunted up the cook tent for breakfast.

Soon we were waiting with other pioneers in bonnets and long dresses. Children, some very young, clung to their mothers' skirts or rode in the covered wagons. Men clad in buckskins, wearing black hats and cotton pants held up with suspenders, walked or rode horseback. One woman, wearing a long dress and bonnet, rode a mule.

We take our place behind the riders, who are positioned behind the covered (horse- and mule-drawn) wagons. It is chilly, with a breeze still blowing, at precisely 7 a.m. when the wagon master yells "Wagons Ho!" Then the creak of wagon wheels and the snorting of horses signals the beginning of our trek through the Blue Mountains along the Oregon

Trail. We leave the valley of the Grande Ronde via the highway between Island City and the freeway ramp to Pendleton.

We walk right along, as we are told to maintain a 3.5 mph pace to keep up with the horses. It makes quite a sight as the covered wagons wind up over the overpass and head up I-84 through the cut into the Blue Mountains. We look across at the steep hillside and ridge to where the actual Oregon Trail went, and try to envision them yoking several oxen to the wagons and pulling them, one by one, up that steep hill.

The brisk walking warms our blood and the sun burns down on the hot pavement. With just a hint of fall in the air, we notice the nine bark beginning to redden on the opposite hill. We walk along gazing down upon the Grande Ronde River glinting in the morning sunlight. We ponder at Hilgard and see in our mind's eye the wagons descending that slope. If we don't maintain that 3.5 mph pace, a "sag wagon" will pick us up and deposit us at the beginning of the walkers. I don't want this to happen, so I keep up the grueling speed.

We begin to climb and the sun burns down with more intensity. I drink lots of water to keep from dehydrating. At 10:30 the wagons come to a halt, and we rest and eat our sack lunches in a wide spot off the road, against a rock cliff, shadeless, treeless and hot. We sit on the hot gravel and rocks, but get little rest. After filling our water bottles at the water truck, we trudge onward and upward. Traffic has been diverted to the left lane, and we have the right for the wagon train.

Far ahead I can see Scotty, age 73, in the lead. Her walking stick clicks against the pavement. She has been walking six miles every morning for months. Marilyn has been picked up by the sag wagon and waves, smiling at us as she passes. Uhlie, Jan and I keep bravely on in this dreadful heat.

We meet many interesting people walking along. An old man from Vermont has hiked the Appalachian trail; a young woman from England will walk all the way to Oregon City. Men, women and children have come from all over the country, who, for their own personal reasons, want to walk this portion of the trail. Some of the wagons and the older man from Vermont have traveled the entire way from the Wyoming border. They are trail toughened, but we are not, except for Scotty.

We begin the long ascent of Spring Creek hill and the end of 15 miles. At the end of our first day on the trail, I am nursing a big blister. The hot pavement, the fast pace and the heat are taking their toll on my feet. Regretfully, I give in—and climb into one of the sag wagons.

Just another quarter mile to Spring Creek and camp. Jan joins me. Uhlie and Marilyn are in another vehicle. Scotty arrives tired and happy, on foot. We are now in the Wallowa Whitman National Forest, in the heart of the Blue Mountains. Hot, dusty and tired, I ride the shuttle bus back to La Grande, where I drive my car forward to the Spring Creek camp. Looking out the window of the bus, it is hard to imagine we walked all those miles.

We make camp not far from some actual wagon ruts of the original Oregon Trail. Jan and I wait in line for a hot shower, provided by the wagon train. Shower stalls with hot water in a long truck, labeled *Oregon Trail '93*. Refreshed and band-aided on my bloody blister, I join Jan, Uhlie, Scotty and Marilyn for supper: hamburgers and all the fixin's.

Then the fun part, an evening program near the circle-up of wagons. We sit in the grass on an open hillside under tall Ponderosa pines. We listen as a historian tells about the section of the trail we will travel tomorrow, and are entertained by three sheepmen, permittees on this forest allotment for 30 years. They obviously work to improve the environment, as the area is not overgrazed and appears natural-looking.

The men sing Irish ballads into the night; all lyrics have the word whiskey in them. Our eyes droop and because dawn will come all too soon, we troop off to our camp in the nearby woods. Snug in my tent, I ponder on the early travelers and how, here in the Blue Mountains, they wrote in their journals about hearing cougar and seeing bear and elk, how they had traveled over a thousand miles across sage and plain, how they must have welcomed these trees. We'd been told that this wagon train had traveled from the Wyoming border 640 miles, 190 of those miles in Oregon. This was their 46th day on the trail.

August 11—Trail Journal, Day Two—I slept fitfully and awake before dawn to a cold, dew-laden morning. Once again I slip into my long dress, apron and bonnet, soiled now from sweat and dust of the trail, pull up tent stakes, load gear in van, and put Scotty's tennis shoes on over my blister. Together the five of us walk up to the cook tent for breakfast.

The song "Trail of Dreams," sung last night by Charlie Rose, who wrote songs commemorating the Oregon Trail, wanders through my mind this morning. *2,000 miles of restless hunger... destiny lay westward.*

Emigrant Springs in the Blue Mountains

Leaving Mark Twain (Mark McKinley) holding sway around the campfire, we stumble off through the woods to our tents and sleeping bags. The night is mild and a sky full of stars blinks through openings in the pines. We are careful lest we walk into a tethered mule or one of the work horses used to pull the covered wagons. We hear their snorting and stomping, but in the dark cannot see them. Earlier, from the campfire, we heard the tap-tap of a horse-shoe hammer as one of the riders, perhaps, was resetting a shoe. Looking heavenward at those jillions of stars, waiting for one to fall, I wish I weren't so sleepy, for there is supposed to be a meteor shower tonight. Once in my tent, I curl up and close my eyes, thinking I'll wake in the middle of the night and then watch the falling stars. Marilyn and "Uhlie" sleep outside, Scotty continues to sleep in the van, and Jan has her tent pitched near mine. Just drifting off into dreamland when (after the campfire program ends) I awaken to a great swishing and zipping, followed by the pounding of tent pegs.

Newcomers joining the wagon train tomorrow are pitching their tents. All around us. Tired children fuss, parents try to shush them, flashlight beams swoop here and there, until what seems like hours, all is still...and the stars fall, silently. Only Marilyn is awake to see them.

After a short but sound sleep, the noises of the night repeat themselves, as these new wagon train participants must register by 5:30 a.m., as we did in La Grande. Their children protest at being dressed by flashlight, tents are zipped and folded, car doors bang and wake up the mules and horses, who bray and whinny. We give up sleeping. It is now day three.

August 12—Trail Journal, Day Three—Emigrant Springs Camp in the Blue Mountains As daylight peeps through the pines, we see that the tents pitched last night around us are gone without us ever having seen them. Surprise! I am not stiff or sore. My blister is raw, but moccasins solve that problem. Am I becoming "trail toughened"? That, I muse, must be how those thousands of emigrants walked 2,000 miles—they became hardened to the trail. Those who didn't, fell by the wayside. "A grave for every mile!"

Soon we, too, pulled up stakes, threw our camping gear into the van and drove, without breakfast, to an area along the route on the Umatilla Indian Reservation. In a clearing in the trees we spotted a member of the Umatilla tribe on horseback waiting to participate in a "friendly protest" confrontation with the wagon train. Dressed in his beautiful beadwork, buckskin and feathers, mounted on his horse on his own land, with the early morning light sifting through the pines.

We walked up a gravel road along the route the wagon train would soon be making on its way for the ceremony. The sight from Vista Point was breathtaking. Blue vistas stretched as far as we could see beyond a wooded canyon; faded hues of blue separations of mountain ranges that led the eye to the far-off Montana Bitterroots. The fresh coolness of an August morning wafted to us the seasonal smells of dry grass and sage. We savored the immense, all-pervading quiet.

The Indians rode silently through tall pines and soon the first covered wagons, drawn by puffing oxen teams, lurched up the steep hill. Wagons were halted, horseback riders gathered round, and then the walkers.

I did my photographing before the ceremony took place. Somehow it didn't seem right to photograph during such a solemn moment. To me those news media people with their huge cameras seemed out of place there. What a world we live in now. Will people sitting in front of the TV, know what this is really like? This time and place, here in the Blue Mountains, and the scene it is recreating from the past?

Antone Minthorn told us how Washington, DC, has denied the Umatillas their interpretive center, so they can tell their story, about their heritage, their culture. It was a moving ceremony that opened with an Indian prayer spoken in the native tongue. The rising sun lit the beautiful colored feathers, the bead work, and the handsome, strong faces of the Umatillas. Then the wagon master and the tribal leader smoked the peace pipe. The sun rose higher in a clear blue sky and the day warmed.

"Like they did 150 years ago," spoke the wagon master, "the Indians will help us get off this hill." And with those words the teams began to pull the covered wagons, and the train was again in motion. As those wagons rolled over the gravel, a fine sun-stirred dust sifted through the pines, and the wagon train made its way quickly down the old road.

Scotty and I joined the walkers, walking to where the train headed off toward the Longhouse fields at Mission and the next camp. Feeling great, still wearing my moccasins, I wanted to continue all the way to Oregon City, but I had signed us up for only two days in the Blue Mountains. Besides, we still hadn't eaten breakfast. We were hungry.

Our adventure was over. Scotty and I met Jan, Uhlie and Marilyn back at the van, and I drove us back over the Blues to La Grande, back to the valley of the Grande Ronde, where we had begun our trek. Again we marveled at the distance traveled on foot. Now we understood how those early emigrants made it. They simply did it, as we had. Awakening each morning, doing what had to be done, the best we knew how. Some survived, a great many did not.

"A grave for every mile," sang out the words of Charlie Rose's song being played on the tape deck in the van, Uhlie's gift to me, purchased at the wagon train camps... "2,000 miles of restless hunger," "The trail of dreams."

Because of those who went before, we live here today. We who traveled only a small part of that famous trail will never forget or fail to respect those early travelers and our own forefathers. At Denny's in La Grande, we order big breakfasts all around and recount our experiences through the Blue Mountains before heading back to our own country, to a land by-passed by the Oregon Trail. Due in part to its geographic isolation, the Wallowa country would not be settled by white homesteaders until the 1870s.

Back we traveled to our homes, where we modern-day pioneers have chosen to emigrate, to live, and to raise our families. For me, returning meant coming home to company, raspberries, CattleWomen and Stockgrowers' doin's, grandchildren, family gatherings, peas to pick, shell and freeze, and hours spent behind this typewriter.

Then it rained and thundered in the mountains, and I recalled the wagon train. Where were they now? I washed the trail dust from my long prairie dress, bonnet and apron, and hung them on the line to flutter in a clean, rain-washed breeze. My blister slowly healed and I am left with wonderful memories, not only of the wagon train itself, but of those special people walking the trail. Somehow, all alike, in that we were living a dream.

August 17—Back on the ranch, our county fair is history, as is the annual CattleWomen's meeting and Stockgrowers' dinner-dance. Our raspberries continue to ripen along with the gooseberries, pie cherries, and huckleberries. Our company has gone home and we are eating newly dug red potatoes from the garden, as well as peas, cabbage and beets. I've frozen some of the first ripe peas, canned bush cherry jelly, frozen raspberry jam and peas.

Now it is raining again, and it snowed in the mountains yesterday. There is a feeling of fall in the air already, and our maple tree's leaves are beginning to turn. Our brief, beautiful and frantic summer is all but over.

August 25—There is frost here on Prairie Creek this morning. Hough's sprinklers leave glittering ice paths on the alfalfa.

September, my month, is nearly here.

August 31—The wine bright days of Indian summer are upon us. And what lovely days they are! After a summer of storms, which brought cool and unseasonable weather, perhaps we'll have a glorious fall. A full moon will rise tonight, which will make the second full moon in August the blue moon. There wasn't even any frost this morning, only a heavy dew that sparkled along the ditch banks.

It snowed in the mountains last week. Backcountry campers got cold, among them a group encamped up Hurricane Creek, near where that trail connects with the Lakes Basin at Moccasin Lake. That they were not happy campers came via an SOS call over a short wave radio. If someone was riding in, could they please bring blankets, gloves and a hot water bottle?

Linde's husband, Pat, who works for Jim Steen (a Wallowa County backcountry outfitter) would be helping move that camp to Frazier Lake on Thursday, and since the nights were still very cold, he wondered if maybe Linde could ride in with the requested warm gear. Linde called me Wednesday evening, asking if I would like to ride in with her.

Because I had spent all of that day making sauerkraut, and pickling beets, and had my column typed and in the mail, I said, "Why not!"

Thursday morning found the two of us riding up the West Fork of the Wallowa River into the wilderness. We looked a sight! Linde had layered the blankets under her saddle. She looked like something straight out of "the Arabian Nights." Both of us carried packs on our backs while mounted on our horses. Behind my saddle, rolled up in a heavy jacket and slicker, was my bedroll. In Linde's pack rode the gloves and hot water bottle. Mine contained lots of clothes (to wear to bed) and a toothbrush. My saddle bags held a bottle of water and a package of trail mix.

It was a morning made in heaven: sunny, clear, frosty, crisp and tingling with fall. My mare walked up the trail as if she had done it all summer. Wild purple asters grew alongside the trail, and sunlight spilled down upon huge patches of goldenrod. Ripe huckleberries, thimble berries, and wild raspberries grew close enough to pick from the saddle.

The trail followed the rushing white waters of the West Fork, into which flowed various smaller streams that our horses splashed through. There wasn't a cloud in the sky, and we sang songs to the accompanying clip-clop of our horses' hooves. We gazed up at aspen thickets growing on open mountain sides, rode by the Chief Joseph Trailhead, and, after three miles, and passed the Ice Lake cutoff.

We rode through thick spruce, and across rock slides where several elusive pikas scolded us. We clumped across old wooden bridges that spanned other creeks flowing out of the mountain snowbanks. We pulled into Six-Mile Meadow around 1:30, dismounted, nibbled on a light lunch from our saddle bags, and rested.

Around 3 p.m. the approaching pack string, consisting of five guests and the crew, splashed across the West Fork into Six-Mile Meadow. Pat was pulling four mules, as was Shelly Steen. Counting mules and saddle horses, it made quite a string of animals. I guess there's nothing prettier than a pack string going down the trail in the Wallowas. After breaking camp up Hurricane Creek, they had ridden through the high Lakes Basin.

Because of the continuing cold nights, it was decided to make camp at Eight-Mile Meadow rather than Frazier Lake. This proved to be an adventure for me, as I hadn't been any farther up the West Fork than Six-Mile Meadow, when I cooked for Manford Isley's pack outfit one September nearly 17 years ago.

Linde and I fell in behind that pick string, riding our mares, looking like a cross between a dude and a mule. We were a welcome sight to those unhappy campers. For the next two nights they would sleep warmly. Jim Steen's daughter-in-law, Shelly, 24, slim and pretty, led off through the trees, crossed the river and pulled in to an opening near a meadow bordered by a meandering stream.

This would be camp. The opening provided a breathtaking view of the high mountain range to the east. Water trickled down over the granite formations, seeping from under melting snowbanks that glistened in the late afternoon sunlight. There followed such a flurry of activity.

While Pat tended to the pack and saddle animals, Shelly began setting up ridge poles for the large wall tent that would serve as a cook tent. Marilyn, Brenda, Linde and I also pitched in to help set up camp. We set up folding tables, a butane stove, arranged pack boxes around the inside of the tent. Mules were hobbled and turned loose to graze, horses were tied to a tie line strung between trees, until it was their turn to graze. Coolers containing food were dug into and supper was started, wood was gathered for the campfire.

By the time our sleeping tents were pitched, the sun had gone down over the high western mountain and a bitter chill filled our meadow. We built the fire up with huge chunks of dead wood, donned jackets and gloves and kept on working. Linde and I helped the kitchen crew and soon the spaghetti was ready. Then the water was heated, and I did the dishes. Outside, the moon rose and filled the sky with cold light. The horses grazed, the mules brayed, and the fire crackled. It was home!

In my tent I put on everything I'd brought along: long johns, jeans, sweat pants, three sweat shirts, down vest, ski mask, gloves and a warm scarf around my neck. Then I crawled into my light sleeping bag and zipped up my one-man tent. I wasn't cold, but a heavy frost began to cover everything outside. The stars were so bright, and there were so many.

I was up at 6, still bundled to the teeth, letting my shivering mare graze the frosted meadow and drink. Soon Pat got a fire going, and Shelly and Brenda started breakfast. Marilyn wrangled and saddled horses and mules. Linde and I helped wherever we could. We ate hunched over the warmth of the campfire, and after the dishes were done, we took off up the trail to explore even higher country.

Pat led a pack mule that carried lunch. We were headed to Frazier Lake and more adventure. The dudes, feeling much better now thanks to more blankets, gloves and the requested hot water bottle, were all in a good mood, and it was a lovely morning again. We rode through thick lodgepole thickets and then broke out into areas of rock slides bordered by high meadows and quaking aspen.

The sun warmed. Brilliant Indian paintbrush and every type of wildflower there ever was flourished in that Alpine zone. Higher and higher we climbed, our horses' hooves clattering over the rocky trail. We crossed and recrossed water in this "land of winding water." The sound of rushing water was forever in our ears as most of it roared over falls and fell from hundreds of feet above from the last snowbanks.

We rode past a weathered sign, *Polaris Trail,* and noticed a dim trail leading off through high ferns and wildflowers. High above we could see the traversing trail that led to the top of Polaris Pass, all in solid, loose rock. Higher still, alongside the West Fork, we looked down upon a snow bridge, where the river disappeared and reappeared under a huge bank of snow.

In the openings grew the wild blue delphinium, higher than our horses' heads. Then Frazier Lake appeared, fringed by wildflower meadows and Engelmann spruce, peaceful, calm, and sparkling in sunlight. We splashed across boggy meadows laced with watercress and came to the trail again. We passed the Glacier Lake cutoff, and came to Little Frazier Lake. Here grew the blue gentian and pink elephant heads and pink and white heather bells.

We rode up the long zig-zag trail to Hawkins Pass and looked down upon the South Fork of the Imnaha, right where it is born. Upward towered the massive mountains, still wearing snow. We crossed several large snowbanks on the way up, Hawkins Pass having just recently been opened. We ate lunch there in the pass on this perfectly lovely day, at 8,400 feet elevation, before returning to the Glacier Lake cutoff. While the crew returns to camp with the dudes, Pat, Linde and I ride up that steep trail to Glacier Lake.

The ride up that wild trail to the lake and to the summit of Glacier Pass cannot be adequately described. Mere words fail. There at 8,200 feet at the lake, we gape and stare at one of the loveliest sights we'll ever see, on one of the nicest days we'll ever have in the Wallowas. At 8,500-foot

Glacier Pass, our horses stop to catch their breath, and we gaze down toward Moccasin Lake.

It is late evening when we reach camp, but we agree the effort was worth it We'll never forget this day.

September 7—Through the screen door in the front room I can see Hough's two large "bread loaf" hay stackers at work. A cloud of alfalfa smoke pours forth from their backs as they roar up and down the field across the road, on this hot September afternoon. Unlike those wet first cuttings, these second cuttings are going up beautifully.

The lack of morning frost and hardly any dew are making this seem like the summer we never had. All the farmers are smiling. Haying in our valley is such a beautiful operation; that is, when the weather cooperates.

Nowadays there are so many ways of putting up hay. Here on our ranch we continue with the conventional bales, but many others have resorted to more modern methods. Driving around the valley you'll see round bales, large compressed bales, and the bread loaf stacks, like in the fields of our neighbors, the Houghs.

The stacks I like best are on our Prairie Creek neighbor's ranch, where Hank Bird continues to put up his hay loose, as the early settlers did. Cutting, raking and stacking the loose hay into long loose stacks, with a farm hand on his tractor. To me, this method makes sense. Low overhead, easy to feed, if you don't have to transport the hay, and, too, they lend a pastoral touch to the agricultural area of Prairie Creek.

Hank Bird's long stacks also remind us that the early settlers put up their hay with swing pole derricks powered by horses. All over Eastern Oregon these Jenkins stackers stand as sentinels in the fields, while modern practices go on all around them. I love to see the stackers, but one of these days they will wither away.

I once visited an old equipment show in Baker City, where an old man had reconstructed a miniature model of a working derrick, an ingenious invention that worked for many years. They were made strong, too, proven by the fact that they have lasted through many Eastern Oregon winters. In his youth, the old man hayed with horses and a swing pole derrick.

A small sprig of snowberry reposes in a bottle on the kitchen table as I type, a reminder of our recent Labor Day "mini-vacation" on the upper reaches of the Imnaha River. When I look at the small white snowberries hanging there in clusters on the branch, I am transported back to sitting on a stump above the rushing waters of the river, reading a book; no phone, no TV, no pressing ranch duties, no community responsibilities, just the soothing sound of the river, the company of my dog Daisy, and the snowberries, with the warm morning smell of ponderosa pine, and autumn waiting in the wings.

Doug and I took off that Friday afternoon. I drove the pickup and he the mini-motor home. We headed up Little Sheep Creek to Salt Creek summit, down past Lick Creek and on toward Gumboot. At the bottom of Gumboot we turned up the Imnaha River and encamped at a favorite spot along the river above Ollokot. I just love Wallowa County place names. They all have stories.

After setting up our picnic table and lawn chairs, we both relaxed for the first time in weeks. I had brought along Teresa Jordan's new book, *Riding the White Horse Home*, which I highly recommend to all ranch wives. Until recent years, Teresa, a fourth generation rancher, has lived the life she writes about. Her country was the Iron Mountain country in Wyoming, but it could be any remote ranch in the West.

She writes so honestly about her family in such a sensitive way, a way that we who still live on ranches and make our sole living as ranchers can identify with. It is gratifying to read the works of a talented contemporary writer who represents the less than two percent of us still in agriculture.

There on the upper Imnaha, however, our ranch seemed almost non-existent. Ben, who is leasing our cattle this year, has every thing under control, and Doug and I help only where necessary. The seed potatoes will be ready to harvest around the first of October, and demand much intensive care.

We had looked forward to getting away, a little grouse hunting, camping, and exploring new country. In a county as vast as ours, we need only to jump into the four-wheel-drive and take off. Adventure awaits.

We were up at dawn Saturday morning, driving up around McGraw, hunting for grouse. Nary a bird did we see, not even a feather, and no scratchings or any sign at the springs. Nothing. But did we ever "limit out" on huckleberries! In less than half an hour we had nearly a quart, enough for sourdough hotcakes for the next two mornings.

It was late in the morning when we returned to camp, where I mixed up those pancakes and fried some of our fresh pork sausage and eggs. I can still taste that breakfast, eaten in the fresh air there above the river. We spent our days just lazing around, reading, hiking. Doug did a little gold panning, and I did a little fishing. Nothing serious.

Family and friends stopped in, visited and had supper with us. Linde and Pat were there Saturday evening, having camped up at Indian Crossing, where they were repairing fences and corrals for Jim Steen's outfitters service before hunting season. We barbecued steaks, mushrooms, peppers and corn on the cob over the outside grill. We feasted also on sliced Imnaha tomatoes left by daughter Jackie and her family, and blackberry cobbler, baked at home.

On Sunday evening, a friend stopped by with an old client of Doug's from the days when he operated a guide service from his Dug Bar Ranch. Lynn had come every hunting season to Dug Bar for 15 years. We invited them to supper that night.

Over grilled lamb chops, we were very entertained by the two of them recounting old "hunting stories" of an era that is no more on the Snake River. That wonderful system of private ranches is now included in the National Recreation Area, and the Snake rolls on, as do the stories that have been told of its history.

Sunday morning found us back up on McGraw, turning down the road that led to the old fire lookout. The road dead-ended four miles farther, but the drive over ruts and rocks was worth it. Five head of elk appeared in front of us, then disappeared, in the way of wild things, into the brush. We parked at the road's end and stared out at those miles of unpeopled places.

The fresh morning air hummed with insects there in the first rays of the rising sun. Feed was everywhere this year, owing to the summer rains, but we saw no sign of livestock, which seemed odd. Even the elk would prefer to have cattle grazing the area, for they like nibbling the tender shoots that sprout after cattle have grazed. The tall, rank grasses have no appeal for them.

We walked up past a salt lick to a high ridge, and peered down at the backwaters of Hells Canyon Dam far below, almost obscured by autumnal haze and the sheer distance of Hells Canyon. It was so quiet. We stopped later to read a weathered sign that told how Captain Bonneville and his party had crossed the Divide there after making their laborious way up from the Snake River and crossing over into the Imnaha. In the dead of winter! They had left Boise on Christmas Day 1833, 100 years before I was born.

We stopped short of a locked gate where only horseback riders or hikers could proceed. Beyond lay a vast country beckoning: P.O. Saddle, Barton Heights, the old Marks cabin, Freezeout. Someday we'll return.

September 14—All I could see were two long, pointed white ears with dark spots on them, and a young boy riding behind those ears. Seating capacity had been quickly filled and there was standing room only at this year's annual horse and mule auction at Hells Canyon Mule Days. To my left, amid this throng of standing humanity, a hand shot up, bidding.

The hand was Doug's. I wondered what was going on. He hadn't mentioned anything about buying a mule. The bids were all in. *Sold.* The ears and the boy disappeared behind a heavy swinging door...and we owned a mule.

After returning to the Mule Days dance for a few dances, we left for the ranch. It was raining. The next morning dawned cold and windy, and fresh snow blanketed the Wallowas. Driving into Enterprise to haul home Doug's purchase, I wondered if this "ghost mule" was a molly or a john.

Doug pulled the bill of sale from his pocket, which answered the question. It read: *one white/paint molly mule.*

It was still very windy and cold when Doug walked to a far pen to find, halter, and lead our new white mule to the loading ramp. I finally got a good look at her. She had nice feet, legs and withers. She appeared gentle, and sported a few gray spots on a white body. She was seven years old. I named her "Snowberry," which seemed fitting considering the fresh snow on the mountains. On the slopes of the mountains grows a wild berry, known as a snowberry or grouse berry. During the fall, right now in fact, the bushes are covered with small white berries.

And now, as I type, Snowberry seems right at home with Foxy, my young Appaloosa mare. Perhaps this molly mule will help fill the void left by my faithful old mare Cal, who is now in horse heaven. She had ring bone, an incurable disease that made it impossible to keep her for a riding horse.

I'd raised her from a young filly and she carried me over many Wallowa County miles, mostly behind a bunch of cows, trailing from winter to summer range. I ride her daughter Foxy now, but Cal will remain in my heart. She was truly a faithful cow-horse, as well as a friend.

There is a heavy frost this morning and the thermometer on the carport registers 26 degrees. The geraniums next to the house survived, but I wonder about the Alder Slope garden. My green beans are just coming on and the corn is not yet mature.

I went up there yesterday simply to enjoy the wildflower patch, which is a riot of golden California poppies, three shades of bachelor buttons,

and colorful Icelandic poppies in shades of red, pink, salmon, orange
and white. Autumnal light drifted over pink cosmos and other flowers
too numerous to mention. My sweet peas climbed the old wooden fence.
Some had been blown down by the wind. I picked a large bouquet and
gave it to my friend Grace, and said goodbye to summer.

I canned sauerkraut this morning, what turned out to be an especially
good batch. The jars sit cooling on the table next to me as I type.

Last week my uncle Marshall, who lives with his wife, Billie, at
South Lake Tahoe, called to wish me a happy birthday. Marshall is very
interested in stargazing and has an observatory of sorts in his home. He
said that on the 13th and 14th, Venus, the morning star, would be doing
a "dance," and if I wanted to see this, I should arise at 5:30 each morning
and see for myself.

Uncle Marshall was right. On the morning of the 13th, Venus was
situated very brightly under the waning moon. And this morning, the
14th, Venus twinkled high above the small fingernail moon. A very lovely
sight! A few minutes later and clouds covered them both, as daylight
seeped into the dawn sky. I don't know what caused this third brightest
heavenly body to act this way, but who cares?

Also on the 13th, I arose in the middle of the night to see the northern
lights, another wonder of the universe that makes our earthly struggles
seem small in comparison.

On my 41st birthday, while cooking for a dude outfit camped at
Horseshoe Lake, I hiked alone to Razz Lake. In 15 minutes I had caught
my limit of trout on a fly line, the only visitor to that high, remote lake
on that September 9.

On my 57th birthday I bought a mule.

On my 58th birthday, Linde and I climbed 8,874-foot Ruby Peak; and
on my 60th, last week, she and I rode to Aneroid Lake. Next year we
have set our sights on Sacajawea Mountain, which has been our goal
since climbing Ruby Peak, but somehow our plans always went astray.
Part of the fun of living is arising each morning with something to look
forward to. I'm betting next year we'll get the job done.

It was another one of those warm fall days when Linde and I unloaded
our horses at the trailhead above Wallowa Lake. Soon we were riding up
the steep trail to Aneroid Lake and entering the wilderness, where we
left the noisy effects of man behind and appreciated the solitude. Indian
paintbrush, ripe huckleberries, thimble berries, snowberries, wild blue
asters, and surprise syringa still bloomed along the trail.

We rode through high meadows with creeks wandering through
them, always amid the sound of rushing water. We passed Roger Lake,

a small clear jewel surrounded by trees, and finally came into view of Aneroid Lake, sparkling in sunshine.

We tied our horses to the hitching rack in an old log corral. Then we found some wooden weathered chairs to sit in and stared out at the rugged mountain. Patches of winter snow still clung to crevices that filled steep talus slopes. A small creek raced through a wildflower meadow into the lake. Linde produced a fine lunch and we ate and relaxed in that quiet setting. Then we visited old "Silvertip's" cabins. Lots of history here.

Many years ago, Charles Seeber came to Wallowa County because his father thought the altitude might cure his tuberculosis. Seeber settled at Aneroid Lake when he was a young man, and did ultimately spend many years there. He was not only cured, but lived to a ripe old age. After his bushy head of hair turned quite gray, he was to carry the nickname Silvertip.

Silvertip developed the Aneroid Lake area, making it into an outstanding resort in its day. He built all the cabins, which stand to this day, which is even more remarkable because all building materials had to be brought in by pack mule. He fashioned chairs, tables and other furniture using materials at hand, mainly logs. Logs stood on end were made into steps. The cabins sport hand-hewn shakes and the logs are as sturdy today as the day they were built.

The supplies were packed in with a pack string, and Silvertip rented out the cabins and operated a store there. Today it is owned by a private company and maintained in such a way as to be a credit to the owner. It is a fine example of how deeded land in the wilderness can be managed properly, enhancing the wilderness itself by being there. Red's Horse Ranch on the Minam and the Minam Lodge are other good examples.

Today, Silvertip's dream and his fine handiwork stand to remind the younger generation of what one man can do. This is a remarkable tribute to mankind, and should be left as it is, to enjoy. The only visitors we saw were a couple celebrating their 25th wedding anniversary, reading quietly down by the lake. We hadn't met a single person on the trail, as we rode the six miles out to Wallowa Lake and returned home.

That evening, my family surprised me with an outdoor barbecue up at Pat and Linde's place.

September 20—My kitchen is a potpourri of autumn this morning: sauerkraut in the canner, applesauce simmering, huckleberry buckle in the oven, and a large crock of seven-day sweet pickles adds its spicy, vinegary odor to the mix. Cloudy and cold weather makes inside tasks more appealing this morning. My typewriter stares at me, but I'm more in the mood to putter in the kitchen.

After gathering up a box of windfalls from our old, gnarled apple tree, I spent a good part of the morning peeling them. Peeling apples allows for good thinking time, and through the kitchen window I can contemplate the soft light filtering through the reddening young maple's leaves. Recent frosts have caused them to turn overnight.

I can take time to enjoy the little birds flitting in and out of the raspberry patch. One small wren flies directly to the window sill, perches there a minute, cocks his head and stares right at me. For an instant we communicated. Beyond the raspberry patch rises East Peak Mt. Howard and Bonneville. Silent sentinels, named after a general and a captain who trod here so long ago.

I think about how swiftly the years have passed, are passing, and how much I enjoy these seasonal changes, how much they affect me in a positive way. How sad, it seems to me, that many people become so wrapped up in today's accelerated world that they scarcely know what season we're in.

Taking time to contemplate and enjoy nature is, to me, one of the joys of living. It is, in fact, living. Rushing here and there certainly isn't. The huckleberry buckle, by the way, was a variation of Ellen Stevenson's recipe in a recent Agri-Times. Wonderful! The sauerkraut fermented in its golden juice in a crock in the basement and turned out to be an especially good batch this year. Crisp and salted just right.

The apples on this old tree are an unknown variety, planted long ago by an early homesteader, but they cook up into the most wonderful applesauce. The seven-day sweet pickles are a recipe that I've used for years. No fail. But they do take time and patience. Today I will boil the spicy syrup to pour over them, and on Wednesday I will can them. These are old-fashioned tasks, performed rituals of autumn.

The heavy frosts deepen, and soon I shall have to dig the keeping onions, dry them in the sun, and store them in the basement for winter use. The corn didn't quite make it, but there are enough kernels to feed the pheasants and quail, which need food too.

The sunflowers grew and grew. They must be 11 feet tall or more. Their brilliant yellow blooms follow the sun until their heads become too heavy, and then they simply droop with the effort. They, too, will provide seeds for the birds this winter.

We are enjoying the new red potatoes, which are growing quite large, and the beets, carrots and parsnips. The squash, green beans and nasturtiums have succumbed to the killing frosts, as has the blazing, glorious wildflower patch. What joy it brought to all who saw it. I tried to capture its brief beauty on film, but somehow a photo can't do it justice.

The sweet peas have withered along the wooden fence, and the lovely pink cosmos are blackened by frost. Having a garden teaches us so much about birth, life, and death. It happens so easily, no fanfare: here today, gone tomorrow. It also teaches hope, as new seeds spring from the old in the spring, and spring is eternal, as eternal as the equinox, which will have happened before I finish typing this column.

Last week was special. Rosalie Sorrels spent last Thursday night with us. This wonderful lady, born the same year I was, who just turned 60 herself, is Idaho's famous folk singer. Rosalie is known as the "Travelin' Lady," and she has been captivating regional, national and international audiences for three decades. She is a great one-woman show with her storytelling and singing talent, and her humanness. Perhaps that is the reason for her success: she relates to people from all walks of life.

Her book *Way Out in Idaho* is a wonderful collection of songs and stories about Idaho, and she has made and sold albums and tapes. She lives very simply, in a cabin built by her father along Grimes Creek, which is near Idaho City. I met Rosalie at one of our Fishtrap Writer's conferences, and she made a lasting impression on me. I've enjoyed her books and played her tapes often.

Rosalie and I talked non-stop while I prepared dinner of fresh garden vegetables and steak that Thursday evening, and then she and Doug and I continued with that conversation all through dinner. She told us that her birthday party lasted two weeks and 200 people came. Does that tell you something about her personality? People pitched their tents near her cabin or brought trailers. They barbecued, sang around the campfire and visited. She cooked for them on an old wood cookstove that sits outside with a roof over it.

Many friends make their way to Rosalie's remote cabin, and I can see why. Doug and I attended her performance at the OK Theater that evening. Those who couldn't make it missed a great show, a unique show.

The next morning was such a lovely one, all blue and gold with sunshine and crisp with frost, so I took Rosalie up to the garden to see the wildflower patch, not yet blackened, and to meet Bill. She loved it. After days on the road, it relaxed her to get out into the country among its people. Rosalie left with her guitar, and a bouquet of flowers given to her at last night's performance. She drove alone in her car over the mountains to Kennewick, where she was scheduled for a book-signing that evening.

More company drove in from Portland, so I fixed lunch, all the while trying to pack my suitcase to leave at 12:30 for Spokane. Linde arrived, busy herself trying to leave, and we picked up daughter Ramona and granddaughter Carrie, and were finally off.

By 8 p.m. we were seated in the Spokane Opera House watching "Cats," a wonderful musical and dance production based on *Old Possum's Book of Practical Cats* by T.S. Eliot. What a life: one night Rosalie Sorrels at the OK Theater, the next Cats.

We had so enjoyed our drive through the lovely, golden Palouse hills. The grain had been harvested, leaving golden fields surrounded by neat, tidy farms that lay connected to quiet towns. After being swept into Spokane with its crowds of humanity and traffic, we were overjoyed to find our motel would be relatively quiet and situated along the river.

The Cavanaugh River Inn was lovely; petunias, marigold, impatiens, zinnias and bright red geraniums blazed from flower beds surrounded by well-kept lawns. We ate dinner outside on a patio fenced away from wild Canada honkers and domestic ducks and geese, who entertained us while we ate. The river swept past and the growing city was visible on the opposite bank.

The Spokane riverfront is undergoing a facelift. We were able to walk the few blocks from the inn to the opera house, across a lovely bridge that spanned the river, to Riverfront Park, where more flowers and maple trees lined the pathways. None of us had ever been to Spokane before and this introduction was truly a treat.

The next morning we ate breakfast at the International House of Pancakes, then stumbled onto an open air country market where we wandered among booths of local gardeners' beautiful, fresh bounty. Such a colorful place: freshly picked peaches, apples, plums, tomatoes, onions, herbs, squash, green beans, watermelon, loaves of bread and delicious rolls, ethnic foods, and even musicians playing. Among the heads of dill and cauliflower were mounds of freshly picked sweet corn. I purchased some to take home, and it proved to be most delicious.

September 29—If it weren't for cottonwood leaves turning yellow, blackbirds flocking together, golden grain falling to the harvester, my frost-killed flowers, and potato digging in progress, one might wonder if we were not in the middle of summer. Recent afternoon temperatures have soared into the high 70s and mornings, although cool, have lacked any frost for nearly a week now. The air is balmy, dry and still. There are no clouds to mar the bluest of skies. It's almost like September is holding its breath for October.

Days such as this frustrate me. I am miserable with longing to flee to the mountains, to wander around in their glorious midst during these rare days of Indian summer. However, life doesn't always let one do what they want, when they want. Other commitments come first.

Succumbing to this wanderlust last Saturday morning, however, Helen, Scotty and I, thanks to Helen's planning, I were soon swaying along as we were pulled steadily up in our Wallowa Lake Tramway gondola cage to the top of 8,150-foot Mt. Howard. With our lunches tucked in our day packs, we had not a care in the world; the lovely day stretched before us.

Wallowa Lake came into view first, encircled by its perfect moraines, followed by the awesome peaks composing the drainages of the West Fork of the Wallowa River. The vast county we live in sprawled below. Beyond the lake lay the small towns of Joseph and Enterprise, flanked by the rolling prairie hills out north and the gradual slopes of the Wallowas to the west. The long, narrow valley, sandwiched between mountain and plateau, disappeared into hazy blue horizons.

Mt. Joseph, with its constantly eroding sides, exhibited a different character than the one seen through my kitchen window. A few patches of winter snow clung stubbornly to clefts in the mountain's massive slopes. We could see lakeside activities far below, including the annual Alpenfest, become insignificant amid the sheer heights of mountains. Tomorrow would be the last day the gondola would operate this season.

What a glorious day it was, clear enough to see for miles in any direction. After we came to a rather abrupt stop at the terminal, a young man opened our cage door and we stepped out into the rarified air of Mt. Howard. We had been lifted into the alpine zones in 15 minutes. We immediately struck off up a trail, taking in the view of our beautiful country, picking out where each of us lived in that panorama spread below. On some high promontory overlooking those awesome peaks, we munched our lunch and felt as free as an eagle that soared above in the pure, blue sky.

Returning later in the afternoon, we sat on a deck overlooking the valley, sipping cold fruit juices before boarding our car to the lake. Suddenly Helen cried, "Look!" and we followed her gaze below us into the wild eyes of a bobcat. It simply crouched there, watching us descend the mountain.

Earlier last week, friend Grace and I bumped along dirt roads in her Jeep out in the north end of our county, off McCubbin Road, following written directions to Kathy and Jay Hadley's sheep camp. Kathy and her husband work for the Krebs' sheep outfit, and she is the one I did an article about a couple of years ago in the fall, when they were camped in the long meadows that border the north highway. We found their camp with the herder's wagon, the sheep bed ground, and salting place, but no herders or sheep.

Leaving some fresh beets and a cabbage from my garden at the wagon, Grace and I jounced farther on old logging roads looking for Jay and Kathy, with no luck. The roads forked and angled crazily off into the thick timber. We were afraid we might become lost in the maze, so retraced our route back to the Sled Springs work camp and then out to the highway. On the other side of the road we found picnic tables, and here we ate our lunches in the hazy autumn sunshine. There on the breaks of Joseph Canyon, the yellow jackets tried to steal bits of our lunch.

I had left a note at the sheepherder wagon for the returning herders, saying we were sorry we had missed them. A few days later, I received a long letter from Kathy thanking me for the vegetables and wishing she had been there. Kathy is a good letter writer, which is becoming a lost art these days. She writes,

I'm sitting here on an old stump at the edge of McCubbin meadow by my sheep. It's afternoon. The sheep started down off the mountainside and headed for water here. Only there were about 400 head that got down the slope a little different way and wouldn't get through a logjam of lodgepole deadfall.

I had to get around them and chase them back up through the logs to the ridge top. They hit open ground and started to run, scared by the dogs. Tried to send Ginny and Skeeter around the top, and chased after, jumping over belly-high logs on Rog, Kathy's horse. Got around the lead and turned them. Roger hit a hive of bees and got stung and took off bucking. Got the sheep turned down and tried to follow tracks down. The rest of the herd had long since trailed out.

Down through a thicket of Christmas tree-sized lodgepole. A thick green mass of boughs. lodgepole. A thick green mass of boughs. "I could hear my loud brass bell way down in the bottom. Finally got them together again a minute ago and sat down to write a hello to you.

Typical afternoon. Yeah, they're on the march again, and baaaaa-ing. I've got to see where they are heading. Back in a minute.

And then the letter goes on after she returns, telling some of her experiences with coyotes, bears and even a cougar. Kathy is alone a lot with her 1,200 sheep. A pretty awesome responsibility, which she takes seriously. I really enjoyed her long letter. It was just like visiting with her. Some of it she had written that night in the wagon.

I think about her now, out there with her sheep, as I try to write this at my kitchen table with myriad interruptions associated with ranch life and potato digging going on around me. Kathy lives a unique life, and does it well. The Krebses are lucky to have her for a herder. Perhaps later on, in the fall before the sheep are shipped to Ione for the winter, I'll have an opportunity to visit her again.

Various people who read this column find their way to our ranch. Like Wayne and Joann Chambers, who live and farm in Albany, Oregon. They raise peppermint, dill, fescue, wheat, clover, sugar beet seed and filberts. Joann says they enjoy hiking too, and were visiting the eastern part of our state, so decided to look us up.

They left us a box of filberts, which contained recipes for using these delicious hazelnuts, and yesterday I baked a batch of hazelnut cream cheese brownies. Although the recipe took a little time, the result was a delicious cookie, soft and chewy, full of flavor, and loaded with filberts.

The annual mule deer buck season opens Saturday morning, and son Todd has borrowed my mare Foxy to set up camp in the mountains. Hopefully, grandson Josh and he will have a good time this weekend. It is Josh's first year to hunt. How I envy them in their high camp.

September 30—A couple of months ago, a school teacher from nearby Baker County, Sheryle Martin, called to ask if I would mind conducting two one-hour sessions on writing for an outdoor school scheduled at Wallowa Lake around the end of September, with some wonderful school children from Haines and North Powder.

I agreed and, armed with an informal lesson plan, I drove up to the lake yesterday. It was a beautiful drive, as the lake was quiet and all the tourists gone. Yellow cottonwood leaves drifted down upon the blue-green waters as numerous waterfowl made V's in the water. Instead of people and car noises, you could listen to the blue jays and hear the sigh of the wind in the pines.

The children were just returning from a hike when I arrived, and I was a little early so I joined them for a presentation by a meteorologist, who showed a film on flash floods and talked about the weather, after which the students seated themselves on the lodge steps and we held our classroom outside, to talk about their experience outdoors, and about what they had seen on their hike.

I tried to make the students aware of the sights and smells and sounds around them, prompting them to write and think about them.

They listened attentively. I read to them some of my columns, which they seemed to enjoy. I asked the students to tell about themselves, which proved to be entertaining to all.

Today when I drove up, the children greeted me with, "There's that cool lady," and immediately came to sit down on the steps, as quiet as can be, begging me to read to them again, which I did. Then I handed out paper and pencil and asked each girl and boy to write me a story. The children, in their early teens, all took off in different directions and concentrated very hard on writing.

In this age of TV and automated this and that, it is sad to me that today's young people don't write as much as we used to.

One young boy took a long time writing his story. Finally he shyly handed it to me. By Justin B. 9/29/1993,

When I listen to you reading about yourself it's almost like it's happening right in front of me. I feel that way when I read good books also. But only some of them. But your writing makes me feel that way too. When the other people come to talk to us everyone is bored. But when you talk to us everyone is very interested in what you're saying.

Well, thank you, Justin. It was a neat experience for this writer to have met all of you from Haines and North Powder. You are good neighbors and we all enjoy living here in Eastern Oregon. Don't forget what I told you: read, read, read, and write. You can do it! There is a whole new world waiting for you inside the pages of books.

October 2—The seed potato harvest is in its second week and the cellars are filling. Prolonged dry, warm weather has permitted farmers to get their grain harvested and late cuttings of hay are still going up. It has been so hot and dry, in fact, that the fall is beginning to resemble those drought years.

October 4—Indian summer's colorful palette deepens more each day, and the needles of tamaracks growing on the steep mountain slopes begin to lighten. Autumn is for us vagabonds, who have tasted former wild freedoms and become restless to again walk the trails, see new country and satiate our hunger. Goodness, such poetic talk from a ranch wife, but all too soon the cold fall winds will sweep down out of the north, the rains will turn to snow, and the frosts will deepen. Something inside urges, *go now before it is too late!*

Last Saturday morning in the pre-dawn hours, Linde and I answered that call, which led to an adventure that lasted all that day and into the night. At 5:30 a.m., Linde and I were shouldering our day packs and leaving the Hurricane Creek trailhead, our only light from the stars and the moon, swimming far above to the right of Twin Peaks, whose silvery glow illuminated Falls Creek, the quaking aspen thickets, and distant snowbanks overhead.

Soon the roar of the falls could be heard. It was warm. There was no frost, not even any dew. Fallen leaves on the trail crackled underfoot, and tall dry grasses brushed against our legs. We could smell the dampness. The trail was steep and the exertion of walking soon had us shedding our light jackets. Daylight seeped slowly from the east and the valley below, and suddenly Twin Peaks was awash with a golden pink glow, and our moon slid over the Hurricane Divide. Now we could see the yellowing willow thickets bordering Falls Creek as it splashed down from LeGore Lake and the peaks above.

Sacajawea Mountain came into view south and west of us, still in shadow. We switchbacked our way to a mountain mahogany patch, a familiar landmark on the trail to LeGore. I was thankful for my father's often-used walking stick. It was to save my life several times that day and night. We entered a high trembling aspen grove, which led to a tiny creek that tumbled down to join Falls Creek, now far below us. Sunlight crept slowly down the mountain sides and by the time we chugged our way up to the old LeGore cabin we were in the morning sunshine.

"Hey, LeGore," we yelled, "put the kettle on for tea!"

There is little left of the old miner's cabin now, and not even his ghost or his brother's did we see. We didn't have hot tea, but did eat some breakfast from our day packs and take refreshing gulps of water from our bottles, after which we photographed some of the area. Rested, we climbed the steep trail that would be the last real trail on our journey upward. From then on, we knew the country; at least at first, until we got up considerably higher.

We found a small meadow browned by recent frosts, and a few purple-blue gentians provided the only color. Linde startled a lone blue grouse beside the creek. We rested, photographed, and gazed up toward the jumble of giant boulders we would have to pick our way through to yet another, higher basin.

Eventually, gasping for breath, we emerged into that beautiful high meadow, rimmed by high ridges and Sawtooth Peak. Our main goal was to scale that peak, which rose 9,174 feet into the cobalt sky above us. After more gulps of water, we followed the creek until it disappeared underground. We continued along the course of it and knew its source was an enormous snowbank to the south of the basin, where we headed. We climbed up onto that high ridge at its lowest point, angling across loose scree and moving rocks. My walking stick saved me. Linde was the first to reach the ridge top, which was narrow and jagged.

"Oh my golly," she exclaimed, for it was the first time she had seen the other side.

Far below glittered the little potholes below Francis Lake, all blue-green, and beyond stretched the vast drainages of the Lostine. On the horizon were the Elkhorns and the Blues. Because we were so temptingly close to LeGore Lake and Twin peaks, I suggested we climb father up along the high, rocky ridge top and get a better view, and then return to scale Sawtooth. Soon we were standing on a narrow hogback, in the same spot I'd stood to photograph LeGore Lake nearly 20 years ago.

On one side, far below, was LeGore Lake, the highest lake in Oregon, and on the other side of the saddle was Francis Lake. On the Francis Lake side were numerous sheep trails that wound underneath us. Soon we saw movement and here came a huge ram and an ewe. Rocky Mountain sheep fed just below us.

October 5—It rained. Not much, but enough to dampen the ground and calm the dust in our potato fields, and enough to make frost on this clear, crisp fall morning.

I watched an early weather report on TV and, as usual, the coldest spots in the Northwest were not recorded. Walking out in the frosty grass to peer on the post that holds up the clothesline, I see that our temperature is 28 degrees. On TV the coldest was 30.

But then Joseph isn't on the map, at least as far as weather is concerned. It is, as a burgeoning tourist area and a haven for an influx of artists, but the truth about our weather is seldom found in travel brochures. If that fact were known, perhaps our rural county would not be invaded by all these new people who want to live here. Would they still want to do so when, in fact, on many occasions we have had the chilly distinction of being the coldest spot in the nation?

As I finish the final typing of this column at my kitchen table, I make frequent visits to the cow pasture, or look through my binoculars. Startch picked this beautiful blue and gold autumn day to calve. I'll keep you informed. Currently, the big concern in our rural areas is the continuation of our rights as private landowners. We ranchers, as part of the entire Western agricultural community, are under the gun, so to speak, in managing our natural resources.

We are the buffer against a changing West. We hold the last frontier. Like our cattle during a storm, we are backed up in a corner. Which way to turn? What choices and decisions should we make? How do we proceed? Up the fence line, cross it, go back. The biggest challenge of our time, and the future of our young agriculturists is on the fence line, but I have faith in us. Agriculturists have handled crises before. It is not "just luck" that we people of the land have managed to stay in business through droughts, depressions and other numerous disasters. It took commitment and work and plenty of smarts.

Now is the time for all of us to show that we can manage, have managed, and will manage the resources entrusted to us, in such a manner only people who love the land can. And so will our young agriculturists of the future. But this will not come about without sacrificing time, as we must keep informed, and that is hard when we need to be home doing the work. If you don't stay home and do the work, you can lose your ranch that way for sure. Oh my!

Most importantly, it is a time to be united, not divided, for if we are to save what we value most, we need all the help we can get. I feel a new breeze blowing over the West, a refreshing breeze called hope. Former National CattleWomen's president Gerda Hyde of Chiloquin, Oregon, has always stressed: "Tell our story. Let those masses of people, generations away from the farm, know who we are, where we've come from, and where we are going." Chances are most of them have come from the same roots. But generations of city life has made them forget.

We must inform and educate. It is our only hope for survival, and preserving a way of life that could possibly be the salvation of our entire country. Some of us are going to have to clean up our act.

And our water, and do a better job of managing our lands. Show that we can. Set good examples. Stay home and do the work. Perhaps good will come out of this if we all work together.

Off the soapbox.

Barring unforeseen breakdowns or other numerous complications, our potato harvest just might be finished as early as tomorrow. Yeah!

Last Saturday morning might have been the opening of general mule deer buck season in Wallowa County, but it was potato digging as usual on this ranch. Since it was also daughter Ramona's birthday, and she was working on the digger, grandchildren Adele and Ryan helped me bake a cake, make a corsage of sweet peas and bachelor buttons, and a picnic lunch.

At noon we piled into the car and transported our "birthday party" to the potato field. Because it was windy, cold and sprinkling rain, all the workers were huddled in their rigs warming up. We held our party there in the dirty field, and lit the candles away from the wind. The dirt-covered smiles made it all worthwhile. And I was remembering back in 1951, having just turned 18 and giving birth to this daughter.

Later that evening, Ramona, her husband, Charley, and I attended "Landmark," a theatrical magazine for rural America, at the OK Theater in Enterprise. I had so hoped Doug could attend too, but it was 6:30 before he returned from the potato field. And then the bulls got out!

The Vigilante Theatre Company, which produces "Landmark," believes that its theater should relate to the lives of the people where they live. They searched and researched for the material, some they wrote themselves, and the result is this wonderful production. Four young men and women staged a drama of how country life is today, and they deserve a wider audience.

Quoting from a note from the editor, printed in the program, *Less than 100 years ago, over 80% of the people in our nation were directly involved in agriculture. Today the figure is near 3% or less.*

However, it is still the largest industry in the state of Montana and important to their entire region and the world. People come and go. The world grows smaller. And though the natural joys and difficulties are still present in farming and ranching, the country life just ain't what it used to be. Theatrical material on this new kind of life is not exactly abundant.

The Vigilante Theatre Company is sponsored by the Montana "Agriculture in the Schools" program and believes its efforts "provide a better understanding of the contribution of agriculture to our lives and to the nation's economy." Through the medium of theater, singing and acting, this small traveling troupe is bringing more understanding to our city cousins. It was good to see our local farmers and ranchers in the audience. During these times all of us need a little ego boosting and a good laugh.

The change in the weather and the much welcomed moisture made for a successful buck season weekend for our family. Grandson Buck shot his first muley on Imnaha, Uncle Charley hunted his own place and bagged a buck; grandson Shawn, home from college for the weekend, got his venison somewhere in the vast outback of Wallowa County, as did son Todd.

Todd took along his two sons, who, with their cousins Shawn and Buck, have some good huntin' stories to tell. Cousin Rowdy shot his buck during bow season. Yes, we have a lot of young'ns growing up who love being out in the outdoors and love the taste of venison. Eighteen-year-old Shawn, who is doing his own cooking at college, will welcome the addition of some meat to go with his Top Ramen noodles.

Sunday morning early found old hand Mike McFetridge, Doug and me riding the steep moraine to gather our fall calving cows and their new calves. Only they didn't want to be gathered. What a time we had, riding and searching that wet, cold timbered tract, which runs halfway up the side of Mt. Howard and down along the east moraine of Wallowa Lake. This 1,600 acres of high mountain meadow and timber is enclosed on the bottom side by a 16-foot-high elk fence.

October 13—Our lawn is littered with fallen willow leaves, the last blooming snapdragon droops forlornly against the house, and fall mists encircle the mountain peaks. It is a cool and cloudy morning here on Prairie Creek. That familiar, damp, fresh smell after a rain in autumn lingers in the air. Like the first bite of a crisp apple, I want to savor it.

Wild geese fly over regularly now, often landing in neighbors' grain fields to feed. Every morning numerous sparrows, chickadees and one lone towhee have been busy in the old apple tree. They appear to be engaged in some sort of feeding frenzy, pecking among the split apples clinging to the higher branches of the tree, perhaps storing food in their bodies for winter, or at least stopping over at this bed and breakfast on their way south. At any rate, I enjoy them. They are always so happy.

One morning a black hood and a contrasting chestnut side showing white underparts caught my eye in the tree. I ran for my bird book and identified him as a male Rufus-sided towhee. Having never seen the likes of him here, I look forward each morning to his cheery arrival and will miss him when he flies on.

Hopefully, the potato crew will finish digging seed tomorrow. After recent rains and mountain snows, we had some heavy frosts, but lately mornings have been free of any frost at all. I look up at old snow-covered Sawtooth Peak imagining our tracks are snow-covered, too. Linde and I timed that one just right!

Yesterday I helped Bill add to his winter's supply of wood. An old logging road in the Canal burn has been opened for woodcutting. We drove about a mile in to where son Todd had felled a dead tamarack the day before. It had rained on the way up Salt Creek summit, but sunlight sparkled on the wet grass by the time we arrived, and it was cool and nice to do all that hard work.

And wood gathering is hard work. I found that I could still wield a splitting maul and a wedge, and still enjoy the familiar crack of a huge chunk of wood splitting in two. Each round was so large I had to split them into six chunks, so they would be light enough to load on the pickup. We worked late into the afternoon; when we finished, a large load of split, seasoned tamarack was neatly stacked on the truck.

It was pleasant there in the burn. Even though the blackened trees stood all around, so too was there life. Water trickled from numerous springs in the area, the grass was high and golden, and a few live tamaracks were turning yellow. Mountain ash bushes were loaded with brilliant orange berries, on which birds were feeding. Crows, huge black birds, cawed all around.

All over the burn, thousands of new little trees, vigorous after our wet summer and nurtured by the burn itself, stretched upward in the freedom of light and air. The short daylight hours were fading when we pulled out of the old logging road, and numerous deer began to appear. A local rancher's cows and strong big calves ambled up the highway; there has been no shortage of feed this year.

Cutting, splitting, hauling and stacking wood another one of those autumn rituals that we here in the Pacific Northwest perform before winter. For us in rural areas, an ample supply of hay, a sufficient wood pile, a canning cupboard and freezer full of summer's bounty are just like money in the bank, and the product of our labor warms us twice. Our fall calvers and their new babies have already trailed down from their high moraine pastures for the winter. How I enjoy seeing these healthy calves nearby.

Yesterday morning I walked around our "country block" and spied the calves of all colors dozing in the autumn sunlight. I had a wonderful walk, accompanied by my little dog Daisy, visiting neighbors along the way. It was one of those blue-gold mornings. October's snow covered the high country, and yellow cottonwood leaves drifted down to float upon the creeks. The hike got me in shape for the afternoon wood-cutting. Since I am the self-appointed caretaker of our road, I picked up trash thrown out by motorists.

My trash catch of the day consisted of one glove, two feed sacks, four beer cans, baling twine, someone's wood permit, and a tangle of small wire. No office gave my orders; there was no feasibility study and no payroll, just legs to walk me and hands to do the work. Refreshing to know there are things we can still do to improve our environment, without have to wade through all that staggering paperwork that seems to be strangling our present-day society.

The grandchildren are all in school, which limits grandma's time with them. Why, I even had to go fishing in the creek by myself. Twice! Each time I caught a nice mess of rainbow trout on grasshoppers, using the kid's pole and the unorthodox method of fishing that, according to my husband, shouldn't catch fish, but does.

I enjoy watching the grandchildren in their sports events, which include Chelsie's volleyball, Rowdy's football, and James' soccer games. My grandchildren are the berries in my bonnet. I am so proud of every one of them.

The yellow keeping onions are stored in the cellar and boxes of apples from Bill's trees wait in the root cellar until we find time to press them into sweet cider next week. Linde and I dug the carrots last week and they, too, are stored for the winter. Such a satisfying thing, a garden. We are enjoying parsnips, and potatoes. Cooked alongside a nice beef pot roast, they are hard to beat.

When these golden autumn days are replaced by the beginning of a long cold winter, I will be working on my forthcoming book. A promise I've been keeping to myself for a long time. And that time has come. I am going to master my little word processor so the job ahead, although not easy and all new to me, can be made easier. Or so everyone tells me. To allow myself more time for this project, I will be writing a column every other week, rather than weekly.

We received a letter yesterday from sister Mary Ann, who is in her second year of serving in the Peace Corps on the island of Dominica. Having recently moved to the village of Scott's Head, an extinct volcano, she writes to entice us to come visit.

To further lure us to her island, she enclosed recent photos she'd taken of the area. Her hillside home, which looks out over the Atlantic on one side and the Caribbean on the other; the blue-green water of Soufriere Bay, white surf, mango and plantain trees, green jungle surrounding the tiny settlement of Scott's Head, and she herself, looking healthy, posing with the natives.

How far removed she seems from Wallowa County's snow-capped mountains, with autumn all around, and winter coming on, this feels like home to me; the place I love. Another of my kindred spirit sisters, Caroline, did go over there earlier and says it is an adventure. Doug says we might just have to go see for ourselves. Time will tell.

October 19—Joyce Edie, who says she has been writing a column for five years, and writes "Round the bend" for Agri-Times, says that when writing a column you have only a certain amount of space and therefore must know "when to shut up." She also says "it's not professional either and to stop it right now." Thank you, Joyce. I needed that. I have been writing this column for more than ten years, and have certainly been guilty of what you refer to.

Joyce is right about editors being nice. Perhaps they are too nice in my case, and rather than edit out my "rambling on and on" they choose to print every word, even if it spills onto the next page. Unlike Joyce, I am never in a quandary about what to write, but rather finding time to write. Therefore, it's hard to shut up once I get in front of the typewriter.

Quite simply, I love to write.

Anyway, here goes...and I promise to do better and stay within my column inches, whatever they are. Now, where was I? So much to tell, and already I've used up valuable space with "much ado about nothing." Speaking of which, the movie version was wonderful! Our Fishtrap Gathering and the local OK Theater presented "Much Ado About Nothing" one night last week.

Even local students, who received English credits for attending, were turned on by this spirited version of Shakespeare's popular comedy. I guess that's one of the joys of living here: we can attend cultural events or we can travel 30 miles to the small settlement of Imnaha and partake in a bear and rattlesnake feed. Quite the opposite from Shakespeare, but then not really, when you stop to think about it.

It was raining pretty good when we left last Saturday morning to drive down along Little Sheep Creek to Imnaha. The canyons are colorful this time of year, what with the yellowing cottonwoods scattered along creeks, and the brilliant red splashes of sumac everywhere.

The "fall gather" is on, weaning time is here, and Wallowa County hands are "all-weather cowboys." Therefore, a little rain didn't faze the local populace at the Imnaha Store, namely Dave Tanzey and his crew, who were busy spit-roasting a bear carcass when we drove by on our way to the rodeo. Neither did it interfere with the rodeo, the first ever held in the spanking new arena constructed by more locals, who had obviously spent many hours sinking railroad ties and picking rocks in a flat that lay just south of the Imnaha Store and Tav.

The arena was built on land formerly owned by local rancher Don Hubbard, who generously donated the three-acre site for the community's enjoyment. Gray clouds clung to canyon rims and the Imnaha flowed past.

The rain ceased when Toby Stanley carried the American flag around the arena, while a portable loudspeaker carried the strains of "I'm proud to be an American" over the flat, the young lad riding his horse, dwarfed by canyons that stretched to the sky, while a small group consisting of the dwindling population of cowboys and ranchers who make their living on the Imnaha held their hats over their hearts. Truly a touching scene.

The first event was preceded by a prayer, led by one of those cowboys, my son-in-law Bill, in which he thanked those who worked to stage the rodeo, the donor and those who built the arena. And then the fun began! The sun broke through the clouds during the musical tires. They had egg races, keyhole races, barrel races and pole bending.

Two-year-olds up to old hands like former Snake River cowboy Jim Blankenship took part. Jim, by the way, won the pole bending. The audience was sprinkled with Warnocks and Markses, descended from some of Imnaha's first settlers. And among the contestants, the younger generations competed with the same vigor as their elders. Old-timers Clyde Simmons, Wilson Wilde, Jim Stubblefield and Mary Marks looked on with amusement.

George Kohlhepp provided thrills and spills when his horse bucked during each event, but George is a cowboy, reared on the Snake and Imnaha. He simply climbed back on as if it were the normal thing to do. Toward the end of the rodeo, the horse settled down.

Everyone helped everyone else. They were community; the children belonged to all. Absent was the serious competition that has ruined professional horse shows. The only requisite was to have a good time. At 1 p.m. we broke for lunch and walked down to the bear and rattlesnake feed, where a record-breaking crowd jammed the store and spilled out onto Imnaha's main (and only) street.

In addition to three bears, around 100 rattlesnakes were crisp-fried for the occasion. Dave and Sally Tanzey and their crew served up quite a feed, which included macaroni salad, baked potatoes, bread, beans, and Imnaha tomatoes. Barbara Warnock pushed her way through the feasting throng to sell squares on the cow chip lottery, the proceeds of which are donated annually to the Finch Memorial Scholarship, awarded each spring to an Imnaha student.

Accompanied by daughter Lori and her family, who drove over from Pendleton to share in the festivities, we returned to the rodeo. Somehow grandchildren Ryan and Lacey found themselves in the midst of a chicken scramble, wherein wild jungle fowl, donated by the Warnocks, downriver, were released into the arena, at which time all heck broke loose and stayed loose for the duration of the rodeo.

Those chickens could fly like pheasants, and they simply sailed right over the fence and landed in trees or hid in the tall grass bordering the river. Grandchildren Buck and Mona each managed to grab one before they all escaped, and returned carrying a mad rooster and a squawking hen by the legs. Until the end of the rodeo, children could be seen climbing trees or hunting down the remaining chickens. Every so often one of them would emerge triumphant from the bushes, carrying a chicken with a herd of youngsters trailing behind.

Ranchers' wives competed in the events, too. The Imnaha women came from up Camp Creek, the upper Imnaha, and Freezeout Creek. These canyon women knew how to ride, like Vicky Marks, Pam Royes

Like the river along which they live, the generations of Warnocks roll on.
Pictured here at the Imnaha Junior Rodeo is young Clancy Warnock with
his dad, Dan. Clancy is the newest generation of this family descended
from the first settlers on the Imnaha River in Northeast Oregon.

Old hands Clyde Simmons, left, of Imnaha, and Snake River cowboy Jim Blankenship enjoy the Imnaha Rodeo. Blankenship won the pole bending.

The Holstein milk cow wonders what all the fuss is about.

and Jackie Matthews, who competed with the children they are rearing there. A very gentle, placid, non-nervous-type Holstein cow was led into the arena and turned loose in the cow chip lottery square to do her thing. Only she didn't, at least not while we were there. But she must have later, because we heard on the local radio that she did.

On Sunday Doug, Pat, Linde, Bill and I gathered up all the apples we've been storing and, using a borrowed cider press, pressed more than 30 gallons of delicious cider.

Yesterday, Doug and I drove to Clarkston, Washington, to attend his sister Betty's funeral. It was a lovely service for a wonderful lady. Betty's spirit will live in the hearts of all fortunate enough to have known her.

Returning home, we listened to her voice talking on tapes she'd recently made. Winding down Rattlesnake Grade, we were transported to another time and place, to the family ranch down on Joseph Creek, and Betty's remembrances of her happy growing-up years in that isolated canyon.

October 26—Heavy frost covers the bluegrass growing along the irrigation ditch in the horse pasture. The air here on Prairie Creek chills when drawn deep into the lungs. The fall-calving cows and calves, being driven down the road to the chutes this morning, exhale steam into the frigid air. The sun has burned its way up over the coyote-colored hills into a flawless autumn sky.

Doug, Jim and Seth will be helping Ben brand and work the calves. The din of bawling mother cows comes to me from the corrals as calves are sorted from cows. My mare remains saddled waiting for Linde, who will arrive shortly, and then we will trailer our horses to Bear Gulch and ride up to that area between the Sheeps known as the Divide. For years we have talked of doing this in the fall, and now we are actually about to leave. Because Ben has plenty of help, I needn't feel guilty.

Yesterday morning I took an hour's lesson from Karen at Blue Mountain Computer on how to operate my new laptop word processor. After an intense session, I drove directly back to the ranch, set up on the kitchen table and practiced.

At the end of two more hours of concentration, I willingly accepted Linde's invitation on the phone to go for a hike. It was a glorious afternoon. Cottonwoods are at their peak of color and their golden leaves flutter against a cobalt sky. The air was chilly, but we were soon walking briskly enough to stay warm. We hiked about two miles through timber, then broke out onto the ski run road that leads to Ferguson Ridge. Our destination was friends who are building a new home up there.

Rust-colored tamaracks punctuated the evergreen thickets and ice-encased low-lying limbs, wet from McCully Creek's splashings, rattled above the sound of running water. Chief Joseph Mountain, still blanketed by the season's first snowfall, gleamed in autumn sunlight. And I didn't have my camera! We returned along an irrigation ditch to Linde's house. Returning to the setup on my kitchen table, I was able to master a bit more of this complicated thing, with a much clearer mind.

October 27—Linde, who had run into several snags getting away yesterday, didn't arrive here until late morning, so by the time we unloaded our horses at the trail head, it was nearly noon. Our mares, feeling a bit frisky because of the frosty morning, soon settled down and we found ourselves deep in canyon country climbing a faint trail that follows a small creek up through the bottom of Bear Gulch. In the early days, an old wagon road followed this route, and every so often the trail would turn into a dim road. Another lovely autumn day in a succession of them.

Canyon country, rims on either side, and beyond. Endless and alike, but not really, in that each bend in the trail brought a fresh surprise. The cold creek, fed by springs that seeped from hillsides and mossy rocks, gurgled contentedly. Cottonwoods stood out among the willows and brush that grew there, boldly gold.

Enormous ponderosa pines grew everywhere, and we were startled by the unusual vine-like trailing plant growing practically in the creek. Its leaves were purple, an uncommon color in the wild, and on this purple-leaved plant grew shiny red berries. Leafing through my wildflower book over breakfast this morning, I think they might be a Bane berry.

The only sound in the gulch, other than the soft footfalls of our mares' hooves on fallen leaves and running water, was made by numerous crickets that must have been hidden in the dry fall grass. There was ice on puddles in the trail, and frost remained on the shaded norths.

The day warmed. As we rode higher and higher into more open country, the sun was most welcome. We stopped near a sunny hillside, tied up the horses and ate lunch. It was nearly 1:30. Then upward we continued through endless country, not thinking of how many miles we were putting behind us. We came to where the trail forked, and took the left fork to follow the creek, and soon we found ourselves in a great open grassy bowl, at the end of which stood a lonely homesteader cabin.

How peaceful it was there, nestled against the barren hillside, with just a splash of color from a nearby clump of quaking aspen and some red ninebark. Here the trail ended, so we followed a cow path that led to the high Divide, from which we could glimpse the hazy blue Wallowas to the west and the Seven Devils to the east.

Looking around at the country, it seemed logical to follow the cow trail to the bottom of the gulch, which we did, sliding down a steep canyon side that eventually connected with our trail. Soon we came to another fork, which led to Downey Gulch, and oh how I wanted to ride up that dim road to the top, but it was well after 4 p.m. and the short October daylight would be even shorter in Bear Gulch. So we rode back down the canyon, realizing we would still be traveling a lot in the dark.

After the sun disappeared over a rim, the brief twilight faded and it got darker and darker, until suddenly we looked up to a glow behind a rim to the east. The moon! Moonlight riders we were, able now to see shadows cast by our moving horses, and imagining cougars and bears behind every rock and bush. When the moon was hidden, as it often was, by a high outcropping of rim rock, we simply let the horses pick their own way, which they did quite nicely. We just had to reach out occasionally and keep low-hanging thornbush from scratching our faces.

The sight of Linde's truck and horse trailer parked at the trail's end was most welcome. We stiffly dismounted and loaded our horses, after which I made a quick phone call from a neighboring ranch house to Doug, who was pretty relieved to know we were among the living. Linde's husband had come out earlier from elk camp, so Doug treated us all to pizza in Enterprise. What a day!

Needless to say, bed felt pretty good last night, and this morning finds me here at the trusty typewriter at the kitchen table writing about these experiences. Not feeling comfortable enough, just yet, to enter this into the word processor, where I could possibly hit the wrong button and lose it.

Doug is out hunting his cow elk, the second chance, which coincides with opening morning of the first general bull season for Rocky Mountain elk. Confusing, isn't it. Odd that in all our riding yesterday we never saw one elk camp, nor one elk.

November 8—After venturing forth into a frosty dawn this morning, carrying a teakettle of hot water to thaw out my chickens' water, the warmth of the wood cook stove was very comforting when I returned to the house. Glancing at the thermometer on the way in, I noted the temperature: 15 degrees. Our old Monarch range gulps the wood and rarely goes out now, except at night.

Yesterday I butchered the last of the stewing hens and simmered one on the stove all day. That particular hen must have been older than I guessed, because I'm still cooking her today and she is finally falling off the bones. Chicken and dumplings for supper. A homey, cozy fragrance of celery, onion and simmering chicken fills my kitchen as I write.

The remaining cottonwood, aspen and willow leaves are all but gone, wafted away during last week's wind storm. Some Western larch (tamarack) still wear their golden needles, but they, too, are falling. Colorless November is here. But today it is bright, crisp and sunny. And the nights are cold, still and star-filled. Darkness comes early now, and much of our northern day will be spent indoors.

Linde has been gone more than a week now, visiting relatives, so I haven't been on any wild adventures. Reluctant to bid October goodbye, I did a lot of traipsing around, photographing the lingering color. Two cottonwood trees on upper Prairie Creek were particularly outstanding, outlined against snowy Mt. Joseph.

Seven-year-old James invited me to eat with him in the school cafeteria one day and then attend his Halloween parade and party. I enjoyed it immensely and the experience reminded me of long-ago Halloweens with my own children, their mothers and fathers. It was fun. Afterward we picked up Adele and went fishing.

The next day, we picked up granddaughter Becky and all went on a hike and picnic in the woods, after which we drove to Wallowa Lake. We had the place all to ourselves! The children ran with glee into thick layers of golden cottonwood leaves. The four of us shuffled through drifts, stirring them up as we ran, catching some as they fell in a golden shower, a sight I'll always treasure.

My three grandchildren tripping along under that golden canopy through which a dome of cerulean blue could be glimpsed. The children laughed for the sheer joy of being alive, responding to the beauty around them. The crystal cold lake sparkled through the trees as we ran out onto the deserted beach. The children's shoes soon filled with sand, so they took them off and ran with abandon along the beach.

Sunlight backlit Becky's auburn hair and Adele's blonde ponytail. James tagged behind the girls as they waded out to a log and stood on it, feeling the fresh air wafted over the lake, not minding the icy cold water. They made sand castles, played hopscotch, and reveled in the solitude. A small flock of mallards bobbed up and down near the shore, and several white sea gulls grouped themselves nearby.

Where the Wallowa River empties into the lake, the children floated leaves. The air was crisp, the sun golden, and for two hours they played. As the sun sank lower and disappeared behind the mountain, it turned bitterly cold and the children raced to put on their shoes and jackets and we were soon in the warmth of the car. I took them home and returned to the ranch, revitalized by the children. Seeing them today brought back memories of my own childhood, shuffling through fallen oak leaves along a cold creek in early winter.

That evening Doug and I joined the potato crew for a dinner at Vali's at Wallowa Lake. It was the first fall in nearly 14 years that I didn't plan and cook a big harvest dinner for the potato crew. The Halloween hunter's moon was something to see the night before the full moon, as it rose cold and huge over the eastern hills.

On the last day of October, Doug and I drove to the hills in hopes he would spot a cow elk on our summer range. No elk, but we had an enjoyable ride. Slate-colored clouds boiled up in a stormy sky, and out in the Zumwalt hill country all there is is sky and rolling, high plateau, so the sky is what you notice.

The clouds were layered, with the ones closest to earth moving rapidly in the direction of the wind, and the darker strata appearing not to move at all. We saw several bunches of does and fawns, and on Salmon Creek our lonesome cows trailed along forlornly, single file, in a hopeless search for their calves, weaned two days before and trucked far away over the Blue Mountains. From the road they looked like ants against the enormity of those tawny, frosted hills and that dark roiling sky.

Driving home, we saw a coyote running across a field, dodging chaff piles before simply melting into the hills. A ham I had left roasting in the oven during our absence filled the kitchen with warm smells. I lit a candle in a jack-o-lantern. It was Halloween. But we are just too far out in the country for the little goblins—no trick or treaters.

November dawned cold, 18 degrees. I spent the week working on my book. I've finally figured out the little word processor and use it for printing my manuscript, but I knead sourdough bread, gather eggs, feed cows, or pick up grandchildren, and those typewritten words are still there waiting when I return. I can't trust this other thing just yet. Experience and time will surely erase my fears. November evenings are long, a good time for reading, and I've just finished *Arctic Daughter* by Jean Aspen.

Curled up next to the fire in our warm home is a good spot to read of such cold adventures. My mother and stepfather returned from their trip to New York, which mom describes in her journal as an adventure, especially crossing the U.S. by Amtrak, which at 83 she took in stride. She and Bill are old hat at getting around in New York, so they had a great time.

One night last week, Doug and I attended granddaughter Carrie's

Drama Club production of "Our Miss Brooks," which made us laugh. Very well done. What a comedy.

Grandchildren Ryan and Lacey from Pendleton spent last weekend with us while dad went elk hunting. Again I hauled children to the lake so they, too, could experience the deserted lake shore. The leaves were browner and the air colder, but that did not deter the children's pleasure. Grandma huddled under a blanket while they played.

I guess if I were going to add something to Joyce Edie's list, it would be: "Shuffle through leaves with children in the fall.

November 23—We are in the midst of our first real winter storm. The temperatures slid below the 8-degree mark this morning, and it is snowing. We awoke yesterday morning to about three inches of fresh snow, and now, as I write, another layer is being added to that. On our lawn the white, dry stuff measures more than 10 inches. With Thanksgiving only a day away, our thoughts ride with the newlyweds, granddaughter Tammy and husband Matt, who are making their slow way northward to be with family.

Last we heard they had made it safely, albeit a little hairily, to Ontario. This seems to be the year for Wallowa County women elk hunters. Stories abound locally about their recent success. We understand that a young mother on upper Prairie Creek, who had an elk tag for the first bull hunt, went up on the Divide with her husband and brand new baby.

After the husband took off on foot hunting, she remained in the truck to nurse her child. After attending to her baby's needs, she laid the infant on the seat and stepped outside to stretch. Suddenly, here came a big bull elk. So this ranch wife calmly reached in the truck for her rifle and shot the elk dead. Presently a game warden appeared on the scene and saw that the bull was properly tagged, after which the amazed officer enlisted the aid of another hunter to help the young woman dress her kill.

Then there is Connie Dunham, our Wallowa County CattleWomen president, who arose early to hike up a hill, to a stand on their ranch, and shoot herself a six-point bull. Grandchildren James and Adele's mom bagged her big bull in the Chesnimnus unit, and Nancy Beach, out north on Paradise Ridge, shot a humongous seven-point, one of the largest bulls ever taken out there. Female luck held through cow season, too, as Linde bagged her first elk on the second day of the Chesnimnus hunt and I tagged mine that same day. And now, we have our own story to tell.

Same as last year, Bryan Wolfe drove over from Hermiston the night before opening morning of the Chesnimnus cow hunt, and Fred Hubbard, my girlfriend's husband from Auburn, California, had also driven up for the hunt.

Dark and early Saturday morning we were all up puttering around in the kitchen. I prepared sausage gravy and baked biscuits in the wood stove oven. Meanwhile, Bryan and Doug worked the sandwich detail. I was amused to see that Doug cut the meat loaf that second morning while Bryan spread on the mayo. Apparently those farmer-ranchers couldn't agree on how thick meat loaf should be sliced. One thing for sure, their lunches were most welcome by the time we got around to eating them both days.

Again, Venus shone brightly in an opening of pale blue sky sandwiched between a salmon sunrise. Becoming just light enough to see when we broke over Dorrance grade. There is nothing so lonely as our November hills. Perhaps its only the moaning of the wind, or simply the vastness of rolling grasslands and sky that evokes this feeling.

We drove to the same spot as yesterday, glassing the surrounding country frequently. Again it was Linde's good eyesight that caught movement, which appeared to be several head of elk bedded down about three miles distant. We glassed several herds of deer between the elk and us. After an "adventure" that I won't elaborate on, after a long day and thanks to our husbands, we finally packed out our cow elk, a quarter at a time, to the pickup.

Linde and I packed out head, heart and liver, plus hunting gear. The men secured the meat on a long pole, which they hoisted onto their shoulders, before hoofing it over a snowy trail to the pickup. It was well past noon when our two tired guys finally ate their lunches. Pat says that if we shoot elk again in a place like that, he'll vote for gun control.

Eventually reuniting with Bryan and Fred, we returned via the Zumwalt road to the ranch, after which Bryan headed over the mountain ahead of the snow storm and Fred, Pat and Doug skinned out the quartered elk. Too tired to cook, we all went into the Top Hand Cafe in Enterprise for supper, where we retold the preceding story. Perhaps in ten years the story will become even more exciting. I wonder if Doug and I will still be hunting elk in ten years.

Last night for supper I fried the elk heart and baked some delicious squash that Bryan brought over from Hermiston. Fred, who is still with us, unable to leave due to the storm, say she'll be here Thanksgiving. The more the merrier. Again our modest home will bulge, as the last count was 27. We'll all have much to be thankful for this Thanksgiving: family, good friends, meat for winter, and memories in the making.

December 7—My new ultra lite word processor was all set up, plugged in, ready to go this morning, when the electricity went out. So here is me sitting in front of the faithful Smith-Corona and feeling grateful, as well, for the old Monarch wood range, which provides for cooking and heating. It seems old things still prove to be the most reliable when one lives in a high mountain valley all winter.

Gusting winds that blew all night and into today probably knocked out the power somewhere along the line. I've alerted PP&L, which should soon solve the problem.

Partly hidden behind gauzy snow clouds, our mountains look like a mirage this morning. As I write, snow has begun to fall here on Prairie Creek. Thick flakes whiz past my window, driven by the wind, reducing my world to a restless blurred whiteness.

I have been alone since Saturday, when Doug and son, Steve, left to attend the national seed seminar in Portland. They are due to return tomorrow. Not having to cook has given me more time to work on my book, which, although progressing, is proving to be more of a project than I anticipated.

In addition to keeping the home fires burning, so to speak, I bundle up each morning, accompanied by my dog, Daisy, and venture out in the cold to chore, which, in the winter, consists of forking hay to my two milk cows and their weaned heifer calves, carrying water to the laying hens and feeding them, splitting and hauling wood to satisfy the Monarch's voracious appetite, and checking the potato cellar switches, as per Doug's instructions.

I was in a baking mood this morning, so tried out a new pie recipe. Berries and cream, using frozen huckleberries and whole milk cream for the filling, which turned out delicious, and the fragrance released from those huckleberries brought back memories of picking them way up on McGraw during grouse season.

The box of persimmons that Fred brought up from Auburn during cow elk season are ripening, so am drying some and decided to fill the cookie jar with persimmon cookies. They are good keepers, and full of raisins, nuts and dates. Good for visiting grandchildren.

It is comforting to be able to pick up the phone, dial a friend, and hear a voice over the frozen miles.

"Is it snowing on upper Prairie Creek?" or "Have you got your fire built on Alder Slope?" Or, in 83-year-old Grace Bartlett's case, "Have you been out to feed your horses yet?" Phones link loneliness and soon loneliness leaves.

I was talking to daughter Ramona when suddenly she exclaimed, "What was that?" and hung up. Later I found out the wind had knocked out a window on their back porch. Ramona found a hammer and nails and nailed a big board over the hole until husband, Charley, got home to fix it right.

Last week, after Thanksgiving and all that feasting, Linde and I decided to put on the cross-country skis and give it a try.

The snow was perfect, and although the temperatures hovered around zero, we bundled up and had a great time. Our weather has since moderated and the snow has settled with an icy crust on top, not good for skiing. So, to get in some daily exercise, we go for brisk walks along the county roads instead, often cutting through fields and snowy pastures to get to our destination.

The daylight hours shorten and once we had to flounder through knee-high snow following a ditch back to Linde's to beat darkness, but being out that time of the evening has its own rewards. We watched the purple-pink sky of a December sunset deepen behind the Seven Devils Mountains to the east; we watched the ranch house lights blink on and felt the chill of a winter night coming on.

One day last week we struck out here and walked the road to visit neighbor Ardis Klages. It was a lovely morning, all dazzling white and blue, and we walked and talked, in the way of friends, our dogs running alongside, sniffing out mouse and weasel tracks. We found Ardis preparing a noon meal for her men in her recently remodeled kitchen. Ardis can look out upon the snowy Wallowa chain, which is foregrounded by the Klages' frozen fields dotted with cattle and, perhaps, take note when her husband and son head home for dinner. She says they have their big meal at noon. Ardis has baked a pie earlier, and is fixing herbed potatoes to go with baked salmon steaks.

Linde and I perched on high stools at the kitchen counter and visited while she cooked. When we returned home, a layer of clouds had switched places with the blue sky, and bitter cold settles in again.

One afternoon, we hiked from Linde's house on upper Prairie Creek up the ski-run road and into the woods beneath Ferguson Ridge, to visit Dick Williams, who is building a home up there. It was quite a long walk, but we discovered we were in better shape than we thought. In no time, we were enjoying a grand tour of the Williamses' new home, one that Dick designed himself. It was especially interesting to Linde and me as we had seen the home site before even a road was built into the woods, and now here was a house! Dick was the fellow who rescued us when Linde's car got stuck in the snow when we were skiing last winter.

In last Sunday's Oregonian there was a fine article on Imnaha school teacher Gary Wagner, a Wallowa County native who grew up here before venturing "outside" for further education. He became a very fine teacher, one of Oregon's best, but lost his wife to cancer, and now years later has returned to live here with his two sons. The best part is that he is teaching at the two-room Imnaha school where two of my grandchildren have him for a teacher. It was so refreshing to read about something positive, rather than the sensationalism that seems to dominate today's media coverage.

The electricity has been restored, and my column is finished.

The wind still howls, however, and it looks as though we are in for a snowy evening. Christmas looms and, to get into the spirit, I've placed a pine wreath made by granddaughter Carrie over the old horse collar mirror. When Doug returns, perhaps we'll go tree hunting.

Our CattleWomen's annual Christmas party is Thursday, and we look forward to the children's school programs. Christmas is magic for children, and this grandma would like to wish all children, everywhere, a very merry Christmas!

December 21—On this first day of winter, I am leafing through my daily journal wondering what to write about. I came across the following, written at day's end when I curl up in a chair by the old Monarch and reflect on the day's events. I thought that perhaps, for those of you who are housebound for one reason or another, you'd like to go for a walk with me.

In the midst of busy holiday preparations, I frequently strike off across the field in the direction of a neighboring hill for a brisk hike, my dog at my heels. Daisy knows what the word "walk" means. Her tail wags, her eyes light up with anticipation, and she is eager to be off.

Up Tenderfoot Valley road we go, through a hole in the fence, as we know all the places to cross, into Hough's frozen alfalfa field. Crunch, crunch, we come to an irrigation ditch and walk gingerly across a wooden head gate where ice is jamming, cracking, melting and grinding under us. We cross through another fence, where we are temporarily free from fences and pause at the bottom of a steep hill. Our way is pockmarked with badger, red-digger and coyote dens; waist-high golden grasses and weeds in earthen tones of coyote, rust, tan, and burnt sienna. It is like uncovering fall.

Small patches of snow lay in a worn, frozen cow path that winds up through a draw. I inhale the clean air in great gulps, deep into my lungs. It is like a drink of cold spring water, pure and exhilarating.

We walk slowly up the hill, following the cow path. Rocks in various formations, left from ancient volcanic residues, begin to appear. Powdery blue sage and dry burdock rattle against my boots and stick to my jeans. We climb higher, loving this aloneness of space, sky and far-off mountains locked in winter silence. I turn around to gaze up toward old, eroding Sawtooth, remembering when Linde and I stood atop the peak in October. Daisy sniffs into every badger hole, running ahead and then back to make sure I am coming.

On top I remove my scarf and savor the feel of cold air on my scalp. Warmed from the exertion of climbing, the cool refreshes. I reflect that on this date 34 years ago, I was confined to a hospital bed, where I had given birth to my third child, a girl. Today, free from child-rearing, I have looked forward to this time for myself, while remembering with affection that time as well. There is a time and a season for all we do.

We cross a rockjack at another fence, which leads to a frozen stock pond, all hushed and quiet. Ancient, leafless, dormant willows repose high and dry on hummocks clustered at the southern edge of the pond. I envision next spring's hatch of wild honkers.

But today there is no life, no squirrels, no birds, only a solitary hawk soaring high overhead. We walk northward along the frozen shoreline, then down a hill toward an old apple tree, all that remains of an abandoned homestead, to a gate that leads to Echo Canyon road.

The sun silently slides behind Chief Joseph Mountain, and I know it must be 3:30. The short winter day is fading, and the familiar cold is settling in. Hough's black Angus cows stand in a cud-chewing row, watching curiously as we pass. Vapors escaping their nostrils, so they look like woolly buffalo on Prairie Creek. Off in the direction of Wallowa Lake, in that glacial pocket, a layer of cotton hovers over the open waters of the lake. Several tendrils have escaped and are enveloping Bonneville Mountain and East Peak, while other wisps trail off toward McCully Basin.

I quicken my step, button my coat, and wrap the scarf securely around my head and neck. On Tenderfoot Valley road again, a great clamoring echoes over the still chill of Prairie Creek, and outlined against shadowy snowy peaks fly 30 honkers, V-ing their way across the December sky. My heart leaps for joy. The geese skim the willows and cottonwoods along the creek, which are to me in winter so honest, vulnerable, brave and enduring. Daisy and I hasten home in the chilling twilight. We have savored the afternoon.

Last Thursday morning I picked up our phone to dial the neighbors and invite them to join Doug and me for dinner the next night. Then I began to cook. I combined grated raw potato, carrots and raisins in an old recipe given to me by Gladys Yost years ago. It is a carrot pudding that is then steamed in a coffee can for three hours. Cooked a lemon sauce to pour over. Baked an apricot pie and a berry and cream pie.

The next morning I joined other Fishtrap board members in our county library and pasted address labels on a bulk mailing, then home by noon to put a ham in the oven and continue preparing for 21 people who were coming to dinner. Doug got into the act, stringing lights along our fence and on the fir tree in the yard. The wonderful mix of food, holiday cheer, and mostly the people themselves, contributed to the evening's success, and we spent a delightful evening eating and getting to know our neighbors, the inhabitants of Tenderfoot Valley Road.

What a great group lives along our road. Their backgrounds are as diverse as the food I prepared. Lois and Don Hough, at the end of the road, were here. They, like Doug and me, are semi-retired from ranching and, like us, unable to let go completely.

The Lockes, Gardner and Tappy accompanied by son Tim, and Tim's girlfriend, who is from Ecuador and only speaks Spanish. The Lockes are a well-traveled, interesting family, spent considerable time in the Peace Corps in Ecuador. Gardner and I talked about far-off places like Chile, which was better than any geography lesson, and considerably widened my perspective on the world.

From farther up the road came the Waters family, Larry, wife Juanita, and mother Dorothy; as did the young Brinks, the newcomers to the road, who brought their three children. We had invited daughter Ramona and son-in-law Charley, who speaks fluent Spanish and was able to converse with Tim's girlfriend. Pat and Linde also joined our group. Linde, originally from Germany, mixed right in with our international gathering. Plunked down here on our part of planet Earth, we, from different cultures, have chosen to live.

December 23—With just two days left till Christmas, there's really no need of being in a rush. The thing to do is clearly to go fishing. Really. That's what we did. Accompanied by friends Linde and Pat, Doug and I headed down the long, winding road to Dug Bar on the Snake River to go steelhead fishing.

It was crisp, clear and eight degrees when we finally got on the road. Our neighbor's horses and a mule had broken in with ours the night before, so we spent considerable time fixing fence and chasing animals. The sun was tinting canyon rims early-morning gold as we turned downriver from the small settlement of Imnaha, and began the long drive to the road's end at Dug Bar, where our boat was parked near the landing.

We wound down past Horse Creek and Corral Creek, crossed the Cow Creek bridge, then passed McClaran's ranch and headed up the steep, narrow road to Doug's old permit land, which used to join the deeded land at Dug Bar. This land is now in the National Recreation Area. Near a livestock watering trough, fed by a spring, we spotted around 20 head of bighorn sheep. What a sight they were, grazing near the road, obviously attracted by the plentiful feed left from cattle grazing. The wild sheep appeared unafraid of us and calmly continued grazing the steep canyonside.

It was nearing 10 a.m. when we backed up to the boat to transfer our gear before launching into the Snake. The breeze created by the boat's movement was cold as we motored upriver, but we were prepared with scarves around our heads, gloves, layers of clothes, and blankets to drape over us. Doug, at the helm, looked colder, but he, like us, was bundled up as well.

We hadn't met a single soul during our 60-mile trip in, and it appeared as though we were the only boat on this section of the river. The air was fresh and full of that cold-water river smell. It was exhilarating, being there in December. We pulled into an eddy near Deep Creek and made several casts. No luck. Then up past Van Pool's, on the Idaho side, and fishing from the boat.

Doug landed, or rather boated, a nice one.

Pat lost a lunker, but we saw it splash above the swirling waters of the Snake before it unhooked itself and swam away. We pulled into a quiet sandy cove further upriver, collected a small pile of driftwood, lit a fire, and grilled Pat's fish. This is Doug's specialty. He had brought along butter, garlic salt, and a handmade grill to support the fish over the fire. The fish was soon cooked to perfection and we wasted no time diving into that epicurean delight...with our hands! Never has anything tasted so fresh and delicious.

The Snake swirled past us, luminous, blue-green, roiling in whorls in the silence created by the cold of a late December day. Far from the madding crowds, enjoying the basics of food, warmth and companionship, it was the best Christmas present we'll ever imagine, surrounded by the natural world, which to us includes cattle, several of which we could see grazing on the Idaho side.

We shared that special part of our world with a pair of bald eagles, which flew from a tall pine across the river to hunt rodents on the dry, grassy hillside. On a nearby sandbar, numerous waterfowl, including wild Canada geese, gabbled contentedly to themselves. And when we were in the boat again, many species of wild ducks flew upriver. We tied up at Roland Bar, just below where Jim Blankenship's weathered ranch buildings and house still stand today along Cat Creek, next to a good spring where numerous walnut trees continue to grow.

What a peaceful spot, and what a sad thing that these wonderful, well-run ranches are now out of private ownership. The owners' good stewardship is the reason the canyon is so special today. The canyon belongs as much to the cattle, sheep and ranchers as it does to recreation and wildlife. In fact, the reason that the wildlife flourishes is because of the decades of grazing native grasses, which keeps them healthy for all life, wild as well as domestic.

Winter days are even shorter in the canyons, and we headed back toward Dug Bar when the sun disappeared behind the ridge known as Teaser. A flamingo sunset tinged the clouds, which outlined dark, dinosaur-backed ridges separating the high grassy benches of Cow Creek, Lightning Creek and Horse Creek.

"The cream of cattle country," says Doug. We celebrated the end of a perfect day at the Imnaha store where, after three people left, we were the only ones there. After a bite to eat, and backing up to the warmth afforded by the barrel woodstove, we headed up Little Sheep Creek to Prairie Creek.

We live by creeks and rivers in this land of winding waters. It would seem they are not just place names to us, but rather, places to live, to visit and enjoy, and to know intimately.

Several days ago, Doug returned to Dug Bar, this time with a boat-load of grandsons and a son-in-law. Another good time was had by all, especially grandson Buck, who caught a nice 28-inch steelhead and added a wonderful memory of being with grandpa and daddy on a cold December day in his young life. It is a treasure no one can ever take away from him.

Back in front of my word processor, my book is coming right along. Thanks to all of you who have offered encouragement.

The greeting on our Christmas card, which is a photo of our snow-covered home, reads, *Wishing you a world of Peace.* Happy New Year!

Shown here is proof that even Santa Claus must do the chores. The rather trim Santa was feeding cattle for rancher Dwayne Voss on Prairie Creek.

1994

January 1—Last night we said a quiet goodbye to 1993, and this morning a happy hello to 1994.

The weather on this first day of the new year can't seem to make up its mind. First it snows, then rains; a little freezing rain fell, followed by fog; now, as I work my new word processor, the sun has burst through the clouds. May you all have these bursts of sunshine in your lives this new year.

January 11—Transplant a Wallowa County ranch woman to a suburban neighborhood in Auburn, California, and she soon transforms even that atmosphere into her more familiar habitat. This mild, clear January morning finds her in front of the portable Smith Corona, seated in an immaculate kitchen looking down upon the smog-fogged Sacramento Valley. Time has covered the rolling oak-studded foothills of her youth with other homes like the one she occupies.

Well, almost, for in this not-so-humble abode, a bowl of sourdough bread is rising on the floor in a shaft of sunlight; and outside, off a high wooden deck, in the bare branches of an oak tree which escaped the subdivision, draped in an unorthodox manner, hang her socks, to dry, as there appears to be no clothesline in the small yard and she does not believe in dryers when the weather is nice, nor even when it isn't; at home she hangs long johns and socks behind the old wood stove.

Apples wait to be peeled and made into a pie for Tom's birthday, and the last issue of Agri-Times, minus "Janie's Journal," reposes on the kitchen counter. "She" is me, Jane, who has recreated a bit of Prairie Creek here 800 miles from home. Now, I can write!

Doug and Fred, who is retired, left early this morning to check out the antique shops that line old Highway 49. Named after the famous gold rush of '49, the highway wends its way along the base of the Sierra foothills, and like pretty places all over the West, its route is now covered with more "shops" than ranches.

When people living in the California cities become too frazzled, they flee to the foothills where they prowl the shops and purchase "country things" to take back to the city. "Country" still exists on the surviving ranches, like over White Rock way, where my cousins, the Smiths, Mehrtens and Wilsons, continue to ranch in the tradition of Egbert and Isaac Wilson, who crossed the plains in the mid-1800s to settle along Carson Creek and put down their roots.

The ranches of these descendants appear isolated, but each year, like a cancerous growth, suburbia creeps closer. The bones of my great-grandmother, great-grandfather, grandmother and grandfather repose in a pioneer cemetery near which a modern freeway carries hordes of city dwellers to the playground called the Sierra Nevada. That playground used to be summer cattle range, and still is in isolated areas, but few people are aware of this, and numerous restrictions imposed in the past decade have limited grazing rights. But in those grazing areas, "open space" is left.

Doug and I drove over to White Rock yesterday to have dinner with the Smiths and the Mehrtens, descendants of those early pioneering Wilsons. Baby calves dozed on green grass in sunshine. Carson Creek, full from recent rains, flowed slowly past, as it has since Egbert and Isaac arrived. The old ranch house, built in 1937, immense, sturdy and true, constructed with pride, wood and brick, looms before us as we travel the dirt road to the ranch.

Sue's Catahoula cattle dogs raise a ruckus when we step out to open the gate. Aggie, soon to be 86, is sweeping the long wooden porch when we drive in the yard. She smiles. The years don't seem to matter much to Aggie. Widowed for years, she reared two sons and carried on. Now son Chuck and wife, Sue, run the ranch.

Inside the old ranch house Aggie has been baking bread. "In a coffee can," she says with a smile. "Recently a son recalled how I used to bake it that way to make sandwiches for his lunch pail, when he was little. Everyone liked it so well, I just kept making it that way."

Aggie had also baked a pan of her famous chewy bars. Sue, who was just finishing chores, came in to help prepare the rest of the meal. George, well into his 80s, joined us at the long oak table that in years past has served many generations of this family. Aggie and George are the survivors of the Smith family. Ray and Edna passed on some time ago.

They are an inspiration to me. There is a perpetual sparkle in their eyes that gives away an inherent sense of humor that has endured over the years. Hard work, coupled with a closeness to the land, has only softened the lines in their faces. They are among the lucky ones who love their work and accept with quiet dignity that which fate has dealt them.

After we ate and the dishes were done, we drove over to the Wilson ranch where acres of range spread out before us. More newborn calves nursed their mothers or lay asleep, clustered in groups, babysat by one cow while the others grazed. We watched for Chuck on the long-winding gravel lane. He would be horseback, checking calving cows.

The three-story ranch house was built well over 100 years ago. It still stands today, with the rose bushes and trees planted long ago still growing in the yard. Here we met more descendants, distant relatives of mine, before returning to Auburn.

One week into our yearly pilgrimage to California, we've only called home once, to learn it was 10 degrees and several inches of new snow had fallen. Hard to comprehend down here. On the way down we spent one night at Rose and Ernie Gnos' cabin on Donner Lake. Our experience seemed a far cry from the ill-fated Donner party, whose attempt to cross the Sierra in dead of winter ended in tragedy. Our winter stay was pure luxury.

That evening, Ernie presided in their spacious modern kitchen. While we perched on bar stools, watching, he prepared an Italian dish. As aroma of sauteed mushroom, olive oil and garlic floated to our nostrils, Ernie galloped around his kitchen like his TV counterpart. Outside we could see snow piled up on the decks and hear a creek splashing underneath an ice bridge. Inside, a cozy fire fed by eucalyptus wood brought from their Dixon ranch burned slowly in the rock fireplace. From the dining area we looked through a solid glass wall to other snow-covered cabins that line the north shore of Donner Lake.

The next morning, while Ernie went skiing, Rose took us on this enormous tram, which held 118 people, in nearby Squaw Valley. This windowed contraption swept us to dizzying heights to a nearby 9,000-foot mountain, on top of which we were unloaded like so many cattle into a hallway that led to an enormous building erected on the mountain. Inside its massive construction were restaurants, shops and ski rentals. Outside this gargantuan edifice, built in the midst of the winter-locked Sierra, we could gaze in wonderment at the surrounding mountains, into whose midst we had been suddenly transported—in six minutes!

Around us, in competition with the scenic grandeur, were other human marvels, such as a turquoise-colored swimming pool and spa, a bungee jumping-off place, an ice rink, and last but not least the ski slopes themselves, where skiers in their '90s colors glided with seeming ease over a fresh six inches of powder over a larger base.

For me, these marvels of modern man weren't to be overshadowed by the natural world and I focused my camera on distant Lake Tahoe, the familiar lake of my youth that reflects the sky, and its 100 miles of shoreline. From this distance, one could look upon and enjoy the lake and surrounding vastness for what it was. Distance and winter hid the terrible over-building that has ruined the once peaceful shores of Lake Tahoe.

Virtual cities have replaced the ranches I knew as a child, where I helped gather cattle on an old horse named Pedro in the swampy grasslands that bordered the lake. From inside the glassed-in restaurant we gazed out at the panorama before us. On that clear morning it was beautiful. We sipped herb teas and smelled espresso, another mark of the '90s, while gazing out the immense glass windows.

The round loaf of sourdough bread is ready for the oven. My niece, Lori, and husband Tom, are at their jobs; Kyle in school across the way and Kayla at daycare. What wonderful hosts they are, and what a nice family, too. We are so lucky to have them in our family.

January 18—Two-year-old Kayla, a very vocal member of the family we are staying with here in Auburn, is my sister Mary Ann's granddaughter. One she hasn't seen much of, since she's been living on the island of Dominica, way out in the Eastern Caribbean somewhere.

Kayla's mother says she is going through the terrible two's, that rebellious stage where only her ideas are important and everything else is not OK. If she wants something changed or brought to a halt, she screeches, "S'top it!" This little voice can bring an entire family to its knees. When I see what is happening to my beloved California in the way of over development, over-population, and over-everything, I feel like Kayla: "S'top it!"

Incredibly, among this maze of humanity that has gravitated to the Golden State since we've been in Oregon, we are still able to seek out and find relatives like my Uncle Johnny, who continues to live in the old three-story house my grandpa built to rear his and grandma Wilson's seven children in. There it stands, with failing dignity, among the convenience stores, schools, and sprawling subdivisions.

The long poultry houses sag, and today no one is left who even knows what they once were, there in Rio Linda, the beautiful river, which was once a great poultry area.

Inside the house, my uncle Johnny resides alone, like a living relic of those times, surrounded by memorabilia of his and California's past; composing music, often late into the night, at age 85. He refuses to leave, even when relatives suggest he move to a smaller place, one easier to clean; he stays where grandma and grandpa's ghosts haunt the rooms. Perhaps he, like the house, will just fade away.

We visited uncle Johnny on our way back from Lodi, where we traveled to find granddaughter Tammy and husband, Matt. We found the younger generation eager to get on with their lives, making a move to a house in the country. Both are happy with their jobs and the accelerated life of the '90s Californian.

Uncle Johnny, dressed in a worn suit, greeted us through a locked door, then let us in. He led us to the old familiar living room-turned study, where he asked us to move in close so he could hear and see us better. Then he regaled us with tales of earlier times along Carson Creek in El Dorado country, where he was born. These fascinating stories have been passed down from generation to generation. I went home and wrote them down for my children.

We managed to see nearly all the relatives in a two-week period. On our last day in Auburn, a Sunday, we packed a picnic and accompanied two sisters and a brother-in-law to La Trobe, where more ancestors sleep in oak-shaded pioneer cemeteries. Here we spent an idyllic day along the banks of French Creek.

It was nearly 70 degrees there, seemingly removed from the not-so-far-away and creeping-closer Folsom suburbia. After spreading a blanket in sunlight on green grass under ageless, leafless water oaks, we built ourselves huge Dagwood sandwiches and nibbled fruit. Then, while Doug and Duane panned French Creek's bedrock for gold, we three sisters took a jaunt up the creek to a remembered spot we visited several years ago.

First we climbed a knoll to the rock foundation that is all that remains of the old Smith house. A few narcissus poked their way through oak leaf mold and several unidentified thorny trees grew where the yard had been. After climbing a nearby hill, we dropped down to follow a deer trail along the creek, which led to a rocked gorge where water and the drip of time had carved beautiful stone into sculpture. Water disappeared through holes in the rocks, then emerged to fall in tiny waterfalls, where little pebbles ground together in a most happy way. The rocky gorge was grown over with Toyon berry, chaparral, manzanita, scrub oak, poison oak, and hung with green ferns that sprang from mossy rocks.

We lingered there, wanting to photograph, but there wasn't enough light. It felt damp and cool, which was good because we had exerted ourselves to get there. We found a quiet pool, took off our shoes and socks, and dipped our feet in the icy, healing waters of French Creek.

We were all quiet as our feet dried on a sunlit rock, contemplating

skaters skittering around the pool's surface. These minute swimming
insects seemed terribly territorial as they attacked each other, but perhaps
they were mating. Annie Dillard or Thoreau would know. It didn't seem
to matter. The evolution of the creek continued without our knowing.

How, I thought, can we save these primitive places? I had a terrible
vision of it becoming some millionaire's back yard, or worse yet, a
state park, where masses would trample the fragile place. Today it is a
rancher's property, grazed by cattle, which has allowed the native flora
to flourish and the creek to do its thing, which simply is to be.

I want to say, let's get behind our ranchers and support them, so there
can be these little islands of joy where those of us who like to contemplate
skaters can go. A place to think, perhaps not finding answers but at
least having the privilege of nature's quiet places. Those of us born with
creeks in our childhood need them. All people need them, but don't
know it yet. As the crow flies, only minutes away from French Creek,
California children are growing up knowing another kind of ranch.

We passed one this morning. The Briggs Ranch, it was called. An
enormous, pretentious, modern community-living complex, with upscale
homes built behind rocked walls, and a grand entrance patrolled by
guards. Perhaps this Briggs Ranch was once a real ranch, but certainly
not now. S'top it!

With the sun sinking behind the El Dorado hills, and gold remaining
after the 49'er gold rush still in French Creek, we left and soon re-entered
the other world of California, the insane rush of traffic in and around
the interstate freeways that never sleep.

But in that cacophony of the '90s, amid sirens, cars and humanity,
we found a little eatery called the Roseville Gourmet, run by a most
delightful family, who hired a cook who knew his Chinese food. After a
day spent traipsing around in fresh air, we ate heartily of that gourmet
food. I must admit, we tasted the best of California's two worlds.

And now, as I write here in the Silver Queen motel, in the old mining
town of Tonopah, Nevada, those California crowds seem non-existent.
Doug and I traveled through miles of desert today, open spaces of sagebrush, juniper, sand, mountains, alkali flats, playas, and land-locked
lakes…all under the vast, blue Nevada skies. Tomorrow we follow our
map southward toward Las Vegas, with all its glitter, a place we've read
about but have never seen.

We will hopefully bypass this man-made spectacle and continue on
to Arizona, where we hope to see an old Prairie Creek neighbor, Max
Gorsline, and his dog Mel. We'll look up Ralph Tippett, too, another
snowbird who travels these long distances to warmer climes each winter.

As for me, who doesn't mind cold, I am anxious to return to Wallowa County, and winter. Do some cross-country skiing and get on with my book, which is waiting for me. As we pass Las Vegas, I shall shout out the window of our speeding car: "Stop it!"

January 23—A deep purple darkness began stealing over the vast Arizona desert, etching tall Saguaro cactus against the fading evening light as we sped westward toward the small settlement of Wenden. After spending the night in Tonapah, Nevada, we were tired from the long hours of driving, yet feeling lucky after surviving the crush of Las Vegas traffic. That town has gone insane. To my way of thinking, things there are totally out of hand.

Later, we'd been held up by more construction on the Boulder Dam project, another of man's marvels that now must somehow generate even more electricity to satisfy the needs of a burgeoning Las Vegas. Blue Lake Mead appeared as an oasis amid the dry canyon-like setting.

Where, oh where, will all the water required for Las Vegas' future come from, to flush all of these toilets, water all of those lawns, and wash all those teenagers' hair…on a daily basis? I couldn't help but wonder. We'd enjoyed the Joshua Tree Parkway, where we'd driven through miles of scenery that was straight out of "Arizona Highways." When we pulled into Wenden, population 300, elevation 1,800 feet, in the county of La Paz, we located a pay phone and Doug called our old friend Max Gorsline, who was expecting us.

We invited him to join us for a bite to eat in Wenden's only eatery. Over enchiladas we visited Max, who is still recuperating from a serious lung condition. Afterward, only a short distance away, we retreated to Max's small trailer parked next to several other Wallowa County inhabitants-turned-snowbirds, where we wearily visited until my eyes drooped and Ralph and Doug's cousin Enid returned from Wickenburg.

Bed had never felt so good as we bunked down in Ralph and Enid's cozy little cottage. The mild desert night enfolded us and we slept the sleep of weary travelers.

The next morning we thought we were back in Wallowa County, leastwise in the kitchen, because Enid served us sourdough biscuits with sausage gravy. We polished the meal off with more hot biscuits and wild black cap jam. Around 5 that morning I'd heard coyotes, even through the bedroom walls…in stereo.

After breakfast Doug and I piled in with Ralph in the pickup and headed up into the nearby desert mountains to try our luck at gold panning. For me, who had never been to Arizona, never seen so many varieties of cacti growing in such profusion, never felt such warm January sunshine, it was an exciting new experience.

Fascinated with the flora of the desert, I eagerly learned to identify teddy bear cholla, ocotillo, saguaro, creosote bush, and the green-limbed palo verde, to name a few. I took notes and photographed as Ralph's pickup bounced and jounced into arroyos and washes that laced the wild desert. We finally parked near a dry wash, where we unloaded the pickup of its mining paraphernalia.

I had been looking for a road runner, but never could spot one. Many species of desert songbirds twittered among the palo verde, however, and several ravens voiced their raucous caws above us in the clear desert air. The hillsides, lined with dry washes, showed evidence of former flash floods that occurred when desert rains, like a sort of natural sluice, washed the gold down to lodge in bedrock crevasses. Palo verde and saguaro provided the only shade.

It was around 80 degrees, in January yet! I helped unload shovel, pick, rake, scrapers, wire brushes, buckets and a water jug, while Doug and Ralph lifted the dry gold-pan sluice, an ingenious contraption constructed by Ralph, out of the pickup. The gold is "dry panned" with a bellows, used to pump and reduce dirt and gravel to a fine powder, which is then blown by Ralph to reveal flakes of gold or nuggets that are too heavy to withstand the blowing.

Ralph, 80 years young and just recently having suffered several "little strokes," took up his pick and began to loosen some gravel in the wash. He scraped it into a bucket, which he then poured through a coarse screen, which eliminated the larger rocks.

I helped turn the crank that operated the bellows, above which the material vibrated down a series of wooden steps onto the ground, where it formed a pile of tailings. The sun bore down and a slight breeze rattled the dry ocotillo, but it was a dry heat, not at all unpleasant. After working up a sweat, our efforts produced several flecks of dark Arizona gold, and gave us an insight into dry panning on the desert. It was good exercise!

At well past noon, we ate a tailgate picnic, and Ralph commented that a miner has a picnic every day.

Yesterday, a Saturday, taking Max with us, the five of us drove west to Quartzsite, to the big granddaddy of all flea markets and rock shows. The dawn sky was about the color of a ripe cantaloupe, with a few thin clouds forming over pale blue. This light, filtered through those clouds, lit up mountains that bore names we couldn't pronounce, but it was very lovely to see them etched that way in interesting shapes all around us.

When Quartzsite came into view, we couldn't believe our eyes. Acres and acres of RV's spread out into the creosote bushes, covering an area adjacent to the "Main Event," as it was called. After finding a place to park, we all took off in different directions, losing ourselves in rows upon rows of vendors selling everything from turquoise to hand-carved wooden figures.

The crowd was a melting pot of humanity, mostly retired people but with a sprinkling of younger ones, from all over the U.S., to buy, sell, trade, or sight-see. I succumbed to one merchant selling handmade stoves, who was at the moment roasting a turkey and sending mouth-watering aromas into the air. The stove folded up into a compact box that could be carried up on a pack mule or put in a boat. I could envision me cooking on it along the Snake River or up in some remote corner of the Wallowas.

Doug found little treasures of his own while Max and Ralph and Enid had returned to the car to rest, so I wandered into an aisle where a dark-haired young woman was playing an old, worn, dusty fiddle. Accompanying her on guitar was a bearded man.

The woman's free-flowing hair stirred gently in the desert wind. She wore no makeup to spoil her natural beauty. Her eyes closed often when she fiddled, and she seemed to bare her soul through her music. The couple used no sound system and the simple melodies floated through the desert air. The couple appeared to be very poor. A rusty can lay there on the ground for donations and money for two tapes they were selling. During a break between songs, I asked the girl how long she had been playing the fiddle.

"Since I was 10," she replied.

"I can tell," I said. The sound of her music was so incredibly lovely, it brought tears to my eyes. I purchased one of their tapes, then returned later to photograph the couple.

In the afternoon we found a place near the car to eat, so Max and Ralph could join us. A cousin of the Gatlin brothers, one Johnny Gatlin, belted out country western while his slim wife barbecued ribs. We sat on bales of hay and got those ribs all over our faces, and stomped our feet to Johnny's songs. It was "finger-lickin'" good. We saved the bones for Max's dog, Mel. We "tasted" Quartzsite, in more ways than one, on that warm January day in Arizona.

February 1—After traveling 4,400 miles through five Western states and being away from Prairie Creek for a month, it is good to sleep in a familiar bed again, to gaze out upon our mountains, and be HOME!

Great piles of snow line upper Prairie Creek roads, backgrounded by Chief Joseph Mountain.

Doug and I pulled into Enterprise late on a Saturday afternoon, having spent the last night of our trip in Ontario, Oregon. So many memories. Ones that stand out in retrospect include watching the full moon rise over the desert mountains at Furnace Creek in Death Valley; walking around in the evening light, which reflected mountains, in pools at Badwater, the lowest point in the Western Hemisphere; seeing the Death Valley museum at Furnace Creek, beautifully done; spending the night at Stovepipe Wells; and arising the next morning to see the Panamint mountains dusted with snow.

Interesting story about how Stovepipe Wells got its name. It seems some early prospectors were exploring in the valley, found water, and marked the spot with a stovepipe.

We drove north through that unbelievable valley of unnatural history and ended up at Scotty's Castle, another wonder that still blows our minds. It was one of those clear desert days, and the gushing spring that made settlement possible there still runs.

Originally the place was a ranch owned by a Mr. Johnson, who established a lifelong friendship with Death Valley Scotty, who claimed to have struck it rich in a gold mine there. Not a speck of natural gold was found, but Scotty convinced Mr. Johnson that there was truly a bonanza waiting to be mined and that he should finance the venture.

When Johnson came west to see his investment, he found no gold, but being in bad health, he rode horseback with Scotty and trudged around the desert, ate heartily, breathed the clear air and soon became robust and healthy. Eternally grateful to Scotty for this transformation, Johnson continued to support Scotty's dreams, which in fact included the beautiful castle, if you will, that stands today. Johnson said he was repaid in laughs, as Scotty was quite a character, who gained worldwide fame for his daring exploits.

There are so many interesting and beautiful things to see in the castle, I can't begin to describe them to you. After a tour through this impressive structure, I gazed up to a nearby hill where across marked Scotty's grave. A winding path led to the spot, so I walked up the hill. There was a cold breeze blowing the palm trees below, and looking down toward the castle, then out across that vast expanse of Death Valley, was one of the most exhilarating experiences of my life.

Etched on a large desert rock was Scotty's epitaph, which went something like this. *Never say or do anything that will hurt someone, never give advice (they won't take it anyway), and enjoy life.*

We drove out of the park via Scotty's Junction and headed off for lunch in Tonopah. Lest you think the world is becoming too populated, take the road from Tonopah to Ely, Nevada. I guarantee you won't think the West is anything but arid for miles and miles, but the desert grows on you; open space and unpeopled places are relaxing and good for the soul. We slipped some easy listening music in our tape player, and the miles disappeared.

The black shape of a prancing bull on an occasional sign denoted that we were in open range country. We saw some of those rugged range cattle, the object of so much controversy, rustling a living from the harsh environment of the desert. We learned many live off sagebrush and, in Arizona, were told they eat the pods off some sort of bush that is highly nutritious. Seems to me that when a critter can turn that kind of flora, which doesn't require much water, into a product that nourishes our bodies, it can't be all wrong. Especially when nothing else seems to survive out there, except antelope, jackrabbits and coyotes, which coexist with the cattle.

When we got to Ely, we ordered steak sandwiches, being in cattle country. They were delicious. We also passed by a few oil wells, their grasshopper-like pumpers sucking the earth's juices, so we could drive our car through the arid West. Another thing that struck me as we were traveling along was that the towns that flourished were surrounded by a resource, like range for cattle, fertile land for raising hay or crops, or timber and mining. When these resources weren't being utilized, the towns dried up and were claimed again by the desert.

Then there was Las Vegas, built for all the wrong reasons. "Family Fun" their signs proclaimed. Family? When they provide plastic video centers for the children, while their parents gamble and drink, is that family fun? Sorry, this writer doesn't buy that.

I'll continue to teach my grandchildren about rocks, plants, sky, and the beauty of our earth. And while I'm at it, I'll give a pitch for conservation and caring, not reaping the land for profit only, but loving it, and respecting the right for every living thing. Plastic? No wonder our children are spiritually hungry. Better that they could be taught to get "high" on scenery.

When we pulled into Baker City, Doug dropped me at the Oregon Trail Interpretive Center on Flagstaff Hill while he went antiquing.

I spent a glorious two hours absorbing the exhibits, which were upstaged by the scenery afforded through the huge glass windows. The Powder River Valley lay below, backgrounded by the snow-covered Elkhorns. It was breathtaking. There were very few people there on that January Saturday, and I was privileged to sit by two children in the Blue Mountain exhibit, where we watched a special program performed by residents of the Baker City area.

Clothed in Oregon Trail attire, members of this talented group took their places by the campfire of a wagon train encampment, and transported us back in time. I got as much satisfaction watching the faces of those children as I did the live performance. Growing up in a world of TV, plastic and materialism, their rapt attention proved once more that our youth are starved for basic things like stars, dirt, a bit of sagebrush, and the sounds of a fiddle, families singing together, and the quavering wail of a coyote.

And, on that note, I leave you to return to my book, cows, chickens and cross-country skiing.

February 15—It didn't take long to get back into the Wallowa County routine. Since I was starting to wear those breakfasts of elk steak, gravy, fried potatoes, and sourdough biscuits that Enid fixed while we were staying in Wenden, Arizona, it was imperative that I revert back to cold cereal, skim milk and grapefruit...and cross-country skiing!

On Super Bowl Sunday we tried out the new stove I had purchased in Quartzsite. It passed the test on barbecued ribs. We had in daughter Ramona's family and Bill, from Alder Slope. Bill brought back my dog, which he had been caring for in my absence. Daisy was ecstatic to see me again, and immediately we resumed our daily walks.

Speaking of which, I received a letter from Blanche Strey, of Lacy,

Washington, and she says, *Thank you Janie for that brisk walk. It carried me from the halls of Panorama Convalescent Center to your hill. I, too, once climbed to the top of a hill, with dogs Bob and Mike. And we loved the 'aloneness of space, sky, and far-off mountains, locked in winter silence.' And there always seemed to be a 'solitary hawk, soaring overhead.'* Love, Blanche. *P.S. Miss your column in the off weeks.*

It is because of people like Blanche that I continue to write. Thank you for the nice note, and I hope to keep transporting you out of that convalescent center.

Because I'd turned my two milk cows out with the main herd before we left, I walked up on the hill one afternoon into the midst of the fall calvers and their calves. Calling, "Here Startch, here Startch," until, very slowly, there was movement among the cud-chewing cows, and my old black and white Simmental/Holstein matron got to her feet and wove her way through the milling cows.

Followed by her daughter, she headed my way. Walking toward the barn, I turned to see my two very pregnant cows following behind. After I opened the gate to their pasture, they ambled over to their feeder and begged for some hay, so I tossed them a few flakes and filled their salt box with mineral.

The Barred Rock pullets are laying less now in the cold weather, but appear none the worse for wear while I was away. Ben had seen to that. I lined their nests with straw, filled their can with oyster shell and scrubbed out their automatic warm water bowl. Skip and Chester, the two roosters, have made a truce and as long as Skip doesn't enter Chester's territory, all is well. Our one surviving barn cat, old Scotty, crawled into a box we put out with a hole in one end, and gave birth to four kittens yesterday. In tomcat country, one never has just one cat for.long.

Once more involved in community, I found myself attending morning meetings, planning the catered meal CattleWomen will serve for Winter Fishtrap, serving on planning and advisory committees that hope to help guide Wallowa County's future.

Like all pretty places in the West, our area is faced with major decision-making now to ensure we don't go astray down the road. We can all complain about the present state of things, but unless we are willing to donate some of our time and energy to helping solve some of these problems, we have no right to criticize those who are.

It felt really good to sit down at my piano again, and play early of a morning. Music restores the soul and allows us to be creative in our own way. So does cross-country skiing, which has been fabulous. Linde and

I are ready to don skis whenever the weather is right, and soon we are out in the woods, sliding and gliding along some snowy forest trail. One morning three other local gals joined us and we made a six-mile loop. The snow was nearly perfect, the air crisp and pure, and conversation spiced with laughter followed in our wake.

On a recent zero degree morning, Linde and I found ourselves in another one of our famous adventures. After leaving a nearby trailhead, we decided to strike off up a mountain, hoping to find a shortcut to the top. A group of snowshoers encamped on a level spot away from the main trail must have thought we were nuts.

We waved as we passed their camp, and began to herringbone, side-step, and otherwise struggle to the place where we knew there was a logging road. The snow was deep, powdery and drifted, and covered downed logs and trees. The going got real tough. We saw where the snowshoers had descended a steep chute, and we avoided these steeper routes and began making short traverses back and forth up the snowy hill. Working every muscle in our bodies, sweat soon formed under our clothes, as we were then in bright sunshine.

Once I fell when one ski sank into a deep hole alongside a fallen log and wedged tight under it. I was able to struggle free and wearily make my way up to Linde, who had finally located the elusive road. We skied over waist-high drifted snow and made our way slowly to the top. And there were the Seven Devils Mountains of Idaho, gleaming under the most polished blue sky imaginable. After consuming a granola bar and a drink of water, we started down the other side, this time following a ski trail.

What had taken us two hours to ascend, took us 15 minutes to descend. We fairly flew down that familiar trail. It was pure pleasure and worth the effort we'd exerted earlier. We had little time to spare, because I had promised to be back in time to watch grandson Bart while mom and dad went fishing with Doug on Snake River. Nordic skiing is a wonderful sport. Even for grandmothers!

Last Sunday evening, Pat and Linde made their way through our drifted roads and together we drove the 30 miles to Imnaha to attend the annual sweetheart dinner put on by the Imnaha Christian Fellowship. The ladies outdid themselves on the prime rib dinner, which was served up with baked potatoes, corn, salad, bread, jam, pickles, horseradish, and the most impressive array of homemade pies you ever saw. Skip Royes, who relinquished the previous year's honor, crowned Jim Blankenship as the 1994 sweetheart. And Clyde Simmons was there to harass Jim.

As in the past the skits and songs performed by the small community left us with a warm feeling in our hearts as we drove home in a rain that turned to snow about Lightning Creek. The rural settlement of Imnaha is composed mainly of ranchers' families, and it seems to me we need to preserve these cattle communities, for their people. They are pretty special.

February 25—Meanwhile, back at the ranch, our cows began dropping baby calves in snowy pastures. Wallowa County calves are a hardy lot. It wasn't below zero or anything, but wet and cold enough to be pretty miserable for newborns.

I had made reservations on the 23rd for four other gals and myself to spend the night on a high ridge in a ski shelter hut. Little did we know there would be a record-breaking snowfall during our stay. I was up early choring and getting ready to leave with Linde and Susanne Gadola around 10 a.m. Stanlynn and Carol would leave the trailhead around 3 p.m. My waterproof pack was stuffed with a sleeping bag, a pan of frozen lasagna, a loaf of sourdough bread, a bottle of water, and a toothbrush.

It was snowing when we drove to the trailhead, parked Linde's jeep, and began our trek. Snow lay deep in the road, and we had to break trail, which was exhausting. When we turned off into the woods and began to climb, we took turns in the lead.

Linde and I brought our two dogs along, and they followed in our tracks because snow rose over their heads alongside the trail. The snow continued to fall and, really, it seemed pretty nice being out there. We weren't cold. The soft stillness, the drooping, white evergreens, and the sound of our sliding and swooshing skis was making it an adventure. Susanne carried snowshoes on her pack in case someone lost or broke a ski. We marked our trail in so Stanlynn and Carol would know which way to turn at each fork in the trail. New snow continued to fall, quickly filling our tracks. At the last fork, a weak sun burst forth enough to cause spruce trees to cast shadows. The respite from the falling snow was brief, and again the skies opened up.

Soft, feather-light flakes floated down upon our silent world. Our packs felt extremely heavy by the time we made the final ascent to the hut. The valley far below seemed non-existent. We were on a giant hogback, peering into a curtain of snow that limited further vision. Huge drifts continued to pile next to the hut, and we stuck our skis and poles in them before entering the shelter.

Soon we had a crackling fire going in the barrel stove and were melting snow for water. We were home! Let it snow.

After resting a bit, Linde and Susanne skied down to meet Stanlynn

Roadside winter art on Prairie Creek.

and Carol, who, as it turned out, had an easier time because our trail was still mostly broken.

Before I joined them I found a snow shovel and shoveled out a path to the outhouse and the sauna. The snow was over my waist. We built a fire in the sauna tent stove when everyone arrived. After early darkness stole upon our ridgetop, we lit the lantern and ate lasagna, warm sourdough bread, and Linde's crisp carrot and celery sticks. Then Carol produced some imported chocolates...yum.

After the dishes were done we retreated to the sauna tent where a hot fire waited. We had good intentions of rolling in the snow after a sweat, but quickly changed our minds after stepping out into the steadily-falling snow, and settled for rubbing a bit of snow on our arms. We laughingly made our way back to the hut, fed the fire and hit the bunks. Since I was closest to the fire it was my duty to feed it during the night and let Stanlynn's large dog, Bear, out, then in.

The next morning we stared out into a white void, and pushed higher and deeper snow away from the door of the hut. After breakfasting on Stanlynn's fruity oatmeal, we packed up and left. It was exhausting work skiing back to the trailhead, and still snowing. It took us four hours of slogging through soft new snow with no semblance of a trail to find Linde's car buried at the trailhead. At one point, Stanlynn donned snowshoes to break trail, but they, too, sank in the waist-high snow.

Linde and I left our packs in the car and skied down to where Stanlynn and Carol were parked, and buried too! What a relief to see Linde's worried husband, Pat, waiting with his chained-up truck to rescue us.

Returning to the ranch I found one of my milk cows had dropped a big heifer calf in the deep snow, so I spent more than an hour bending over the chilled calf with a heat lamp and giving it colostrum from a bottle. She is now none the worse for the experience, and I am again milking a cow.

February 28—Looking out my kitchen window on this last day of February, I spot a pair of returning robins. Perched on the pole fence alongside the raspberry patch, they survey the huge drift of snow that all but covers their future treats. Will they stay here or will they fly on to easier pickin's?

Such an active past two weeks this has been. What with planning the Saturday evening meal we CattleWomen catered for Winter Fishtrap, attending the weekend writers' conference itself, skiing...and calving season.

Fishtrap opened with a Friday evening pizza feed at Vali's Alpine

Delicatessen at Wallowa Lake, followed by introductions of this year's participants, including John Rember, who attended the first summer gathering six years ago, writing about the changes he's seen in his part of Idaho and watching the changes taking place here in Wallowa County. Other visiting participants who explored the theme "Recreation and the West" included Angus Thuermer Jr., editor of the *Jackson Hole News* in Jackson, Wyoming; Emily Swanson, a member of the Montana State Legislature; and Jeanne Thomas, education/tour coordinator for the museum at Warm Springs, Oregon.

During the weekend sessions we became more familiar with the history of Jackson Hole, and the Teton and Yellowstone National parks. Angus vividly described the rapid development of Jackson Hole, which led to its subsequent demise.

Emily Swanson explained how the elk in Yellowstone Park have learned to react to humans and "get smart" when hunting season rolls around. Managing wildlife inside the parks is affected by private lands outside the park.

"Elk, deer and grizzlies can't read signs that mark park boundaries," she said. Emily was in sympathy with the ranchers who had quietly and successfully managed their lands all these years, only to find themselves in a dilemma not of their own choosing, wondering how and when it will end. Most of the big ranches around Jackson have been replaced with subdivisions, and many once lovely "beaver slide hay meadows" are now destination resorts.

Jeanne Thomas was wonderful! A great-grandmother at age 55, a woman who went out and educated herself, learned the English language, reared her children (who educated themselves) to become successes in their chosen fields. And you can see why, when you get to know Jeanne. She is about as down-to-earth as one can get. Before Jeanne left, her wish was to shake everyone's hand, and I think she accomplished this by Sunday. Her warm personality, sense of humor and dedication to preserving tribal legends, languages and traditional ways impressed all of us.

The next morning I was up at dawn to feed my livestock before driving to the Eagle Cap Chalet at Wallowa Lake for breakfast with fellow Fishtrappers. The catered breakfast was such a treat, and we visited while stuffing ourselves with muffins, fruit, and quiches. When the afternoon sessions were over I hurried across the river to the Methodist Camp kitchen where the CattleWomen, under the able direction of friend Linde, were preparing the evening meal. Everything was under control, so I helped Betty Van set tables for 80 people while Linde, Pat, Gay and

Ramona dealt with beef tri-tip, salad, sourdough breads, vegetarian chili, and lemon dessert.

Outside the lodge it was snowing, adding to the already deep drifts. Several mule deer ambled past, and peered through the windows at our preparations. We slid fiddle music into a tape player and soon the gathering gathered around the roaring fire in the old stone fireplace, which awoke flies from their winter slumber to crawl lazily around the windows. A good conversation piece that was definitely Wallowa County.

After returning to the Eagle Cap Chalet meeting room the next morning for breakfast, we reconvened at the Methodist Camp lodge for open mic readings, of which I was first on the agenda, reading a short essay I'd written on recreation and the West. After lunch another successful winter Fishtrap writers' conference came to an end, and we came away with the good feeling of having made new friends, understanding different cultures, and better able to guide and share in our own area's destiny.

March 9—March came in like a soft spring lamb on Prairie Creek. It didn't even freeze the night before, and now our barn lot is a soupy mix of manure and snowmelt. My milk cow's heifer calf is growing daily, as is her grafted bull calf. Despite two calves nursing her, I continue to milk a gallon of milk from this Simmental/Holstein cross cow every morning and evening.

Down in the calving fields, newborns sun themselves in this unseasonable March warmth. Those earlier babies didn't look as contented the day I returned from that skiing adventure. Being born into a world of sixteen inches of new snow was somewhat of a shock. It was really something to see when all of that snow went off, in less than 24 hours.

Daisy and I, taking our daily walk, were sidetracked at every turn by running water. Barrow pits ran full, rushing water ate at the county roads, and every cow path leading down a draw turned into a raging creek. On the prairie itself, lakes formed and great wetlands appeared, where wild ducks and geese cavorted happily. As the warm breath of the chinook swept across the land, the snow receded, turned to water, pooled a while, and was gone.

Daisy and I continue our daily walks over Hough's hills, and we spotted the first waxy buttercups today, cheerful drops of gold upon the drab March landscape, near a rock outcropping where the afternoon sun warmed the earth enough to bring the harbingers of spring to flower.

Lavender and golden crocuses blooming alongside our house inspired me to clean out the flower beds. March is usually a season of blizzards, wind, rain showers and cold blustery weather. I think it isn't over yet, and expect April will get even with us.

March 18—On a Saturday early in the month Doug and I drove over the Blues, pulling a stock trailer behind our pickup. Doug let me off at Blue Mountain Community College, and he drove on to Hermiston to purchase a bull at the annual C&B production sale. While waiting for daughter Ramona and granddaughter Carrie, whom I would meet there, I wandered leisurely around the campus.

It was a warm, mild morning, and the greening grain fields that provide much of Pendleton's wealth rolled into the distance. College campuses fascinate me. Having never had the opportunity to attend college, I have always deemed it a privilege to do so. It upsets me somewhat to see so many young people take it for granted. Wandering into a theater where a young student was playing the piano for a day-long music competition that day, my faith in young people was restored. After listening all afternoon to talented teens sing, I was impressed even more.

Granddaughter Carrie, representing her high school, performed in the vocal competition. As I listened to her sweet 16-year-old voice singing an Italian song, I couldn't help thinking of my father, Carrie's great-grandfather, who had a Caruso-like voice. His only audience was a milk barn full of cows and his children, like me, who, at the time, failed to realize what a great voice he had. Perhaps daddy's voice has manifested itself in our Carrie. It was wonderful being there, listening to Carrie and others like her, who are developing their talent. Seeing the joy in their faces as they sang was just great.

Since the weather hasn't been conducive to cross-country skiing lately, Daisy and I have resorted to our daily walks. Sometimes we are joined by Linde or Scotty, and sometimes Scotty and I walk around Wallowa Lake, which is in its "off season" and quiet and peaceful. Thank goodness we still have an "off season" here in Wallowa County.

After our brisk walks, we go swimming in the indoor pool at the Eagle Cap Chalets, another off-season privilege. Occasionally I drive to Alder Slope to check on Bill, clean out the screens on the trout ponds, and hike around listening to the music of running water and startling the white tail deer. The bluebirds have returned to Alder Slope and their bright blue flashes are a joy to behold.

Last week two grandchildren spent the night. They amused themselves with the new kittens, which now have their eyes open and are quite cuddly. In the afternoon James and I hiked over to the irrigation ditch, where ice still hung in large shelves over the water. We broke off huge chunks of it and floated icebergs. We came home all muddy, but as James exclaimed, "It was worth it, wasn't it, grandma?" Sure was.

Not much more to report here, although there is lots of news these days in Wallowa County. A mill closure, which will affect one of my married sons, and the ongoing battles of grazing rights, resource management, health care, new growth, and education. But in a world that seems to be going insane, I find that to remain sane we need to not ever loses our sense of wonder about the first buttercups, baby kittens, and children, or we won't be able to effectively deal with everything else.

March 30—The transformation has begun. Snowy white has given way to frosted brown, and now, the first, faint greening. Although spring has officially occurred on our calendar, this eternal season is just now making a visual appearance upon the land.

Other signs point to spring here on the ranch. Ben's son Seth has been harrowing the fields, Doug has been burning dead grass, and a pair of honkers are nesting near the irrigation ditch. During the recent full moon, Startch, my infamous milk cow, decided to calve. After bedding her down in a warm stall every night for a week, she finally gave birth to a big bull calf in those final hours before dawn. Arising early that Sunday morning, I could tell right off Startch had accomplished her labor. Only there was no calf!

Puzzled, I opened the gate so she could go for water, and there, wandering around near the irrigation ditch, was her calf, shivering and still covered with amniotic fluid. It looked as though it had been born into a motherless world. As close as I can figure, the old cow must have positioned herself next to the only crack in the side of the stall when she was ready to deliver. The slippery calf apparently slithered through that opening and found himself in the cow pasture.

Startch proceeded with motherhood. She licked her calf dry, and with the patience of age, ambled (calf following) to the farther end of the cow pasture, where she calmly discharged her placenta. I carried a forkful of alfalfa hay down to her and saw that the calf was nursing. I returned to the barn, where I let the other calves in to nurse the other milk cow. Since then we have acquired two more calves, and now six calves are being raised on these two cows. A pretty profitable venture, but for the first two weeks, labor intensive on the part of the milk maid.

Just the day before, we had trailed the fall-calving cows to the hills, which meant 17 miles in the saddle. A little much for grandma, after a winter of not riding. So after chores, we cowboys and cowgals (Pat,

Linde, Sarah, 87-year-young Mike McFetridge, and I) headed out to the old Dorrance place on Crow Creek, where our cows were penned for the night and anxiously awaiting our return.

Saturday morning we'd had our usual struggle keeping the cows from turning back to their bawling calves, which were being weaned in the corrals at the ranch. It took all hands, and then some, to persuade those cows to continue down the road. One quick, young cow did turn, and the rest of the herd followed, but after much hard riding and yelling, we finally got them lined out.

Once we hit the graveled Cow Creek road, things went smoother. Mike rode ahead to block the inevitable open gates, which led to farm ground and pastures all along the route. Buttercups bloomed profusely, hawks circled above in a flawless blue sky, and we saw an enormous bald eagle perched in the middle of a field, hunting mice. As the endless hills stretched ahead of us, Mike and I were remembering previous drives when quite often it snowed, just as we rode up through Crow Creek pass. That Saturday, however, was just about perfect, with just a bit of breeze.

Ben showed up at noon driving the pickup, with a lunch his wife, Jackie, had prepared for us. We munched fried chicken and hoagie sandwiches before climbing back into the saddle to catch up to our disappearing herd. Snow banks, usually numerous in March, were scarce. Cows and horses watered up at a snowmelt pond alongside the road, and by 3 o'clock we had the herd corralled near the old pink barn. We unsaddled our horses after Ben arrived, fed them oats and hay, penned them for the night, and hayed the cows. After the ride home it was chore time, after which I fixed supper, put Startch in the barn, soaked in the tub and fell into bed.

Early the next morning I found Startch's big calf, and Linde, Pat and Mike drove in to give me a ride out to Crow Creek, where the cows appeared to have forgotten all about motherhood. Their familiar spring range beckoned, and they could just about taste that grass after a winter diet of hay. I always wish for my camera when those cows are making their single-file way up Dorrance gulch. Looking back at the distant, snowy Wallowas, separated by miles of rolling high plateau, is such an impressive sight; a sight that is disappearing in our West, they say. But the cattle business is very much alive in Wallowa County.

As we rode up and over the grade and gazed upon the vast Zumwalt hill country, it came to me again how fortunate we are to make a living here. It all seems so right, somehow, utilizing the grass, which year after year sustains our cattle, which sustain not only us but many others as well, without ruining the land. Buttercups lined the roadway. Dry

Hands from all over the county help out on branding day on Big Sheep in the Imnaha canyon. This outfit is being leased by Kirk Makin of Enterprise.

Salmon Creek, experiencing its yearly joy, was wet. Green bunch grass pushed its way up through the old. The ageless hills respond to the seasonal changes, as they have for eons.

With a contented smile creasing his face, old hand Mike, an amazing cowboy seemingly as old as these hills, looked out upon another spring transforming the land he loves so well. Mike and Pat split the herd, turning half in the Johnson pasture while Linde and I drove the other bunch to Butte Creek. I barely got ahead of them before they reached the gate, so anxious were they to commence grazing.

Presently, we saw dust rising in the distance; Doug driving the cattle truck. We loaded the dogs in the dog catcher and returned to the ranch.

Before Mike left to ride home with Pat and Linde, he squeezed my hand, his unspoken words, "Well, we made it one more spring, didn't we?" I guess that's all any of us can do these days: make it one more spring.

April 12—We are experiencing a typical Wallowa County spring, which is to say the weather lately has been unpredictable, and fickle as April can be. Just when things begin to really green up, along comes another storm, dumping soft snow all over Prairie Creek...again. In the warmer canyons, the sarvisberry is in bloom, and in secluded settings of the Imnaha, the first brandings are under way.

My camera and I were there, at one held up Big Sheep recently, where cowboys, cowgirls, dogs, children, horses and grandmas converged. It is like tasting a slice of the old West, which is yet very much a part of the present West. After the little calves were separated from their mamas, lending a constant bawling sound to the scene, cowboys who had trailered their mounts from miles around advanced, loops built, to begin headin' and heelin' the calves. The unsuspecting calves were held between the mounted riders to be branded, castrated (if they are bulls) and vaccinated, before being turned loose.

There is just as much activity going on with the ground crew, which is there to administer branding iron, needle and knife. Blood and dust co-mingle with scorched hair in a scene as old as the West. I capture it on film from the bed of a hay truck amid that rugged canyon setting beside Big Sheep Creek, running full of snowmelt just past the corrals.

By 1 p.m. the first batch of calves were reunited with their moms, and Liz and Kelly had the barbecue fired up and were soon feeding the hungry crew. Although there are more modern methods of handling calves these days, in many instances Wallowa Countians stick to the old ways: neighbor helping neighbor, combining work and play.

The next day was Easter Sunday. Arising early, I stumbled out in the dark to let my two cows in the barn to nurse their six calves; fed everything hay, including my mare; watered and fed the chickens; then changed from overalls to skirt and made the 7:30 sunrise service at the Joseph Methodist Church.

The Sunday sky was gray and curtains of spring snow showers hung over the Wallowas, but inside the old stone, stained-glass-windowed church, it was warm and glowing. Not only with light, but with friendly people, all dressed in their Sunday best, including a daughter and her family who had driven 30 miles to sing in the community-wide cantata. The blending of those familiar voices in song was very uplifting. A superb program staged by our neighbors from all over the valley. Everyone got into the Easter spirit, a rebirth not only of the season we call spring, but a resurrection, a living force that drives us all.

Back home to the tantalizing aroma of ham baking in my oven, which Doug and I loaded, along with colored eggs, potato salad and banana cream pie, into our car. The gathering of the clan, this year down at daughter Jackie's place on Camp Creek, is an annual tradition. We feasted on Jackie's fresh-from-the-oven bread, roast turkey, Ramona's barbecue ribs, the ham, salads and desserts, then worked it all off with a baseball game. First, though, the older children hid eggs and the younger ones went on their excited hunt.

Golden forsythia, as well as tulips and daffodils bloomed at that lower elevation. Cottony clouds floated over rim rocks, alternating cool and

Little Amber Shear, whose daddy works for the outfit up Big Sheep Creek in Wallowa County, smiles for the camera at a branding.

warmth. Young and old played side by side, including grandma, who hit left-handed into left field and managed to clear all four bases, even though she didn't slide as son Todd would have her do. From little Ryan to tall Shawn, children and parents took their turns being up to bat. Two of the more adventurous grandsons abandoned the outfield, and being akin to mountain goats, hiked straight up one of those steep canyon sides.

Because our family has extended itself so, we had ample players for two teams. Occasionally the ball sailed off into the nearby creek, and the horses, which normally use the flat for grazing, fled to the nearby hill and became our spectators. We used feed sacks with rocks on them for bases, which made it nice for sliding. Wherever their paths in life may lead these youngsters, they'll always remember such simple pleasures; creating memories to comfort and sustain.

Returning home on top to windy, blustering snow squalls, the day itself fast becoming a memory, tucked away in the subconscious, to be brought back over the years and savored. Doug is farming, preparing the hill land to plant to a hay crop. The last of the cows are calving, and hopefully by May 1st they'll all be trailed to summer range.

Twice daily, I tend my growing calves, which are becoming increasingly difficult to separate from the cows. They are like little leeches, and I've resorted to various tactics to make them release those teats. With the twins, I can pick up a hind leg and drag them, kicking, into the other pen. The larger ones I propel by placing one hand under the chin and the other on the tail. Developing muscles uncommon to grandmothers, I am looking forward to turning all six out with the cows, which might be sooner than expected.

Two of my sisters are driving up for a week's visit, and that means making time for adventure!

May 10—There is supposed to be an eclipse of the sun taking place as I write this morning. The past few days have been summer-like, except the land still wears a brilliant green cover, and everything is a-bloom. Linde and I really felt the heat yesterday, when we began planting the Slope garden. By the time we roto-tilled, extended a row of raspberries, and seeded a row of lettuce, two rows of peas, and some spinach, we were seeking the shady porch. Over a fruit jar of cold spring water we looked out over our labors and rested.

On the way home we stopped at the Alder Slope Nursery, where Linde got carried away with all the growing things offered there. Our little pickup resembled a moveable garden service, what with a roto-tiller

Chief Joseph Days Queen Josi Botts, left, poses with her court, princesses Shannon Vernam, center, and Carrie Snyder.

Popular couple Bud and Ruby Zollman will be grand marshals for the Chief Joseph Days parade.

surrounded by potted plants.

Early on the morning of April 29, with a heavy frost coating the meadows, we saddled our horses and gathered the spring calving cows and their calves, turned them onto the Liberty road, and began the long seasonal trek to the hills.

Old hand Mike McFetridge, Ben, his son Seth, and Linde and I spent all day pushing those tired little calves and worried mama cows out to East Crow, where they spent the night in a holding pasture. The day quickly warmed, becoming downright hot by the time we made it through the Crow Creek pass. As usual, the slowest calves bunched up in the rear, where some had to be hog-tied and given a ride in the pickup so they wouldn't hold up the drive. Much of our time while still in the valley was spent on foot, leading our horses and pushing calves, and my boots weren't made for walking.

It was definitely the day designated "Turn out to grass." Huge semi truck and trailer rigs bulging with cattle wove slowly through our trailing herd. We saw yearlings, destined for the B&H ranch on Chesnimnus Creek; Shorty Lathrop and his crew waved from loaded cattle trucks, as did Larry Fleshman and the Ketscher family. The Crow Creek road was a virtual traveling cattle thoroughfare.

However, we appeared to be the only ones trailing the old way, and as the day wore on...5 p.m., 6 p.m., trucking cattle began to take on a greater appeal. Long after our neighbors were finished for the day, we were still plugging along.

Around noon, we ambled along in back of the herd, munching lunches, then climbed back into the saddle, making those long, slow miles disappear. Early on I had resorted to a "tin dog" (a pop can filled with gravel), which was hurled into the herd to speed things up. We became hoarse, yelling, "Hey, girls, come on babies."

Mike's dog, Sam, old and hard of hearing, wasn't much help, and the cows continually fought Ben's dog and spent much time bellowing and being protective of their calves. Often, tired calves would crawl through a fence along the route, then husky Seth would have to run them down, grab a hind leg, and push them through again. We were all very hot, dusty and tired by the time the last calf wandered into the pasture at East Crow. The old wire gate looked pretty rickety, and I didn't like the "homeward bound" look in one cow's eye as we patched up the gate. That cow's calf had been hauled to the front earlier, and she hadn't mothered-up yet.

Early next morning, under cloudy skies, on our way out to resume the drive, we met that cow! Farther on, more cows and calves. Our hearts sank. Every inch along the way had been sorely earned, to no avail. Expecting the worst, we were cheered to see half the herd still grazing in the holding pasture, along with our horses (which we had envisioned high-tailing it to Salmon Creek). Apparently these hadn't discovered the torn-down gate.

It began to rain, a warm steady patter, which is great for cattle country. We donned slickers, caught and saddled our horses, and by the time Ben, Mike, Linde and I gathered the herd and had them started on the road, Seth, driving the cattle truck, had caught up to us driving the errant cows and calves. We left the lead cow grazing along the road. Seth caught her calf and hauled it back to the cow. Ben and Seth would deal with them later.

Meanwhile, it began to pour. Water dripped off my old Stetson in a steady stream. We weren't cold...yet. The calves, broken to drive now, were traveling better, and due to the coolness we made better time than yesterday. No traffic that Saturday either, but we received the word via the Crow Creek telegraph that a bunch of yearlings was heading our way. Luckily we met the cowboys and cowgirl, who say they will stall the cattle at the Dorrance place until we pass by. We sure didn't need another wreck.

Heading up Dorrance Grade, rain turns to snow. I am warmly clad, but Linde was cold, so I loaned her my ski hat and produced an extra pair of gloves from the pickup parked at the Dorrance place. We plodded on. Halfway up, who should appear but Doug, bearing goodies: hot coffee, tea and freshly baked maple bars.

A lost bear hunter pulls up behind Doug, wants to know where Zumwalt is. We all visit there in the snowy rain, warming ourselves with hot drinks. The cows are nearly to the top when we finish. Doug, having been rained out of farming, made points with us that day. On top we were hit with wind-driven snow, which chilled to the bone, and our visibility was limited. Presently, Ben appeared in the cattle truck and easily persuaded us to warm up inside the cab and eat our lunches. I spotted a cow making her way back, and before we knew it, Mike was out in the storm turning her back.

Linde and I continue to marvel at this 86-year-old cowboy who can still do a day's work and smile through it all. The three of us climbed back into our wet, cold saddles and rode forward in search of our phantom herd. Doug soon appeared and insisted Mike get in, and loaded up his horse. It was really getting cold and Mike was pretty chilled. That left Linde and me to finish the drive, which we did, without incident.

And wouldn't you know, just as we turned the last of the herd into the pasture at Deadman, it quit storming.

Twenty-five miles in two days. Due perhaps, to the cooler weather, I wasn't as tired as the day before, or maybe just in shape.

Envisioning a day of rest, until I remembered a promised fishing trip with the grandchildren. I never break a promise to children, so we spent a great day at Wallowa Lake, then home to the ranch to play baseball, do chores and tell stories.

One day last week we drove with daughter Ramona and son-in-law Charley to La Grande to meet with a very surprised daughter Lori and family for a birthday dinner at Ten Depot Street.

On Mother's Day morning, Doug and I went mushrooming and found enough morels for one meal, then joined a branding on Sheep Creek hill, where we helped son-in-law Charley work his calves. Mother hot day, and by the time we finished, everyone was pooped. Family members all pitched in. A special Mother's Day, as the children remembered me in one way or another.

In spite of all their tribulations, families are powerful support systems and we in the ranching community need all the support we can get these days.

May 21—The familiar snow shape of a horse, known locally as "Tucker's Mare," is hidden from view this morning due to low-lying rain clouds which wrap themselves around the mountains. It is the season for thunderstorms. Great purple clouds gather and drive drenching rains before them across the valley. Rainbows sprout during short bursts of sunlight, arching their colorful bows above the brilliant green countryside.

Nearly a week now of scattered showers has stimulated grass-growing. In the hills and canyons, wildflowers are riotous... yellow cous, lupine, larkspur, camas, balsamroot, mule ear; the rocky plateaus are pink with low-growing phlox. Rain-washed skies were robin's egg blue, with great mushrooming clouds growing, casting moving shadows across acres of grasslands last Monday when we rattled out in the truck to work the spring calves.

Mounting our horses, we rode the north pasture, gathering together the scattered cows and calves. It is always such a sight, seeing those moving cattle against the wildflower-flecked hills, to be savored and never taken for granted. No dust that Monday, and no heat, unlike last May, when we branded in nearly 80-degree temperatures.

Normally quiet, Salmon Creek was soon inundated with the sounds of bawling cows and answering calves as we sorted calves from cows. Soon

12-year-old Buck Matthews of Imnaha, and Doug Tippett of Prairie Creek, help rope calves for a branding on the Cross Sabres Ranch near Joseph. Many ranchers continue to work their calves in the old way, and a good cow horse is a valuable tool. Ramona Phillips and hired hand, Ted, work with the ground crew.

the branding fire was crackling. I pushed, one by one and sometimes, if they were small calves, two by two, the calves up the long wooden chute that leads to a squeeze chute and calf table. There were only four of us that day: Ben, his son, Seth, Doug and me. Ben and Doug branded and castrated, while Seth gave shots.

Every so often one of those clouds activated Mother Nature's irrigation system, but the cool was not all unpleasant. When 50 calves wore the X brand, we climbed into our trucks and ate lunch while a passing shower turned the corral to mud. Then back to work.

After pushing many calves up that chute, I soon learn to "read" each calf, and label them: Kicker, gentle, stubborn, and watch out for flying little hooves. When the pen emptied, I'd hurry and fill it again, so as to be ready with another calf by the time the men were finished. I find that the less one stirs up the calves, the better, and things went pretty smoothly until one decided to turn around or back out of the chute.

By 5 p.m. we had worked 143 calves, and I was able to rest while the men sprayed the cows. We turned the mothered-up cows out of the corrals and drove them back to their summer range. Their bawling gradually faded away in the distance, and again the air filled with the sound of blackbirds, and of Salmon Creek gurgling past.

Peace restored; a curling wisp of smoke from the branding fire and a muddied corral were the only evidence we'd caused all that commotion. We unsaddled our horses and turned them loose in the horse pasture. Doug loaded up a stray yearling heifer that had wandered in with our cows and we delivered her back to her range. The "mountain oyster" buckets were overflowing and promised a good feed for supper later in the week. We noticed fresh snow lying in the Crow Creek road on our way home.

Back to the ranch and a fire in the wood cook stove, warmed up leftovers for supper, and that long-awaited soak in the tub. Due to the continued rains we've been unable to finish branding the other bunch of calves. One of these days, I suspect, I'll be helping trail the fall calvers to their summer range on the east moraine of Wallowa Lake.

Our Slope garden is up, what we planted anyway. Been too wet to plant much more. We keep busy attending grandchildren's school functions, concerts, plays, end-of-school programs and the like. Then there is lawn-mowing, meetings, and the busy-ness of spring. Shafts of sunlight sift down upon the Wallowas now as I write. It is good to see them again. Fragments of cloud wreath the peaks, which are covered with fresh white snow.

And life goes on outwardly beautiful in Wallowa County, although there is much turmoil as to what the future holds for many of its inhabitants. Meanwhile, enjoy the beauty that is given freely and be thankful for being alive.

June 6—A warm rain that began in the night and continued until noon today has left Prairie Creek freshened and green. Such a grass year! Acres and acres of it, waving in a clean, cool breeze this afternoon. Grass pollen outlines puddles left by the rain; and on the timbered slopes of the mountains, pine pollen drifts like smoke.

June…a lovely time when the rains come. Among the hills that separate prairie from canyon it is the hot pink, wild geraniums' turn to bloom. Along the irrigation ditches, wild daisies are beginning to dot the green with white and yellow.

My childhood chum Sandra and her husband, Fred, spent last week with us. Sandra and I grew up together in the foothill country of Northern California's Placer County. Living about four miles apart, we spent our summers walking back and forth on country roads, visiting each other and sharing dreams of our future, while growing into young adulthood. Now, 45 years later, we keep in touch and catch up on our lives. Often, after supper, Sandra and I would take long walks around the ranch.

The morning after Sandra and Fred's arrival, Sandra and I were in the

Slope garden, setting out Walla Walla sweet onion plants and hilling in a long row of seed potatoes. That evening we all drove to Imnaha to attend the end-of-school program. As usual, grades 1-8 put on an original play, one that only a small, isolated community's children could create. We were greatly entertained. The audience, sprinkled with babies of all ages, assured a future for the two-room school beneath the rim rocks. At one point, a small child, wanting to be part of the act, ran up on stage and made his own loud statement, which caused gales of laughter.

But there was pathos, as well as mirth, when the three graduating eighth graders gave short talks before receiving their certificates. For you see, next fall these students, products themselves of the canyons, will have to leave their world as they now know it to attend a much larger school "on top," which in turn leads to the world on the "outside."

Graduating Luke read, "I will miss my friend Buck, being in school with him and going for hikes in the canyons."

Luke and Buck grew up together, living a sort of Huckleberry Finn existence while their dads cowboyed for most of the cattle outfits up and down the river. This is a way of life they'll never forget. The audience, made up of the small, close community, sensed this emotional milestone in their lives. Wherever Buck and Luke, and all the other Imnaha children, may wander down life's path, a part of them will forever remain on the Imnaha, that sense of place permanently ingrained in their very being. Driving those 30 miles home that evening, we saw the full May moon show its partial eclipse from the top of Sheep Creek hill.

The next morning Sandra and I pretended to be tourists in my own town and "did" the shops in Joseph. It was a lovely sunny day as we wandered into the art galleries and gift shops, many of which I'd never been in. Amazing how our little "cow town" is changing. A matched pair of Morgan horses pulled a carriage up the street, giving tourists a "Western experience." So many changes, I scarcely knew where I was!

We lunched at the Blue Willow in Enterprise, a small eatery set next to an aspen grove and creek. We visited over home-style vegetable soup, salad, fresh fruit and warm, fragrant bread just out of the oven.

One such evening we observed a pair of killdeers and their four young babies. At sunset, as the air became cooler, the mother bird would call for her young, fluff her feathers, lift her wings, and from all directions the little fluffs of feathers would run, snuggling under her warmth. When mom wanted time off to eat, she merely called her mate, who then took his turn brooding the tiny birds. We surprised a pair of wild mallards swimming in the creek, and numerous hawks flew into the tall cottonwoods growing there.

Later in the afternoon I met with a committee to go over the submissions for the summer Fishtrap fellowships. Last week we had read and digested 34 manuscripts, taking notes. Sandra listened in, much entertained.

After supper that evening, Fred and Doug went kokanee fishing on Wallowa Lake while Sandra and I planted a wildflower patch in our front yard. The next evening we took Fred and Sandra to the Enterprise FFA pancake feed and plant sale. We returned stuffed with pancakes, sausage and eggs, and carrying petunias and several tomato plants, which the FFA members had raised in their greenhouse.

At 6 a.m. on opening day of fishing season, this grandma was on the shores of Kinney Lake with a son and two grandsons. It was chilly at that early hour, but we beat the crowd and found a good place to fish. When James' dad had to leave for work and Josh had to weigh his 4-H lamb, that left just James and grandma. We had pretty good luck and between the two of us limited out on rainbows and catfish.

An extra treat was provided by a lone beaver that swam around the lake, whacking his large, flat tail and generally entertaining the fishermen. On the far shore a family of wild honkers fed on the grasses growing there. And all around us was the lush Prairie Creek springtime, with its wild flowers, rushing waterways, waving grasses, and gorgeous clouds sweeping shadows over the Wallowas.

In spite of untangling lines, keeping track of worm cans, and lugging a lunch, the experience was worthwhile when James' smile lit up his young face as he pulled in a fish.

Later that afternoon daughter Lori, husband Tom, and two children arrived to spend Memorial Day weekend with us. That evening, over a steak dinner at Vali's Wallowa Lake Delicatessen, we celebrated Lori and Tom's 12th wedding anniversary.

The next day found us, Doug included, up at Kinney Lake again, with even more children.

On the first day of June, Linde and her visiting company from California, Dr. Johnny and wife Claire, helped us plant the remainder of the Slope garden. Earlier in the week Bill and I had planted eight rows of sweet corn, enough for the pheasants and white tail deer...and us.

It was inspiring to watch that elderly couple, who really got into gardening that day. Dr. Johnny, despite Parkinson's disease, hoed and pounded stakes while his wife, in her 70s, seeded beans, carrots, beets and squash. The friable ground, damp and warm, made it a very pleasurable task. Gardening, not only good for the soul, made us hungry, so

Dr. Johnny treated us all to lunch in town. And now this rain will be bringing up all we planted.

The fall calvers have been trailed to the moraine pasture, the final bunch of calves is branded, Steve is planting seed potatoes in a rented field, and yesterday I took several grandsons fishing again.

It will soon, and suddenly, be summer, when more company is expected. Among the company will be sister Mary Ann, home from her island after a two-year stint in the Peace Corps. But today there is a fire in the old Monarch and fresh snow in the high country.

June 23—Normally this column is in the mail by Thursday, but most of my busy week has been devoted to gardening and grandchildren, both of which require nurturing, cultivation, and love; that is, if one wishes to realize any amount of satisfaction from either one.

Summer finally arrived, bringing warm nights and hot days, which have contributed greatly to the garden's rapid growth. We are now enjoying fresh spinach, radishes, lettuce, and green onions, as well as the perennial herbs which I use a good deal in cooking. The grandchildren, also benefiting from sunny summer time, have been fishing, sleeping in a tent on grandma's lawn, and boating. So, between hoeing, irrigating, and traipsing around with a fishing pole, not to mention cooking, my column is behind schedule this week.

For a Father's Day inspired by the warm weather, I decided to throw a big barbecue, and invited family and friends to gather on our lawn for a feast. Actually, I couldn't wait for an excuse to roast a turkey in the new outdoor stove we'd purchased at Quartzsite, Arizona, last January. One taste of the stove salesman's roasting turkey had sold the stove to me!

Now I tried to follow the directions and duplicate his efforts. Allowing ten hours of slow cooking, I prepared the bird in the morning, feeding the fire with briquettes and apple wood chips throughout the day. Between tending the fire, I baked sourdough bread, cherry pie, peach and raspberry cobblers, and fixed salads.

Early that evening, I lifted the lid to a juicy turkey, roasted golden! Joined by our large, extended family, we enjoyed what we'd waited for all through the long winter months. In our high mountain valley, the days are numbered where we can eat outside. Buck and Josh hand-cranked a big batch of ice cream which was scooped out on the fresh pie and cobblers.

Ben and Seth are making silage, using green chop, cut from the meadow grass on the hill. Tomorrow they will begin swathing the lower field to make hay. There was new snow in the mountains when last I wrote, but it has again melted. Irrigation is a way of life now. Pipe changers can be seen out early of a morning moving both hand and wheel lines.

One evening last week, a neighbor called to say she had a box of freshly picked cherries for me. The next morning I got in and canned 14 pints, made preserves, and built a fresh cherry pie. Then I pitted enough to freeze for future pies.

The next day, armed with gardening equipment, Linde and I weeded the Slope garden, which, at the moment, is beautiful. We used the mower and weed eater to clear grass away from a house I hope to sell up there. It was hard work, and when we finished, it was early afternoon, and we were beat.

Last Tuesday Doug and I, along with two grandchildren, attended a grass-weed-riparian area tour here in the county. It was a long day for the children, but very worthwhile, I thought. Two busloads of us jounced along Wallowa County back roads and viewed various examples of management practices being carried out by local ranchers. All of which, hopefully, enlightened several agency people present as to what land owners are doing to better manage their lands, in terms of conservation and looking to the future.

It is a VERY frustrating time for the less than two percent of us still engaged in the business of agriculture. It seems our many questions are never answered in a straight forward manner, but rather, in terms of jargon, which we really don't understand. Likewise, agency people are equally frustrated, being at the mercy of an even more complicated bureaucracy.

When something needs fixing on a ranch, the rancher goes about fixing it. However, when they deal with government regulations, often-times the problem is out of hand before permission is granted to proceed with any solution. And, nearly always, old-fashioned common sense never enters the picture. One thing that is used for everything is paper. Papers covered with graphs, charts, statistics, and numbers, many of which many of us can't begin to grapple with.

But a rancher accepts a problem as a challenge, works out a solution, and goes to work until he achieves results. The rancher, too, has the advantage of BEING there on his land, every day, season in and season out. He knows intimately what ails it, what is good for it, and what must be eliminated or continued in the way of management. Because he has learned by trial and error, the results show up ultimately in either a profit or a loss. If he cannot make a profit, or at least sustain his operation, he is soon out of business. It is that simple.

What works for him, stays; what doesn't, is changed. It seems to me then, that ranchers, who know the country and its individual needs, and who have survived droughts, low markets, and increasing regulations, are in the best position to manage these lands as they have in the past. Granted, mistakes have been made, but from what I observed, steps have been taken to rectify them, and the ranching community is striving to sustain their resources, as well as those on public lands. 'Nuf said. But after a day of viewing some of our older, established ranching operations, and seeing how permittees on the forest lands have been improving ranges, watersheds, and riparian areas, the land seems to be in good hands.

As we drove by acres and acres of well-managed ranges, and viewed sheep and cattle grazing long, grassy meadow, dotted with man-made ponds, I was pretty proud of our local ranchers. Some of the most scenic areas in the county lay in the vast outback that stretches to the Idaho and Washington borders, and it will remain scenic as long as it is managed by true stewards of the land, they whose very livelihoods depend on that good management. Couldn't ask for a more efficient system than that. For the sake of our future generations, some of whom may wish to continue in the honorable profession of ranching, I hope many of our modern-day issues can be resolved in meetings like these.

Education of the general public and agency officials, whose roots have strayed so far away from the land, need help in seeing what appears so obvious to us. We live in frustrating times, when it seems there is no light at the end of the tunnel, but when our city cousins feel hunger in their bellies, it might be too late for the western rancher as we know him today. I guess all we can do is continue to educate the masses, and hang in there.

As we were eating our brown bag lunches under some silver cottonwoods, there along Crow Creek, at Mack and Marian Birkmaier's ranch, we all agreed this way of life is worth fighting for. Not only for the younger generation, taking over now, but for the betterment of society as well, because an entire western culture is at stake here, a culture holding onto the last vestiges of an independent way of life, which is traditionally about as American as you can get.

July 8—My house, which has been overflowing with company for nearly a week, is empty for the moment. The annual summer Fishtrap Writer's Conference begins this evening with a dinner at Wallowa Lake. Beginning on the morning of the 4th, I have been taking a writer's workshop conducted by Jonathan Nicholas, columnist for the Oregonian, and his wife, Vivian McInerny, an award-winning journalist. It is listed in the Fishtrap brochure as a workshop on *Temporary Brilliance: Writing for the Recycling Bin.* Sounded interesting, and I have much to learn about this craft of writing, so I signed up early.

Our expected company arrived last Saturday. We knew from phone calls that 2-year-old Kayla had broken out with chicken pox the morning before they left. Everyone here had had them, so we didn't think that would pose a problem.

On Sunday night, everyone except sister Mary Ann, just home from a two-year stay in the Peace Corps, Kayla, and Kayla's mom, Lori, drove up to the Wallowa Lake moraine to watch the county's 4th of July fireworks.

Monday morning at 9 found all of us who had signed up for Jonathan and Vivian's class seated in a small cabin named "Wallowa" at the Wallowa Lake Camp. Right off the bat we were given an assignment: We were to have a 600-word essay ready by 8:30 the following morning for the New York Times! The subject was to be about this area we call home, Wallowa County. Ideas began immediately forming in my mind. The "Temporary Brilliance" was kicking in, spurred by Jonathan's inspiration and pointers on column and newspaper writing.

He gave us copies of five of the nation's leading newspapers to peruse, to select one article to critique in front of the group. In reading the Picayune Tribune, the New Orleans edition, I found nothing on the front pages but O.J. and similarly depressing stories. I didn't want to waste my temporary brilliance, which would end up in the recycling bin, on those subjects.

At noon I joined other workshop participants on the lawn to eat my brown-bag lunch, then returned to the reality of my life on Prairie Creek, a reality that had to be tended to before I could continue with any journalistic brilliance. But let me tell you, it took brilliance to complete what had to be done before, at 4:30 a.m. the next morning, I quietly tip-toed out to the kitchen carrying my word processor, and began that 600-word assignment.

What greeted me back at home that afternoon was a phone call from 8-year-old James, whom I had promised to take to the lake to try out his birthday present, a two-man raft. Everyone else was too busy to take James, it seemed, so grandma had promised and it was most important that I follow through.

I picked up James, his little sister Adele, and granddaughter Lacey, and, stuffing the inflated raft into the back of our van, we headed to Trouthaven on the west shore of Wallowa Lake. The raft was small and had a pair of oars, but there was no rope or anything for me to hold onto while the children rafted. None of the children had ever rafted, much less paddled, but as is often the case in my life, I was saved...by another grandma!

Carol Hearne, owner of Trouthaven resort, fastened a long rope on the oar lock and we played out the rope and let the children practice paddling. Passing motor boats, towing water skiers, caused big wakes which threatened to swamp the raft, but the children had a ball.

After 3 p.m. I returned the children, after buying them all ice cream in Joseph, and carried on with my day and night, which included 35 guests coming for an outdoor family 4th of July picnic on our lawn. The daughters and daughters-in-law, plus other members of our large extended family, brought salads and beans, and I provided roasted chicken, barbecued beef and the makings for hand-cranked ice cream.

Our California relatives were looking forward to joining their Oregon cousins. Soon carloads of relatives arrived, spilling forth their contents of children. We had two sets of Loris and Toms, and the Pendleton Lori and Tom couldn't find anyone to feed their 4-H lambs so they brought them along in the horse trailer. We were a loud, boisterous group. It was, luckily, a nice evening, a bit coolish when it came time for the fireworks, but sparklers rained colorful sparks into the night, children whooped and hollered, and the smoke was intense.

It was nearly 11 p.m. before all the celebrating ceased, and I wearily fell into bed. Before dawn that next morning I wasn't functioning too well, but I did manage to put words on paper and turn it into Jonathan a few minutes after 8:30. He says to me, after all the aforementioned, "You're pushing the deadline, aren't you?"

At that moment I was glad of the note I'd written to him, which accompanied the article, wherein I'd described what I've used as a theme statement (journalistic jargon) for this column. So be patient, readers, and I'll return to the ranch writing next time.

Tuesday morning our class was conducted by Vivian. Her assignment: a profile on a person we knew, to be turned in the next day. So that afternoon, amid the total chaos of the chicken pox kid, feeling good now, running around; the TV going full bore; and people talking, I sat M.A. down at the kitchen table and proceeded to interview and "profile" her. It took real concentration but I came up with a semblance of a profile.

The next morning, Jonathan critiqued our New York Times articles and added further to our "brilliance" as newspaper columnists. That night I cooked a big dinner here for our house guests, and each night

M.A. and I drove back up to the lake to attend the open mikes, which were wonderful.

Vivian and Jonathan wrapped up our class yesterday, which was very stimulating and productive, and, as always, new acquaintances were made and new ideas were shared. I brought two young women out to the ranch to eat lunch in the yard and we shared more about our lives. One gal, from Milton-Freewater, and her husband operated a 4,000-head Holstein replacement heifer operation. We talked cows. The other gal was from Seattle.

Last night I read M.A.'s profile at the open mike, and now while our California extended family is off to the lake and the paddle boats and picnics, I must wind up this column and be ready for this evening back at Fishtrap.

The Icelandic poppies are blooming furiously, brilliant red in the afternoon sunlight. A recent rain dampened Hough's hay, but today it is being fluffed up by raking. Luckily, Ben got most of ours in before the rain.

July 19—Why is it, as the years slip by and our children have children, time seems to escape us? Is it because we have so much more we want to do while we still can? For me, time is measured in summers. The lazy, hazy days of summertime are not by any means lazy, at least not here in Wallowa County. Each day is precious; so little time to squeeze in all those outdoor projects before the first snow brings bitter cold, before the Icelandic poppies and vegetable gardens are reduced to a blackened tangle by the first killing frost, which can come as early as August. Maybe that's it. We want to LIVE, like the poppies and garden, before we die.

"Human life," my mother once said, "is only a heartbeat in eternity."

Bill George called the other evening. "Janie, the deer are coming in at night and nibbling the raspberries, nipping the peas, and they've pulled up two cabbage plants."

Since Linde and I have put so much work into this beautiful vegetable garden, we weren't ready to let a couple of mule deer yearlings use it for a playground and feeding area. So, this morning, armed with an electric fence charger (provided by Doug), plus wire, insulators and steel posts, we strung a hot wire above an existing pole fence.

The very old, falling-down fence had to be resurrected before we could put in the steel posts. When the hot wire was strung, we tied old rags onto the wire, which will hopefully further deter the deer, or at least give them enough of a jolt to discourage their using our garden for such nightly frolicking.

Since Bill has no dog now, as old "Speedy" died last winter, the deer have become very brave. Of course, having been fawned and raised there in the adjacent woods and grown up on the browse provided by the nearby swamps, they naturally think this is home. However, although we leave plenty of corn on the stalks in the fall for the pheasants and quail, and there are wind fall apples galore for the deer, we planted this garden for us. The surrounding fields and alder thickets provide ample browse for these young mulies; it isn't as though they were starving.

While Pat wielded the weed eater around the perimeter of our garden, Linde and I labored over the fence. The high-altitude sun bore down on us, and sweat trickled down beneath my wide-brimmed straw hat. We laughed as we stood back to survey our morning's work. There was definitely a feminine flair about it.

It was nearly 2 p.m. when we finished. We had taken one rest since early morning, to enjoy cold slices of watermelon. I treated everyone to lunch at the Blue Willow. We sat out on a picnic table under the shade of several young aspen trees that grew beside a small stream where a mother mallard and her half-grown ducklings swam. A cool breeze cooled our summer-warmed bodies, and the homemade bread, fresh fruit and pasta salad really hit the spot.

My sister Mary Ann is still with us, though her daughter, Lori, Lori's husband, Tom, and their two small children left for home at the end of that hectic 4th of July and Fishtrap week. Two-year-old Kayla still wore her chicken pox spots. M.A., attempting to readjust after living on a small island out in the eastern Caribbean for two years while she served in the Peace Corps, has decided Wallowa County might just be a good place to get over the inevitable culture shock.

The fast-paced life of her Auburn, California, home didn't appeal to her after the lackadaisical lifestyle she'd become accustomed to on the island of Dominica. She stays on with us here, absorbing life on a Prairie Creek ranch. Each day must seem like an adventure. All around her the haying is going on, frantically at times. Even last night, into the night under the light of the moon, we could hear Ben finishing a pasture next to the chicken pen, and the far-off *chunk, chunk* sound of Dan Butterfield, baling late into the night.

It is very hot and dry, with day after day of sun and dry winds, and I have been photographing hayfields. Baling is mostly done when the cool of evening descends on Prairie Creek, and now with the growing July moon, I think of the ranchers out there, alone in their beautiful hay fields. They must feel like artists do at a finished painting, when they look at the long rows of bales against the mountains in the moonlight.

Up in the rented ground on upper Prairie Creek, the seed potato crop is up and the rows are filling. Rouging has begun and Doug, astride his rouging cart, slowly drives up and down each row, looking for diseased plants. Every year it becomes harder to find people willing to rouge seed potatoes.

On a whim last Sunday, Doug suggested we load up the mini-motor home and camp out for a night on the upper Imnaha River. There, along the river in a comfortable campground, we parked our home on wheels and pretended we were just traveling through, like the few other campers there were doing. The experience proved to be very restful, and provided a respite from the constant irrigating and yard-tending routine back home, not to mention meetings, family involvement and the ever-present telephone.

I packed along Mary Clearman Blew's latest book, *Balsam Root*. That evening over grilled T-bone steaks, fried potatoes and onions, and a salad made with our fresh garden lettuce, we watched a pair of pine siskin finches feed on leftover crumbs.

The next morning we feasted on a late breakfast of sourdough pancakes flavored with the season's first huckleberries, which Doug had picked on the way in. We went for walks, I fished, and we all tried our hand at gold panning. Doug and I spent the night under the stars, while M.A. opted for the motor home. I was lulled to sleep by the soothing river sounds.

On Saturday, daughter Ramona, granddaughter Carrie and her two girlfriends, plus M.A. and I, hiked up the Hurricane Creek trail to Slick Rock. Indian paintbrush and other July wildings grew profusely alongside the trail and sprinkled the high meadows. It was another hot day and we were pretty warm when we arrived at the falls at Slick Rock Creek. The girls wasted no time in peeling off their clothes to the bathing suits worn underneath, and this grandmother joined those three teenagers under the falls, barefoot and fully clothed!

At first it took my breath away, but then it was heavenly. I found a pool that had formed, over eons, in solid rock, and I simply sat there with the spray of the falls on my face. Gazing up at the azure sky, cool after a long hike, and feeling 16! I found it very fulfilling there on that terrace, perched on the sheer rock face of Slick Rock, my first-born daughter and her daughter beside me.

Three generations enjoying the wild freedom offered up in this special place. Perhaps we'll be better able to cope with our lives down there in the valley below, where our homes shimmered in the July heat. During that moment in time, life was sweet!

Shannon Mitchell, Tanya, Andrew, and Rachel Gorbett, in the Chief Joseph Days Junior Parade, are all grandchildren of Ed and Helen Jones of Enterprise, and are from a family displaced by logging bans and mill closures.

Goat ropers in the Chief Joseph Days Junior Parade, Emily and Lee Ann Maasdam, and cousins Ethan and Jake, pose with their goat.

August 4—The searing summer of '94 marches into August, with day after sweltering day of heat and thunderstorms. Our summers without heat (last year, for instance) are hectic enough. Add soaring high altitude temperatures to stress-inducing activities, such as water shortages; the relentless, heavy ranch work, such as haying and irrigating; and events such as Chief Joseph Days, with its influx of hundreds of visitors, the inevitable summer company for those of us who live in scenic valleys.

Throw in a county fair, fruit to "put by" for winter, gardens to tend, and grandchildren, if time permits, and the problem becomes having too little time to enjoy.

It is the same every summer, except this summer is by far the worst one experienced in the 26 years I've lived here. In the intervening years, I have watched, with other permanent valley residents, the ever-changing face of our local culture, the recent rapid growth of upscale homes, and the influx of retired people with outside incomes who can afford to move here and stay, while our own children struggle to live here on a daily basis.

But isn't life itself a struggle? Wherever we choose to live? Seems to me, we must take what we are given and go with it. There can never be a "paradise place." Only we ourselves create paradise by shaping our environment to our own ideals, which include commitment to family, community, and to sustaining our precious resources for future generations. It means things like lending a hand to those in need and being a good neighbor, which have shaped our rural cultures.

All of these things take a great deal of effort, but if everyone committed himself to the task, we wouldn't have to build jails or spend thousands of dollars on mental health services. And mostly, we wouldn't have our children running the streets. This is our one national shame!

If I were forced to live in a city far-removed from my beloved Wallowa country, I would probably be spearheading a committee to plant trees and flowers, or preserve open space for those children. But just the thought of breathing polluted air makes me ill, and like a wildflower, I'd probably just wither and die. And so, too, would my children, who have never lived in town.

Here's a headline in our local weekly paper: *Cattle Ordered Off Public Lands in County.* Federal appeals court in San Francisco rules logging and grazing violates the Endangered Species Act. This is just a news article to the tourists who visit our scenic area, but the realness of those printed words will affect my children, all of whom are engaged in agriculture.

It has already affected my youngest son, married, with four children to support, now recently out of a job as a result of the Boise Cascade mill closure in Joseph. He was employed briefly as a ranch hand and is now out of work again, and looking for a job and a place to move his family. In the meantime, he is finding work as a firefighter, now helicoptered with his chainsaw to put his life on the line to protect our natural resources.

Special interest groups were privy to banning logging that was his livelihood, and now he goes off to this dangerous task, without even his wife and children knowing where, or how, he is. He is not alone. Young men have gone to fight fire from all over the Northwest

My son, just 30 years old, once was a faller in the woods, then a ranch hand after receiving a degree from a two-year community college, before he became a mill worker. Most important, he is a husband and father, and member of our Wallowa County community. Like many, he will work at anything to live here, even if it means barely scraping by. This recent grazing ruling is scary. Real scary. It will impact all of our children and their children, not to mention all our generation who live here for the place, not the amenities.

We ranchers are especially stunned and grasping for straws, any straw, to save our way of life and our very culture, which includes one of the last places where family values hold stubbornly to tradition. On ranches, families actually eat their evening meal together, moms and dads come from their fields and cattle operations in work clothes, to watch school plays or sport events, neighbors haul neighbors' kids' livestock to the fair.

Folks help folks. When they don't, the valley weeds them out, because when winter comes you need all the friends you can get. But now tempers flare like fires after lightning zig-zags through the long, hot August nights. There is tension in the air, everyone holding his breath. The air is unbearably hot; gardens wither and some are dying, due to water shortages. So are second cuttings of alfalfa, because the streams running out of the mountains have dried up.

Gardens like ours on the slope, which are lucky enough to have water, flourish in the heat. Zucchini runs rampant, corn is as high as my head, the green beans are outdoing themselves, and every berry that ever there was is ripening all at once. If my husband brings another berry into the kitchen to be preserved, I'll scream, because there are still berries in the freezer from last year.

I should be thankful, and I am. We give much of it away, but when summer's stresses appear, and all you want to do is get into the mountains, it is a bit much. Gardening must be done in the cool of early morning, or late evening. Anything requiring energy must be done then, but can't always, so we blunder on, dreaming of winter, a time of rest.

Ben, bless him, has finally finished haying and ag-bagging. He and his children did it by themselves. Doug has been helping a lot in the potato fields. Far from being retired, when work needs doing, he is there, like all of the senior-citizen ranchers hereabouts. The reality is that the average age of ranchers and farmers is over 60!

Outwardly, our valley is incredibly lovely. Late-summer golden grains ripening, green irrigated pasture land, dry sear hills, cloud shadows floating over hazy blue and snowless mountains, baled hay in many shapes dotting the fields, and fire and heat combining to make spectacular sunsets and sunrises. Inwardly the stress builds, like the afternoon thunderheads over the valleys and canyons. Dramas being played out in places like Imnaha, Prairie Creek, Chesnimnus, Crow Creek, Eden, yes, and even Paradise.

And out in the forests the cattle shade up with their spring calves, swat flies with their long tails, only emerging in the cool of the evening to graze. They don't know that 10,000 of them in our county alone will have to be gathered in the heat, their calves sold before they are ready. Beautiful cows, held and selected for their mothering ability as a result of many years of breeding, will be sold for hamburger! Cowboys would have to push sweaty horses into thickets in country that is so vast and terrain so steep, it will take days.

Let's hope this doesn't happen, but if it does, we'll just start over again, like those before us who endured droughts, market collapses, and other hardships. Although Doug and I don't run cattle on any public land, our neighbors' hurting hurts us. It affects the jobs of our children, and will significantly impact the entire county. Tourism can never bring those cattle dollars! And the people who own the hardware store and the new espresso bar will feel it.

This morning there is a feeling of fall in the air, and where yesterday our eyes scanned the horizon for the telltale signs of new fires, there is relief from the intense heat. It is a very sad time in the Wallowa Valley right now, but tomorrow is a new day and the creative personalities of the special people who inhabit this valley will triumph. I can feel it in my bones.

Our county fair is next week, and the grandchildren have 4-H and FFA lambs, steers and horses. And grandma just might enter some zucchini, and a photograph. Life goes on.

August 10—One very hot day at the Wallowa County Fair, I judged the horse herdsmanship. It was a tough job, let me tell you. I had no idea how serious these 4-H horse clubs are. Their exhibits were creatively decorated with flowers, photos, and name signs. Their horse stalls were kept immaculate. The North End kids won. Hurrah! Those wonderful young people living on ranches in an area with place names like Lost Prairie, Flora, and Paradise.

At times in the heat there in the show barn, when the sheep judge was really working those showmanship entries, the fair got pretty intense. You could feel it in the stands, and feel it in the young people, but these children cut their teeth on adversity, and the land has shaped their character, as it has their parents; they could stand the heat.

The judge was special. He really liked young people. He knew about sheep showing and sheep, and he looked each member in the eye and talked to them, and got their attention and they learned. They all won! We need more like him in our schools. He cared, and the children knew it. It seems so simple, yet so difficult.

I'm willing to wager that this judge didn't get paid very much on Wallowa County's limited fair budget, but he must have been well paid in satisfaction. Down the road, these young people will make him proud. We all had to agree that this crop being raised now is pretty special. The future of our beautiful country is in their hands, and I feel safer knowing this.

After work, we played; just another part of the culture of hard-working ranch folks. On the last day, the children exhibited their sense of fun! With chicken and pig scrambles, with wheelbarrow races, egg tossing, hog calling contests and playing volleyball on the lawn.

Our wonderful young people with healthy minds and bodies are our most precious resource, and they played off those show ring tensions. Seven of my grandchildren entered the fair.

Daughter Lori called with great news. It seems Lacey, over at the Umatilla County Fair in Hermiston, sold her lamb to Wallowa Valley Simmentals for $3.50 per pound. Bryan and Lou Ann Wolfe had something to do with grandpa buying Lacey's lamb. This was Lacey's first year to show in 4-H, and we understand she is hooked. Because our fair ran at the same time, we were unable to attend. Good show, Lacey.

Trying to keep track of all those grandchildren was a lost cause. Most of the time I was confused. I ran into other equally confused grandmothers who just missed seeing their grandchildren show or couldn't find when and where they were supposed to be. In my case I get confused often, because when I don't see a grandchild over a month, they grow into these young adults I don't recognize any more. But, bless them, they are kind and they love me.

I was very proud of their efforts, and mostly proud of their parents, who supported them. I was doubly proud of my eldest son, whom I have watched mature from a young 4-H'er to a father, with 4-H and FFA'ers himself, and who now uses his years of experience to be the livestock chairman of the fair. His oldest son, now a junior at the University of Idaho, visited with me at the fair. What a nice young man you are, Chad. Wherever in life you go, a part of this place will go too.

The fair is also a place for old-timers to gather and tell of the days that are no more. If you want to learn about a place, listen to children and old-timers. They tell you. Like Chuck Gavin, who never missed a day at the fair, who is a retired extension man and former showman himself.

He goes back as far as my father, in that he was at the World's Fair when it was held at Treasure Island in San Francisco. My daddy showed a Guernsey show string there when I was but a babe. Wish I'd listened more when he told about it. Too late now, but Chuck filled me in.

Fairs get in your blood. Joe Beach, who suffered a stroke more than a year ago out there in the "North End" on his ranch on Paradise Ridge, was at the fair that last day. Joe's one of those tough Wallowa County people I talked about earlier. He is walking on his own again. He sure enjoyed coming to the fair, and it was nice of his wife, Patty, to bring him, and nice of his grandchildren to help. Things must be pretty dry out there now, but Patty said she has a garden, and the view looking down to the breaks of the Grande Ronde is still pretty much Paradise.

Joe filled me in, too, on that late '30s World's Fair that I didn't listen enough to my daddy about. It was pretty special. Joe never forgot that World's fair. He'd gone down with busloads of FFA kids from all over Oregon. Clear from Paradise to San Francisco, it must've been something, as special to Joe as when we Placer County foothill kids showed our 4-H livestock at the Cow Palace in San Francisco in the late '40s. We'd never been to the big city.

Yep, Joe, I understand. From Hungry Hollow to San Francisco.

I could write several columns on county fairs, but as usual words keep marching across this screen until I stop. And I must tend to green beans, and zucchini. The garden's plumb out of hand.

Members of the Tomahawk 4-H Club of Imnaha all showed horses at the Wallowa County Fair. From left are Mona Lee Matthews, Sara Borgerding, Hope Royes, and Cory Garnett.

18-month-old Taylor, daughter of Prairie Creek ranchers Dub and C.J. Darnielle, shows off her lamb during the pee-wee showmanship classes.

Homemaker of the Year award at the Wallowa County Fair went to Becky Wolfe of Wallowa, wife of rancher Gordon Wolfe and mother of two.

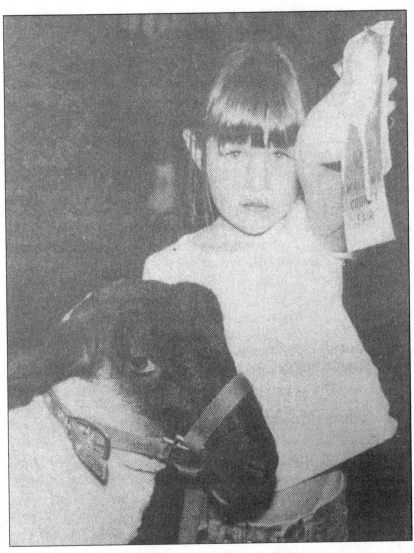

Amber Shear, 4, shows off the blue ribbon she won in the pee wee showmanship class at the Wallowa County Fair. Amber's parents work on ranches in Prairie Creek and Big Sheep Creek.

Late August—Moving steadily, with the dawn sky of a new day, a helicopter hums directly over our ranch house on this noticeably cooler morning, before melting into a flaming sunrise that resembles the imagined gates of heaven, rising above Hells Canyon, the deepest gorge in North America, which gashes its ancient way northward only a few "crow miles" east of our ranch.

The persimmon sun, flaming like the fires raging in the Hat Point area, settles into a thick purple layer of smoke edged with real clouds that are shot with light. More streams of light cascade from Heaven's gate. And...those real clouds hold the promise of rain. September, you are a catharsis to all who live here. Your season signals the end of this long, crazy summer. The land sighs and relaxes, and so do I.

Those creative, intelligent minds of our permanent inhabitants, many of whom are descended from our first settlers, continue to give us hope, providing solutions to meet head-on the myriad problems posed by government restrictions.

Meanwhile, we ranchers and loggers have been dealt another bad hand, the latest threat to our existence: FIRE. Guess I didn't knock on pine trees hard enough, because what we all dreaded, happened, in the early hours Sunday morning. I remember waking up with goose bumps, looking out the bedroom window, toward the dry eastern hills, lit up by the lightning-charged sky, and knowing the inevitable consequences of those strikes. Tinder-dry forests and summer range land, so parched, even the oldest old-timers admit—the worst dry summer they've known.

At least 62 fires were ignited. Although most of the smaller smokes were quickly extinguished, the Wallowa-Whitman, Hells Canyon Recreation Area, and private bunch grass range was on fire. Private citizens, ready for this, became heroes, when it came to protecting their own. At the outset, every man in our large, extended family was involved in one fire or another. At one point during that fateful Sunday, only the women and children were left to run the ranches.

Stories trickled in from all over the county. Marge McClaran, who was already in practice for feeding firefighters from when fire had broken out earlier on their Lightning Creek (lower Imnaha) winter range, again prepared meals, this time for the Gill Ranch fire that consumed much of their summer and fall range "on top."

Like I've said before, these people cut their teeth on adversity. Everyone in agriculture knows this to be fact. My oldest son, Ken, had, earlier that Sunday morning, borrowed Doug's pumper to fight fire in the Green Basin fire, which was on private land in the Lostine Canyon country. When Doug decided to drive the 24-mile gravel road out to our

Salmon Creek range to check on conditions there, I herded four children and carried on with ranch chores.

Returning later that afternoon, driving in a hurry, leaping from his pickup amid a cloud of dust, Doug ran to the phone.

"The whole Chesnim country is on fire," he said, and then we called the ranch owners who owned lands in that vast Zumwalt prairie which lies north of here. All that valuable fall feed, the nutritious bunch grass, was burning.

Fortunately, because of the drought and extremely dry conditions, the prairies were grazed down, but many fields were being saved for weaning calves. A lightning strike on the Gill ranch had ignited a wildfire that swiftly swept westward, leaving a blackened mosaic in its path.

Within minutes, Doug had organized a crew and equipment was loaded, including two dozers, water tanks, pickups. shovels, wet burlap bags and other gear. I fixed food and lots of coffee, and called the State Forestry Department to register our men and equipment, as they would be protecting private lands.

Then—the waiting game. We women anxiously watched the horizon as the merciless hot, dry winds blew from Hells Canyon in the east. We took care of the children and carried on. One young ranch wife changed wheel lines in the potato field and ran a swather while I watched her two children. And, of course, we worried, like women before us have worried in these same situations in the past.

My oldest son, meanwhile, was dispatched from the lower valley fire to the fires on Zumwalt. Although he arrived too late to save much of the Gill Ranch range, he was able to save some of it before going on to the other fires, five of which raged and billowed up from the nearby timbered Chesnimnus. Our range, to the south, was spared. Pat operated one dozer, and Doug the other, working into the night and early morning hours building a fire line in the Alder Creek area.

Marge McClaran fed weary firefighters at Pine Creek. Her son, Scott, working with the State Department of Forestry, did a commendable job of organizing the fire protection on private lands. Marge's husband, Jack, relayed messages from his Enterprise home. Communication was essential in a land so far removed from settlement. CBs and two-way radios were invaluable tools.

Marge started up the jeep on Pine Creek and generated enough power to call Jack. Nearly 60 miles separated that remote cow camp from civilization. The McClarans and Tippetts are used to that, though, as are the Lathrops, Youngs, Ketschers, Yosts and other ranchers who operate those outback areas of Wallowa County.

The next day, Linde and I went back out with the men to drive back trucks, and ended up on fire watch all day. The endless winds continued and new fires spurted up, or old ones came to life. We watched the burning lines, which dramatically stopped that Gill ranch fire just short of the Pine Creek cow camp, where Marge fed us that night.

Our weary crew was made to feel welcome: meat loaf, beans, and bread never tasted so good. Thank you, Marge... and Jane Wiggins, too!

September 3—It is cold—Hurrah! Cold enough for a jacket when I go out and feed the chickens, salt the cows, and feed the dogs and cats. The kittens are growing and playing, and I have time to watch their antics. I have time to contemplate the sunflowers I planted beyond the Icelandic poppies. Their golden faces are turned toward the cloud-cloaked sunrise that was yesterday morning's Heaven's gate, over Hells Canyon, where weary fire crews will find some relief.

The other fire, known as the Twin Lakes fire, is still visible from my kitchen window. Burning in the country to the south of us, it has burned through more heavy fuels for days. It will take more rain to put these two big ones out.

Amid all of this adversity being thrown at us, to make us tough, there are little gold coins. My oldest daughter, Ramona, and her husband Charley, celebrated their 25th wedding anniversary here on the ranch that Saturday evening before the fires. It was a lovely golden evening, and more than 30 family and friends, including children and dogs, had a wonderful time.

I will forever remember Lacey and Ryan's little new puppy, Max, running through a throng of kids and into the house with seven helium-filled balloons tied to his collar! He was nearly airborne. Max was purchased at the petting zoo at the Umatilla County Fair for 25 cents. He was the life of the party.

Thanks to the efforts of family members, the occasion was a complete surprise to the deserving couple, who, like many before them, have weathered the storms of matrimony and life together. They are survivors, like the small Gill homestead out there on the lonely Zumwalt Prairie.

Happy anniversary, Ramona and Charley! Better times are ahead. Our only hope is to pool together for what we love and value the most, our way of life, our valley, and every canyon, creek, prairie and glorious mountain in the Wallowas, in this unique frontier of the West, where our hearts will always reside.

September 16—In my mind's eye I'll always remember the day I watched the fire burn on the Chesnimnus. Standing there on Young's, looking across to that charred surreal landscape, gazing down into the still smoking timbered draws of the Alder Creek drainage, my heart was gladdened at the sight of several bluebirds pecking around the ashes for charred grasshoppers. Later, on the way to Pine Creek that evening, we spied a lone pup coyote hunting gophers, unafraid as we passed. No one shot at him.

Near the same vantage point where two early settlers, brothers Joe and Tom Gill, had built a fire lookout, we looked more than 100 years later upon a scene that must have been repeated often over the intervening years. Joe and Tom had witnessed the range wars of the sheepmen and cattlemen, like we are witnessing the range wars between the government and the grazing permittees.

The scene that day, etched in my memory, was of Bill Bailey's black cows and calves grazing unconcerned amid patches of unburned grass while smoky dust devils spun themselves out across the charred, blackened grassland. The wind made the same lonely sound it must have made in the 1880s, winnowing the grain for the Gill family after all available hands had harvested their meager 20-acre crop by hand.

Across from us lay the cremated remains of the old Gill barn. Gone are its hand-hewn beams and adjacent log corral. All that remains are the still-hot ashes of a very hot fire. History, burned by nature, leaving only the story. Falling down, but triumphant, the old Gill homestead cabin has withstood more than 100 years of harsh winters, searing summers, other prairie wildfires, and relentless winds.

Two live, green-leafed, ancient cottonwoods told the story of why the Gills had settled there: water. Even in this extremely dry year, a fresh pond was full, with green grass bordering it. The bluebirds and the pup coyote must've come to it and similar rancher-made ponds to slake their thirst. The little shack stood bravely, though cows had gotten into it when trespassers had carelessly left the door open, and storms had lashed it, sun had beaten into its rotted logs, and snows had covered it. But it had survived, while all around...everything blackened.

The shack was a survivor, like the descendants of those Zumwalt hill people, many of whom own that same land today. The land is their legacy, and ours too, because they have maintained it with love. It is theirs and therefore ours too, because their traditions and culture is allowed to live on in the land. These people shaped the land, and the land shaped them.

And that is why the land is still the same as it was more than 100 years ago, except that it has been improved with more ponds and better management.

I visited with many of the landowners out there that day amid the charred remains of that vast Zumwalt prairie. From our own fire watch position, we could see numerous dark purple funnel clouds rising from the eastern horizon that forms the rim of Hells Canyon. Freezeout, Saddle Creek, Horse Creek, and Granny Camp transformed, as we watched, into a sterile moonscape. Fuel loads, years in the building, were torched by lightning, a fire waiting for a happening that finally happened in the searing summer of '94.

Today we hear on the news that this Freezeout fire is the highest priority fire in the Northwest. We can't recreate in the Hells Canyon National Recreation Area this Labor Day weekend. All roads to that area are blockaded. Meanwhile, another fire in the West rages on. My youngest son is still on that one. Twenty miles northeast of Boise, I think, though not sure; haven't heard from him in days.

Back here in Wallowa County his wife and children are moving, without dad, to another house. They are lucky. They have a house to move into, and daddy has a job, even though it's dangerous. A grandson, a junior at the University of Idaho, is also fighting fire. I hear he is now at Memaloose and Hat Point area on the big one. Steep terrain there, but Chad has always liked the outdoors.

Doug is weary, as is Pat, and all the other firefighters, of the logistics as well as actual suppression. I am weary of the summer, too, all of it. But for now our grasslands in the Zumwalt appear safe. The rain has come, the balm of cool September soothes the land, and that "dry fear" is gone. Last night, thunder reverberated from mountain to hill land, but we were relieved to hear it accompanied by the sound of rain.

September 22—A late September sun, still hidden by our neighbor's hill, floods Echo Canyon with golden light and illuminates Hough's irrigated pastures, torching the bread loaf haystacks and igniting Black Angus cows and calves, its path of light moving silently, steadily southward. Resembling a great round space ship, the blinding sun emerges from its hiding place beyond the dry hill to continue its heavenly voyage, navigating today the autumn equinox.

My scraggly row of sunflowers hearken! Their drooping, sleepy heads come to attention and their sunny faces brighten and turn toward the rising sun...Save for one. Why?

As each new day dawns, my life seems already charted on some sort of predestined course. And, like the odd sunflower, I can't look directly at the sun. Guess that's what makes life so interesting and exciting: the anticipation of wondering what's next. For me it all has something to do with fall. My time. When sunlight falls at softer angles, a change from summer's harsh overhead glare.

This morning's September light spills onto a bowl of ripening pears from Imnaha, which reposes on my kitchen counter top. Suddenly, it's a painting! Still life.

Looking out our living room picture window I see that a light frost glitters along the irrigation ditch in the horse pasture. Precisely at sunup, a chill breeze wanders over Prairie Creek and a coyote pup struggles with his emerging voice. From farther down the valley, an adult coyote encourages the youngster's efforts.

Small birds waken to the warmth of a new morning, and begin to flit from sunflower to sunflower, feeding as they cling to heavy golden faces with tiny feet. Coyotes and birds break the dawn's silence of Prairie Creek like the start of a concert. The sun is the conductor, and waves a baton. A cow bawls for her calf.

A pair of red tail hawks silently wing their way into the heights of the ancient yellowing willows, whose roots are embedded along the irrigation ditch in the bull pasture. A V of wild honkers slices the indigo sky overhead. It is a blue and gold morning.

Across the road, Hough's third-cutting alfalfa, lying in windrows, releases its dew-laden aroma. "Skip" and "Chester," my two roosters, crow, on cue, with the rising sun. My wildflower patch stirs, bachelor buttons, Icelandic poppies, cosmos rejoining in light. The frost didn't leave the bottom. They are safe one more day. Golden California poppies, still furled in chill, wait for more warmth to open. Brilliant red and salmon pink geraniums spill out of blue granite-ware kettles, loving this Indian summer.

The day has begun. I sip my friendly cup of Postum and scribble these words in pencil on a notepad. So I can look out the window. Canned pears and seven-day sweet pickles cover my kitchen table. Herbs from my Slope garden dry on a newspaper on the front room floor. Dill pickles cure in a crock. There are newly dug potatoes in the cellar, and dried keeping onions on the back porch.

Strawberries love our frost-free fall, and continue to grow large and sweet. I can't bear for them to go to waste, so this morning I will make yet another batch of freezer jam to give Skye Krebs and wife Penny when they accept the Grassman of the Year award at the annual meeting of Wallowa County Stockgrowers. Krebs runs sheep on summer range in Wallowa County.

Every morning for a week now, Doug, armed with a lunch, a wood permit and his shotgun, has driven north to Wallowa County's vast outback, wooding and grousing. At night he returns smiling, happy and triumphant, bearing a small jag of wood and at least one, and sometimes three, blue grouse. We've had two good feeds of fried grouse and sourdough biscuits.

One evening we had Duane Wiggins (Jane was out of town), and Ralph and Enid over for supper to share in the wild fare. Fall is the season of plenty here in our valley. Corn on the cob every meal, new potatoes, pickled beets, crookneck squash, carrots and Imnaha tomatoes.

Zucchini, anyone? In our small towns of Joseph and Enterprise you better lock your cars, else you might find the front seat filled with zucchini. No kidding.

Which reminds me that if you're looking for an outstanding recipe for zucchini bread, go find one of Judy Wandschneider's cook books, *Cookies and Conversation,*, from Pika Press. It's the best one I've run across yet, and I've tried lots of them. The recipe calls for whole wheat flour, honey, wheat germ, raisins and nuts; good for you, and so tasty.

Our summer-without-end continues with week after week of yo-yo temperatures that climb into the 80s by afternoon and plummet into the 30s by dawn.

September is my time, but the pull of Indian summer's charm is not conducive to writing. I turn into a vagabond and head over the nearest hill; but even without writing, I find my time so taken with too many things. It is frustrating, but of my choosing. As we grow older, our friends, naturally, fall into the category of aging, and it is hard (for me, at least) to think of them really ever growing old.

When you take the time to really know them, you find these special people still possess young spirits and hearts, so you don't notice the aging body that holds the mind. You see only the mind, and their eyes hold you.

I always remember my own grandmother, Mary Myrtle Wilson, who lived to be over 101, saying at age 90-something, pointing to her heart, "Here beats the heart of a 19-year-old." That was her secret of longevity. She never considered herself old, and these friends of mine don't either! But their bodies are wearing out. And so is mine, but come Saturday I hope to be able to climb Sacajawea Mountain.

October 1—4 a.m—Surrounded by brilliant stars, the remnant September moon hangs suspended in a rain-cleansed, pre-dawn sky. Yes, rain. After a seemingly endless summer, we awoke the other morning to the refreshing sound of water dripping from the eaves. A life-giving rain had come in the night, and by morning our thirsty land had been somewhat appeased. Albeit short-lived, this gift of moisture was truly welcome.

Yesterday morning's misty beginning soon gave way to a warm, dry day, followed by an evening so mild we left the bedroom windows open all night. No frost yet to speak of, so the Alder Slope garden is still producing the most luscious sweet corn we've ever tasted. And the marigolds, planted there to discourage insects, are brilliant, as are the Sensation mix cosmos that won "Best of Show" at our August Wallowa County Fair.

The wildflower patch out front here on Prairie creek continues to provide joy to my heart, as do the geraniums, petunias, hollyhocks, and sunflowers. What an unusual year! Flowers all over the county are so happy, having been allowed to bloom and bloom, as if they were in the Willamette Valley west of the Cascades rather than in this high mountain valley.

The reason for being at my word processor at 4 a.m. is that this is opening morning of mule deer buck season. Doug has a tag, which means he will be leaving soon to drive to Imnaha, and I want to go too! We plan to visit relatives' and friends' deer camps, do a little fishing, and generally enjoy this Indian summer day. If Doug should bag his buck, that would be a bonus, and fodder for a future column.

But the really exciting news is that yours truly, along with 14-year-old Tanya and friend Linde, climbed Sacajawea Mountain! For me it was the realization of a long-time dream.

Sacajawea is named in memory of the young Shoshone Indian girl who guided the Lewis and Clark expedition during its "Corps of Discovery." Clark had nicknamed the girl "Janey," which is the spelling that was used in my name when I was a young girl. Sacajawea has long been my heroine. After having moved here in 1968, I would gaze up at this beautiful mountain, which rears its massive self next to the equally magnificent Matterhorn, and long to climb to its soaring summits.

After 26 years, my sought-after dream materialized. Sacajawea and its companion peak, the Matterhorn, are the two highest peaks in the Wallowa chain. Their steep ramparts, composed of talus, loose scree and weathered, barren rock (of which I know not the proper names), this mass of solid rock soars upward to pierce the sky at nearly 10,000 feet.

Due to this drought year, the mountains' flanks were completely (and unusually) devoid of snow. Normally, this time of year, one may be caught in an early snowstorm. We timed our climb just right. Linde had planned the trip for years, but always before, inclement weather or obligations here below the mountain thwarted our plans.

This time, it was all a go, and meant to be. Doug and Pat even agreed to go. Not to climb the mountain, mind you, but help pack us in and set up base camp.

So, last Saturday morning, the five of us left the Hurricane Creek trailhead on horseback, with the two men each pulling a pack mule. Our faithful molly, Snowberry, and Pat and Linde's faithful mule, Tank, carried our camp and food.

The golden, crisp fall morning soon warmed to the usual summertime intensity, but a cool breeze blowing from the high country cooled us. When we arrived at the high basin meadow where we planned to set up camp, we discovered much to our dismay that the creek was dried up. But we continued on to where I'd remembered springs, and suddenly the creek ran with clear, cold water before disappearing in the rocks.

Our camp was soon set up at the foot of Sacajawea; our frosted, golden meadow, ringed by evergreens, rimmed in by the Hurwal Divide on one side and Sacajawea on the other. It was a camp made in heaven, and one that had been in my mind's eye for all these years. I had to pinch myself that it was really happening.

The trail in had been steep with switchbacks, and our horses and mules had to stop often to rest, especially my mare, who hadn't been ridden all summer. Poor Foxy. At 1:30 p.m., camp having been set up and lunch eaten, Linde, Tanya and I decided to tackle the mountain. We'd climb until 5 o'clock; then, no matter where we were, we'd turn around and descend. Not smart to be caught on the mountain at night.

Following directions from various sources as to how to climb the peak, we stumbled onto a trail of sorts, which led upward to a high, rock-strewn basin. We chose a ridge to the right to begin our ascent, as the trail had disappeared into a gully. Higher and higher we climbed, over loose rock, solid rock, and washouts that had been carved over time by snowmelt.

From the narrow, rocky ridgetop we gazed around in awe, then looked DOWN! My stomach still lurches at the memory of that sight. We discovered a goat trail, which seem to follow the ridge top, and kept on it.

Stopping to catch our breath, we noticed a huge smoke billowing up from the direction of Standley, which later turned out to be the beginning of the large Fox Point fire. We looked southward to see the Twin Lakes fire flaring up again in that unseasonable, summer-like weather. We gazed in wonder over to the massive summit of the Matterhorn, and seemed on the level with the red-rocked Hurwal Divide.

Grasping for a foothold and a handhold, we reached the first summit.

While catching our breath, we gazed across to a string of peaks that seemed to rise forever. We recognized the Eagle Cap among them, as well as other familiar landmarks we'd climbed. Weary, sweaty and thirsty, we rationed our water. Often we had climbed on hands and knees (me mostly, as I was the oldest member of the expedition). The late September sunlight was fading, and the sun itself had disappeared behind the summit. Soon it was 5 o'clock.

Reluctantly, with the final summit so close but still so far, we rested before beginning the slow, steep descent. I managed to capture some of those indescribable vistas on film before scrambling down that mountain of moving rock to the basin, far behind my younger companions.

Mere words cannot do justice to the climb, nor the trip, but I must be ready for the hunt. Morning is coming, just as life itself does..too fast to squeeze in all I want to do.

We wearily trudged back to camp where barbecued steaks, potatoes, homemade bread and salad never tasted so good. We spent a restful night there in the basin, touched by the colors of fall, and lulled to sleep by the sound of the clear, cold creek.

The next morning we breakfasted on fried grouse, shot by Doug and frozen and carried in by the mules, plus huckleberry muffins baked at home. Tanya was a happy camper and a delight to have along, not to mention a great mountain climber. This trip will be stored away for the winter of my life.

And now, to address this day and this envelope, which contains my forever-late, past-the-deadline column.

October 17—One of the rewards of writing this column is hearing from those who read it. All manner of people respond, but the one who haunts me is 95-year-old Blanche Strey, who lives in Lacy, Washington. This column is dedicated to you, Blanche.

On September 20, 1994, she wrote, telling me how much she enjoyed my journal of September 16, wherein I had written about the Gill ranch fire, and kindled a spark in her memory. For you see, Blanche and her soon-to-be-98-year-old husband, Bill, used to live in the same "hills" I often write about. The couple owned a ranch near what is known as "The Buttes." In her letter Blanche wrote,

I am reminded of the one time I was at the Gill ranch. It was one of our first years at the ranch. Clyde Harsin instigated the gathering, and a sister of the Gill brothers and her husband came later in the day. I have a picture of some group, some place. Cliff and Ethel Wade were there and we were the only other women in the picture. We had a picnic lunch. And Tom and

Joe (Gill) tossed their tobacco sack to each other throughout the day. My sight is no better. Bill is quite frail. I was so happy the fire did not reach the Buttes. Love, Blanche and Bill.

Several times, I have gone through back files of the Wallowa County Chieftain searching for Blanche's columns. Either I ran out of time, or found I had been looking through the wrong years. This morning I was lucky. Elane Dickenson, a reporter for the Chieftain, just happened to have one of the files out that contained Blanche's columns.

Blanche, who way back then wrote "Kitchen News" (and a ranch woman's views) under the pen name of Dorcas Jane, lived on a ranch north of Prairie Creek. Though more isolated and farther from town than we are, she wrote about a life that had many similarities to mine. More than 60 years span that time frame.

Actually the Zumwalt country was more settled then, with families living in every draw and by every spring. Today, most of the old buildings have disappeared. A few gray, weathered ones tilt and sag, and each winter more fall victim to fierce prairie storms. Blanche and Bill's house, which used to sit farther up the draw, was moved down toward the road, and is one of the remaining homes.

The country itself hasn't changed much. Cattle still graze the native grasses under the Buttes, as they have for 100 years. The seasons, so well described by Blanche, still come and go. It is an immense high plateau where sky and hills meet, silence and the wind are friends, and the winters harsh. The country grows on you, and when you are out in it on horseback or on foot, just you and the land, it becomes a part of you. It definitely shaped Blanche and Bill's life, and in their waning years they think of it with a bittersweet longing.

So it was with fascination that I poured through each week of those 1944 editions, reading words written by Blanche fifty years ago. For instance, from the Thursday, June 22 edition,

The annual miracle of the apple blossoms has come and gone in a gorgeous display, with a series of scenes acted in costume. Deep pink, then palest flush, and bridal white. Three old plum trees in a row cling to life, each with a few green branches among stark limbs. Almost I could wish that the apple trees might blossom forever and never bear fruit. They are so lovely. But that would mean no apple dumplings, which would never do.

My mother bakes her apple dumplings in a sugar-cinnamon syrup. And though I strive, I have yet to achieve that same sweet sticky sauce, which surrounds each mound of crust-covered apple slices. I don't hold with the cored-whole-apple school of dumplings.

Later, in the same column, she adds,

Keep thinking of that soldier boy who just wanted to go home and sit on the front porch. He had no yen for excitement, far places, or elaborate entertainment. I wish he might see our lilacs washed with rain; the red hen and her seven buff chicks dashing out between splashes for a scratch or two; the milk cows, Jerz and Buttercup, meandering along the pasture trail lined with blue lupine.

Blanche paints a word picture here that is very familiar to all who have been in the hills. And she knew what that soldier boy missed most.

In the August 3, 1944 edition,

Monday—Visioning the clothes on the line before 10 o'clock, I put water on to heat as soon as the hotcake griddle came off the stove. But the gasoline washer was possessed of inertia, and one solid hour was consumed in futile stepping and stomping. Finally the thing took off with a loud sputter and clamor. With the threat of wash board looming, the roar made sweeter music than any stringed instrument I've ever heard played.

Hay hands ate canned pears and molasses cookies instead of pie. The whole dinner was on the frugal side, and thank goodness for wash-day beans.

Back to Janie's Journal—This morning I canned sauerkraut. Darlene Turner and I made a joint effort of dealing with the cabbage she raised in her garden. And because of the kraut, this column, and ranch *deja vu*, after reading about Blanche's dumplings, I decided to bake them for supper.

I admit I come from the whole-cored-apple-school, but I used slices instead of whole apples, covering them with crust and surrounding them with a cinnamony, honeyed syrup. They were wonderful, and made the kitchen smell homey when Doug came in all dirty and tired from the potato field. Thanks, Blanche. It was a delicious way to deal with the box of apples daughter Jackie brought up from Imnaha.

As Dorcas Jane, Blanche wrote about those 16 years she and Bill lived on their ranch. In the newspaper office this morning I read on and on, and as the morning disappeared and I scribbled with a borrowed pen, I found more similarities.

Blanche loved to read and, like me, would often mention a good book in her column. And, like me and Rosemary Green, she felt just a bit guilty about reading during the day, so she would read standing up, doing other things, leaning on the wood box, stirring a pudding, suffering a little, lest she become comfortable. All this just to read, to feed her hunger for learning.

Sometimes Blanche would stay up late at night, "having the readingest time." And then the next day be so tired, to tackle her hard ranch chores.

Blanche and Bill sold their ranch in October 1944, and lived that fall and winter in a cabin at Wallowa Lake. It must have been an autumn like the lovely one we are experiencing now. Blanche continues to write her column,

As if to shame us for leaving, Wallowa County has burst into a golden revelry. Golden days ornamented with all of the tints and shades of gold. Tamarack gild the mountain slopes, and gold leaves cast sun-mottled shadows. In winter, spring and summer, the Wallowa Lake region has an unequaled beauty. But right now, in the gold of the year, its command of appreciation is greater for me.

For me, too, Blanche.

Beneath this paragraph, a poem,

Then one break day, we wake to find October
Sans raiment gold, sans everything—and sober.

And on this golden morn, I captured on film some of October's raiment. Maple trees lining the streets of Joseph; new snow on the mountains; blue sky, orange mountain ash berries, and along the creeks colors reflected in clear, cold water. Floating cottonwood leaves, and frosted meadows.

I think of Blanche Strey, of the 1930s and 40s, and of Blanche Jane Tippett of the 1990s.

Gold October, beans on the Monarch range, dumplings in the oven, milk cows in the pasture, bandy hen on eggs, reading books in bed at night (every night), grandchildren, and winter coming on.

Timelessness in a world that exists off the beaten path, away from the touristy, arty world of Joseph. Wish Blanche could come for a visit. I'd love to show her around.

Whenever Doug and I drive past the old Strey place, out there beneath Findley Buttes, I think of the two of them and wonder what they looked like then. I've never met them, but through Blanche's letters, columns, and a phone call, I've come to know they were not so very different from us and others who continue to plug away at this old lifestyle, here in Wallowa County.

It is a lifestyle that has endured for many years. Though we complain sometimes, we ranch wives love our lives, hard work and all, and when we reach (if we reach) Blanche and Bill's age, perhaps we too will look back on these times as the happiest of our lives.

Oh yes, Doug did get his Buck. And we had a marvelous day. Too much to write about.

Last Saturday night, after a day of digging spuds (for Doug, that is), we drove down to Troy to attend a benefit dance. We spent the night in our mini-motor home, and next morning enjoyed seeing the "North end" all glorious and painted with October. Wish you could have seen it too, Blanche and Bill.

October 31—My childhood chum Sandra and husband Fred visited us from Auburn, California, this past week. She and I spent a blustery, rainy day wandering up and down Joseph's main street, visiting the many art galleries. By late October, when cold settles down below the Wallowas, the tourists have disappeared, so we have the place pretty much to ourselves.

A heavy downpour sluiced down the streets of Joseph, music to our ears after a droughty summer, as we sipped hot flavored lattes and visited about old times. On a whim, we signed up for a tour of the local bronze foundry, and found it to be a most educational experience. Feeling like errant children, we returned at dark to the ranch to fix supper for the men.

On Sunday morning, after chores, I fried trout and sourdough huckleberry pancakes on the old Monarch wood range. We spread Sandra's apple butter and real maple syrup on the pancakes. What a treat.

It was raining again when Sandra and Fred left this morning, and the Prairie Creek wind blew in great gusts. Tradition has it that Sandra takes our Christmas card photo, regardless of the weather, and we forget until they are ready to leave...every year.

Usually our card portrays Doug and me clad in heavy coats, huddling in the cold under our snowy mountains. It wasn't much different this time. Teeth chattering, we posed in the front yard with the tawny-colored hills providing the backdrop for this year's photo.

Each year we appear a little older through the camera lens, bringing Christmas wishes to those who live outside our valley. This November's first impending snowfall draws the curtain on glorious Indian summer, and signals the beginning of winter.

November 1—After all the little spooks and goblins went to sleep last night, the rain turned to snow, and this morning the first white dusting of it covers everything here on Prairie Creek. Resembling Jerry Palen's Flo, bundled in scarf, big boots and winter coat, I shuffled out through the white stuff to chore. My two milk cows, Startch and Stargirl, plus the newly purchased Holstein heifer, Hollyhock, huddled together for warmth under the overhanging eaves of the old barn. A coverlet of snow clung to their bony backs and occasionally a big glob of it melted down their shoulders.

With my eager dog, Daisy, and a parade of cats in tow, I reached the hay shed, where I rolled a bale of hay closer to the gate before snipping baling twine with pliers and forking flakes into their large wooden feeder. The cattle are always impatient, and invariably block my approach to the feeder with their large bodies. After they are fed I carry several flakes of fragrant meadow hay into the barn, where the first-calf heifer waits for her breakfast. This Simmental/Holstein daughter of Stanch receives a can of rolled barley in addition to her hay.

In a far dark corner, black as night, curled in straw, slumbers Spook. No, Spook didn't appear on October 31, but Halloween was only a week away when this jet-black bull calf made his rather untimely way into the world. You see, he wasn't planned. Here's his story.

It all began last January, when Doug and I went south, and turned Startch and her big black baldy heifer calf out with the fall calving cows and their calves in the hill pasture above the house. Roaming with the fall calvers, to breed them back, was this big black Simmental bull. Not a heifer bull.

My well-developed heifer soon found herself with calf. Only it was her secret. In the spring we turned my two milk cows' heifers out on summer range with the rest of the replacement heifers. At that time I did notice that the black baldy looked pretty bloomy, but didn't think much about it.

Our long, hot summer progressed, and one day as Ben was riding out there in the hills checking the cattle, he noticed the heifer, who was definitely springing. She had this nice little udder forming, and her tummy was protruding. Her secret was out! Doug and I made a game out of guessing when she would calve. When Ben was out in the hills salting the cattle, around the middle of September, he hauled the heifer back here to the valley ranch.

I began feeding her a little hay, and keeping a close watch on her. Then, one blustery late October afternoon, the heifer appeared uneasy. She kicked at her belly and paced nervously back and forth across the small pasture lot next to the calving shed. A storm seemed to be building, so that evening I drove her into the calving shed, bedded her in straw, and returned to the kitchen to finish preparing supper.

I checked on her just before bedtime. Nothing.

At midnight I awoke from a deep sleep. Outside, the wind was stripping rusty leaves from the ancient willows in the calving shed pasture lot. The smell of rain was in the air. I turned the light on in the calving shed and walked over to the heifer. Two huge feet and hooves protruded. I observed her for a while, taking note that she had been in labor for some time. The straw around the stall showed signs of struggling. Not much progress, and I knew she just couldn't get the job done by herself. My soon-to-be-young-mother wasn't even a two-year-old yet.

Doug, who had been late for supper, returning from the potato field after a week of working late every night, trying to get the seed potato harvest in, was fast asleep. I dreaded having to wake him in the dead of night. He so needed his sleep, but the heifer needed help. I had no choice. Gently I shook him awake. And, without a word, he dressed and together we silently drove to the calving shed.

After we got the heifer in a chute, Doug took one look and decided that if she needed a cesarean, we better call the veterinarian. I was dispatched to the kitchen to wake yet another tired, busy man in the middle of the night, but the young local vet on call was very nice and said to bring the heifer right in. He'd be at the clinic, several miles distant, in Enterprise, waiting for us.

So, clad in P.J.'s under barn chore clothes, I helped load the laboring heifer into the truck and we headed to town. It had already begun to rain, and we rode in silence through the black night. Lights glimmered wetly through the rainy windshield, leading us to the vet clinic at the north end of town. We soon had the heifer unloaded, two feet still visible, and coaxed into entering another chute. After assessing the situation, the vet seemed to think the heifer, with a little assist, could have the calf normally. She was a healthy, roomy gal.

With the aid of a calf puller, those two huge feet preceded the body of a large, black bull calf, which slithered onto the floor in a rush of amniotic fluid. At first the big calf couldn't breathe, so Doug and the vet draped him over a panel and suctioned his nostrils and throat with a vacuum, at which time the calf gulped into his lungs that first breath of life-giving air. The vet milked a bowl of warm colostrum milk from the relieved heifer, and tubed the baby bull, which attempted to struggle up on slippery feet.

It was by now nearing 2 a.m. on a spooky night. On the way home, Doug named the calf. And now, the morning after Halloween, Spook is a healthy, robust week-old baby, and mother is just fine. His untimely birth, what with winter coming on, justifies his access to the warm barn. His gentle teenage mom is a good milker, and one of these mornings I'll coax her into a stanchion with some rolled barley and we'll have us some house milk. End of story.

November 16—Why would anyone want to drive over Tollgate in a windstorm, with ice on the road, blowing snow whirling off the trees and onto the windshield?

Well...you see, at the base of the Blue Mountains, amid that fertile pea farm ground, there lies the small town of Weston. And last Monday night, in the Memorial Hall, there was a turkey dinner. Cranberry sauce, mashed potatoes, dressing, gravy and homemade rolls and pumpkin pie; all served up by the W-M High School Spanish Club.

The nice folks in Weston were putting on their annual Chamber of Commerce turkey dinner, and Doug and I had an invitation. Actually, it was several months ago when Sam Tucker called me one afternoon on behalf of the Weston Chamber to ask if I would be the speaker for their annual dinner. He said that in years past they had invited dignitaries from all over, and for three years there were these folks in Weston who had wanted to have Janie Tippett as the speaker. So, to make these persistent people happy, he was asking me to PLEASE come.

Not only did Sam invite me, but he insisted I set the date for the dinner so it wouldn't interfere with any of my plans. How could I refuse? I marked November 14 on my calendar, which worked well, as it was before my cow elk season and Thanksgiving.

Doug and I left around mid-morning last Monday, me behind the wheel, to drive over Tollgate. I drove slowly up and over the summit, savoring the beautiful winter white on evergreens, the blue sky, and the occasional glimpses of the vast plain below.

Trying not to let the blowing snow and icy conditions interfere with my pleasant thoughts of traveling through the Blue Mountains, we were soon heading down Weston Mountain into the vast farming area that surrounds Milton-Freewater and Walla Walla. There was still plenty of autumn color on that side of the Blues, and the temperature was noticeably milder. We tended to some business in Walla Walla, ate lunch, and browsed around some antique shops before heading over to Weston that evening.

Colorful maple trees, leaves intact, lined Weston's tidy streets, and the small town was pretty quiet. Since we had arrived an hour earlier than the scheduled dinner, we wandered into the Long Branch restaurant and ordered tea for me and coffee for Doug. The place, reminiscent of Miss Kitty and Festus, was adorned with old photos and memorabilia of Weston's past. The wind swirled loose leaves around the street in front of Memorial Hall as we climbed the steps of the old building and entered a large, warm room.

Here we met Sam Tucker and Jennabelle Vincent, both of whom had corresponded with me about the chamber dinner. They proved to be as charming in real life as they were on the phone. Virgil Rupp, editor of Agri-Times NW, walked in with his wife, Rosemary, and the talk was of Virgil's successful elk hunt. One could tell we were in the heart of the Blue Mountain agriculture and sports area, amid people who were proud of their history and heritage. I copied that information from the Weston Chamber of Commerce's stationery.

After being served a delicious turkey dinner, we were entertained by a young boy by the name of Brander Richmond, who performed a piano solo. Wow! Could that boy play, and without music yet. His fingers fairly flew over the keys as he managed some pretty serious classical music. Then it was my turn. These people had asked me to be their speaker.

In the Long Branch, I had jotted down some notes, but not being fond of speeches myself, I kept pretty much informal, sort of like visiting. That morning I had grabbed a copy of an article I'd written this past summer at the Fishtrap Writer's Conference, an assignment in Jonathan Nicholas' workshop. It was supposed to be an article on Wallowa County, suitable for the New York Times. I had dashed off a copy on my printer, and in my haste that morning, I had forgotten to separate the sheets. As I read, I realized this folded-up article began to unfold on the audience side of the podium.

It must have been quite amusing to the people listening and watching. But they were most kindly folks, and seemed to enjoy what I had to say. And, believe me, I appreciated their smiling, friendly faces staring back. Thank you, Weston Chamber of Commerce. Both Doug and I considered it a treat to visit your special community in Eastern Oregon.

The drive home late that night was uneventful, thank goodness. The wind was still blowing snow, and we met only two vehicles crossing over Tollgate at that hour. We made it back to the ranch before midnight.

The next morning Ben shipped the spring calves, and Doug drove one of the trucks. The four steers, just weaned off my milk cows, went down the road with the big bunch.

Last weekend I had walked out into the midst of the weaned calves, and located (or rather, she located me) my milk cow's heifer, which I will raise for a replacement animal. Since she is such a pet, the heifer followed me out of the corral, after which I turned her in with the milk cows. My herd, counting "Spook," numbers six head now, which I tend to each day. They are part of my morning chores.

Linde and I have resumed our walks, regardless Of the weather. One day we hiked up through the snowy woods. Our dogs, ecstatic at the thought of rambling over the countryside, bounded over logs, sniffed squirrel holes, and rolled in the snow. We came out on a road that led up toward Ferguson Ridge, followed it until we came to where some friends had recently built a house.

It was a wonderful walk and we had a nice visit at the end of it with our friends, before returning home. Another day we took a hike up under the base of Chief Joseph Mountain. May as well get in shape for cross-country skiing, as conditions are improving daily.

Thanksgiving is nearly upon us, when 25 family members and neighbors will fill our home with happy voices and big appetites. It will be good to see the grandchildren. They've been so busy with school functions, I haven't seen nearly enough of them lately. We here on Prairie Creek hope all of you have a wonderful Thanksgiving day, and thanks again, Weston Chamber of Commerce, for inviting us to your annual dinner.

November 30—Great rags of cloud, torn by a roaring south wind, swept across the eastern hills as I peered out our front window just at daybreak this morning. Intermittent rain and sleet, which fell all night on top of snow, paints an icy glaze the surface of the road, and everything else here on Prairie Creek. A neighbor, driving by in his pickup, travels at a snail's pace and appears to be driven by the wind.

The way to the barn is a skating rink, and I laughed as Daisy and the four cats ran ahead of me, sliding into each other. The old mother cat simply stood still and let the wind push her sideways nearly to the barn!

Last evening, during the wind and sleet storm, I donned slicker and boots and, armed with the milk pail, made my way to the barn, where I let the young first-calf heifer in. I'd shut the calf up in a stall all day, so the heifer would have plenty of milk for the both of us.

She came in readily and I locked her into the stanchion and gingerly eased on the hobbles. She struggled just a little, then went to eating her barley and allowed me to milk her for the first time. Ate age 61 it felt good to still be able to break a first-calf heifer to being milked. Although I must confess, I was a little nervous about putting on those hobbles.

I continue to receive interesting letters from readers, and the latest one, from Grace Harvey of Pilot Rock, deserves mention. Grace, 81, says she is envious of all my energy, but from her letter I'd say she has plenty of that herself. She says her horses are being wintered down by Pendleton, so now she has more time to do the many things she put off all summer. Enclosed in Grace's letter was a poem, written by her friend Virginia Jones.

Going Up to Grace's

When life's frustrations my spirit embraces,
I jump in the pickup and go up to Grace's.
While I drive along wondering why life is so tough,
My eyes savor green velvet moss on the bluff
And around the next bend where the clear waters run,
I see an old homestead asleep in the sun.
Then on up the canyon and through a green gate,
Where hot tea and warm friendship always await.
We'll put on our jackets and walk up the hill,
Then poke up the woodstove to take off the chill.
Or saddle the horses and ride down to see,
Where the bear tore down part of the old apple tree.
Time passes swiftly, we lose track of hours,
Just talking travels, books, grandkids and flowers.
Sunset the gray skies with golden replaces,
And I'm thankful and glad that I went up to Grace's.

Just reading that poem makes me want to jump in my pickup and go up to Grace's.

Our cow elk hunt was very successful, even though we were beginning to think it was just a sightseeing tour of winter in Wallowa County's vast outback. Bryan Wolfe and son Jeff had driven over the night before, and in sleeping bags on the living room floor slept two excited grandsons, Josh and James. Josh had a cow tag, and brother James, age 8, was along for the adventure.

I fed my cows and tended the chickens in the dark on opening morning, while Doug tended to sourdough hotcakes on the wood cookstove in the warm kitchen, and Bryan put together the traditional meat loaf sandwiches for lunches.

Dawn was just brightening the eastern horizon when we left, in two four-wheel drive pickups, to travel out the long Zumwalt road. We gazed out upon the snow-covered hills and watched a flaming sun rise over the dark purple Seven Devils Mountains in Idaho. Amber light spread across the frozen landscape as we looked for the dark shapes that would be elk. Nothing.

Before the Steen Ranch we turned down toward Vance Draw and entered the snowy timbered country, where the snow became deeper in the road, and we searched for elk tracks.

We made an excursion out on Cold Springs Ridge, passing several cold hunting camps, but didn't see that anyone was doing anything more than trying to stay warm. Smoke swirled up from the wall tents and an occasional face peered out at us. The road on Cold Springs ridge was drifting in because of the wind.

It was really something to look down at the canyon to the east and see the big snow cornices hanging over the edge, with the flowing snow curling around them. While we could, we turned around and drove to Buckhorn for another view of winter, in an area that is closed much of the year. Gazing down at the awesome breaks of the Imnaha and the Snake in that biting cold wind was an adventure in itself.

Back in the warm pickups, we listened to the 4-H radio auction wafted to us across the frozen miles from Enterprise. Unbeknownst to me, Bryan was bidding on my sourdough bread, using his cellular phone. What an age we live in!

Parked alongside the road overlooking Pine Creek, we ate our lunches and glassed for elk. We sure hadn't seen many tracks. We drove on down toward the Chesnimnus, just about ready to call it quits, when Doug spotted eight cow elk crossing the creek. By the time everyone jumped out and headed for the bank of the creek, the elk had retreated up a steep, timbered side hill. Josh, running to get a shot, picked out a cow in an opening, and shot. He connected, and after the shooting stopped we had three elk down. Then the work began.

All but Josh's cow were down on the steep, slippery, frozen hillside, above the creek. Josh's had gone down and crossed the creek. James and Josh were so excited they could barely contain themselves. James splashed across the cold creek following the older hunters, and after much grunting, gutting, tugging and pulling, the three nice cow elk were dragged, with the aid of Bryan's four-wheeler, to a spot where they could be loaded with a hoist into the back of our pickup.

The enjoyment of the trip, for all of us, was watching the two boys. Josh, age 13, had shot his first elk, and James got in on the entire hunt. After a long drive home in the wind and snow, I fixed a hot supper while the men skinned the three elk out in our shop. A big job. James' dad came over after work, and helped. As the years go by, the telling of that story by those two boys will no doubt improve with age. Lucky boys.

Thanksgiving was wonderful. A huge golden roasted turkey fed 25 of us, and our house was crammed with relatives and friends. I set up tables in three rooms, and used the wood cookstove to cook and serve up the hot dressing, rolls, and mashed potatoes.

The children ran around outside, creating second appetites, and then the pies were brought out. Pumpkin, homemade mincemeat (made from elk), granddaughter Carrie's pumpkin cake, daughter Lori's cookies. It was amazing how it all disappeared. Sorry, Roger Pond, this family hangs onto its traditions, and as long as this grandma can hold out, the family seems to want to gather here. One day, perhaps, it will be the daughters' turns.

Yesterday I baked Bryan's sourdough bread, and today Doug is delivering it when he attends the Winter Farm Fair in Hermiston. It is a bad time to be on the roads. Yesterday I worried about the children traveling to and from Lewiston to put granddaughter Tammy and husband, Matt, on the plane. All made it safely, but winter travel in our area is no fun.

As this south wind roars outside, I see that it's warmer breath is melting the ice. Meanwhile, I savor the warm closeness of the old Monarch as I write.

December 12—Prairie Creek is cloaked in frozen fog this morning. The leafless willows that line the ditch in the bull lot wear whiskers. Hoarfrost coats the wire fence around the chicken pen, feathering the long golden grasses and weeds that stick up through the snow. My line of vision is limited to the immediate yard outside the window as I write. The mountains are non-existent. Dark shapes of cattle wait patiently just across the fence for their morning feed of silage. The fog and cold are silent.

In fact, winter is mostly silent here, which is peaceful. But in other parts of the county there is much merry-making going on. After the chores, the families come to town to watch school Christmas programs, and on Saturday evening they turned out in droves to attend a cowboy Christmas ball. Cloverleaf Hall overflowed with children, cowboys, mothers, grandmothers, grandpas, kissin' cousins and even Santa himself. Cowboy poets performed, some quite young, and there was a table piled high with cookies and punch and a chair for Santa. It was definitely a family affair.

There was more Christmas spirit at historic old Wallowa Lake Lodge last week. Decorated with two Christmas trees, there was caroling, a delicious ham dinner, and more entertainment by various talented members of the community. It didn't matter that people had to leave their warm homes and travel over snowy roads in bitter cold temperatures.

There is a strong sense of community here, and it is seen again at the church sings, one of which I attended recently. It may be cold outside, but it is warm inside where people gather during the holiday season. Our CattleWomen met last week too, way up a snowy road under Ruby Peak at the home of Steve and Trudy Allison. Inside the warm log home, we nibbled on traditional holiday goodies and watched deer wander around the snowy yard.

Speaking of snow, it is just about perfect for cross-country skiing and Linde and I have been out most every day. We simply find a snowy woods and make our own trails. The air is so cold and fresh, and the exercise gives us the stamina to cope with the busy holidays. Hearing the slide and glide of our skis, and seeing the evergreens drooping under snow, we look for deer and elk tracks, and read the tales in the snow, where an owl swooped down to catch a mouse. It is good for the soul to simply be out in that silence. This is winter in Wallowa County.

The small town of Joseph was quiet last Sunday morning, except for Joseph High School, where a horse trailer full of Christmas trees was parked. FFA members were selling the fragrant trees which had been cut at a tree farm over in the Willamette Valley. Doug and I selected a tree along with many other neighbors who were there, all smiles in the frosty air. Our tree is still fragrant in the living room and twinkling with lights.

We will have grandchildren here for Christmas, along with their parents to celebrate the season. May your hearts be filled with gladness of Christmas and let there always be a song in your heart. Because we in the ranching community will need all the songs we can sing to survive the coming years. Merry Christmas from Prairie Creek.

December 29—Just like the wind, which shifted this morning from a warmer southerly direction to a colder northern one, the season shifts toward a new year. We had a wonderful Christmas, due in part to our new tradition of taking off on a fishing trip the day before Christmas Eve. Having baked six loaves of Tannenbaum Brot (Christmas tree bread) and delivered them to friends and relatives, wrapped presents for 18 grandchildren, purchased ingredients for our prime rib Christmas dinner, watered the Christmas tree on a daily basis, attended umpteen school and church programs, and written the yearly Christmas card letters, I was ready for a little diversion.

Mother Nature cooperated and slid in a few warmer days without wind or blizzard, so on the Friday before Christmas, Pat, Linde, Doug and I piled into the 4-wheel-drive and headed down Sheep Creek to Imnaha, thence downriver to Cow Creek. It was a bright, crisp, sunny day, and although the canyons were devoid of snow, heavy frost glittered white on the norths and in the shaded draws. We saw lots of deer out feeding or laying on benches soaking up sun.

It was noon when we arrived at the Cow Creek bridge, so we drug out some cheese and crackers and enjoyed a tailgate picnic before assembling our fishing gear. Doug had hauled his Honda down, so he soon *put-putt-ed* down the trail, which here enters the rugged Imnaha Gorge.

I took off on foot, wearing a daypack that contained water and spare fishing gear. Armed with my pole and a determination to walk the five miles to Eureka Bar, where the Imnaha joins the Snake, I set a brisk pace. Linde and Pat would fish and be along later. I was anxious to hike to my favorite fishing place, where I had in the past hooked two big steelhead, which led to an even bigger story. On one occasion the fish, and the slippery rock that shelves into the river, had conspired to do me in, but I was determined to actually land a fish there, not to have the fish land me.

It was a wonderful experience, being alone there in the gorge. The cold winter smell of the river, the clear, fresh, unmoving air, the echoing sound of the river running, the feel of the frozen trail beneath my feet, and the anticipation of what lay around each bend. The trail looped around, sometimes at river level, then climbed up and through patches of blackberry bramble to follow narrow, rocky ledges that looked downward to the cold running Imnaha. Preserved red sumac leaves lay scattered in the trail, and clusters of greenish, white berries hung thickly on leafless poison oak.

My faithful dog, Daisy, loved this escape too, and would run on ahead, sniffing the trail for animals that had preceded us, then come racing back to see if I was coming. Once we startled a beautiful wild duck of some sort, which wore a rust-colored coat of feathers. The lone duck seemed to own the canyon. He would fly up at our approach, then we'd spot him swimming again farther downstream. Magpies and hawks flew around the higher crags, and an ouzel (dipper) sounded his familiar song above the roar of the rapids. Whenever the river eddied or pooled, it was filmed with ice. There was very little sunlight in the gorge, but the golden-tipped rim rocks above provided weak winter light.

Daisy and I were warmed by the exertion of hiking by the time we arrived at my favored fishing hole. I carefully made my way to the river's edge, clamoring over giant icy boulders that shelved into the water. Casting my line outward into the current, which eddied around a large rock, I expected the familiar yank and pull of a steelhead but felt only the shudder of a riffle against my bait. Not so much as bite.

Oh well. For those of us who go fishing, we know fishing isn't the ALL of it. That day the canyon itself was my greatest catch. After several unsuccessful casts, I reeled in an scrambled safely back up to the trail, and continued downriver to Eureka Bar. The sun was sinking as I walked on, glimpsing the rugged reaches of the far-off hills that border the Snake on the Idaho side.

The last rays of the December sun lingered, providing the remaining light of day. On and on, we walked, until finally we were opposite the old mine entrance that tunnels through rock to the Snake River side. After huffing and puffing my way up and over a high wooden bridge, I gazed down at the Snake. Far below on a rocky shore I could see Doug, his Honda parked nearby.

After walking down to where he fished, (he had no luck either), I looked at my watch and saw that it already was 3 p.m., time to start back if I didn't want to hike in the dark. Even if Doug had offered to give me a lift on that Honda, I would have declined. Remembering those high, rocky points that drop straight down to the river didn't appeal to my sense of safety. So Doug took off, fishing along the way before disappearing entirely, leaving Daisy and I alone with the cold canyon trail. But I wasn't cold, not when hiking at the speed needed to beat darkness.

Around 4:30, in the dusk, I could make out the flicker of a small campfire, and knew we were close to the trailhead. The smell of wood smoke drifted down toward me and the cheery flames drew me on. After warming up a bit and marveling at the beauty of the black and quiet canyon, we headed up the long gravel switchback road to Imnaha, where Sally Tanzey fixed us a bit to eat at the store. Ten miles is good for the soul, especially during the rush of Christmas.

Earlier in the week, we had traveled to the small settlement of Imnaha to attend the school Christmas program, which was, as usual, worth the 60-mile round-trip drive.

The children of Char Williams' upper classes had written their own scripts, constructed their own stage sets, with the aid of lots of duct tape, and managed to pull the production off amid more than a few giggles. Small country schools, isolated from the mainstream of modern life, seem to foster particularly creative children, and often their patient teachers are amazed at what these young minds come up with.

Santa made his annual appearance and each child sat on his knee and voiced Christmas wishes before receiving a bag of nuts, oranges and candy. It is said a community helps with the rearing of its children. There under the rimrocks, the children of Imnaha belong to all. As the years roll on and we see a batch of young'uns grow tall and poised, learning readin', writin' and 'rithmetic, and even musical inst'ruments, we look at the little ones on their parents' laps and know it won't be long until a new generation begins all over again.

One thing for sure, some of these children may leave the canyon, but the canyon will never leave them. It is there, like the cold waters of the Imnaha and the rim rocks themselves, locked in their souls forever. What a gift.

Grandson Buck, the only eighth grader, will be going out "on top" to high school in Joseph next year, but Buck will cope, and even know how to play the trombone, thanks to this little two-room school and its special teachers over the years.

Happy new year to all of you from Prairie Creek!

This dark brown jenny, shown with her three-day-old offspring, was bred to a paint stallion to produce this buckskin molly hinny. The animals are owned by Jim and Vivian LaRue of Enterprise.

1995

January 4—This morning we left the ranch on Prairie Creek, our car thermometer registering zero degrees as we drove toward the lower valley along the Wallowa River. The skies and roads were clear and we were actually on the road, heading south on our yearly jaunt to visit relatives and enjoy a respite from the ranch chores and cold.

We lunched at Farewell Bend, where the old Oregon Trail left the Snake after having followed that river for days along its westward route. Two bald eagles stared at us from a large Russian olive growing near the river. Clouds rolled in from the southwest as we entered Oregon's Owyhee country.

We stretched our legs at Jordan Valley before eating up the long miles to McDermitt, on the Nevada border. Then, more long sagebrush-filled distances led us to the glittering lights in the Nevada desert, which would be Winnemucca.

At the old Hotel Winnemucca we ate a Basque supper, family style, while seated at a long wooden table with other travelers. We joined right in, not ordering, simply helping ourselves from a tureen of steaming soup, then dipping chunks of sheepherder bread in the rich meat stock, before going on to salad, followed by bowls of beans, pasta, lamb stew in gravy, and finally, a T-bone steak.

We washed it down with glasses of full-bodied red wine as we visited our fellow supper guests. The wonderful herbs and garlicky odors of Basque cooking followed us out into the high desert night.

The next morning we awoke to four inches of fresh snow, with the white stuff still falling. The wet snow melted quickly, as we sped on toward Reno. A big storm that had swept over the Sierra was gathering itself for another attack when we pulled into Boomtown. Snow flakes swirled in the wind as we walked to our car, and headed up toward Donner Pass.

At Truckee we took the Donner Lake road and arrived safely at Ernie and Rose Gnos', where we were expected for the night. Delicious smells wafted from the kitchen, where chef Ernie held sway. After spending a morning on the ski slopes at nearby Squaw Valley, Ernie was preparing a treat for us.

He and Rose are part of a large farming and ranching operation in Dixon, California, and semi-retired enough to spend time at their Donner Lake cabin, which, in reality, is more than just a cabin. A fire was crackling in the stone fireplace, and a floor-to-ceiling glass window looked out on snow-buried neighboring cabins.

While Rose tossed a green salad at the table, Ernie served up roast lamb smothered in seasonings, served with homemade sausage, simmered in sauerkraut. Carrots, onions, parsleyed potatoes and french bread completed the menu. A real treat. While we visited over a light dessert of caramelized apple slices and coffee, we learned that a skier went missing that night not far from where we were. We could envision him out there under all that snow, and were relieved the next morning to find out he was finally rescued.

After a comfortable night there along the shores of Donner Lake, we took Ernie and Rose to breakfast at a small eatery along the lake shore. Ernie, dressed in ski togs, left afterward for his favorite run at Squaw Valley. Since another storm was predicted to hit the Sierra by late afternoon, we wasted no time driving over the summit, which proved fortunate because we encountered rain at Colfax, and it hasn't let up since.

Leaving the freeway at Auburn, we visited my folks and found them in good health. Mom, at 84, still looking young, attending her meetings, watercolor painting classes, reading and walking every day. Bill, into aerobics and baking bread. He had a batch of whole wheat bread that he was kneading when we arrived.

Increasing rain and lashing winds assailed us as we drove to Caroline and Duane's, where we settled in. Yesterday was my baby sister Kathryn's 49th birthday and Mary Ann had driven down to join us, so we celebrated the day here at Caroline's by cooking her a special dinner, playing games, visiting, and generally enjoying ourselves, which isn't hard to do. It just happens when we four get together.

I had brought some pasta, a gift from friend Linde, so we cooked fettuccine. I baked sourdough bread sticks using my sourdough, and Caroline and I built a high lemon pie for the birthday cake. Duane and Doug enjoyed the food but fled the rest of the time. Four women together is a bit much!

When all is said and done in this world, these close associations with family and friends should remain at the top of our priority list. It takes a certain amount of effort to keep relationships alive, and we should never take them for granted. Rather, we should treasure them.

More adventures await us, but first we must wait out this storm. Daughter Ramona called from Prairie Creek and it seems the "Pineapple Express" blew in there too. She said it was raining. In January yet!

January 9—The thermometer on sister Caroline's porch registers a balmy 62 degrees on this Monday morning here in Auburn, California. A clump of yellow perennial daisies blooms next to a small potted evergreen, still wearing Christmas lights. A furious wind whips the tall, swaying young eucalyptus trees, which seem foreign somehow in these oak-studded Sierra foothills of my youth. I can see pyracantha bushes, laden with bright orange berries, as I type. A tiny humming bird sips at a swaying feeder suspended from the carport.

Overnight the grass seems to have taken on a tropical greenness, due to this so-called "Pineapple Express" that blew in shortly after our arrival. Caroline and husband, Duane, live near Auburn-Folsom road in a rural area that is now just a stone's throw away from the city limits.

There remains a bare hill above the house, and due to the many planted trees, one isn't aware of the many homes nearby. Interesting to me are the trees planted years ago by my father. Especially the cedar, growing full and tall and the enormous digger pine, which was but a tiny seedling when daddy so lovingly planted it in the red granite soil.

A large pond, filling rapidly due to persistent rains, is home to several wood ducks and other wild waterfowl. Blue jays squawk in the trees, showing bright flashes of blue as they fly from limb to limb. A mockingbird appears to lay claim to one of the pyracantha bushes, and spends considerable time defending it from other birds. And as I peer through the pond-side shrubs I see pussy willows! Up toward the hill a mixed bag of breeds and sexes of cattle grazes its way between the trees.

Sister Caroline has left for work, as has her husband. Doug is meeting a friend and will spend the day visiting an old gold mining operation, so I have this cozy little house all to myself.

January 18—Filtering through a layer of high, thin clouds, the weak January sun lays a warm path across the carpet here in sister Caroline's living room. Several chunks of seasoned live oak glow orange in the tiny stove next to where I write. The wood ducks are back this morning, swimming in and out of reeds and rushes bordering the pond.

Doug is off to Reno for the day, a little over an hour away, across the Sierra Mountains, which are, for the moment, passable. Since last I wrote we have been in the midst of one of the worst rain storms California has experienced in a long while. When I was a child growing up in these foothills, I remember occasional thunderstorm deluges, when the creek known as Doty's Ravine, which flowed through our ranch, ran bank to bank, sometimes flooding the flats, but my memory fails to bring back anything resembling this past week!

That warm "Pineapple Express" sent wave after wave of tropical storms washing over the Golden State. Torrential rains fell in sheets, blinding motorists, turning roadways into waterways, and you should have seen the creeks. It didn't even have to be a creek, merely a natural drainage between low hills. All that water had to go somewhere.

Within hours, tiny watercourses turned into raging torrents of water searching for a place to run. If it couldn't drain, it flooded. Even ditches became creeks. Roads were blocked by water-logged oaks and digger pines which blew over in the high winds. Boulders and red granite-like soil was deposited along the back roads. And it rained and rained, until Dry Creek (ironically) made national headlines in nearby Roseville, where sister Kathryn lives, and where hundreds of homes were flooded.

During the worst of the storms, Kathryn was out in her little pickup helping neighbors haul sandbags. Yesterday President Clinton was there in Roseville, talking to the folks affected by the floods. In nearby Rio Linda, that same Dry Creek inundated even more homes, and the president talked to the people there in the Methodist Church, where a lovely carillon has been dedicated to the memory of my grandmother, who died at the age of 102.

"Rio Linda," the river beautiful, wasn't. And now the waters have subsided, and the flotsam and jetsam are all that remain to show where the water levels were. Road crews are out and about repairing damages, as California picks itself up again, after burning, quaking, and now flooding. A cycle that has been going on for eons.

Last week we packed our bags and took up residence with my girl-friend Sandra and her husband, Fred, who live at the end of a high ridgetop above Auburn. From their large living room window we could see the comings and goings of each new storm.

And when the nights were clear enough, we could see lights all over the Sacramento Valley. At sunset the vast flood plain gleamed among the settlements. We played Scrabble, solitaire, cribbage, listened to music, and watched movies. We cooked, ate, washed dishes, and managed to squeeze several long walks in between storms. We burned up two wheelbarrows full of oak wood in the fireplace and I read several books, played the piano, and forgot what day it was. Nice.

There were rainbows when the sun shone through glistening rain, and in Sandra's yard I picked carnelians and found the first blooming narcissus. Each day, great flocks of wild geese flew overhead, searching for feeding areas. One morning, a four-point black tail buck came bounding down off the hill and disappeared into the nearby woods, and blue jays and mockingbirds got drunk on orange pyracantha berries.

As the "wolf" moon rose, the skies cleared and I imagined what it would be like back at home on Prairie Creek, with that same moon glowing softly, illuminating our snowy Wallowas. I often wonder, too, about my faithful dog Daisy and hope she isn't missing me too much.

Some days we lunch with mom and Bill and my sisters. Yesterday we took sister Kathryn to lunch in Roseville, where we found ourselves seated in a small Spanish eatery, listening to south-of-the-border music, and enjoying Mexican food. One day Sandra treated me to lunch at "Awful Annie's" in Auburn, where we munched on "Awfully" good sandwiches while staring out from a tiny covered balcony under dripping locust trees.

Doug occupies his free days antiquing, visiting and playing cribbage. Each morning he arises early and drives to his favorite doughnut shop, shades of Kohlhepp's Kitchen, where he works the Sacramento Bee's crossword puzzle and kibitzes with the locals. It is not a bad life, but I do miss Wallowa County and the daily challenges encountered there. And of course the cross-country skiing.

One day last week my stepfather, Bill, took me with him to his step aerobics class. I wore my "long janes," bright red long johns, a gift from Doug for Christmas, and in doing so started a new fad among the exercise class participants.

Bill and I, by far the oldest members in the class, didn't miss a beat. While his were in step with the class, mine merely kept time to the music.

One night last week Sandra took me to a practice session of her singing group, called the "Sweet Adelines," in Auburn, where I was welcomed and given music to join in harmonizing with this large, 50-member group. It was fun, and the only other guest had recently moved to the area from Pendleton and knew me through this column! Small world.

Yesterday Doug and I drove to Folsom where we visited an ailing, elderly cousin in the hospital. We had quite a time finding Aggie in that large facility, but we were glad to have made the effort. Cousin Aggie, in her late 80s, smiled in recognition as she lay nestled in several pillows, recovering from pneumonia. In spite of losing her sight and hearing, Aggie's spirit was intact.

Later, we drove to the old Smith ranch on Carson Creek. Leaving the last subdivision behind, we drove through the familiar White Rock hills, green now with new spring grass. I noted with a pang of nostalgia that this world, too, was changing. The country looked old, like Aggie, and just beyond the large ranch house and barns, new subdivisions crept even closer. I imagined hearing the steady drone of Highway 50, which winds its way over Echo Summit.

High on a hill, at Clarksville, sleep my grandmother and grandfather, as well as numerous other relatives. Judging from the looks of things Carson Creek had gone on a rampage of its own. Its waters had risen up and over the bridge to rush headlong down between low-lying hills. Fence posts, limbs, sections of fence wire, and all the flotsam of Carson Creek's past had been washed on down the meadow.

While visiting Aggie's brother, George, at the ranch, he told us four feet of water had covered their road, leaving them stranded during the worst of the storms. Aging too, George came out on the porch to visit.

An old windmill creaked in a soft breeze, while cows and new year calves grazed the green native grasses, much as they have for years. Chuck and Sue, the younger generation, were both out working, so we weren't able to see them.

The old red brick ranch house seemed empty and lonely without Edna, long deceased, and now Aggie in the hospital. We remembered past visits, sitting at the long dining room table, eating Aggie's Mock Ravioli, coffee can bread, and chewy cake, while connecting past to present. Soon there will be only memories.

January 31—Is this a dream? It seems so. I am typing this column on an electric typewriter situated in a small office space inside a kitchen of a home in Sedona, Arizona. Through large glass windows, which command a splendid view of red rock cliffs, blue sky and a mixture of pinyon pine and juniper, I would rather gaze than write.

The house itself is of the desert. Walls, furniture and art work are a blend of Arizona's past and present. Although not your ordinary abode, it is typical of the new Sedona, where, like Wallowa County, retired folks are moving in and building the house of their dreams.

How Doug and I came to be here is because sister Mary Ann is house-sitting for the owners, who are off to New Zealand. The house seems enormous—immaculate and expensively furnished—a far cry from what we are accustomed to.

This morning Doug noticed tracks in the carefully manicured yard. "Javelina," he said. Several wild pigs had visited in the night, which is not surprising because this community has been built out in the desert amid the wildlife habitat. Doug and I have really been seeing the country. And finally, after nearly three weeks of rain, we are enjoying the sunshine.

As we exited California we spent one night with my uncle Marshall and aunt Billie Wilson in South Lake Tahoe, where we were treated royally and met their next-door neighbors, Lolly and Keith, who read Marshall and Billie's Agri-Times. There was plenty of snow there. but it had settled enough to let me get in a good hike.

Leaving the Sierra, we drove up Spooner Pass and down into Nevada's Carson Valley, where we looked up a distant cousin of mine who is married to Frederick Dressler, a well-known fifth-generation rancher in the area. Lola Mary and Frederick's home stands next to the older (more than 100 years old) home of Fred Sr., who at age 95 still makes the major decisions on the ranch.

We spent the night in Hawthorne, Nevada, where it rained all night and into the next day. The next night found us in Searchlight, Nevada, and by the next morning it had cleared, and the desert skies remained that way for the duration of our trip.

While driving along south of Parker, Arizona, in the middle of the desert, Doug exclaimed, "Look there," and lo and behold there was this young man riding a camel, and leading three more with pack saddles!

Nothing would do but I had to leap out of our car, run over the wet sandy desert, dodging cactus and creosote brush, in my haste to intercept this unusual pack train. I was rewarded with an interview and several photos.

The handsome young man's name was Howdy Fowler of Tularosa, New Mexico, and he and his camels were on their way to completing a trek of 1,700 miles. Why? Because this expedition is dedicated to "Peanuts" Lewis of Tucumcari, New Mexico, who was killed by a gang. He died on February 1, 1994.

Howdy said he'd gotten plenty wet the past few days, but was now enjoying the sunshine. A yellow cur-hound he'd found in Texas took time out to rest, his long tongue lolling out as he panted from the sun's warmth. Howdy told about when the dog had held down a wild hog so its tusks wouldn't hurt him, and how faithful a friend he had become over the long miles.

The camels had been imported and untrained, so the first week out, Howdy had spent a good deal of time being bucked off. He rode a large camel, using a saddle that sat against the back hump; the animal grunted and seemed anxious to get moving again, while the three pack camels

Not your ordinary pack string—this is Howdy Fowler, on the camel, of Trail Dust Ministries, snapped outside of Parker, Arizona. Fowler's expedition draws attention to the responsibilities of raising children.

assumed that ancient pose, staring off across the desert as if they had always been there. The darker and larger of the three went to nibbling sagebrush, as we talked.

Howdy said the camels can go two weeks without water. I wanted to visit longer but knew Doug was waiting for me along the highway. As the caravan ambled slowly off across the Arizona desert I snapped another picture, and Howdy waved.

"God bless you," he said.

As we drove toward Quartzsite, Arizona, I thought about Howdy and his "Trail Dust Ministries" and hoped his expedition would do some good, and make parents aware of the responsibility of rearing a child who can contribute to society rather than destroy it.

It was 70 degrees at Quartzsite as we spent the afternoon walking up and down the outside aisles of one of the world's largest rock and gem shows, and flea markets. Oh, my, this place, like Las Vegas, is getting out of hand. Acres of RV's filled the desert and traffic was so congested we had a hard time of it.

While strolling among the laden tables and booths of every kind of ware imaginable, I heard the familiar strains of fiddle music I'd heard last year. It was Jeanine, looking thinner and just as poor. She and Roger

Ralph Tippett, left, and Doug Tippett stand next to a giant saguaro cactus near Wenden, Arizona.

were playing away out there in the warm desert sunshine. An old coffee can lay in the dirt at their feet for donations. Again I listened, enraptured by those haunting notes as they poured from Jeanine's very soul.

It was late afternoon when we pulled into Salome and found a small motel. A flaming sunset backgrounded tall palm trees and Saguaro cactus in the small courtyard near our room. We gave Doug's cousin Ralph and Enid a call, and learned that their company had deserted their bed.

"Didn't suit them," said Enid, so we were invited to move to Wenden the next day. Our three-day stay at Ralph and Enid's was spent soaking up the warm Arizona sunshine, eating sweet, tree-ripened oranges, taking long walks around the small town, visiting other Wallowa County folks who winter there, and eating Enid's famous sourdough biscuits.

It was pretty hard to take, but we survived. Doug helped Ralph scrape off his bee boxes, and scouted the desert for gold prospecting, and when we left we were loaded with oranges, honey, and plenty of pleasant memories, but no gold.

Early Monday morning, with January just about to say goodbye, we headed north toward Prescott. We drove through peaceful valleys nestled high above Wenden, up in the snow zone. One such place was called Peeples Valley, where cattle grazed a melted meadow. The unseasonable warmth was melting everything. We had agreed to meet sister Mary Ann at the old mining town of Jerome, which lay on the other side of a steep, winding mountain road above the town of Cottonwood.

We met M. A. at the state park, where we toured the mansion museum. The mansion had been designed and built in 1916 by "Rawhide" Jimmy Douglas, using adobe bricks made on the site. It boasted a wine cellar, billiard room, marble shower, steam heat, and, much ahead of its time, a central vacuum system.

James S. Douglas began development of the Little Daisy Mine in 1912, and by 1916 Jerome had two bonanza mines. Copper and a rich ore vein kept the mine going, but after the Depression and low grade ore deposits reversed the fortunes of the town, the "Little Daisy" shut down permanently in 1953. The town is still there, perched on steep hillsides, and is being rebuilt to house tourist shops and eateries.

Although crumbling in places, the place is fascinating to see, and the large machinery, crude by today's standards, remains as a legacy to those who worked the mines, which are honeycombed under the town.

It was dark when we drove into Sedona and found a motel. Upon awakening the next morning we were pleasantly surprised to see the beautiful red rock formations that looked out over the town.

February 5—We left Sedona, Arizona, on that bright, beautiful morning, and drove up lovely Oak Creek Canyon on our way to Flagstaff. From there we took Highway 180 to the Kaibab National Forest, and soon after found ourselves at the south rim of the Grand Canyon.

Here we mingled with two busloads of tourists, who were snapping pictures of each other against the skyline of Grand Canyon. All they would see. or remember, of one of the wonders of the world would be the taking of the photos and looking at themselves in the photos, which would include only the sky for a background! I found this endlessly amusing.

We drove on toward the desert view, where, quite alone, we gazed at the panorama below. I was so impressed that, when we visited Glen Canyon Dam later in the day, I purchased Wallace Stegner's *Beyond the Hundredth Meridian*, which is fine reading after having just viewed that fascinating canyon country.

On the wall in the visitors' center overlooking Glen Canyon Dam I read, *The finest workers in stone are not copper or steel tools, but the gentle touches of air and water working at their leisure with a liberal allowance of time.* That liberal allowance of time had created the spectacular canyons, and in just a few years man had created this dam. Really makes one think.

We left the Grand Canyon and traveled many miles through the Navajo reservation to Page, and then took 89 to Kanab, Utah. After many more miles, which led us up into snow country at Long Valley, we headed west across the 10,000-foot summit somewhere in the Dixie National Forest, where in the darkness we glimpsed snow banked above our car and great groves of naked aspens...and passed only two vehicles, one of which was stuck in a snowbank.

It was late when we pulled safely into Cedar City for the night.

We continued westward the next morning to the Nevada border, and headed north to Ely, Nevada, after which we ate up the miles of sagebrush mountain country to Jackpot, where we spent our last night.

After having traveled through six Western states and added 5,000 more miles on our car's odometer, we managed to see a big chunk of the West. Arizona and Utah's red rock country is lovely in its own way, but nothing compares to entering our own beautiful Minam canyon. The way of the heart leads forever homeward.

February 7—The sun streams, deceptively warm, through the window next to where I write. Outside the window, the sun's rays strike the frozen crystal flakes left by last night's snowfall, transforming them into cold, glittering diamonds. It is 15 degrees now in late afternoon, and it is predicted to dip below zero by morning.

I can see the fall calvers trooping slowly down their packed, snowy trails to the heated water trough for a drink, while their calves trail dully behind. The old Monarch snaps and crackles, and a pot of beans simmers in a mixture of garlic, onion, seasonings, and ham hocks. It is that kind of day. And it is wonderful because, after a month of being gone, we are home! We pulled in on a Friday evening, and Daisy was so excited to see me, she hasn't calmed down yet. The barn cats all survived, and the new black calf, Spook, must've grown a foot.

My old milk cow, Startch, wasn't at the barn to meet me. Ben had called while we were in Arizona to say she had died of natural causes. In reviewing her record I discover she has raised more than 30 calves in her lifetime, and her progeny are continuing to perform admirably in the calf-rearing department.

I will miss her, but it helps knowing she won't have to suffer any more cold in her arthritic bones this winter. A few of my hens continue to lay, thanks to Ben, who faithfully tended to my chores.

The weather was unseasonably warm while we were gone, so there was only a semblance of a snowdrift left in the raspberry patch. And, up until Saturday, it remained so. However, we who live here in Wallowa County know it's still a long time until spring. In one respect, it was as if we hadn't been gone at all, as we plunged back into our familiar lifestyles here on Prairie Creek and the community.

On Sunday afternoon we attended the cowboy poetry gathering at Cloverleaf Hall and listened to special guest Bill May, who traveled all the way from Steamboat Springs, Colorado, to perform. Brother to local wheat farmer Helen Stonebrink, Bill recited and sang some of his original pieces before he and Helen staged a regular jam session, which you could tell brought back pleasant memories for the both of them.

This grandma was pretty proud, because the youngest performer was none other than grandson James. The gathering, staged by one of the local Granges, benefited the restoration fund for the pioneer Hurricane Creek Cemetery. And the week just kept on like that.

One evening we drove to Imnaha for dinner with daughter Jackie's family; there were also a final meeting of the Wallowa Lake Basin Advisory Committee, a CattleWomen's meeting, and a Nez Perce park planning meeting, among which I sandwiched the gathering of items for a yard sale on Saturday.

Our family is about to bust its buttons over granddaughter Carrie, who has been selected to represent Oregon in the National Sound of

America Honor Chorus. The group will perform in some of Europe's finest concert halls on its 25-day tour, but that means she will need a lot of financial assistance, hence the yard sale and other planned money-raising events.

Wouldn't you know, the day of the yard sale it began to snow, and turn very cold. Linde helped and we held it in our shop where Doug laid out plywood tables and fired up the barrel stove.

Linde and I had priced the items the night before, collected from several families, and she and Pat joined us for supper. I prepared a recipe clipped out of Agri-Times for Savory Stew, which I highly recommend. Dessert of blackberry cobbler put us in mind of summer, when the luscious wild berries ripen in the lower canyons.

Last evening we made the 60-mile round-trip to the Imnaha church to attend the annual Sweetheart Roundup. What an affair it was, complete with real-life mannequins, attired in Western wear. Bridles and other horse tack decorated the walls and miniature bales of hay and horseshoe sculpture served as table centerpieces.

In keeping with the Imnaha tradition of good rib-sticking food, church members served prime rib, baked potatoes, salad, homemade rolls, and their specialty: homemade pies of the finest quality.

The meal was followed by a program which got off to a rousing start when Skip Royes galloped on stage with his stick horse, shook the dust from his hat, and looked for "the little gal he'd left there two years ago," whereupon the audience broke into gales of laughter. You see, Skip is a real-life cowboy.

He launched into a line about how canyon girls never forget their man, and surely his love would appear from behind a rimrock, where she had been waiting for him. And lo and behold, she was. His real-life, slim, blond wife strolled on stage singing, "I want to be a cowboy's sweetheart," looking for all the world like she had just stepped out of a Rodgers and Hammerstein musical. Singing right on key, Pam delighted the audience with her sweet voice, which even managed a yodel or two.

Outside, beneath a misty moon and snow-dusted rims, the canyons of the Imnaha provided a "for real" backdrop for Pam and Skip.

February 27—The robins are back, the first wet and wobbly calves peer at a snowless pasture, and the buttercups are up. Actually, I think some of the robins didn't bother to go south at all during our mild winter, and the baby calves haven't had it this good in years here on Prairie Creek; but Linde and I had to go to the lower canyons of the Imnaha to find the first buttercups.

It was a spur of the moment decision. We'd drive to Cow Creek and see if it were possible to drive, at least part way, up the seven-mile dirt road to the ranch. It was a frosty, clear morning, and we got an early start. Frost whitened the meadows that border Little Sheep Creek, and ice crusted its waters. The rising sap in the Red Osier dogwood contrasted sharply with the colorless landscape.

When we arrived at Imnaha, near where Sheep Creek empties into the river, the sun was just breaking over the eastern rimrocks. Its warm rays spilled down upon Barry Cox atop a large haystack, where he was tumbling bales down onto a truck, which he would feed to his herd of mustangs. Here in this isolated corner of Oregon there still is a West. A West that belongs to the cowboy.

As we drove downriver our hearts were gladdened by the sight of bunches of baby calves running and bucking for the sheer joy of being alive; hundreds of them, there along the river, in the sunshine, while their mamas munched hay in the long wooden feeders alongside the road. The river itself has been fenced off to protect its waters from pollution, and the setup is neat and tidy. When the grass is ready in the grazing allotments, the cows and their growing calves will be turned out to utilize an area that is otherwise unsuitable for any other purpose.

The canyons are already greening, due to the recent moisture and mild temps. Beyond, rising in multi-hued colors, march the canyons. Because it was a weekday, traffic on the narrow, rim-hugging road was absent. There was a lot of water swirling its cold way down the Imnaha to join the Snake, and we guessed its milky color was due to an early snowmelt.

At Cow Creek we stopped briefly to visit with Jack McClaran and daughter-in-law, Vickie. We had seen Jack's son, Scott, working cattle on horseback on the way in. We asked permission to drive up Lightning Creek, and inquired as to road conditions. I was driving our little four-wheel-drive Luv pickup, so Jack didn't see any problem.

We left Cow Creek and drove back to the bridge to locate the locked gates leading to the Lightning Creek ranch. We drove up that canyon about three miles or so, parked the pickup, shouldered our day packs, and traveled the remaining distance on foot.

Frost coated the shadowed bottoms and the creek splashed merrily along beside us. Never having been up this particular canyon, I was impressed by the openness of the area. It was lovely and quiet, save for the water and bird song. We were glad to have abandoned the pickup when we came to a rotting bridge, which was about to succumb to time.

There were numerous gates, and in places the road was very rutted and muddy as the ground thawed. At one point, we briefly left the road and took a cow path shortcut that wound steadily uphill. Looking back from whence we had come, there was this wonderful view of distant rims backgrounding the canyon we were ascending.

Asking Linde to pose alongside the trail with our dogs so I could get a shot with my camera, I became so engrossed in capturing the scene, I bent down to steady my arms and plunked myself down into a large cactus plant. Ouch! After extracting nearly 30 thorns, we continued on up the trail. That photo better be good.

On and on we walked, until we came to a sunny hillside clearing and there is where we spotted the first buttercups. Their waxy, yellow blooms were so welcome because it spelled spring to us.

Farther up on a rise, under the rimrocks, stood the hay barn, a garden spot fenced against the deer, a root cellar in back of the house, and an irrigation ditch dug to divert water from the creek to water the garden in summer. I didn't want to ever leave. It was absolutely quiet, save for the happy sound of birds and the gurgling creek.

A faint, fresh, cool breeze blew up the canyon and the sun shone on a perfect late February day. We sat on the old porch and ate our lunches, relaxing before exploring a trail beyond the meadow, which led to the Summit Trail...16 more miles, according to the weathered sign. It struck me then, as it has in the past, just how vast is this country, and the sheer space of it.

It was already afternoon when we began our walk back. Again we noticed the buttercups. It was as though even more had popped into bloom during our absence. Near the mouth of the creek we were startled by six wild sheep, leaping from ledge to ledge as easy as you please. Driving up the long switchback road to Imnaha we saw herds of sleek mule deer, their bellies swollen with fawn. The winter had been kind to them this year.

We visited daughter Jackie on our way down, and now we stopped to call on Myrna Moore and her children, Jake and Jenny, at Bear Gulch. We have been sharing our books with them. Myrna is looking forward to planting her garden and purchasing a milk cow soon.

After steaming cups of herb tea and rich slices of freshly baked lemon pound cake, we drove back out "on top." Another wonderful day in Paradise.

March 1—This past weekend was our fourth annual Winter Fishtrap Writer's Conference. This year's theme was, "Violence." Listening to writers Patricia McConnell and Mikal Gilmore talk about their lives and the resulting books they have written, I am ever so thankful for the upbringing I had.

I learned early on to appreciate and draw strength from our wonderful outdoor world. If every child had that opportunity to see beauty, to learn to be alone and think without conflict, there wouldn't be the need for so many jails. No matter what life throws at us, it is easier to bear if we know that somewhere there is beauty and life is good, and one has only to seek it. And mostly, it's free.

Violence in our society is escalating, and it is up to each one of us to make a difference in young lives. If we only touch one life, the effort will be worth it in bettering our society.

There are different kinds of artists in this world, and one mother I know is one without her knowing it. She and her husband have created several works of art, which take the shape and form of their extraordinary children. Reared in an atmosphere of discipline, love and respect, these children are singing their way into everyone's hearts.

Claudette Wieck has painted her own smile on their faces. Recently I purchased a flour mill from Claudette's Kitchen Kneads. Yesterday morning she came over with a bag of wheat for me to grind. After raising a houseful of children, occasionally sprinkled with visiting grandchildren, Claudette looks as young and radiant as ever. Motherhood has certainly agreed with her.

The freshly ground whole wheat flour, still warm from the grinding, is mixed with sourdough, potato water, mashed potatoes, a little honey, salt, and white flour to produce some of the best bread we've enjoyed. And the wheat germ and all the goodies are baked into the bread.

Bread, like children, must be kneaded, sweetened, and shaped, not sparing good ingredients, so the product will nourish us. If all children received such nurturing, we could channel our tax dollars toward education rather than jails.

March 13—The Wallowas were alive with the "Sound of Music" last weekend. Rodgers and Hammerstein, that is, as sung by the Wallowa Valley Players. This ambitious project, directed by Louise Kienzle and backed by members of the local community, was a smash hit. Enterprise High School's multipurpose room, which serves mainly as a cafeteria and is used for myriad school functions, was never so packed as it was for the three performances. The production, months in the making, starred all local talent.

The opening scene set the mood, when the nuns, attired in authentic dress, sang in the Nonnberg Abbey. The show-stealers were the Von

Trapp children—Liesl, Friedrich, Louisa, Kurt, Brigitta, Marta, and precious little Gretl—Wallowa Valley children who arise each morning to stare up at their own version of the Austrian Alps.

Of course, the fact that granddaughter Carrie was cast as Liesl provided an unending source of pride to this writer. But then all of the children are so special, to all of us, and they easily captured the audience's hearts.

The amount of effort that went into pulling this thing off blows the imagination. There were rancher fathers, in spite of calving time, hammered together stage additions; local women sewed seven changes of costumes; artists painted backdrops; mothers applied makeup and ferried children to rehearsals day after day, and sometimes late into the night); and volunteers set up lighting, played pianos, donated props and loaned a hand wherever needed. This was a vast community effort, and applauded by the community.

After the Von Trapp family escaped into the mountains to travel to Switzerland, roses were handed to the large cast, and they lined up for a standing ovation. And then men, women and children, many from the audience, acting as one body, dismantled the stage in just one hour!

Daughter Lori and family had driven over from Pendleton to attend the Sunday matinee. After helping with the cleanup, we all drove to the Top Hand Cafe for a bite to eat. Snow that had fallen the night before was already melted when we returned to the ranch. A bright spotlight moving through our cows told us Ben was out checking the mothers-to-be.

Although Startch wasn't here for the event, she became a great-grand dam…again. I had been checking this first-calf heifer closely for nearly a week, when finally one morning, stealing a moment from bread baking, I ran out to the barn lot to find her in labor.

Two front feet protruded, and the heifer, lying on her side, was moaning and groaning. I could see that it was a big calf, so I ran for Doug, who grabbed a ketch rope and a pair of pulling chains on the way out the door.

Together we observed for a while, then he suggested, because the heifer knew me better, perhaps I could approach her, secure the rope around the two front feet, wait for a contraction and give her an assist. I did, and heaved for all I was worth. The heifer paid little attention to me, and soon the head and shoulders appeared.

Both the heifer and I were tiring, and the hips seemed to be locked or caught up somehow. I wrapped the rope around my middle and sat down, pulling steadily. Finally, *whoosh!* A large black bull calf slithered onto the snow, whereupon the heifer got up and left.

Doug and I drove her back toward the calf, which was steaming in the snow, and the new mom began licking her baby off. After I iodized the navel, we left her to her task. Later I went out and bedded the calf in some straw, and saw that it was already nursing.

This morning the new baby is running around the pasture, looking forward to spring.

March 15—There are three eagles (two golden, one bald) perched in one of the ancient willows that grow in the calving pasture. They are very fat and cumbersome, due to gorging themselves on placentas. Ranchers are seeing them all over Prairie Creek, another example of Western ranchers contributing to the health of wildlife. Numerous birds feed near livestock, elk follow the cattle's grazed-over ranges, and wildlife congregate around water holes built by ranchers. It is a natural part of the Western environment.

Ranchers' fields provide nesting sites for a large population of raptors in Wallowa County, a place where it is relatively quiet, removed from the housing developments, with fresh running water and plenty of rodents. Ranchers welcome wildlife.

A small yellow crocus alongside the house is blooming, and the tulips are up. The grass grows greener after each snowmelt, and the little creeks and ditches are running full. I have ordered baby chicks and garden seeds.

After a fresh snowfall this week, the temperature fell enough to hold the snow above timberline, so Linde and I dropped everything, put housework on hold, drove up the ski run road, and donned skis. Because the road wasn't plowed, we skied up to the McCully Creek Trailhead and on up the trail, which gradually climbed along the creek.

The sun shone with such warmth that we soon shed jackets and stuffed them into our day packs. We ate our lunches alongside the trail, then continued a quarter mile farther, until the sun's warmth began to melt the snow. We waxed our skis and turned around. What had taken us more than two hours to climb, took us 15 minutes to descend. We fairly flew down our own ski tracks. Fun!

The following days were mild, however, and the warmer winds and rain have melted our ski trails. March became briefly angry with us, for the wind blew for three days, and tales ran rampant of cats blowing past windows, camp trailers being hurled into the air, and barn roofs being blown off. But now, the wind has died down at last. All through this violent weather, preparations for the Sound of Music went on. The show, like all life, must go on.

When we can't ski, Linde and I take long walks around Alder Slope, where spring is evident in the swamps, pussy willows are out, and great flocks of migrating birds sing for joy. Ducks fly up from irrigation ditches, and baby calves romp over the fields. Ruby Peak is just under us, and Idaho's Seven Devils Mountains beckon. Our dogs are in heaven, chasing squirrels.

One such day we took some homemade soup up to Bill's, and after a long walk we visited him over bowls of delicious chowder.

This morning we visited Max Gorsline on upper Prairie creek. Linde brought a crock pot of Crazy Shirley's soup and homemade bread. After a morning of listening to Max reminisce about early Wallowa County, we enjoyed the hearty soup. As I write, great gray and white clouds form and move across an unsettled sky. Mountain snowfields gleam in openings of sunlight. Edelweiss, edelweiss…my homeland forever.

March 20—At some moment during this day, in our part of the world, the rhythmic tide of the seasons flows into the vernal equinox. We've been seeing the signs for quite some time now: flat and sun-colored buttercups blanket Hough's hill, hawks build nests in tall cottonwoods along the creek, crocuses burst through the snow, and we find birth everywhere, the pastures throbbing with new life.

Birds sing of spring, and calving time brings to mind Sue Wallis, a wonderful cowgirl poet I met last week when I attended a workshop sponsored by our Fishtrap Currents program. Sue hails from Deeth, Nevada, works for the Western Folklife Center in Elko, and has authored a book entitled *Another Green Grass Lover.*

At a gathering of poets that included her husband, Rod McQueary, plus local talent, Sue recited her version of a myth she created from Saint Brigid, the patron saint of pregnancy and childbirth.

"You see," said Sue, "there was a wild bunch that lived in the first century, and they had good horses, and chariots, and iron weapons. So they whipped everybody in sight, until they controlled a territory nearly as big as the Roman Empire." Sue said their entire culture revolved around poetry.

The druids educated themselves by memorizing massive amounts of poetry. Their business was the grazing of cattle; they lasted the longest in Ireland and called themselves the Celts. At any rate, Saint Brighid's feast day falls in the early springtime of lambing and calving.

Sue's poem touched a chord deep in my being, and when, on Saint

Patrick's Day, we were seated with friends around a table brimming with corned beef and cabbage, I read Sue's poem. It seemed appropriate not only for the Irish, but for the season here in our valley.

Loving and strong women stand in her shadow,
Fierce Brighids in these lonesome hills—
Women of learning tend to their cattle,
shoe their horses, pound their anvils, and doctor from saddles.

. . . well, you'll just have to purchase the book to read the rest.

Seated around a small wooden table at the Joseph Library, poets in the form of Wallowa County cowhands and cowgirls came shyly to the workshop, conducted by Sue and Rod. Carrying portfolios soiled with dirt and age, they found the courage to recite what they had written from their hearts, what had come to them while on horseback in the lonely canyons or tending cattle far out on Crow Creek.

That morning I hastily jotted down a short poem about trailin' cattle to the hills, which I will use in a later column. One strappin' young lad recited a poem he had written about his life on the rodeo circuit. That out of his blood, Tony is presently cowboyin' for an outfit up Big Sheep.

It was truly a great experience for all of us to be among kindred spirits, and the workshop extended the feelings generated at all of our Fishtrap Writer's Gatherings.

On Thursday evening we Fishtrap board members treated Rod and Sue and the local poets to a homemade potluck upstairs in the Enterprise Community Church before the performance at the OK Theater. Those who weren't there missed a very special evening.

We went to bed that night listening to the drum of rain on the roof. Around midnight I awoke to a strange sort of silence. Snow, seven inches of new snow blanketing Prairie Creek by the next morning. Our whitened world lingered for a few days, until the sun's warmth, mixed with a chinook, melted it slowly into the ground. What a grass year we should have. The ground is saturated.

Another night last week, which was quite a social week, which is just another sign of spring in Wallowa County, I attended the mass honor choir at the Joseph High School gym. Schools from all over, including La Grande, Elgin, Prairie City, Pine Eagle, Wallowa, Enterprise and Imbler, staged a mass concert.

After each choir sang in turn, the combined voices of more than 200 filled the gym with song. Boys and girls from small town Northeastern

Oregon arise early each morning before school and practice. Their final song told how they sing softly while the stars fade from the night.

"We are singing, singing...can you hear?" We in the audience heard, but can those who were not in attendance hear?

Budget cuts affecting these wonderful drama and choir programs in the schools are threatening their very existence. In times like these, when young people are subjected to so much violence and negative thinking, they were singing to "our sweet world." It would seem the soul-lifting experience of music, and the need for self-expression through drama, could provide these youngsters an opportunity to discover themselves, and in doing so project that positive image to the sweet world they sing of.

Times haven't changed all that much since that long ago time of the Celts, when Brighid's people memorized massive amounts of poetry; and stories about birth and new life, told by the women to their daughters, were passed down through the generations. Pain and joy...joy and pain. Perhaps there is a message of hope here: from the pastures of cattle, the OK Theater of Cowboy Poetry, and the high school gym in Joseph...our children are singing, singing. Can you hear?

While I was typing this column, my milk cow Stargirl calved, a nice bull. He was already up and nursing when I went out to check her!

March 27—Slate-colored storm clouds brew, but the sun is winning on this breezy afternoon. The new green of emerging grass has been dulled by frosty mornings, when chocolate-colored puddles freeze solid and lingering snow doesn't melt on the norths.

Our calving pastures are divided into three sections. The east enclosure holds the about-to-calve cows, the west one is full of pairs, and the now-empty middle pasture used to hold the late calvers. The "girls," as Doug refers to them, are calving in a pretty even pattern this year.

My now-deceased old matron, Startch, became a grandmother again, as she has in past springs, when her daughter, Stargirl, dropped her big bull calf last week. Ben had a little orphan, who was bumming milk from any cow she could, so I grafted the grateful little heifer onto Stargirl.

Another first-calf heifer birthed twins and didn't have enough milk, so now I have three calves on this large Simmental-cross cow. She has a fine udder, with easy-to-milk teats. Whenever I need house milk, I simply take mine before turning the calves into nurse. There is always plenty of milk for all of us, including the barn cats, who wait not-so-patiently at their milk bowl.

After a fresh snowfall last week, daughter Jackie and grandchildren

Buck and Mona spent the night, and the next morning, after I arose before dawn to chores, we loaded the car with ski equipment, fried chicken, deviled eggs and fresh fruit, and drove over to North Powder, where we turned off toward Anthony Lakes Ski Resort.

It is such a beautiful drive up that long valley with its old barns and split rail fences. Soon we began to climb in earnest up the steep, winding road to the 7,100-foot base of the Anthony Lakes ski lifts. The road was in good shape and we lucked out, because the day before, high winds had caused the closure of the chair lift.

But that Thursday of spring break, the sun came out from behind white clouds that floated in a cerulean sky, and there wasn't a breath of wind. The children, joined by other Imnaha friends Luke and Hope, didn't miss many rides on the chair lift all day. Rosy-cheeked and smiling, they zoomed down the mountain slopes, dodging snowboarders and loving it.

Around noon we drug out the picnic and ate at a sunny table located in the ski lodge, where we could view the slopes through large floor-to-ceiling windows. For three years I had promised them this trip, and for once it finally worked out. Eleven inches of fresh snow from the night before made for perfect skiing.

My early garden seeds arrived in the mail, and so did those baby chicks. Twenty-five Barred Rock pullets, nearly a week old now, are eating and drinking under a cozy heat lamp in a large wooden box in the calving shed. Grandchildren James and Adele spent considerable time last week playing with the chicks and helping me feed and water them.

The vegetable seeds are sprouting on a sunny table set up in the living room. Alaskan leeks and celeriac are just peeping through their peat pots. Later, I will start the pickling cucumbers and a cold climate muskmelon indoors, giving them a head start in the garden, which can't be planted here until June.

Daisy and I usually take our daily walks up on Hough's hills between morning and evening chores, following cow trails that wind through buttercups and the emerging green shoots of grass widows. Irrigation ditches, freed of ice during the day, are full of wild mallards and muskrats. I can look southwest from the barren hills to the mountains and view the entire Wallowa chain, all snow-covered, brilliant in the sun, locked in cold silence.

The social activity of the previous week has slowed, so there is time for reading good books, which I devour in the evenings. There's also time for catching up on correspondence and beginning the spring house cleaning, and I can always make time for cooking, which is a pure joy for me. Sometimes, I cook too much for the two of us, so I give it away to some of the married children, whose lives at the moment are frantic. I've even had time to work on my book!

Granddaughter Carrie's FFA senior class left this morning for its annual agriculture, educational tour of California. To raise money for this trek, they held a pork barbecue and sold items constructed in their woodworking class, at an auction recently.

The talented youngsters, under the direction of Vo-Ag instructor Scott Lathrop, crafted such objects as bookcases, mailboxes in the shape of cows and dogs, bells with deer horn handles, storage chests, and pine planters complete with primroses. A beautiful handmade quilt was also auctioned off. Needless to say, the money was raised.

Linde and husband, Pat, have been gone this past week, so she and I haven't been on any daring adventures lately and, of course, the spring chores keep me pretty close to home. Shipping seed potatoes will begin shortly, and then I suspect our phone will be ringing with drivers wanting directions and other related matters.

Time to walk down the lane for the mail, and gather the eggs.

March 30—The days have been warm and sunny. Friend Scotty and I drove up to deserted Wallowa Lake State Park and hiked around the campground, dodging tame deer and enjoying the "off-tourist" time. Afterward, we swam in the heated indoor pool at the Eagle Cap Chalets.

Refreshed after our swim, we found a picnic table where, quite alone, we ate our lunches overlooking the lake, where two pairs of merganser ducks, a few migrating loons, and several resident honkers gabbled softly. These were the only sounds. No traffic... very restorative. We are making it a weekly thing now. Linde is under the weather, having contracted a flu bug somewhere. Hopefully, she can join us next time.

After spending all day (between chores) cleaning out that room, Doug treated me to dinner at our local Elks Lodge. The food was super! We rated chef Tom Swanson's prime rib a perfect ten. Methinks wherever Tom cooks, hungry people will follow. Not alone in my thinking; the place was packed.

It is a treat having Stargirl's fresh milk. Daughter Jackie and family stopped by last evening, and stayed for a bowl of clam chowder, chock full of potatoes and clams, and swimming in rich whole milk.

April 3—Doug brought our two horses in from the hills and shod them last week, and we were all set to haul them down to Big Sheep for a branding last Saturday morning. Only it rained, then snowed, so the branding was canceled. I had made plans (and cookies), when, as so

While Daddy shields the flame from a breeze, Mom lights the candles on Buck's birthday cake, which sits on a stump way out on Sleepy Ridge.

often happens in this part of the country, our actions were determined by the weather.

So, what does one do when the weather keeps an outdoor gal indoors? Clean out closets. This long-delayed project stretched into Sunday. I unearthed enough dusty junk, which had to be sorted through, to fill five cardboard boxes.

In so doing I was swept back in time. Long-forgotten scrapbooks surfaced, full of photos and clippings of my Sourdough Shutterbug 4-H Club. The children, all grown, with lives of their own, smiled back at me from trips we'd taken all over the county... Hat Point. Pine Creek, east moraine. Kinney Lake, Brownie Basin, Sleepy Ridge. and Red's Horse Ranch, to name a few. They posed around campfires, peered from tents and sleeping bags, and hiked against awesome rugged peaks.

I recalled the time Scotty went with us. I was driving "old green." our faithful Dodge ranch pickup, the children and gear in the back, up that precarious road to Hat Point.

We spent the night there on the edge of Hells Canyon, our feet draped over the rim, watching the stars pop out and looking down at the gleam far below which would have been the Snake, flowing past Johnson Bar.

I'd given the 4-H'ers a lesson in outdoor cooking. The menu was stuffed green peppers, to which the children responded with ugh! But when those fragrant, steaming, hamburger-filled baked peppers came out of the cast iron dutch oven, smothered in cheese, they ate every scrap and wanted more. We always roasted marshmallows after dark, and told stories.

The next morning, after the members did some photographing and Sam Heiny broke his own record and consumed 11 sourdough pancakes, we drove out on Sleepy Ridge, where daughter Jackie, husband Bill, and their then two young children, Buck and Mona, were camped in a tent, herding cattle. The family had packed in with horses and mules.

We weren't sure we could find them, but I knew approximately where they would be. So we left the road, struck a cow path. and drove between trees, with only inches to spare, until Scotty, who threatened to abandon me, almost did. Finally, in a little clearing bordered by tall stands of ponderosa pines, we found the wall tent. This turned out to be an adventure... and a necessary one.

Because, you see, grandma had baked a sourdough chocolate cake for Buck's third birthday, and like the mail, that cake had to be delivered. The frosting was a little smeared, due to the jostling received in the pickup, but way out there on lonesome Sleepy Ridge, we lit the candles and sang "Happy birthday" to Buck, who will be 15 this summer!

I think often of my 4-H'ers…Becky Jones, Kurt Ehrler, Chad and Rowdy and Chelsie Nash, Willie Zollman, Eric Johnson, Brian Freels, Ryan Hook, and all you other members who over the years have made me proud. What times we shared, what sights we saw, and what freedom we felt on all those wonderful campouts and hikes.

Looking at the old photos, I realized again how fast the years are slipping away: Shuffling through more papers and mementos made me tired, just being reminded of all those projects I was once involved in. Reminders of CowBelles, seed potato promotions, history group projects, photo club. And then there were all those greeting cards. It was obvious, going through all those boxes: I am a clipper! My goodness, I clipped articles on everything…and kept them.

Naturally, they all had to be read before carting them out to the burning barrel. Now the room is neat and tidy, the memories stored away for another rainy day, and my backpacking and camping gear is stacked in one spot. Where I can find it.

Ben is preg-testing the fall calvers today, so in a few days I'll have a cowboyin' job. We'll be weaning the calves and trailin' mamas to the hills. Oh boy!

April 11—Living here in Wallowa County provides such a potpourri of life; at least it does for me. Take last week, for instance. Tuesday found me at a branding up Big Sheep Creek, where most of my day was spent vaccinating 225 calves, which were roped and tied by several cowboys (including son Todd and husband, Doug), then branded, ear-tagged, and de-horned before being turned loose.

Wednesday, Scotty and I hiked up one of the trails leading out of Wallowa Lake, after which we swam in the warm, restoring waters of Eagle Cap Chalet's indoor pool.

Thursday, after chores, which included straining my bucket of house milk, feeding baby chicks, and haying my milk cow "herd," Doug and I mounted our saddled horses and headed the fall calvers out to the hills.

Leaving the bawling, weaned calves behind, we made our way out the familiar route taken each spring and fall, which leads north into the high, rolling plateau grass country. We left the cows penned in a large corral, eating hay Ben had hauled out to the old Dorrance place on Crow Creek, nearly 20 miles distant.

That evening, after chores and a long-awaited tub bath, I picked up Linde and we enjoyed a musical interlude in Mike and Allison Kurtz' lovely home. Laura Zaerr strummed her harp in front of a massive stone fireplace, with candle light glowing softly onto her instrument.

What does a retired hardware store owner and last year's grand marshal of Chief Joseph Day do to keep from being bored? Bud Zollman helps with brandings, such as this one on Big Sheep Creek in the Imnaha Canyon.

I sought out a comfortable chair, sank back, closed my eyes, and became lost in Laura's beautiful music. The harp, lovely to behold, was simply another piece of furniture until Laura's fingers 'caressed the strings. Then something magical transpired, as the room filled with celestial music. The notes floated in the air.

Never having heard a harp up close like that before, I was transfixed, especially when Laura played a piece she had composed herself, called Crystal Lace, which described her feelings of the first snowfall in autumn. It was! And in listening, I could hear in other tunes the sounds made by the wind in the hills, and the soft spring rain...it was that kind of music.

I purchased two of her tapes and listen to them often at day's end, when I am winding down.

The next morning found us bright and early at the old pink barn on Crow Creek, letting the cows out and heading them up the grade that leads to our summer range. While Doug drove the pickup on ahead to the ranch, I trailed the cows to Wet Salmon.

It was a nice morning, coolish but no wind, until we topped the hill above the ranch. Then a fine rain, blown by the lonely hill wind, began to dampen me. Doug helped from then on, joining Daisy and me as we pushed the tired cows up the meadow and into the far pasture.

Meanwhile, the skies really opened up and we were thankful for oilskin slickers. To me it was beautiful, even in the rain and wind—pastures all greening, ponds brimming with water and wild mallards, hawks nesting, and meadowlarks singing "spring is coming." A carpet of yellow bells, buttercups and cous bloomed among the emerging grasses.

Saturday evening found Doug and me perched on the edge of our seats in the Enterprise High School gym watching a "smoker," a series of boxing matches put on by the local Lions Club to raise money for scholarships for deserving students. I am not into boxing, but grandsons James and Rowdy were in two events.

Could this be my little James sitting in a corner of the ring, wearing boxing gloves, a mouthpiece and headgear? It was. And as James coolly lost, grandma alternately peered from behind the program to see if he was still OK.

Then Rowdy, a high school junior born with a killer instinct, won his match. I was glad when it was over, and was shocked to find myself rooting for Rowdy. Guess I wanted him to stay in control so he, too, wouldn't get hurt. Grandmas are like that.

I composed the following poem for the recent cowboy poetry work-shop sponsored by our Fishtrap Currents program, taught by Sue Wallis and her husband, Rod. I had jotted down these lines that morning after chores, and taken the poem with me to the workshop. Although it is written about trailing cows and calves, it seems appropriate now.

You will note the word "couses," which I added to rhyme with houses. It's really not plural for the popular Indian root plant, also called biscuit root, but anything goes in poetry.

Trailin' Cattle to the Hills

Long about the first of May,
Cattle lose their taste for hay.
So cows and calves are gathered fast,
And headed toward the hills, at last.

The mother cows know where to go,
But convincin' baby calves goes slow.
The mothers trail away ahead,
While their offspring lag behind, instead.

The patient cowboy in the drag,
Throws tin dogs at calves that lag.
The long miles become longer,
And them calves don't get any stronger.

Grass widows, buttercups, and couses,
Bloom in open space, devoid of houses.
Hawks circle the sky above,
And ground squirrels make love.

Climbing Crow Creek Pass, wouldn't you know,
The clouds open up, and it begins to snow.
All this the cowboy does see,
As he rides along, composing this song,

Only the cowboy is really a cowgirl
...named me!

April 18—Flakes of dry snow float in the wind as the unzipped clouds spill their contents over Prairie Creek. The snow melts on the green grass, but without sunlight the grass is gray, like the sky. The whole day is gray, and matches my mood. I am trying to be cheerful, but it is hard. As if to match the grayness, negative things happen.

I won't go into too many details here; but take this morning for instance. After milking the cow, and finishing my morning chores, I gulped down a bowl of cheerios (in hopes it would make me cheery), so as to face the day, which began by meeting with the plumber on Alder Slope to assess the damage done by a renter this winter to my pellet furnace.

After that was done, I showed him another problem under the kitchen sink. Then it was back to the ranch to call for an estimate on replacing a damaged linoleum, the result of a frozen pipe this winter. The woes of being a landlord. When this rental is finally in shape, it will look better than our own home!

Looking to the brighter side, I whipped up a sourdough chocolate cake and some sourdough bread for granddaughter, Carrie's 18th birthday, which is today. I decided to bake two loaves of bread while I was at it, and as I took the fragrant loaves from the oven, there came a knock at the door. Neighbor, Chet Hanks, who lives down along Little Sheep Creek, was standing there holding a carton of pale blue and green Aracuna eggs to put under my setting hen.

In return for the eggs, I gave him one of the hot loaves of bread. His smile brightened my day. A month or so ago I traded Chet a pecan pie for a new rooster. Alas, Chester, my old rooster, is now in chicken Heaven. I named the new rooster Chester, too, after our friend Chet.

Doug, who came into the kitchen as the sourdough cake was coming from the oven, made his usual remark about "How come you are giving this cake away?" Poor, abused husband!

The chicks aren't babies anymore. They are all feathered out, and will be moved to new quarters in the chicken house this weekend. The leeks and celeriac are threatening to burst through their peat pots, and I have now seeded the pickling cucumbers indoors.

Last Saturday was the last day of steelhead season, so Doug and I drove down to Witherite's Hole on the Imnaha. It was a lovely day, and Jerry and Myrna were out working up their garden spots. There was a crisp breeze blowing off the rims, and the river roiled past clear and high. Although we got several bites from hungry trout, nary a steelhead did we hook.

The next day, Easter Sunday, I was milking my cow when I should have been joining the 40 or so people down on Imnaha for the sunrise Easter service, high on a scenic canyon bench. As the small group of worshippers huddled around a campfire, the glorious day dawned above the Imnaha.

Children and adults, their voices raised in song, were echoed by other canyon dwellers—coyotes, who joined the chorus, just as the sun burst over the eastern rims.

It is a lovely time in the canyon country now, almost a miracle in itself to those of us "on top." There are LEAVES on trees. Golden showers of forsythia, resembling artist's brush strokes, brighten yards. Violets escape flower beds and cover lawns with fragrant shades of purple. Bleeding hearts, lilacs, daffodils, and other old-fashioned flowers bloom in country profusion.

Inez Meyers is gone now, but her garden lives on, and her spirit dwells there. And in the wild canyons themselves, sarvisberry bushes are at their peak. Their white, clustered petals resemble clouds that have fallen onto the green, steep terrain.

Most of our large, extended family was busy with spring activities and others were moving, so there wasn't much of a turnout for the annual Easter picnic this year. Daughter Jackie baked a turkey and I brought down a ham and some deviled eggs. After we feasted, the cowboy dads, so tired from the busy days of branding and calving, rested, while we women and children went "stalking" the wild asparagus.

The walk was lovely, and grandson, Buck and friend, Luke, spotted the first tender shoots growing near an old homestead site. Gnarled, blooming apple trees, a spring, and a nut tree of some undetermined origin, were all that remained of the homestead.

The views, upriver and down, were breathtaking there on the old home site, situated on a level spot between two creeks, which splashed merrily down to join the Imnaha. The river being so close, we could hear the sound of its swirling waters.

By the time we combined our asparagus, we had enough to fill one large bag, and the day warmed enough to shed our jackets. My only regret was that all of the family wasn't able to share the day. Everyone is so busy, as spring accelerates. I almost hate to see summer come, knowing what it always brings. Meanwhile, we'll enjoy our county while we can, before the hordes of tourists invade.

Time for evening chores.

April 27—When I awoke Tuesday morning, it was to the sight of my sister Kathryn standing on a small balcony and looking out across the Warm Springs River, where the rising sun punctured dark clouds and created a golden wash across the Oregon high desert. The first sound I heard was the bubbling song of the meadowlark.

Next to me in the queen-size bed, daughter Ramona slept on after our long drive yesterday, as sister Caroline in the next bed stirred and, like me, awoke to the meadowlark. After talking about it for two years, we were actually at Kah-Nee-Ta, the resort perched on a high bluff under wild, rugged rimrocks in the heart of Central Oregon.

Owned and operated by the Confederated Tribes of Warm Springs Reservation, Kah-Nee-Ta, far-removed from towns, offers a peaceful getaway. I had visited here in the past with friends, and since dreamed of returning with family.

Bird book in hand, Kathryn and Caroline, who are really into birding, were soon peering through binoculars and exclaiming over each newcomer, when suddenly Kathryn uttered "Shush." And there beneath our balcony, nibbling its way across the lawn into the sagebrush was a cottontail rabbit. Just then, a large magpie swooped down and stole away crumbs we had scattered on the railing for the smaller birds, which had descended in droves once they discovered us eating our breakfast muffins.

Having arrived the day, tired and warm after a long drive, Ramona and I could hardly wait to dive into the pool, which was heated by the natural hot spring waters. We were thus engaged when Kathryn and Caroline checked in.

That evening, quite alone, we four picnicked on a hill below the lodge—fried chicken, deviled eggs, sourdough bread, fruit, oatmeal cookies, all washed down with mango juice. In spite of two conventions going on in the massive lodge, other people seemed non-existent and we felt as if we were the only guests. The evening was so mild, we lingered outdoors until nearly dark, then strolled into the dining area to order dessert and coffee. Huckleberry parfait and huckleberry and pecan cheesecakes. Sinful!

We had good intentions of climbing the hill behind the lodge and watching the sun rise Tuesday morning. No matter we weren't there for the actual rising, because we were justly rewarded with a balmy morning as we made our way up footpaths lined with golden arrow leaf balsamroot, pink phlox, and a tiny five-petaled flower resembling Arizona baby blue eyes.

Crossing a saddle at the top, we hiked down into a sagebrush-filled basin, surrounded by high rock outcroppings. It was quiet, so we could hear coyotes calling in the next canyon and chukars talking near a tumble of large rocks. Morning cool released the scent of sage, and ravens, shiny and black, hung in air currents overhead.

At the top of a rocky crag, we looked down upon the Warm Springs River to the lower village, where a cluster of tepees shone white in the early morning sun. We drove back to the small settlement of Warm Springs to visit the museum, which is nationally renowned for blending real economic progress with traditional values. The museum is beautifully done...in circles.

As I walked slowly around the museum I jotted down quotes from the interpretive exhibits:

"The elders teach us how to be a community, where each person counts and is heard. The elders arc living treasures who preserve and perpetuate our heritage. Elders teach by example..." What a wonderful world it would be if, in our own society, elders were revered like "treasures," I thought.

Wandering on around the large, circular exhibits, I had the feeling of being transported back to Warm Springs culture, where people moved with the seasons, root digging, berry picking, hunting deer and antelope, fishing, staying inside for the winter, telling stories. Their books were stories, passed down orally from grandmother to grandchildren.

"Family has always been important to Indian culture. Children are taught with love, respect and patience." Love, respect, patience. Those three words, if used in the upbringing of our young, could eliminate the need for jails. In an age of escalating child abuse and disregard for the elderly, there could be a lesson here.

It couldn't have been a lovelier April day. White clouds drifted in an azure sky as we carried our picnic to a secluded spot along the creek next to the new museum. The scent of sage mingled with that of budding leaves on alder and cottonwood. Sounds of running water and bird song filled the air.

We returned via the winding desert road to Kah-Nee-Ta, where we spent the warm afternoon soaking and swimming in the lower village pool, which was hotter, being fed by the natural hot springs there. We lounged, soaked up sunshine, and drank deeply of the pure desert air, before driving up the hill to our rooms.

More swimming before treating ourselves to dinner in the Juniper Room. As we watched, a coyote slipped downhill, past a dead snag, and melted into the tall desert grasses. We gorged ourselves on red snapper, prime rib, salads, Indian fry bread and huckleberry jam. Oh my!

At dusk we climbed the high rocky trails to see if we could spot the coyote. No luck, but we did hear the chukars chuckling to themselves before roosting for the night, and from our high perch above Kah-Nee-Ta we exclaimed over the lighted doorways, burning bright orange, as reflected from their painted entrances: an arrowhead-shaped lodge with hundreds of orange campfires glowing in the dark!

Stars appeared above as we swam in the warm pool, and we gazed upward at those "pretend" campfires. Kathryn and Ramona rented a funny movie, but Caroline and I were in dreamland before it was halfway through.

Wednesday morning we bade our tearful goodbyes next to a rock alongside the parking lot where a passerby had snapped our group shot with Kathryn's camera against the balsamroot-covered hillside. Back to families and jobs in California for Kathryn and Caroline, and back to Wallowa County for Ramona and me.

Driving through Central Oregon we stopped in Shaniko, where this ghost town is coming back to life. We visited the historic, newly refurbished Shaniko Hotel. Upon entering the lobby, we were a few minutes early for the antique shop's opening, but a kindly proprietor let us in, saying the woman who ran the shop would be there shortly.

After she arrived, Ramona purchased a collectible and asked if she would take a check, to which the obliging lady answered with a smile, "Sure, and if it isn't any good, I'll tell Janie Tippett!"

To which, in surprise, Ramona replied, "Well you can ask her right now, because there she is, and she is my mother!"

After a good laugh, we learned that the pleasant lady was a ranch woman and had gone to college with Doug at Washington State University, and remembered when he was on the rodeo team there. Small world.

We were introduced to one of the Farrells, who fell in love with the old Shaniko Hotel and purchased it in 1985. The restoration has been beautifully executed and looking around the rooms made us want to return for a longer visit. I walked across the street and purchased a stamp from postmaster Patricia Mobley at the tiny post office. As I licked the stamp and affixed it to a postcard for a friend, I visited with a native about planting his vegetable garden.

Upon leaving, Patricia handed me a copy of some historical information. Reading it later, I chuckled at Shaniko's colorful past.

"A wild and woolly place with a population of 600 in 1910 and growing fast. In those days Shaniko never had a cemetery, because nobody died a natural death. Those killed in gun battles were left for the coyotes and those that drank themselves to death were poured back into the keg, and a yeast cake was added and left to work again."

As we drove up 97 to the Columbia River, it reinforced again how lucky we who live in Oregon are, especially those of us east of the Cascades.

Daisy wriggled all over to see me, and Doug survived my cow and chicken chores. Good to be home, but the memories of Kah-Nee-Ta will continue to cheer the four of us in our declining years. Tucked away in memory to smile at when the going gets rough and comfort is needed.

May 1—For some reason this first day of May seems reminiscent of when Mt. St. Helens erupted. The same moist and cloudy skies, greening grass, and receding winter. I remember the fine gray ash settling on our car, and wondering. A brisk wind blew over Prairie Creek earlier this morning and hawks appeared to be hang-gliding in the air movement. All over the prairie, hawks can be seen...Swainson's, Ferruginous, and Red Tail, mostly.

Daisy and I took two long walks yesterday, and in every cottonwood and willow we passed under, a hawk, sometimes a pair of them, would stare down at us. Some were mating and others are already setting on eggs, which have been laid in large stick nests in the leafless trees. The faint, pale green of emerging leaves gives the illusion of a gauzy veil, but the nests are obvious at this stage of spring.

Speaking of hawks, I have just finished reading Marcy Houle's book *The Prairie Keepers*, Addison-Wesley, wherein the author describes her two-year study of raptors in the vast Zumwalt country, part of which is our spring, summer and fall range. It is a country where winter holds sway for more than six months of the year; a silent country where, as Marcy found out, things go on, year after year, in much the same way, regardless of cattle grazing, which Marcy attributes to the total overall health of the prairie. She has done a wonderful service to the ranchers and told the story with great sensitivity.

I did get a chuckle out of Marcy's description of an ornery Black Angus bull with long horns and a ring in his nose. I've yet to see a real Angus that wasn't polled, and a ring in his nose...well, perhaps it added spice to the story.

She does give the local ranchers fictitious names, but when it comes to my old friend Cressie Green, she sticks with the truth. Once, another friend, Grace Bartlett, and I accompanied Cressie on a trip to her beloved roots near Elk Mountain, to visit her childhood home, and it was one of the highlights of my life. One of the last chapters in the book is a wonderful tribute to a remarkable woman.

Our old "mama kitty" delivered herself of the usual spring batch of kittens with relative ease. Five of them, in assorted colors, match the roving tomcats we glimpse in the neighbor's fields. Each morning and evening I milk a warm, frothy bowl of milk for her.

The growing Barred Rock pullets have been moved to larger quarters in the chicken house, and separated from the older laying hens. "Cheryl" the banty hen is setting on her clutch of Aracuna eggs in the hen house.

Our living room resembles a greenhouse, with budding plants everywhere. I now have cucumbers and cantaloupe sprouting. Cabbage plants are outside "toughening up" before being transplanted into the slope garden, and on Saturday I purchased some varied-colored Impatiens, which have been transplanted into a large kettle. The tulips and daffodils are all in bloom alongside the house. Sunday morning they stuck their shivering heads up through the snow, a wet snow that melted quickly and added more wonderful moisture to our grass lands.

Due to circumstances I won't elaborate on, we are going out of the seed potato business. Raising any sort of certified seed is stressful, and at our age, Doug and I don't need any more stress in our lives. Besides, this will free us to go fishing and camping…I hope.

In two days we start the cows and calves to the hills. Looking forward to those peaceful miles in the saddle. If I can have my druthers, though, I would hope for sunshine, but that is only for "fair weather cowboys," and if you are a real cowboy or cowgal, you take what you get. Guess in life we survive by "taking her as she comes."

May 6—Grandchildren James and Adele visited today, and we watched the running of the Kentucky Derby. We had several racehorse enthusiasts here for the occasion to bet on the race. Everyone put a dollar in the pot, then drew names of the horses out of a hat. Little Adele picked the winning horse and won the jar of money.

Earlier, in a freezing wind, James and I had checked out the fishing holes in the irrigation ditches. Just checking, because the season doesn't open until the end of the month. James and I can't wait!

May 8—On Wednesday of last week we began trailing cows and calves to the hills, "we" being Ben, his daughter Sarah, Doug and me on horseback, and our faithful friend Scotty, who walked the entire 22 miles! They don't make them any tougher than this 73-year-old native of Scotland, who can be seen walking six miles from the town of Enterprise every day of the week.

Brandishing a long walking stick, attached to which was a plastic bag full of beer cans she'd picked up along the route, this indomitable woman pushed tired calves out of borrow pits and chased them out of chokecherry thickets. Scotty held her good humor until the last stretch, which climbed a slight hill, before the cattle were turned into what we call the Johnson pasture. It had begun to rain and Scotty isn't fond of mud. Tired as she was, she pushed those lagging calves to their limit.

Doug and I were in the saddle early that first morning, riding down to the bottom pasture where the spring calvers were waiting for their morning feeding of hay. Scotty lagged behind on foot, waiting for us to gather and turn out the cows on the long dirt road that leads north to our spring range.

Sarah and Ben circled the herd to try and get them headed toward the gate, but when cows don't want to head in a certain direction, they won't, and that morning they didn't. The calves scattered in all four directions, with cows bawling after them, creating mass confusion, it was decided Ben would ride back and return with a pickup full of hay. After which the herd, acting as one body, followed Ben directly out the gate; we relaxed, which was short-lived, because driving cows and young calves is a pain.

The cows, beginning to graze alongside the road, were soon strung out in an uneven line, momentarily forgetting their calves trailing forlornly in the rear. They would suddenly remember their missing calf and come bawling back, searching and sometimes mothering up.

Consequently we had this "army" of footsore baby calves bringing up the rear as we trailed out the Crow Creek road, where the long miles stretch ahead through the pass before winding around toward East Crow. Cloud shadows dappled the hills, hawks sailed above, meadowlarks sang, bright, pink grass widows trembled in a cool breeze, and because of all that rain, the landscape was an intense green. There was always the threat or rain, so we were clothed in our oilskin slickers.

As the cows grazed the lush grasses alongside the road, that odor of bruised grass mingled with cowhide and wet earth. Their bawling, the clean smell of rain-washed hills, and the creaking of saddle leather on a sweaty horse triggered the familiar senses of past drives. And it was good. Each hoof print left by the cattle and our horses left water seeping into the track.

Scotty kept asking how much farther, and Ben delighted in kidding her, pointing to a high hill and exclaiming, "Up that road, clear to the top and on the other side." Scotty would groan, until she saw the smile on my face, which meant she'd been had again.

Very little traffic on the Crow Creek road that day. We passed Tom Birkmaier doing a little maintenance work on the one telephone line that provides his only link with civilization out thereon the "crik." An occasional Forest Service rig wound its way slowly through the cattle, and Paul Yost waved on his way out to Chesnim.

When we stopped to let the cattle rest, we dug into our saddle bags for mashed sandwiches. Along about 5:30 we drove the last tired calf into the holding pasture at East Crow, unsaddled our horses, turned them loose with the cows and calves, and climbed into the pickup with Doug and rode the 15 miles back to the valley ranch. Scotty said she would see us in the morning, and we knew she would be there.

Morning came, and soon we were on our way out to the herd. It was mild and moist, and while walking down across the creek to catch my mare, I noticed the far hills were lost in mists. We led the horses back to the pickup, gave them some oats and saddled up for another day of riding. Unlike the morning before, the herd gathered up nicely and straggled out onto the road in pairs.

We pushed them to the old Dorrance place, and when we reached the pink barn corrals we let the cows graze and the calves lie down. As I drove back with Doug to East Crow so he could bring the cattle truck forward, I ate my lunch while driving the pickup back. Then it was up the long Dorrance gulch road to the top.

Golden balsamroot and bright pink phlox brightened our way. The creek known as Dry Salmon was wet. Very wet, with runoff flowing down the draws. In fact, the hill country was saturated, which should make for a great grass year, especially important after these past several drought years.

It's always a good feeling to turn the cows and calves out on their spring range. We will let them rest a couple of weeks before returning to brand and work the calves, spray the cows and turn the bulls in. While trailing the cattle I occasionally glimpsed two of my "milk cow herd pairs." No more feeding hay. Hurrah!

May 27—This morning I awoke to Chester's crow, the songs and chirping of meadowlarks and robins, and the occasional bawl of a cow: all the familiar ranch sounds here on Prairie Creek. After painfully pulling myself up from my all-night position of lying on my back, I hobble like an old woman to the kitchen where I fix myself a cup of steaming Postum.

Doug has gone outside already and I am alone. I slide a tape in the tape player and soothing music fills the room. I open the front door to the living room and let May rush in. A breeze, laden with all the fresh

Queen of Chief Joseph Days is Erica Gilliland, left, shown with her court, Bridget Brown, middle, and Katie Lewis.

Dave and Darlene Turner smile as they learn they will be grand marshals for the 50th annual Chief Joseph Days parade.

scents of spring and this lovely season, comes full upon me. It is my healing. I notice lilacs beginning to open, late pink tulips, budding, and dandelions bursting open in the morning sun.

My faithful dog Daisy, hearing the front door open, comes into the yard to be petted. Daisy knows what happened to me a week ago this morning. She was out there on Salmon Creek when my mare went to bucking, and moments later when Ben was bending over me as I lay crumpled there in the dirt, the wind knocked out of me and a numbing pain creeping over my right side. Funny, isn't it? How one minute you are in control, then, *wham*.

This morning I will not walk out to the barn, bucket in hand, to milk my cow and let the calves nurse. I will not walk up the familiar, worn path to the chicken pen and talk to the little banty hen who has hatched out five tiny chicks. I will not feed and water the pullets and laying hens.

There are so many things I won't be doing this spring, like planting a vegetable garden and flowers, and going fishing with my grandsons. What I will be doing instead is concentrating on resting and healing.

"Slow and easy," says the doctor. Slow and easy, like this pecking on the typewriter with my left hand so as not to move my right clavicle, which is cracked, nor disturb my right rib cage.

It hadn't seemed much different than the first day of any other spring branding; up early to chore and pack a lunch, and the long ride out to Salmon Creek. Doug, already on the tractor turning sod in the lower field when we drove by on the way to the hills, waved as we passed. It was a lovely May morning, a light frost sparkling on green meadows now devoid of cattle.

It was still early when the three of us drove into the Salmon creek place, caught and saddled the horses, and began riding toward the meadow where we would gather in the cows and calves. The dogs were feeling good, running around chasing each other, when I noticed my mare becoming nervous around Ben's dog, who is what we call a cow-eating fool. So I gathered up my reins and the next thing I remember is a rough ride on the back of my bucking horse.

I was OK until I lost my stirrups. And the next thing I remember was hitting the ground, groaning with the wind knocked out of me, a pain creeping up my right side. The rest is a blur of a pain-filled day, riding 30 miles in a bumpy cattle truck to the hospital, being X-rayed, diagnosed with a broken clavicle and possible internal injuries, fitted with a brace across my shoulders, and after Doug was summoned off the tractor, finally allowed to go home.

Only, we were soon back to the hospital as the pain in my rib cage intensified, and an 60-mile ambulance ride later, I arrived at the Grande Ronde Hospital and its waiting CAT scan.

After two days in La Grande, I am home at the ranch, where I will watch May melt into June, and spend six weeks attempting to mend.

Thanks to granddaughter Tamara, who typed this on my word processor for me. And if I can find another volunteer, there will be a column next week.

May 31—Yeah! I'm back at the word processor. Granted, it isn't without discomfort, or even pain, but I have the doctor's permission. The past two weeks have been very frustrating for a person who participates so actively in life.

When misfortune hits a marriage, it doesn't take long to find out the true caliber of one's spouse, and I must say mine passed with a 10. Not only has Doug tended to my needs, but also those of the yard, garden, chickens, washing and cooking…all in addition to the myriad problems associated with the disposing of a cellar-full of potatoes, broken down equipment, and other daily challenges faced by today's rancher-farmer. Not an enviable task.

Take yesterday, for instance, when he wearily came into the house, caked with dirt and grime, a result of spending most of the day under an old silage truck, repairing a drive line. He washed his hands and began mixing up a batch of sourdough biscuits, still wearing the oil and dirt-stained clothing. Now I know many women would absolutely throw a fit over the thought of this, and Betty Crocker would turn over in her grave, but when you are married to a man of the soil and you've been outside working yourself, enough to understand that the truck must be repaired so the potatoes can be hauled, you don't complain about something so trivial.

In the neatly filled garden spot, a newly planted vegetable garden is sending up the first, tender shoots. Linde came down and got the bedding plants I'd so carefully tended for two months, and transplanted them in her garden. I had to give up on the Slope garden this year, but I dream of being up there, hoeing the black soil, but that is life. And life does go on.

The banty hen's little babies are healthy and growing, and my milk cow's three calves have been turned out with her. Doug buys milk at the store now. The baby kittens provide no end of amusement as I watch their tumbling antics from the porch. The doctor has given me permission to slowly exercise my right arm, using it until the pain makes me stop, which is happening right now, so will take a rest.

Last week our calendar was marked for various events that weave the pattern of our large family's daily lives. *I am caught in the web of the family,* as my mother writes. How true. We've all looked forward to the small 1st-8th grade Imnaha end-of-school program, more so this spring, because grandson Buck was the only 8th grader. This grandma was determined to go, fractured clavicle or not.

I was still very ouchy under my rib cage. In fact, my entire right side still feels like I've been run over by an elephant. So, still wearing my fashionable open-down-the-back hospital gown, I slipped into a denim dress, which couldn't be put on over the right sleeve, had Doug button me up as far as was decent, and covered the upper part of my body with a white shawl.

Did I look like the old matriarch, or what! But I survived the 60-mile round-trip to Imnaha, loved being outside the confining walls of our home, enjoyed the play written by the upper classes, and watched my strong young grandson receive his promotion to 9th grade. This fall Buck will ride the bus up to join friend Luke at Joseph, where the world will begin to change more than a little for this young lad.

After partaking of homemade cake and punch, we drove back "on top." The canyons never looked lovelier and I never enjoyed them more. The next night I performed a repeat of my fashion statement, and we sat on hard bleachers, me with a pillow to support my aching shoulder, and experienced another proud moment as granddaughter Carrie received her high school diploma.

On Saturday many relatives and friends converged here, and soon balloons and crepe paper festooned my convalescent living room, surrounding me with an instant party. The honor guests were granddaughter Tammy, her husband Matt, and the soon-to-be great-grandchild that is due in July. In other words, we had a baby shower, where the men and women were both invited. The occasion was also a wedding anniversary for daughter Lori and son-in-law Tom, as well as a graduation party for Carrie. Oh my!

On Sunday afternoon I was driven in our van up to daughter Ramona and husband Charley's ranch on Sheep Creek hill, where there would be a branding. The family all appeared again, along with friends, and I was vastly entertained from my vantage point in the car. My family, performing a very real Wild West drama beneath the splendid backdrop of the snow-clad Wallowas.

The day was perfect, a cool breeze blew over the hills, wild flowers waved in an ocean of grass, children rode off with their parents to bring in the cows and calves, daddies roped alongside daughters, and everyone pitched in. Very gratifying for a grandmother to observe.

When the dust cleared and the last calf was headed, heeled, brought to the branding fire and worked, and the cattle turned out to their grassy fields, Ramona, who has had a week of graduations and what-have-you, brought out the barbecue grill and soon everyone ate hungrily of hamburgers, salads and beans.

Luckily, Doug had fixed us all sourdough pancakes that morning, because it was late in the afternoon before everyone finished. A little excitement was thrown in when a yearling elk wandered over the hill and joined the cows and calves. Nothing would do but our cowboys had to try to run it down. The elk was entirely safe, however, because when it discovered several thundering horses approaching, the distance between cowboys and fleeing elk widened dramatically.

Tammy's husband, Matt, from California, got a real taste of some of the last Wild West that day, a West they say is disappearing. Too bad, because our family and friends demonstrated that day what much of the West was built on: hard work, play after work, and the feeling of a job well done.

With all its foibles, there is nothing stronger than family and friends helping each other, sticking together through hard times. When we lose that part of the West, it will be a loss to community. This kind of Wild West performance will never be seen on TV or in a movie. But the everyday drama of Western culture that never makes the headlines is still being played out in remote places like Wallowa County.

Hurting again. See you next week.

June 7—Sitting here in front of my word processor, not entirely free of pain but feeling less of it than last week, I gaze out at verdant spring which meets winter a mere mile or two from our ranch. The contrast is startling. Lush waving prairie grass, freshly washed after two days of mixed rain and snow, stops just short of frosted, timbered slopes, which draw the eye upward to barren, snow-swathed peaks. Viewed in early morning sunlight, our blinding white Wallowas dominate the landscape, prairie green and mountain white.

Mornings have become a regular ritual accomplished in slow motion; cup of orange juice, hot shower, a cup of Postum while lounging in my bathrobe, dress, fix some oatmeal, and wash yesterday's accumulated dishes, mostly with my left hand. Taking time to savor the morning, as seen through my picture window. I love being able to watch the changing moods of Prairie Creek, seeing the rain curtains sway in the wind and work their way up the valley, listening to thunder. I sense the earth drinking and the grasses brightening. I imagine the wildflowers, refreshed now around Kinney Lake, where on Sunday Adele, James and I talked "papa" Doug into taking us fishing.

What a treat to see and feel that lovely spot. James and I have dreamed of it all winter. I perched on a rock, oblivious to the coolish breeze, just enjoying watching the children and Doug fish, and even providing assistance when needed, untangling lines and replenishing worms) James not only caught a fish, but he and Adele captured a toad, which they later turned loose near their dad's pond. These are simple outdoor pleasures that the children had looked forward to all this long winter and cold spring.

Fields of wildflowers, cattle grazing, milky snowmelt water flashing down the ditches out of the mountains, and everywhere green, green, green, backgrounded by the snow-covered Wallowas. Even though I was later to pay the price for such exertion, it was worth every ache and pain.

Having spent the better part of the past three weeks here on the ranch, with its peaceful atmosphere, has been wonderful. How I savor the days. And take time to contemplate moving clouds, watch the unfurling of brilliant, pink phlox in the wildflower patch, take short walks with Daisy, gather the eggs, walk down and see my calves on the milk cow, and enjoy the iris, bleeding heart, pansies and impatiens blooming just outside the living room door.

I enjoy watching the garden Doug planted come up, although it is frustrating not being able to pick up a hoe. The strawberries are blooming and the raspberries about to. It is as if the 10-mile distant town of Joseph, with its booming tourist attractions, doesn't even exist to our quiet road.

Dramas continue to unfold within our large and extended family, and I can only sit here, absorbing it, as informed, unable to play any other role, except to support, worry, wonder, rejoice, and sometimes weep. Such has been the role of grandmothers for years; such will always be their fate.

Then there are phone calls, cards in the mailbox, flowers, food at the front door, and welcome hugs from my wonderful grandchildren, all of which have contributed to my recovery. Speaking of phone calls, I have received several from fans who read this column. Like 84-year-old Kenneth Boyer of Haines, who like others, want to share their own experiences.

Kenneth told me he used to feed a team of Belgian work horses, and when he unhitched them from the hay wagon, he and his son would hop up on the pair of draft horses and ride to the barn, where they would unharness.

"Well," said Kenneth, "One time this 1,800-pound, three-year-old dumped me." Kenneth, 70 at the time, suffered a punctured lung, several broken ribs, and a shoulder broken in three places! Ouch. Undaunted, in the way of Eastern Oregon cowboys, Kenneth mended, and was soon back riding. At age 75 he was testing out another coming three-year-old Belgian.

"Riding her around," he said. "She was gentle and all was going just fine," when suddenly "My border collie dog, which I had acquired from another Baker County cowboy, Dan Warnock, slipped out from under a wagon and spooked my horse." Another fall, more injuries, but I'll wager that at 84 Kenneth is still riding.

My old friend Mike McFetridge, now nearing the 90-year mark, didn't ride with us this year when we trailed the cattle out to grass. I received a nice supporting card from Mike, too, bless him. He knows all about this cowboy life.

Received a cheering call from Wallowa County's number one cowgirl, Ruth Baremore of Wallowa, who must be near the 70 mark and continues to work cattle horseback. Ruth related how once when she was out to Promise, her summer range, a dog spooked her horse and she was bucked off. Luckily she wasn't hurt then, but Ruth has been hurt. A milk cow kicked her in the face, and her shoulder was broken, too, from a horse accident. She said the work had to be done and soon she was back in the saddle.

Ruth knows about emotional hurt, too: the death of a husband, a family to rear, a ranch to hold together, and the death of a grandson. Ruth doesn't spend any time feeling sorry for herself, however, and always has a smile for me. A very special lady. And like many other Wallowa County ranch women, an inspiration.

Old friends, some who go back a long way, like Betty Hammond, call. My neighbor down the road, Lois Hough, appears at the kitchen door laden with fresh-cut flowers, homemade cookies, a jug of orange juice and a smile. The neighbor wife to the south, Tappy Locke, calls and gives me advice on exercising my right arm. Tappy, at age 61 like me, took a fall from her horse coming down the Ice Lake trail one summer. She knows about broken shoulders.

Tappy still rides, but Lois quit last year. She says the horses on their ranch don't get ridden enough and just aren't dependable. Smart gal. Lois, Tappy, and Ardis Klages (another ranch-wife neighbor) fall into that over-60 category of "average" ranch wives who still actively participate in the ranch operations. On Prairie Creek, we seem to greatly outnumber the younger ones.

Another top cowgirl, now in her later years, Mary Marks of Imnaha, called. She related similar experiences while spending all those years riding the upper and lower reaches of the Imnaha alongside her late husband, Kid.

Kate Wilde called, another Imnaha friend who used to live up Big Sheep and out here on Prairie Creek. She reminded me that husband, Will, not too long ago was mauled by an angry cow and broke several ribs. Will is over 80 now and going strong, thanks to Kate's good care and cooking.

Myrna Moore and daughter, Jenny, from down Bear Gulch, stopped by to return some books and visit. Myrna says she thinks about being bucked off whenever she rides the rimrocks working cattle. We agree; it is always on our minds. It is the way we choose to live.

Other friends share their stories, which are entwined with our high-risk lifestyles. This rugged country breaks, mends, and shapes us. We, therefore, become products of the land. Hardened by cold, taught patience by tragedy, awed by the beauty we behold each day. We pay a price for our lifestyles here.

Doug's brother, Jack, and wife, Blanche, from Clarkston pay a visit. Their lovely bouquet of fresh roses lasted more than a week. Doug's sister, Barbara, brought out a small turkey all roasted with veggies, and a loaf of homemade bread. Jim and Ethel Chandler, who operate a bed and breakfast in Joseph, sent down a fresh seafood linguine.

Now I'm back to cooking the meals, and Doug is glad, even though it takes much longer than it used to.

June 19—Heavy wet clouds, which have produced cold and misty rain all morning, slowly dissipate as soft breezes stir the air enough to separate them. The hot June sunlight burns holes in the moist canopy as patches of the cleanest, purest blue briefly appear. After being housebound for three days, I take advantage of this weather break, knowing it won't last.

Standing on our front lawn I breathe deeply of rain-cleansed air before wandering over to lean on the wooden pole fence that serves to corral my wildflower patch. I savor the sweet fragrance being released by an extraordinary flower which I've been referring to as some variety of phlox. It is presently blooming so profusely pink that it has created a solid mass of color. So lushly does it grow, weeds don't stand a chance.

I can't seem to identify this prolific volunteer in any of my wildflower books; it originated in a packet of Western wildflower seeds planted several years ago. While Doug views this runaway plant with alarm, I simply enjoy its free gift of beauty. Volunteering next to this brilliant pink jungle are my Icelandic poppies. As they did last year, these vari-colored beauties will bloom well into summer.

Also reseeding themselves, via the Prairie Creek winds, are the bachelor buttons and golden California poppies. These two varieties completely fill the north end of my patch. This unchecked, unweeded, unfertilized jumble of joy, which I know is God's gift to me, is my "ego" system. Good medicine.

One cloudy and cool morning last week, Linde and her twin sister, Inge, who is visiting from Greece, whisked me to nearby Wallowa Lake where we three began hiking up the Chief Joseph trail. Lagging in the rear, feeling like a child just out of school, I was extremely sensitive to the forest and acutely aware of the seasonal changes which have always excited me. It must have been amusing to Linde and Inge when I exclaimed so about everything.

"Oh! Look, the first Calypso! The wild strawberries are blooming, the wood's violets are over here," and then I would traipse off the trail to follow an irregular line of calf brain mushrooms pushing their way through the forest duff.

The trail forked and soon we were walking above the wild, roaring snowmelt waters that cascaded down out of the mountains to form the west fork of the Wallowa River. After weeks of imagining what it would be like here, I was suddenly in the midst of it. I almost forgot about my injuries until the nagging pain returned, and then I would have to lean against the railing of the wooden bridge that spans the river, or sit on a log until the pain subsided.

We returned via a solid rock pathway that formed a steep gorge carved by the river. I was always taking side trips to better see clusters of lavender penstemon, which grew in terraced clefts above the roaring river. Intermingled with the penstemon were Golden Arnica and red-orange Indian paintbrush. We stood on a narrow shelf that protruded above the cascading white water falls opposite the Boy Scout camp, and watched the wild water tumble down to its frothy pool. Then we scrambled down off the rocks and made our way slowly back to the trailhead.

Earlier that same morning, I had suffered through the painful process of typing this column. And a few days before, I had swept, mopped, and waxed my kitchen floor, not to mention baking two rhubarb pies and doing all the dishes and cooking again.

When I returned from my exhilarating hike, I sat down and wrote a long letter in longhand to one of my sisters. I slept well that night.

The next morning, our 17th wedding anniversary, I was in so much pain that I could hardly pull myself up from bed. Doug fashioned a sling for me out of one of his shop rags, and then he drove us up to Linde and Pat's for breakfast. Even though I was in pain most of the time, the meal was such a treat, and a sample of Pat and Linde's "Thistle and Shamrock" Bed and Breakfast.

Linde had cooked a breakfast casserole consisting of sausage, eggs, bread cubes and cheese. With it she served hot bran muffins and a large tray of fresh fruit. It was a misty, cold morning, and through the windows next to where we ate, the upper Prairie Creek woods looked surreal. Several Rufus-sided towhees and a blue jay came to the feeder on the deck, entertaining us while we lingered after breakfast.

Linde and Pat's bed and breakfast is just opening this summer. They cater mostly to horse people, who come here to ride the many trails that lead into the mountains, so they provide accommodations for horses as well.

Encouraging letters and cards continue to fill our mailbox. Thank you, Agri-Times readers, from the bottom of my heart. I love hearing from you, although I find it distressing not being able to thank each one of you individually.

I recently received a letter from Carole McCarty of Kamuela, Hawaii, who writes that she was born and reared in Pendleton, attended two years of college in La Grande, and has lived in Hawaii for 30 years, but her heart still longs for Eastern Oregon. Taking time from tending her acre of plants, flowers, birds and squirrels, Carole's 85-year-old mother forwards my Agri-Times column to Hawaii. Carole says my writing provides an escape for her and she visualizes the seasonal changes and "goings on" in Eastern Oregon through my pen.

Carole, an illustrator, sent me a copy of her latest work, a children's book, entitled *Tutu Nene and Nele,* which is a charming story about the rare Hawaiian goose, Nele, that lives in the Volcanoes National Park.

Another letter that touched me was from 65-year-old Erna Kagele, who with her husband, Melvin, son and son-in-law, farms near Ritzville, Washington. Erna says, "I laughed when you talked about Doug fixing dinner with his dirty clothes on. We farmers are like that. Like my neighbor said, 'Dirt built this house and dirt won't hurt it', or many other things."

Erna also wrote that she turns "green with envy" when I write about taking all those hikes and walks. Well, just come on over some day, Erna, and we'll take one together. I might be a little slow for a while, but I do have lots of time.

Thanks also to Uncle Marshall and Aunt Billie Wilson way off there in South Lake Tahoe. They subscribe to Agri-Times so they can keep track of our family. Their phone calls and cards are very cheering. Since I am now back to square one in the rehabilitation department, I am limited again in so many things, all of which are my loves—playing the piano, taking photos, writing, hoeing in the garden, rolling out pie crust.

On Father's Day, the family descended here on the ranch, Daughter Ramona, the organizer of the family, planned it all. Everyone brought food. We enjoyed a barbecued salmon that granddaughter Tammy and husband Matt brought up from California recently; potato salad, Angie's famous beans, and numerous desserts, which included a mincemeat pie made by Doug the day before. Seated in a kitchen chair, I led Doug through the crust-making process. It was quite an experience for the both of us. The pie turned out great.

Never having had the opportunity to receive a formal college education, I feel I deserve some sort of degree in homemaking. After baking literally thousands of pies over the years, raising a family, and "doing" for family since I was 17 years old, it seems to me this should count as an education. Or at least be recognized as a career.

Methinks homemaking, motherhood, and all the myriad domestic skills in which millions of women in our generation are accomplished should be recognized as one of the most important roles a woman can play.

June 27—Suddenly... it's summer. And what a summer. After weeks of cloudy, cool, oftentimes rainy weather, our short growing season has arrived. Overnight, hay is ready to cut, the standing-still vegetable plants in the garden have changed from a pale yellow to a healthy shade of green, and the air here on Prairie Creek is filled with bits of floating cotton, which drifts down from ancient trees that border the numerous irrigation ditches. The merest breeze releases great showers of this fluff.

These warm mornings I watch with fascination Hough's hay fields, as explosions of pollen drift over the mature red-colored grasses. It is like watching a prairie fire begin... pollen smoke. The new warmth has unfurled bright red Icelandic poppies and brilliant blue bachelor buttons in my untended wildflower patch. June bearer strawberries are ripening, and we've been enjoying the first green onions and radishes from Doug's well-kept garden.

"Tucker's Mare," that legendary snow shape of a horse, outlined high upon a Wallowa peak, is now visible through my kitchen window. Surrendering to high altitude heat the snow is slowly evaporating from the high places, creating a purple and white mosaic. As summer progresses the white will all but leave and the purple will persist.

An artist some years back visited our valley in August and saw the landscape as Alizarin crimson, or some such watercolor. Now I see what he saw, as the mature grasses and distant mountains really do take on that hue. In the lush, irrigated pastures grow great patches of Ladino clover, the air fragrant with its sweet scent. It is a heady time.

It is also haying time and prolific crops are falling to the swather. Ben and son Seth have begun to cut the mature grasses in one of our hayfields this morning. They will green chop it for making silage, which will be stored in large plastic bags for winter feeding. Our neighbors to the north, the Stilsons, are already in the field compressing large "bread loaf" hay stacks.

Ranchers glue themselves to the evening and morning weather reports on TV. Shall we cut? Will it rain? Will it stay warm enough for the hay to cure? What to do? In our high mountain valley, it matters. We only get two cuttings.

The grass growing outside our pole yard fence is up to my shoulders. As I write, I can see the waving reddish heads, full of seeds, pleasing to the eye, creating an illusion of living amid a vast grass prairie. These varieties of wild grasses growing around the chicken pen and beyond the raspberry patch are so tall that they all but obscure the mountains, at least from my vantage point.

Doug has turned my milk cow and her calves into this area to graze down what will later become a fire hazard. Following the cow around are two young bulls, one of which we hope has already bred her. So far the cattle have scarcely made a dent in the grass.

Yesterday morning I began therapy exercises to release my "frozen" shoulder. Ideally, I am not supposed to attempt any anti-gravity activities. Like this typing, which I accomplish very slowly, resting my arm frequently on the arm of Doug's desk chair. It still hurts. And I MUST be better for the Fishtrap writers' conference, which begins next week, as I am signed up for Teresa Jordan's workshop.

Teresa is the author of *Riding the White Horse Home* and *Cowgirls*. Our popular Wallowa Lake Gathering is now in its eighth year, and continues to grow. This year's theme is "Orphaned in Eden/Search for Family in the West." Ought to produce some interesting and stimulating discussions and writings. I can't wait.

All during this long, damp spring of my confinement, I've dreamed of returning to the hills. I pictured in my mind's eye the vast Zumwalt country, blanketed with its abundance of wildflowers and native grasses, maturing now in the sudden heat. I could envision our cattle, sleek and fat, grazing those lush acres. Last Sunday, my wish was granted. Doug packed a lunch, and we were off to the hills, driving north on the long, graveled Crow Creek road.

Near Beck's place on East Crow the roadway was lined with brilliant pink wild roses. At the old Dorrance place Crow Creek meandered through its verdant green meadow, as it has ever since Church and Minnie Dorrance reared their family there. The morning was warm and as we made our way slowly up the steep, rutty grade, I remembered my last ride there, clutching my right shoulder in pain, bumping along in the old cattle truck with Seth at the wheel.

I spied several mule deer does, bedded in the thornbush thickets below the road. Their tiny spotted fawns lay hidden in tall grass. On top, the Wallowas loomed behind us while before us the familiar rolling hills stretched to the horizon, colored by the most massive display of wildflowers I've ever seen. Yellows dominated, with lupine and larkspur blue and pinks of Clarkia and sticky geranium added to the pallet.

The sight took my breath away, and so did the wonderful quiet, the utter stillness of the land. A faint breeze carried the mingled scent of wildflowers. The air was heavy with it. A golden eagle soared before us and landed on a rocky outcropping. Hawks were everywhere. Dry Salmon Creek was still wet! The stock ponds were full and our cows and calves were lost in a sea of grass.

The calves I would have helped brand that fateful day had doubled in size, due to the milk now being produced because of that grass. How, I thought, could a place so lovely have been the scene of an incident that would change my life so drastically?

As we drove away from our Salmon Creek place, I painfully snapped a photo of the scene. Wet Salmon Creek, bordered by thornbush and willow, winding its way through the swampy meadow, tucked away between the folds of the wildflower-strewn hills.

We drove up and down the hilly, rocky road, crossed Pine Creek and came out on the Zumwalt road. Where prairie meets timber, we drove past the old Steen ranch, then out to Thomason Meadows and on out to Buckhorn where we picnicked. Before us stretched one of the most beautiful sights in the West. The drainages of Horse Creek and Lightning Creek, their sharp ridges flowing out onto great flat benches, where bunch grasses provide wonderful livestock range.

Idaho's jagged crest of the Seven Devils rose to the east, and northeast, Montana's Bitterroots glimmered in the haziness produced by great distances. The breaks of the Imnaha and the Snake rose and fell in an endless succession of blue/purple separations. And we were the only ones there! Daisy and I took a brief walk and I was able to snap a photo of Indian paintbrush growing on the steep hillside which sloped downward from where we had eaten lunch.

Returning over the long miles back to the ranch, the Wallowas growing closer as we approached the valley, I asked Doug to stop so I could shoot my last film frame. So I'll always remember this day, and how the hills looked. Summer's heat will soon cook their beauty.

July 13—This bright, clear morning sparkles with leftover moisture from last evening's passing thundershower. The wildflower patch, refreshed and brilliant, with red, pink and orange Icelandic poppies, fairly glows in the early-morning sunlight. As I write, the first puffy clouds appear, multiply, join, and soon the blue sky is filled with them. The billowing white formations form more rapidly over the Wallowas, as the energy of more thunderstorms builds within them.

Between showers, the air is warm, breezy and dry, and ranchers and farmers bale hay into the night, playing a game with Wallowa County's fickle weather to see which will win. Ben so far is winning, but only because he, Seth and daughter Sarah, spend every spare minute of every day at the task of swathing, raking, baling and repairing the inevitable breakdowns.

Doug, in addition to cleaning up around the potato cellar, which is now for sale, has been helping bale hay. Seth and Ben have also been preserving some of this hay crop in the form of silage. When you stop to think of the amount of work involved, you have to admire our ranchers, farmers, hired men and young people out there in the fields this time of year.

I love haying time. I love seeing the long swathed rows of freshly-mown hay in the fields. It fills my senses with its lovely textures, its sweet scent, and I like the comforting *put, put, put* sound made by our little tractor, as blond, pony-tailed, 17-year-old Sarah makes her rounds pulling the hay rake. She looks so young and proud and strong, and I wonder if she is filling her senses like I am.

Marc Jaffe pulled into Wallowa Lake last week, bringing with him his wife Vivienne, daughter Eva, and son Benjamin. The family paid Doug and me a visit Saturday evening. It was a wonderful exchange, eastern people visiting our West. Marc has been coming to our Fishtrap Writer's conference since it began and is, in fact, on our advisory board.

The Jaffes subscribe to Agri-Times, which makes its way back to Berlin, New York, and Marc wanted his family to see our ranch and experience some of the things I write about in my column. The children instantly fell in love with our five kittens and my dog, Daisy. We took a walk up on the hill, where we could look down and see Ben haying.

Vivienne and Marc loved seeing the pastoral scene of Prairie Creek, and 15-year-old Eva was entranced with the beauty. Benjamin, much to Daisy's delight, ran around like young boys do, with the dog ever at his heels. Vivienne shares my enthusiasm for the wildflower patch, and we discussed seeds, planting and such. It was fun having them here. I only wish I'd been up to cooking a nice meal for them. Perhaps next time.

The next day, beginning around 8 a.m., Doug saddled his horse and hauled him up to help son-in-law Charley at a branding for the Cross Sabres Ranch. Other family members and neighbors straggled in throughout the day, until there was a full crew.

It was one of those cool, early July days when great cloud shadows move silently over the green hills. For brief moments, overcast skies would part and the sun would burst forth to lay a golden path over upper Prairie Creek. Add the ever-present mountains, still splotched with snow, an old red octagonal barn, and cowboys working cattle; the whole created a splendid subject for the photographer. Ignoring the pain, I raised my arm into position and shot a complete roll of film.

Brief rain showers didn't discourage younger granddaughters, who rode off on their horses across the green hills. When they returned they were wearing wildflowers in their wet hair and had decorated their horses' bridles with sprigs of purple lupine. And I was out of film!

Daughter Ramona had prepared barbecued beef sandwiches from roasts she had cooked the night before. When it began to rain pretty steadily, she decided to feed the crew, and we all rode over to their nearby ranch to eat inside. Busy Ramona had also prepared macaroni salad and brownies, enough for nearly 20 people. The good food and the camaraderie of everyone working together provided the only pay that day. It also provided an opportunity for the ropers to hone their skills.

After eating, the crew resumed the branding until 8 o'clock that evening, when the cows finally were turned out with their branded calves. I stuck it out the entire day, as there is nothing more entertaining for a grandmother and mother than watching her children and grandchildren at a branding. Grandson Bart and I sat in the comfort of the car most of the day, except when I felt the urge to photograph.

Early Monday morning found me in Teresa Jordan's writing workshop, which was held in the Eagle Cap Chalet conference room at Wallowa Lake. In spite of my shoulder acting up, I wasn't going to miss this opportunity to learn all I could from a writer I admired greatly. Our class was full of visiting writers from far-flung places in Oregon—Long Creek, McMinnville, Brothers, Hood River, Ontario, Portland, Pendleton, Umatilla, Seaside, Union—as well as Walla Walla and Trout Creek, Washington.

It was extremely interesting listening to their stories, learning what had brought them to Fishtrap. Ellen Morris Bishop, rancher, journalist, geologist, photographer and writer, was there. After class the second day I invited Ellen out to the ranch, where she met Doug and we visited in the quiet of our yard. Then we drove up to Alder Slope to pick up a book from a friend, which Ellen wanted to read.

I became acquainted that first morning with Becky Hyde, a young, beginning writer, who was attending her first writer's conference. Becky, the daughter of well-known ranchers Doc and Connie Hatfield from Brothers, Oregon, is married to the youngest son of Hawk and Gerda Hyde of Chiloquin. After our first session I detected a lost look in Becky's eyes—that country girl look. She was missing the ranch. So I invited her out on Wednesday.

Teresa and her husband, Hal Cannon, collaborated on their workshops. Hal was teaching song writing, inspired by images, and Teresa taught connecting prose, or poetry, to images. So our projects, to be completed by Thursday, would be presented by the class, jointly, combining music, words and images.

Becky was working with a black and white photograph that depicted her and her young husband on their wedding day. She needed a quiet place to work, so here on the ranch Becky worked all afternoon on her piece, which turned out to be an essay about her wedding boots. It was wonderful. I predict a great future for this bright young woman. And may she continue to tell the rancher's story, and by doing so preserve our heritage.

It was a special treat getting to know these talented women. Yesterday, Thursday, our class presented its "projects," which were all unique in their own way. Magic just seems to happen when two very genuinely kind, talented instructors inspire a group of creative minds for four days. I am sure none of us will ever forget that finale workshop. It was extraordinary. The power of images, words and music unfolded for all to see.

Last night, Fishtrap paid tribute to Alvin Josephy and wife, Betty, in honor of their 80th birthdays. Much was said for the deserving Alvin, who has devoted his life to recording the American way of life, but it was his wife, Betty, who in her brief moment at the mike brought tears to my eyes. Not a writer herself, but a mother, grandmother and supporter of a writer husband, she shared her feelings about the importance of family. This, after a wonderful tribute given by the two Josephy daughters.

In keeping with this year's theme, "Searching for Family in the West," Betty was right on. No family is without its problems, but we women know what it means to be so recognized by one's children for the strengths we so diligently strive to give our young. And to see that strength come out, as it did last night, makes all the tears worthwhile.

July 18—Slate-colored clouds float over the eastern hills. Their dull colors backdrop my wildflower patch, which is brilliant in contrast. Reds, blues, golds, and pinks appear more vivid this morning. It rained most of the night, a soft, warm rain. The wild roses are happy, and daisies line the irrigation ditches and dot pastures with clumps of white. It seems more like June than July.

Doug's vegetable garden is lush, peas are blooming, onions, radishes, and leaf lettuce produce enough salads for us and the neighbors. Potatoes, carrots, beets, and cabbages resemble pictures in seed catalogs. Not a weed to be seen. Gooseberry bushes hang heavy with pale green berries, while strawberries continue to ripen in frightening quantities. Doug, Ramona, and Linde compare notes on preparing freezer jam.

The full, July moon, swimming behind wet clouds tonight, will brighten the long rows of corn in Bill's Alder Slope garden. This is the summer I will simply enjoy. Enjoy walking among the vegetables, gathering them, cooking them, savoring them…with my left hand. I am resigned at last to this more passive role, the hoe-less role.

The Barred Rock pullets have begun laying their first small brown eggs, and Cheryl's chicks are half grown. Two of them have feathers on their legs like their little Banty mom. The raspberry kittens are a joy, living beneath thick foliage under the rows of raspberry canes and appearing in the cool of evening to cavort about the yard.

Editor Virgil Rupp parked his little camper pickup in our yard during the Fishtrap Writer's Conference last weekend. He enjoyed waking from his comfortable bed to beautiful Prairie Creek and my wildflower patch. And Doug and I enjoyed visiting Virgil.

Early Monday morning found me at our local hospital, undergoing physical therapy. Angie, who administered the treatments, is ordering a special arm harness to wear, which should alleviate the painful process of being at this word processor.

By Tuesday I was experiencing a real let down after a week of "WORDS." Written words, many of which I wrote myself, and spoken words, which flowed from the lips and hearts of writers. As I listened to works from western writers in an audience that included Eastern ears, such as Marc Jaffe and Alvin Josephy, thoughts of my own began to surface. "Orphaned in Eden, Search for Family in the West"...a very complex subject. Just a tip of the iceberg was broken off into the waters of thought, and that tiny chunk of thought will undoubtedly float about until it dissolves into a fermenting sea.

Here then are my thoughts on the subject of family, which don't necessarily swim in the mainstream of thought. See what being around literary minds does? I felt that the elusive object of the search, in other words, family, was never properly defined.

What is a family? To me, it always was. I mean, it always did exist. I was born into it. Complex as it seemed, in my mind and in the minds of countless others of my generation, family was a very real, tangible thing. Family worked better than any other way that I could see.

However, a large segment of "The Western Family," in reality, is composed of people not from the West, but from the Midwest, the East, and numerous foreign countries. Therefore, very few of us share a truly Western heritage. And there we were, all mixed together in a great melting pot of cultures, preparing to explore "the Western Family," or the search for same. Or something.

As we prepare to enter a new century, the present time of the '90s is entirely different from the '50s, when a person born into a loving family had a pretty good chance of making it in this world. Now, with the age of technology, will the child of the next century, still requiring the same basic needs as that child of the '50s, receive the necessary nurturing?

I found the subject overwhelming, when it should have been simple. Especially for me, born into an established line of generations who had already defined family as a way of life that couldn't have existed without the strength of family.

Enter our keynote speaker, Stephanie Coontz, who talked about *The Way We Never Were,* the title of her book. What did she mean...the way we never were! When our large, extended family was as close to the image of the traditional Western family as any family could be.

I am a third-generation Westerner, as my great-grandmother came West in 1874. I have never been East. My children are fourth generation Westerners, and their children, my grandchildren, are the fifth generation born here in the West—and they are staying too. And a sixth generation child, due momentarily, will be born as far West as the wagons rolled. This new babe will be born into a large, loving family. She won't be orphaned in Eden. This child won't have to search. But, the West she will enter is no longer Eden. Someday, perhaps this long-awaited great-grandchild of mine, who will wear my name (if it is a girl), will help reconstruct Eden. And the strength of his or her birthright could be the vehicle to help bring this about. I wish I could live long enough to see my great-grandchild's future world.

Her young mother, although college-educated, has already put motherhood ahead of career. She knows, because of her upbringing, that family means more to our young people now than it ever has, and this new infant will need all the strength it can muster as he, or she, meets the challenges posed by this upcoming generation. Families, in our case, worked and are still working, and providing a great support system, as well as role models for those outside the family structure. Five generations of family standing firmly behind this unborn infant. No orphan, this child. Five generations that did their own searching in the West, and because established. *The Way We Never Were* does not apply here.

So you see, this writer had a hard time coming to grips with Stephanie's presentation. As I listened to contemporary writers expound on the state of the '90s, I was able to see outside my own cozy cocoon of family, even see my own family in a different perspective. Ours, no different from others, is not without its problems. How we deal with those problems is what counts. We've always relied on the support system to survive family crises.

Author Craig Lesley, who wrote *Winterkill* and *Riversong,* and has just come out with a new novel about a single parent, entitled *The Sky Fisherman,* cited examples of people in small communities who are adopting orphan children; Alvin Josephy, well-known writer-historian of Native American cultures, remarked that the raising of children was the responsibility of the entire village.

One fact stands out clearly: when a child is born, it needs care, nurturing, and LOVE, lots of it. If things go awry, and it is shown neglect, abuse, and lack of nurturing instead, that child grows up with a deep anger inside, not knowing about beauty or how to give love, and becomes confused and learns to hate. That child learns how to survive by his wits, learns how to lie, cheat, steal, and comes back as an adult to haunt our society and help destroy it.

Listening to Stephanie, I understood that it is up to all of us to redefine family, but still use the same principles that worked in family, so that a child born into this world of "The way we never were" can grow up in a world of the way we should be. Because the reality is that today's families are being torn apart, to the point where families like ours, are rare. Children are reared by single parents, grandmothers, day care providers, nannies, baby sitters, brothers, sisters, or adopted parents.

But I am heartened. Not all doom and gloom, I see many present generation parents who have already begun to shift back to family...putting more emphasis on being a family, realizing that the future of their children depends on the stability of the children they have opted to bring into the world. In other words, taking parenthood seriously. The big problem now is dealing with the monster which has been created.

I guess all we can do is help with children's projects within our own communities, and help those less fortunate see that there is a better world out there by opening doors, reading to them, involving them, showing them the beauty around them, inspiring, and most of all caring about them in a way that can effect a positive change in their lives. The needs of our children MUST come first. If we never were...perhaps we'd better be. We all need to shed prejudices and accept the fact that different lifestyles are here to stay.

After listening to the rather lengthy dissertations, I loved folk singer, songwriter, cowboy poet Hal Cannon's short response: "We need more songs." And George Venn, who simply recited a poem about a child torn between two families: his mother's, where he lived, and his father's, where he visited. Listening to George's well-composed words, I understood, as only a grandmother whose own heart has been hurt can, as she observes the life of her precious grandchild as he makes his way in a very confusing world.

Here again, I thought, family can offer support and love, and provide the necessary ingredient for that child to see that life is sweet. And thanks to songs and poems, and stories, we can all tell about our lives here in the West, and perhaps...someone will be listening. And we can find answers to what we are all searching for here in Eden.

July 21—Summer has given us a break. After nearly a week of heat, which we Wallowa Countians aren't used to, July has decided to cool us off with a "born-in-the-mountains" breeze. As afternoon thunder-heads build, the air is further cooled by showers. That is, if you happen to be under one of those swiftly moving clouds. For instance, take yesterday, when our hometown of Joseph had water running down the streets, and thunder rolled off Chief Joseph Mountain, while out here at the ranch on Prairie Creek, only a light rain fell.

And while Ben, wife Jackie, and daughter Sarah worked all afternoon into the evening, hauling hay to the stack yards and barn, thunder pealed and lightning sliced dark clouds.

All of my former tasks are being performed admirably. I do all the cooking now, and the dishes, and some watering of my wildflowers, but no lawn mowing, hoeing, or anything requiring the use of two arms. I am back to daily evening walks with Daisy, my faithful friend and dog. Am late with this column due to having been involved in a very emotional week, which is not over yet.

For starters, I jump every time the phone rings, because my great-grandchild, due today, is expected to make his or her appearance. My continuing medical problems required that I undergo a CAT scan yesterday, and friend Linde took me in for that.

Then, on Tuesday morning, after an hour of physical therapy, I drove up the street from the hospital to hold our month-old new grandson, Ethan Douglas. I made him smile as I cuddled his strong body in my arms. Later that day, I learned that our dear friend Bill had fallen and had been taken by ambulance to our local hospital in Enterprise. I drove over to visit him, then walked over to the adjoining nursing home to see Aunt Amey Wilson, who had just that day been transferred from the Willamette Valley Care Center to her beloved Wallowa Valley.

As I took this frail, old woman's hand into mine and talked to her, she finally recognized me and said: "I'm home." Yes, Aunt Amey, you are home. When those of us who love this place have to leave for any reason, returning is akin to heaven. With all its cold and hardships, this mountain valley will forever be home.

July 28—Still feeling like a bird with a broken wing, I continue on with this surreal summer. No grandchild yet. This babe is taking its time. Meanwhile, the young mother-to-be (my granddaughter) and the grandmother-to-be (my daughter) waits. As does the great-great-grandmother at her home in Auburn, California (my mother). And yours truly sits by her phone way up here in Northeastern Oregon, nearly a thousand miles away. The unborn infant calls the shots.

Our friend Bill, now in his 80s, was transferred this past week to Walla Walla, where he underwent surgery for a fractured upper leg. Poor Bill. He just returned to our local hospital last evening, having survived his third surgery in the past few years. Proving the outdoor life is good for you, Bill has certainly been a fine example of living the good life.

My own days are filled with doctor and therapy appointments. It is a summer of becoming intimate with the medical world, with waiting rooms, consultation rooms, therapy rooms, full of doctors, nurses, therapists, aides, and other patients. The "other patients" have brought a new awareness to my life, friends and acquaintances over the nearly 30 years I've lived in the valley. A parade of aging people. some gracefully, some not so gracefully. But aging, the way we all do.

I've always plunged headlong into life before, scarcely taking time to contemplate the fact that I, too, am growing older. Now I am forced to consider.

Yesterday, before seeing a hone specialist. I was required to fill out endless forms. *When were you born? Have you had prior medical problems? Social Security number? Driver's license? Full name, employer, and how did your accident occur? Over and over, each of us patients fill out forms for each new doctor. My birth date is permanently embedded in my memory: 9/9/33.

In spite of all that is being done, pain is my constant companion, and one I would just as soon discard. Even sitting at the word processor, typing out this column, is pain. Therapy is pain, but I must continue if I want to regain any former function.

Our fall calvers on the high east moraine overlooking Wallowa Lake are dropping their first calves. Literally. Awakened in the middle of the night by a phone ringing. The local sheriff: "There is a baby calf in the barrow pit, alongside the Wallowa Lake highway, and the mother is trying to get through the fence.

Doug dresses, drives the pickup up there, loads the big black baldy calf, returns to bed, and reunites mother and baby the next morning. The calf had fallen out of his steep pasture!

This morning a friend traveling the same road notices another baby calf wandering in the middle of the road. Calls. By the time Doug drives up there, the calf has crawled back through the fence to its mother. That time of year.

Doug returns home late every evening, weary from tearing down an old shed near the potato cellar in Joseph. He and a crew have been working to clean up the property in there so it can be sold. A big job. One of the hired men fell and broke a bone in his leg a couple of days ago. Agriculture is hazardous to your health.

Summer wears on. The raspberries are ripening so thick, even the robins don't make a dent. I fixed the first tender zucchini for lunch today. Since Doug is gone so much of the day, the watering of the gardens, lawn and flowers is now up to me. A full time job. Accomplished slowly. I also gather the eggs, cook, do the dishes, and spend much of my time in self-therapy. Ouch.

Ben, aided by his family, has finished haying the first cutting. They are now busy with the irrigating, checking calving cows, salting the cattle in the hills, mending fence, and repairing machinery. For Ben and his family, this ranch is a seven-days-a-week job, and it shows. The place is beautiful. Ben and others like him all over the valley are to be admired. And never taken for granted. They are dedicated.

To escape the drudgery of therapy and depressing news, I look forward each evening to long walks around Prairie Creek. So does Daisy, who jumps with joy at the mere mention of the word "walk." Quite often, as the golden evening light washes across the lush, green fields, I glimpse a solitary white-tail doe. She comes bounding off our hill above the house, leaps the fence, crosses the road and disappears into the tall grasses that border an irrigation ditch in Hough's field. There she is protected.

One such evening, Daisy and I climbed through the fence and began our walk across Hough's irrigated alfalfa field, where the second cutting is lush and brilliant green. Along this path of high grass, where the doe lives with her fawn, we wandered. All of a sudden there was a swish of grass and the doe jumped up in front of us and cleared the fence that separates the alfalfa from a field of oats. The fawn, lying perfectly still, doesn't move an eyelash. The doe, white flag flying, bounds off a few yards, stops in the high waving oats and watches us.

The scene is rare and beautiful. The old, weathered posts holding up the barbed wire fence, the contrast of pale green oats heading out with the lush alfalfa, the high water grasses dividing the two fields, the sunset-tinted sky, the cool mountains, breathing so close, the nearby hills (where Daisy and I are headed)...and the silence. Broken only by the caw of a crow, and the rushing water in the irrigation ditch. The sights and smells of a prairie, which, in evening after a hot day, is magical.

I decide to complete the route taken so often before my horse wreck. Can I do it? Once the decision is made, Daisy and I must overcome obstacles, like how to cross a deep irrigation ditch. A board placed there earlier in the spring has been swept away by high water. I find the board and, using my good arm, make another foot bridge. We cross.

The holes in the fences, worn by the cattle, have been mended by Hough's hired man. We must walk down each fence row until we find a rock jack to climb over. Obstacles overcome. Like life. We do it! And emerge victorious at the base of the hill. How often these past weeks I have thought about the lupine blooming there, mingled with sage and yarrow, and mature cheat grass.

Daisy is ecstatic. She runs from badger hole to squirrel hole, she swims in the ditch we are following, she rolls in the crooked cow path that leads up the draw. We enter another field through a wire gate, and in that ditch we startle a wild mallard hen and her young. Hough's Angus cows graze placidly, and stare silently at us. We amble past stack yards full of bread loaf hay, fragrant in evening cool. The sun is setting. Long streaks of golden light fall upon the prairie. In a pool of water left by flood irrigation, I spot a lone lesser yellow legs. What a thrill. I was drawn to the rare bird by its call.

Walking slowly home, I pondered as I often do, about how these ranches provide a haven for wildlife, and for us who love them. These peaceful open spaces, where hay grows, where pastures provide fodder for grazing livestock, where families struggle to eke out a living. How long will it last? In a world driven by the dollar, how long will it last? In the end we must think of what is best for the land. Right now it is in good hands. What does the future hold?

Must get this in the mail so I can watch grandchildren in the Chief Joseph Junior parade this morning. I hope that in next week's column I can report becoming a great-grandma!

August 5—It's a boy! On the last day of July my great-grandson, a healthy, bright-eyed babe, was welcomed into our large family. Clayton Lauchland, weighing 8 lbs, 2 oz. Those oft-repeated statistics carried over miles of phone line connecting myriad aunts, uncles, cousins and others of Clayton's extended family. Welcome to our world, my child. We up here in the far corner of Eastern Oregon can't wait to hold you.

Daughter Lori and family drove over from Pendleton that last weekend in July to spend Chief Joseph Days with us. We managed to take in several events, which included the Shriner's and Chamber of Commerce breakfasts, the big parade, the Sunday rodeo, the Christian cowboy church service held in the rodeo arena, and the Indian dances.

The breakfast, now held on the site of the now dismantled Boise Cascade mill yard, gives us busy Wallowa Countians a chance to socialize with friends and neighbors. While we enjoy a hardy breakfast of steak, eggs and pancakes, listen to Wanda Sorweide play the organ, gaze at our familiar mountains, we all remember the mill that used to employ many of our locals. Not so long ago, but the one thing in life that is for sure is that everything changes.

Like these breakfasts, which used to be held outside on Main Street Joseph, where today another mini-mall, "Hurricane Creek Plaza," is going up. Our young people are now employed at other jobs. The lucky ones found jobs here; others had to move out of the county. So, where large stacks of logs once stood and gave off their familiar pine scent, we ate our outdoor breakfast and took time from our busy schedules to visit. It seems during our hectic Wallowa County summers we ranching families never have much time to socialize. Chief Joseph Days provides that opportunity.

After the big parade on Saturday, we ambled up and down Joseph's Main Street, noticing mini-reunions taking place along the sidewalks. Actually, a person could stand in one spot and wait, and sooner or later an old friend or acquaintance would happen by. Then, after much handshaking, hugging, joke-telling and laughing, the recounting of experiences would ensue.

We ran into family here and there, having recognized daughter Jackie riding her horse with the 1975 Chief Joseph Days court; granddaughter Chelsie throwing water from the Enterprise FFA float; and grandson Buck riding his horse with the Imnaha Rodeo Club entry. Grandchildren, recognizing us through the throngs of tourists, ran up for hugs. Neighboring ranchers, dressed in clean shirts and jeans, smiled and waved as we passed on the street. It is always the best part of the celebration, meeting up with familiar, dear faces.

On Saturday afternoon, son-in-law Tom and grandson Ryan and I attended the Nez Perce ceremonial dances, which were held on the Joseph High School football field. It was a cold afternoon and clouds scurried across the face of Chief Joseph Mountain and a cold wind blew the eagle feather headdresses and fringed buck-skin leggings of the Nez Perce as they danced to the steady beat of the drum. A very inspiring sight, one I never tire of. Always admiring the fact that these people are keeping their culture alive.

Thanks to elders such as Horace Axtell, and others like him, the Nez Perce traditions are being perpetuated, so the younger generations will have the opportunity to carry them on. As I've often mentioned, I admire greatly the way these people respect and learn from their elders, and the way they treat their young, loving them and letting them be children.

Along that line, I must quote a letter received recently from a friend, Cora Stubblefield, who is the postmaster of the little post office in Monument, Oregon. Cora writes that she is sorry to hear of my accident, and wanted to comment on my column in which I wrote about "family," the theme of our past summer Fishtrap Writer's conference.

Cora writes, *How wrong some families are, in these times. Our family has very strong ties. We have had a real shocker. July 12 my husband, George, was diagnosed as having acute leukemia. It's been hard, but, as you said, in a family crisis, the five grown children and prayers support us and keep us going.*

The one thing I don't like in this modern world is that children are not allowed to be little kids. They force them to grow up too soon. Also parents and teachers aren't the role models that I grew up with. Having had Craig Lesley and George Venn as visitors in our home, I know what you are saying about them. They have both been very helpful to our youngest son, Robert, who is working on a novel.

Having had the pleasure of meeting Cora's son Robert at past Fish-traps, and knowing he has since received his MFA from the University of Montana, I wish him luck. Am looking forward to seeing your first novel in print, Robert.

We need these voices from Eastern Oregon. Another letter from a fan, Claudine Smith:

Hi! I'm an 83-year-old grass seed farmer's wife, who has been a fan of yours for a number of years now. I enjoy your column in Agri-Times so much, but just never had the nerve to tell you...until you spoke of laboriously using your left hand, that did it. Nine years ago I had a stroke on my right side and since have to do everything with my left hand, hence the poor writing, but I'm thankful for what I can do.

Well, I thought you wrote beautifully, Claudine. She goes on to say they are family-oriented, too. This past year they had their 100-plus-year-old farm house remodeled on the inside to retain the historical value. Her husband, John, was born there, and so was his father. Their daughter, Carolyn, and family moved there from Portland, so the farm place will stay in the family. *Please keep up the column,* she writes, *We love it.* Thanks, Claudine, and all you other people out there who continue to inspire me.

Doug and crew are busy every day now, tearing down an old shed near our potato cellars in Joseph. The raspberries show no mercy and continue to ripen. My childhood chum Sandra, who drove up from California this week, is at the moment picking them. We have been freezing berries and making batches of freezer jam, so much it almost resembles Knott's Berry Farm in our kitchen. We also water the gardens, which seem to be enduring the intense heat of August.

Yesterday we took a carload of grandchildren up to Wallowa Lake for a promised treat at Russell's, followed by swimming and fishing; then returned to cook a large dinner for the demolition crew. It was so hot that by day's end yours truly was fading fast. Our county fair begins today, and the Tippet family reunion, held here this year, is next weekend.

Good old summer-time. Sandra and I go for walks in the cool of evening and morning, and catch up on our lives, which, we agree, in our retirement years seem to be more complicated than when we were rearing our children. Such are the "golden years."

Friend Bill, recovering from his recent surgery, is back in his cabin on Alder Slope. Son Todd and his two sons, Josh and James, will pack in with horses to Francis Lake this weekend. Those two happy little boys were so excited yesterday, that's all they could talk about. Sure hope they bring me some fish. Wish I could stow away with them.

On the first day of August, Linde drove me to La Grande for another x-ray. Then that evening I was scheduled to judge the photography section of the Union County Fair.

Granddaughter Lacey called from Hermiston this afternoon to tell us she received a blue ribbon for her lamb at the Umatilla County Fair.

Yesterday it was the monthly meeting of our Fishtrap board, held in our front yard here at the ranch. It was very pleasant out under the trees and it didn't rain until the meeting was over!

The Tippetts will arrive for the weekend beginning tomorrow. This reunion, planned by the younger generation, should be fun. Hope it doesn't rain. Such is the summer of '95.

August 11—Never go far from your jacket. We who live in Wallowa County generally learn this from experience, which is the best teacher. One might add, never go into the back country without rain gear, even if, when you leave the trail head, it is a searing 85 degrees. My youngest son, Todd, and his two young sons, Josh, 14, and James, 9, were tired and hot by the time they drove up the long Lostine canyon road to the jumping off place for their long horseback ride into remote Francis Lake, in the rugged Eagle Cap Wilderness.

With a nine-mile ride before them, they proceeded to pack their gear onto a pack horse, taking jackets but not rain gear. After all, the skies were clear, it was hot, and it was August. The "dry" month, the best month to camp in the high lakes.

Upon reaching Francis Lake late that Saturday afternoon, they set up camp and went directly to fishing. Their luck was good, that first night was mild, and their long-awaited trip was proving to be worth the time and effort it took to get there. Another party left when they arrived, so the father and sons had the lake to themselves. Not many hikers and backpackers make it all the way into this wild lake.

I had taken son Todd on a similar two-day pack trip to Francis Lake when he was a young boy. He never forgot it. The unspoiled beauty of the place, its nearby peaks, clear, sparkling lake, and mostly the fishing, remained in his memory over the intervening years. A snapshot of my

10-year-old son holding a native Eastern Brook trout, which he had caught himself in that cold lake, reposes on my dresser to this day. It was only natural that he should one day return with his sons.

It was all they had hoped for. They watched Rocky Mountain goats feeding high above them on the rugged steep slopes of the high divide that separates Francis Lake from LeGore Lake. They cooked their freshly-caught trout on a camp stove, and watched the stars come out in a crystalline sky.

On Sunday night they crawled into their sleeping bags that last night of their campout, pulled a large tarp over them and slept the sleep of tired, happy campers. On Monday morning I awoke here on Prairie creek to look out at a cloudy sky. Then around 6 a.m. the overcast skies let loose with a cold, steady rain. Temperatures plummeted. My eyes sought out the Wallowas, which were cloaked in cold mist. I knew it would be snowing at Francis Lake.

I was a worried mother and grandmother. I had been there, and knew how high the country was and how the horses would have to be gathered in a blizzard. The wind was now blowing with such force that the corn stalks in Doug's garden were bent over. Because they had only one pack animal, my son and his sons had packed only the barest of necessities, which didn't include rain gear.

Upon awakening to that downpour of cold rain, Todd did what only a father could do. As the three were soon soaked to the skin and freezing, he told the boys that they would have to move and keep moving, or they would die. That revelation scared them into action and they helped catch horses, saddle, pack, and leave the lake, pronto.

By this time it had begun to snow. Not just a summer storm, but a fall blizzard. Visibility was reduced and the boys and Todd were freezing, with a rugged ridge to ride over and a steep, unprotected high trail to descend. The frozen trio walked, leading their horses, those first eight miles, until the snow turned to rain; only then did they mount their horses.

James told me later, "Boy, grandma, the heater in dad's pickup sure felt good." And grandma sure felt good when she learned her loved ones had made it safely out of the mountains. Except for a few sore muscles, all three seemed to have survived the ordeal quite well. Methinks rain gear will always be a priority on future trips into the wilderness.

When last I wrote, we were dealing with summer's heat. Now we are wearing jackets to the fair! Sandra, who has been cleaning house (seriously), has been such a blessing. Never has my house shone with waxed floors, clean windows and washed rugs all at one time. Especially not during the busy month of August.

Doug has been berry, berry busy. Not only has he been tearing down a building, but berry picking. Last Sunday he drove to the upper Imnaha and came home with huckleberries, then turned around and drove clear down to Pack Saddle Creek to pick blackberries. Between the raspberries, which won't quit ripening, and the gooseberries in the garden, we are nearly berried in berries.

Because Sandra and I have been so busy lately, we decided to take a day to play. We rode the Wallowa Lake Tramway to the top of Mt. Howard on that first clear day after the storm. Fresh snow on the high peaks had vanished, but large snowbanks from last winter still dotted the high ridges. As we rode a gondola car up the steep rise to the 8,250-foot summit, we glimpsed rushing waterfalls on the opposite mountains. Sandra marveled at this first-time trip, gazing down on the lovely, glacial-carved lake that glimmered far below.

After unloading at the summit, we hiked trails to various overlooks, from which we could view breathtaking sights. One such sight led our eyes downward toward the checkerboard valley where lay Prairie Creek, its green belt winding through folds in the hills. Willows lined irrigation ditches, and we searched for, and found, our ranch.

From another view point we gazed across at the vast, rugged peaks that form the chain of the Eagle Cap Wilderness Wallowas—Sacajawea, Chief Joseph Mountain, the Matterhorn, and far-off Ruby Peak. It was a glorious, clear morning. Colorful wild flowers, such as mountain heather bells, Indian paintbrush and penstemon, greeted us, wetted by melting snow-banks. After our walk, we sat near the snack bar and gazed out at the mountain tops, so close, and ate our sack lunches while chipmunks and golden-mantled squirrels, their cheeks fat with peanuts, cavorted about the area.

The weather was perfect: not too warm, nor too cool. The day was made for us. On our return ride we glided down the mountain to the lake, where we found our car and drove back to Joseph. In the peaceful setting of Tom Swanson's Deli, we sipped a cold drink and treated ourselves to a nectarine and peach torte, which Tom talked us into sampling, after which Tom gave us a personal tour of the newly opened wildlife exhibit, which is beautifully done. For those who will never get into the wilderness, this exhibit, which is a privately owned collection, affords an opportunity to view wildlife in their natural surroundings. It is most impressive.

Sandra and I are still making raspberry jam and trying to keep up with the zucchini, peas, beans and beets. Our county fair is in full swing, and I drove to the fairgrounds in Enterprise almost daily to watch my many grandchildren show their animals. As usual, I am very proud of all their efforts as well as those of their parents, who support them. Many hours put in by volunteer 4-H leaders and vo-ag instructors and parents are paying off.

If you want your faith restored in our youth, attend a county fair. It is always gratifying to visit with old-time fair-goers like Chuck Gavin, retired extension agent, and Hazel Johnson, who support and enjoy watching yet another crop of youngsters show their stuff.

August 18—Our porch thermometer registered a frosty 32 degrees this morning. Green beans and squash got nipped, but the zucchini and corn seem to have escaped any visible damage. The wildflower patch, revived by recent rains and thunderstorms, has taken on new life. Bachelor buttons are especially vivid this bright, clear morning. For several days we haven't seen much of the sun, and jackets are a must, but I refuse to start a fire in the wood stove. It is, after all, SUMMER!

So, here I sit at my word processor, wearing a jacket in the middle of August.

Ben and Seth swathed one field of grain hay and began cutting a second, when the skies clouded up. There are numerous fields of beautiful grain hay down around Prairie Creek, and we are all hoping for a warm breeze and some sunshine to dry things out. Already there is a familiar feeling of fall in the air. It's more than the crispness which comes with early frost; it's an elusive, undefinable something, to those of us in tune with the seasons.

Perhaps it's the blackbirds flocking together, or the sounds of wild honkers V'ing overhead every morning and evening now. Or the redness of rose hips, adorning bushes whose stems were so recently covered with pale pink petals. Maybe it's the clarity of the rain-washed air, the sight of apples weighing down branches of old gnarled trees in abandoned orchards scattered all over the country, or the ripening of the wild berries: huckleberry, blackberry, thimbleberry, grouse whortleberry, elderberry, and gooseberry. At any rate, summer seems gone and autumn beginning.

Down in the calving pasture, the first-calf fall calvers are nearly calved out. The newborns, their bellies full of milk, frolic in green grass, as opposed to our March babies, whose mothers birth them, wet and steaming, upon the snow. Up on the high east moraine of Wallowa Lake, the old cows are nearly through calving too. Their off-spring grow healthy and strong, due to abundant milk produced by their dams as a result of a bumper grass crop growing all during this wet, cool summer.

All this is in juxtaposition to last year when drought conditions created sparse dry grasses, and dust raised in the fields and along the country roads was baled into the hay. Forest fires raged in Hells Canyon, and in our hills and forest. What a different summer! But not different in that August is always hectic, rain or shine. My childhood chum Sandra found out just how busy the summer can be. Especially during fair, which was also the weekend of our Tippett family reunion. August is always the time of ripening. Raspberries, peas, squash, beans, beets, cabbage must be put by for winter. From-morning until nightfall we were on the run. Doug and crew were gone all day tearing down the large shed at the potato cellars, so we always had a hot meal on the table when he returned.

Thanks to Sandra, we emerged sane, and even managed to have fun coping with each new daily crisis. My shoulder continues to heal, due in large part to spending hours in therapy.

On Saturday of the family reunion, we hurriedly accomplished obligations here on the ranch, and Doug left early to go elk hunting in the hills. It was opening morning of his landowner-preference tag hunt!

Sandra and I headed for the fair in time to see the pee wee showmanship class. After granddaughter Adele showed her lamb, we ran over to the dog showmanship class, being held outside on the lawn, in time to watch grandson Buck show his dog. Along with poodles, cockers, and you name it, there was our Buck leading his cow dog, King, around the ring. Later that day, we learned that Buck won the championship in intermediate dog obedience with King. The 4-H dog project is one of the fastest growing projects in our county, and these young people do a fine job of training their pets.

Since it was noon, we joined the throngs at the food booth and ordered a famous fair hamburger, served up by volunteer 4-H members and leaders. After which we were further entertained by more grandchildren who were participating in the lamb, pig and chicken scrambles, wheelbarrow races, and an egg toss. For us grandmothers, it is a time to watch our offspring's offspring have fun at the fair.

After a week spent grooming, working with and showing their animals, that last day is set aside for fun and games. Amazingly I was able to pick out granddaughters Chelsie, Becky and Adele and grandsons James, Josh and Rowdy among the crowds of youngsters.

The lamb scramble was hilarious. Five wild, leaping lambs were turned out of a trailer to flee in front of a herd of youngsters, who bore down upon them, brandishing halters. When the tanbark dust cleared, five rumpled children emerged, dragging their lambs to the appointed corral. Same deal with five squealing piglets, which, at first, were oblivious to their fate. Chickens crowed, flew and fled. Feathers and dust mingled, and tattered children appeared from the melee clutching squawking fowl of every description. It was bedlam, and a standing-room-only crowd of relatives and friends cheered the youngsters on. Such is the energy of youth.

Volunteer leaders, my eldest son included, who had helped organize the activities were showing signs of wear after a week of fair…but not too much wear to join in the fun. When the last feather settled and the last squeal faded away, Sandra and I looked at our watches. It was 3 o'clock. We were a bit sheepish as we drove back to the ranch. After all, the family reunion was scheduled for 4 o'clock! Not to worry. The visiting Tippetts had everything under control.

They began arriving bearing steaks, freshly picked corn on the cob, new potatoes, tomatoes, french bread, salads, green beans, and one family, who owned an ice-cream parlor, brought a tub of fresh huckleberry ice cream. That had been the understanding. We would supply the place and they would supply the food.

Doug, who elk-less returned from Salmon Creek, had set up bar-becues, a sheepherder stove and picnic tables. By 6 o'clock everyone began lining up for the feast. The sky clouded up, the wind began to blow, rain drops spit upon the hot briquettes, and the family bundled up. No matter, nearly 50 people enjoyed visiting and eating. Mothers with small children fled to the warmth of the house, while boys and men and the not-so-young shot off potato guns and drank cowboy coffee. Camp trailers filled our bull pasture, and every bed in the house was filled with bodies. Others left for local motels.

The next morning was grand. Bright sunshine brought the mountains into clear focus, and children ran around enjoying the ranch. There was a great picking of raspberries, horseshoe pitching, and kitten taming. Not to mention hiking, horse petting, and chicken scrambling. Bob and Wayne Tippett presided over the breakfast of sourdough hotcakes, sausages and eggs, which was cooked outside and eaten on the lawn. While family reminisced and poured through family albums, others got re-acquainted. Everyone was reluctant to leave.

My chickens settled down after the last child left, and Daisy came out of hiding as the last relatives were leaving. It was a wonderful reunion, and yours truly had little to do but be hospitable, which was easy with such nice people.

Sandra drove south early Monday morning, and although I missed her immediately, I was far too busy to dwell on it.

Most of that day was spent with five grandchildren. We baked a birthday cheesecake for one of the daddies, picked raspberries, and went fishing over the hill. At day's end, after the children returned to their homes, it was as if summer had vanished. The fair was over, the reunion was history, and all the myriad activities that cram a Wallowa County August were coming to a close.

This week has flown, and here it is Friday again, and I'm just now finding time to do this column. Perhaps things will slow down a bit...but I wouldn't bet on it.

August 24—It is a fat time in Wallowa County now. Apples and berries continue to ripen, as do those vegetable gardens that escaped the recent frosts. Down in the canyons of the Imnaha, the sweet corn is ready, and Doug purchased a bag of fresh ears this week from Jerry and Myrna Witherite, who always have a very productive garden. Nothing compares to the sweetness experienced by that first juicy bite of freshly-picked corn. It is like tasting summer.

I have finally finished "putting by" the raspberries. Neighbor Glenna Isley came by the other morning and picked a bucket full. The rest are up for grabs, or offered to the robins, which have taken up permanent residence in the patch. The half-grown kittens alternate their time between the back porch, the raspberry patch, and the hay stack on the hill. Their energetic old Calico mother faithfully hunts the fields, dragging her daily catch of gophers to her lazy kittens. Ben and his family have been busy between thundershowers, trying to get the grain hay up.

Every rancher here on Prairie Creek stopped in the middle of baling yesterday afternoon, when a sudden rainstorm, accompanied by flashes of lighting and peals of thunder, came racing over the valley. Mother Nature is the only one who can bring hard-working men to a complete halt!

We did experience a few days of familiar August heat before our cool summer reappeared. Today is flattish again, with leftover clouds floating in a hazy blue sky. A breeze that is almost cold wanders over Prairie creek, which still resembles June more than late August. Since the trails into the high country have been opened, I have been hearing reports from friends about how lovely the back country is, especially Hurricane Creek, which is one of my favorite places to hike. It has been very frustrating for one who longs for a bit of wilderness now and then.

So, last weekend, I fixed myself a sandwich, filled my water bottle, beckoned to my faithful Daisy, and drove up to the Hurricane Creek trailhead. Earlier in the year, before my accident, I had ordered a small dog pack for Daisy. The day before this hike, I had buckled the light pack on her back and went for a short walk around the ranch. Daisy seemed not to mind the thing and it fit perfectly.

After tucking my sandwich in one pocket and the water bottle on the other side of my little pack animal, I zipped up the pack and we were off up the trail. Not having to carry a daypack across my tender collarbone was nice, and just as my informants had said, there was green everywhere, wildflowers were still blooming, snowmelt seeped down every draw, and large snowbanks clung to shaded clefts among the highest peaks.

We crossed over Falls Creek, walking gingerly over a series of logs that previous hikers had placed, then continued on up the worn trail, which follows the winding course of Hurricane Creek. Rushing white water filled my vision, clear, sharp air filled my lungs, and I suddenly felt stronger. After a steep climb, I paused to rest where I could look down upon the tumbling creek and gaze ahead at my favorite mountain, Sacajawea.

There I met a most interesting gentleman, who, like me, loved hiking the high Wallowas. He was from La Grande, he said, and drove over often to climb his favorite trails. We had such a good time talking about where each of us had been, and recounting our experiences over the years. Often, I think, people who meet on these trails share a common bond, forming an instant kinship with each other. A shared joy of having experienced wild, quiet beauty. It is a very special thing. Although this fellow was in his 70s, years of outdoor life appeared to have prolonged his youth.

We parted as he went on ahead at a faster pace, while Daisy and I took our time. Later I glimpsed him across Hurricane Creek, near the Thorpe Creek trail. He had taken off his hiking boots, put on waders, and forded the cold waters so he could hike up to the Thorpe Creek basin. We had both talked about this being a good access to Sacajawea. A huge fallen tree had spanned Hurricane Creek there for years, but last winter's snowmelt thaw had finally swept it down-stream, and with it, taken the only crossing.

Not feeling up to making the cold crossing barefoot, Daisy and I made the loop from the Thorpe Creek trail and joined the main trail again, which led to Slick Rock. The day was warming up fast, and this was, after all, my first long hike since my injury. I decided not to push my luck, and we turned around before the final climb to where Slick Rock Creek joins Hurricane Creek.

Daisy and I made our way back slowly, pausing often to rest. We passed through a sunny meadow and stopped at Deadman Creek, where we could gaze up at the still snow-pocked chasms of Sacajawea. Good thing my sandwich was wrapped in a plastic bag, because my faithful little pack animal laid down there in the creek to cool off!

Sitting there on a large fallen log, I ate my lunch, sharing some with Daisy, who, after all, packed it in for me. Yellow cinquefoil, orange Indian paintbrush, and wild purple asters stirred in a cool breeze that wandered over the adjacent meadow. The trickling waters of Deadman Creek were soothing, and looking far above in the direction of a small, high lake of the same name, I could see water cascading down in a thin white stream.

Quite often Deadman is dry by mid-August, so there aren't any waterfalls, but this year high snow banks are still melting and it was a delight to see. I had remembered, in my mind's eye, the steep talus slopes, and the stark, rugged beauty of the barren Hurricane Divide. A wild, unspoiled sight, one that gives me strength.

I met friends on the trail. One gal, on horse-back, had shared other high lake adventures with me. When Daisy and I returned much later to the trailhead, I was hot and weary, but still somehow renewed. We had stopped to rest on a high grassy bank above the rushing creek. Under several tall tamarack trees that provided shade, I lay on my back, resting upon a bed of kinnikinnick and wild strawberry, and contemplated those trees.

Trees teach us patience. They stand tall, never moving from one place to another, living out their lives in one spot, enduring all seasons, especially the freezing cold of our Wallowa County winters. Now they appeared happy, sighing in the breeze, with clean, pure air cleansing their boughs. Through their green canopy of needles, I glimpsed a patch of pure blue sky. Suddenly, all was right with my world.

Back home I took a long nap and awoke refreshed. Hopefully, I can work in more of these restoring hikes during our long, lovely Indian summer. Doug and crew have finally finished tearing down the old potato shed, and the equipment auction is scheduled for September 14. Then, perhaps, Doug will have time for some long-deserved R. and R., fishing and grouse-hunting.

During August's golden twilight hours, Daisy and I take walks along our country road. A couple of evenings ago, as we were returning to the ranch, a shaft of light broke between dark rain clouds, just long enough to create a fragment of a rainbow. It was as though a giant bar had been thrust into Hough's hill, a vivid rainbow bar. The "bow" was lost in cloud. A dark wavering line of honkers flew cross the bar, and soon they too dissolved in cloud.

August 31—The chill of this late August morning is wearing off and being replaced by the season's warmth. The hot, high altitude sun warms the cold zucchinis growing under their lush squash foliage. It awakens the last of the Icelandic poppies and bachelor buttons, and unfurls the California poppies, which continue to give me joy as autumn approaches.

The land relaxes as September nears, as though the frantic activity previously performed upon its fields, pastures and gardens is nearly over. How it must look forward, like many of us, to the slower pace and rest of winter. Ben, who shows the strain of responsibility and back-breaking work, also looks more relaxed. It was good to see him at the annual Stockgrowers' dinner-dance last Saturday night, holding his pretty blond wife, Jackie, mother of their four children, against him, dancing around the floor of Cloverleaf Hall.

Doug and I joined Jack and Marge McClaran and Biden and Betty Tippett for a most delicious steak dinner. In addition to the traditional steak and taters, we attempted to sample many of the other gourmet offerings served up by the caterer and the cowboy, Sheryl and Ken Roberts, which included ham, carved by the cowboy; many salads, condiments, an old trunk filled with homemade breads; jams, jellies, fruits, beans, and myriad vegetables prepared with fresh herbs; and, for dessert, huge strawberries drizzled with both white and dark chocolate.

The cowboy theme ran through the artfully arranged food, and it was almost too beautiful to eat. It was so much fun just to walk around, taking it all in visually, like digesting wonderful artwork, which, in fact, it was. We did justice to the food, visited, and then attempted to dance it off. By 9 o'clock I began to fade, and by 10 the coach turned into a pumpkin, so we returned to the ranch, leaving the younger cowboys and cowgirls to carry on.

At one point during the evening's festivities, which included the awarding of the Grassman and Cattleman of the Year, Jack McClaran turned to Doug and remarked, "How many years have we been coming to these things?"

I would wager it would be quite a few indeed.

Jack watched as the Grassman of the Year was awarded to his son, Scott, and the Cattleman of the Year winner, Sonny Hagenah, of Lostine, walked up to receive his trophy. Down through the years many local stockgrowers have received these annual awards. Many have passed on, and it seems each year the crowd is thinner. There aren't as many young people taking the old folks' places. A few, but mostly they see how hard their parents have worked, and sought different occupations. Also they see the changes and challenges as a bit overwhelming, especially when they can take an 8-5 job, have a vacation once in awhile, benefits for their families, and avoid the risks involved in ranching and farming.

But then I looked around and saw that there were, indeed, some young ones who are dedicated and willing to sacrifice to continue a way of life they love, and all of us in agriculture here in Wallowa County continue to carry on for our way of life. It certainly isn't for outstanding profit. Not with the risk-taking gambles with the weather, market, and outside forces working against us. The young ones who survive will have to be creative, thrifty and flow with the times to stay in business. I applaud all who continue to accept this challenge being posed by the '90s. Go for it.

Another reason I was fading was that it had been a long day. Which really began the night before at a social evening at Pat and Judy Wortman's ranch home out of Enterprise. Another traditional stockgrowers' get-together, where all of us producers of livestock relax and recount the busy summer season in an informal atmosphere, outside on Pat and Judy's porch and patio. Everyone brings favorite finger food and we sort of graze around the tables loaded with tasty tidbits and try not to gorge ourselves. Actually, we are getting in training for the next day, which ends with the above described meal in Cloverleaf Hall.

Saturday morning finds all of us seated in the VFW Hall in Enterprise breakfasting on the VFW ladies' eggs, hash browns, sausages and hot biscuits. Then, still seated, we listen to the state of affairs of those of us who raise the food to feed the masses, which seems to deal more with the salvation of salmon than of beef. But let me tell you, the salvation of salmon has much to do with the salvation of beef. I won't go into that here, as all you have to do is pick up any publication these days and read of the continuing story.

Like I said, the challenges of the '90s cannot be taken lightly. They aren't going to go away, and must be dealt with. Kudos to those who have fought the good fight. We can't thank you enough, you people who attend myriad meetings, defending our way of life, like our Oregon State Cattlemen's Association president, Mack Birkmaier, who took his Crow Creek expertise to high places and affected change.

And his wife, Marian, who typed his letters, supported his efforts, and many times accompanied him all over the country these past two years. But Marian will be glad to have her husband back. Bet she misses those years out on quiet Crow Creek, when she and Mack were rearing their family and tending those cows, on their land and on public land.

Thanks to Mack and others like him, those cattle are still allowed to graze the public lands here in Northeastern Oregon, as they have for years.

What would our national forests be without a few "slow elk" wandering around, cleaning up the grasses and growing big, healthy calves so our city cousins can enjoy a steak over Labor Day? Think about it.

At noon we CattleWomen found ourselves at the Wallowa Lake Lodge, just like old times, attending our annual luncheon meeting. It was another gourmet meal. Oh my! Such a selection of mouth-watering buffet. I so enjoyed visiting past Oregon State CowBelles presidents Fern Wolfe and Marilyn Johnson of Wallowa, and seeing faces I haven't had time to see all during our long, busy summer. It is gratifying to see a young CattleWoman, Angie Ketscher, going in as Wallowa County CattleWomen president. Angie and husband Ross are among the younger generation of ranchers in Wallowa County.

Yesterday Doug, Wolfgang (Wolf) Moser and I made sauerkraut out of the cabbages I planted, before I got bucked off, in Bill's garden. In less than an hour from the time we cut them in the garden, the shredded cabbage was layered with salt and beginning the fermenting process in large crocks. Doug carried the crocks down into our basement this morning, and in a week I will check them to see how they are coming.

Wolf, who is from Germany, loved being part of the kraut-making this year. When I was laid up, he and wife, Sally, went up to the Alder Slope garden and hoed around the cabbages for me. Using my old kraut cutter, Wolf shredded 15 heads, while Doug washed and cut the cabbages into halves and cored them. It was a lovely afternoon, and the fall feeling in the air made it a pleasant task, performed under the shade of our willow tree in the yard.

This weekend we plan to escape to the upper Imnaha country and partake of a little relaxation and recreation, and pretend we are senior citizens enjoying our golden years.

September 7—A light rain that began falling in the night has continued throughout the day. And now in late afternoon a cool breeze begins to sweep away the thick wet clouds and trailing mists, which hover over the mountain tops. As this misty mirage disappears, I run to my kitchen window and let my gaze wander up toward the McCully Creek basin where I know it will be like winter, and see that I am right. Our backcountry is covered over with a blanket of early snow. Chief Joseph Mountain comes out of hiding, its massive skyline also painted white. Does this mean an early winter?

Wild geese continue to fly across our flaming autumn sunset skies in large V's, honking their way south. Noisy blackbirds cover power lines along our country roads. Row after row of them blacken the fences. Then, acting as one body, these birds swoop, circle and glide before alighting in our hayfields to feed upon grasshoppers and other insects.

Doug's garden continues to bear prolifically. While we were gone during the Labor Day weekend, the zucchini grew to gigantic proportions and Early Sunglow corn began to ripen on the stalks.

Golden jars of canned Alberta peaches cover my kitchen table, alongside three gallons of garlic dill pickles. Seven-day sweet pickles are doing their thing in a crock on the kitchen floor, and the sauerkraut is fermenting in two large crocks downstairs.

Using the leftover ripe peaches, I baked a fresh cobbler yesterday. How I enjoy the fall of the year, which is the time of "putting food by" for winter, when all the delicious, nostalgic smells drift through my kitchen and fill my senses, as well as those of the visitors who happen by when I am pickling, canning or baking. To me it is not work, but rather a privilege, especially since now I can use my arm again, with only a minimum of discomfort.

The other day as I was in the midst of dill pickles, I answered a knock at our back door. There stood Eddie Wallace, grinning. "I'm here to catch the old hens," he said. Since my young Barred Rock pullets are really into laying now, there is no sense in feeding these older hens, especially since most of them have quit laying. As in the past, the stew pot is their ultimate fate. Last year Eddie and wife, Carol, who live out north, turned them into chicken 'n' dumplings, which is one of Eddie's favorite dishes.

Doug, who had left earlier that morning to cut a load of firewood for our Monarch range, came driving in just as Eddie and I were in the middle of the "hen catching."

One of my banty hen's youngsters, a small gray rooster with feathers on his legs, became very excited when he found himself surrounded by squawking hens, and proceeded to fly to the top of our high chicken wire fence...where he hesitated only a moment before trying out his wings to fly completely over the pen. Meanwhile, Daisy, whose chief occupation around here, besides taking walks with me, is to sit outside the chicken pen and salivate at all those "birds," took off after the hapless rooster.

The little fellow fled to the safety of the garden, where he should have stayed, but instead he decided to slip through the hog wire garden fence and disappear into the woodshed. Daisy was right there to grab him. Small gray feathers clung to the jaws of my little dog's mouth as I convinced her this was NOT helping me catch hens. After being released from the Jaws of Death, the squawking rooster quit the flats and disappeared over the nearest hill.

When the ten hens were all caught and put into Eddie's wire cage in the back of his pickup, and actually driving off down the road, I searched in vain for my bewildered bird. Later that afternoon, I tied Daisy to the yard fence and let my pullets out to eat grass and fluff in the raspberry patch dirt.

That evening when the young hens went in to roost, I found the small, shaken rooster snuggled next to his little banty mom! Meanwhile, Chester, who will be entered in the Great Rooster Crowing contest at Weston, Oregon, Pioneer Days next spring, got in lots of practice for the upcoming event. My goodness! He must've crowed 50 times during the disruptive reduction of his harem.

Doug and I enjoyed a marvelous three-day Labor Day holiday, relaxing on the upper Imnaha River. We secured a camping area away from other campers, next to the woods, where we were right above the river with a picnic table and fireplace under some giant ponderosa pines. Due to our cool summer the upriver grasses were still green, and there was an absence of the usual late summer dust. Weather-wise we couldn't have asked for a nicer three days in a row.

It was pretty hard to take. Huckleberry sourdough pancakes cooked on a sheepherder stove every morning, and lazy afternoons reading a good book, as I took Craig Lesley's *Sky Fisherman* along. Sleeping in our mini-motor home with the sound of the rushing Imnaha in our ears. Sitting around the campfire in the evenings and moonlit nights. Cooking fresh garden produce and grilling steaks outside for supper. Enjoying the company of two good friends, Bud and Ruby Zollman of Joseph. We picked huckleberries way up high, past McGraw, in a place we just happened onto, and took long drives looking over the country, including taking in the view of Hells Canyon from the new scenic overlook.

We drove out toward P.O. Saddle and looked down at the backwaters of Hells Canyon Dam; gazed down from Saulsberry Saddle to the breaks of the Snake. Awesome country. Big country. Indian paintbrush and purple penstemon still colored the high, rocky ridge tops, where we saw nary a grouse. We drove over a rough road to read a weathered sign which told of Bonneville's crossing there in 1833, one hundred years before we were born! We tried to envision that weary, cold and hungry expedition in such rugged, unforgiving country, caught in winter.

Mainly though, what I love in this vast canyon country is its silence, a commodity that is fast becoming scarce. Silence and open space. Out there on those lonely ridges which form the breaks of the Snake, there are miles of open space and acres of silence, and unpeopled places that stretch to the horizon from any direction you may choose to look. And it does this wild heart good. In all of us there beats a wild heart, even if we don't know it. It simply takes a wild sight to unleash it. Those of us who live close to the land know this and that is why we choose to live, continuing to struggle, to preserve our lifestyles here on ranches in the West. It certainly isn't for profit!

Meanwhile, back at the ranch, Ben (bless him) had worked during the holiday and gotten the second cutting alfalfa all baled. He piled the beautiful green bales into a stack before the rains came again. Hopefully, he too will be able to take a little rest this fall, when the work's all done.

And now, the September sun has burst through wet clouds. In Doug's garden a row of colorful sunflowers turn their glistening heads toward its warmth. It is good to be alive.

September 20—Cycle Oregon cycled through on its way to Halfway last week. As these 2,200 pedaling people entered our valley, the local population swelled proportionately. What is it about small towns when they learn big crowds will descend en masse? Such preparations. But then it takes preparation to feed the daily calories required for cyclists pedaling 75 miles per day…especially when you are talking Eastern Oregon terrain. Not to mention altitude.

They spent a night in Joseph, encamped on the high school hill overlooking the town of Joseph and almost able to touch Chief Joseph Mountain. The sight of all those small, colorful tents pitched against the skyline was mind-boggling. Cycle Oregon was treated that night to a gorgeous harvest moon rise over the Seven Devils in Idaho, a cowboy poetry program in the Harley Tucker Memorial arena, and a star-sprinkled clear sky that welcomed a September sunrise. I attended the poetry readings because this grandmother had two grandchildren performing. I plunked myself down in the grandstand and was soon surrounded by cycling multitudes who had shed Lycra for more casual wear and jackets.

Our September days may be warm, but you'd better change into something warm when the sun sinks over the Wallowas. The ones who came in shorts left first, and as the program progressed, the effects of climbing up and over Tollgate, and chugging up Fishtrap Hill out of Elgin began to show. Those tired hikers wanted to crawl into their tents and silently steal away to dreamland…and dream of the 75-mile ride to Halfway, via the loop road, on the morrow.

As a result there weren't many left to hear grandson James and his sister, Adele, do their thing, but this grandma, although she hadn't ridden all those miles on a bike, but had put in a good many on the ranch, stuck it out and stayed until James recited his cowdog poem.

Sitting next to me was a 60-year-old gentleman from a suburb of Portland. He filled me in on Cycle Oregon, which I found fascinating. He said the average age of the participants was over 40, and many were in their 60s, 70s "and over"! He also said after Cycle Oregon '95 was over, Cycle Oregon 96 would be filled in less than a month!

This whole affair was the dream-child of Jonathan Nicholas, who had opened the meeting there that night in the arena. Since I have become acquainted with Jonathan through our Fishtrap Writer's Conference and taken a workshop with him, this proved to be a very interesting revelation to me.

Early the next morning, I jumped into one of the ranch pickups and with my dog Daisy in the back, drove to the end of our county road to watch Cycle Oregon pedal past. Momentarily forgetting I had sauerkraut and pears to can, a column to get in the mail, and housework up to gazoo, I smilingly waved at the cyclists, who all wore smiles too, and waved and honked their little horns, or rang bells on their bikes. How I envied them the route they would take, and their freedom of the open road.

Yesterday, my friend Grace gave me a copy of the Oregonian which had Jonathan Nicholas' column in it wherein he had written about Cycle Oregon "experiencing" rural Eastern Oregon. Jonathan wrote of the "gold coins" encountered on that scenic route that spanned the miles connecting Athena to Fossil.

One quotes, *There was the dawn in Joseph, the sun came up over a valley glowing with pristine promise.* And another, *Time is one thing folks have in rural Oregon. Time to sit out on the front porch and wave as strangers ride by. Time to stop and celebrate a sense of community vast as the landscape we call wonderful, the landscape they call home.* Nice, Jonathan. Full of the gold coins you taught us to use in writing.

And here is me, one of your students, living in that *Valley glowing with pristine promise.* Watching you cycle past, waving, and taking time to get to know you and the other cyclists, who absorbed a bit of our rural culture here in Eastern Oregon. Most, at least the interesting people I met, were impressed that we are all dependent on natural resources, that the health of Eastern Oregon reflects the health of Western Oregon.

Back at the ranch, the Booker Auction Company pulled off our used potato equipment sale in its traditional professional manner. The last of the machinery is being loaded out today. It was a pleasure to meet all the Bookers and a big thank you to Merle's father, who brought us some watermelons and corn from their garden in Washington.

It was a very hot September morning for the auctioneers, who cried their way through the selling of Doug's old trucks. With just a tang of nostalgia, we said goodbye to "Big Red" and "Old Stinky," cumbersome trucks that we gals had to fill with spuds year after year as we sorted on the big, clanking, dirty diggers alongside.

Last weekend I took grandchildren James and Adele camping. It was a promised outing that had been postponed so many times, due first to my injury, then to other conflicting dates, that James was saying it would NEVER happen. But grandma made it happen. First we had to take James to his soccer tournament, purchase some groceries, load the motor home, can the pear butter, and on and on, and on top of everything, I was coming down with a summer cold…and it was hot, very hot.

We finally "got gone" around 2 p.m. and followed Cycle Oregon's route out of the valley, up and over Sheep Creek Hill, turned toward Salt Creek summit and down Gumboot to the Imnaha River. We made it to Ollokot Campground around 3:30 and then everything got easier. We had the entire campground to ourselves, and selected the campsite I had pictured taking the children to when we camped at Ollokot on Labor Day.

Wanting to give the children a real camping experience I didn't fill the water tank at home. I let them pump it from the well there and carry it to our camp. We hunted firewood, cooked over an open fire, and ate outside on a picnic table. We told stories, roasted marshmallows, and fell into bed early that night, happy but tired campers.

The next morning dawned a bit cooler. We slept in and went fishing after breakfast. It did my heart good to watch nine-year-old James cast his fly rod over the Imnaha, and even catch a fish. Mostly though, he could watch the water as it flowed past and listen to the sound of it, absorbing it all, and dream a little without a schedule to adhere to.

Little blond Adele collected rocks and berries, content in that wonderful wild place. I could picture Cycle Oregon passing by here, and wondered how they must have felt experiencing this special place. We took a walk in the deep woods and identified berries and wildflowers, watched two yearling mule deer feed in the meadow next to camp, and took Daisy, who loves to camp too, for walks. We dawdled when it was time to go, not wanting to leave.

Deciding to return to Prairie Creek via the Imnaha River Road, we drove the long miles to the small settlement of Imnaha, where we had a snack at the newly opened Imnaha River Cafe. We were the only ones there, as it was past the lunch hour. Here we recounted the "gold coins" seen on that long trip down the gravel road to Imnaha: the ruffed grouse (brush pheasant) which crossed the road in front of us, the five-point mule deer buck standing in the river to drink far below us, the abandoned homestead shacks and apple trees laden with fruit. And the canyon. And the river. We passed only three vehicles in more than 30 miles.

Because it was Sunday and we thought Daisy deserved a treat, we fed her a hot dog in a bun, right there in the motor home while it was parked next to the restaurant.

The children thought this was pretty hilarious and began to laugh. We laughed a lot that trip. Children need all the laughter they can get these days. We all do.

Doug and I leave for Pendleton this afternoon, that is, if I finish this column in time, to attend the Oregon Cattlemen's convention.

September 29—Taking a breather from pulling beets in the garden this morning, I gazed up toward our ever-present mountains to see old Sawtooth's flanks spotted with new snow. Resembling the color patterns of Paint Indian ponies, other familiar peaks swam in and out of focus, thick layers of snow clouds swirling around the entire Wallowa chain—blue mountain ridges wearing white spots. I recognized Twin Peaks, Ruby Peak, Montana, Howard and, briefly, Chief Joseph Mountain, before the swirling white clouds snatched them from me.

I can envision the cottonwoods beginning to color now along the Upper Imnaha trail, that lovely wild trail that leads to the forks of the Imnaha River. The North Fork is near where I used to cook for Isley's deer camp nearly 20 years ago. The colors will be changing way up there at our old camp on the Middle Fork too, and I remember an October snowfall that painted the peaks white, as seen from my cook tent.

I remember how the sun glittered on the golden cottonwood leaves and trembling aspen thickets, there against that backdrop of snow-dusted peaks. I remember too the warmth of the sheepherder stove in my large cook tent; the happy sound of mules braying at daylight, the sound of hoof beats coming up the trail, and the laughter of returning hunters as the packer-guides led mules lashed down with those legendary Upper Imnaha mulies.

Jim Steen, one of Wallowa County's finest outfitters, purchased Isley's outfit and along with it the hunting territory, which included the jump-off place at Indian Crossing. Jim, like the rest of us who love that wild Upper Imnaha country, is now part of that country.

Perhaps the cottonwoods there along the North Fork will glow a little brighter this fall, and perhaps when Jim's ashes were scattered from a plane piloted by his son, a few of them settled on Bonner Flat. Such a place! I can envision it now, with its golden, frosted grasses, growing in that great high meadow with bright streams trickling through it, scattered with evergreens, under an immense sky. A very special place is Bonner Flat.

Jim, brave until the end, passed away in Portland while awaiting a lung transplant. Doug and I attended memorial services for him at his ranch outside of Joseph. Jim had many friends, and their cars lined the gravel lane that leads to his and wife Connie's place. They came from Idaho, where Jim was born, and from every corner of our large country.

The day was cloudy and gray, except when, briefly during the simple service, the sky opened up to reveal a patch of clear blue, before a chill wind, hinting of the winter to come, covered it up again. We joined a long caravan consisting of cars and nearly 50 mounted riders, and formed a procession making its way slowly to the nearby Joseph landing strip. Then Jim's son Shawn took the saddle bags off his horse, which contained his father's ashes, and walked slowly over to the waiting plane with his brother, Scott.

Jim's wife Connie climbed into another small plane and they both took off. The clouds shed a few tears for Jim as the two planes circled briefly overhead and faded away in the dull gray skies, winging their way toward the Upper Imnaha. Goodbye, Jim. And goodbye, too, to those days gone by, when outfitters such as Manford and Jim led their long pack strings up that high, beautiful trail.

Cowboys know how to live, and how to die, I thought. Jim knew how to live, and although he died prematurely, he lived life to the fullest. He rode the mountain trails, he floated the Snake, he knew the lonely canyon country's silence. He wasn't afraid of death, and now he is part of the country he loved so much. We should all be so lucky.

Doug and I had a wonderful time at the Oregon Cattlemen's Association convention in Pendleton. We stayed with daughter Lori and son-in-law Tom at their mini-ranch out of Pendleton, along Wild Horse Creek. It was a jam-packed four days.

We managed to squeeze in granddaughter Lacey's livestock show, which was held next to the convention center on the Pendleton Round-Up grounds. A proud grandpa and grandma rooted for our 4-H'er as she garnered the reserve champion sheep showmanship award. While we were attending the final banquet and roast for the outgoing OCA president, Wallowa County's own Mack Birkmaier, Doug's bid, which he'd given to Lori, was the one it took to purchase "Tinkles," Lacey's Suffolk market lamb. I also managed to find time to take several long walks with grandson Ryan, who loves to hike with grandma.

Lacey Jo Seely, Pendleton, grins happily after winning the reserve champion ribbon in 4-H sheep showmanship competition at the Pendleton Junior Livestock Show with her lamb, "Tinkles." Lacey's grandparents, Doug and Janie Tippett, purchased the lamb at the auction.

It was a pleasure to renew old friendships with people like Gerda Hyde of Chiloquin, which I did during the social hour in the Happy Canyon Pageant area.

And what a treat to listen to storyteller Raphael Christy as he presented some of Charley Russell's yarns. Christy is an award-winning historian who has been presenting this program, accompanied by slides of Russell's works, for 10 years. The place was packed and the evening was beautiful.

Several Lorenzen and Rew ranch Red Angus cattle were tied there against the backdrop of Happy Canyon with the colorful sunset skies of Eastern Oregon overhead. Mack Birkmaier's roast was highlighted by the presentation of a custom-made saddle by Ray Holes of Grangeville, Idaho. Months in the planning, this surprise was pulled off without the family knowing about it. Wallowa County attended en masse, and were by far the largest, and the rowdiest, delegation there.

That Saturday night of Mack's roast, his Wallowa County neighbors supported and honored him. The gift of the saddle was the brainchild of Doug, who enjoyed the evening immensely. Doug had welded a stand for the saddle out of some horseshoes that he'd painted black.

Mack, speaking at an earlier meeting of the membership, emphasized that because fewer people belong to OCA, it is imperative that the young people carry on because many of the older members are retiring or passing on. It was brought out that economics is a factor with the young people—they can't afford to travel and attend meetings, plus they need to keep their ranches running, stay home and do the work. Mack stressed that we in the industry need to showcase good stewardship.

"Walk a little lighter on the land," he also said. "We are judged every time someone goes up the road." He said we need to be credible and tell the truth about our way of life.

In other words, we are being watched, and the masses perceive us as they read about us, and how they observe our comings and goings. "Lean and mean," he said, "but let's not get mean. This is so important... Our communities are at stake."

Mack ended his talk by saying it is the people who hold the community together, their strengths and willingness to volunteer for organizations such as the OCA.

"The people I've worked with these past two years are the best darn people on earth."

It was an emotional ending to Mack's term in office.

It was gratifying to see Mack's family all there that Saturday night at the Red Lion Inn. That's what it's all about: our ranching way of life. Families working to preserve a way of life that, in turn, sustains the health of a community.

Now to address my pickled beets. Must can them, then get this column in the mail so I can go with Doug to Imnaha tomorrow—see if I can spot a buck for him, as I did last year. Maybe we'll take along the fishing poles and try our luck down at Cow Creek; that is, if we don't run into a buck on the way.

October 19—So much LIVING, and so little time to record it!

To catch you up, Doug bagged his mule deer buck out on our summer range. He didn't see one he liked the opening morning when we drove to the Cow Creek bridge on the lower Imnaha, although we did see several legal bucks and more than 30 deer that day. While I did just a little hike down the gorge trail, Doug got in some serious fishing and returned with a nice steelhead.

The next weekend I prepared a meal around that delicious fish and we transported a "Movable Feast" up to Ramona's, surprising her on her birthday. I had spent the day cooking. The sourdough was very active, so I baked a chocolate cake and two loaves of french bread with it. Then I prepared coleslaw and rice pilaf. Everything tasted so good, and Pat and Linde, who were working in the rain to complete a roofing repair job, joined us in the surprise.

On Friday the 13th, Eileen Thiel and I left Joseph before daylight, and drove to Boise, Idaho, where we boarded a plane for Denver. Eileen is a seed potato grower's wife and writer, and for months we had been planning this trip to attend the Women Writing the West conference.

Heavy frost glittered cold upon the landscape that morning and as daylight seeped into the Minam canyon, soft muted tones of autumn came into focus through the mist along the river. Burnt umber, ninebark red, tawny grasses, tamarack gold. Indian Summer had returned.

Flying on jets is not my thing, but to get to Denver, attend the conference and return in a minimum time, we had no other choice. As I also found out, I do not do airports. Eileen left me off at the Boise terminal, curbside, standing guard over our carry-on-soft-bag-luggage, coats, and lunches, which I soon stuffed into the bags, when I realized we wouldn't have time to eat them before take-off. Then she drove off to find a long-term parking space.

I waited…and waited, and nervously looked at my watch; it was nearly time to board our plane, when, looking a bit harried, Eileen finally appeared. We lugged our cumbersome bags into the terminal and half-galloped to our gate, where we had our luggage checked for bombs and our tickets stamped, just in time to board Delta for Salt Lake City, where we would have a layover before catching a connecting flight to Denver. Whew!

Then it was up, up and away, over the great Snake River plain, looking down on fertile farmland stretching for miles east of Boise. The winding river reflected the sky as it snaked its way through rocky gorges and leveled off upon the plains.

Early autumn snow covered a far-off mountain range, and rain water, resembling tiny glass mirrors, dotted ancient volcanic lava flows. Miles of rugged, unpeopled places stopped short of agricultural lands which created a mosaic of circles. Great circles of color, where diversified crops, recently harvested, contrasted sharply with irrigated greens. Far below I could see a lone farmer working his field, a tiny trail of dust lingering in his tractor's wake.

Suddenly we were over the fringes of the Great Salt Lake, where white saline deposits outlined numerous estuaries. Great Salt Lake, that enormous body of water...there under the Wasatch mountains. When we landed at the Salt Lake airport, I could smell the salty air.

Inside, looking out large glass windows to the air terminal, we ate our soggy sandwiches as we waited to board our flight to Denver. Denver...what an airport. What a trip! Mind boggling. Miles of indoor shops, eateries, dining high up, along a walkway that looks out at the sky...and small, computer-operated trains that zoom past at terrific speeds, stop to let you on, then zoom-zoom you to where you hope you want to go. We actually made it out into the open air and located DASH, an airport shuttle, which DASHed us to Denver, 25 miles distant.

We were exhausted when we were, at last, settled into our room on the seventh floor of the Comfort Inn in downtown Denver. After resting, we walked via an enclosed glassed-in promenade to the adjoining Brown Palace Hotel. This edifice, completed in 1892, is listed in the Register of Historic Places, and is a Denver landmark.

We let our country eyes sweep upward to the six tiers of cast iron balconies, then to the stained glass ceiling which cast light downward in the huge hotel lobby. The stone used inside the lobby is Mexican onyx. It was a place of wonder to us. A young man was playing at a grand piano, which sat next to a marble table on which reposed an enormous vase of fresh-cut flowers. Chandeliers reflected a soft glow of light.

We decided to eat in what is now the Ship Tavern, which they say was a tea room during Prohibition, and probably, in the Gay '90s, served as a ladies' hair dressing salon. This grand hotel, built with money from early cattle barons and mining magnates, is kept in splendid shape. Eileen and I were quite taken with it all. We had to pinch ourselves to make sure it wasn't all a dream. Over Caesar salad, fresh shrimp, and hard rolls, we thanked our lucky stars for allowing that Friday the 13th to be so special.

The next morning, under blue skies and a warm Indian summer sun, we walked seven blocks to the Convention Center where we wandered around in a book-lovers paradise. The Rocky Mountain Book Festival was in full swing. We listened to a couple of panel discussions and spent the day browsing the numerous displays, which offered everything from food preparation to ethnic dancing, in addition to books.

That evening, back in the Brown Palace Hotel, we registered for our WWW conference and proceeded to meet many interesting women from all over the U.S. who are writing about the West. Eileen and I found ourselves among the minority of women who actually live in the West, and write about it, too. Most attendees, we found, were from Texas, New York, Maryland, Florida, and places in between.

We struck up instant friendships and shared writing experiences over a scrumptious salmon dish baked in some sort of tender crust, served with green salad and a slice of potato quiche. There was such an array of table ware we couldn't possibly use it all. Elegant dining in Denver's Brown Palace Hotel! We were a long way from Joseph, Oregon.

The next day we convened in a meeting room at the Comfort Inn where we participated in several round-table discussions, which were followed by an annual meeting of our organization. It was a wonderful conference and gathering of women writers, who presently number more than 200.

After meeting so many women authors who had numerous books already published, I was naturally curious about their lifestyles and learned that writers are a busy, interesting, intense group of people, who somehow make time to write, because they must. I understood.

I'll never forget the ride in DASH back to the Denver airport that Monday morning...watching a brilliant pink sunrise color the autumn skies and light up the Rocky Mountains which loomed near the city. Speeding along the freeways eastbound, we watched the airport building's seven teflon peaks, which represent mountain peaks more than 14,000 feet high, rise suddenly on the horizon.

We said goodbye to the mile-high city, where we took so many lasting memories away with us, as we flew over the white-washed Rockies, winging our way home to our own paradise in Wallowa County. It was a relief to arrive safely, albeit a bit tattered, and greet Doug, who had just pulled in with a load of wood for the old Monarch.

Daisy went bonkers, as usual, and the next morning I couldn't wait to drive to upper Prairie creek, where I greeted my oldest granddaughter, Tamara Jane, and beheld my beautiful new great-grandson for the first time. Tammy and baby Clayton had flown into Boise on that Friday-the-13th afternoon after Eileen and I had already taken off.

As I cuddled and rocked my precious two-month-old great-grandson to sleep, I realized that the Brown Palace Hotel, with all its glamour and luxury, could not hold a candle to this.

The next day found me attending the American Forest Congress round table in La Grande, held on the Eastern Oregon State College campus where, during a break, I enjoyed meeting with granddaughter Carrie, a student there.

As for my vision of American forests, I would like to quote Charles A. Lindbergh, pioneer aviator and environmentalist: *The human future depends on our ability to combine the knowledge of science with the wisdom of wilderness.*

These three Wallowa County ranch couples all recently celebrated 50th wedding anniversaries. From left are Maxine and Don Kooch, of Enterprise; Mary and Wilmer Cook, of Alder Slope; and Rena and John Freels, of Joseph. Their ancestors homesteaded in the area.

November 7—November signals the change from Indian summer to much colder months here in Wallowa County, when chill Prairie Creek winds swirl frosted brown leaves across our lawn, and rattle dried corn stalks in the garden. This morning, colorless November suddenly replaced colorful October, and all that remains of the color is preserved in the photographs I took a couple of weeks ago, and the cottonwood leaves I pressed between the dictionary for decorating the Thanksgiving table.

So, too, change our lives. My friend Bill, who spent more than 30 years on Alder Slope, is adjusting to change. Having recently sold his cabin and acreage, a place he loved dearly, but could no longer care for, he now resides in a newly constructed "assisted living" facility located across from the Chief Joseph rodeo grounds.

Rather than looking out at familiar Ruby Peak, 81-year-old Bill stares out his newer window to a line of leafless cottonwoods growing along a ditch bank...a past favorite place for the visiting Nez Perce children to swim and cool off during the annual Chief Joseph Days celebration. The facility is built in an open area where many Nez Perce camped in the past. More changes.

Moving slowly, so as not to disturb his hurting leg, Bill makes his way in a walker down the long hall to the dining area, where he is served three meals a day. No longer does he have to painfully start a fire in the wood stove during these frigid mornings, nor does he have to stumble up out of his chair to fix something to eat. All his needs taken care of.

Well, sort of. All except the need to gaze out from his cabin toward Ruby Peak, and watch the seasonal changes as the tamaracks lose their needles, and the snowline creep down the mountain.

Bill's change is also my change, for our family has been going up to Bill's place for 27 years. With joy I have planted and cared for gardens there, planted ponderosa pine and Douglas fir, stocked trout ponds, changed sprinkler pipes, and mostly just spent hours sittin' and visitin' over many cups of tea on the cabin porch, listening to the birds sing in the apple trees, watching hawks glide over the slope and the baby quail appear from under the squash plants.

Now, we visit in Alpine House. A big change.

Son Steve, too, is experiencing change. He is moving to Idaho Falls, where he has accepted a job with a construction company. Because we are out of the seed potato business, the ranch can no longer support another family. As in many rural areas of the West, the old-timers are fading away.

Having lived long, productive lives, men like Truman Poulson and Wilson Wilde have gone over the divide to where there is no winter, only Indian summer. These two old cowmen/horsemen have seen plenty of changes. Truman was born in 1900 and Wil in 1908. Doug and I attended both of their memorial services, which left us with a good feeling, having been reminded anew about their interesting lives. Both men were "true blue" Wallowa Countians.

The frantic pace of getting ready for winter has slowed somewhat here on the ranch, at least for me. Elk mincemeat is frozen, potatoes, carrots and onions are stored away, sauerkraut is canned, and yesterday Doug butchered the last of the old hens. We had chicken and dumplings for supper. Yum!

I had left the hen simmering on the wood cook stove all day while I attended a museum board meeting in Joseph. Speaking of the old Monarch, it burns all day now, and it seems there is always something bubbling away in my dutch oven. This old stove, which used to reside at Dug Bar on the Snake River, has a voracious appetite, but feeding it creates a cozy sense of home.

I weaned the milk cows' three calves last week, and since Stargirl still has gobs of milk, I opted to dry her up slowly, so it wouldn't hurt.

That means I am back to milking again. It feels so good. When one is hurt as badly as I was, it is a pleasure being able to squeeze hard enough to milk a cow.

I am also back to forking hay to her and the young Holstein heifer, Hollyhock. Best therapy yet! In other words, I'm once again into chores: packing water to the laying pullets, haying the stock, milking, and feeding Daisy and the barn cats. That early morning exercise gets my blood going.

There has lately been snow on the ground, so it is a chore just to get into all of those clothes! For several days in a row the temperature hovered around 10 degrees, with one morning dipping to 7... *brrr*. The irrigation ditches froze over and our bright landscape faded to a dull November brown. It has warmed some today, and rain is in the forecast. The sky is leaden and a brisk wind is causing the last of the frozen willow leaves to let go.

Tomorrow Ben and his crew will begin hauling the calves in from the hills and delivering them to a local cattle buyer. Lucky for us, the mama cows far out on Salmon Creek will be out of earshot. It is weaning time...We have been hearing the familiar bawling lately as the sound from Hough's weaned calves floats up the long meadow to our ranch.

The fall calvers and their babies have been trailed down off the high east moraine and they are happily grazing the hill hay field as I write. Sometimes the little calves slip under the electric fence and come right up in the yard, whereupon Daisy obligingly chases them back in the pasture.

One crisp fall day last month, Linde and I drove down in the canyons to Bear Gulch, where we helped Myrna Moore pick apples. For sorting and picking, Myrna gave each of us a box of sweet Golden Delicious apples, then invited us in for a bowl of soup. Vicky Marks and her daughter, plus 14-year-old Jenny Moore were there too. We women had a nice gabfest over lunch in the modest little house there at the mouth of Bear Gulch where it joins Little Sheep Creek.

Fall in the canyons is so special, and so are the people who live there.

The fall calves are branded and worked, and soon it will be time to begin feeding hay. There is still sufficient grass out in the hills for the spring calvers, so they will stay for a while longer, until it snows and they have forgotten their calves.

Elk hunters, pulling contrivances of every possible description, have made their yearly pilgrimage to our area. They are camped all over our outback trying to track down the elusive wapiti. The tourists, however, have fled to warmer climes. In Safeway this morning I actually met people I knew!

Fall means attending high school sports functions. Doug and I were there to cheer for the hometown teams and root for Ben's daughter, Sarah, and our granddaughter, Chelsie, at a recent volleyball tournament. Even though the girls were on opposing teams. Our woodshed is full (thanks to Doug, who made many trips out north for pine and tamarack) and our large hay stacks are proof of the hours of work Ben and his family put in to secure winter cattle feed. Let it snow!

During the last golden days of October, I often drove to my place on Alder Slope, where a son now lives with his family, parked my car, and walked with Daisy around the country block, a considerable distance. We took our time, visiting neighbors along the way and marveling in the beauty of the slope, which rises to meet timbered mountain sides that lead to barren peaks.

Golden tamarack contrasted sharply against the evergreens. Snow-clad Ruby Peak, encircled by clouds, rose above us. Red rose hips and white snowberries decorated the country lanes, and as we passed by the Alder Slope Pioneer Cemetery I wondered what those early settlers would think about the changes coming to our slope today.

Change was just a part of their everyday lives. Change from horse-drawn carriages to automobiles, from candles and lamps to electricity, from open range to fenced-in pastures; and now they sleep, like Wil Wilde and Truman Poulson.

I filled my lungs with the sharp cold air, and looked down at the flat where the town of Enterprise went about its daily business, then turned eastward toward the shining Seven Devils range in Idaho. In spite of changes, I mused, life is still what we make it, and being able to walk in beauty reminds me nothing else really matters that much. The good things in life really are free.

Tomorrow I am looking forward to spending the day with two grand-children. What more could a grandma ask for!

During my visit to Bear Gulch, Jenny Moore shared with me this poem, which was published in Agri-Times with the following editor's note: *Jenny Moore, 14, lives far from a city, is home-schooled, and wants to be a writer, says her friend and mentor, Janie Tippett. "In this age of teenagers being so mixed up, here we have a child of the 90s who listens to the beat of a different drum," Tippett said.*

Gifts

I would like to write a simple song
Full of praise and happy light,
To sing all day long
And through the night.

A song to sing through all time,
A poem that would never grow old,
But I have not the skill to rhyme
All the beauty of the summer warm and winter cold

And sun and moon above
Into a song and make it right,
So just try to tell of the things I love,
All of the many wonders bright.

A hot sun on a clear day,
Green leaves against the blue,
The rainy chill of early May,
And summer blossoms too.

A wild wind blowing,
Long grass quivering,
A witch's moon glowing,
Aspen leaves shivering.

A golden cloud made of angel's wings,
Swallows playing in the evening sky,
Bounding joy of which the lark sings,
A baby robin learning to fly.

Early morning sun,
Dew on the grass,
A glad feeling in everyone
As the breezes pass.

Stars at night, cold,
Above an enchanted land of snow,
Wintry sunsets bright
Casting everywhere a golden glow.

Sights and sounds and wonderful things,
And the joy of each new day,
Magic laughter and butterfly wings,
I love them, that's all I wish to say.

The great earth and good brown sod,
The open sky and twilight dim,
Were all given to us by God,
And we thank Him.

By Jenny Moore
Bear Gulch, Imnaha
Wallowa County, Oregon

November 21—I simply must learn more about this word processor. After having typed 10 paragraphs this morning my phone rang, which necessitated another phone call, at which time Doug walked into the room where I was seated in front of this thing, all of which resulted in a lengthy discussion concerning the two phone calls. Ranch stuff.

As all of the aforementioned transpired, this screen in front of me went blank. When I finally returned to my work, I pushed the wrong key, or something, and wouldn't you know. What I have previously written is wiped out, not only from the screen, but from this life. My words now reside in na na land, where all lost word processor material will never be known to anyone.

Because I didn't even name the document (because it didn't ask me to, for heaven's sake) it can never be retrieved. My inspiration is gone, along with my fading memory, which brings to mind a card I received in yesterday's mail from a new friend, Gwen Peterson, a ranch wife and writer from Big Timber, Montana.

Gwen is the author of a very amusing book entitled *The Ranch Woman's Manual*, wherein she offers advice in hilarious detail to help ranch women cope with their everyday lives. Gwen has been there, and there is a ring of truth in every word she writes.

Rather than sit down and cry, she wrote this manual so the rest of us could survive by laughing. She writes of dealing with wire and panel gates, with husbands during the sorting of cattle, with summer company, canning, and all the myriad tasks we ranch women are expected to handle.

Gwen writes, *Going to write a book: How to Be Elderly, if I don't get too old; too many irons in the fire and the flame is dwindling.* I met Gwen during the WWW conference in Denver last month. She is a very funny lady, and those of us still engaged in ranching need all the humor we can find.

Now, where was I? At age 62, I find my flame dwindling too, and on this cold November morning, so is the old Monarch's. A pause while I feed its flame with some tamarack. This past week, not any different from other weeks in any given season, has been hectic.

On Thursday I hosted our Wallowa County CattleWomen. A large turnout filled nearly every chair in the house as a young Angie Ketscher conducted her second successful meeting. We so welcome these younger generation members to our organization. It is refreshing to have their new ideas and youthful vigor. The flame is dwindling in us older Cow-Belles—whoops! I mean CattleWomen—too.

I had baked a wild blackberry cobbler that morning, and decorated the kitchen table with fall leaves. It was most enjoyable visiting after the meeting with old friends, many of whom had driven long distances to attend.

Friday was spent cooking. Two loaves of sourdough bread, large meatloaf, lasagna casserole, and pumpkin pie. That evening Bryan Wolfe, accompanied by friend Pete from Hermiston, drove in just in time for the meatloaf supper, after which the re-telling of previous elk hunts ensued, a past-time nearly as engaging as the actual hunt itself.

Before dawn the next morning found me in the kitchen presiding over sourdough waffles, sausage, eggs and coffee, while Doug handled the traditional meat loaf sandwiches. Then we were off, heading north in two rigs. Friend Linde, who had responded to Bryan's wake-up call on the phone, joined us for breakfast and rode with Doug and me. Bryan and Pete followed as we sped through the frosted hills along the lightening Crow Creek road.

A lovely salmon sunrise colored the eastern sky, and the weather was unusually warm for the middle of November. The air was positively balmy. Because Linde's husband was camped down on Lightning Creek with more elk hunters, and she had drawn a cow tag for the Chesnimnus unit, she opted to hunt with us. In fact, it was Linde who shot the first cow (elk that is).

We had left Pete off to stalk a herd of 400 head, which were reportedly in the area, and after bumping our way uphill through one of our pastures, we spotted the herd, which was, at that point, fragmented, and grazing its way slowly in a southwesterly direction. What a sight! Seeing that many elk amid the vastness of the Zumwalt Prairie.

Because they eat like our cows, it is like supporting that many more cattle on a limited range. The elk love being with and following the cattle, because that is where the tenderest shoots of grass grow. Due to the warmth following recent rains, new grass is greening the hills as if it were spring.

After Linde shot her cow, we drove around toward what we call the Johnson pasture, where we ran into another splintered bunch of elk. All of us, with the exception of Doug and Pete, limited out. After considerable grunting, the men gutted and loaded up the large cow elk, and we drove to our ranch on Wet Salmon Creek, where we dove into those meat loaf sandwiches.

Meanwhile, back at the valley ranch, the men, aided by Linde, skinned and quartered those three large elk in our shop, while I started a fire in the wood cookstove, slid the lasagna casserole in the oven, fixed a tossed salad and garlic sourdough bread, gathered eggs, walked out to get the mail, and washed the hearts and liver.

More hunting tales over supper, and after supper. But let me tell you, it was nice to have Pete here. He did all the dishes after every meal!

On Sunday morning Doug baked sourdough hotcakes on the wood stove, Pete and Bryan pitched in on the lunches, and the three of them left for a second hunt to fill Doug's and Pete's tags.

Meanwhile, I left that same morning for Walla Walla, catching a ride with other Fishtrap board members to attend a meeting at the Alumni Center at Walla Walla College. The weather continued unusually mild and partly sunny, which made for a nice trip...and another good elk hunt for the guys, who were grinning broadly when I returned that night. Both Pete and Doug had bagged their cows.

My milk pail was brimming over with bleeding hearts and livers, for luckily my cow is now dried up, and Pete and Bryan had treated Doug to supper in Joseph. The hunters left on Monday morning, loaded down with with a lasting supply of meat and memories. It was fun having them here, and I missed Pete doing my dishes.

Yesterday afternoon I helped Doug and son-in-law Charley load the purebred calves, which were then hauled to our corrals here to be weaned. Luckily our bedroom is mostly sound-proof.

I have done the shopping for the Thanksgiving turkey (a 20-pounder). Twenty-two coming for dinner! Therefore I must get this column out in the mailbox, because tomorrow I will be cooking and baking all day. And, like Gwen, my flame is dwindling.

December 5—Prairie Creek is quiet, cold and calm this morning, recovering from a fierce, frigid windstorm. The hard-frozen ground appears swept and barren, no snow, no mud, sterile, as if nothing could ever grow there again. To match the mood, the sky is colorless. Only the Wallowas, with their purple-blue slopes and snowy ramparts, seem alive. Their cold breath sends shivers down my neck. The swirling snow "banners" of yesterday have been blown into white sculpted cornices or driven into icebound crevices.

Christmas is upon us. There is no turning back. This year it happened the day after Thanksgiving, when I drove into Joseph to run a few errands and ended up Christmas shopping. Wallowa County loves Christmas. It is as if, when the deep cold comes, those bright holiday decorations radiate warmth.

An increasing number of our senior citizens have been going to Arizona for the cold months. Many left before the first snow storm. For those of us who stay, life is never dull. Far from it. Linde, Ramona and I, accompanied by various children, attended the Eugene Ballet's wonderful performance of the Nutcracker. This talented traveling troupe set up in the Enterprise High School gym, and danced to a full house.

Then there are those holiday bazaars, like the Handcrafters of Wallowa County, who hold their annual event in Cloverleaf Hall. If you aren't in the Christmas spirit by then, you're really a scrooge. Colorful booths fill every available space of that community hall at the fairgrounds. Familiar faces smile back from each of those booths.

Hope McLaughlin, looking like a Christmas decoration herself, dressed in an old-fashioned high necked dress with a colorful pin, fashioned from buttons, at her throat; wearing laced boots, Hope sits in a chair sewing potholders. She is making the potholders out of scraps left over from sewing the lovely quilts that hang on the wall behind her. Hope is industrious; her fingers are never still. And she, like all artists, expresses herself in her handiwork.

Hope's husband Harold, always ready with a smile and a joke, greets us amid the wooden creations he has made in their home, which sits high on a hill above Alder Slope. Stools, folding tables, cutting boards, checkerboards, and small, polished jewelry boxes. I purchased an apron, sewn by 93-year-old Marie Burdette, and three of Hope's potholders.

I visited with "northender" Myrtle Wolf, who says, "There are still some of us left out there," referring to what is known as the ghost town of Flora, where her family lives. "But," says Myrtle, "the old-timers are passing on. Each year there are fewer of us." Myrtle, surrounded by her lovely embroidered pillow cases and quilts, still wore her ready smile.

Doug and I ate supper Friday evening there in Cloverleaf Hall, enjoying not only the home-style roast beef meal cooked up by the Imnaha Grange ladies, but the camaraderie of friends and neighbors.

The next day, Saturday, friend Linde hosted a get-together at her lovely log home on upper Prairie Creek for the purpose of making Christmas decorations. It was such fun gathering there, friends from Prairie Creek, Imnaha, Bear Gulch, Alder Slope, Joseph and Enterprise. At a large round table women and children chattered away, while fashioning angel ornaments out of noodles and macaroni.

One mother brought freshly baked gingerbread men, and little hands were kept busy frosting them. Granddaughters Adele, Becky and Mona Lee became engrossed in several projects. It was really entertaining watching a child's imagination express itself in so many ways. We munched cream puffs, cookies, carrot sticks, pretzels and other snacks, and drank apple cider. The warm feeling of chinked-log interior lent itself to the old-fashioned spirit of Christmas, and fat flakes of snow floated past the windows.

There was a lot of laughter, and exclaiming over each other's decorations. I had made forays up Little Sheep Creek the day before, gathering bundles of snowberry, rose hips, and juniper to make a wild wreath. Thanks to neighbor Karen Coppin, the wreath was a success! Morning stretched into late afternoon, and because this gathering was so successful, we vowed to make it an annual occasion.

Before our thermometer dropped, about three days ago, Daisy and I took advantage of the mildness and continued our daily walks about Prairie Creek. We often take the familiar route through Hough's field and up a draw to the hilltop, where one can view the entire Wallowa chain and the prairie below as it stretches toward what we call "the hills."

We were, in fact, in the hills, and a coyote flushed out of the sagebrush right in front of us. Five white tail does grazed, unconcerned, until we were practically upon them, then went bounding away, flags flying in alarm, before resuming their feeding. Up there under that immense sky we were all safe: the coyote, the deer, Daisy and I, and the wild honkers flying overhead.

Yesterday Doug and I attended our local livestock auction where we sold some calves, along with a few of son-in-law Charley's. I reminisced with lower valley rancher Wayne Wolfe about the days of the big sales, when cowmen who came from all over the county, many of whom are now gone. Wayne commented that there didn't seem to be any in-between ranchers anymore. They were either very young or very old, and the old were quickly dwindling.

But the familiar cry of the auctioneer, the smell of cattle, and the presence of stockmen is still a vital part of our culture here. This country grows fine cattle. It would be nice if the wealth of the grass equaled the wealth of the market.

Last evening, Doug, son-in-law Charley and I attended a slide program, "Of Steamboats and Copper Mines," presented by historian and writer Carole Simone Smolinski. The program was held up on the hill above Enterprise, at the Wallowa Mountain Visitor's Center. A recent donation of photographs taken at Eureka Bar in the 1890s has been made available to the public, and slides were made from those revealing photographs.

Doug and I have trekked many times down that trail to the site of what was known as the mining community of Eureka. There, near the confluence of the Imnaha with the Snake, was built an impressive mining venture on which thousands of dollars and the sweat of many men were spent. Records indicate nothing was ever realized, at least as far as being equal to the frenzied effort it must have taken to establish that remote community.

That community came alive for us that night: the boarding house, blacksmith shop, numerous tents, and an intricate system which transported the raw material from the mine, over the Imnaha River to the smelter plant built on a rock foundation near the bar.

Carole's voice transported us back to a fascinating era of our county's history. Doug, who ran a guide service for 15 years out of Dug Bar farther upstream, added his own personal recollections of Eureka Bar.

And now, as I write, the snow has begun to fall. Methinks we'll have a white Christmas. At the end of my busy days, sitting by the fire I only have time to quickly scribble entries in my daily journal. Hope all of you have a wonderful holiday season.

December 20—We bundled up and drove the 30 miles to Imnaha in the dark, cold canyon night to attend the school Christmas program. The new church, which sits on a hill overlooking the small settlement, serves not only as a place of worship but for school functions as well.

The pews were full of mothers, fathers, grandparents, aunts and uncles, many of whom make their living somehow connected to cattle ranching. Fathers came in late, still wearing work clothes, hay clinging to them, after driving steep, lonely roads to attend the school program.

From kindergartner Marshall Cox to the only eighth-grader, granddaughter Mona Lee, the small school performed in its traditional manner. Poems were recited, instruments played, songs sung and the entire community was proud of every child, not just their own relatives.

Santa arrived, right on schedule, amid jingle bells and a great flourishing of *ho, ho, ho!* The future generation of Imnaha inhabitants lined up to receive bags filled with oranges, candy and nuts. We always leave this little school feeling good about the world.

December 21—This year, I baked six of the traditional Tannenbaum Bot, the fruity, nutty Christmas tree loaves, to deliver as gifts. Tonight Doug and I drove to the Enterprise High School gym and watched granddaughter Chelsie play basketball for the Savages, who won.

December 22—Six degrees, *burr…* on this first day of winter. Clear, cold and sunny. Visited our friend Bill at the Alpine House in Joseph. Gave him a loaf of Christmas bread. Also visited Aunt Amey in the Wallowa County Nursing Home.

One of the barn cats joined Daisy and I for a walk in the last sunlight of this shortest day of the year. We had to walk fast to stay warm.

December 23—Clear, cold, nine degrees, and an inch of hard-crusted snow on the ground. Purchased the prime rib and trimmings for Christmas dinner. Saw so many familiar faces in Safeway, I was a long time getting out to the car! Grocery shopping is a small town social event.

Daisy and I and a different cat made the long loop up Hough's hill to the top, then down the fence line to Echo Canyon road. Wonderful hike in the December air. We observed several hawks out hunting mice, and a kingfisher and eight mallards in the irrigation ditch. Ice is forming in pretty patterns alongside the waterways, and snow crystals crunch underfoot.

Back home, I put a large bowl of sourdough to rise for bread. Tonight Doug and I will visit friends in Joseph for some Christmas cheer.

December 26—'Tis the day after Christmas, and the ranch is strangely silent. Where yesterday the voices of many children mingled with those of their parents, a portion of our combined seven children and their offspring, today's silence seems almost overwhelming. Like Christmas day, today is sky blue, crisp cold, and the sunshine bright with just enough snow on the ground to glitter.

The Wallowas, serene and cold, alternate between shadowy blue and blinding white, as the sun follows its brief path across the December sky. The winter solstice has come and gone and imperceptibly, the days will begin to lengthen. It was only 3:30 when the sun slipped behind Chief Joseph Mountain on Christmas day, and the children playing on the hill quickly made their way indoors, where they consumed great quantities of pie and warmed up by the fireplace and wood cook stove.

Twenty-three members of our large, extended family, some of whom had driven long distances—from Wyoming and Idaho—sat down to demolish 20 pounds of prime rib, Yorkshire pudding, mashed potatoes, gravy, sourdough bread, tossed green salad and a sampling of grandma's pickled beets and cucumber pickles. We sat 10 in the dining area and 13 in the living room.

I had spent the day before Christmas baking three loaves of sourdough bread, and mince, raspberry, and blackberry pies. I spent Christmas morning fussing over the two large roasts, one of which was baked in the wood stove oven. Cooking is one of my favorite pastimes, and seeing people enjoy what I've prepared is reward enough for the effort, but today it is nice to just "do" for Doug and me.

Son Steve left earlier this morning to return to Idaho Falls, and Doug has gone to town. The house is mine. The only pressing thing I must do is get this column in the mail and feed the ever-hungry wood stove. It was five degrees this morning and I find the snapping of the seasoned tamarack comforting as I look out at our cold cows munching hay in long, frozen paths that wind their way over our hill pasture.

Like cowboys and ranchers all over our valleys and canyons, Ben has been out feeding. Many are out with a pick and shovel these mornings, breaking ice in the creeks and ditches so livestock can drink.

The days leading up to Christmas were completely filled. I had to "steal" time for my daily walks with Daisy. Doug and I enjoy having friends and neighbors over for dinner when the house is all warm with holiday decorations. One day a week or so ago, I roasted a leg of lamb and served it with potluck dishes brought by other friends. We had a wonderful evening, and wondered why we always wait until Christmas to get together.

And now, as I finish this column, the day beckons. Daisy and I must follow the path to Hough's hill and take advantage of the sunshine to see what new adventure awaits us there.

The new year will be well on its way next time I write. Until then enjoy life and look forward to what 1996 will bring.

Spring break week brought out the fishermen and school kids. Shown here with his first steelhead is Josh Nash. Cousins, from left, James Nash, Lacey Seely, Adele Nash, and Ryan Seely, cheered him on. That's Grandpa Doug Tippett at right.

1996

January 8—Eucalyptus, catalpa, and tulip trees frame my view of the Sierra foothills from brother-in-law Duane's office here in rural Newcastle, California. This house, where Duane and my sister Caroline live, sits back off the county road, next to a wild area of blackberry bramble, ponds, and a nearby granite gravel pit.

Doug is off to what is left of the ranch where my three sisters, one brother and I were reared. Running through the oak woods is a small waterway, referred to as Ditch Creek, where gold left over from the '49ers has settled into bedrock crevices. Doug, clad in hip boots and armed with his pick and shovel, is spending this warm, sunny day panning his way along the creek.

Sister Caroline has left for lower Auburn, where she works on the staff of a regional magazine, and Duane left earlier for his job in Sacramento.

The house is mine.

Last evening Duane and Caroline, who are not as intimidated with word processors as I am, proceeded to set me up in Duane's office so I could get this column out. So, here goes...

When we drove out of the Wallowa Valley last week it was a balmy 45 degrees. After stops in Baker City, Farewell Bend, and Jordan Valley, we crossed the Nevada line to McDermitt. Darkness fell across the desert as we pulled into Winnemucca, secured a motel, and joined other guests at a long wooden table in the historic Winnemucca Hotel. Basque cooking filled our senses and our stomachs as we attacked a variety of dishes ranging from soup, salad, bread, rice, stew, beans...to steak, served last! and washed down with chilled red wine.

Sunny sagebrush vistas stretched ahead the next morning as we sped toward Reno and the new Sierra of California. After daughter Ramona won a jackpot at Puckerbrush, Nevada, population 28, thus assuring her plane ticket home, we stopped next in Sparks so Ramona and Doug could go antiquing. Reno offered even more of the shops they love to browse in, so we toured the Biggest Little City in the West, which can no longer lay claim to that title.

We made one more stop in Boomtown before being swept along in the traffic crossing Donner Pass, then rapidly descended the snowless mountains to Colfax and an enchilada supper with Arnold Solis, who runs a Mexican food and antique establishment, and who always remembers us as "Those Oregon folks."

After leaving Ramona at my mother's apartment in Auburn, we arrived rather bedraggedly here at Caroline and Duane's. And now our annual vacation is well on its way.

Granddaughter Tamara and our new great-grandson drove up from Lodi the next day, and we actually got that five-generation photo taken! Doug was the photographer and my stepfather, Bill, whistled and waved a toy so baby Clayton would smile for the momentous occasion. Ramona left with her daughter and grandson to travel to Lodi, and we haven't seen them since.

California weather, juxtaposed to what we've been viewing on TV of the eastern U.S., seems positively summer-like, and we are loving it while we can. Sunny day follows sunny day, and Caroline's primroses and pansies are blooming.

On Saturday we joined 20 other family members and friends in Roseville to celebrate my youngest sister, Kathryn's, 50th birthday, and it was so warm the party was held outside.

Since we five kids were all raised on a dairy, cows are in. And can you believe what game we played for the party? Pin the teat on the udder! Amid gales of laughter, young and old alike were blindfolded, twirled around, and sent to tape a teat. This utterly ridiculous activity won Doug a prize for coming the closest to the right spot.

Yesterday morning, we met old friends Sandra and Fred at the IOOF Hall for a $2.50 breakfast that included all the pancakes, eggs, and bacon or sausage that we could eat. It was a treat as well to tour the historic Odd Fellows Hall there in Old Town Auburn. After loading a hastily put-together picnic lunch, all four sisters and various spouses drove down to our old ranch, where brother Jim and wife Joyce live. Here we spent the day roaming around the woods and fields of our youth.

Sister Mary Ann, who lives in Mom's small house there on the ranch, was our guide as we strolled toward a pond built by Jim years ago, for resident wild geese and ducks to raise their young. We ambled through damp shadowy woods, where oak trees, denuded now of leaves save for the live oaks, grew in all shapes and sizes.

We soon crossed Little Ditch Creek and came to neighbor Walter Allen's fence line. M.A. had called ahead for permission to walk there. After much giggling and struggling through a barbed wire fence, K. being the youngest of the group at 50, we emerged onto a decomposed red granite road, where we were almost immediately greeted by the property owner himself.

Eighty-six-year-old Walter drove a very decrepit pickup with a friendly, tail-wagging farm dog riding in the back. More than 40 years have elapsed since we "Bachman children" grew up neighbors to this solitary old man. M.A. and K. rode on the open tailgate of Walter's sputtering pickup, while the rest of us, who included my girlhood chum Sandra, walked up the winding road to where several old ramshackle buildings perched on a hill. Small irrigated flats nestled between the hills. Oaks and huge granite rocks dotted the area. New green grass colored the countryside.

Walter parked his pickup beside a large assemblage of flat rocks, where native Digger Indians once kneeled with stone pestles to grind acorns into meal. What remains of this ancient dwelling place are more than 20 holes in the flat rocks, which now harbor frog eggs waiting to hatch in the collected rainwater. After photographing our contemporary group standing atop this ancient kitchen, I ambled over to Walter and listened to the telling of stories passed down from his grandparents about this very place. Fascinating stories about where there used to be an old stage stop.

"Where those trees are," said Walter, looking toward some pointed-topped evergreens, "My grandfather was born there, and so was I. They had trouble getting along with the miners, so they moved over there."

That warm afternoon, as I gazed out across Walter's fields at history rotting away as we spoke, I took in the nearby creek of my youth, known as Doty's Ravine, where I learned to dog paddle. I remembered the old apple orchard growing across the creek, which used to provide a small part of Walter's living.

A solitary man who never married, Walter eked out a simple living with a few sheep and a small dry-land vineyard known for the quality of its wine grapes. White-haired Walter, sitting in his old pickup with his dog in the back, blended in with the falling-down fence leading up to the rusted, tin-covered barn, and the house he has finally abandoned for a mobile home.

Slowly, savoring the sunny afternoon, we made our way back through the woods, past a Hereford cow seeking out the newborn calf she had left hidden behind a patch of scrub oak, to the cow pasture meadow and up a slight rise to the familiar house. I felt my father's presence there in the many trees he had planted, and in his fascinating garden, which now runs rampant with ivy and myrtle. We all felt a sense of coming home.

Hungry now, we produced our picnic and devoured new-crop navel oranges, summer beef sausage and crackers, and topped it off with hot raspberry tea and the lemon-raspberry bars Caroline and I had baked the night before.

After driving to the old pioneer Manzanita Cemetery to share our nostalgic day with Daddy, we drove home beneath a California sunset that bled with the colors of persimmon and orange. It was a perfect ending to a special day.

January 22—Patches of blue appear in a cloudy, rain-washed sky as a cold morning breeze wanders among the foothills here in rural Newcastle, California. Like the wandering breeze, Doug and I have been moving from one location here in Placer County to the next. My word processor, however, did not wander with us, but remained hooked up to Duane's printer. Therefore, I have returned to type words to screen and attempt this column.

Our wanderings have taken us to sister Mary Ann's, where we stayed on the ranch where I was raised, thence up to friend Sandra's to visit a few days before settling into my mother and stepfather's apartment here in Auburn. Mom and Bill are attending an elder hostel in Santa Rosa this week, so we are apartment sitting.

After Doug dropped me off here at Caroline's to work on this column, he headed up Highway 49 to spend the day in Grass Valley and Nevada City. These past two weeks have been crammed with experiences that now seem blurred together. I remember traveling the winding road from Auburn down to the American River, then up the equally crooked road to Cool, where we stared out at the not-so-populated countryside of oak trees and cattle ranches, and passing through Coloma where, in January 1849, gold was discovered by a miner named Marshall.

Farther up toward the Sierra we spent the day in Hangtown (Placerville) wandering in and out of the many small shops that make up the new "old town." Shops to lure the tourists, like the old hardware store where you must search behind the fancy kitchenware to find paints, tools and other hardware. Here we saw ranchers in work clothes shopping beside tourists. Shades of Joseph.

We ate our lunch in a small eatery that featured fresh seafood chowder and french bread baked that morning in a bakery on the corner. Out on the narrow streets we could see our breath in the frosty air, and locals talked about snow down to 2,000 feet. Returning to the river before making the final steep ascent to Auburn, we noticed mountain bikers, hikers, and kayakers loading up after a day in the outdoors.

While visiting Sandra and her husband, Fred, if it wasn't raining, Sandra and I would spend the time walking along the long ridge top where they live. A deep canyon plunged off the ridge to the east of their house, filled with toyon, manzanita, chaparral, digger pine, blackberry patches and wild grape vines. On one of our walks, I was able to capture on film four jennies, wild juvenile female turkeys. Black-tail deer graze the Hubbards' yard and we would often return from a walk to find three yearlings there nibbling the bushes.

When it rained, Sandra and I curled up on the sofa by the fire and leafed through high school annuals, reminiscing about the '40s and '50s when we grew up in these foothills and rode the bus to Lincoln schools. We had lunch one day in lower Auburn, at "Awful Annie's," at a small table perched on a porch overlooking black oak and barren fig trees.

One bright and sunny morning, I joined Sandra's hiking group, which consisted of 11 senior citizens, for a jaunt above the American River canyon. Following a path along an old irrigation canal, we came suddenly face-to-face with a bobcat, which then leaped on down the trail and disappeared into a thicket of toyon berry. Just minutes away, a flock of wild turkeys flew downhill in front of us.

The now-sprawling city of Auburn was just minutes away. Wildlife, like the country folk, must adapt to change. We were told that the wild turkey population is increasing. On my walks around the ranch where I was reared, I once spotted several of them scratching in the cow manure or hunting among the dead oak leaves for acorns.

While staying there at sister Mary Ann's, many childhood memories surfaced. Memories of walking, as a child, those 240 acres, alone, memorizing every hill, stream, tree and rock. Today, hidden among the oak woods that surround the hill we knew as "Big Top," are 15 homes.

My brother, Jim, runs his cows on the remaining pastures and open space in the woods. He and his wife, Joyce, have reared their family there, and now, they too are gone. But they, like us girls, return. Jim built a pond that is fed by a branch of Ditch Creek, and today wild honkers flock there for protection and food. Each morning Mary Ann walks out to feed them their daily ration of grain.

Doug has added to his gold collection by patiently panning in Ditch Creek. One Sunday, all four of us sisters, accompanied by Duane and Doug, piled into our cars and headed over the hills to El Dorado County to spend a day along French Creek. It was cold and foggy, and even thicker fog shrouded the country near La Trobe as we drove up and over the narrow "roller coaster" hills to French Creek. Over the last rise, where we spotted more wild turkeys, the fog lifted.

The skies, far from blue, still contained high fog, and a damp cold penetrated French Creek. We warmed up by taking brisk walks before spreading our picnic on the hood of Caroline's car. Doug panned in the creek, where years ago a distant relative of mine, a prospector by the name of Justice, worked this very spot for the elusive yellow gold. Remains of the old Smith house, a crumbling rock foundation on the adjacent hill, bears silent witness to those who came before.

French Creek hasn't changed much over the years. Cattle graze the green hills and hawks glide silently overhead. We gals were gladdened by two pair of western bluebirds, watching as their bright feathered bodies flitted through the spreading oak trees.

That evening, more fog settled into the populated valley surrounding the city of Roseville, as we found a Chinese restaurant, where we enjoyed a tasty meal.

Baked sourdough bread yesterday in mom's oven. Caroline brought me some of her well water, as chlorinated city water kills the yeasty bacteria in sourdough. Sure is a switch to heat the house with the touch of a thermostat, feed what I normally give to my chickens to the garbage disposal, and not have Daisy here to munch bones.

January slides by as Doug and I look out of mom and Bill's apartment window to see new snow blanketing the Sierra...and we think of home, wondering what winter is like in our part of the world. We'll soon find out, weather permitting, as we head up over Donner Summit and point our car northward toward Wallowa County.

February 6—Daisy, leaving a flurry of dry snow in her wake as she sped from her warm nest in the barn, nearly knocked me over. My little dog didn't run out and greet us as we drove into the ranch, and understandably so. It was 20 below zero! But when I whistled for her, she momentarily forgot the bitter cold and radiated a warm welcome home. We had been gone nearly a month.

The farther north we traveled on the last day of our trip, the lower our car's thermometer registered. So many memories to store away; to bring back and savor, such as the day we drove with sister Kathryn to Lodi to visit granddaughter Tamara, her husband, Matt, and that first great-grandson, Clayton. Previous rains had left standing water between the numerous wine grape vineyards, where pruning had been halted by the weather.

Following Tam's directions, we pulled up in front of a tidy, old-fashioned, 100-year-old farm house which has been lovingly kept up by the original owners. Tam and Matt, now renting the house, have it fixed up all homey and clean. Tall walnut and oak trees surround the house, and one ancient oak had the largest wisteria vine I've ever seen twining around its trunk. It must be a lovely sight when those blooming lilac clusters droop from that tree in the spring.

The main attraction, however, was the baby, and we spent most of our time "Clayton watching." The object of our attention obliged willingly, and entertained us with all of the things six-month-old babies do.

Another day, Mary Ann drove us to Sacramento to visit our Auntie Carol Nunn, after which we stopped to see an aging uncle who had recently been hospitalized due to a broken ankle. Seeing this beloved uncle there in the hospital bed lent a sad note to that day. Better to remember Uncle Johnny as the music-writing, creative fellow we've always known.

On the last weekend of our stay, Mary Ann, Sandra and I joined 13 other hikers on a jaunt down an old stage road that takes off above Auburn, and winds down to the confluence of the middle and north fork of the American River. Again, it was one of those beautiful January days sandwiched between rainy, foggy ones.

It was my first experience dealing with mountain bikers. They zoomed down the trail with breakneck speed, big tires bouncing off rocks and splashing through mud puddles.

"Biker coming," we called to the hikers ahead. The riders appeared to be having a wonderful time, at least those going downhill. Judging from the pained looks and sweaty faces of those making their tortuous way uphill, I didn't think they were quite as happy. However, when one spends five days a week behind a desk, staring at a computer screen, I was told, the experience is not only great, but necessary.

On Super Bowl Sunday, we sisters, not being football fans, all congregated at the ranch and spent the day together. While a cold, wind-driven rain soaked the foothills, we made a kettle of soup on M.A.'s wood stove. Each sister brought an ingredient and added it to the pot.

We sipped the Super Sunday soup and then piled into Caroline's car and, in the rain, toured what is known as the Thermalands country, which lies northeast of the Mt. Pleasant District where we were raised. Sunshine broke through wet clouds, and the greening, open country, dotted with oak trees and streams, glistened with raindrops. Creeks ran bank to bank, and at Camp Far West, a man-made lake, water overflowed into a rocky gorge from the spillway into Bear River. Misty spray catapulted into the air as we walked a wet trail to view the falls.

While driving through open range where no fences separated cattle from the narrow country roads, the sisters informed me that large developers had already made plans to build subdivisions here. And now I am reminded of a quote from Thoreau, an excerpt from his 1860 journal, *Almost all our improvements, so called, tend to convert the country into the town.*

We said our goodbyes to all the family, stopping one final time to see mom and Bill on the way out of Auburn. They had returned safely from their elder hostel, where they reported having an interesting and informative week. We thanked them for letting us stay in their apartment, where for one week we had lived a lifestyle about as different from our Wallowa County one as could be possible, and enjoyed it. We had to admit to them, however, that we weren't quite ready to exchange ranch life for city life.

The stormy Sierra, having provided a mere six-hour window of clear weather, permitted us to sneak through on bare roads. Winter snows lay deep on Donner Summit, which was an extreme contrast to a month ago. Donner Lake, an ice-blue jewel, lay at the base of the snowy summit.

Meanwhile, back here on Prairie Creek, nearly a week has passed already and life goes on. The days are longer and the bitter deep-freeze chill has relaxed. As I write, the cows tiptoe across the icy surface of the thawing snow to come to water. The spring calvers, bellies swollen with calves, wait for motherhood. Ben has done his usual fine job of caring not only for our cattle, but for the chickens, barn cats and dog as well.

Slowly, the news trickled in. The death of another old-timer, Chet Lewis; friend Grace hospitalized with pneumonia; grandson James calls: "I've got the chicken pox, grandma." More changes to our small town of Joseph. Kohlhepp's Kitchen has been sold. Now under the new name of the Cheyenne Cafe, the gathering spot for old-timers has seen a facelift.

Linde called and set up a cross-country ski trip to nearby Salt Creek Summit, where it was 10 degrees warmer than Prairie Creek. On that weekday we were the only skiers and the cold quiet of Wallowa County's backcountry was perfect for skiing.

On Sunday Doug and I drove out of the Wallowa Valley to the 60-mile distant city of La Grande where we met daughter Lori and her husband, Tom, and their children, Lacey and Ryan, at The Pizza Hut for lunch before attending the matinee performance of "The Secret Garden." Every seat in McKenzie Theater on the Eastern Oregon State College campus was filled. Afterward, we met with granddaughter Carrie, who was in the cast.

Driving home under a muted, full moon, the pale light of which shone on the Minam River, allowed us to see bunches of deer along

Highway 82. At the moment, a chinook's warm breath is causing a great melting here on Prairie Creek.

February 13—The sound of two wild honkers flying low over our wall tent woke me. Their honking was the only sound, save for the swirling, sliding current of the Snake as it flowed past Dug Bar. After dressing in the warmth given by our Duckett Sheepherder stove, in which a fire had been kindled earlier by Doug, I opened the tent flap just in time to watch the sun fire the high rims with gold.

A hard frost covered the ground, and it would be nearly 8:30 before the sun spilled over the high eastern rim onto Dug Bar. The Snake, jade-colored, flowed just beyond our camp. Walking uphill to the Forest Service outhouse, I remembered when Doug and I were first married, the all too brief time we spent living in the house here on the Dug Bar Ranch. The house, painted a different color now, still stands under a grove of locust trees where nearby Birch Creek empties into the Snake.

Returning to the tent to mix up sourdough pancakes, I see the two geese have landed in the eddy. At the barn, cowboy Bill, who works for the Hubbard Ranch, is saddling up his horse and packing a mule with salt. By the time we are eating hotcakes, bacon and eggs outside in the sunshine of a beautiful canyon morning, we can see Bill making his way on horseback, pulling the mule up the steep trail to Dug Bar. His two cow dogs surprise a herd of mule deer, which then leap to an adjacent bench and curiously stare at the passing procession. We are witnessing a bit of the old West, which is still very much a part of the present West, at least here in the Canyon country of Wallowa County.

Last Sunday, listening to a favorable long-range weather forecast on our TV at the ranch on Prairie Creek, we decided to spend a week camping and fishing at Dug Bar. It turned out to be a wise decision, as day after day of mild, sunny days ensued. We ended up living there in our snug wall tent for six days.

It was pretty hectic that Monday "getting gone," as we had to have our income tax book-work completed before we left, as we planned on coming out on Thursday to meet with our accountant. By the time we loaded our camping gear and hooked the boat to the pickup, it was already afternoon, and we had a 30-mile drive to Imnaha, then another 30 miles of winding dirt road to Dug Bar. Daisy, perched on the tarped duffel in back of the pickup, grinned with anticipation.

The sun had long since disappeared behind the high western rims when we pulled into our camping spot at the head of the bar. Gas lights glowed softly from the windows of the house, and were most welcome, because human habitation in the remote, ragged canyon is very scarce. We'd negotiated the washout at Corral Creek and survived the deep, muddy ruts that filled the narrow road as it hugged the high rims above the Snake. At one point I had to run ahead and throw rocks out of the road, due to our boat trailer's limited clearance.

Bill, lonely because his wife was out "on top" purchasing supplies, and wasn't due in until Thursday, walked down and gave us a hand setting up the tent, It was dark by the time we had a fire popping in the stove, a lantern lit, and hamburgers sizzling in the fry pan for supper. Shortly afterward we crawled into our bedrolls and slept the sleep of happy campers.

The next morning I found a card and some heart-shaped chocolates waiting for me on the camp table—from my Valentine! We spent our days fishing from the boat, which Doug piloted up and down the river.

Monday evening, while I tended the sourdough biscuits, Doug returned with fish enough for supper, which were cooked along with some venison loin we'd brought in. I made a salad and baked those biscuits in the small oven of the Duckett stove. We had invited Bill for supper, and he was so impressed with the biscuits that he wanted to know how to begin a starter of his own. It was cozy in the tent; we had chairs, a table, and pack boxes that doubled for more work space.

In the clear, frosty night air, stars glittered so bright, we thought we could feel them. And stepping outside to see the soft glow of the lantern-lit tent, is another picture I'll store away in my mind's eye.

After camp chores were done that first morning, Daisy and I hiked up the Snake River trail that took off just beyond the barn. The day was clear and sunny, with nary a breeze to rattle the dormant hackberry, bunch grass and sarvisberry. The ground was frozen on the shady norths but thawing in the sun-filled sections, still dozing with the smell of spring. I paused often on the steep trail to take in the scene below and catch my breath.

The view became more interesting at every switchback. Ranch buildings clustered under locust trees, a gray horse running around the pasture, missing the one Bill was riding, the river running high, winding out of sight between towering canyon walls that stretched forever, and our tiny wall tent pitched alongside the lone hackberry tree. In the river I spotted Doug piloting the boat through Warm Springs rapids.

A golden eagle flying downriver, cattle with new calves grazing a faraway grassy bench, and outlined against the sky the nine deer Bill had spooked earlier, their long mule ears pointed toward Daisy and me.

Up we chug to a wire gate and fence line. I climb over a rockjack and continue toward Dug Basin.

Far below, the white water of more rapids near Deep Creek comes into my line of vision as the trail levels out, following its high course above the river. I want to keep going, but must get back to camp and fix lunch. Recrossing the rockjack, something bright yellow catches my eye. A buttercup! Then, looking around on that high saddle, I see more. Spring is coming to the canyons.

On Wednesday, son-in-law Charley and his young, good-looking ranch hand, Greg, drive in and spend the night with us. While Doug takes them fishing downriver toward Eureka Bar, I set the sourdough biscuits to rise and boil up some spuds to fry later. Our visitors brought in some beef steaks that we would barbecue over coals outside.

That evening, the four of us feasting in that wild setting, we had to agree, "It just don't get any better than this!" While Greg read the instructions, Charley struggled with the setting up of his daughter's pop-up tent. After many laughs, the tent was somewhat secured to the ground, and our two guests survived the night.

The next morning we treated Charley and Greg to our familiar fare of sourdough pancakes. Then, while the men fished downriver, I puttered around camp, read a book, took a short walk with Daisy, and enjoyed the solitude afforded by the canyons.

We packed up what we needed after lunch, leaving the camp there, and drove out "on top" where I arrived with no time to spare to drive to Enterprise and preside over a Fishtrap board meeting. There had been no time for a bath, so I attended with sourdough dried on my clothes and feeling a bit grubby.

The next day, after we met with our accountant, we noticed a few clouds banking over the mountains as we refilled our supplies. We pulled out of the ranch on Prairie Creek at 4 and headed back to the river. We made it without incident, and ate our late supper by lantern light before tumbling into bed, with the sound of the Snake in our ears.

A light rain pattered on our tent the next morning, and white mists trailed over the river and hung in the draws, but it was warm and there was an absence of wind.

It turned colder, however, as we fished the confluence of the Imnaha with the Snake, when the rain became serious. We were pretty soaked by the time we returned in the boat to camp. But then, like it does in the canyons, the sun came out between showers and life was glorious again.

That afternoon, Daisy and I hiked the Nee-Me-Poo trail, which follows the retreat route taken by Chief Joseph and his Wallowa band of

Nez Perce, until another rain shower turned us back.

Bill and wife Diane, who had returned late Thursday night, invited us to dinner that last evening. Bill had hinted that if I brought the sourdough biscuits, they'd provide the rest of the meal. So we carried a pan of biscuits uphill and baked them in the same old gas stove we used when Doug owned the ranch. Bill barbecued and we enjoyed a tasty product of the canyon grass: beef. Pretty hard to beat.

A rainbow arched over Warm Springs rapids as we loaded up and left the next morning. As we would around those high rims, I glanced down at Dug Bar and wished we didn't have to leave. What a wonderful adventure it would be this year, without the seed potatoes to worry over, to be there and watch spring spread across the canyons.

Doug and I attended the Sweetheart dinner at the Imnaha church that evening, but that is another story.

February 20—Back up here "on top" at the ranch on Prairie Creek, our mountains wear a fresh blanket of snow and more rain is forecast. The first baby calves are appearing in the calving pasture, and Ben is busy.

March 11—Because there is so much to write about between columns now, I don't know where to begin. Should I write about the emerging buttercups, the returning robins, the new calves…or brag about grand-daughter Chelsie's basketball team's win? Big Time. They won the state class 2-A championship. Our local radio announcer even shed a tear or two over that final, emotional game in Pendleton. Knowing Enterprise would travel en masse to that championship game, his comment was: "Would the last person to leave Enterprise, please turn out the lights!"

Then there was our Winter Fishtrap Writer's Conference, held at the Eagle Cap Chalets at Wallowa Lake, and of course more cross country skiing adventures. One morning I awoke to see a small Palomino mare in our horse pasture. Doug surprised me with a new saddle horse…her new name, Sorpresa, Spanish for surprise.

Two of my milk cows, Hollyhock and Stargirl, are back at the barn, and the chore of feeding them each day is added to taking care of the chickens, my new mare, and checking on the other three milk cows, which comprise my small herd.

One first-calf heifer just calved yesterday, but the two kept by the barn are just springing. Ben brought me an orphan bull calf whose mom was sick, and the vet brought him into the world after her death. He'll do fine on a bottle until Stargirl calves.

Last Saturday I drove to Imnaha and went fishing with grandson Buck, who had just climbed to the top of a high rim above his house to hunt for sheds. Sheds are antlers left lying around from elk and deer. Buck and his two friends Gabe and Luke had found several that morning.

It is fun being with 15-year-old Buck; he always has good stories to tell. Did I know that Imnaha was plunged into total darkness one night?

"No," I replied. "How come?"

"Well," said Buck. "The PP&L men came down, and found a placenta hanging over the power lines! And the whole settlement was without power." It seems an eagle carrying a cow's placenta must have dropped it in flight. Easy to believe, as there have been bald eagles all over Prairie Creek lately, gorging themselves on the leavings of birthings of hundreds of calves.

Linde and I made an effort to get ourselves in shape for a big back country ski trip, by skiing around Ferguson Ridge for several days in a row. Finally, when we had tended to the logistics, we waved goodbye to Linde's husband Pat, who had driven us to our jumping-off place at Salt Creek summit.

"Any last requests?" he called, as we skied out of sight.

Nearly 12 miles separated us from my car, parked at the McCully Creek trailhead, and the morning was perfect. Clear and crisp with deep, powdery snow covering the trail. It was slide and glide alongside the frozen canal. Huge snow cornices hung over the far edge of the canal.

We were in the old burn of the huge Canal fire, now a scene of beauty. Fire-blackened trees, reduced to straight poles, cast shadows on the clean white snow. A scene created by heat and cold…fire and ice. When the barren tree shadows fell from above the canal, their dark shapes curved softly to accommodate the curve of the hill. A log across the canal was a work of art where a lone snowshoe rabbit had crossed it.

The Seven Devils mountain range in Idaho came into view, owing to the bareness of the burn. Far below, in the blackened timber, we could hear the drumming of a great northern flicker, the only sound in that vast white wilderness. The trail was level and in full sun for the first few miles, and then we were treated to evergreens laden with snow, which afforded shade. We began to shed layers of clothing.

A slight whisper of a breeze sent showers of snow sifting down from the burdened limbs. Diamond sparkle's of snow dust wafted through the sunshine filled air. Finally, we came to a downhill section and zoomed around corners, loving the wild freedom of the woods and the feel of cold air blowing our hair back from our faces. Numerous creeks splashed under icy, snow-sculpted bridges, and under great fallen logs.

At one point the sun's warmth caused a great melting in the bank above the road, where a spring seeped from the ground. Red Osier dogwood's sap was rising and its thin limbs seemed to turn a deeper shade of cranberry as we watched. You could hear the trickle of water, see the red soil thawing and. oozing, and smell the letting go of winter to spring.

Beginning to experience hunger pangs, we searched for a fallen log, brushed the snow off, spread our jackets, and in the sunshine ate our lunches. Our two dogs collapsed in the snow, and rested. While we had been skiing in a forward motion, they had been running up and down the trail, or sniffing out snowshoe rabbit tracks. When I lagged behind Linde, who is 10 years my junior, here would come Daisy checking on me.

Resuming our trek, we skied down a steep draw and crossed Cabin Creek, which flowed from high places. Down another final draw, carved by the waters of Ferguson Creek; and then up a long hill to see the ragged crest of the Seven Devils, their snowy ramparts etched against the blue horizon above Hells Canyon.

Finally, a marker sign, *8 miles*, which meant approximately four more to go. Eventually we broke out on a high curve that afforded a splendid view of the Findley Buttes, and the cut that is Little Sheep Creek's course to Imnaha through the canyon country. Farther north the vast Zumwalt Prairie stretched all the way to the timbered Chesnimnus and Washington state line.

Closer to home, we could pick out our ranch and Kinney Lake. We felt so lucky being there on that high ridge, the only skiers on that Friday. Soon we were following our old ski trails, which wound above the Ferguson Ridge ski area. The blisters forming on our heels hadn't yet broken by the time we reached the McCully Creek trailhead and my car. A wonderful ski on a perfect day.

At our Winter Fishtrap Gathering, I listened to writer and former smoke jumper Clay Morgan speak about writing. He said, "When you write, there must be a story, and most importantly, your subject must be in some sort of danger, or else you lose your reader's interest."

In a way, I disagree with Clay. I think there is so much danger woven into modern writing that the real danger is in not being able to enjoy reading about something pleasant. Clay may be right, but if he is, the book I am working on will never sell. But I think people are hungry for adventures that fill the senses, especially narrative written firsthand about the outdoors.

Our Winter Fishtrap's theme was FIRE, and Sid Goodloe came all the way from his Carrizo Valley ranch in New Mexico to wow us with his knowledge of using fire as a management tool on his ranch. Not a fan of Smokey Bear, Sid, small of stature, large on personality, spoke with a Texas A&M drawl that left no doubt in our minds as to what he was saying. Clad in boots, hat, belt buckle, Levis, and silk kerchief at his throat, Sid painted word pictures, brought to life by slides, of his world of pinion, pine and juniper-turned-savannah.

Stephen Pyne, professor of American studies at Arizona State University West in Phoenix, a leading authority on wildfire and author of numerous books, provided an overview and a history of fire through the ages. What a treat meeting and getting to know Stephen. At the moment I am reading his book *Fire on the Rim,* which deals with his 15 years as a firefighter on the North Rim of the Grand Canyon.

What would we do without fire to use as puns? It was indeed a fiery gathering, and brought to our cold winter conference a diversity of subjects dealing with enough heat to warm us for months to come.

April 2—This was not a good morning. First off, after I let the three calves nurse Stargirl, I ran Hollyhock and her calf into the small enclosure next to the milking parlour. No problem there. I let Stargirl out and left her three calves in the barn. Everything was going too smoothly.

With the aim of letting "Venus" out of the calving shed, where I had been keeping her with her two necked-together calves, I walked across the ditch and opened a large wooden panel gate. Taking care not to let the baling wire, which served to secure the gate, touch the hot wired fence, I left the gate open.

My husband believes in hot wiring everything. It is threaded around my chicken pen, and literally encircles the ranch. I managed to make it safely through that obstacle, only to be thwarted by another, a metal gate this time, with two latches that slid into openings on a metal post. The bottom latch was engaged; the top, not. Another pieces of Wallowa County rawhide secured this gate too, which opened into a series of corrals.

I struggled to no avail to disengage the bottom latch. In the nearby barn I found a steel post to use as a lever, so the latch would unlatch from the uneven gate. It wouldn't budge. Exasperated, I struggled until Ben, passing by with a load of hay, came to my rescue. And, in the way of men, as they stand before a helpless female, Ben gave one mighty jerk and the gate flew open.

I drove the cow Venus and her two calves out of the barn. Rather, I drove the cow out, and dragged the two calves, or they drug me, through the barnyard gunk. The calves and I were gasping for air by the time I shoved them through the gate into the pasture with the other two milk cows. Before dealing with the wooden panel.

In my haste, I had forgotten about the hot wire, and my hat touched one, and my hand was on the baling wire, closing the gate, when it too connected with the hot fence. Yikes!

I went to my knees as the jolt ran through me. Jump-started and mad, I left the gate closed, but not tied, and after haying the cows, headed to the house.

Covered with barnyard, I stuck my head in the kitchen doorway and told my True Love that it wasn't the livestock business that would do me in. It was the facilities! Smart man that he is, he chose at this time not to respond. Eventually I cooled down and he dealt with the gate…and things have been pretty good ever since.

In a few days, we will remove the swivel collars from the two pairs of necked-together calves, and not until next spring will I have to deal with this aspect of grafting calves onto cows.

About twice a week I milk a gallon of house milk from the Holstein/Simmental Stargirl, who fills my milking stall with her bulk. After three other gals dropped out on us due to other commitments, Stanlynn, the llama lady, who owns the Hurricane Creek Llamas guide service, ed with me into the Big Sheep Shelter from Salt Creek Summit.

The weather was perfect and although I was a bit different skiing on corn snow, we had a very pleasurable trip in, carrying packs containing our sleeping bags on our backs. My faithful dog, Daisy, equipped with a dog pack, carried all my food. Good dog.

We spent the night in the outfitter's tent, which contained all the comforts of home (almost), cooked our meals, read by lamp light, and went to sleep, lulled by the soothing waters of Big Sheep Creek flowing just below camp.

At one point we entertained ourselves by reading the adventures of former visitors, written in a log book. Many mentioned the mice. One party wrote: *Final count…6 mice, 2 knees, and a blister.* Others elaborated on heavy snows, star-filled nights, gourmet food and wonderful accommodations. All had a good time.

So did we, and wrote: *0 mice, 2 wonderful times, and all knees and joints intact.*

We awoke to silence. It was snowing. A fine snow, with a prediction of a blizzard working its way down from the north. So we opted to pack up that morning, and head out. The corn snow had frozen during the night, and the new snow on top was treacherous because of the ice beneath. But we managed to make it safely out to the trailhead just after the blizzard hit. On the trail out we passed a group of six skiing into our shelter for a four-day stay. Two men were pulling sleds, one of which had a fresh pineapple lashed on top. What a picture that made in the blizzard. It snowed several inches that day, and the next it was bright and sunny. How we envied that group of men and women, far back there at the headwaters of Big Sheep Creek.

Today is a grass-growing day, and the Wallowa snow fields are blinding in their whiteness. Tomorrow I will be on horseback most of the day, as we take the cows the final lap of their annual trek to the hills.

April 8—"This is the day that the Lord has made, I will rejoice, and be glad of it." These words drifted out over what is known as Kate and Wil Wilde's bench, situated high above the snowmelt-swollen waters of the north-flowing Imnaha. As the rising sun spilled down over the eastern rimrocks, the singers' voices mingled with those of numerous meadowlarks. Mixed voices, young girls and boys, their parents, and a sprinkling of grandparents, rejoicing in a near perfect Easter Sunday morning.

A small campfire competed with the sun to ward off an early morning chill, and red-stem filaree bloomed pink between patches of scab rock. Stuck in the ground, a crude wooden cross provided the only prop. The service was short, and ended with four teenagers presenting a scriptural skit and the gathered congregation singing "Amazing Grace."

To those of us privileged enough to be there, it was an unforgettable experience. No doubt about it, He was there. I drove down with grandson Shawn, home on leave after graduating from Marine boot camp, to be with family for the sunrise service.

Then it was a 30-mile drive back to the Prairie Creek ranch to take a ham out of the oven and join 34 members of our large extended family out on what is known as Ramona and Charley's grass ranch. We spread a picnic under the wide, sunny skies, and became children again. With the snowy Wallowas looking down, we tossed horse shoes, hid and hunted Easter eggs, and gorged ourselves on roast turkey, ham, numerous salads and homemade bread, topped off by a large cake honoring Shawn.

We then spent the long afternoon playing a rousing game of baseball. After 9-year-old James and 13-year-old Becky chose up their teams, the grassy hills rang with the excited voices of young and old alike. Big girls braided wildflowers in little girls' hair. Grass widows, yellow bells and buttercups are out now, and this grandma's heart overflowed with gratification.

What a spring this is! So much going on, I scarcely have time to record it. There have been brandings up Big Sheep Creek, with outrageous scenery backgrounding the activity. The canyons are alive with blooming sarvisberry bushes, yellow forsythia, and showers of fruit blossoms. Grass is greening, trees are leafing, and birds are singing. I snapped rolls of film during a recent branding, because so many of the cowboys and cowgirls were my children and grandchildren. All had a job to do, and made the work fun.

During spring break week, we had the grandchildren here from Pendleton. Lacey and Ryan joined their cousins, and Doug and took them fishing on Imnaha. We all cheered when 15-year-old Josh caught a nice steelhead. After picnicking with two carloads of children we managed to survive the day, and even squeezed in milk shakes at the Imnaha Cafe.

This morning Doug and I helped Ben trail the fall calvers out of the valley. The weaned, bawling calves have been left behind here in the corrals while their mamas can't wait to graze the Salmon Creek hills. Meanwhile, my own burgeoning cow herd is content, but not without days of sweat, mud and patience. After much trial and error, I now have eight calves nursing four cows, with one more heifer to calve and graft an extra calf on.

April 21—One sure way to make it snow in April in Wallowa County is to mow the lawn, or set a banty hen on a clutch of eggs. She'll hatch during a blizzard every' time. Cows know this too, and the stirrings in their bellies give way to birthings during, or just before, a spring storm. One thing about spring snows; they are short-lived, and moisture in any form is welcome. Dry-land grain fields, and the acres of hill and canyon range drinks and stores the precious water for the dry season to come.

Opening the chicken house one such snowy morning, and closing it quickly behind me, I heard, above the roar of the Prairie Creek wind, small cheepings. My little banty hen was hatching out five varied-colored chicks, which are sired by one, or all three, of my roosters.

Speaking of roosters, I am encouraging Chester III to crow as much as he likes, for you see, he is entered in the Great Rooster Crowing contest in Weston, to be held on June 1. Instigator and organizer Ruby Kirk hopes there are many entries in what is becoming THE annual event in the small town of Weston, Oregon.

Ruby writes, *This year I have arranged to have a loud speaker system, as I had trouble making myself heard over the crowing.*

Rain, sleet, snow or hail has not thwarted the hikes Scotty and I

While three cowboys on horseback hold the calves steady, a ground crew bands, vaccinates, and dehorns. Shown here at a recent branding on Big Sheep Creek in the Imnaha canyons is a crew helping Kirk Makin, who runs cattle there. Entire families have a job to do. Horseback are Buck Matthews, Doug Tippett, and Bud Zollman. Ground crew are Greg Johnson, James Nash, Mona Matthews, Jackie Matthews, Bill Matthews, Hope Royes, Kirk and Liz Makin, and Riley Makin. Even the smallest youngster has a job.

take once (and sometimes twice) a week around Wallowa Lake. It is our favorite time up there, no tourists with their RV's and noise. Not that we have anything against them, but if one really wishes to enjoy the beauty of the lake, April and late fall are the times to experience serenity along with spectacular scenery.

Most of the cabins and homes are vacant then, and walks along the rivers flowing into the lake are especially refreshing. Some take you into wilderness, only steps away up a nearby trail. The trails, when not covered with snow, are carpeted with soft pine needles, and the crystal clear waters of the West Fork of the Wallowa River tumble down from high places in torrents and under wooden bridges that span the stream.

On a recent April morning, Scotty and I, along with our two dogs, decided to walk up the Chief Joseph trail. We appeared to be the first hikers this spring. There was the smell of wet moss and emerging ferns, and brilliant buttercups bloomed on the sunny exposures. Rock chasms yawned below us as we climbed a narrow ledge and gazed down upon frothy pools, where blue-green waters cascaded from the mountains.

Up over rock slides we climbed, where our dogs were teased by the shy Pika, small rock rabbits, which let out a high-pitched cry before ducking safely under rocks just as the dogs reached their hiding places. Patches of snow lay in the trail, high altitude sunlight, warm and steaming, the shadow of a cloud, glimpses of Wallowa Lake through tall pines.

We broke out on a high switchback and looked back to see the snowy heights of Mt. Bonneville, illuminated in brilliant sunlight. We approached a roaring falls, where a creek races straight down toward the Boy Scout camp. We stood on the wooden bridge, absorbing the energy of falling water.

Some days we walk from the head of the lake to the foot, noticing hawks sailing over the east moraine, and returning waterfowl bouncing up and over the wavelets. Large numbers of mule deer feed on the new bunch grass growing on the glacial drifts that comprise the great moraines. Deer are skylined against the high, perfect lateral moraine, the grassy sides of which are waiting to burst into a golden carpet of Arrowleaf balsamroot in late May or early June.

On the lake shore, dormant syringa is beginning to bud, and the giant cottonwood's leaves are greening. The lake and its basin is a very special area, beloved by all.

Other mornings, we hike to a picnic table at the foot of the lake and eat our lunches, seated behind a grove of aspen with the lake at our feet. And always, after a hike, we swim. Not in the lake mind you, but at the wonderful indoor pool provided by the Eagle Cap Chalets.

Mike and Bev Hayward, owners of this establishment, have done a masterful job of providing tastefully built log cabins and apartments to serve the tourists. Locals can enjoy the amenities during the off-season; the pool, that is. Nothing is more refreshing after a brisk mountain hike than a swim in an indoor pool, followed by a soak in a whirlpool hot tub. Again, we have the place to ourselves, and relax while our dogs collapse under the car and dream of chasing pikas.

My last cow, a second-calf heifer, calved yesterday. She waited until the mini-blizzard hit, then let the big "black baldy" bull calf out into the world of snow. Today he is running around, bellering in the sunshine of a perfect day.

Things are easier at the barn these days. I let Stargirl's three calves in to nurse morning and evening, and milk her for what house milk we need. The other two cows have accepted their extra calves. If only cattle prices would come up, I might realize a profit this fall. Nine calves on five cows isn't bad.

Weather or not, spring is here in Wallowa County, and as usual, the calendar fills up before the page is turned to a new month.

Last evening I attended, as a member of the press, the annual coronation dinner-dance of the Chief Joseph Days royal court. Mad cow disease didn't spoil the appetites of the huge crowd who partook of Jerry's catering of a prime rib dinner. The meat was cooked to perfection and the entire meal was delicious.

Emcee for the gala event was none other than our ex-Oregon Cattlemen's president, Mack Birkmaier. With his down-home, Crow Crik humor, Mack enlightened the crowd with amusing anecdotes and stories gleaned from his Joseph Creek growing-up years. He began with a story about my hubby, who also grew up on Joseph Creek. Perhaps you've heard a version of this popular story before, so I won't retell it here. Just ask someone who attended last night's function and they'll gladly pass it along.

On the serious side, Mack encouraged everyone concerned about the future of the cattle business, which supports and enables us to attain a sense of community so special here in Wallowa county, to defeat the stream initiative. If this dangerously worded bill should make its way onto a ballot, many well-meaning people would vote for it, not knowing the ramifications such a bill would have on the entire agricultural community.

As I hike along the streams and rivers of Wallowa County, I can't help but remember that there are thousands of cattle in our area, yet our streams, spring runoff and an occasional exception not included, run as clean and as sparkling as any in the state. In the urban areas, where subdivisions are going up at an alarming rate, the waterways are littered with pop cans, foil, and plastic, and fouled with human refuse.

Given a choice, I'd choose cows over condos any day.

May 2—I ventured out to chore into a frosty morning, a biting wind blowing out of the north. Then Doug saddled my new mare, Sorpresa. I stuffed a water bottle and two oat cakes in my saddle bags, and climbed aboard. It was all day in the saddle, as we trailed the cows and calves out to their summer range, a distance of 24 miles.

Friend Scotty, who wanted to go along for the hike, appeared on schedule, and walked the 14 miles that first day. Whip in hand, she urged calves out of barrow pits, and was a great help. Being 74 didn't slow her down one bit. The morning continued cool, verging on cold, which was excellent for trailing cows and baby calves. My easy-riding new little mare was full of vinegar. The long miles stretched ahead as we turned onto the Crow Creek road.

Other ranchers, including Doug McDaniel, Makin and Lathrop, passed us, hauling cattle in trucks. Identical twin sisters Sharon and Sherry helped also. Dressed alike: same chinks, shirts, boots, and slickers, it was impossible to tell them apart. These two gals, who grew up near Sisters, Oregon, moved to Wallowa County years ago, and have spent most of their lives in the saddle. They were good help. If a calf lagged or became sore-footed, it was roped and lifted into a pickup, which appeared at intervals, with Seth, Ben's son, at the wheel.

At noon we sought a sheltered spot along the gravel road, and hunched down out of the wind and ate our lunches. I was thinking about our friend Bill, who would be leaving Alpine House right then with his son and family to move to Smith River. No time for goodbyes...we wish Bill luck in his new home.

After trailing the cows and calves into the pasture at East Crow, we unsaddled our horses and turned them loose with the cattle. Then returned with Doug, who had appeared with the pickup to transport us back to the valley.

The next morning frost lay heavy on Prairie Creek, but there was an absence of wind. Scotty showed up and Doug drove his carload of female cowboys out to East Crow where we saddled up and gathered the cows and calves, and turned them out on the road to finish the final 10 miles. This is the life.

The air is fragrant with all the springtime odors of the hills. The smell of water running in Crow Creek, dark, loamy soil, bruised grass, under cow's hooves, chokecherry leafing out, a hint of mint, wafting from the waterways. And the sights. Prairie Smoke, the cloudy pink bloom that will mature into a billow of smoke-colored puffs. Sunshine and cloud, ever-changing light. A scattering of dry snow flakes, the splash of a beaver's tail in the swamp alongside the road. A crumbling homestead, lonely, children's graves enclosed by an iron fence. The snorting of my mare, the shuffle of cow's feet in the gravel, the bawling when mom is separated from her calf.

The old Dorrance place with its aging log cabin, and "pink" barn comes into view, then Seth and Ben there to turn the cattle up the grade. Suddenly we are surrounded by a wild garden of phlox, and farther up the grade appear the first balsamroot, their yellow sunflower-like blooms mingling with the new bunch grass. Heavy-bellied mule tail does shyly hide among the thornbush thickets below the road.

Sherry and Sharon rope two lagging calves and Seth appears to load them in the sag wagon. At the top we let the herd drift, and eat our lunches in the sunshine. In the distance behind us, the snowy Wallowas; and before us the vast high plateau that comprises the grassy Zumwalt Prairie.

Not a soul do we meet on this road. We ride past where the one-room Dry Salmon Creek School once stood. Today the cattle drink, as Dry Salmon Creek is wet, flowing happily along. Turning up the final pull toward Deadman, the first flakes of snow sift through the sunshine. Then, in as long as it takes to tell it, the sky darkens, the snow thickens, and the air is cold. Soon visibility is limited to the cow directly in front of my horse. White builds up on our horses' tails, on our slickers, and our mittened hands.

Grimly we urge the cattle on. Scotty, silent in a white world, trods resolutely onward. Down the long, sloping hill to Deadman the wind whips snow into our faces, and our sunny lunch stop is only a dream. At last we push the last calf through and Seth shuts the wire gate. Fortunately, in only a matter of minutes Doug appears and we load the horses and head for home. In the warmth of the pickup our heads nod and sleep is ours.

After my horse accident last May, I wondered if I would ever ride again. Once a cowgirl, always a cowgirl.

May 7—For the first morning in a long while there was an absence of frost. Tulips, stunted for days by cold, have unfurled into a glowing row of red on the eastern side of our house today. Another sign of spring: kittens. Our aged mama kitty "kittened" behind the broom and mop holder on the carport, as she always does. Three black babies, mewing.

Then we noticed one of her grown, pregnant daughters with her. On closer inspection, we realized this offspring was nursing her mom. Every time we passed by the porch, we tossed her out. Then lo and behold we discovered more kittens, squirming around the first batch.

Yep, daughter birthed hers on top of mom's. The old matriarch, approaching the end of her nine lives, must have made arrangements for this "kitty commune" in the event old age caught up with her before the kittens were weaned. The mothers take turns hunting gophers and nursing their combined brood of five. All are thriving.

Several mornings later, through the open window over my kitchen sink, I heard more mewings. Following the sounds, I realized they were coming from a 10-gallon, rusty milk can that was shot full of holes and used in the summer for a flower planter.

Another daughter of the old mama kitty had chosen this safe spot to raise her three kittens! Kittens, anyone? Guaranteed hunters.

Life is everywhere now, the land pulsates with it. However, one life was recently extinguished. Friend Jan Bailey lost her husband after a bravely fought battle with leukemia. I attended Ron's graveside service on an April afternoon at the nearby Prairie Creek Cemetery.

It was an unsettled day, great clouds forming, casting their darkened, moving shadows scudding silently over the green and fallow farmland that is upper Prairie Creek. The ragged crest of the Seven Devils range swam in and out of focus. Like life…shadow and sunlight. Death, it seems, comes as surely as birth, as surely as the spring storms that sweep over the Wallowas.

It was a moving service. So right. There were tears shed as the clouds shed the sleety rain…and everyone felt cleansed. A clump of people gathering, shivering in the Prairie Creek wind…yet warmed by words.

My 86-year-old mother and her husband, Bill, after four days of sightseeing along the way, drove in safely from Auburn, California, on a Friday. They looked terrific. Mom and Bill hadn't visited Wallowa County in nearly ten years.

That first evening, after supper, I took both of them to a poetry reading at the Bookloft in Enterprise. Neighbor Sara Miller read poems dedicated to William Stafford, and several she had written herself. It was a very enjoyable evening, and a nice way to celebrate National Poetry Month.

Arranging to visit mom's grandchildren and great-grandchildren, not to mention connecting with their spouses, was quite an undertaking. The grandchildren, now with graying hair, have children who are now grown and a few are off to college.

One cold, windy morning I took them to Joseph High School, where they were able to see great-granddaughter Chelsie perform in a track meet, as well as meet her father, Ken. We invited Ramona's family over one evening for a roast chicken supper, and another time we traveled to the springtime canyons to visit daughter Jackie's family, who lives along the Imnaha River.

On a Sunday afternoon we caught up with grandson Todd and his family on Alder Slope. Bill and I got in several walks, and once we swam in the indoor pool at the Eagle Cap Chalets at Wallowa Lake. Mom, too, jumped right in, agile as ever, while her husband swam laps around the pool.

I was able to exercise my culinary hobby and cooked gourmet meals: poached salmon, sourdough bread, and blackberry cream pie. I had fun with baked tomato pasta and antipasto salad. They claimed it was the best food they'd had on the entire trip. And Jackie's Imnaha beef steaks, barbecued by Buck and Mona, were a special treat as well.

Mom worked on a watercolor of a bouquet of tulips and daffodils I'd forced to bloom indoors. An accomplished watercolorist, she recently completed a showing of her works in Placer County, California. When we were growing up on the dairy, mom was too busy with the dairy work to paint, but she is making up for it now.

When the folks left, it was a real letdown, but mom says they'll be back when she turns 90. Hope it's before that. After they left I took a long walk over Hough's hill, and was comforted by the showing of wildflowers. Acres of Prairie smoke, cous, yellow bells, shooting stars, and carpets of phlox, ranging in color from pale pink to magenta.

May 15—After a warm rain soaked Prairie creek—again—I ventured out to the barn, clad in raincoat and boots, and thought the landscape resembled pictures I'd seen of Scotland. Through the muted green mists appeared my enormous Simmental/Holstein cow. Glistening with moisture, a dandelion protruding from her mouth, she brought to mind a poem memorized in grammar school.

Blown by all the winds that pass,
and wet from all the showers,
she walks among the meadow grass
and eats the meadow flowers.

With the vast segment of our population so far removed from the land, and therefore cows, perhaps it would help in communicating through poetry. Robert L. Stevenson sure reached a lot of people with that one.

Stargirl's vast, damp hulk warmed the barn with her presence, and the froth fell from the mouths of her nursing three calves. After I pulled them off, this gentle giant of a cow licked her offspring tenderly through the stanchion she was locked into.

The dandelion had fallen into the feed trough and mingled with rolled barley. As I unlocked the stanchion, and opened the milking parlour door, the old wooden floor boards creaked under her weight as she slowly made her way outside, where she let out a long sigh. Lots of work converting grass to milk. Lots of grazing and cud-chewing...and patience.

From another poem of Stevenson's, memorized about the same time,

The world is so full of a number of things,
we should all be as happy as kings.

Looking out at Prairie Creek that misty morning, I could understand what Robert L. was trying to convey.

It is time to pick up nightcrawlers, which ooze their slimy way across the barnyard, and pack them in dirt for fishing season; and time to wander the woodlands in search of tasty, elusive morels. Speaking of which, Linde and I began what started out to be a wild morel chase that turned into a mushroom bonanza. The long hike was worth the effort as we finally stumbled into a sunny opening fairly bulging with morels.

We had hiked up our old ski trails on Ferguson Ridge, keeping a lookout for mama bear and her cubs, startling mule deer does, and following cow-like tracks of elk, filled with water near the boggy springs. We were thrilled with the first tiny Calypso, that dainty pink orchid-like flower with a yellow throat. Open areas were painted lavender with grass widows. Thunder clouds circled above but never wet us as we stood on that high ridge and surveyed the valley, which led to the undulating hills veiled in gray rain showers.

When we spotted a stray morel, our energy increased and onward we wandered, uphill, downhill, across foaming McCully Creek and lesser rills. Until finally, when our small buckets were filled, I used my raincoat to carry the excess.

May 16—Doug and I joined an Extension tour that departed Wallowa early in the morning. After filling up the Moffit tour bus at Island City, our driver and tour guide, Dale Victor, drove south toward Baker City, where we then headed in a westerly direction that led to Sumpter.

Enlightening us along the way, Dale related how the town of Auburn, just out of Baker City, had at one time been the largest city in Oregon, owing to the gold mine there. We also learned that the entire valley, with its wandering Powder River, was once filled with beaver, which were later trapped out.

We pulled into the Sumpter Valley railroad site, where the original steam engine and five miles of track had been restored. The track runs through the dredged areas where a dredge, which cost approximately $350,000 to build, produced $4.5 million in gold between 1935 and 1954. The dredge, also soon to be restored, was enclosed behind a fence that we were allowed to walk around to view this hulk that dredged six miles of tailings and weighed about 1,240 tons.

That day, in the rain, the ghosts of those men who operated this monument to men's dreams stood strangely silent, and small fish in the pond it floated in made dimples that competed with the falling rain.

Dale drove us to the small town of Sumpter, built after five confederate soldiers from Civil War battlefields set up their camp at the confluence of Cracker and McCully Fork creeks. The town grew slowly as mining, lumber and ranching merged as industries. Today, Sumpter has a population of around 130.

We were let off the bus to wander around between rain showers, ducking into old stores and interesting buildings, before meeting at the Sumpter Cafe for a wondrous feast, served in a rustic chuck wagon. After a buffet of ham, turkey, mashed potatoes, gravy and umpteen salads, we boarded the bus in a pouring rain to continue touring the gold country surrounding the area.

After a gain in altitude to more than 7,000 feet we reached the ghost town of Granite, another gold mining community, perched on a steep mountainside. I was interested in the story of a former resident, '49er Jimmie, who had only one companion, a rooster with which he shared all meals. It is said this rooster often perched on the edge of the bean pot, pecking himself some supper.

Back in the bus, with the windshield wipers strumming a *wish-wash*, we peered out at the miles of wet forest until Dale topped out and informed us we were now at the headwaters of the North Fork of the John Day River.

That vast drainage shows on the map as being uninhabited, except for trees, meadows, creeks, and numerous species of wildlife. In the summer it is grazed by livestock.

We stared out into small, wet meadows, where elk grazed in the rain, and creeks rushed to rivers, as the warm rain filled tributaries and the melting snow seeped silently out of the high country. We approached Tony Vey meadows—miles of meadow—which was a cattle ranch, the small buildings dwarfed by the immensity of the country.

Nearby, Starkey Creek rushed to join the Grande Ronde, and all at once we were in Starkey, a wide spot in the road that consisted of a general store. Soon we were back on Highway 82 and headed back to La Grande. Driving home, we noticed our own rivers were swollen and running over the banks.

Balsamroot bloomed, the green landscape shimmered through the rain, and again I thought of Stevenson's poem—"We should all be happy as kings." The world is always there, waiting for us to enjoy.

May 21—It is a time between storms. Already the gray curtains of rain sway in the wind over the Wallowas, and the taste of wet is in the air. Doug is roto-tilling the garden for the second time, in hopes of setting out the Walla Walla onion plants and cabbages before the next deluge. Our hayfields are knee-high, the grass growing so fast and so profuse it is frightening.

My three milk cows' calves' udders are swollen with milk, and their seven calves are roly-poly. For two weeks now we have been planning to brand those calves we trailed to the hills, and each time the date is set, it storms. But the hill country is a sea of grass…and that's what cattle raising is all about.

On Mother's Day we helped son-in-law Charley brand. Branding has become a traditional Mother's Day activity. Great wandering clouds sent shadows scurrying across the green hills as relatives and friends arrived with pickups pulling horse trailers and carrying border collie dogs.

The branding was special for me on this Mother's Day. Great-grandson Clayton was in the thick of it, decked out in wranglers, belt buckle and hat, looking forevermore like his mother and grandmother before him when they were nine months old.

He rode his first horse and gaped in awe as his uncles roped calves, his mom and aunts gave shots, and his grandpa and grandma branded, de-horned, castrated and ear-tagged. Like all young cowboys, he ate when he was hungry and slept slumped over aunt Carrie's shoulder when he was sleepy. Trucks and trailers were used to form a corral to hold the cattle, so Clayton spent a good deal of time in the pickup with great-grandma, watching the goings-on from the open window.

This littlest hand didn't lack for attention. The Johnsons, down the road, trailed a herd of cows and calves past the branding on their way to where their cattle will summer on the Divide. Off the beaten paths here in Wallowa County and all over Eastern Oregon, despite ailing cattle prices, this traditional Western lifestyle is carrying on…as it has for more than 100 years. And the country is still incredibly beautiful.

After the last calf was released to dash back to mama, we all headed over to the ranch house, where Ramona had previously prepared a humongous pan of enchiladas, fruit and tossed salad, cake and ice cream.

June 10—There are times when life becomes too serious, and then you must do something for the sheer nonsense of it. Such was my participation in the Great Rooster Crowing Contest, held recently in conjunction with the 104th annual Pioneer Picnic in the small town of Weston, Oregon. Surrounded by fertile farm lands and dominated by the

This sign adorns the site of the Great Rooster Crowing Contest in Weston.

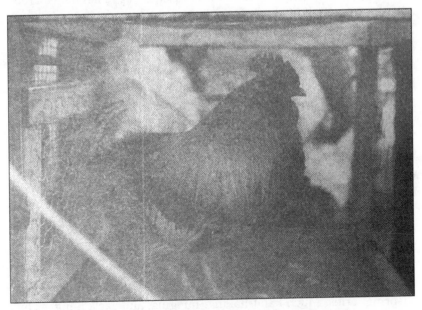

Resting between crows, this rooster eyes his competition.

large Smith Frozen Foods plant, Weston each year celebrates the return of its pioneers in their tidy park, situated in the middle of town.

Doug and I had gotten an early start. Good thing, as Chester escaped his wire cage twice, taking flight in a large field, and each time, with Daisy's delighted help, I managed to run him into the chicken pen and hook him by the feet. But after the third time, I decided to capture his son "Mr. Hanks" and go with him instead.

The Great Crowing Contest was turning into a Great Catching contest, with the roosters winning, and we hadn't even left Prairie Creek. We placed "Mr. Hanks" in the back seat of our van, covered his cage with a tarp, opened the side wings for air, and took off for Weston, which lies over a mountain range west and north of here.

As we traveled to Elgin and then over Tollgate, we heard not a sound from Mr. Hanks. Upon entering Weston we cruised down Main to the park where a sign proclaiming the picnic led us to where we were supposed to be. The picturesque park could have been any small town in the West. There was the mouth-watering aroma of barbecuing beef, the sound of a small band, two trumpets, one clarinet and a trombone, flags flying, children and old folks, young married couples, and dogs.

A few civic-minded young pea farmers were taking time out from their busy lives to help with the barbecue, setting up tables under a roof adjacent to a small kitchen. Several women hovered over and served homemade pies, whole or by the slice, pies piled high with whipped cream, and oozing fruit juices. Various crafts and homemade quilts were displayed around the park. We'd noticed yards lining Main street were blossoming with yard sales, the flotsam of people's lives reposing in the sun.

After making our way to the shaded end of the park, we unloaded Mr. Hanks, located a fountain and filled his water container and gave him some feed. My rooster at this point was crouching in a corner of his wire cage, thinking it was still night time, and acting a bit confused. He'd never been to town before. Mr. Hanks was the first rooster to arrive.

Doug covered him up again and then we strolled over toward a group of people waiting in line for the barbecue. As the four-member military band played on, children escaped their parents and careened around and through everything, like children do at picnics. Old-timers talked in soft voices over lunch, or arrived aided by walkers or leaning on their offspring: arms. Much handshaking. hugging, and exclaiming, as old friendships were renewed.

While waiting in line I introduced myself to a young farmer whom I remarked looked like a pea farmer. He was, he said. The newer generation of the Perrine Farms pea operation. He asked how I knew, to which I replied that after attending umpteen potato conferences, and working in feed and seed at the Wallowa County Grain Growers for years, I could tell any farmer in his field. He laughed.

The handsome Mr. Perrine, fit from farming, mentioned that Ruby Kirk was his mother-in-law. Ruby was the one who had phoned, urging me to enter Chester in the crowing contest. I'd only corresponded by phone or mail and never met her. Just then this 75-year-old dynamo of a woman appeared, and we met Ruby, who was sprinting around issuing orders, attending to details of the contest, scheduled for 3 that afternoon.

"There are 33 roosters entered," she said, laughing all the while. My kind of woman, doing something for the foolishness of it.

"This thing is getting out of hand," she chuckled.

Doug and I chowed down on the sweet corn-on-the-cob, barbecued beef sandwiches, and coleslaw, then contemplated long and hard over those pies before choosing a slice. After checking on Mr. Hanks, who appeared to be still thinking it was night, we ambled down the street on this perfect June day to peruse the yard sales.

The day warmed and, after returning to the park, we spread a blanket next to Mr. Hanks under a leafy maple and took a nap. But not for long, as the roosters began to arrive. Banties, Barred Rocks, Rhode Island Reds, fighting cocks, and one huge Brahma rooster that crowed and crowed with a low gurgling sound. Soon, roosters of every color and description filled cages that covered long planks placed on sawhorses by Ruby's tireless husband and helpers, who appeared a bit overwhelmed by the incessant crowing.

One rooster made a break for it, but I grabbed our blanket and saved the day by herding him behind Mr. Hanks' cage, where he was plucked by the feet and plunked back into his cage. The roosters' cages were covered on top with various kinds of material, which didn't stop their crowing, and soon bedlam reigned as some 30 roosters *cock-a-doodle-doo*'ed in every note on the musical scale.

Each rooster's name was affixed to the cage with the owner's name on the back. Beyond Mr. Hanks were two roosters named Bud and Bud Light.

Meanwhile, Ruby was "recruiting" tally keepers, cajoling curious onlookers and grabbing anyone she could, until she had 33 "volunteers." One for each contestant, who would sit on long wooden benches and stare at the bird in front of them and record every crow...for 30 minutes. When time was up, the cards would be tallied and the trophy awarded to the rooster that crowed the most during that time.

"Ladies and gentlemen, remove your covers," yelled Ruby's husband, and *swish*, off went the pieces of material from the tops of the roosters' cages.

Mr. Hanks, who had been completely covered, owing to Doug's thoroughness, blinked in the bright light of day, stood and shook his feathers, and did NOT crow. The two very aggressive roosters on either side of him strutted their wings, as if to attack him. Intimidated by his sire back home, this yearling of mine simply cowered in the middle of his cage and said nothing! He was hungry and thirsty, as he thought this night would never end, so this big *galunk* of a rooster went to pecking his food and put his gawky feet into the water carton, promptly knocking it over…and didn't crow a lick.

All around him, the place was beginning to sound like the poultry department of the State Fair, when Ruby raised a megaphone to her lips and yelled, "Go!"

Whereupon all those roosters let loose, or rather continued the crowing they'd been doing a pretty good job of already…with the exception of Mr. Hanks, who alternately crouched or pecked his food, throwing weird looks at the two roosters next to him. It was hilarious. The poor soul assigned to Mr. Hanks nearly strained his eyes and ears listening for a crow that never materialized.

As each rooster crowed, his fan club would cheer wildly. One small banty nearly strangled every time he crowed.

Suddenly, what appeared to be the total populace of Weston assembled on the lawn facing the roosters. Doug, who sat in the car until the contest was well under way, appeared and just shook his head in disbelief that otherwise sane people would turn out for such foolishness. I was in hysterics, as was everyone else. Ruby finally shouted through her horn, "Time's up!"

And when the cards were tallied, that little but mighty banty by the name of Blade, who nearly broke his crow, won, crowing 75 times in 30 minutes. Blade's owner is James Erler. Second place was Darrell, who crowed 68 times. Marvel Eaves of Enterprise transported her own rooster over the mountain to the contest, where he placed third, crowing 53 times, followed by Gordon Reinhart's entry with 50 crows. Ashley Tubbs' rooster came in fifth, crowing 48 times.

Mr. Hanks and six other entries never so much as uttered a sound. His sire, Chester III, would have given them a run for their money, as he gets excited easily and he would have been excited that day. It was hard to be serious as I interviewed and photographed the event. Soon

Doug loaded his out-of-control wife and her silent rooster into the car, and headed back over the mountain to home.

Later, when I let Mr. Hanks loose in the chicken pen, he crowed! Traitor.

June 25—What begins many conversations in Wallowa County? Same old thing: the weather. Of which they say only fools and newcomers attempt to predict. Trying to outguess Mother Nature, when it comes to planting gardens hereabouts, is an occupation in itself.

Take last week, for instance, when those of us who always wait until the first of June to plant those tender frost-susceptible vegetables, such as corn, squash, beans, tomatoes and the like, awoke to a killing frost. Twenty-six degrees! And here it is nearly July. How were we to know it would be the coldest recorded temperature on that date for the past 100 years?

Doug kept the sprinkler going that night, and by morning his beans, corn, potatoes and squash were imprisoned in ice, and the garden fence resembled an iced lace tablecloth. When the ice melted, we turned off the sprinkler and those tender plants were pretty burned, but are slowly coming out of it.

Doug replanted some of the seeds, which are yet to sprout, and now we have had rain, the first moisture in June, and warm sunshine, which is almost tropical-like, and the flowers and vegetable gardens are responding favorably.

That is, until the next disaster. Hail or high wind...or snow.

One must be an eternal optimist to garden, however, and this writer is pretty eternal. The garden I had going on Alder Slope, on my property being leased to one of my sons, really got hit. So I replanted what was susceptible and, after discovering the Alder Slope Nursery was sold out of what I needed, found the necessary bedding plants in La Grande, when Doug and I drove out yesterday to attend a team-roping event that son-in-law Tom was participating in.

This morning, armed with shovel and hoe, I transplanted marigolds, cherry tomatoes, and replanted what had earlier frozen. Although it is late to hope for anything in our short-season valley, the eternal optimists, which is the gardener's true spirit, still awaits the harvest. And, in the meantime, enjoys seeing things grow and hoe-hoe-hopes for the best!

Doug and I helped Ben, Seth and Sarah brand our spring calves in the hills. It was perfect weather, with clouds building but not spilling on our day. I spent two days alternately working the chute gate and pushing calves up the long wooden chute to the calf table.

Linde Irwin looks towards the high peak, Sacajawea, visible from the Hurricane Creek Trail.

At noon, we spread our picnic on the green grass, and rested. June is a lovely time out on Salmon Creek, and the grasses waving in the wind resemble swells on the ocean. Wildflowers abound. It is a time for lupine, wild roses, sticky pink geranium, and a host of yellow wildings that elude description. Some of these grow out of scab rock, and spill from cracks in solid rock. Penstemon, in shades of blue to lavender, color the landscape.

Early on the morning of June 10, Linde and I, accompanied by our two dogs, shouldered our day packs at the Hurricane Creek trailhead and headed into the wilderness. Several miles up the trail, we spied a high meadow above a falls and made that our destination for lunch.

Our first challenge was in crossing Falls Creek, which had turned into a rushing torrent due to warm temps melting higher snow. Using our imaginations, we rigged up a bridge that hung precariously in the roots of a fallen tree, and spanned a roaring stretch of water to the opposite bank. As we made our way up the steep incline following a waterless gulch, we jumped a doe and twin fawns, which bounded off into some scrub fir. Brilliant Indian paintbrush and blue forget-me-nots dotted the areas.

Reaching the falls via a route that is not a marked trail, we gazed upward to see this amazing amount of cascading water falling from the basin we hoped to reach. I did some photographing of the falls, the spray

Janie Tippett and Daisy head for a high basin under the Hurricane Divide.

of which wetted us nearly through. On a whim we decided to attempt climbing up a rock chimney to reach the area we wanted to see. It was a handhold, foothold situation and a little tricky, but at last we emerged at the top and found ourselves in a mountain mahogany thicket that grew on a steep hillside.

Following a game trail, we zig-zagged our way to the basin we had glimpsed below, and when, gasping for air, we pulled ourselves to the top, the sight took our breath away. Never in all my rambles over the Wallowas have I beheld anything so lovely. We were looking down at a high basin, or hanging valley, in which three streams, flowing over solid rock, converged below to spill over the falls.

Snowbanks glistened where the snow melted and ran into the streams. One shining creek seeped down from a high, remote lake. The awesome Hurricane Divide lay above us, and seeing motion below, we beheld nearly 30 wild mountain sheep, several already with lambs, bounding away single file up toward the solid rock face where the creeks spilled down.

Wildflowers waved in the breeze, and warm sunshine flooded the basin. We sat there in that high, wild setting and ate our lunches, and stared at the sheep, which had climbed to a high ledge between two creeks, bedded down, and were staring at us.

Not desiring to return via the rock chimney we opted to cross the creeks in the basin, find our way up the opposite side of the falls, and follow another game trail that ultimately took us safely back to the main trail. In the time Linde and I have left in the world, we will always keep that special place locked in our hearts. And when this weather straightens out we'll be heading off for another adventure. Happy trails!

July 2—Suddenly awake, I found myself staring up into the nearly full June moon as it floated free of Suicide Point, high above the receding waters of the Snake. Our boat, secured earlier to a large boulder on the Oregon shore at Salt Creek, had gently rocked us to sleep. The original water bed, I mused.

As I gazed up at that immense volcanic formation, through which a rocky stairway-trail had been carved, it brought to mind Grace Jordan's book, *Home Below Hells Canyon*, in which she describes the cliff-hanging experience of traveling the Suicide Trail horseback.

In the gently rocking boat, I was soon back in dreamland, until, once again, I was suddenly wide awake. This time the boat was grating on rock and I spotted Doug, oar in hand, shoving the boat away from the rocky shore and out into the dark water of the Snake. The moon had disappeared over the high western rims toward Imnaha, but its glow lingered enough so that I could make out Doug's figure struggling with the boat.

Due to the dams above Hells Canyon, the water flow is regulated as needed for the generating of power. If Doug had not been aware of this fluctuation, we would have been left high and dry, stranded on some ugly boulders by morning. Doug soon had the boat secured fore, to a scrub hackberry, and aft, anchored in the Snake. Planets and glittering stars decorated our bedroom ceiling, the Snake spoke softly, and we slept.

Yesterday, because the weather from now on would be too hot for camping on the Snake, we had decided to make the trip to Dug Bar and camp upriver before towing the boat out. After an early start that Friday morning, we drove the long, winding road that winds its rim-hugging way for 30 miles past the small settlement of Imnaha and comes to an abrupt end at Dug Bar.

As we traveled from above 4,000 feet to 1,000 feet, we witnessed the end of spring and beginning of summer. Observing local flora and fauna was fascinating as we went from cool syringa-scented canyons to the warm air of the Snake River, drenched with the scent of yellow blossoms and sweet clover.

We glimpsed numerous half-grown chukar chicks, accompanied by mama chukar; soft-eyed mule deer does, switching flies in the shade of sumac and cottonwood gulches, knowing their fawns were hidden nearby; a lone cow elk, so fat that her hide jiggled when she ran. Lower river cactus continued to bloom, grasshoppers provided fodder for chukars, and numerous song birds. Canyon sides were swathed in golden goat weed, and occasional mariposa tulips imposed their pinks.

It was nearly noon when we finally got the boat launched and loaded with our camping gear. As Doug piloted the boat upstream, we left the world behind and became nomads. Hungry, we pulled into Deep Creek and built some sandwiches from the cooler box, then slowly continued upriver, stopping often to fish. While Doug napped, I pulled in a big whitefish, which I released.

We passed Van Pool's and Roland Bar, and Jim Blankenship's old place…abandoned now, taken over by thistles. We passed mother merganser ducks, trailing large hatches of ducklings, bouncing up and down over the waves made by our passing boat. Things appeared pretty quiet at Copper Creek, and the shade provided by large, leafy cottonwoods and cool lawns was inviting. It was really warming up.

Gliding past Kirkwood, we noticed quite a few tourists visiting the historic ranch once owned by Len Jordan. Sign of the times…these once-viable, producing ranches are now tourist attractions, where we ranchers are viewed as former colorful inhabitants, and even the machinery used to farm and put up hay is now classified as museum pieces.

Just opposite Suicide Point, we pulled up to a campsite at Salt Creek, where we left most everything in the boat except what we would cook for supper, which we packed up to a convenient picnic table on a level spot beneath some crooked hackberry trees. The waters washed at a somewhat sandy beach below us, and the rugged outcrop of Suicide reared its jagged crest across the river. Nearby Salt Creek splashed down from a steep canyon above, and a faint trail led through thistles to an old log double cabin.

That evening I fried hamburgers and cooked corn on the cob over a small propane stove. As all of the floaters and boaters had gone downstream for the night, we had that stretch of the upper Snake all to ourselves. Well, almost. A friendly mule deer doe and two yearlings shared our camp. Actually, it was their home, and we were the guests. One yearling, a young buck in the velvet, was very curious. They grazed contentedly just beyond, under a rim while we ate.

Listening to the birds sing that evening I decided the canyon belongs to the birds. How happy they were! Some music. There was the varied descending call of the familiar little bird that also frequents the high Wallowas, the *chuck, chuck chuck*-ing of the chukars, the cawing of crows, the happy sound of swallows, and numerous other birds I couldn't begin to identify. In the fading light of the canyon their chorus diminished with the coming of darkness, but lingered on in my dreams.

We were up before the sun had time to climb up and over the Idaho side of the canyon. Several feet of wet rocks separated us from the boat, and as I made my slippery way to the beach, I noticed a large sand bar exposed now below camp. Again, with the coming of dawn, the bird song filled the canyon. Accompanied by the soft lapping of the water, as the tide washed in again, looking at the sand bar I could see Doug's tracks being washed away.

Doug said, "Have you checked the sourdough?" and I could tell by the smirk on his face that something was up. Lifting the loose-fitting lid on the plastic pail that served as a crock, I peered down to see numerous earwigs swimming in our pancake starter. But appetites are keen on the Snake, and those were the best pancakes ever. Here's the recipe:

Night before, mix flour and creek water with starter in plastic pail. Cover with plate, so earwigs can crawl in. Next morning, fish out sourdough-drunk earwigs, donate them to the birds, and add egg, oil, pinch of baking soda, and a bit of sugar and salt, mix well, bake on hot griddle and serve with maple syrup and strawberry jam. Voila! Salt Creek Sourdough Earwig Pancakes.

Since we were on no set schedule, we packed up the boat and headed upstream to Temperance Creek, where we went ashore to visit the old Johnson ranch. Sad. I can certainly understand how it must have been heart-wrenching to leave such a place. What a fine sheep outfit it once was. Those last days of June were warming up and the rushing waters of Temperance Creek created a sense of cool.

We remembered the old house, long since burned down, and walked past the newer one, uphill to the sheep shed, from where we could view the long sweep of the river and the ever-present canyons stretching to the sky. The last sheep grazing outfit in the Hells Canyon National Recreation Area is now history, and the rancher and his family are added to the legacy of the Snake. Somehow the caring for the land will never be the same as when those who loved it and lived there, in all seasons, managing these canyon ranches.

After boating upriver to just under Hat Point, where we craned our necks to look up toward the steepest gorge in North America, we turned around and headed back down the Snake, carrying old and new stories with us. Doug caught some bass at Sheep Creek, and I'd caught a huge carp and a sucker earlier. No keepers, but that carp really put up a fight.

That night we slept in the boat at Dug Bar and watched the June moon rise over the Idaho breaks of the Snake. Pretty nostalgic, especially for Doug, who spent many years ranching and guiding there.

That elevation reminded me a little of my childhood home in the Placer County foothills in summer. The shimmering heat, damp morning dew, smell of dry grass, humming of insects, and butterflies, which flew everywhere. Gossamer orioles nest hung from locust trees and bright flashes of yellow/orange sailed through the leaves.

That night I covered the sourdough with a paper plate and then a plastic plate. No earwigs, and the water of Birch Creek, coupled with the pure Dug Bar air, created pancakes so light they nearly flew off the griddle.

We left early to beat the heat, pulling the boat slowly up the steep, rocky road without mishap until, chugging up the Horse Creek grade, we had a flat tire on the boat trailer.

At Corral Creek we picked some wild golden apricots from a tree growing on a steep hillside. They were the sweetest cots we'd tasted in a long time... and like our trip, their flavor will be savored for years to come. It is haying time now, and the prolonged, hot, dry days are providing perfect haying weather. Ben and his family have nearly finished one field, and Doug is swathing another one this morning.

July 24—There was a chipmunk perched on top of the woodpile this morning. How did it get there? Did it ride in with Doug when he hauled a load of firewood earlier this week? Or is it just passing through? We have never seen a chipmunk here on the ranch before. I left a few cantaloupe seeds scattered on a chunk of tamarack for it. And if our cats don't make a meal of this cheerful little newcomer, we'll enjoy its company.

"Tucker's Mare," the snow shape of a horse, has melted down to where it looks more like a white mare than it has all spring and summer. Daily I watch for it in this withering heat, as the high altitude sun eats away at the remaining patches scattered among the high Wallowas.

Numerous streams dashing down out of the mountains are still full of icy snowmelt. This accumulated water is filling Wallowa Lake to capacity, and below the dam at its foot, the overflow is diverted in a series of irrigation ditches that thread their way through fertile farmlands where the water is pumped into a vast network of sprinkler systems. Therefore, Prairie Creek is green. In the days before settlement, this area was a continuation of the sagebrush dry hills that border it.

This ample snowmelt, combined with fertile soil, warm growing weather and dedicated irrigators, has produced one of the most bountiful hay crops in years. Yields and quality are high, and so are the stacks appearing all over the valley this July. Ben, driving the tractor pulling a loader/stacker, swept up the last bale of meadow hay in the north field when Daisy and I took our twilight walk last evening around the ranch. Earlier I had photographed that field, when row upon row of fragrant, dewy bales dried in the morn.

I can hear Hough's large hay stacking machines chugging up and down the fields, compressing, shaping, then spitting out large "bread loaf" stacks. Soft round bales repose in other fields, or are arranged neatly in round pyramids.

To the south of us, Hank Bird continues to put up his hay the old way. After it has been cut, raked and cured, the hay is stacked (with a farmhand) into long, loose stacks. Driving by the other day, I noticed a fellow working on top of the loose hay, tamping and shaping the stack with a pitchfork.

In the nearby town of Joseph there are artists creating bronze sculptures, many of which depict our Western way of life. Out here on Prairie Creek, we have men like Hank Bird who sculpt works of "living art" out of their daily lives. There is a certain serenity to Hank's long hay stacks, a serenity lacking in our modern, machined, money-mad world. Looking at those hay stacks reminds me of Wallowa County's rich heritage that shaped its culture. Once upon a time, every rancher put up hay that way, using swing-pole derricks, powered by horses and men.

The young wild honkers must be learning how to fly now. Silent all spring, the geese are making themselves evident again. Early of a morning, and again in the cool of evening, we hear them winging and honking their way to our fields, where they land to graze the high grasses growing alongside the irrigation ditches.

My three milk cows and their combined seven calves have been turned into a small lot east of the house to graze the tall grasses. Gargantuan ancient willows, their thirst slaked by an irrigation ditch, provide shade where my "herd" can chew their cuds and cogitate away the long summer afternoons. What a life.

Mr. Hanks and Chester III awake everyone at daylight, and their harem of hens continues to lay brown eggs while they attempt to stay cool. The raspberries are dangerously close to ripening and I've made so many batches of strawberry freezer jam that the recipe is permanently embedded in my memory. The kittens, like others before them, have discovered the afternoon shade of the raspberry patch, and appear in the evening to tumble about the lawn.

My wild, out-of-control flower patch is riotous with color. Wafted on the Prairie Creek wind last fall, some of those Icelandic poppy seeds took root in the strawberry patch! Doug, who prefers order in gardens, is having a fit, but the poppies are winning. And the blaze of orange, red, white and lavender breaks the monotony of an otherwise green strawberry patch.

His vegetable garden, rows as straight as a ruler, weeded to perfection, is, like Hank's hay stacks, a work of art. We have been feasting on fresh lettuce and green onions and anxiously awaiting those first peas and new potatoes. And guess what? There are two zucchini nearly ready to pick.

Meanwhile, up on Alder Slope, I drive at least twice a week after I've finished errands in Enterprise, to work my own garden. His and her gardens...our children wonder about us. On Alder Slope, among a serendipity mixture of marigolds, herbs, corn, potatoes, chard, lettuce, beets, petunias, purple beans, carrots, peas, crookneck and zucchini squash, and a long row of mammoth sunflowers, I hold sway.

Daughter-in-law Angie, who works all day in Enterprise, loves the garden, as does son Todd, who is a cowboy by profession. The grandchildren delight in picking the produce, and understand that "Grandma has to have flowers in her vegetable garden."

On the subject of gardens, I received a phone call a few months ago from Tamara Fritze, who said she was working on her Ph.D. at the University of Idaho and doing a dissertation on gardening. Alex Kuo, who teaches there and with whom I'd taken a workshop at Fishtrap a few years ago, had recommended that Tamara interview me. So, about a week ago this delightful young woman appeared at my door.

After showing her our gardens here, I drove Tamara up to Alder Slope to visit the gardens there. She was observant and obviously quite taken with all she saw. After I introduced her to 82-year-old Wilmer Cook, she listened in awe as he described how he and wife, Mary, get down on their hands and knees and slowly make their way up and down the rows of their huge garden, weeding as they go.

Their weedless garden, watered and thriving, contains fruit trees and long rows of raspberries, strawberries, and numerous garden vegetables. On the eastern edge of the garden, several hives of bees hummed with activity as the pollinators buzzed among the blooms, making honey as they worked. Outside the garden fence, Wilmer and Mary's two Jersey milk cows grazed the lush pasture.

Looming above all, the eroding crest of Ruby Peak with the last of its snows melting, looked down on this quiet, pastoral scene, a scene Wilmer's father before him must have viewed many times. Continuity here, and at Ted Juve's across the road, where, as a potter, he too farms and cares for the land that was his father's and grandfather's.

I hope Tamara was able to grasp that simple theme. I don't know much about dissertations, but I do know it is good what Wilmer and Mary, and Ted are doing. Somehow, caring for a small acreage, sub-sisting mainly on what is produced there, radiates outwardly to the community...and the world.

In the future it may be the only thing that matters.

August 6—Living on a ranch and being a country columnist means I must roll with the seasons, for it is the seasons that dictate my life. My days aren't planned, they simply happen. Take this morning, for instance. After arising early to jump into the shower, tend to the chickens, feed the dog and cats, fix a bite of breakfast, and confer with Doug as to what he had planned for the day, I murmured to myself, "Sit thyself down in front of the word processor and DO your column."

Meanwhile, the sun streamed across the hills and warmed up Prairie Creek, temperatures having dipped to 32 degrees during the night, so

Deborah Shear won her showmanship division with her first prize Suffolk lamb at the Wallowa County Fair.

naturally I had to first inspect the garden. Then, while pausing to admire my poppies, backlit in morning light, I remembered the Wallowa County Fair, which reminded me of the premium book I'd opened to the Floriculture Division over breakfast.

Back in the kitchen, concentrating on the book, I read, *Entries in perishable products accepted between 7:30 and 10:30 a.m,* which is today!

Yesterday morning had found me at Cloverleaf Hall entering a few photographs in the non-perishable department, which, I told myself, was enough to satisfy this yearly urge to exhibit at our local fair.

WRONG.

Ever since I was a young 4-H'er, fairs have been in my blood. More than 50 years of county fairs! So, there I was, lovingly snipping away in my rampant flower patch, choosing a colorful assortment of bachelor buttons here, a spray of blue flax there, a few Shasta daisies, and gobs of those brilliant poppies. Then back to the premium book.

Lot 7, under the heading of "Memories," described in Class 1. Arrangements: Using an antique or collectible. After contemplating the old blue granite-ware coffee pot reposing on top of the Monarch range, I artfully arranged my posies and filled the pot with water. The effect was perfect, and I was having so much fun.

I threw an apologetic look in the direction of my word processor, loaded my flowerful entry into the car, and headed for Cloverleaf Hall. Waiting in line to fill out my exhibitor's tag, I chatted with other ranch wives about the temperature this morning, and wasn't it typical of Wallowa County to have frost every month of the year?

There were others entering the "Memories" class, and they were all cleverly thought up. We were all very interested in each other's flowers, and asked questions about different varieties and this and that like gardeners do when they get together. One friend, who lived out north, said the grasshoppers were eating her plants. I stopped to admire a beautiful display of grains and grasses being entered by a local farmer.

After leaving Cloverleaf Hall I got to thinking about my Alder Slope garden. Not too worried about a killing frost there, but just wanting to be in the midst of it on this perfectly gorgeous morning. Fifteen minutes later, there I was, hoe in hand, savoring it all, looking up at Ruby Peak, then out over the valley toward the Seven Devils in Idaho.

The plants were thriving in that black loam soil, and the sunflowers were over my head. I felt like planting myself there, taking root, not coming inside until a killing frost. But soon I was off, returning to Enterprise, where I purchased a book at the Bookloft, visited some friends, sipped a cup of coffee, and munched on two apricot-oatmeal bars for my lunch.

Returning to the ranch, I read my mail, gathered the eggs, and dealt with the two heaping bowls of freshly picked raspberries Doug had left on the kitchen counter before heading for the hills to check our cattle. By the time I finished yet another batch of freezer jam and packaged the remaining berries for the freezer, made a phone call to friend Linde to plan a hike, and watered the sweet peas, my afternoon was slipping away...along with my energy.

But this is FAIR week...and the cool weather we experienced these past few days has gone back to Alaska. The days are perfectly delightful, and I don't want to be stuck in front of this word processor. So I finally sat myself down and this is what I came up with.

Last week, six of us gals hiked up the old stock drive to Murray Saddle, on what is known locally as the Bill George trail, then attempted to climb Ruby Peak via a route described in local author Fred Barstad's new book, *Hiking Oregon's Eagle Cap Wilderness*.

The route we chose was NOT the right one for our varied group, and two gals turned back after we scrambled up a narrow, cliff-hugging sheep trail. The remaining four of us gained the ridge top and ate our lunches in a high saddle which afforded a sweeping view of the valley below. A huge snowbank clung to the windswept north face of the barren mountain, just under where we sat.

The weathered, rock-strewn ridge that led upward to the northern approach to Ruby Peak was still a considerable distance away, and we still had a rough climb ahead. At over 8,000 feet the air was thinner and a cool breeze began to waft a few thunderheads our way. Then we got to thinking about our two companions waiting for us at the Gap. Had they made it safely back?

Climbing up on a high rocky point, I could see a safe route down and we opted to descend at that point. Scrambling and sliding, hanging onto scrub fir, we soon found ourselves crossing miniature wet meadows, green and boggy, where perfect little pink Elephant Heads grew along patches of wild onion. Below and to the south lay the larger meadows where Silver Creek is born and its cold waters tumble down through a pristine basin before turning northwest toward the Lostine.

More relaxed now, we crossed the irrigation ditch and ambled through myriad growths of Indian paintbrush, alpine forget-me-nots, and wild daisies. It was springtime in the mountains! And there ahead of us were Debbie and Nicki, safe and enjoying the day. It was warming up.

It had been a pretty strenuous hike and there were a few blisters, so we took the steep, shorter horse trail route and soon arrived a bit spent back at Linde's car. Over a cool, refreshing drink on the deck of a new Joseph eatery, we gazed upward to the snowbank and couldn't believe we had been there only hours ago.

Chief Joseph Days and the Fishtrap Writer's conference are history. Ben has finished swathing the grain hay, and those windrowed rows of nutritious winter fodder for our cows will soon be ready to bale. Irrigation goes on and Sarah, a pretty senior at Joseph High School this fall, is here early of a morning and later in the evening to help change sprinkler lines.

August will disappear faster than July as the days shorten toward fall. As the seasons roll, so rolls this life of a rancher-wife-columnist.

August 27—Our mountains are only faintly defined on this late summer morning. I must peer with concentration to determine their ridge lines. The familiar chutes and eroding escarpments appear fused together in a smoky blue haze. Distance obliterates Bonneville Mountain, but I know it is there, shrouded in settling smoke that surrounds Prairie Creek and all of Northeastern Oregon.

An autumn-like breeze stirs the red-tinged tassels of Early Sunglow corn, and slowly moves the heavy layers of gray cloud northward. Directly above I can see patches of purest blue. The air, flowing from the south. is cool and moisture-laden. There are droplets of water on my sweet peas. and a hummingbird, suspended in whirring flight, probes their sweetness for breakfast.

The coolness is a relief from the days of burning heat that brought anxiety each afternoon as rising temps and winds fanned enormous canyonland fires to the east of us. We have been surrounded by FIRE.

One of the season's first fires began west of where Doug and I camped earlier this summer along the Snake River. It became known as the Salt Creek Fire, and was to burn thousands of acres before it was contained. As usual, the fires are given names. Names that have been placed upon the land before they gave fires names. Salt Creek, Heaven's Gate, Sheep Creek and Deep Creek. All burning in the Hells Canyon Recreation Area, that vast ungrazed area that lies in the steepest gorge in North America.

On the Idaho side of the Snake, the Seven Devils, a familiar landmark as seen from Prairie Creek, has been lost in smoke for days. Devils Tooth, Tower of Babel, She Devil, The Ogre, The Goblin, He Devil and Devil's Throne, these seven jagged peaks with names that form a kinship with fire.

Our neighbors Pat and Linde, after spending nearly two weeks on the Salt Creek fire, returned home for a mere hour before being called out on the Bull fire, another lightning-caused fire that rages still, located somewhere in the drainages of the North Fork of the John Day, where, from a mountain top, Linde calls from a cell phone to relay messages.

I can picture them in that huge fire camp, through the yellow haze that fire creates through sunlight...while their summer slips away. Meanwhile back home, granddaughter Carrie operates their bed and breakfast, waters the gardens, tends the chickens and dogs, all of which is sandwiched between working for her dad, changing sprinkler pipes, swathing and baling hay...and saving money for her sophomore year in college.

We ranchers who own dry grasslands where our cattle are grazing on summer range, hold our breath and pray that no new lightning strikes hit out north on the Zumwalt. Many of us have pumpers loaded on ranch pickups and food packed, and stand ready to defend our private lands. There has been a tenseness in the valley, especially during the late afternoons when the hot breath of August rattles the ripening grains and the sear grasses tremble. It is as if the searing sun's rays could ignite on its own.

Last night we could not sleep, as the clouds sweeping silently in from the south were supposed to have lightning riding with them. Through our open bedroom window I could feel the soft presence of rain. So warm and sultry was the starless night, this morning's moisture was a mere dewdrop on the sweet pea vines.

Last night's August moon swam through dark, damp clouds, and before midnight, a cool breeze wafted to us a potpourri of scents...mint, freshly raked hay...and smoke. Our neighbor Greg Brink had just swathed his mint field when Daisy and I took our evening walk around the ranch, and Ben was raking the second cutting of alfalfa and clover hay on the hill.

Yesterday our ranch echoed with the sounds of grandchildren who, in spite of the fire, enjoyed a summer day. Ten-year-old James and his eight-year-old sister Adele were here. Then I provided taxi service for 13-year-old Mona Lee and her friend Lea to and from volleyball practice at Joseph High School.

While the teenage girls were gone, the younger children tied baling twine together and fashioned phone lines. They climbed the willow tree in the yard, spending time in their leafy world, where all children need to be at that stage of their lives. They played with the kittens, picked raspberries, pulled carrots from the garden for lunch, made up their own play and brought back memories of rearing their father and aunts and uncle.

Children's needs never change, I mused as I watched them. They need grandmas, trees to climb, food in frightening quantities, kittens. and time. Time to simply be children and enjoy summer.

About a week or so ago, after the day's heat had spent itself, Doug and I drove down along the lower Imnaha River to pick blackberries. There was a peacefulness there, the soothing sounds of the creek running under tangled berry vines, grasshoppers chewing dry grasses and weeds, the steady buzz of crickets, basalt radiating the day's stored heat, and the sound of berries plunking into our buckets.

Later, ambling along the narrow, dusty road away from alder, elderberry and cottonwood that flanked the creek's steep course, I gazed upward to the east toward the breaks of the Snake to see great billowing clouds of smoke. The Salt Creek Fire.

"Must be heading in the direction of Lord Flat," Doug had commented earlier. I tried to envision those steep acres of dry, grassy canyon land as the monster fire grazed it, leaving a blackened mosaic in its path.

I noticed chukar tracks in the dust at my feet and I watched carefully for rattlesnakes near the creek. Scattered poison oak leaves were already turning the color of fire, and come October the sumac's glow will paint the canyon country with its own fall flame.

Later, after dark, we ate fried chicken with blackened fingers at Dave and Sally Tanzey's Imnaha Store and Tavern.

The next morning my kitchen counter was littered with Surejel, sugar, blackberry juice. strainers, berry seeds, berry-stained bowls and pots and pans…and finally five pints of jelly, that happily all sealed. The remaining berries were packaged for the freezer, with enough left for a bubbling hot cobbler that came out of the oven at noon.

These hot days and warm nights, combined with constant watering and hoeing, have encouraged my Alder Slope garden to flourish beyond my wildest hopes. The giant sunflowers must be nearing ten feet now, and are just beginning to form heavy heads. Purple beans, cucumbers, tomatoes and corn are in a race with time to ripen before the autumn's first killing frost.

Doug's garden is the same, and I am afraid to look at the cabbages. It is time to make kraut, before their large heads split open. My canning cupboard is filling with pickled beets and jelly, and the freezer groans with berries. My hunter-gatherer husband brought home some huckleberries one day when he was making forays into the woods to restock our woodpile.

The cows on the moraine have been birthing husky calves for some time now, and the season is ripe with fall wood in the woodshed, hay in hay stacks, and food put by. Those are the things that count in our high mountain valley. May it always be so. For our grandchildren's sake.

September 4—A cold rain fell last night on our thirsty forests, canyons and hills. Come morning the Wallowas were cloaked in clouds. Alaskan air flowed down upon us, and we knew, if it cleared off in the night, there would be a good chance of frost by morning. So, there I was, bending over a row of green beans, picking them before they could be ruined by the first fall freeze. As I pulled the long green beans from the tangled vines, a chill wind rustled the corn stalks at my back.

Straightening up at the end of the row, I glanced toward the mountains to see the most amazing sight. Where there had been barren ridges, pockmarked here and there with dirty patches of snow, there now lay the clean mantel of the season's first snowfall. A few trailing clouds wreathed the mountain's snowy summit, which stood out in the bold brilliance of that suddenly sunny morning. The sky was scoured clean by the storm, and blues ranged from robin's eggs on the horizon to cerulean directly above.

That did it!

Hurriedly, after storing my beans in the bunkhouse fridge, I donned hiking boots, grabbed my daypack, beckoned to Daisy, and we were off to catch up to Linde and two other gals, who were already hiking up the trail to Slick Rock Creek.

Earlier I had declined an invitation to go hiking, thinking the beans and several other commitments were more important, but that was before I saw those mountains. Every vagabond will understand that on such a September morn, we MUST be out. I could already taste the air after the first rain and feel the first snow. I knew what it would be like up that trail, and I wasn't getting any younger. The beans could wait.

When Daisy and I left the trailhead, the other three were an hour ahead of us. As the sun came streaming through the woods, every leaf and blade of grass sparkled with leftover rain. The narrow path was damp, and all the combined scents of summer saturated the air. Blue jays squawked, Hurricane Creek dashed its cold way over water-worn rocks, warm sunshine released the vanilla-like essence of ponderosa pine, moss revitalized by moisture was green and alive, and above us the high timbered slopes of Chief Joseph Mountain were dusted with snow.

When we came to Falls Creek, I remembered with what difficulty Linde and I had crossed it earlier in the spring, when it was a rushing snowmelt torrent. Over the summer, when the creek quieted, previous hikers had arranged a series of logs across the creek, which made the crossing easy. After hiking a steep stretch of trail that afforded a view of the winding creek's course, which led the eye to the first glimpse of Sacajawea, I paused to catch my breath and glory in the scene before me.

This favorite mountain's barren talus slopes were shining under melting snow, while the peak itself was ermine white. We broke out of the forest into a meadow, dry now save for a few scattered cinquefoil spotted with yellow blooms. Here, I gazed up Deadman Creek and the awesome Hurricane Divide. Little creeks, still fed by snow banks, glistened as they tumbled over solid rock to the basin above' the falls. It was just as I imagined it would be, standing there in my bean patch earlier.

We passed the cutoff to Thorpe Creek and continued on up the trail toward Slick Rock. Daisy began to wag her tail. She had spotted Linde's dog coming down the trail ahead of the gals. They were returning, and very surprised to see me. Joining them, Daisy and I without a pause walked briskly back to the trailhead.

Minutes later, Linde and Michele were helping me pick purple beans in my Alder Slope garden. I covered the tomato plants and prayed it wouldn't freeze that night, as this was only the first picking of beans and cucumbers were forming, and corn was ripening. I gazed long and fondly upon my summer's efforts; the garden never looked lovelier.

By morning it could be history, but it got down to only 32 degrees that night and Doug kept the sprinkler going here on Prairie Creek, and my Slope garden escaped the frost! Linde and I snapped the beans at her place, and together we loaded the pressure canner.

September 11—Grandson Rowdy married his Kasey in a very touching ceremony held at the Elgin Christian Church on Saturday. Special for this grandmother, as the occasion brought out nearly all of our family during a busy time of year. It was gratifying to see the generations roll on...each year a little faster.

After the wedding reception and a barbecue held out at the Rysdams' rural home, Doug and I took the route over Tollgate to Pendleton to visit daughter Lori and her family, who live along Wild Horse Creek. It was hot the next day and we relaxed in the shade of lovely old trees in Lori and Tom's yard, and were treated to yet another barbecue, only this one featured a large ice cream birthday cake. And Doug and I, who celebrate birthdays one day apart, along with grandson Ryan, turned another year older.

Returning home that evening, Doug and I stopped to visit the Oregon Trail Interpretive site at Spring Creek. It was quiet and peaceful there, as we walked the paths and read the signs. As we viewed the wagon ruts, we could hear the creak of iron and wooden wheels, see the dust rise, and envision the difficulty of crossing steep slopes, strewn with rocks and covered with fallen trees.

It brought back memories of my participation in the recreation of that rugged portion of the Oregon Trail. Walking in the heat of summer through the Blue Mountains had certainly given those of us who accomplished the trek more respect for our early pioneers.

Doug and I had a wonderful Labor Day weekend, camped along the Upper Imnaha River at the Ollokot Campground. Sort of a tradition for us. Friends Bud and Ruby joined us with their camp trailer. We spent our days lazing in lawn chairs, walking along the river, reading, searching for Duck Lake, grouse hunting, picking the last huckleberries, seeing new country, cooking over the sheepherder stove, and growing older.

Returning to the ranch we noticed that Ben had the second cutting baled, our neighbors were harvesting grain, and the garden was all ripening at once. Suddenly, it was fall.

Today Ben and Doug are shipping the yearling fall calves to a feedlot, the gardens are living on borrowed time, the grandchildren are back in school, and the blooming sunflowers in the Slope garden are outdoing Jack's beanstalk. One of my banty hens is setting on a clutch of eggs…again, and "Mr. Hanks" is crowing a lot these days, because he is now KING OF THE ROOST. But that is another story.

This reminds me of Doug's birthday card to me. It says it all, *You are a story I want to keep reading for a long, long time. All my love to you at the beginning of a new chapter.*

September 24—After two nights of killing frosts, the squash plants have been reduced to smelly puddles of blackened vines, the beans are history, and the corn stalks appear to be dried. The lush red clover, alfalfa, and meadow grasses that my three milk cows and their seven calves have been grazing, have lost their luster. Sweet peas struggle valiantly under the protection of the roof's overhang.

The two young Northwood maples' leaves have rusted overnight and a few frozen berries hide under the rows of reddening strawberry plants. New snow dusts the highest peaks, as our neighbors finish harvesting grain and baling second and third cuttings of hay. Our first-calf heifers have all calved out, and their offspring dash across the fields during these early fall days.

Seasoned tamarack cracks and pops in the old Monarch range again, and when I am not simmering a kettle of applesauce, canning sweet pickles, I'm most likely out in the gardens, pulling onions up to dry, or digging potatoes for a stew. It is the time of year for hardier meals.

Last Saturday was a busy and happy Grandma's Day. 10-year-old grandson James called earlier in the week to say he needed someone to take him to his soccer game that morning. And, he added, "Grandma, do you suppose you could take me up to check my gopher trap line?" So, as the sun rose on that bright, clear, frosty-cold morning, I was already on my way to Alder Slope to pick up James.

It seemed that everyone in James' family was going off in different directions that day. Dad off to work, sister Becky to a game, sister Adele and stepmother Angie off to enter the Imnaha Rodeo, brother Josh bow hunting with cousin Buck, and James to his soccer game. After surveying the damage done to my frosted garden, James directed me to Sacette's alfalfa field, about four miles distant, where we left the car parked alongside the county road.

We walked down a tiny path worn by James' comings and goings, crossed a small ditch of running water, and climbed through a fence where he had stashed his little shovel, wire probe and a dull pocket knife. James gathered up his tools and we made our way uphill through ankle-deep alfalfa, which had begun to thaw and was very wet.

The air was crisp, but the sun soon warmed us. The scene was pastoral: cattle and sheep grazing, a pair of draft horses slurping at a water trough across the road, golden stubble fields, irrigated green pastures, small farm houses, old barns...all dwarfed by the immensity of the nearly 9,000-foot mountain known as Ruby Peak.

We soon came to the first gopher trap. James' trap line had been marked with orange flagging tied to wire stakes which marched up the field. He pulled up the trap, an open-ended black plastic cylinder, which held a very fat, and very dead, gopher. James cut off the gopher's tail, stuffed it into his pocket, and buried the dead rodent. Then, using his probe, found another fresh tunnel and reset the trap. The field was pockmarked with gopher mounds.

The second trap yielded another gopher, and James said, "You bring me good luck, Grandma," but the remaining eight traps were not sprung.

We trudged through the now-soaking grass back to the car, and returned to James' house, where he ran to the woodshed to collect a cottage cheese carton containing more gopher tails. The total count is now up to 13. Then we drove to Sacette's ranch house, where James was paid 50 cents per tail for his efforts.

Leaving the magic world of Alder Slope, we entered a different world where 300 children from all three Wallowa County schools had converged to play soccer. I let James out, then tried to find a place to park, after which I made my way through throngs of parents, siblings and an occasional grandparent like myself, responsible for a young one that day. After team picture-taking and warm-up exercises, which were followed by a group photo of all 300 players, the youngsters were let loose to play soccer.

Meanwhile, clouds rolled in on the clear day, and a chill wind blew out of the north. We spectators huddled under blankets and shivered while rooting for our kids. I had to hand it to the volunteer coaches and refs, as well as the mothers who provided food and drink for the young players.

It was already afternoon when James and I returned to the ranch, where we found Papa Doug out in the garden picking corn. Soon we were on our way to Imnaha for the renowned Bear and Rattlesnake Feed and community rodeo. It was much warmer in the canyons. By the time we arrived at the famed Imnaha Store and Tavern, and made our way through the revelers to the chow line, the bear was gone, but there were a few remnants of fried rattlesnake.

James sampled the rattlesnake, while Doug and I settled for salads, rolls, Imnaha tomatoes and what appeared to be a sort of end-of-garden stew. The main street of Imnaha, which is the only street, was jam-packed with people who came from near and far for this unique event. We were even too late to purchase a square in the Cow Chip lottery.

"All sold out," said Barb Warnock and Jean Stubblefield. Proceeds for this fundraiser go to the Imnaha school scholarship fund. We walked up the road to the rodeo grounds, which is built on land donated to the community by local rancher Don Hubbard. Here, young and old competed for the pure enjoyment of it. No one takes these competitions too seriously. The main idea is to have fun.

This year, adults and young people have white-washed the arena's fence and added an announcer's booth. We walked in and sat on logs just in time to watch James' younger sister, Adele, run the barrels on her dad's horse, Cowboy. Then it was Angie's turn. Even the school marm, Char Williams, competed, as did the Imnaha school bus driver, Grant Warnock, as the canyons rose all around, to the east, west, north and south, their rims brushing the clouds.

Returning by late afternoon to Prairie Creek, James and I had a little daylight left, and my little trapper wanted to set some muskrat traps in the creek. So there we were, as the sun slid out of sight over the western ridges of the Wallowas, when a familiar cold came down hard from the mountains and a breeze sprang up, rustling the old cottonwood's leaves.

A trout broke water near a willow root in the creek, orange-red clusters of rose hips were reflected in the sunset water, a red tailed hawk screamed, and a large soft owl flew silently from his perch above us. A few cold grasshoppers clung to high, golden grasses at creek side, and we just soaked it all in, knowing we were witnessing the season's change on this eve of the autumnal equinox.

We made our way back through the hay field to the warmth of the house, where I cooked a hearty hot supper for the three of us. James savored every bite of the fried fresh beef heart, corn on the cob, tomatoes and new potatoes from the garden.

Driving my grandson home that night, a half moon sailed in and out of the clouds. James was fascinated by its movement, so we stopped to stare at the night. I explained that it was only the wind moving the clouds which made the moon appear to sail.

Minutes later, under that same moon on that cold night, James and I, using a flashlight, poked into squash plants to pick the last crooknecks and zucchini before another frost did them in. We flashed the light up into the faces of the enormous drooping sunflowers, which appeared almost magical under that frosty sky.

Lucky is the grandparent who can spend quality time with a grandchild. Daughter Ramona is flying out of Lewiston today to be with her first grandchild. May she, too, enjoy her day, when she plans to take year-old Clayton to the ranch where I and my three sisters and brother were raised, so he can learn about creeks and rocks and country places. I wish all children could experience the outdoors. We wouldn't need all of these new jails if children could see beauty instead of ugliness.

And now we look forward to a long Indian summer. There wasn't even any frost this morning!

October 9—Peering down into that vast ocean of cloud while cruising at 33,000 feet above the Rocky Mountains, I caught occasional glimpses of snow-dusted peaks through fragmented blue holes, a welcome change after more than an hour of viewing undulating, arid plains. My stomach lurched as the huge plane lost altitude and prepared to land at the Denver airport. Suddenly all those miles of unpeopled, Western landscapes were replaced by miles of human settlement. From the time I deplaned and entered the airy labyrinth of the Denver airport, and returned two days later, I would be totally consumed with the modernness of man and his effect upon the land.

Built with mega-millions, the Denver airport is a realization of civilized dreams. It represents Colorado's sky, light and space...so much space, with so many directions to go, that a country gal is overwhelmed, but I had been there last year with my friend Eileen and was therefore somewhat familiar with the procedure of finding my way out of the place and procuring a shuttle to whisk me to the 25-mile-distant city of Denver. I allowed myself time this year to ride an escalator to the skywalk eateries, plunk down my suitcase, choose from the vast selection of ethnic foods, and sit there alone and take it all in.

After a light lunch, I made my way outside to Island No. 3, as directed, to wait in the dry Colorado sunlight for my Super Shuttle. Soon I was driven in a van full of other travelers through fierce traffic to the Comfort Inn in downtown Denver. I shut my eyes as our driver swerved, veered and careened to avoid hitting others all traveling at great speeds in several lanes.

The Women Writing the West conference would begin that evening in the Brown Palace Hotel. After riding the elevator to the 15th floor of the Comfort Inn to my room, I looked out the window to gaze down at tiny people on sidewalks and tiny cars speeding along miniature streets.

Searching for a piece of sky, I craned my neck upward past the 55-story, glass-windowed Republic Plaza building to see the waning moon situated calmly in a blue sky.

Several autumn-yellowing trees appeared to grow out of the cement below the plaza. I could see and hear no bird song and no cattle, rolling hills, mountain peaks, or silence. Just the song of Denver, a city that never sleeps.

Later, walking across the glassed-in promenade that connects the Comfort Inn to the Brown Palace, I gazed out at the 107-year-old brown-stone Protestant Church, which stood next to the Museum of Western Art. While riding an escalator in the hotel, I turned to see a slightly-built woman behind me. Her face reflected the harsh Colorado sun. She wore jeans, a Western shirt, and a wide, friendly smile.

This was my introduction to Peggy Godfrey, writer, rancher, mother and cowboy poet. We became instant friends, and soon I was to meet others who form this network of Women Writing the West, a wonderful group of women from all over the U.S., Canada and Australia, who had flown to Denver for the second annual mini-conference.

In addition to running her own sheep and cow-calf operation near Moffat, Colorado, Peggy Godfrey does contract haying and hires out as a hand on the Double Bar V Ranch at the north end of the San Luis Valley, one of the highest and harshest ranch lands in the world. She was in Denver to make several appearances in galleries and perform her unique brand of poetry. Peggy has published three books, including "Write 'em Cowboy," and seemed to know everyone. And she savvied livestock, so we got along just great.

Friendships were rekindled during the three-day conference, and new acquaintances were made. I met author Harriet Rochlin, who narrated her slide presentation, "Jewish Women in the Early West," and filmmaker Doris Loeser, who presented her PBS film, *I'll Ride That Horse,* a marvelous documentary on early women rodeo riders. Doris had interviewed one of the famous Greenough sisters, Alice, who still lives, and was able to supply much of the film's narration.

Saturday morning we were taken on a tour of the historic Brown Palace Hotel, built in 1892; a place where we could feel the presence of former cattle barons. Next stop was the Museum of Western Art, where we gaped at original Charley Russell's and Fredric Remington's. Then we took a taxi to the convention center, to spend the day at the fourth annual Rocky Mountain Book Festival, joining throngs of book lovers who perused miles of booths of books and listened in on panel discussions centering around life in the West.

At 5 p.m. some of us attended an Indian author's book-signing back in the Museum of Western Art.

That evening, after an elegant Brown Palace dinner, we listened to speaker Teresa Jordan of Deeth, Nevada, another Fishtrap friend and a former rancher from Wyoming's Iron Mountain country. Teresa, who is married to folk lyricist-singer Hal Cannon, is the author of *Riding the White Horse Home, Cowgirls,* and *Graining the Mare.* Her new book is soon to be released.

Teresa spoke about "The Stories That Shape Us." It was a wonderful evening and our table was the rowdiest one there, as we had Peggy, who just can't help being herself. So there we were, women from many states gathered in the Brown Palace lobby until nearly 11, telling stories that shaped all of us.

The next day we met in round table discussions with publishers, agents and authors. After a short business meeting, we adjourned and all went our separate ways to fly home. My suitcase was weighted down with books. How could I resist "words" written and autographed by my new friends?

Another rancher/writer, Gwen Peterson of Big Timber, Montana, rode the shuttle with me on that Sunday afternoon to the airport. We said goodbye in that vast terminal after she pointed the way to Concourse B, where my flight to Boise would soon depart.

It was dusk when the plane landed in Boise, and darkness fell as I sped along the fast freeway toward Ontario. I steered north, leaving traffic and noise behind as I neared Northeastern Oregon. As I wound my way down the grade and into the still Minam Canyon, it was nearing midnight and I was able to relax, knowing I was nearly home.

Now, as I look back on that experience of traveling alone and meeting so many people from all parts of the country, it makes me so much more aware of how lucky we who live here are. I did find in my travels that people are just people, and all responded to a smile.

The next day Doug and I worked my seven milk cow calves, and I attempted to get back in the swing of ranch life.

The following day found us horseback on the steep east moraine of Wallowa Lake, gathering our fall calvers and their babies. We have had the most glorious Indian summer, but it has made for extremely dry forests, hills and canyons. We could really use some moisture.

A fence was broken in one place, probably by elk, and some of our cows had crossed over into Gorsline's, so Doug and I rode over into that part of the forest looking for cow tracks. Suddenly my new mare pricked up her ears, and up the trail in a thick copse of firs, a bull elk bugled.

Tamaracks are turning gold on the slopes of the Wallowas now, and even though it was a long, hot trip trailing those cows and tired calves to the ranch, I wouldn't have missed it for anything. I thought of my new friend Peggy, who told me, "Cowboy is a verb." It sure is, I mused; today we "cowboyed."

Ben took us to lunch at the Wagon Wheel in Joseph after, even though it was well past the noon hour.

I accompanied Doug on the opening morning of buck season, to get in on another adventure. My hunter husband bagged a nice four-point on our own property. The fresh venison is delicious.

Two weeks ago, Doug and I, friends Bud and Ruby and son-in-law Charley pulled our boat to Dug Bar and motored down the Snake fishing and picnicking. The days aren't long enough to accomplish all we'd like to do, and life slips away, like Indian summer will, into winter.

This morning I stopped at our local hospital to offer support to daughter Ramona, who was sitting at the bedside of her eldest son, Bart, while he received blood transfusions to sustain his fragile life. Unlike his cousins, Bart has never been able to hunt, fish, hike and do all the things country boys do. But looking down at this special grandson, at his pale, thin hands clasped together for strength, I thought of the indescribable gift he has given our family: the gift of himself, to humble us and make us appreciate life.

October 24—Here it is Thursday already, and I am just now getting to this column, the only excuse being that I wanted to wait until after opening morning of our cow elk hunt, so I could tell a hunting story. Although this won't be much of a hunting story, it will still be a story.

After arising in the dark yesterday to a cold, drippy dawn, we rushed around flipping sourdough hotcakes, doing chores, and throwing a lunch together, then drove to the other side of the ranch where Doug proceeded to load fence material into the back of the pickup.

It was at that point I began to realize our day would not be entirely devoted to hunting. Doug had drawn an antler-less elk tag for the Zumwalt area, while mine was a landowner preference, which meant my cow elk would have to be taken on our hill range, within the boundaries of our private lands. Doug could hunt the entire Zumwalt unit, which extended far beyond our private property. This, therefore, dictated our day.

It was already light by the time we drove out the long Crow Creek road, then headed in a northeasterly direction toward Butte Creek. A few road hunters appeared to be ahead of us. The narrow dirt road was greasy with mud from the rain. To the south the Wallowas swam in and out of focus, and dark curtains of cloud hung over the snow-frosted Chesnimnus country. We saw nothing in the way of wildlife when we stopped to glass the surrounding hills, so we drove back toward Salmon Creek where Doug dropped me off to "hoof it" over a thousand-acre piece of property.

"Hunt the brush patches," he said. "You might be able to scare up an elk." Leaving him to repair a fallen-down rockjack, Daisy and I took off, walking through the old corrals, where, over the years, we have branded spring calves and worked cattle. We climbed a slight rise to a wire gate, over the same ground I had lain, broken and bruised, on that fateful morning more than a year ago.

As we ambled slowly up the long, dry meadow, Maud, Snowberry, and Mildred, our three mules, followed close behind. Perhaps they were lonely. Animals out in that vast open country don't see humans very often, especially this time of year. These mules will winter here, pawing through the snow to subsist on the nutritious bunch grasses that remain beneath the frozen terrain.

Standing out darkly in the leafless thornbush thickets, stick nests of hawks were easily seen. Wet Salmon creek was dry, but ponds built over the years contained sufficient water to satisfy the needs of livestock and wildlife.

Daisy and I followed the creek's course into another pasture, and found ourselves in a narrow bottom blanked by steep hills. The thornbush was thick here and leaves had been stripped bare by the fierce fall windstorm that swept though our country last week. Early snows had fallen tumbling temperatures, but now this warmer rain had freshened the hills. The sun never quite managed to break through the thick layer of clouds.

My .243 rifle was slung over one shoulder, binoculars swung from my neck, and a water bottle protruded from a pocket of my heavy coat, which also contained an apple, bullets and my hunting license and tag. My hiking boots were caked with black soil that clings like clay when it is wet. In other words I was weighted down with the trappings of a hunter. Nevertheless it felt good to be out there, walking. Although as time went on and I didn't spot any elk, I realized it would have been more enjoyable without those burdensome objects.

We made our way slowly past a pond, where in the spring I had seen a wild mallard and her ducklings, to an opening in the thornbush patches. Shuffling along, a porcupine was nibbling shoots of blue grass. Calling Daisy to my side, I watched as the fluffy gray creature fed on the only green around. We came to another line fence, crossed the dry creek bed, and slowly made our way up a long, steep hill. Walking backward most of the time, I was able to glass the opposite hills for any elk that might be hiding in the brush patches. All was silent.

Among our hills is one of the few remaining places where one can actually listen to the sound of silence. The entire Zumwalt came into view as I climbed higher, and to the north rose Greenwood Butte and the snowy Chesnim; northwest, the cleft in the canyon which would be Joseph Creek; to the south, the white Wallowas rose into the dark sky...so much country, the gentle breeze whispering through miles of golden grassland.

After reaching the hill top we continued down the other side into Deadman to another, nearly-full pond, bordered on one side by aspen trees. It was here I found the first fresh elk sign. The aspen's leaves were still green, very unusual for this time of year. Like Prairie Creek, I thought, where willows and cottonwoods haven't turned yet, and probably won't at this late date. Rather they will turn brown with the freeze and blow away in the wind. Normally colors peak by mid-October.

Making our way down Deadman's dry wash, carved over the years by spring snowmelt, we walked through an open gate where our heifers had obviously recently passed by. The only life I had seen, other than the porcupine and mules, had been our cattle. They might as well have been slow elk. An occasional hawk flew overhead, and numerous squirrel and badger holes marked the terrain over which we traveled. Daisy and I appeared to be in an endless world of dry bunch grass hills. Hills that ended in sky.

After chugging up yet another hill, we followed a familiar cow path, one I had driven cattle over many times. Horseback, paying attention to gathering cattle, you don't notice the details of the land.

That day I was really getting the feel of our "hills."

Author Marcy Houle wrote a book about this country, titled *The Prairie Keepers*. While walking these hills and draws to study the habits of hawks, Marcy referred to the Zumwalt as one of the last wild grassland prairies in North America. It also provides habitat for one of the largest concentrations of raptors in the U.S. Even more amazing is that these lands are privately owned.

Marcy gives credit to the stewardship of local ranchers, who have managed to keep this area productive as well as wild by balancing the needs of nature with the grazing of cattle. Topping another hill, I glassed our pickup along the far road where Doug was still repairing fence. Fence maintenance on these vast acreages is a never-ending job, even more so during hunting seasons when frightened herds can lay an entire section flat.

Elk follow cattle, as they prefer tender grazed-over grass to rank ungrazed grasses. They slake their thirst at the same ponds, and lick the salt put out for cattle. Elk prefer quiet, peaceful places where they can bed down, unmolested by civilization. Ranches provide that haven.

By the time Daisy and I made our way back to the pickup it was well past noon, and we had traversed over a goodly portion of 2,000 acres. If I had known I wouldn't see any elk, I would have left that heavy rifle in the pickup. But then again, I mused, if it weren't for my elk tag, I wouldn't even have been out there that time of year. I would have been in my snug, warm home, seated at the word processor, writing this column, not pressured by a deadline.

After eating a sandwich, we drove to another section of fence where Doug went to work replacing more fence material. For miles these fences march: Rockjack, stay, stay, stay, stay, rockjack, up and down the hills.

After a brief rest, Daisy and I walked up the road toward Zumwalt. What a joy it was to suddenly come upon 10 pair of bluebirds, their brilliant bodies brightening the stark landscape as they perched on weathered fence posts. They eyed us silently before flying off to hover in air currents, beating their wings. Their presence made my day.

Driving homeward along the Zumwalt road, we watched as a new storm brewed over the Wallowas. Our CB radio squawked with fragmented accounts of other hunting stories. It was cold and windy when we returned to the ranch to build a fire in the Monarch, warm up some leftover pork roast, baked squash, and cornbread for supper, and hit, the hay.

And now, at dawn on this Friday morning, as I do the final typing of this column, I look outside to see a good three inches of snow has fallen over Prairie Creek during the night.

November 5—From the Cardiovascular Intensive Care Unit (CVICU) waiting room here at St. Alphonsus Hospital, I look out large windows, four stories up, watching a moving river of lights wending its way along the highway that led us here a week ago today. It is 7:30 a.m. Boise time, and dark clouds fill the sky as dawn seeps over a busy city. The CVICU lies beyond heavy metal doors, and in Room 410 lies my husband.

Doug experienced the first warnings of his heart attack while lifting a rock onto a rockjack way out there on Salmon Creek, while I was elk hunting. He had kept it to himself as the pain in his chest had subsided.

The recurring pains persisted, however, and after he informed me on Friday, I wasted no time rushing him to the nearest medical facility. Our local hospital was able to stabilize him, and the following Tuesday daughters Ramona and Lori and I were en route with him to Boise. A catheterization revealed minimal damage to the heart, but myriad narrowed arteries. He was one of the lucky ones. The tests also showed the slight damage that occurred in 1983.

"However," said Doug's heart surgeon, "to prevent future attacks, I recommend bypass open heart surgery." Since the CVICU was booked, Doug's surgery was scheduled for 7:30 a.m. Saturday. The three of us gals had checked into the nearby Roadway Inn within walking distance of St. Alphonsus.

Time dragged on for me, but not for Ramona and Lori, who "did" the shopping malls. One day, to pass the time, I tagged along. Walking through malls is not my favorite thing, but it was a welcome change.

Halloween came and went. The hospital was free of pumpkins, ghosts and black bats. A grandson and his young mother, who live in Boise, visited, and 17-month-old Ethan brightened our hours.

I took long walks around the huge grounds and discovered a memorial rose garden dedicated to the sisters who served St. Alphonsus from 1894 to 1994. Even though the roses had spent their beauty, it was quiet there and I sat alone on a wooden bench watching a magpie search for crumbs. Large flaming maple trees lit up the green lawns. Their foliage was so bright it was as if someone had plugged the trees into a light socket.

Looking down from Doug's room when the morning, and later, evening light lit them was a treat I looked forward to.

Finally, Saturday morning came. Son Steve flew in from Phoenix, and Bob and Merilee Tippett, from Pasco, Washington, arrived, as Merilee's mother was there on the same floor for her surgery. The world shrinks. We walked across the frosted lawn as a half moon and stars glowed in a dark, clear sky. We formed a "prayer ring" around Doug's bed and they wheeled him off the surgery.

We visited with Doug's nephew. A family reunion we say. We waited and waited. A green-clad, slippered fellow emerged.

"He's on the pump," he said, and disappeared. At last...Dr. Barnes appeared, looming over us in the waiting room, looking weary after seven hours of surgery.

"We did an eight-way bypass," he said. "He is a very strong man. Everything went just fine." When we were finally allowed to see Doug, he was still under anesthesia and appeared more dead than alive. Tubes running from every body opening bleeped and burbled, and monitors sent colored rhythmic scribbles across the screen, over his head. It was a scene right out of "Star Wars."

An hour later, a breathing tube down his throat, he could only signal with his strapped-down fingers. He wanted to know, he wrote on paper with a marking pen, when would the tube come out of his throat? The nurse told him one more hour. Then this tough rancher husband of mine made a thumbs up signal. He'd make it, his eyes said.

Doug's recovery has been remarkable, thanks to his good physical condition and his positive outlook. The prayers of family and friends played a big role.

That Saturday was a beautiful fall day here in Boise, and I took a walk under Idaho's blue skies to relieve the tension. Looking up toward the fourth floor of the new heart wing where Doug lay, his heart stopped for the surgery, I noted a white fluttering in the clear sky above. A V of wild snow geese flew over the north tower. It was as if, from that moment on, I knew Doug would be OK, and indeed, he improves daily.

The daughters have returned to their families, Steve has flown home to Arizona, and I have adjusted to my life here. Today the lawns are littered with golden maple leaves and at home it has snowed again.

Last night around 1:30 a.m. the "Life Flight" helicopter landed on the roof of St. Alphonsus. This morning over breakfast in the hospital cafeteria, I visited with the wife of the man who had been air-lifted from Jerome, Idaho, suffering a serious stroke. He was in surgery, she said. He'd been attending a livestock auction when it first began. "And," she added, "he didn't tell me!"

"Sounds familiar," I said.

"He's only 55," she replied.

We sat there, two ranch wives miles away from our familiar homes, worried about our hard-working husbands, wondering what the future will bring. Sharing and comforting each other to get through each day.

I find people endlessly fascinating. Take Domingo, for instance, the cattleman and sheepman we met the first night here, who was in visiting one of his Basque sheepherders, recovering from heart surgery.

"Wonderful man," says Domingo. "He doesn't speak English. A good worker, knows sheep. Works hard, plays hard. I herded sheep once myself in the mountains. Happiest days of my life. Man is closer to God up there with the sheep."

The herder lying in bed looked from Domingo to me as we talked about raising garlic and baking sourdough bread.

After a week of city noise and sterile hospital rooms, I long for Prairie Creek. Mostly I long for the quiet. Doug is walking up and down the halls now. Hopefully, by next week we can return to the ranch. After my horse wreck over a year ago, Doug was my nurse. Now it is my turn. These are the threads of our lives with which we stitch our marriage together.

November 26—As she was traveling over the Blue Mountains with her family to spend the weekend with us, granddaughter Lacey crafted a "Dream Catcher" to help pass the time. What is a "Dream Catcher"? It is a slender, looped willow twig secured with a sinewy thread, which is also used to weave a web that is stretched between the willow loop. Woven in the web are tiny turquoise-colored beads, and hanging from the bottom of the "catcher" are three bird feathers.

It is an old Indian custom that the net of the dream catcher catches dreams. I was so taken by Lacey's creation that I purchased this one from her. It hangs above me as I work here at my word processor, catching dreams that form in mind, to be put on paper.

My days are so full I can scarcely find time to write, so in the middle of the night, I slip from my side of the bed and quietly make my way to the front room. Two nights ago, around 3:30 a.m., I was thus engaged when I looked up through the dream catcher to see the full November moon.

When I focused my eyes on the net of the catcher, two moons filled the beaded net, yet when I focused on the moon, it became one again... a bit of magic to brighten my solitary hours, and provide a subject with which to begin this column. In the midst of life's travails we all need dream catchers to sift our thoughts and substantiate the fact that life, in spite of its ups and downs, is, after all... sweet.

Doug continues to improve on a daily basis. Today being bright, crisp, clear and sunny, he didn't return from his daily walk when I was expecting him. A friend had come to visit and hadn't passed him on the road, so I became alarmed and we jumped in the car to track down my missing husband. We found him walking around the block... four miles! He was relieved to see us, as he had a little less than half of the distance yet to travel.

It has proven to be an adventure cooking all these low-fat meals. Daughter Ramona gave me a new baking cookbook, which features applesauce, mashed banana, prune puree, lecithin, non-fat buttermilk, and yogurt in place of shortening or butter. The end products, laden with whole wheat flour, wheat germ, oat bran and rolled oats, are so nutritious we are both full of new energy and losing weight.

We continue to eat plenty of meat, only it isn't fried in fat, but broiled, boiled, or stir-fried. All those canned peaches, pears, cherries and berries are wonderful to have in the canning cupboard, and of course we still use the sourdough.

Pretty amazing, this modern heart surgery. Doug has received numerous cards and letters welcoming him to the "Zipper Club." When he left St. Alphonsus Hospital the staff gave Doug a red heart-shaped pillow to hold against his chest when he had to cough. Not only did the pillow protect his chest incision, but everyone who visits Doug signs their autograph on the heart. However, all of the myriad chores Doug used to do are now my responsibility. It has been a challenge, but we will make it somehow.

Thanksgiving is two days away. Turkey day. Speaking of which, the turkey that is, I have a tale to tell. It began earlier in the fall, when I delivered some freshly-dug potatoes from my Alder Slope garden, to my son Ken's family. In their yard I was quite taken with grandson Rowdy's "herd" of free-roaming turkeys and inquired about the possibility of purchasing one for our Thanksgiving dinner.

Things like Doug's heart attack and elk season intervened, and I put the idea on the back burner. Two nights ago, grandson James called.

"Grandma, do you have Rowdy's turkey there yet?" came the 10-year-old voice over the telephone line.

"No," I replied. "Come to think of it, I don't."

In the meantime, Rowdy had butchered several turkeys and there were only two left. Then in the middle of the week the turkeys shrunk to one. When I called over there to see if I could pick up mine, son Ken thought I had already picked up the turkey, as there was only one strutting about the yard. It seems Mr. Coyote had himself a Thanksgiving dinner!

Anyway, on a cold, foggy evening I fetched the surviving turkey and turned it into my chicken house to await death row the next day. Yesterday, I was at the school to pick up James, who rode home with me to do the terrible deed of readying this massive bird for our feast. I won't go into the gory details, but the death blow was swift, and I'll wager this turkey suffered far less than did his litter mate, who met his fate in the jaws of a coyote.

After scalding and picking and gutting the bird, James and I cleaned up the mess and came in to fix supper. It had been a long day in a succession of long days. But when we sit down to our turkey, all stuffed with homemade dressing and seasoned with sage from the garden, accompanied by mashed potatoes, gravy, candied yams, fruit salad, rolls and pumpkin pie, we will not only be thankful for the turkey, but for heart surgeons, grandchildren, family and friends.

Although I walked a goodly portion of our summer range on Butte Creek, Salmon Creek and Deadman I was unable to fill my L.O.P. cow elk tag. I wasn't alone. The elk, which were so numerous in years past, seemingly vanished from the Zumwalt this year. Grandson Josh and friend Linde and I did enjoy our tromping around the cold, still hills in November, but other than a porcupine, two coyotes, a white weasel, and our cattle, horses and mules, there wasn't a sign of life anywhere.

We survived a bad snow storm, followed by warm chinook-type winds that blew down several trees around the ranch and left us without power for several hours. Today, high, thin clouds decorate a startling blue sky. Although temperatures are in the 30s, the sunshine is most welcome, especially after freezing rain and fog.

In the midst of that storm, a few of our cows, their calves weaned already, decided to come home. They managed to break through a gate and came straggling into the valley two days later. The others remain in good shape, grazing the dry bunch grass, after the chinook melted the snow.

Here on Prairie Creek the air is filled with the sound of "goose music," as the wild honkers land to feed on leftover grain in our neighbors' fields before continuing on in their long, wavering strands overhead toward Wallowa Lake, where hundreds of geese, including snow geese, seek the sanctuary of the off-season waters of this quiet glacial lake.

Ben sold our calves and my milk cow's bunch. It will soon be time to trail in the remaining cattle, and then begin the long winter of feeding hay.

December 9—As one storm after another sweeps across our part of Northeastern Oregon, man and beast alike must contend daily with cold snow, high winds, and now, rain…which is melting the snow. Yesterday, however, there was a brief break in the clouds, and a spring-like breeze drove ragged snow clouds apart enough to expose a weak December sun. Daisy and I wasted no time going for a stroll down our country road.

Seizing this opportunity to escape the myriad, and inevitable, holiday preparations, I took in great gulps of storm-scoured air and filled my senses with what was around me, which included a confused nightcrawler oozing its way across the road, a juvenile hawk flapping its way into the air from its perch in an old cottonwood, and several wavering V's of geese honking their way cross Prairie Creek.

During these storms, ducks and geese by the hundreds have been converging to feed on the exposed grasses in our fields, as well as neighboring grain fields. A few Sunday hunters were out and the rural quiet was broken by the occasional report of a shotgun.

It was snowing to the west, on the slopes of Ruby Peak, and sunlight sliced through a cloud break to create a rare December rainbow. It made my day!

Linde and I got in two days of cross-country skiing before the big melt. To get our "ski legs," we drove to Salt Creek Summit and skied several miles in perfect snow, before another winter blizzard hit. Later that week, we skied up past the Ferguson Ridge ski area, and that day had a pretty good workout. There is no better sport than Nordic skiing to get the blood going. Now we must wait for new snow and colder temps.

Doug continues to improve daily, and because his lifting is still restricted to 10 pounds, the splitting and hauling of wood is my chore. He does do dishes, however, and I must say this sharing of household duties is a nice change.

Ben started the remainder of our cattle in from the hills last week, after an unusually severe storm threatened to drift the roads shut. It was time, and the lead cows knew the way. They spent the night corralled along the Crow Creek road, where Ben hauled hay out to them.

That next morning the temps hovered around zero as Doug and I hauled my mare out to Salmon Creek, where she will winter with our other two horses and three mules.

We passed our corralled cows eating hay where they had bedded down for the night. Ben's saddle horse was in among them. It wasn't easy negotiating large drifts that were forming in the road near Salmon Creek, but our four-wheel-drive made it.

After unloading the mare in a whirling white wind storm, we made sure the other horses and mules were close by, so she could see them. They will have a large area in which to roam, and during bad weather the animals can come down around the old barn for protection from the merciless winds. Our horses and mules winter just fine by pawing through the snow for the nutritious bunch grass, the same grasses that have sustained horses in Wallowa County for well more than 100 years.

There is nothing quite as desolate as those Zumwalt hills on a cold December day during a snow storm, however, and I was relieved when we gained the safety of the Crow Creek road. As we stopped to load Ben's horse, left behind as Ben was trailing the cattle in a warm pickup, I thought of son Todd and his friend Scott riding the windswept Divide country for strays on such a day.

Later Todd was to share one of those cold experiences, about how he sent his two dogs down into a draw to bring out some cattle, and how he couldn't see but a few feet ahead in the cold, blowing snow. How the wind blew with such force it pushed his horse sideways. He waited there, on his horse, looking toward the draw when after a while, through the white void of shifting snow, there appeared the cattle. The dogs were bringing them up!

Cowboys, along with their faithful horses and dogs, are the unsung heroes of a diminishing way of life. You won't see these fellows in town much; they are too busy. The pay is low and the hours long, but they continue to work at the life they know and love, to support their families.

This way of life is as old as the history of Wallowa County...and only the tough survive. Many of these younger ones dream of a ranch of their own one day, but find it increasingly difficult to realize those dreams in our modern West. The West they envisioned is being replaced with second homes and an emphasis on tourism. Local art galleries are full of bronzes and paintings depicting the Western way of life...the cowboy, his dog, his horse...but few realize the reality of such lives.

I mused on these things as Doug and I, in our warm pickup, plugged holes along the route our cows took to the ranch that day. Christmas draws near. On Saturday Linde and I drove into Enterprise to purchase a Christmas tree from the FFA chapter. Linde wanted a tall tree, and I wanted a small one. By the time we got there, after driving slowly over icy back roads, the tall ones were gone. I purchased three smaller ones for various members of our family, and then we drove slowly up the ice-covered Alder Slope road to pick up some grandchildren.

We later attended the annual Hand Crafter's Bazaar at Cloverleaf Hall in Enterprise.

It might have been blustery and cold, with the snow blowing every which way outside, but we found a different scene entirely inside the hall. No wonder the children wanted to be there. Santa Claus, all whiskered and smiling, greeted us as we entered. Several old and young fiddle players made old-fashioned music, and wonderful smells wafted from the kitchen, where the Imnaha Grange ladies were serving their famous roast beef dinners and homemade pies. Booths, brimming over with fudge, handmade quilts, wreaths, toys, rugs, and hundreds of other hand-crafted items, completely filled the Community Hall. Christmas was in the air. The children took their time shopping for small gifts, while I visited old friends and ran into family.

After lunch we left to drive back to the ranch in the storm, where the kids and I tackled that tree. Adele and James decorated into the afternoon, and I supplied the hot chocolate not only for them, but for another grandson and his friends who stopped in to warm themselves after duck hunting. Perhaps some of the ornaments aren't spaced just right, and the angel is a little askew, but who cares? The children had such fun, and that is all that matters. They even made stockings to hang over the fireplace mantel for Daisy and the cats.

When the children's father stopped by to pick them up, I fixed yet another round of hot cocoa to warm up the cowboy. After which daddy bundled up his young'uns and loaded them into the truck where his horse and two cow dogs had been waiting patiently.

And so it goes here on ranches all over Wallowa County. Feed the livestock, feed the fire, keep warm, and support one another, to survive these long, cold winters of our lives. Merry Christmas to all of you...and may the new year bring health, happiness, and high cattle prices.

December 23—The winter solstice has come and gone. And even though the lengthening days aren't noticeable yet, just the fact that the sun will slip quietly over Chief Joseph Mountain a wee bit later than 3:15 lifts our spirits.

Two days away from Christmas finds Prairie Creek muted in cold fog. Willow limbs, raspberry canes, chicken wire fence, haystacks, and barn cats wear whiskers of white hoarfrost. Even I, taking my morning walk with Daisy, am covered with it. Eyelashes, hair, cap and mittens all wear the frozen breath of Prairie Creek, a silent white land, shrouded in fog. There are no mountains, no hills, only frosted black cows grazing frosted brown grass.

The warm breath of our weaned heifer calves creates a halo of steam over the hay feeder as they eat their breakfast. *Auk...Auk...Auk*, a lone crow breaks the silence from an invisible willow growing alongside the creek, its solitary call echoes across the snowy pasture.

Daisy and I, trailed by various barn cats, make our way up Echo Canyon to a bridge that spans an irrigation ditch. Resting after a brisk uphill climb, I gaze down into the open channel of water which slides between ice-laced shelves. Sculpted by freezing and thawing, these icy fringes are works of art. Amoeba-like dark water spreads and contracts beneath these thin ice sheets. I stare in fascination, seeking solace and diversion from the demands of the season.

Refreshed on that first day of winter, I returned to what must be done. I walk in all weather, and no two days are alike. As I sit here in front of my word processor, watching the early morning light seep across Prairie Creek, there are no mountains to the south and west; no hills to the north and east; my world has shrunk to the chicken house, woodshed, and barn. What appears to be frozen frost floating in the air may, in fact, be snow. Not having listened to any forecasts this Monday morning, I feel in my bones we will have a white Christmas.

Our days have been filled with holiday happenings. School Christmas programs, open house get-togethers, friends over for supper, baking and cooking, final shopping, wrapping gifts, and planning Christmas dinner here for 18... all of which must be woven into our daily ranch life.

Saturday night, Doug and I drove the 60-mile round-trip to the Imnaha church to attend a special Christmas service. Lots of singing, and a creative play, staged by the Imnaha Fellowship youth group, put us in touch with the real spirit of Christmas.

Because Doug is not supposed to split wood yet, I was pleasantly surprised one morning, after pushing the wheelbarrow up the snowy path to the woodshed, to find a pile of split tamarack. Elves? No. Ben. Bless him.

That next morning I baked him an apple pie.

Then there was the time our cows broke through a fence and got into a haystack. Ben was out of town, but neighbors Tom Butterfield and Karl Patton came to the rescue. By morning our grain hay would have been demolished, but thanks to Tom and Karl and their border collie dogs, we were able to handle the situation. I mixed up the sourdough that evening and delivered both neighbors a loaf of warm french bread the next morning.

Our ranch home provides a sort of "halfway house" for the Imnaha boys who are on the Joseph High School JV wrestling team. Because these wrestlers must travel such long distances to compete with other Eastern Oregon teams, it is often in the wee hours of the morning when they return to Joseph. One such dark and cold morning, I awoke to the sound of grandson Buck's old pickup chugging up our lane, and later, when we got up, we were greeted by three slumbering bodies sacked out in our living room.

Naturally, Buck's grandma fixed a breakfast of sausage gravy over hot biscuits before sending them on their way back to the canyon. Over breakfast I enjoyed listening to their stories of traveling to Culver, near Madras and Redmond, and how each of them fared in their matches. I find 16-year-olds fun to be around. They keep us young.

Ran into neighbor Marian Birkmaier in the grocery store yesterday. She and I were both shopping for Christmas dinner, lots of family coming, and we were standing at the meat counter selecting our prime rib roasts when along came another neighbor, Ardis Klages. So there we were, three Prairie Creek rancher-wives spreading cheer to each other, not mentioning the fact we were spending far more money for the finished product than what we received for our calves this fall. We laugh and say: We raise it, we support it, and we eat it. "Beef, it's what's for dinner."

By the time you read this, we will already be three days into 1997. Whatever changes the new year brings, we look forward, not backward, with hope.

Index

Doug Tippett appears too frequently to be included in the index.

Photos of Doug appear on pages 291, 347, 440, and 459.
Photos of Janie appear on page 475.

9 781733 483

Ranch wife, camp cook, photo-journalist, and amateur histor
Janie Tippett continues her thirty-one years of newspa
columns chronicling the lives of cattle ranchers and hay farm
in the remote hills and canyons of rural northeast Oregon.

In this third volume, she trails cattle to the hills, attends lo
rodeos and brandings, cares for her garden and the ranch
Prairie Creek, explores Nez Perce history, visits her husba
Doug's historic Dug Bar ranch on the Snake River in H
Canyon, competes in the Great Rooster Crowing Contest
nearby Weston, and collects oral histories from local old-tim
about Wallowa County's past.

Janie's journals capture the complicated struggles of the m
and women who love their vanishing way of life.

Janie Tippett, 1995

In 2010 Janie published *Four Lines a l*
about homesteader Mary Marks in
Imnaha country.

Her writing and photos have appeared in
Wallowa County Chieftain, *Agri-Times NW*,
Oregon Magazine, *Go! Magazine*, and *Sig*
Mountain, as well as in anthologies from B
Creek Press and Fishtrap, among others.

Lucky Marmot Press
Wallowa, Oregon
www.luckymarmotpress.com

ISBN 978-1-7334833-4-6

9 781733 483346